PROFESSIONAL
Baseball
Franchises

PROFESSIONAL
Baseball
Franchises

FROM THE ABBEVILLE ATHLETICS

TO THE ZANESVILLE INDIANS

by Peter Filichia

Facts On File
New York

PROFESSIONAL BASEBALL FRANCHISES:
FROM THE ABBEVILLE ATHLETICS TO THE ZANESVILLE INDIANS

Copyright © 1993 by Peter Filichia

Facts On File, Inc.
460 Park Avenue South
New York NY 10016
USA

Library of Congress Cataloging-in-Publication Data
Filichia, Peter.
Professional baseball franchises : from the Abbeville Athletics to
the Zanesville Indians / Peter Filichia.
p. cm.
Includes bibliographical references and index.
ISBN 0-8160-2647-5
1. Baseball—United States—Clubs—Registers. 2. Baseball—Clubs–
–Registers. 3. Baseball—United States—Clubs—History.
4. Baseball—Clubs—History. I. Title.
GV875.A1F45 1993
796.357′64′0973—dc20   92-12766

A British CIP catalogue record for this book is available from the British Library.

Facts On File books are available at special discounts when purchased in bulk quantities for businesses, associations, institutions or sales promotions. Please contact our Special Sales Department in New York at 212/683-2244 (dial 800/322-8755 except in NY, AK or HI) or in Oxford at 865/728399.

Text design by Ron Monteleone
Jacket design by Victore Design Works
Composition by Facts On File, Inc.
Manufactured by R. R. Donnelley & Sons
Printed in the United States of America

10 9 8 7 6 5 4 3 2 1

This book is printed on acid-free paper.

CONTENTS

To Anthony DiDomenico
who taught me how wonderful baseball could be

ACKNOWLEDGMENTS

My profound thanks to Jerry Jackson, acknowledged by the Society for American Baseball Research (SABR) as the guru of the Minor Leagues, without whom this book could not have been completed.

Special thanks to SABR (Morris Eckhouse, Executive Director) and its members, especially Eli Babcock, Dave Beisel, Eduardo J. Blanco, Sr., John Dowling, Rusty Eichblatt, J. Thomas Hetrick, Leo Hirsch, David Kemp, Mike Keough, Greg McFarland, Jorge C. Menendez, John F. Pardon, David Pietrusza, the Selters, Eric Wunderman and Heidi A. Zeimer.

Thanks to Bill Deane and Gary Van Allen at the National Baseball Library at the Baseball Hall of Fame, Cooperstown, New York. There I also found helpful information compiled by Al Becker, Cappy Gagnon, Al Glynn, Bob Hoie, Jim Laughlin, Vern Luse, Bob McConell and Ray Nemec.

Also thanks to Linda Konner, John Harrison, Douglas J. Cohen, Cathy Kiliper, Anthony Levaggi, Rick Lidinsky, Arthur Foisy, Elaine Foisy, Richard Adler and Jerry Ross.

HOW TO USE THIS BOOK

◆

This book lists every city in which Major or Minor League ball has been played professionally in an established league since baseball began as an in-earnest business in 1869.

Let's take a sample listing:

WATERBURY, CT

Waterbury Huskies (aka Frolickers)
Eastern Association (B), 1914; re-named franchise. Had been WATERBURY CONTENDERS, 1913. Disbanded with league after 1914 season.

And let's examine each line closely:

WATERBURY, CT

Waterbury Huskies (aka Frolickers)

The city/state head is on top, with the team's city and nickname listed directly below on the first line. Whenever a team was known by two nicknames, the lesser-used nickname is included second in parentheses with an "aka"—"also known as"—notation. It may be a mere dimunitive of the first (the "Cardinals" are often known as the "Cards"), or a completely different name, as in the case cited above.

There are quite a few "aka's" in the listings, because many sports teams were known by two or even three names. For example, a recent SABR (Society for American Baseball Research) newsletter, in discussing the 1991 Minnesota Twins' and Atlanta Braves' rise from last place to first place, mentioned that this happened once before—to "the 1890 Louisville team (Colonels, Cyclones and/or Eclipses)." The name varied "depending on your source."

Indeed, in the late 19th and early 20th centuries, Minor League baseball was not given the substantial coverage it receives today in *USA Today* or even metropolitan newspapers; its team names were sometimes blithely awarded by the reporter covering the game. Searching through yellowed newspaper reports (as this writer did for several blinding hours) often yields one, two or three names for a given team. Considering that even today one can't find a team's nickname in the standings of the clubs—teams are simply listed as "Baltimore," "Boston" and "Cleveland," and not "Orioles," "Red Sox" and "Indians"—one must often rely on what the reporters called the team in the stories describing yesterday's game.

Sometimes the reporters simply played fast-'n'-easy with the team names. Just as today's Baltimore, Boston and Cleveland clubs are often dubbed "the O's," "the Sox" and "the Tribe," so too did sportswriters invent or corrupt names of clubs. Baseball fans of yesteryear will recall that when a newspaper was not able to fit the word "Washington" or "Senators" in the headline of a one-column article, the story would often be bannered "NATS FALL TO YANKS" or "SOLONS BOW AGAIN." While the Washington Senators were sometimes called "the Nationals," they were never officially dubbed "the Solons." All of these variations are noted in this encyclopedia.

Another problem is that many stories written about late 19th and early 20th century teams were penned by writers who weren't sports reporters by profession; indeed, the profession didn't exist during the infancy of the sport. Few knew then that such games and teams would be of interest to late 20th century readers. When one sees that the 1913 Zanesville team was known as the "Flood Sufferers," one has to wonder if that's what the president of the team officially named his club, or if the reporter was taking a literary license in honor of a recent deluge. A writer compiling information on baseball clubs 100 years from now might assume that the Mets were really called "the Amazin's" because some New York sportswriters, when the team was seemingly unbeatable in 1986, enjoyed calling the club by this sobriquet rather than use its formal name.

The best solution seemed to be to include as much as possible from those old newspaper clippings or magazine articles, as well as listings in the *Baseball Blue Books*, an annual series that has been published continually since 1909; but the series didn't routinely list every nickname for every team until recently.

In fact, for many other teams you won't find a nickname at all. "Some of these teams never had nicknames," reports Bill Deane, head librarian at the National Baseball Library at the Baseball Hall of Fame. "It wasn't an automatic thing back then for a team to be called by a nickname. Some just liked to be called 'the so-and-so baseball club' or even 'the so-and-so nine.' " When a team was unnamed—or if the statisticians, researchers and fans who belong to SABR cannot find a name for a given team—it is simply listed here with the city name and no nickname afterward. In short, what's included here is only what has been proven accurate.

Major League team names are included in capital letters—as are Negro League teams. Granted, the stadia and statistical information for Negro League teams was decidedly minor, but that was because of baseball's prejudice before 1947, and not because of the abilities of those playing on the teams. The rationale of this author is that since Negro League players are now eligible for the Hall of Fame alongside Major League players, the teams also deserve equal billing. If they're good enough for Cooperstown, they're good enough for Major League typeface in this encyclopedia.

Mexican League teams list (when applicable) both the Spanish name and, in parentheses, the translated American name; for example, one Saltillo team is referred to as both the "Peroneros" and the "Parrots."

Onto the next line:

> Eastern Association (B), 1914; re-
> named franchise.

Here we see the league in which the team played. As for the teams currently operating as of press time, they are flagged (still in existence as of 5-1-92). Sometimes you will find on the line immediately below the league the name of yet another league; that simply means that the team joined a new league the following year, or that the league went through a name change. If the league was once known as an association—or vice versa—that fact is noted by a slash (/).

The letter in parentheses—in this case "B"—represents the Minor League level assigned to it by the National Association of Professional Baseball. The practice of branding a league with such a label was established in September 1901, and began for the 1902 season; thus, any team that played before that time has no such legend next to its league name.

Until 1963, the Minor League level ranks began with AAA (the highest regarded level) and descended to AA, A, B, C and D, with three notable exceptions: the Twin Ports League in 1943 was labeled E (lowest of all); the Southern Association and Texas League between 1935 and 1945 were labeled A-1 (a ranking higher than A but lower than AA); and from 1952 through 1958 the Pacific Coast League was labeled "Open" (here noted as "O"), because it was being groomed as a third Major League. Once the Dodgers and Giants left New York, this plan was abandoned, and the league returned to the AAA status it had before the "Open" classification.

Some teams are flagged "(R)", which represents a rookie classification for first-year leagues,

Next in the listing are the years in which the team operated. Sometimes a team switched cities in the middle of a season, or started playing late in a season; if so, that team is flagged with a "mid"—i.e., mid-1953.

This is followed by a description of how the franchise evolved. If the team was operating during the first year of a league's existence, it's known as a "charter franchise." Sometimes a league would start, fold, then reopen a year or two later; when this occurs, a team is still considered a "charter franchise" if it operated during the first year of the league's re-entry.

There are also "expansion franchises." For example, in 1962, the National League added two new teams to its eight-team roster—the New York Mets and the Houston Colt '45s; these are known as "expansion teams." If, however, a team merely replaced another that folded—and the league stayed with the same number of teams as the year before—then that new team is a "new franchise."

If a team moved from one place to another—the way that the St. Louis Browns moved to Baltimore to become the Orioles in 1954—then it's a "relocated franchise." And if a team simply decided to change its name—the way the Waterbury Contenders (see example on p. ix) became the Waterbury Huskies—then it's a "renamed franchise."

One last notation about "charter franchises": virtually all Minor Leagues suspended operations after 1941 through 1945 because of World War II. Once these leagues restarted in 1946 or 1947, they are considered here "new leagues," and their franchises in the first year of postwar operation are called "charter franchises."

Onto the next line:

> Had been WATERBURY CONTEND-
> ERS, 1913.

The cross-references to the team's previous name are in small capital letters, followed by the last year the team existed under that name. This line only appears when a team was relocated, renamed or became another team. If the team does not have a city name, then the city where the cross-reference can be found has been supplied in parentheses.

> Disbanded with league after 1914
> season.

This line tells what finally happened to the team.

So here they are: the good (Amigos, Angels, Apostles), the bad (Brigands, Cannibals, Convicts) and the ugly (Boogers, Cobblestone Throwers, Fever Germs)—the Bunnies, the Clowns, the Cokers, the Crybabies, the Debutantes, the Fairies, the Gasbags—all the way to the Zoos and the Zulus. Play Ball!

KEY TO TEAMS
WITHOUT CITY NAMES

(MAJOR LEAGUE AND NEGRO LEAGUE TEAMS ARE IN CAPITAL LETTERS)

"Actives" teams (See READING, PA)

Arizona teams (Listed under Arizona; located in MESA and PEORIA)

Arkansas Travelers (See LITTLE ROCK, AR and MONTGOMERY, AR)

Athletics of Philadelphia (See PHILADELPHIA, PA)

Berwick, PA (See BANGOR, PA)

Carolina Mudcats (See ZEBULON, NC)

Central Oregon Bucks (See BEND, OR)

COLE'S AMERICAN GIANTS (See CHICAGO, IL)

COLORADO ROCKIES (See DENVER, CO)

CUBAN STARS (See CINCINNATI, OH)

FLORIDA MARLINS (See MIAMI, FL)

FLORIDA TROPICS (See MIAMI, FL)

FOREST CITY OF CLEVELAND (See CLEVELAND, OH)

Forest City of Rockford (See ROCKFORD, IL)

Fox Cities teams (See APPLETON, WI)

Foxcroft, ME (See DOVER, ME)

Gallipolis, OH (See POINT PLEASANT, OH)

Gate City (See POCATELLO, ID)

Gray's Harbor, WA (See ABERDEEN, WA)

Haines City, Fl (See BASEBALL CITY, FL)

Hawaii Islanders (See HONOLULU, HI)

HAYMAKERS OF TROY (See TROY, NY)

High Desert teams (See RIVERSIDE, CA)

Iowa teams (See DES MOINES, IA)

Kane County Cougars (See GENEVA, IL)

Lewis-Clark Broncs (See LEWISTON, ID–CLARKSTON, WA)

Long Island (See MASPETH, NY)

LORD BALTIMORES (See BALTIMORE, MD)

Magic Valley Cowboys (See TWIN FALLS, ID)

Maine Guides (See OLD ORCHARD BEACH, ME)

MARYLAND OF BALTIMORE (See BALTIMORE, MD)

Midwest Dodgers (See DUBUQUE, IA)

MINNESOTA TWINS (See MINNEAPOLIS, MN)

Missions of San Francisco (See SAN FRANCISCO, CA)

Mohawk Colored Giants (See SCHENECTADY, NY)

Narrows Rebels (See PEARLSBURG, VA)

NATIONAL OF WASHINGTON (See WASHINGTON, D.C.)

Northampton team (See CAPE CHARLES, VA)

OLYMPIC OF WASHINGTON (See WASHINGTON, D.C.)

"Orphans" (See BRENHAM, TX)

Osceola, FL (See KISSIMMEE, FL)

Peninsula teams (See HAMPTON–NEWPORT NEWS, VA)

Prince William Cannons (See DALE CITY–WOODBRIDGE, VA)

Quad Cities teams (See BETTENDORF, IA–DAVENPORT, IA–MOLINE, IL–ROCK ISLAND, IL)

Queen Anne Colts (See CENTREVILLE, MD)

Redwood Pioneers (See SANTA ROSA, CA)

Rhode Island teams (Alternate name for PAWTUCKET, RI)

Rio Grande Valley teams (See HARLINGEN–SAN BENITO, TX)

Rutherford County teams (See FOREST CITY, NC)

Southern Oregon teams (See BEND, OR)

Texas Midland (See PARIS, TX)

TEXAS RANGERS (See ARLINGTON, TX)

Tidewater teams (See NORFOLK–PORTSMOUTH, VA)

Treasure Valley Cubs (See CALDWELL, ID)

Tri-Cities teams (See ALABAMA CITY–ATTALLA–GADSDEN, AL)

Tri-City teams (See KENNEWICK–RICHLAND–PASCO, WA)

Tri-City teams (See LEAKSVILLE–SPRAY–DRAPER, NC)

Tri-County teams (See GLENS FALLS-SARATOGA SPRINGS, NY)

Triple Cities teams (See BINGHAMTON, ENDICOTT and JOHNSON CITY, NY)

Twin Cities teams (See MARINETTE, WI–MENOMINEE, MI)

Twin Cities teams (See MONROE, LA–WEST MONROE, LA)

Twin Cities teams (See SHERMAN-DENISON, TX)

Valley Rebels (See LANNETT, AL)

Vermont Mariners (See BURLINGTON, VT)

Vermont Reds (See BURLINGTON, VT)

WESTERN OF KEOKUK (See KEOKUK, IA)

Zanesville Swamp Foxes (See MARION, OH)

TEAM LISTINGS BY CITY

ABBEVILLE, AL

Abbeville Red Sox
Alabama–Florida League (D), 1936; charter franchise. Disbanded during 1936 season.

ABBEVILLE, LA

Abbeville A's
Evangeline League (D), 1935–1939; new franchise. Disbanded after 1939 season.

Abbeville A's
Evangeline League (C), 1952; new franchise. Disbanded after 1952 season.

Abbeville Athletics
Evangeline League (D), 1946–1948; (C), 1949–1950; charter franchise. Disbanded after 1950 season.

Abbeville Sluggers
Louisiana State League (D), 1920; charter franchise. Disbanded with league during 1920 season.

ABERDEEN, SD

Aberdeen Boosters
South Dakota League (D), 1920; charter franchise. Disbanded with league after 1920 season.

Aberdeen Grays
Dakota League (D), 1921–1922; charter franchise. South Dakota League (D), 1923; charter franchise. Disbanded with league during 1923 season.

Aberdeen Pheasants
Northern League (C), 1946–1962; (A), 1963–1971; charter franchise.

Disbanded with league after 1971 season.

ABERDEEN, WA

Aberdeen Black Cats
Washington State League (D), 1910; renamed franchise. Had been GRAY'S HARBOR GRAYS (ABERDEEN), 1906–1909. Disbanded during 1910 season.

Aberdeen Black Cats
Washington State League (D), 1912; new franchise. Disbanded during 1912 season.

Aberdeen Black Cats
Northwestern League (B), 1915; new franchise. Disbanded during 1915 season.

Aberdeen Black Cats
Pacific Coast International League (B), 1918; charter franchise. Disbanded with league during 1918 season.

Aberdeen Pippins
Southwest Washington League (D), 1903–1904; charter franchise. Disbanded with league after 1904 season.

Gray's Harbor Grays
Northwestern League (B), 1906–1909; charter franchise. Became ABERDEEN BLACK CATS, Washington State League, 1910.

Gray's Harbor Loggers
Northwest League (A), 1977–1980; renamed franchise. Had been GRAY'S HARBOR PORTS (ABERDEEN), 1976. Disbanded after 1980 season.

Gray's Harbor Ports
Northwest League (A), 1976; expansion franchise. Renamed GRAY'S HARBOR LOGGERS (ABERDEEN), 1977.

ABILENE, KS

Abilene Reds
Central Kansas League (D), 1910; renamed franchise. Had been ABILENE RED SOX, 1909. Disbanded after 1910 season.

Abilene Red Sox
Central Kansas League (D), 1909; new franchise. Renamed ABILENE REDS, 1910.

ABILENE, TX

Abilene Aces
West Texas League (D), 1928–1929; charter franchise. Disbanded with league after 1929 season.

Abilene Apaches
West Texas–New Mexico League (D), 1939; charter franchise. Became BORGER GASSERS, mid-1939.

Abilene Blue Sox
West Texas–New Mexico League (C), 1946–1955; charter franchise. Big State League (B), 1956–1957; new franchise. Disbanded with league after 1957 season.

Abilene Eagles
West Texas League (D), 1920–1922; charter franchise. Disbanded with league after the 1922 season.

ABINGDON, VA

Abingdon
Blue Ridge League (D), mid-1948; relocated franchise. Had been LEAKSVILLE TRIPLETS, 1948. Disbanded after 1948 season.

ACAMBARO, MEXICO

Acambaro
Mexican Center League (A), 1975–1976; new franchise. Disbanded after 1976 season.

ADA, OK

Ada Cementers
Sooner State League (D), mid-1954; renamed franchise. Had been ADA SOONER STATES, mid-1954. Disbanded after 1954 season.

Ada Herefords
Sooner State League (D), 1947–mid-1954; charter franchise. Renamed ADA SOONER STATES, mid-1954.

Ada Sooner States
Sooner State League (D), mid-1954; renamed franchise. Had been ADA HEREFORDS, 1947–mid-1954. Renamed ADA CEMENTERS, mid-1954.

ADRIAN, MI

Adrian Champs
South Michigan League (C), 1913; renamed franchise. Had been ADRIAN LIONS, 1912. Renamed ADRIAN FENCEVILLES, 1914.

Adrian Demons
Michigan State League, 1895; charter franchise. Disbanded with league after 1895 season.

Adrian Fencevilles
South Michigan League (C), 1914; renamed franchise. Had been ADRIAN CHAMPS, 1913. Disbanded after 1914 season.

Adrian Lions
South Michigan League (C), 1912; renamed franchise. Had been ADRIAN YEGGS, 1909–1911. Renamed ADRIAN CHAMPS, 1913.

Adrian Yeggs
Southern Michigan League (D), 1909–1910/Association (C), 1911; new franchise. Renamed ADRIAN LIONS, 1912.

AGUA PRIETA, SONORA, MEXICO

Agua Prieta Vaqueros (Cowboys)
Mexican Rookie League (A), 1968; charter franchise. Disbanded with league after 1968 season.

AGUASCALIENTES, AGUASCALIENTES, MEXICO

Aguascalientes Broncos
Mexican Center League (C), 1969–1972; new franchise. Renamed AGUASCALIENTES TIGERS, 1973.

Aguascalientes Railers
Mexican Center League (C), 1976; renamed franchise. Had been AGUASCALIENTES VINTNERS, 1975. Renamed AGUASCALIENTES RAILWORKERS, 1977.

Aguascalientes Railroaders
Mexican Center League (C), 1979–1988; renamed franchise. Had been AGUASCALIENTES RAILROAD WORKERS, 1978. Renamed AGUASCALIENTES RAILROADMEN, 1989.

Aguascalientes Railroadmen
Mexican Center League (C), 1989–(still in existence as of 5-1-92); renamed franchise. Had been AGUASCALIENTES RAILROADERS, 1979–1988.

Aguascalientes Railroad Workers
Mexican Center League (C), 1978; renamed franchise. Had been AGUASCALIENTES RAILWORKERS, 1977. Renamed AGUASCALIENTES RAILROADERS, 1979.

Aguascalientes Railworkers
Mexican Center League (C), 1977; renamed franchise. Had been AGUASCALIENTES RAILERS, 1976. Renamed AGUASCALIENTES RAILROAD WORKERS, 1978.

Aguascalientes Rieteros
Central Mexican League (C), 1956; charter franchise. Renamed AGUASCALIENTES TIGERS, 1957.

Aguascalientes Tigers
Mexican Center League (C), 1957; renamed franchise. Had been AGUASCALIENTES RIETEROS, 1956. Disbanded after 1957 season.

Aguascalientes Tigers
Mexican Center League (C), 1960–1962; (A), 1963, 1965–1967; charter franchise. Disbanded after 1967 season.

Aguascalientes Tigers
Mexican Center League (C), 1973–1974; renamed franchise. Had been AGUASCALIENTES BRONCOS, 1969–1972. Renamed AGUASCALIENTES VINTNERS, 1975.

Aguascalientes Vintners
Mexican Center League (C), 1975; renamed franchise. Had been AGUASCALIENTES TIGERS, 1973–1974. Renamed AGUASCALIENTES RAILERS, 1976.

AGUILA, (AQUILA) MEXICO
(See VERACRUZ, MEXICO)

AKRON, OH
(See also CANTON, OH)

Akron Acorns
Ohio State League, 1887; charter franchise. Disbanded during 1887 season.

Akron Akrons
Ohio State League, 1889; charter franchise. Tri-State League, 1890; new franchise. Disbanded with league after 1890 season.

Akron Akrons
Interstate League, mid-1895; relocated franchise. Had been STEUBENVILLE STUBS, 1895. Became LIMA FARMERS, mid-1895.

Akron Buckeyes
Ohio–Pennsylvania League (C), 1905; charter franchise. Renamed AKRON RUBBERNECKS, 1906.

Akron Buckeyes
(New) International League (AA), 1920; new franchise. Disbanded after 1920 season.

Akron Champs
Ohio–Pennsylvania League (C), 1907–1911; renamed franchise. Had been AKRON RUBBERNECKS, 1906. Disbanded with league after 1911 season.

Akron Giants
Inter-State League (B), 1913; charter franchise. Disbanded during 1913 season.

Akron Rubbermen
Central League (B), 1912; new franchise. Disbanded after 1912 season.

Akron Rubbernecks
Ohio–Pennsylvania League (C), 1906; renamed franchise. Had been AKRON BUCKEYES, 1905. Renamed AKRON CHAMPS, 1907.

Akron Summits
Ohio–Michigan League, 1893; charter franchise. Disbanded with league after 1893 season.

Akron Tyrites
Central League (D), 1928–1929; charter franchise. Disbanded with league after 1929 season.

Akron Tyrites
Central League (D), 1932; charter franchise. Became CANTON TERRI-ERS, mid-1932.

Akron Yankees
Middle Atlantic League (C), 1935–1941; new franchise. Disbanded after 1941 season.

ALABAMA CITY–ATTALLA–GADSDEN, AL
(See also GADSDEN, AL)

Tri-Cities Triplets
Georgia–Alabama League (D), 1917; new franchise. Disbanded with league during 1917 season.

ALAMEDA, CA

Alameda
Central California Baseball League (D), mid-1910; relocated franchise. Had been SANTA ROSA, 1910. Became OAKLAND INVADERS, mid-1910.

Alameda
Central California Baseball League (D), mid-1910–1911; relocated franchise. Had been FRUITVALE, mid-1910. Disbanded with league during 1911 season.

Alameda
California State League (D), 1915; new franchise. Disbanded with league during 1915 season.

ALBANY, AL
(See DECATUR, AL)

ALBANY, GA

Albany
Georgia State League (D), 1906; charter franchise. Disbanded with league during 1906 season.

Albany Babies
South Atlantic League (C), 1911–mid-1916; new franchise. Disbanded with league during 1916 season.

Albany Cardinals
Georgia–Florida League (D), 1939–1942; 1946–1958; renamed franchise. Had been ALBANY TRAVELERS, 1935–1938. Disbanded with league after 1958 season.

Albany Nuts
Southeastern League (D), 1926–mid-1928; charter franchise. Disbanded during 1928 season.

Albany Travelers
Georgia–Florida League (D), 1935–1938; charter franchise. Renamed ALBANY CARDINALS, 1939.

ALBANY, NY

Albany
National Association, 1879; charter franchise. Disbanded after 1879 season.

Albany
National Association, 1879; charter franchise. Became ROCHESTER RED WINGS, mid-1879.

Albany
New York State League, 1885; charter franchise. Had been WASHINGTON NATIONALS, 1881. Disbanded during 1885 season.

Albany
Hudson River League, 1886; charter franchise. Disbanded during 1886 season.

Albany
New York State League, 1890; charter franchise. Disbanded after 1890 season.

Albany A's
Eastern League (AA), 1983–1984; relocated franchise. Had been WEST HAVEN YANKEES, 1972–1982.

Became ALBANY–COLONIE YAN-KEES, 1985.

Albany Capital City
Eastern Association, mid-1881; re-located franchise. Had been WASH-INGTON NATIONALS, 1881. Disbanded during 1881 season.

Albany Empires
Alternate name for ALBANY SENA-TORS, 1924.

Albany Governors
International Association, 1888; charter franchise. Disbanded after 1888 season.

Albany Lawmakers
Alternate name for ALBANY SENA-TORS, 1928.

Albany Nolans
League Alliance, 1877; charter franchise. Disbanded with league after 1877 season.

Albany Senators
Eastern Association, 1891/League, 1892–1893; charter franchise. Dis-banded during 1893 season.

Albany Senators
New York State League, 1895; re-located franchise. Became ALBANY SENATORS, 1896.

Albany Senators
Eastern League, mid-1896; relo-cated franchise. Had been TO-RONTO CANUCKS, 1896. Became TORONTO CANUCKS, mid-1896.

Albany Senators
New York State League, 1899–1900; (C), 1901; (B), 1902–mid-1916; expansion franchise. Became READING PRETZELS, mid-1916.

Albany Senators (aka Empires, 1924 and Lawmakers, 1928)
Eastern League (A), 1920–mid-1932; new franchise. Disbanded with league during 1932 season.

Albany Senators
International League (AA), mid-1932–1936; relocated franchise. Had been READING KEYSTONES, 1919–mid-1932. New York–Penn-sylvania League (A), 1937; new franchise. Eastern League (A), 1938–1959; charter franchise. Dis-banded after 1959 season.

ALBANY–COLONIE, NY

Albany–Colonie Yankees
Eastern League (AA), 1985–(still in existence as of 5-1-92); renamed franchise. Had been ALBANY A'S, 1983–1984.

ALBANY, OR

Albany Rollers
Oregon State League (D), mid-1904; relocated franchise. Had been VANCOUVER, 1904. Dis-banded with league during 1904 season.

ALBERMARLE, NC

Albermarle Rockets
North Carolina State League (D), 1948; new franchise. Disbanded after 1948 season.

ALBUQUERQUE, NM

Albuquerque Cardinals
Arizona–Texas League (D), 1937–1939; (C), 1940–1941; charter franchise. Disbanded with league after 1941 season.

Albuquerque Dodgers
Texas League (D), 1965–1970; re-named franchise. Had been ALBU-QUERQUE DUKES, 1960–1964. Dixie Association (C), 1971; charter fran-chise. Pacific Coast League (AAA), 1972–1974; new franchise. Re-named ALBUQUERQUE DUKES, 1975.

Albuquerque Dons
Arizona–Texas League (C), 1932; new franchise. Disbanded with league during the 1932 season.

Albuquerque Dukes
Rio Grande Association (D), 1915; charter franchise. Disbanded with league after 1915 season.

Albuquerque Dukes
West Texas–New Mexico League (D), 1942; new franchise. Dis-banded during 1942 season.

Albuquerque Dukes
West Texas–New Mexico League (C), 1946–1954; (B), 1955; charter franchise. Western League (A), 1956–1958; new franchise. Disband-ed with league after 1958 season.

Albuquerque Dukes
Sophomore League (D), 1960–1961; new franchise. Texas League (AA), 1962–1964; new franchise. Renamed ALBUQUERQUE DODG-ERS, 1965.

Albuquerque Dukes
Pacific Coast League (AAA), 1975–(still in existence as of 5-1-92); re-named franchise. Had been ALBUQUERQUE DODGERS, 1965–1974.

ALCOA, TN
(See MARYSVILLE, TN)

ALEXANDER CITY, AL

Alexander City Millers
Georgia–Alabama League (C), 1947–1951; expansion franchise. Disbanded with league during 1951 season.

ALEXANDRIA, AR

Alexandria
Arkansas State League (D), 1909; charter franchise. Disbanded with league after 1909 season.

ALEXANDRIA, LA

Alexandria
Louisiana State League (D), 1920; charter franchise. Disbanded with league during 1920 season.

Alexandria Aces
Evangeline League (D), 1934–1942; 1946–1948; (C), 1949–1957; charter franchise. Disbanded with league after 1957 season.

Alexandria Aces
Texas League (AA), 1972–1975; new franchise. Became AMARILLO GOLD SOX, 1976.

Alexandria Reds
Cotton States League (D), 1925–mid-1930; expansion franchise. Disbanded during 1930 season.

Alexandria White Sox
Gulf Coast League (D), 1907–1908; charter franchise. Disbanded with league during 1908 season.

ALEXANDRIA, VA

Alexandria Dukes
Carolina League (A), 1978; new franchise. Renamed ALEXANDRIA MARINERS, 1979.

Alexandria Dukes
Carolina League (A), 1980–1983; renamed franchise. Had been ALEXANDRIA MARINERS, 1979. Became PRINCE WILLIAM PIRATES (DALE CITY–WOODBRIDGE, VA), 1984.

Alexandria Mariners
Carolina League (A), 1979; renamed franchise. Had been ALEXANDRIA DUKES, 1978. Renamed ALEXANDRIA DUKES, 1980.

ALLENTOWN, PA

Allentown
Eastern Association, 1884; charter franchise. Disbanded with league during 1884 season.

Allentown
Eastern Inter-State League, 1889; new franchise. Disbanded during 1889 season.

Allentown
Pennsylvania State League, mid-1890; relocated franchise. Had been LANCASTER, 1890. Disbanded during 1890 season.

Allentown
Eastern League, mid-1894; relocated franchise. Had been BINGHAMTON BINGOS, 1892–mid-1894. Disbanded after 1884 season.

Allentown
Tri-State League (B), 1912–1914; new franchise. Disbanded with league after 1914 season.

Allentown
Atlantic League (D), 1916; charter franchise. Disbanded after 1916 season.

Allentown
Central League, 1888; charter franchise. Disbanded with league after 1888 season.

Allentown Brooks
New York–Pennsylvania League (A), 1936; relocated franchise. Had been READING BROOKS, 1933–1935. Disbanded after 1936 season.

Allentown Buffaloes
Eastern League (A), 1931–mid-1932; renamed franchise. Had been ALLENTOWN DUKES, 1929–1930. Disbanded during 1932 season.

Allentown Cardinals
Eastern League (A), 1954–1956; new franchise. Disbanded after 1956 season.

Allentown Cards (aka Cardinals)
Inter-State League (B), 1944–1952; renamed franchise. Had been ALLENTOWN FLEETWINGS, 1940–1943. Disbanded with league after 1952 season.

Allentown Chiefs
Eastern League (A), 1957; relocated franchise. Had been SYRACUSE CHIEFS, 1934–mid-1957. Renamed ALLENTOWN RED SOX, 1958.

Allentown Colts
Pennsylvania State League, 1892–1894; charter franchise. Became EASTON, mid-1894.

Allentown Dukes
Eastern League (A), 1929–1930; new franchise. Renamed ALLENTOWN BUFFALOES, 1931.

Allentown Dukes
Inter-State League (B), 1939; charter franchise. Renamed ALLENTOWN FLEETWINGS, 1940.

Allentown Fleetwings
Inter-State League (B), 1940–1943; renamed franchise. Had been ALLENTOWN DUKES, 1939. Renamed ALLENTOWN CARDS, 1944.

Allentown Goobers
Pennsylvania State League, mid-1895; relocated franchise. Had been POTTSVILLE COLTS, 1894–mid-1895. Became READING ACTIVES, mid-1895.

Allentown Lumber City
Pennsylvania State Association, 1887; new franchise. Disbanded with league during 1887 season.

Allentown Peanuts
Atlantic League, 1898–1900; new franchise. Disbanded with league during 1900 season.

Allentown Red Sox
Eastern League (A), 1958–1960; renamed franchise. Had been ALLENTOWN CHIEFS, 1957. Disbanded after 1960 season.

ALLIANCE–SEBRING, OH

Alliance–Sebring
Ohio–Pennsylvania League (D), 1912; charter franchise. Disbanded during 1912 season.

ALPINE, TX

Alpine Cowboys
Sophomore League (D), 1959–1961; new franchise. Disbanded with league after 1961 season.

ALTON, IL

Alton Blues
Illinois–Iowa–Indiana League (D), 1917; new franchise. Disbanded with league during 1917 season.

ALTOONA, PA

Altoona
Pennsylvania State Association, 1886–1887; charter franchise. Disbanded with league during 1887 season.

Altoona
Western Pennsylvania Association, 1889; charter franchise. Disbanded with league after 1889 season.

Altoona
Pennsylvania State League, 1892–1894; charter franchise. Became LANCASTER CHICKS, mid-1894.

Altoona Engineers
Middle Atlantic League (D), mid-1931; relocated franchise. Had been JEANETTE JAYS, 1926–mid-1931. Became BEAVER FALLS BEAVERS, mid-1931.

Altoona Mountain City
Eastern Inter-State League, 1889–1890; charter franchise. Disbanded with league during 1890 season.

Altoona Mountaineers
Tri-State League (D), 1907–1909; charter franchise. Renamed ALTOONA RAMS, 1910.

Altoona Rams
Tri-State League (D), 1910–mid-1912; renamed franchise. Had been ALTOONA MOUNTAINEERS, 1907–1909. Became READING, mid-1912.

Altoona Unions
Union Association, 1884; charter franchise. Disbanded with association during 1884 season.

ALTUS, OK

Altus Orphans
Texas–Oklahoma League (D), 1911; charter franchise. Disbanded during 1911 season.

AMARILLO, TX

Amarillo Broncs
Western League (A), 1928; renamed franchise. Had been AMARILLO TEXANS, 1927. Disbanded after 1928 season.

Amarillo Gassers
West Texas League (D), 1922; expansion franchise. Panhandle Pecos Valley League (D), 1923; charter franchise. Disbanded with league during 1923 season.

Amarillo Giants
Texas League (AA), 1968–1970; renamed franchise. Had been AMARILLO SONICS, 1965–1967. Dixie Association (C), 1971; charter franchise. Texas League (AA), 1972–1974; charter franchise. Became LAFAYETTE DRILLERS (LAFAYETTE, LA), 1975.

Amarillo Gold Sox
West Texas–New Mexico League (C), 1939–mid-1942; charter franchise. Disbanded with league during 1942 season.

Amarillo Gold Sox
West Texas–New Mexico League (D), 1946–1953; (C), 1954; (B), 1955; charter franchise. Western League (A), 1956–1958; expansion franchise. Texas League (AA), 1959–1963; new franchise. Disbanded after 1963 season.

Amarillo Gold Sox
Texas League (AA), 1976–1982; relocated franchise. Had been ALEXANDRIA ACES, 1972–1975. Became BEAUMONT GOLDEN GATORS, 1983.

Amarillo Sonics
Texas League (AA), 1965–1967; new franchise. Renamed AMARILLO GIANTS, 1968.

Amarillo Texans
Western League (A), 1927; new franchise. Renamed AMARILLO BRONCS, 1928.

AMERICUS, GA

Americus Cardinals
Georgia–Florida League (D), 1935–1938; charter franchise. Renamed AMERICUS PIONEERS, 1939.

Americus Muckalees
Empire State League (GA) (D), 1913; charter franchise. Georgia State League (D), 1914–mid-1915; charter franchise. Became GAINESVILLE SHARKS, Flag League, mid-1915.

Americus Pallbearers
Georgia State League (D), 1906; charter franchise. Disbanded during 1906 season.

Americus Phillies
Georgia–Florida League (D), 1946–1950; charter franchise. Renamed AMERICUS REBELS, 1951.

Americus Pioneers
Georgia–Florida League (D), 1939–1942; renamed franchise. Had been AMERICUS CARDINALS, 1935–1938. Suspended operations after 1942 season, and did not rejoin when league resumed, 1946.

Americus Rebels
Georgia–Florida League (D), 1951; renamed franchise. Had been AMERICUS PHILLIES, 1946–1950. Disbanded after 1951 season.

AMERICUS–CORDELE, GA
(See also CORDELE, GA)

Americus–Cordele Orioles
Georgia–Florida League (D), 1954; new franchise. Disbanded after 1954 season.

AMSTERDAM, NY
(See also: GLOVERSVILLE, NY and JOHNSTOWN, NY)

Amsterdam
New York State League, 1894; charter franchise. Disbanded with league during 1894 season.

Amsterdam Red Stockings
New York State League, 1895; new franchise. Disbanded during 1895 season.

Amsterdam Rugmakers
Canadian–American League (C), 1938–1942; 1946–1951; new franchise. Disbanded with league after 1951 season.

ANACONDA, MT

Anaconda Serpents
Montana State League, 1900; new franchise. Disbanded with league after 1900 season.

ANADARKO, OK

Anadarko
Oklahoma State League (D), 1912; charter franchise. Became ENID, mid-1912.

ANAHEIM, CA

Anaheim Aces
California League (C), 1941; charter franchise. Disbanded after 1941 season.

Anaheim Valencias
Sunset League, 1947–1948; charter franchise. Became SAN BERNARDINO VALENCIAS, mid-1948.

CALIFORNIA ANGELS
American League, 1965–(still in existence as of 5-1-92); renamed franchise. Had been LOS ANGELES ANGELS, 1961–1964.

Orange County
California League (D), 1929; charter franchise. Became POMONA, mid-1929.

ANDALUSIA, AL

Andalusia Arrows
Alabama State League (D), 1947–1950; new franchise. Disbanded with league after 1950 season.

Andalusia Bulldogs
Alabama–Florida League (D), 1937–1938; renamed franchise. Had been ANDALUSIA REDS, mid-1936. Renamed ANDALUSIA RAMS, 1939.

Andalusia Dodgers
Alabama–Florida League (D), mid-1962; relocated franchise. Had been OZARK DODGERS, 1962. Disbanded with league after 1962 season.

Andalusia Rams
Alabama–Florida League (D), 1939; renamed franchise. Had been ANDALUSIA BULLDOGS, 1937–1938. Alabama State League (D), 1940–1941; charter franchise. Disbanded with league after 1941 season.

Andalusia Reds
Alabama–Florida League (D), mid-1936; charter franchise. Renamed ANDALUSIA BULLDOGS, 1937.

ANDALUSIA–OPP, AL

Andalusia–Opp Arrows
Alabama–Florida League (D), 1953; new franchise. Renamed ANDALUSIA–OPP INDIANS, 1954.

Andalusia–Opp Indians
Alabama–Florida League (D), 1954; renamed franchise. Had been ANDALUSIA–OPP ARROWS, 1953. Disbanded after 1954 season.

ANDERSON, IN

Anderson
Indiana State League, 1890; charter franchise. Disbanded during 1890 season.

Anderson
Western Inter-State League, mid-1890; relocated franchise. Had been LAFAYETTE, 1890. Disbanded during 1890 season.

Anderson
Western Inter-State League, mid-1895; relocated franchise. Had been LAFAYETTE, 1895. Disbanded during 1895 season.

Anderson
Indiana State League, 1896; charter franchise. Disbanded with league after 1896 season.

Anderson
Indiana–Illinois League, 1899; charter franchise. Became KOKOMO, mid-1899.

Anderson
Indiana State League, 1900; relocated franchise. Had been COLUMBUS SENATORS (OHIO), mid-1899–mid-1900. Disbanded with league during 1900 season.

Anderson
Central League (D), 1903; charter franchise. Became GRAND RAPIDS ORPHANS, mid-1903.

Anderson
Inter-State Association (D), 1906; charter franchise. Disbanded with association during 1906 season.

Anderson
Northern State League of Indiana (D), mid-1911; relocated fran-

chise. Had been LOGANSPORT WHITECAPS, 1911. Disbanded during 1911 season.

ANDERSON, SC

Anderson A's
Tri-State League (B), 1946; charter franchise. Renamed ANDERSON REBELS, 1947.

Anderson Braves
South Atlantic League (A), 1980–1984; charter franchise. Disbanded after 1984 season.

Anderson Electricians
South Carolina League (D), 1907; charter franchise. Disbanded during 1907 season.

Anderson Electricians
Carolina Association (D), 1908–1912; charter franchise. Disbanded with league after 1912 season.

Anderson Electricians
Palmetto League (D), 1931; charter franchise. Became SPARTANBURG SPARTANS, mid-1931.

Anderson Giants
Western Carolinas League (A), 1972; renamed franchise. Had been ANDERSON SENATORS, 1970–1971. Renamed ANDERSON TIGERS, 1973.

Anderson Mets
Western Carolinas League (A), 1974; renamed franchise. Had been ANDERSON TIGERS, 1973. Renamed ANDERSON RANGERS, 1975.

Anderson Rangers
Western Carolinas League (A), 1975; renamed franchise. Had been ANDERSON METS, 1974. Disbanded after 1975 season.

Anderson Rebels
Tri-State League (B), 1947–1954; renamed franchise. Had been ANDERSON A'S, 1946. Disbanded after 1954 season.

Anderson Senators
Western Carolinas League (A), 1970–1971; new franchise. Renamed ANDERSON GIANTS, 1972.

Anderson Tigers
Western Carolinas League (A), 1973; renamed franchise. Had been ANDERSON GIANTS, 1972. Renamed ANDERSON METS, 1974.

ANGIER– FUQUAY SPRINGS– VARINA, NC

Angier–Fuquay Springs-Varina Colts (aka Bulls)
Tobacco State League (D), 1946; charter franchise. Disbanded with league after 1946 season.

ANNISTON, AL

Anniston Models
Southeastern League (D), 1911–1912; charter franchise. Disbanded with league during 1912 season.

Anniston Moulders
Georgia–Alabama League (D), 1913–mid-1917; charter franchise. Disbanded with league during 1917 season.

Anniston Nobles
Georgia–Alabama Association (D), mid-1928; league (D), 1929–1930; charter franchise. Disbanded with league after 1930 season.

Anniston Rams
Southeastern League (B), 1938–1942; 1946–1950; expansion franchise. Disbanded with league after 1950 season.

ANSONIA, CT
(See also DERBY, CT)

Ansonia
Connecticut State League, 1891; charter franchise. Became DERBY, mid-1891.

Ansonia Cuban Giants
Connecticut State League, 1888; charter franchise. Disbanded during 1888 season.

APPLETON, WI
(Also known as FOX CITIES, WI)

Appleton Foxes
Midwest League (A), 1964; renamed franchise. Had been FOX CITIES FOXES, 1958–1963. Renamed FOX CITIES FOXES, 1965.

Appleton Foxes
Midwest League (A), 1967; renamed franchise. Had been FOX CITIES FOXES, 1965–1966. Renamed FOX CITIES FOXES, 1968.

Appleton Foxes
Midwest League (A), 1970–(still in existence as of 5-1-92); renamed franchise. Had been FOX CITIES FOXES, 1968–1969.

Appleton Papermakers
Wisconsin State League, 1891; charter franchise. Disbanded with league after 1891 season.

Appleton Papermakers
Wisconsin–Illinois League (D), 1909–1910, (C), 1911–1914; new franchise. Disbanded with league after 1914 season.

Appleton Papermakers
Wisconsin State League (D), 1940–1942; 1946–1953; charter franchise. Disbanded with league after 1953 season.

Fox Cities Foxes
Three I League (B), 1958–1961; new franchise. Midwest League (D), 1962; (A), 1963; new franchise. Renamed APPLETON FOXES, 1964.

Fox Cities Foxes
Midwest League (A), 1965–1966; renamed franchise. Renamed APPLETON FOXES, 1967.

Fox Cities Foxes
Midwest League (A), 1968–1969; renamed franchise. Renamed AP-PLETON FOXES, 1970.

ARANDAS, MEXICO

Arandas Union
Mexican Center League (A), 1977; new franchise. Disbanded after 1977 season.

ARDMORE, OK

Ardmore Ardmorites
Western Association (D), mid-1917; relocated franchise. Had been PARIS A'S (PARIS, TX), 1915–1917. Disbanded after 1917 season.

Ardmore Bearcats
Oklahoma State League (D), mid-1924; new franchise. Had been BARTLESVILLE BEARCATS, 1923–mid-1924. Became PAWHUSKA, mid-1924.

Ardmore Blues
Texas–Oklahoma League (D), 1911; charter franchise. Renamed ARDMORE GIANTS, 1912.

Ardmore Boomers
Western Association (C), 1925–mid-1926; new franchise. Became JOPLIN OZARKS, mid-1926.

Ardmore Cardinals
Sooner State League (D), 1954–1957; renamed franchise. Had been ARDMORE INDIANS, 1947–1953. Disbanded with league after 1957 season.

Ardmore Giants
Texas–Oklahoma League (D), 1912–1914; charter franchise. Had been ARDMORE BLUES, 1911. Disbanded with league during 1914 season.

Ardmore Indians
Texas League (D), mid-1904; relocated franchise. Had been PARIS PARASITES (PARIS, TX), 1904. Disbanded after 1904 season.

Ardmore Indians
Sooner State League (D), 1947–1953; charter franchise. Renamed ARDMORE CARDINALS, 1954.

Ardmore Peps
Texas–Oklahoma League (D), 1921–1922; charter franchise. Disbanded with league during 1922 season.

Ardmore Rosebuds
Texas League (AA), mid-1961; relocated franchise. Had been VICTORIA ROSEBUDS (VICTORIA, TX), 1958–mid-1961. Disbanded after 1961 season.

Ardmore Snappers
Western Association (C), 1923; new franchise. Disbanded after 1923 season.

ARGENTA, AR

Argenta
Arkansas State League (D), 1908–1909; charter franchise. Disbanded with league after 1909 season.

ARIZONA TEAMS
(Based in MESA and PEORIA)

Arizona Angels
Arizona League (R), 1988–(still in existence as of 5-1-92); renamed franchise.

Arizona Athletics
Arizona League (R), 1988–(still in existence as of 5-1-92); charter franchise.

Arizona Brewers
Arizona League (R), 1988–(still in existence as of 5-1-92); charter franchise.

Arizona Cardinals
Arizona League (R), 1988–(still in existence as of 5-1-92); charter franchise.

Arizona Giants
Arizona League (R), 1988–(still in existence as of 5-1-92); charter franchise.

Arizona Mariners
Arizona League (R), 1988–(still in existence as of 5-1-92); charter franchise.

Arizona Padres
Arizona League (R), 1988–(still in existence as of 5-1-92); charter franchise.

ARKANSAS CITY, KS

Arkansas City
Kansas State League, 1887; charter franchise. Disbanded with league during 1887 season.

Arkansas City
Oklahoma–Kansas League (D), 1916; charter franchise. Disbanded after 1916 season.

Arkansas City Grays
Kansas State League (D), 1909; charter franchise. Became WIN-FIELD, mid-1909.

Arkansas City Grays
Kansas State League (D), 1910; charter franchise. Oklahoma–Kansas League (D), 1911; charter franchise. Disbanded after 1911 season.

Arkansas City Osages
Southwestern Association (D), 1924–1926; charter franchise. Disbanded with league after 1926 season.

ARLINGTON, TX

Dallas–Fort Worth Spurs
Texas League (AA), 1965–1970; new franchise. Had been DALLAS RANGERS, 1964, and Fort Worth Cats, 1964. Dixie Association (C), 1971; charter franchise. Disbanded after 1971 season.

TEXAS RANGERS

American League, 1972–(still in existence as of 5-1-92); relocated franchise. Had been WASHINGTON SENATORS, 1961–1971.

ARTESIA, NM

Artesia Dodgers
Sophomore League (D), 1961; renamed franchise. Had been ARTESIA GIANTS, 1958–1960. Disbanded with league after 1961 season.

Artesia Drillers
Longhorn League (C), 1951–1953; new franchise. Renamed ARTESIA NUMEXERS, 1954.

Artesia Giants
Sophomore League (D), 1958–1960; charter franchise. Renamed ARTESIA DODGERS, 1961.

Artesia Numexers
Longhorn League (C), 1954–1955; renamed franchise. Had been ARTESIA DRILLERS, 1951–1953. Disbanded with league after 1955 season.

ASBURY PARK, NJ

Asbury Park
New Jersey State League, 1897; charter franchise. Disbanded with league after 1897 season.

Asbury Park Seagulls
Atlantic League (D), 1914; charter franchise. Became BLOOMFIELD, mid-1914.

ASHEVILLE, NC

Asheville Moonshiners
Southeastern League (D), mid-1896–1897; relocated franchise. Had been COLUMBUS BABIES, 1896. Disbanded with league after 1897 season.

Asheville Moonshiners
Western North Carolina League (D), 1909; charter franchise. Southeastern League (D), 1910; charter franchise. Appalachian League (D), 1911–1912; charter franchise. Became MIDDLESBORO COLONELS, 1913.

Asheville Mountaineers
North Carolina State League (D), 1913–1915; charter franchise. Renamed ASHEVILLE TOURISTS, 1916.

Asheville Orioles
Southern League (AA), 1972–1975; new franchise. Became ASHEVILLE TOURISTS, 1976.

Asheville Skylanders
South Atlantic Association (B), 1924; expansion franchise. Renamed ASHEVILLE TOURISTS, 1925.

Asheville Tourists
North Carolina State League (D), 1916–mid-1917; renamed franchise. Had been ASHEVILLE MOUNTAINEERS, 1913–1915. Disbanded with league during 1917 season.

Asheville Tourists
South Atlantic Association (B), 1925–1930; renamed franchise. Had been ASHEVILLE SKYLANDERS, 1924. Piedmont League (C), 1931; (B), 1932; new franchise. Disbanded during 1932 season.

Asheville Tourists
Piedmont League (C), mid-1934–1942; relocated franchise. Had been COLUMBIA SANDLAPPERS, 1934. Disbanded after 1934 season; replaced by relocated GREENSBORO PATRIOTS. Became LYNCHBURG CARDINALS, 1943.

Asheville Tourists
Tri-State League (B), 1946–1955; charter franchise. Disbanded with league after 1955 season.

Asheville Tourists
South Atlantic League (A), 1959–1962; (AA), 1963; new franchise. Southern League (AA), 1964–1966; charter franchise. Carolina League (A), 1967; new franchise. Southern League (AA), 1968–1970; new franchise. Dixie Association (C), 1971; charter franchise. Disbanded with association after 1971 season.

Asheville Tourists
Western Carolinas League (A), 1976–1979; new franchise. Had been ASHEVILLE ORIOLES, Southern League, 1972–1975. South Atlantic League (A), 1980–(still in existence as of 5-1-92); charter franchise.

ASHLAND, KY

Ashland Colonels
Mountain State League (D), 1939; new franchise. Became ASHLAND–CATLETTSBURG COLONELS, 1940.

Ashland Colonels
Mountain State League (D), 1942; new franchise. Had been ASHLAND–CATLETTSBURG COLONELS, 1940–1941. Disbanded with league after 1942 season.

ASHLAND–CATLETTSBURG, KY

Ashland–Catlettsburg Colonels
Mountain State League (D), 1940–1941; Relocated franchise. Had been ASHLAND COLONELS, 1939. Became ASHLAND COLONELS, 1942.

Ashland–Catlettsburg Twins
Virginia Valley League (D), 1910; charter franchise. Mountain State League (D), 1911–1912; charter franchise. Disbanded during 1912 season.

ASHLAND, PA

Ashland
Central Pennsylvania League, mid-1887–mid-1888; expansion franchise. Became EASTON, mid-1888.

Ashland
Pennsylvania State League, mid-1894; relocated franchise. Had been EASTON, mid-1894. Disbanded after 1894 season.

Ashland
Central Pennsylvania League, mid-1896; relocated franchise. Had been MOUNT CARMEL, 1896. Disbanded during 1896 season.

ASPEN, CO

Aspen
Colorado State League, 1889; charter franchise. Disbanded during 1889 season.

Aspen
Colorado State League, 1895–1896; charter franchise. Disbanded with league after 1896 season.

Aspen
Colorado State League, 1898–1899; charter franchise. Disbanded with league after 1899 season.

ATCHISON, KS

Atchison
Kansas State League, 1895; charter franchise. Disbanded during 1895 season.

Atchison
Kansas State League, 1896; charter franchise. Disbanded with league during 1896 season.

Atchison
Kansas State League, 1898; charter franchise. Disbanded during 1898 season.

ATKINS, AR

Atkins
Western Arkansas League (D), 1924; charter franchise. Disbanded with league after 1924 season.

ATLANTA, GA

Atlanta
Southern League, mid-1889; relocated franchise. Had been CHARLESTON SEAGULLS, 1889. Disbanded with league during 1889 season.

Atlanta Atlantas
Southern League, 1885–mid-1886; charter franchise. Disbanded with league during 1886 season.

Atlanta Atlantas
Southern League, 1889; charter franchise. Disbanded during 1889 season.

Atlanta Atlantas
Southern League, mid-1894; relocated franchise. Had been MOBILE BLUEBIRDS, 1894. Disbanded with league during 1894 season.

ATLANTA BLACK CRACKERS
Negro American League, 1938; new franchise. Disbanded after 1938 season.

ATLANTA BRAVES
National League, 1966–(still in existence as of 5-1-92); relocated franchise. Had been MILWAUKEE BRAVES, 1953–1965.

Atlanta Colts
Southern League, 1898; charter franchise. Disbanded with league after 1898 season.

Atlanta Crackers
Southeastern League, 1896–1897; charter franchise. Disbanded with league after 1897 season.

Atlanta Crackers
Southern Association (A), 1903–mid-1918; renamed franchise. Had been ATLANTA FIREMEN, 1902. Disbanded during 1918 season. Southern Association (A), 1919–1961; charter franchise. Disbanded with association after 1961 season.

Atlanta Crackers
International League (AAA), 1962–1965; relocated franchise. Had been JERSEY CITY JERSEYS, 1960–1961. Disbanded after 1965 season.

Atlanta Firecrackers
Southern League, 1892; charter franchise. Renamed ATLANTA WINDJAMMERS, 1893.

Atlanta Firemen
Southern Association (A), 1902; relocated franchise. Had been SELMA CHRISTIANS, 1901. Renamed ATLANTA CRACKERS, 1903.

Atlanta Windjammers
Southern League, 1893; renamed franchise. Had been ATLANTA FIRECRACKERS, 1892. Disbanded with league during 1893 season.

ATLANTIC, IA

Atlantic
Southwest Iowa (D), 1903; charter franchise. Disbanded with league after 1903 season.

ATLANTIC CITY, NJ

Atlantic City
Eastern League, mid-1885; relocated franchise. Had been WILMINGTON BLUE HENS (WILMINGTON, DE), 1885. Disbanded during 1885 season.

Atlantic City
Eastern Inter-State League, 1889; charter franchise. Disbanded with league during 1889 season.

Atlantic City
New Jersey State League, 1897; charter franchise. Disbanded with league after 1897 season.

Atlantic City
Tri-State League (B), mid-1912–1913; relocated franchise. Had been LANCASTER RED ROSES (LANCASTER, PA), 1907–mid-1912. Disbanded after 1913 season.

BACHARACH GIANTS
Eastern Colored League, 1923-1928; charter franchise. Disbanded with league during 1928 season. American Negro League, 1929; charter franchise. Disbanded with league after 1929 season. Negro National League, mid–1934; new franchise. Disbanded after 1934 season.

ATTALLA, AL
(See ALABAMA CITY, AL)

ATTLEBORO, MA

Attleboro
New England League (B), 1933; charter franchise. Became LAWRENCE (MA), mid-1933.

Attleboro Angels
Atlantic Association (D), 1908; charter franchise. Disbanded with league after 1908 season.

Attleboro Burros
New England League (B), 1928; new franchise. Disbanded after 1928 season.

AUBURN, ME
(See LEWISTON, ME)

AUBURN, NE

Auburn A's
MINK (D), 1910–1913; charter franchise. Disbanded with league during 1913 season.

AUBURN, NY

Auburn
League Alliance, 1877; charter franchise. Disbanded with alliance during 1877 season.

Auburn
National Association, 1878; charter franchise. Disbanded with association after 1878 season.

Auburn
New York State League, 1888–1889; charter franchise. Disbanded after 1899 season.

Auburn
New York State League, 1897; charter franchise. Named AUBURN MAROONS, 1898.

Auburn
Empire State League (C), 1908; charter franchise. Disbanded with league after 1908 season.

Auburn Astros
New York–Pennsylvania League (A), 1982–(still in existence as of 5-1-92); renamed franchise. Had been AUBURN PHILLIES, 1980–1981.

Auburn Bouleys
Canadian–American League (C), 1938; relocated franchise. Had been SMITHS FALLS BEAVERS, 1937. Became UTICA BRAVES, 1939.

Auburn Cayugas
Border League (C), 1946–mid-1951; charter franchise. Disbanded during 1951 season.

Auburn Maroons
New York State League, 1898; named franchise. Had been AUBURN, 1897. Renamed AUBURN PRISONERS, 1899.

Auburn Mets
New York–Pennsylvania League (D), 1962; (A), 1963–1966; renamed franchise. Had been AUBURN YANKEES, 1958–1961. Renamed AUBURN TWINS, 1967.

Auburn Phillies
New York–Pennsylvania League (A), 1972–1977; renamed franchise. Had been AUBURN TWINS, 1967–1971. Renamed AUBURN SUNSETS, 1978.

Auburn Phillies
New York–Pennsylvania League (A), 1980–1981; renamed franchise. Had been AUBURN RED STARS, 1979. Renamed AUBURN ASTROS, 1982.

Auburn Prisoners
New York State League, 1899; renamed franchise. Had been AUBURN MAROONS, 1898. Became TROY WASHERWOMEN, mid-1899.

Auburn Red Stars
New York–Pennsylvania League (A), 1979; renamed franchise. Had been AUBURN SUNSETS, 1978. Renamed AUBURN PHILLIES, 1980.

Auburn Sunsets
New York–Pennsylvania League (A), 1978; renamed franchise. Had been AUBURN PHILLIES, 1972–1977. Renamed AUBURN RED STARS, 1979.

Auburn Twins
New York–Pennsylvania League (A), 1967–1971; renamed franchise. Had been AUBURN METS, 1962–1966. Renamed AUBURN PHILLIES, 1972.

Auburn Yankees
New York–Pennsylvania League (A), 1958–1961; new franchise. Renamed AUBURN METS, 1962.

AUGUSTA, GA

Augusta
Southern League, 1898; charter franchise. Disbanded after 1898 season.

Augusta Browns
Southern League, 1885–mid-1886; charter franchise. Disbanded during 1886 season.

Augusta Confederate Yankees
South Atlantic League (C), 1962; (AA), 1963; new franchise. Disbanded with league after 1963 season.

Augusta Dollies
South Atlantic Association (C), 1919; charter franchise. Renamed AUGUSTA GEORGIANS, 1920.

Augusta Dudes
Alternate name for AUGUSTA ELECTRICIANS, 1893.

Augusta Electricians (aka Dudes)
Southern League, 1893; new franchise. Disbanded with league during 1893 season.

Augusta Georgians
South Atlantic Association (C), 1920/League (B), 1921; renamed franchise. Had been AUGUSTA DOLLIES, 1919. Renamed AUGUSTA TYGERS, 1922.

Augusta Pirates
South Atlantic League (A), 1988– (still in existence as of 5-1-92); new franchise.

Augusta Rams
South Atlantic League (B), 1953–1954; renamed franchise. Had been AUGUSTA TIGERS, 1936–1942; 1946–1952. Renamed AUGUSTA TIGERS, 1955.

Augusta Tigers
South Atlantic League (B), 1955–1958; renamed franchise. Had been AUGUSTA RAMS, 1953–1954. Disbanded after 1958 season.

Augusta Tigers
South Atlantic Association (B), 1923; renamed franchise. Had been AUGUSTA TYGERS, 1922. Renamed AUGUSTA TYGERS, 1924.

Augusta Tigers
South Atlantic League (B), 1936–1942; (A), 1946–1952; charter franchise. Renamed AUGUSTA RAMS, 1953.

Augusta Tourists
South Atlantic League (C), 1904–mid-1911; charter franchise. Disbanded during 1911 season.

Augusta Tourists
South Atlantic League (C), 1914–mid-1917; new franchise. Disbanded with league during 1917 season.

Augusta Tygers
South Atlantic Association (B), 1924–1929; renamed franchise. Had been AUGUSTA TIGERS, 1923. Renamed AUGUSTA WOLVES, 1930.

Augusta Tygers
South Atlantic Association (B), 1922; renamed franchise. Had been AUGUSTA GEORGIANS, 1919–1921.

Augusta Wolves
South Atlantic Association (B), 1930; renamed franchise. Had been AUGUSTA TYGERS, 1924–1929. Palmetto League (D), 1931; charter franchise. Disbanded with league during 1931 season.

AUGUSTA, ME

Augusta
Maine State League, 1897; charter franchise. Disbanded with league after 1897 season.

Augusta
New England League, 1901; charter franchise. Became LYNN, mid-1901.

Augusta Kennebecs
New England League, 1895–1896; charter franchise. Disbanded during 1896 season.

AURORA, IL

Aurora
Western Inter-State League, 1895; charter franchise. Disbanded with league during 1895 season.

Aurora Blues
Wisconsin–Illinois League (C), 1911–1912; renamed franchise. Had been AURORA ISLANDERS, 1910. Disbanded after 1912 season.

Aurora Foxes
Bi-State League (WI-IL), (D), 1915; charter franchise. Disbanded with league during 1915 season.

Aurora Hoodoos
Illinois–Iowa League, 1890–mid-1891; charter franchise. Disbanded during 1891 season.

Aurora Hoodoos
Illinois–Iowa League, mid-1892; relocated franchise. Had been PEORIA CANARIES, 1892. Disbanded with league after 1892 season.

Aurora Islanders
Wisconsin–Illinois League (D), 1910; charter franchise. Renamed AURORA BLUES, 1911.

AUSTIN, TX

Austin
Middle Texas League (D), 1915; new franchise. Became TAYLOR, mid-1915.

Austin Beavers
Alternate name for AUSTIN SENATORS, 1895.

Austin Braves
Texas League (AA), 1961; renamed franchise. Had been AUSTIN SENATORS, 1956–1960. Renamed AUSTIN SENATORS, 1962.

Austin Pioneers
Big State League (B), 1947–1955; charter franchise. Disbanded after 1955 season.

Austin Rangers
Texas Association (D), 1923–1924; charter franchise. Renamed AUSTIN SENATORS, 1925.

Austin Senators
Texas League, 1888; charter franchise. Became SAN ANTONIO MISSIONS, mid-1888.

Austin Senators
Texas League, 1889; new franchise. Disbanded during 1889 season.

Austin Senators
Texas League, 1890; new franchise. Disbanded during 1890 season.

Austin Senators (aka Beavers)
Texas Southern League, 1895; charter franchise. Disbanded during 1895 season.

Austin Senators
Texas Southern League, 1896–1898; charter franchise. Texas League, 1899; charter franchise. Disbanded with league during 1899 season.

Austin Senators
Texas League (D), 1905; expansion franchise. Disbanded during 1905 season.

Austin Senators
South Texas League (C), 1906; expansion franchise. Texas League (C), 1907–1908; new franchise. Became OKLAHOMA CITY METS, 1909.

Austin Senators
Texas League (B), 1911–1914; relocated franchise. Had been SHREVEPORT PIRATES, 1908–1910. Became SHREVEPORT GASSERS, 1915.

Austin Senators
Texas Association (D), 1925–1926; renamed franchise. Had been AUSTIN RANGERS, 1923–1924. Disbanded with league after 1926 season.

Austin Senators
Texas League (AA), 1956–1960; new franchise. Renamed AUSTIN BRAVES, 1961.

Austin Senators
Texas League (AA), 1962–1967; renamed franchise. Had been AUSTIN BRAVES, 1961. Became SHREVEPORT BRAVES, 1968.

AYDEN, NC

Ayden Aces
Coastal Plain League (D), 1937–1938; charter franchise. Disbanded after 1938 season.

BAINBRIDGE, GA

Bainbridge
Dixie League (D), 1916–mid-1917; charter franchise. Disbanded with league during 1917 season.

BAJA CALIFORNIA

(See ENSENADA, BAJA CALIFORNIA, MEXICO; MEXICALI, MEXICO)

BAKER, OR

Baker
Pacific Inter-State League, 1891; charter franchise. Disbanded with league after 1891 season.

Baker Goldiggers (aka Miners)
Western Tri-State League (D), mid-1913; relocated franchise. Had been LAGRANDE SPUDS, 1912–mid-1913. Renamed BAKER MINERS, 1914.

Baker Miners
Alternate name for BAKER GOLDIGGERS, 1913.

Baker Miners (aka Kubs)
Western Tri-State League (D), 1914; renamed franchise. Had been BAKER GOLDIGGERS, mid-1913. Disbanded with league after 1914 season.

Baker Nuggets
Inland Empire League (D), 1908; charter franchise. Disbanded with league after 1908 season.

BAKERSFIELD, CA

Bakersfield Badgers
California League (C), 1941–1942; charter franchise. Suspended operations with league after 1942 season, and resumed as BAKERSFIELD INDIANS, 1946.

Bakersfield Bears
California League (C), 1957–1962; (A), 1963–1967; renamed franchise. Had been BAKERSFIELD BOOSTERS, 1956. Renamed BAKERSFIELD DODGERS, 1968.

Bakersfield Bees
California State League (D), 1929; charter franchise. Disbanded with league during 1929 season.

Bakersfield Boosters
California League (C), 1956; renamed franchise. Had been BAKERSFIELD INDIANS, 1946–1955. Renamed BAKERSFIELD BEARS, 1957.

Bakersfield Dodgers
California League (A), 1968–1975; renamed franchise. Had been BAKERSFIELD BEARS, 1957–1967. Disbanded after 1975 season.

Bakersfield Dodgers
California League (A) 1984–(still in existence as of 5-1-92); renamed franchise. Had been BAKERSFIELD MARINERS, 1982–1983.

Bakersfield Drillers
San Joaquin Valley League (D), 1910; charter franchise. Disbanded with league after 1910 season.

Bakersfield Indians
California League (C), 1946–1955; charter franchise. Renamed BAKERSFIELD BOOSTERS, 1956.

Bakersfield Mariners
California League (A), 1982–1983; new franchise. Renamed BAKERSFIELD DODGERS, 1984.

Bakersfield Outlaws
California League (A), 1978–1979; new franchise. Disbanded after 1979 season.

BALLARD, WA

Ballard Colts
Northwestern League (B), 1914; relocated franchise. Had been PORTLAND COLTS (PORTLAND, OR), 1912–mid-1914. Disbanded after 1914 season.

BALLINGER, TX

Ballinger
West Texas League (D), 1905; charter franchise. Disbanded with league after 1905 season.

Ballinger Bearcats
West Texas League (D), 1921; relocated franchise. Had been MINERAL WELLS RESORTERS, 1920–mid-1921. Disbanded after 1921 season.

Ballinger Bearcats
West Texas League (D), 1929; new franchise. Disbanded after 1929 season.

Ballinger Cats
Longhorn League (D), 1947–1950; charter franchise. Disbanded after 1950 season.

Ballinger Westerners
Southwestern League (B), 1956–1957; charter franchise. Disbanded with league after 1957 season.

BALLINGER–WINTERS, TX

Ballinger–Winters Eagles
Longhorn League (D), mid-1953; relocated franchise. Had been LAMESA LOBOS, 1950–mid-1953. Disbanded with league after 1953 season.

BALTIMORE, MD

Baltimore
Eastern League, 1884; charter franchise. Became LANCASTER LANCASTERS, mid-1884.

BALTIMORE BALTFEDS
Alternate name for BALTIMORE TERRAPINS, 1914–1915.

BALTIMORE BLACK SOX
Eastern Colored League, 1923–1928; charter franchise. Disbanded with league during 1928 season. American Negro League, 1929. Disbanded with league during 1929 season. East–West League, 1932; charter franchise. Disbanded with league during 1932 season. Negro National League, 1933–1934; new franchise. Disbanded after 1934 season.

BALTIMORE ELITE GIANTS
Negro National League, 1938–1948; relocated franchise. Had been WASHINGTON ELITE GIANTS, 1936–1937. Negro American League, 1949–1950; new franchise. Disbanded with league after 1950 season.

BALTIMORE LORD BALTIMORES
National Association, 1872–1874; new franchise. Disbanded after 1874 season.

BALTIMORE MARYLANDS
Alternate name for BALTIMORE LORD BALTIMORES, 1873.

BALTIMORE MONUMENTALS
Union Association, 1884; charter franchise. Became LANCASTER IRONSIDES, mid-1884.

BALTIMORE ORIOLES
American Association, 1883–1889; renamed franchise. Had been LORD BALTIMORES, 1882.

Baltimore Orioles
Atlantic Association, 1890; charter franchise. Disbanded with league after 1890 season.

BALTIMORE ORIOLES
National League, 1892–1899; new franchise. Disbanded after 1899 season.

BALTIMORE ORIOLES
American League, 1901–1902; charter franchise. Became NEW YORK YANKEES, 1903.

Baltimore Orioles
Eastern League (A), 1903–1907; (AA), 1908–1911; new franchise. International League (AA), 1912–1914; charter franchise. Became RICHMOND CLIMBERS, 1915.

Baltimore Orioles
(New) International League (AA), 1916–1945; (AAA), 1946–1953; new franchise. Disbanded after 1953 season.

BALTIMORE ORIOLES
American League, 1954–(still in existence as of 5-1-92); relocated franchise. Had been ST. LOUIS BROWNS, 1902–1953.

BALTIMORE TERRAPINS
Federal League, 1914; expansion franchise. Disbanded with league, 1915.

LORD BALTIMORES
National Association, 1872; expansion franchise. Renamed MARYLAND OF BALTIMORE, 1873.

LORD BALTIMORES
American Association, 1882; new franchise. Became BALTIMORE ORIOLES, 1883.

MARYLAND OF BALTIMORE
National Association, 1873; renamed franchise. Had been LORD BALTIMORES, 1872. Disbanded after 1874 season.

BANGOR, ME

Bangor
Maine State League, 1897; charter franchise. Disbanded with league after 1897 season.

Bangor Maroons
New Brunswick–Maine League (D), 1913; charter franchise. Disbanded during 1913 season.

Bangor Millionaires
New England League, 1894–1896; charter franchise. Disbanded after 1896 season.

Bangor Slaters
North Atlantic League (D), 1950; renamed franchise. Had been BANGOR–BERWICK SLATE PICKERS, 1949. Disbanded with league after 1950 season.

Bangor White Sox
Maine State League (D), 1907–1908; charter franchise. Disbanded with league after 1908 season.

BANGOR–BERWICK, PA

Bangor–Berwick Slate Pickers
North Atlantic League (D), 1949; new franchise. Renamed BANGOR SLATERS, 1950.

BARRE–MONTPELIER, VT

Barre–Montpelier Intercity
New Hampshire State League (D), 1907; charter franchise. Disbanded with league after 1907 season.

BARTLESVILLE, OK

Bartlesville Bearcats
Southwestern League (C), 1923–mid-1924; renamed franchise. Had been BARTLESVILLE GRAYS, 1922. Became ARDMORE BEARCATS, mid-1924.

Bartlesville Blues
Kansas State League (D), 1906; new franchise. Disbanded with league after 1906 season.

Bartlesville Blues
Western Association (C), 1937; renamed franchise. Had been BARTLESVILLE MUSTANGS, 1936. Renamed BARTLESVILLE CHIEFS, 1938.

Bartlesville Boosters
OAK League (D), 1907; charter franchise. Oklahoma–Kansas League (D), 1908; charter franchise. Disbanded with league after 1908 season.

Bartlesville Boosters
Western Association (C), 1909–mid-1910; new franchise. Disbanded during 1910 season.

Bartlesville Boosters
Western Association (C), mid-1924; relocated franchise. Had been JOPLIN MINERS, 1924. Disbanded after 1924 season.

Bartlesville Braves
Southwestern League (D), 1921; charter franchise. Renamed BARTLESVILLE GRAYS, 1922.

Bartlesville Broncos
Western League (A), mid-1933; new franchise. Disbanded during 1933 season.

Bartlesville Broncs (aka Broncos)
Western Association (C), 1931–1932; new franchise. Merged with HUTCHINSON WHEATSHOCKERS, mid-1932. Disbanded with association after 1932 season.

Bartlesville Buccaneers
Kansas–Oklahoma–Missouri League (D), 1947–1948; renamed franchise. Had been BARTLESVILLE OILERS, 1946. Renamed BARTLESVILLE PIRATES, 1949.

Bartlesville Chiefs
Western Association (C), 1938; renamed franchise. Had been BARTLESVILLE BLUES, 1937. Disbanded after 1938 season.

Bartlesville Grays
Southwestern League (C), 1922; renamed franchise. Had been BARTLESVILLE BRAVES, 1921. Renamed BARTLESVILLE BEARCATS, 1923.

Bartlesville Mustangs
Western Association (C), 1936; renamed franchise. Had been BARTLESVILLE REDS, 1934–1935. Renamed BARTLESVILLE BLUES, 1937.

Bartlesville Oilers
Kansas–Oklahoma–Missouri League (D), 1946–1948; charter franchise. Renamed BARTLESVILLE PIRATES, 1949.

Bartlesville Pirates
Kansas–Oklahoma–Missouri League (D), 1949–mid-1952; renamed franchise. Had been BARTLESVILLE OILERS, 1946–1948. Became PITTSBURG PIRATES, mid-1952.

Bartlesville Reds
Western Association (C), 1934–1935; charter franchise. Renamed BARTLESVILLE MUSTANGS, 1936.

BARTLETT, TX

Bartlett
Middle Texas League (D), 1914–1915; charter franchise. Disbanded with league after 1915 season.

BARTOW, FL

Bartow Polkers
Florida State League (D), 1920; relocated franchise. Had also represented WINTER HAVEN, 1919. Disbanded after 1920 season.

BARTOW– WINTER HAVEN, FL
(See also WINTER HAVEN, FL)

Bartow Polkers
Florida State League (D), mid-1919–1920; charter franchise. Represented only BARTOW, 1920.

BASEBALL CITY, FL
(aka Haines City, FL)

Baseball City Royals
Florida State League (A), 1988– (still in existence as of 5-1-92); new franchise.

BASSANO, ALBERTA, CANADA

Bassano Boosters
Western Canada League (D), 1912; charter franchise. Disbanded after 1912 season.

BASSETT, VA

Bassett Furnituremakers
Bi-State League (D), 1935–1940; new franchise. Disbanded after 1940 season.

Bassett Statesmen
Blue Ridge League (D), mid-1950; relocated franchise. Had been WYTHEVILLE STATESMEN, 1949–mid-1950. Disbanded with league after 1950 season.

BATAVIA, NY

Batavia Clippers
PONY League (D), 1939–1953; charter franchise. Disbanded with league after 1953 season.

Batavia Clippers
New York–Pennsylvania League (A), 1988– (still in existence as of 5-1-92); renamed franchise. Had been BATAVIA TROJANS, 1966–1987.

Batavia Indians
New York–Pennsylvania League (D), 1957–1959; new franchise. Disbanded after 1959 season.

Batavia Pirates
New York–Pennsylvania League (D), 1961–1962; (A), 1963–1965; expansion franchise. Renamed BATAVIA TROJANS, 1966.

Batavia Reds
New York State League, 1897; charter franchise. Became GENEVA, 1897.

Batavia Trojans
New York–Pennsylvania League (A), 1966–1987; renamed franchise. Had been BATAVIA PIRATES, 1961–1965. Renamed BATAVIA CLIPPERS, 1988.

BATESVILLE, AR

Batesville Cardinals
Northeast Arkansas League (C), mid-1940–1941; renamed franchise. Had been BATESVILLE PILOTS, mid-1940. Disbanded with league after 1941 season.

Batesville Pilots
Northeast Arkansas League (C), mid-1940; relocated franchise. Had been CARUTHERSVILLE PILOTS, 1937–mid-1940. Became BATESVILLE CARDINALS, mid-1940.

Batesville White Sox
Northeast Arkansas League (C), 1936; charter franchise. Disbanded after 1936 season.

Batesville White Sox
Northeast Arkansas League (C), 1938; new franchise. Disbanded after 1938 season.

BATESVILLE– NEWPORT, AR
(See also NEWPORT, AR)

Batesville–Newport
Arkansas State League (D), mid-1909; relocated franchise. Had been MONROE, 1909. Disbanded with league after 1909 season.

BATH, NY

Bath
Western New York League, 1890; charter franchise. Disbanded with league after 1890 season.

BATON ROUGE, LA

Baton Rouge
Cotton States League (D), mid-1928; relocated franchise. Had been HATTIESBURG PINETOPPERS, mid-1925–mid-1928. Disbanded after 1928 season.

Baton Rouge Cajuns
Cotton States League (D), 1902–1906; charter franchise. Disbanded after 1906 season.

Baton Rouge Cougars
Gulf States League (A), 1976; charter franchise. Disbanded with league after 1976 season.

Baton Rouge Essos
Cotton States League (D) 1929; new franchise. Renamed BATON ROUGE HIGHLANDERS, 1930.

Baton Rouge Highlanders
Cotton States League (D) 1930; renamed franchise. Had been BATON ROUGE ESSOS, 1929. Renamed BATON ROUGE STANDARDS, 1931.

Baton Rouge Rebels
Evangeline League (C), 1956–1957; renamed franchise. Had been BATON ROUGE RED STICKS, 1946–1955. Disbanded with league after 1957 season.

Baton Rouge Red Sticks
East Dixie League (C), 1934; charter franchise. Became CLARKSDALE GINNERS during 1934 season.

Baton Rouge Red Sticks

Evangeline League (D), 1946–1948; (C), 1949–1955; new franchise. Renamed BATON ROUGE REBELS, 1956.

Baton Rouge Senators

Cotton States League (D), 1932; renamed franchise. Had been BATON ROUGE STANDARDS, 1931. Disbanded with league during 1932 season.

Baton Rouge Solons

Dixie League (C), 1933; charter franchise. Disbanded with league after 1933 season.

Baton Rouge Standards

Cotton States League (D), 1931; renamed franchise. Had been BATON ROUGE HIGHLANDERS, 1930. Renamed BATON ROUGE SENATORS, 1932.

BATTLE CREEK, MI

Battle Creek

Michigan State League, 1894; new franchise. Named BATTLE CREEK ADVENTISTS, 1895.

Battle Creek

Michigan State League (D), 1902; charter franchise. Disbanded with league during 1902 season.

Battle Creek

Southern Michigan Association (D), 1906–1907; charter franchise. Named BATTLE CREEK CRICKETS, 1908.

Battle Creek Adventists

Michigan State League, 1895; named franchise. Became JACKSON JAXONS, mid-1895.

Battle Creek Belles

All-American Girls Professional Baseball League, 1951–1952; relocated franchise. Had been RACINE BELLES, 1943–1950. Disbanded after 1952 season.

Battle Creek Black Sox

Central League (C), mid-1916; relocated franchise. Had been GRAND RAPIDS BLACK SOX, 1915–mid-1916. Became GRAND RAPIDS BLACK SOX, mid-1916, after one week in Battle Creek.

Battle Creek Crickets

Southern Michigan League (D), 1908, 1910; (C), 1911–mid-1915; charter franchise. Disbanded with league during 1915 season.

Battle Creek Custers

Michigan–Ontario League (B), 1919–1920; charter franchise. Disbanded after 1920 season.

BAXLEY, GA

(See also HAZLEHURST, GA)

Baxley Red Sox

Georgia State League, (D), 1948; charter franchise. Became HAZLEHURST-BAXLEY RED SOCKS, 1949.

BAY CITY, MI

(See also SAGINAW, MI)

Bay City

Northwestern League, 1883–mid-1884; charter franchise. Became EVANSVILLE, mid-1884.

Bay City

Inter-State League, 1891; charter franchise. Disbanded with league during 1891 season.

Bay City

Northwestern League, 1891; charter franchise. Disbanded with league during 1891 season.

Bay City

Michigan State League, 1897; charter franchise. Disbanded during 1897 season.

Bay City

International League, 1898; new franchise. Disbanded during 1898 season.

Bay City

Inter-State Association (C), 1906; charter franchise. Disbanded during 1906 season.

Bay City

Southern Michigan League (D), 1907–1910; new franchise. Became BAY CITY BILLIKENS, 1911.

Bay City Beavers

Southern Michigan Association (D), 1913; 1915/League (C), 1914; new franchise. Disbanded with league during 1915 season.

Bay City Billikens

Southern Michigan League (C), 1911; (C and D), 1912; renamed franchise. Had been BAY CITY, 1907–1910. Disbanded during 1912 season.

Bay City Hyphens

(See SAGINAW, MI)

Bay City Riders

Ohio–Michigan League, 1893; charter franchise. Disbanded during 1893 season.

Bay City Wolves

Michigan–Ontario League (B), 1919–mid-1926; charter franchise. Michigan State League (D), mid-1926; charter franchise. Disbanded with league after 1926 season.

BAY CITY, TX

Bay City Rice Eaters

Southwest Texas League (D), 1910–1911; charter franchise. Disbanded with league after 1911 season.

BEARDSTOWN, IL

Beardstown

Illinois–Missouri League (D), 1909–mid-1910; new franchise. Became JACKSONVILLE JACKS, mid-1910.

BEATRICE, NE

Beatrice
MINK League (D), 1912; new franchise. Disbanded after 1912 season.

Beatrice Blues
Nebraska State League (D), 1922–1923; charter franchise. Tri-State League (D), 1924; charter franchise. Disbanded with league after 1924 season.

Beatrice Blues
Nebraska State League (D), 1928; charter franchise. Disbanded after 1928 season.

Beatrice Blues
Nebraska State League (D), mid-1932–1938; relocated franchise. Had been OMAHA, 1932. Disbanded with league after 1938 season.

Beatrice Indians
Nebraska State League, 1892; charter franchise. Disbanded with league after 1892 season.

Beatrice Milkskimmers
Nebraska State League (D), mid-1913–mid-1915; relocated franchise. Had been SEWARD STATESMEN, 1910–mid-1913. Disbanded with league during 1915 season.

Beatrice Swamp Angels
Nebraska State League, 1892; charter franchise. Disbanded with league after 1892 season.

BEAUMONT, TX

Beaumont
South Texas League (D), 1906; renamed franchise. Had been BEAUMONT MILLIONAIRES, 1904–1905. Became BRENHAM, mid-1906.

Beaumont Cubs
Gulf Coast League (D), 1908; new franchise. Disbanded with league after 1908 season.

Beaumont Exporters
Texas League (B), 1920; (A), 1921–1935; (A1), 1936–1942; (AA), 1946–1949; renamed franchise. Had been BEAUMONT OILERS, 1919. Renamed BEAUMONT ROUGHNECKS, 1950.

Beaumont Golden Gators
Texas League (AA), 1983–1985; relocated franchise. Had been AMARILLO GOLD SOX, 1976–1982. Became WICHITA PILOTS, 1986.

Beaumont Golden Gators
Texas League (AA), 1987; new franchise. Disbanded after 1987 season.

Beaumont Millionaires
South Texas League (D), 1904–1905; renamed franchise. Had been BEAUMONT BLUES, 1903. Renamed BEAUMONT ORPHANS, 1906.

Beaumont Oilers
South Texas League (D), 1906; new franchise. Disbanded after 1906 season.

Beaumont Oilers
Texas League (B), 1912–mid-1917; relocated franchise. Had been OKLAHOMA CITY INDIANS, 1909–1911. Disbanded during 1917 season.

Beaumont Oilers
Texas League (B), 1919; expansion franchise. Renamed BEAUMONT EXPORTERS, 1920.

Beaumont Oil Gushers
South Texas League (D), 1903; charter franchise. Became BEAUMONT MILLIONAIRES, 1904.

Beaumont Pirates
Big State League (B), 1957; renamed franchise. Had been BEAUMONT SHIPPERS, 1956. Disbanded with league after 1957 season.

Beaumont Roughnecks
Texas League (AA), 1950–1955; renamed franchise. Had been BEAUMONT EXPORTERS, 1920–1942; 1946–1949. Big State League (B), 1956; new franchise. Became TEXAS CITY EXPORTERS, mid-1956.

Beaumont Roughnecks
Big State League (B), mid-1956; relocated franchise. Had been TEXAS CITY EXPORTERS, mid-1956. Renamed BEAUMONT PIRATES, 1957.

BEAVER FALLS, PA

Beaver Falls
Ohio Valley League, 1891; charter franchise. Disbanded with league after 1891 season.

Beaver Falls Beavers
Western Pennsylvania League (D), 1907; charter franchise. Disbanded with league after 1907 season.

Beaver Falls Beavers
Middle Atlantic League (C), mid-1931; relocated franchise. Had been ALTOONA ENGINEERS, mid-1931. Disbanded after 1931 season.

Beaver Falls Bees
Pennsylvania State Association (D), 1937; new franchise. Renamed BEAVER FALLS BROWNS, 1938.

Beaver Falls Bees
Pennsylvania State Association (D), 1937–1941; renamed franchise. Had been BEAVER FALLS BROWNS, 1938. Disbanded with league after 1941 season.

BECKLEY, WV

Beckley Bengals
Mountain States League (D), 1937–1938; charter franchise. Disbanded after 1938 season.

Beckley Black Knights
Middle Atlantic League (C), 1931–1934; expansion franchise. Renamed BECKLEY MINERS, 1935.

Beckley Miners
Middle Atlantic League (C) 1935; renamed franchise. Had been BECKLEY BLACK KNIGHTS, 1931–1934. Disbanded after 1935 season.

BEEVILLE, TX

Beeville Bees
Gulf Coast League (D), mid-1926; charter franchise. Became LAREDO OILERS, mid-1926.

Beeville Bees
Gulf States League (A), 1976; charter franchise. Disbanded with league after 1976 season.

Beeville Blazers
Lone Star League (A), 1977; charter franchise. Disbanded with league after 1977 season.

Beeville Orange Growers
Southwest Texas League (D), 1910–1911; charter franchise. Disbanded with league after 1911 season.

BELDING, MI

Belding Champs
Michigan State League (D), 1914; relocated franchise. Had been MANISTEE CHAMPS, 1912–mid-1914. Disbanded with league after 1914 season.

BELFAST, ME

Belfast Pastimes
Maine State League (D), 1897; charter franchise. Disbanded with league after 1897 season.

BELLEVILLE, IL

Belleville Stags
Illinois State League (B), 1947–1948; charter franchise. MOV League (D), 1949; charter franchise. Disbanded after 1949 season.

BELLEVILLE, ONTARIO, CANADA

Belleville
Eastern International, 1888; charter franchise. Became BROCKVILLE, mid-1888.

BELLINGHAM, WA

Bellingham Chinooks
Western International League (B), 1938–1939; new franchise. Disbanded after 1939 season.

Bellingham Dodgers
Northwest League (A), 1973–1976; expansion franchise. Renamed BELLINGHAM MARINERS, 1977.

Bellingham Mariners
Northwest League (A), 1977–(still in existence as of 5-1-92); renamed franchise.

Bellingham Yankees
Northwestern League (B), 1905; charter franchise. Disbanded after 1905 season.

BELLOWS FALLS, VT

Bellows Falls Sulphites
Twin State League (D), 1911; charter franchise. Disbanded with league after 1911 season.

BELMONT, NC

Belmont Chiefs
Western Carolina League (D), 1961; new franchise. Disbanded after 1961 season.

BELOIT, KS

Beloit
Central Kansas League (C), 1909–mid-1910; charter franchise. Became CHAPMAN, mid-1910.

BELOIT, WI

Beloit Brewers
Midwest League (A), 1982–(still in existence as of 5-1-92); new franchise.

Beloit Collegians
Wisconsin State Association (D), 1905; charter franchise. Disbanded after 1905 season.

BELTON, TX

Belton Braves
Middle Texas League (D), mid-1914–mid-1915; charter franchise. Disbanded with league during 1915 season.

BEND, OR

Bend Phillies
Northwest League (A), 1981–1986; new franchise. Renamed CENTRAL OREGON BUCKS, 1987.

Bend Rainbows
Northwest League (A), 1970–1971; expansion franchise. Disbanded after 1971 season.

Bend Timber Hawks
Northwest League (A), 1978; new franchise. Disbanded after 1978 season.

Central Oregon Bucks
Northwest League (A), 1987–(still in existence as of 5-1-92); renamed franchise. Had been BEND PHILLIES, 1981–1986.

BENTON HARBOR, MI

Benton Harbor
Michigan State League, 1893; charter franchise. Disbanded after 1893 season.

Benton Harbor
Indiana–Michigan League (D), 1910; charter franchise. Disbanded with league after 1910 season.

BENTONVILLE, AR

Bentonville Mustangs
Arkansas–Missouri League (D), 1936; charter franchise. Disbanded after 1936 season.

Bentonville Officeholders
Arkansas State League (D), 1934–1935; charter franchise. Disbanded with league after 1935 season.

BERKELEY, CA

Berkeley
California State League (D), 1915; new franchise. Became SAN FRANCISCO, mid-1915.

Berkeley Clarions
Central California Baseball League (D), mid-1910–1911; charter franchise. Had been OAKLAND INVADERS, mid-1910. Disbanded with league after 1911 season.

BERKSHIRE, MA
(See PITTSFIELD, MA)

BERLIN, ONTARIO, CANADA

Berlin Busy Bees
Canadian League, (D), 1912–1913; renamed franchise. Had been BERLIN GREEN SOX, 1911. Disbanded with league after 1913 season.

Berlin Green Sox
Canadian League (C) 1911, (D), mid-1911; charter franchise. Renamed BERLIN BUSY BEES, 1912.

BERLIN, PA

Berlin
Pennsylvania–Maryland–West Virginia League (D), 1907; charter franchise. Disbanded with league after 1907 season.

BERRIEN SPRINGS, MI

Berrien Springs Grays
Indiana–Michigan League (D), 1910; charter franchise. Disbanded with league during 1910 season.

BERWICK, PA
(See BANGOR, PA)

BESSEMER, AL

Bessemer
Tennessee–Alabama League (D), 1904; charter franchise. Disbanded with league after 1904 season.

Bessemer Pipe Makers
Southeastern League (D), 1912; new franchise. Became CEDARTOWN, 1912.

BETTENDORF, IA
(In conjunction with Davenport, IA–Moline, IL–Rock Island, IL)

Quad Cities Angels
Midwest League (A), 1962–1978; renamed franchise. Had been QUAD CITIES BRAVES, 1960–1961. Renamed QUAD CITIES CUBS, 1979.

Quad Cities Angels
Midwest League (A), 1985–(still in existence as of 5-1-92); renamed franchise. Had been QUAD CITIES CUBS, 1979–1984.

Quad Cities Braves
Midwest League (A), 1960–1961; new franchise. Renamed QUAD CITY ANGELS, 1962.

Quad City Cubs
Three I League (B), 1946–1948; charter franchise. Renamed QUAD CITIES PIRATES, 1949.

Quad City Cubs
Midwest League (A), 1979–1984; charter franchise. Renamed QUAD CITIES ANGELS, 1985.

Quad Cities Pirates
Three I League (B), 1949; renamed franchise. Had been QUAD CITY CUBS, 1946–1948. Renamed QUAD CITY QUADS, 1950.

Quad Cities Quads
Three I League (B), 1950; renamed franchise. Had been DAVENPORT PIRATES, 1948–1949. Renamed QUAD CITIES TIGERS, 1951.

Quad Cities Tigers
Three I League (B), 1951; renamed franchise. Had been QUAD CITIES QUADS, 1950. Disbanded after 1952 season.

BIDDEFORD, ME

Biddeford
Eastern New England League, 1885; charter franchise. Became NEWBURYPORT, mid-1885.

BIG RAPIDS, MI

Big Rapids
Northern Michigan League, 1887; charter franchise. Disbanded during 1887 season.

BIG SPRING, TX

Big Spring Barons
West Texas–New Mexico League (D), 1938–mid-1940; new franchise. Became ODESSA OILERS, mid-1940.

Big Spring Bombers
West Texas–New Mexico League (D), 1941; relocated franchise. Had been ODESSA OILERS, mid-1940. Disbanded after 1941 season.

Big Spring Broncs
Longhorn League (D), 1947–1950; (C), 1951–1954; charter franchise. Renamed BIG SPRING COSDEN COPS, 1955.

Big Spring Cosden Cops
Longhorn League (C), 1955; renamed franchise. Had been BIG

SPRING BRONCS, 1947–1954. Disbanded after 1955 season.

Big Spring Cowboys
West Texas League (D), 1929; charter franchise. Had been BIG SPRING SPRINGERS, 1928. Disband-ed with league after 1929 season.

Big Springs Pirates
West Texas–New Mexico League (D), mid-1942; renamed franchise. Had been WICHITA FALLS SPUDDERS, 1941–mid-1942. Suspended operations with league in 1942, and did not rejoin when league resumed in 1946.

Big Spring Springers
West Texas League, (D) 1928–1929; charter franchise. Renamed BIG SPRING COWBOYS, 1929.

BIG STONE GAP, VA

Big Stone Gap Rebels
Mountain States League (D), 1949–1953; new franchise. Disbanded after 1953 season.

BILLINGS, MT

Billings
Montana State League, 1899; new franchise. Disbanded with league after 1899 season.

Billings Mustangs
Pioneer League (C), 1948–1962, (R), 1963; new franchise. Disbanded after 1963 season.

Billings Mustangs
Pioneer League (R), 1969–1976; ("Summer Class A"), 1977–1978; (R), 1979–(still in existence as of 5-1-92); new franchise.

BILOXI, MS
(See GULFPORT, MS)

BINGHAMTON, NY

BINGHAMTON
League Alliance, 1877; charter franchise. Disbanded with alliance, 1877.

Binghamton Bingos
New York State League, 1885; charter franchise. International League, 1886/Association, 1887; charter franchise. Disbanded during 1887 season.

Binghamton Bingos
Central League, 1888; charter franchise. Became HAZLETON PUGILISTS, mid-1888.

Binghamton Bingos
Eastern League, 1892–mid-1894; charter franchise. Became ALLENTOWN, mid-1894.

Binghamton Bingos
New York State League, 1901; (B), 1902–1917; renamed franchise. Had been BINGHAMTON CRICKETS, 1900. Disbanded with league after 1917 season.

Binghamton Bingos
New York State League, 1899; new franchise. Renamed BINGHAMTON CRICKETS, 1900.

Binghamton Bingos
New International League (AA), 1918–1919; charter franchise. Disbanded after 1919 season.

Binghamton Crickets
New York State League, 1895; new franchise. Disbanded with league after 1895 season.

Binghamton Crickets
New York State League, 1900; renamed franchise. Had been BINGHAMTON BINGOS, 1899. Renamed BINGHAMTON BINGOS, 1901.

Binghamton Triplets
New York–Pennsylvania League (B), 1923–1925; charter franchise. Renamed TRIPLE CITIES, 1926.

Binghamton Triplets
New York–Pennsylvania League (B), 1928; 1930–1937; renamed franchise. Had been TRIPLE CITIES TRIPLETS, 1926–1927; 1929. Eastern League (A), 1938–1962; (AA), 1963; charter franchise. New York–Pennsylvania League (A), 1964–1966; new franchise. Eastern League (AA), 1967–1968; new franchise. Disbanded after 1968 season.

BINGHAMTON, ENDICOTT, AND JOHNSON CITY, NY

Triple Cities Triplets
New York–Pennsylvania League (B), 1926–1927; 1929; renamed franchise. Had been BINGHAMTON TRIPLETS, 1923–1925. Became BINGHAMTON TRIPLETS, 1928.

BIRMINGHAM, AL

Birmingham
Southern League, 1885; charter franchise. Disbanded after 1885 season.

Birmingham Babies
Southern League, 1887; new franchise. Became BIRMINGHAM MAROONS, 1888.

Birmingham Barons
Southern League (AA), 1964–1965; charter franchise. Disbanded after 1965 season.

Birmingham Barons
Southern League (AA), 1967–1970; new franchise. Dixie Association (C), 1971; charter franchise. Southern League (AA), 1972–1975; charter franchise. Disbanded after 1975 season.

Birmingham Barons
Southern Association, 1901; (A), 1902–1934; (A1), 1935–1945; (AA), 1961; charter franchise. Dis-

banded with association after 1961 season.

Birmingham Barons
Southern League (AA), 1981– (still in existence as of 5-1-92); new franchise.

BIRMINGHAM BLACK BARONS
Negro National League, 1924– mid-1925; 1927–1930; new franchise. Disbanded after 1930 season.

BIRMINGHAM BLACK BARONS
Negro American League, 1937–1938; mid-1940–1948; 1950; charter franchise. Disbanded after 1950 season.

Birmingham Grays
Southern League, 1892; charter franchise. Renamed BIRMINGHAM PETS, 1893.

Birmingham Maroons
Southern League, 1888–mid-1889; renamed franchise. Had been BIRMINGHAM BABIES, 1887. Became MOBILE BEARS, mid-1889.

Birmingham Pets
Southern League, 1893; renamed franchise. Had been BIRMINGHAM GRAYS, 1892. Became PENSACOLA, mid-1893.

Birmingham Reds
Southern League, 1898; charter franchise. Became MOBILE BLACKBIRDS, mid-1898.

Birmingham Rustlers
Southern League, 1896; new franchise. Disbanded with league after 1896 season.

BISBEE, AZ

Bisbee Bees
Arizona State League (D), 1928– 1930; charter franchise. Arizona– Texas League (D), 1931; (C), 1932; 1937–39; 1940–1941; charter franchise. Suspended opera-

tions after 1941 season, and became BISBEE YANKS when league resumed, 1947.

Bisbee Copper Kings
Arizona–Texas League (C), 1949– 1950; renamed franchise. Had been BISBEE–DOUGLAS JAVELINAS, 1948. Southwest International League (C), 1951; charter franchise. Arizona–Texas League (C), 1952– 1954; charter franchise. Arizona–Mexico League (C), 1955; charter franchise. Became BISBEE–DOUGLAS COPPER KINGS, 1956.

Bisbee Yanks
Arizona–Texas League (C), 1947; charter franchise. Renamed BISBEE–DOUGLAS YANKS, 1948.

BISBEE–DOUGLAS, AZ

Bisbee–Douglas Yanks
Arizona–Texas League (C), 1947; charter franchise. Renamed BISBEE–DOUGLAS JAVELINAS, 1948.

Bisbee–Douglas Javelinas
Arizona–Texas League (C), 1948; renamed franchise. Had been BISBEE YANKS, 1947. Renamed BISBEE–DOUGLAS COPPER KINGS, 1949.

BISMARCK, ND

Bismarck Capitals
Dakota League (D), mid-1922; relocated franchise. Had been VALLEY CITY HI-LINERS, 1922. North Dakota League (D), 1923; charter franchise. Disbanded with league during 1923 season.

BISMARCK–MANDAN, ND

Bismarck–Mandan Pards
Northern League (C), 1962; (A), 1963–1964; new franchise. Disbanded after 1964 season.

Bismarck–Mandan Pards
Northern League (A), 1966; new franchise. Disbanded after 1966 season.

BLACKSTONE, VA

Blackstone Barristers
Virginia League (D), 1948; new franchise. Became HOPEWELL BLUE SOX, 1949.

BLACKWELL, OK

Blackwell Broncos
Western Association (C), 1954; new franchise. Disbanded with league after 1954 season.

Blackwell Colts
Oklahoma–Kansas League (D), 1915–1916; charter franchise. Disbanded with league after 1916 season.

Blackwell Cubs
KOM League (D), 1952; new franchise. Disbanded with league after 1952 season.

Blackwell Gassers
Oklahoma State League (D), 1924; new franchise. Disbanded during 1924 season.

Blackwell Gassers
Southwestern League (D), mid-1924–1926; relocated franchise. Had been NEWTON RAILROADERS, 1924. Became OTTAWA (KS), mid-1924.

BLOOMFIELD, NJ

Bloomfield
Atlantic League (D), 1914; relocated franchise. Had been ASBURY PARK SEAGULLS, 1914. Disbanded with league after 1914 season.

BLOOMINGDALE, NJ

Bloomingdale Troopers
North Atlantic League (D), 1946– 1948; charter franchise. Disbanded after 1948 season.

BLOOMINGTON, IL

Bloomington Bengals
Three–I League (B), 1937; charter franchise. Disbanded during 1937 season.

Bloomington Bloomers
Illinois–Iowa–Indiana (B), 1903–1910; 1912–1929; renamed franchise. Had been BLOOMINGTON BLUES, 1901–1902. Renamed BLOOMINGTON CUBS, 1930.

Bloomington Bloomers
Illinois–Iowa–Indiana League (B), 1931; renamed franchise. Had been BLOOMINGTON CUBS, 1930. Disbanded after 1931 season.

Bloomington Bloomers
Three I League (B), 1935; charter franchise. Disbanded with league after 1935 season.

Bloomington Bloomers
Three I League (B), 1938–1939; charter franchise. Disbanded after 1939 season.

Bloomington Blues
Illinois–Indiana League, 1889; charter franchise. Disbanded with league after 1889 season.

Bloomington Blues
Illinois–Indiana League, 1899; charter franchise. Western Association, 1899; new franchise. Central League, 1900; charter franchise. Disbanded with league after 1900 season.

Bloomington Blues
Illinois–Iowa–Indiana League, 1901; (B), 1902; charter franchise. Renamed BLOOMINGTON BLOOMERS, 1903.

Bloomington Cubs
Illinios–Iowa–Indiana League (B), 1930; renamed franchise. Had been BLOOMINGTON BLOOMERS, 1903–1929. Renamed BLOOMINGTON BLOOMERS, 1931.

Bloomington Reds
Central Inter-State League, 1888; charter franchise. Disbanded after 1888 season.

Bloomington Suckers
Western Inter-State League, 1895; charter franchise. Disbanded with league after 1895 season.

BLOOMINGTON, MN

MINNESOTA TWINS
American League, 1961–1981; relocated franchise. Had been WASHINGTON SENATORS, 1957–1960. Began play in Minneapolis, 1982.

BLOOMINGTON, PA

Bloomington
Central Atlantic League, 1888; charter franchise. Disbanded during 1888 season.

BLOOMSBURG, PA

Bloomsburg
Central Pennsylvania League, 1897–1898; new franchise. Disbanded with league during 1898 season.

BLUEFIELD, WV

Bluefield Blue–Grays
Mountain State League (D), 1937–1942; charter franchise. Disbanded with league after 1942 season.

Bluefield Blue–Grays
Appalachian League (D), 1946–1955; charter franchise. Disbanded after 1955 season.

Bluefield Dodgers
Appalachian League (D), 1957; charter franchise. Renamed BLUEFIELD ORIOLES, 1958.

Bluefield Orioles
Appalachian League (D), 1958–1962; (R), 1963–(still in existence as of 5-1-92); charter franchise.

Had been BLUEFIELD DODGERS, 1957.

BLUE RAPIDS, KS

Blue Rapids Champions
East Kansas State League (D), mid-1910; relocated franchise. Had been HOLTON, 1910. Disbanded after 1910 season.

BLUFFTON, IN

Bluffton
Indiana State League, 1890; charter franchise. Disbanded with league after 1890 season.

Bluffton Babes
Northern State of Indiana League (D), 1909–1910; charter franchise. Northern State League of Indiana (D), 1911; charter franchise. Disbanded with league after 1911 season.

Bluffton Dregs
Ohio–Indiana League (D), 1907; charter franchise. Disbanded during 1907 season.

BLYTHEVILLE, AR

Blytheville
Northeast Arkansas League (D), 1910–mid-1911; new franchise. Disbanded with league during 1911 season.

Blytheville Giants
Northeast Arkansas League (D), 1937–1938; new franchise. Disbanded after 1938 season.

Blytheville Tigers
Tri-State League (D), 1925–1926; charter franchise. Disbanded with league after 1926 season.

BOISE, ID

Boise
Inter-Mountain League (D), 1909; charter franchise. Became BOZEMAN, mid-1909.

Boise
Union Association (C), 1911; charter franchise. Disbanded after 1911 season.

Boise A's
Northwest League (B), 1975–1976; new franchise. Disbanded after 1976 season.

Boise Braves
Pioneer League (C), 1955–1963; renamed franchise. Had been BOISE PILOTS, 1954. Disbanded after 1963 season.

Boise Buckskins
Northwest League (B), 1978; new franchise. Disbanded after 1978 season.

Boise Fruit Pickers
Pacific National League (B), 1904; new franchise. Disbanded with league after 1904 season.

Boise Hawks
Northwest League (A), 1987–(still in existence as of 5-1-92); new franchise.

Boise Irrigators
Western Tri-State League (D), 1912–1913; charter franchise. Union Association (D), 1914; new franchise. Disbanded during 1914 season.

Boise Mountaineers
Utah–Idaho League (C), 1928; new franchise. Disbanded with league after 1928 season.

Boise Pilots
Pioneer League (C), 1939–1942; 1946–1951; charter franchise. Renamed BOISE YANKEES, 1952.

Boise Pilots
Pioneer League (C), 1954; renamed franchise. Had been BOISE YANKEES, 1952–1953. Renamed BOISE BRAVES, 1955.

Boise Yankees
Pioneer League (C), 1952–1953; renamed franchise. Had been BOISE PILOTS, 1946–1951. Renamed BOISE PILOTS, 1954.

BONHAM, TX

Bonham
Southwestern League, 1898; charter franchise. Disbanded with league after 1898 season.

Bonham Bingers
Alternate name for BONHAM BOOGERS.

Bonham Boogers (aka BINGERS), 1922.
Texas–Oklahoma League (D), 1922; renamed franchise. Had been BONHAM FAVORITES, 1921. Became DENISON, mid-1922.

Bonham Boosters (aka Jackrabbits)
Texas–Oklahoma League (D), 1912; charter franchise. Renamed BONHAM TIGERS, 1912.

Bonham Favorites
Texas–Oklahoma League (D), 1921; charter franchise. Renamed BONHAM BOOGERS (aka Bingers), 1922.

Bonham Jackrabbits
Alternate name for BONHAM BOOSTERS.

Bonham Tigers
Texas–Oklahoma League (D), 1912–1914; charter franchise. Had been BONHAM BOOSTERS (aka Jackrabbits), 1911. Disbanded with league after 1914 season.

BOONE, IA

Boone Coal Miners
Iowa State League (D), 1904; charter franchise. Renamed BOONE GREYHOUNDS, 1905.

Boone Greyhounds
Iowa State League (D), 1905; charter franchise. Had been BOONE COAL MINERS, 1904. Renamed BOONE MINERS, 1906.

Boone Miners
Iowa State League (D), 1906; charter franchise. Had been BOONE GREYHOUNDS, 1905. Became CLINTON, mid-1906.

BORGER, TX

Borger Gassers
West Texas–New Mexico League (D), mid-1939–1942; 1946–1954; relocated franchise. Had been ABILENE BLUE SOX, 1939. Disbanded after 1954 season.

BOSTON, MA

Boston
New England League, 1886–1887; new franchise. Disbanded during 1887 season.

BOSTON BEANEATERS
National League, 1883–1906; renamed franchise. Had been BOSTON RED CAPS, 1876–1882. Renamed BOSTON DOVES, 1907.

BOSTON BEANEATERS (aka REDS)
Players' League, 1890; charter franchise. Disbanded with league after 1890 season.

BOSTON BEES
National League, 1936–1940; renamed franchise. Had been BOSTON BRAVES, 1912–1935. Renamed BOSTON BRAVES, 1941.

Boston Blues
New England League, 1886–mid-1887; charter franchise. Became HAVERHILL BLUES, mid-1887.

BOSTON BRAVES
National League, 1912–1935; renamed franchise. Had been BOSTON RUSTLERS, 1911. Renamed BOSTON BEES, 1936.

BOSTON BRAVES
National League, 1941–1952; re-named franchise. Had been BOSTON BEES, 1936–1940. Became MILWAUKEE BRAVES, 1953.

BOSTON DOVES
National League, 1907–1910; re-named franchise. Had been BOSTON BEANEATERS, 1883–1906. Became BOSTON RUSTLERS, 1911.

BOSTON PILGRIMS
American League, 1903–1906; re-named franchise. Had been BOSTON SOMERSETS, 1901–1902. Became BOSTON RED SOX, 1907.

BOSTON PLYMOUTH ROCKS
Alternate name for the BOSTON SOMERSETS, 1901–1902.

BOSTON PURITANS
Alternate name for the BOSTON SOMERSETS, 1901–1902.

BOSTON RED CAPS
National League, 1876–1882; re-named franchise. Had been BOSTON RED STOCKINGS, 1871, 1873–1875. Renamed BOSTON BEANEATERS, 1883.

BOSTON REDS
Union Association, 1884; charter franchise. Disbanded with association after 1884 season.

BOSTON REDS
Alternate name for BOSTON BEANEATERS, 1890.

BOSTON REDS
Alternate name for BOSTON RED STOCKINGS, 1891.

Boston Reds
New England League, 1893; new franchise. Disbanded after 1893 season.

BOSTON RED SOX
American League, 1907–(still in existence as of 5-1-92); renamed

franchise. Had been BOSTON PILGRIMS, 1903–1906.

BOSTON RED STOCKINGS
National Association, 1871, 1873–1875; relocated franchise. Had been CINCINNATI RED STOCKINGS, 1869–1870. Became BOSTON RED CAPS in National League, 1876.

Boston Reserves
Massachusetts State Association, 1884; charter franchise. Disbanded with league during 1884 season.

BOSTON RUSTLERS
National League, 1911; renamed franchise. Had been BOSTON DOVES, 1907–1910. Became BOSTON BRAVES, 1912.

BOSTON SOMERSETS (aka PLYMOUTH ROCKS, PURITANS, SPEEDBOYS)
American League, 1901–1902; charter franchise. Became BOSTON PILGRIMS, 1903.

BOSTON SPEED BOYS
Alternate name for BOSTON SOMERSETS, 1901–1902.

BOWLING GREEN, KY

Bowling Green Barons
Kitty League (D), 1939–mid-1942; new franchise. Disbanded with league during 1942 season.

BOYNE CITY, MI

Boyne City Boosters
Michigan State League (D), 1911–1914; charter franchise. Disbanded during 1914 season.

BOZEMAN, MT

Bozeman
Montana State League, 1892; char-ter franchise. Disanded with league after 1892 season.

Bozeman
Inter-Mountain League (D), mid-1909; relocated franchise. Had been BOISE, 1909. Disband-ed with league after 1909 season.

BRADDOCK, PA

Braddock Infants
Ohio–Pennsylvania League (D), 1905; charter franchise. POM League (D), 1906–1907; charter franchise. Disbanded with league after 1907 season.

BRADENTON, FL

Bradenton Explorers
Senior Professional Baseball Asso-ciation, 1989–1990; charter fran-chise. Became DAYTONA BEACH EXPLORERS, 1990. Disbanded with association during 1990–91 season.

Bradenton Growers
Florida State League (D), 1919; 1921–1924; charter franchise. Dis-banded during 1924 season.

BRADENTOWN, FL
(aka Bradenton, FL)

Bradentown Growers
Florida State League (C), 1921–1923; (D), 1923–1924, 1926; ex-pansion franchise. Disbanded after 1926 season.

BRADFORD, PA

Bradford
Pennsylvania State Association, 1887; new franchise. Disbanded with association after 1887 season.

Bradford
New York–Pennsylvania League, 1890–1891; charter franchise. Disband-ed with league after 1891 season.

Bradford
Iron and Oil League, 1898; charter franchise. Disbanded with league after 1898 season.

Bradford Beagles
New York–Pennsylvania League (D), 1957; new franchise. Became HORNELL REDLEGS, mid-1957.

Bradford Bees
PONY League (D), 1939–1942; charter franchise. Disbanded after 1942 season.

Bradford Blue Wings
PONY League (D), 1944–1949; expansion franchise. Renamed BRADFORD PHILLIES, 1950.

Bradford Drillers
Inter-State League (D), 1905–1908, mid-1914–1916; charter franchise. Disbanded with league after 1916 season.

Bradford Phillies
PONY League (D), 1950–1955; renamed franchise. Had been BRADFORD BLUE WINGS, 1944–1949. Renamed BRADFORD YANKEES, 1956.

Bradford Yankees
PONY League (D), 1956; renamed franchise. Had been BRADFORD PHILLIES, 1950–1955. Disbanded during 1956 season.

BRAINERD, MN

Brainerd Muskies
Northern League (D), 1935; renamed franchise. Had been BRAINERD–LITTLE FALLS, 1934. Disbanded after 1935 season.

BRAINERD–LITTLE FALLS, MN
(See also LITTLE FALLS, MN)

Brainerd–Little Falls
Northern League (D), 1934; new franchise. Became BRAINERD MUSKIES, 1935.

Brainerd–Little Falls Muskies
Northern League (D), 1933; charter franchise. Became BRANDON GRAYS, mid-1933.

BRAINERD–ST. CLOUD, MN
(See also ST. CLOUD, MN)

Brainerd–St. Cloud
Northern League (D), 1905; new franchise. Disbanded with league after 1905 season.

BRANDON, MANITOBA, CANADA

Brandon Angels
Northern League (D), 1908; charter franchise. Western Canada League (D), 1909–1911; charter franchise. Disbanded after 1911 season.

Brandon Grays
Northern League (D), mid-1933; relocated franchise. Had been BRAINERD–LITTLE FALLS MUSKIES, 1933. Disbanded after 1933 season.

BRANTFORD, ONTARIO, CANADA

Brantford Brants
Michigan–Ontario League (B), 1922; renamed franchise. Had been BRANTFORD RED SOX, 1919–1921. Disbanded after 1922 season.

Brantford Indians
Canadian League (C), 1905; charter franchise. Disbanded with league after 1905 season.

Brantford Red Sox
Canadian League (C), 1911–mid-1914; (B), mid-1914–1915; charter franchise. Disbanded with league after 1915 season.

Brantford Red Sox
Michigan–Ontario League (B), 1919–1921; charter franchise. Renamed BRANTFORD BRANTS, 1922.

Brantford Red Sox
Ontario League (D), 1930; charter franchise. Disbanded during 1930 season.

BRATTLEBORO, VT

Brattleboro Islanders
Twin State League (D), 1911; charter franchise. Disbanded with league after 1911 season.

BRECKENRIDGE, MN
(See WAHPETON, MN)

BREMERTON, WA

Bremerton Bluejackets
Western International League (B), 1946–1949; charter franchise. Disbanded after 1949 season.

BRENHAM, TX

Brenham
South Texas League (D), mid-1905; relocated franchise. Had been BEAUMONT, 1905. Became "ORPHANS," in that they did not represent a town.

Brenham Brewers (aka Kaisers and Patriots)
Middle Texas League (D), 1914–1915; charter franchise. Disbanded with league after 1915 season.

Brenham Kaisers
Alternate name for BRENHAM BREWERS, 1914–1915.

Brenham Patriots
Alternate name for BRENHAM BREWERS, 1914–1915.

BREWTON, AL

Brewton Millers
Alabama State League (D), 1940–1941; 1946–1950; charter franchise. Disbanded with league after 1950 season.

Brewton Reds
Southern Interstate League (D), 1903; charter franchise. Disbanded with league after 1903 season.

BRIDGEPORT, CT

Bridgeport
Eastern Association (B), 1913–1914; charter franchise. Disbanded with association after 1914 season.

Bridgeport
Southern New England League, 1885; charter franchise. Became LOCK HAVEN, mid-1885.

Bridgeport Americans
Eastern League (B), 1917–1918; (A), 1919–1923; renamed franchise. Had been BRIDGEPORT HUSTLERS, 1916. Renamed BRIDGEPORT BEARS, 1924.

Bridgeport Bears
Eastern League (A), 1924–mid-1932; renamed franchise. Had been BRIDGEPORT AMERICANS, 1917–1923. Disbanded with league during 1932 season.

Bridgeport Bees (aka Braves)
Colonial League (B), 1947–mid-1950; charter franchise. Disbanded with league during 1950 season.

Bridgeport Bees
Inter-State League (B), 1941; relocated franchise. Had been YORK WHITE ROSES, 1940. Disbanded after 1941 season.

Bridgeport Braves
Alternate name for BRIDGEPORT BEES, 1947–1950.

Bridgeport Giants
Eastern League, mid-1885–1887; relocated franchise. Had been LANCASTER IRONSIDES, mid-1884–mid-1885. Connecticut State League, 1888; charter franchise. Became STAMFORD, mid-1888.

Bridgeport Hustlers
Eastern League (B), 1916; charter franchise. Renamed BRIDGEPORT AMERICANS, 1917.

Bridgeport Misfits
Connecticut State League, 1897; charter franchise. Renamed BRIDGEPORT ORATORS, 1898.

Bridgeport Orators
Connecticut State League, 1898–1901; (B), 1902–1912; renamed franchise. Had been BRIDGEPORT MISFITS, 1897. Disbanded with league after 1912 season.

BRIDGTON, NJ

Bridgton
New Jersey State League, 1897; charter franchise. Disbanded with league after 1897 season.

BRINKLEY, AR

Brinkley
Arkansas State League (D), mid-1908–1909; relocated franchise. Had been POPLAR BLUFF, 1908. Disbanded with league after 1909 season.

BRISTOL, CT

Bristol Bellmakers
Alternate name for BRISTOL WOODCHOPPERS, 1901.

Bristol Owls
Colonial League (B), 1949–1950; new franchise. Disbanded with league during 1950 season.

Bristol Red Sox
Eastern League (AA), 1973–1982; new franchise. Disbanded after 1982 season.

Bristol Tramps
Connecticut League, 1897–1898; charter franchise. Renamed BRISTOL BELLMAKERS, 1899.

Bristol Woodchoppers (aka Bellmakers)
Connecticut State League, 1899–1901; renamed franchise. Had been

BRISTOL TRAMPS, 1897–1898. Disbanded after 1901 season.

BRISTOL–PLAINVILLE, CT

Bristol–Plainville
Connecticut State League, 1891; charter franchise. Disbanded with league after 1891 season.

BRISTOL, TN–BRISTOL, VA

Bristol Boosters
Appalachian League (D), 1912–1913; renamed franchise. Had been BRISTOL BORDER CITS, 1911. Disbanded after 1913 season.

Bristol Border Cits
Appalachian League (D), 1911–1913; charter franchise. Renamed BRISTOL BOOSTERS, 1912.

Bristol State Liners
Appalachian League (D), 1921–mid-1925; charter franchise. Disbanded with league during 1925 season.

Bristol Tigers
Appalachian League (R), 1969–(still in existence as of 5-1-92); new franchise.

Bristol Twins
Appalachian League (D), 1940–1955; expansion franchise. Disbanded with league after 1955 season.

BRISTOW, OK

Bristow
Oklahoma State League (D), 1923–1924; new franchise. Disbanded with league after 1924 season.

BROCKTON, MA

Brockton
Eastern New England League, 1885; charter franchise. New En-

gland League, 1886; charter franchise. Disbanded after 1886 season.

Brockton
New England League (B), 1903; new franchise. Became NEW BEDFORD, mid-1903.

Brockton
New England League (B), mid-1933; relocated franchise. Had been NASHUA, 1933. Disbanded with league after 1933 season.

Brockton B's
Eastern League, mid-1901; relocated franchise. Had been SYRACUSE STARS, 1901. Disbanded after 1901 season.

Brockton Shoemakers
New England League, 1892–1899; new franchise. Disbanded with league after 1899 season.

Brockton Shoemakers
New England League (B), 1910–1913; renamed franchise. Had been BROCKTON TIGERS, 1907–1909. Colonial League (C), 1914; charter franchise. Disbanded with league after 1914 season.

Brockton Shoemakers
New England League (B), mid-1928–1929; new franchise. Disbanded after 1929 season.

Brockton Tigers
New England League (B), 1907–1909; new franchise. Renamed BROCKTON SHOEMAKERS, 1910.

BROCKVILLE, KS

Brockville
Central Kansas League (D), 1907–1908; charter franchise. Disbanded after 1908 season.

BROCKVILLE, ONTARIO, CANADA

Brockville
Eastern International League, mid-1888; relocated franchise. Had been BELLEVILLE, 1888. Disbanded with league after 1888 season.

Brockville Blues
Canadian–American League (C), 1937; renamed franchise. Had been BROCKVILLE PIRATES, 1936. Became GLOVERSVILLE-JOHNSTOWN GLOVERS, mid-1937.

Brockville Pirates
Canadian–American League (C), mid-1936; relocated franchise. Had been WATERTOWN GRAYS, 1936. Renamed BROCKVILLE BLUES, 1937.

BROOKFIELD, MO

Brookfield Hustlers
Missouri State League (D), 1911; charter franchise. Disbanded with league during 1911 season.

BROOKHAVEN, MS

Brookhaven
Delta League (D), 1904; charter franchise. Disbanded with league after 1904 season.

Brookhaven Truckers
Cotton States League (D), 1924–1925; new franchise. Disbanded after 1925 season.

BROOKLYN, NY
(See also NEW YORK, NY)

ATLANTIC OF BROOKLYN (aka BROOKLYN ATLANTICS)
National Association, 1873–1875; renamed franchise. Had been ECKFORD OF BROOKLYN, 1871–1872. Disbanded with association after 1875 season.

BROOKLYN ATLANTICS
Alternate name for BROOKLYN TROLLEY-DODGERS, 1881; 1884.

BROOKLYN BRIDEGROOMS
American Association, 1889; renamed franchise. Had been BROOKLYN TROLLEY-DODGERS, 1884–1888. Renamed BROOKLYN GLADIATORS, 1890.

BROOKLYN BRIDEGROOMS (aka WARD'S WONDERS and FOUTZ'S FILLIES)
National League, 1890–1898; new franchise. Renamed BROOKLYN SUPERBAS, 1899.

BROOKLYN BROOKFEDS
Alternate name for BROOKLYN FEDS, 1914–1915.

BROOKLYN CHELSEAS (aka RESOLUTES and QUICKSTEPS)
League Alliance, 1877; charter franchise. Disbanded after 1877 season.

BROOKLYN DODGERS
National League, 1897–1957; renamed franchise. Had been BROOKLYN SUPERBAS, 1899–1910. Renamed BROOKLYN ROBINS 1914.

BROOKLYN DODGERS
National League, 1932–1957; renamed franchise. Had been BROOKLYN ROBINS, 1914–1931. Became LOS ANGELES DODGERS, 1958.

BROOKLYN EAGLES
Negro National League, 1935; new franchise. Became NEWARK EAGLES, 1936.

BROOKLYN ECKFORDS
(See ECKFORDS OF BROOKLYN)

BROOKLYN FEDS
Alternate name for BROOKLYN TIPTOPS, 1914–1915.

BROOKLYN FOUTZ'S FILLIES (Named for then-manager Dave Foutz)
Alternate name for BROOKLYN BRIDEGROOMS, 1893–1896.

BROOKLYN GLADIATORS
American Association, 1890; renamed franchise. Had been

BROOKLYN BRIDEGROOMS, 1889. Disbanded after 1890 season.

BROOKLYN GRAYS
Alternate name for BROOKLYN CHELSEAS, 1883.

BROOKLYN QUICKSTEPS
Alternate name for BROOKLYN CHELSEAS, 1881.

BROOKLYN RESOLUTES
Alternate name for BROOKLYN CHELSEAS, 1877.

BROOKLYN ROBINS
National League, 1914–1931; renamed franchise. Had been BROOKLYN DODGERS, 1911–1913. Renamed BROOKLYN DODGERS, 1932.

BROOKLYN ROYAL GIANTS
Eastern Colored League, 1923–mid-1927; charter franchise. Disbanded during 1927 season.

BROOKLYN SUPERBAS
National League, 1899–1910; renamed franchise. Had been BROOKLYN BRIDEGROOMS, 1890–1898. Renamed BROOKLYN DODGERS, 1911.

BROOKLYN TIP–TOPS (aka FEDS)
Federal League, 1914; expansion franchise. Disbanded with League, 1915.

BROOKLYN TROLLEY–DODGERS (aka ATLANTICS)
Eastern Association, 1881–1882; charter franchise. Inter-State Association, 1883; charter franchise. American Association, 1884–1888; charter franchise. Renamed BROOKLYN BRIDEGROOMS, 1889.

BROOKLYN WARD'S WONDERS (Named for player-manager John Montgomery Ward)
Alternate name for BROOKLYN BRIDEGROOMS, 1889–1891.

BROOKLYN WONDERS
Players League, 1890; charter franchise. Disbanded with league after 1890 season.

Church City Nine
Inter-State Association, 1883–1888; charter franchise. Disbanded with league after 1888 season.

ECKFORD OF BROOKLYN
National Association, 1871–1872; new franchise. Renamed ATLANTIC OF BROOKLYN, 1873.

NEW YORK MUTUALS
Played in Brooklyn as well as New York City. National Association, 1871–mid-1875; charter franchise. Disbanded during 1875 season.

BROWNSVILLE, TX

Brownsville
Texas Valley League (D), 1928; new franchise. Disbanded during 1928 season.

Brownsville Brownies
Southwest Texas League (D), 1910–1911; charter franchise. Disband-ed with league after 1911 season.

Brownsville Charros
Texas Valley League (D), 1938; charter franchise. Disbanded after 1938 season.

Brownsville Charros
Rio Grande Valley League (C), 1949–1950; charter franchise. Gulf Coast League (D), 1951–1953; new franchise. Disbanded with league after 1953 season.

BROWNWOOD, TX

Brownwood
West Texas League (D), 1905; charter franchise. Disbanded during 1905 season.

BRUNSWICK, GA

Brunswick
Georgia State League (D), mid-1906; relocated franchise. Had been COLUMBUS RIVER SNIPES (GA), 1906. Disbanded with league during 1906 season.

Brunswick Cardinals
Georgia–Florida League (D), 1962; (A), 1963; new franchise. Disbanded with league after 1963 season.

Brunswick Phillies
Georgia–Florida League (D), 1957–1958; relocated franchise. Had been MOULTRIE PHILLIES, 1957. Disbanded with league after 1958 season.

Brunswick Pilots
Empire State League (Ga), (D), 1913; charter franchise. Georgia State League (D), 1914; charter franchise. FLAG League (D), 1915; charter franchise. Disbanded with league after 1915 season.

Brunswick Pirates
Georgia–Florida League (D), 1951–1956; new franchise. Disbanded after 1956 season.

BRYAN, TX

Bryan Bombers
Lone Star League (C), 1947–1948; charter franchise. East Texas League (C), 1949; charter franchise. Renamed BRYAN SPORTS, 1950.

Bryan Indians
Big State League (B), 1954; renamed franchise. Had been BRYAN MAJORS, 1953. Became DEL RIO INDIANS, mid-1954.

Bryan Majors
Big State League (B), 1953; new franchise. Renamed BRYAN INDIANS, 1954.

Bryan Majors
Big State League (B), mid-1955; relocated franchise. Had been GREENVILLE MAJORS (TX), 1955. Disbanded after 1955 season.

Bryan Sports
East Texas League (C), 1950; renamed franchise. Had been BRYAN BOMBERS, 1947–1949. Disbanded with league after 1950 season.

BUFFALO, NY

Buffalo
League Alliance, 1877; charter franchise. Disbanded after 1877 season.

Buffalo Bisons
International Association, 1878; new franchise. National League, 1879–1885; charter franchise. International League, 1886–mid-1890; 1888/Association, 1888; charter franchise. Became MONTREAL, mid-1890.

BUFFALO BISONS
Players' League, 1890; charter franchise. Eastern League, 1891–1898; charter franchise. Western League, 1899; new franchise. Disbanded after 1899 season.

Buffalo Bisons
Eastern League, 1901; (A), 1902–1911; charter franchise. New (1918–1921)/International League (AA), 1912–1945; (AAA), 1946–1970; new franchise. Became WINNIPEG WHIPS, 1971.

Buffalo Bisons
Eastern League (AA), 1979–1984; new franchise. Became PITTSFIELD CUBS, 1985.

Buffalo Bisons
American Association (AAA), 1985–(still in existence as of 5-1-92); relocated franchise. Had been WICHITA AEROS, 1970–1984.

BUFFALO BLUES (aka ELECTRICS)
Federal League, 1915; renamed franchise. Had been BUFFALO BUFFEDS, 1914. Disbanded with league, 1915.

BUFFALO BUFFEDS (aka ELECTRICS)
Federal League, 1914; expansion franchise. Renamed BUFFALO BLUES, 1915.

BUFFALO ELECTRICS
Alternate name for BUFFALO BUFFEDS AND BLUES, 1914–1915.

BUFFALO PAN AMS
American League, 1900; charter franchise. Disbanded after 1900 season.

BURLINGTON, IA

Burlington
Illinois–Iowa League, mid-1890; relocated franchise. Had been GALESBURG, mid-1890. Disbanded after 1890 season.

Burlington Babies
Central Inter-State League, 1889; new franchise. Disbanded with league after 1889 season.

Burlington Bees
Mississippi Valley League (D), 1924–1932; new franchise. Disbanded with league after 1932 season.

Burlington Bees
Three I League (B), 1954–1961; renamed franchise. Midwest League (D), 1962; (A), 1963–1981; new franchise. Renamed BURLINGTON RANGERS, 1982.

Burlington Braves
Midwest League (A), 1986–(still in existence as of 5-1-92); renamed franchise. Had been BURLINGTON EXPOS, 1986–1988.

Burlington Colts
Western Association, 1895–1897; new franchise. Renamed BURLINGTON HAWKEYES, 1898.

Burlington Cowboys
Alternate name for BURLINGTON PATHFINDERS, 1911.

Burlington Expos
Midwest League (A), 1986–1988; renamed franchise. Had been BURLINGTON RANGERS, 1982–1985. Renamed BURLINGTON BRAVES, 1989.

Burlington Flint Hills
Iowa State League (D), 1905; charter franchise. Had been BURLINGTON RIVER RATS, 1904. Renamed BURLINGTON PATHFINDERS, 1906.

Burlington Flints
Three I League (B), 1952–1953; expansion franchise. Renamed BURLINGTON BEES, 1954–1961.

Burlington Hawkeyes
Western Inter-State League, 1890; charter franchise. Eastern Iowa League, 1890; charter franchise. Disbanded with league after 1890 season.

Burlington Hawkeyes
Western Association, 1898; renamed franchise. Had been BURLINGTON COLTS, 1895–1897. Disbanded during 1898 season.

Burlington Indians
Central Association (A), 1947–1949; charter franchise. Disbanded with association after 1949 season.

Burlington Pathfinders (aka Cowboys)
Iowa State League (D), 1906–1907; charter franchise. Had been BURLINGTON FLINT HILLS, 1905. Central Association (D), 1908–1916; charter franchise. Became OTTUMWA, mid-1916.

Burlington Rangers
Midwest League (A), 1982–1985; renamed franchise. Had been BUR-LINGTON BEES, 1954–1981. Renamed BURLINGTON EXPOS, 1986.

Burlington River Rats
Iowa State League (D), 1904; charter franchise. Renamed BURLING-TON FLINT HILLS, 1905.

Burlington Spiders (aka Tigers)
Eastern Iowa League, 1895; charter franchise. Disbanded with league after 1895 season.

Burlington Tigers
Alternate name for BURLINGTON SPIDERS, 1895.

BURLINGTON, NC

Alamance Indians
Carolina League (A), 1963–1964; renamed franchise. Had been BUR-LINGTON INDIANS, 1958–1962. Renamed BURLINGTON SENATORS, 1965.

Burlington Bees
Bi-State League (D), 1942; new franchise. Disbanded with league after 1942 season.

Burlington Indians
Carolina League (C), 1958–1962; new franchise. Renamed ALAM-ANCE INDIANS, 1963.

Burlington Indians
Appalachian League (R), 1986–(still in existence as of 5-1-92); new franchise.

Burlington Rangers
Carolina League (B), 1972; renamed franchise. Had been BUR-LINGTON SENATORS, 1965–1971. Disbanded after 1972 season.

Burlington Senators
Carolina League (A), 1965–1971; renamed franchise. Had been AL-AMANCE INDIANS, 1963–1964. Re-

named BURLINGTON RANGERS, 1972.

BURLINGTON, VT

Burlington
Northeastern League, 1887; charter franchise. Disbanded with league after 1887 season.

Burlington
New Hampshire State League (D), 1907; charter franchise. Disbanded with league after 1907 season.

Burlington A's (aka Collegians)
Provincial League (C), 1955; new franchise. Disbanded with league after 1955 season.

Burlington Collegians
Alternate name for BURLINGTON A'S, 1955.

Burlington Reds
Alternate name for VERMONT REDS, 1984–1986.

Vermont Mariners
Eastern League (AA), 1987–1988; renamed franchise. Had been VER-MONT REDS (aka BURLINGTON REDS), 1984–1986. Became CAN-TON–AKRON INDIANS, 1989–(still in existence as of 5-1-92).

Vermont Reds
Eastern League (AA), 1984–1986; new franchise. Renamed VERMONT MARINERS, 1987.

BURLINGTON–ELON–GRAHAM, NC

Bur-Gra Pirates
Carolina League (C), 1952–1955; renamed franchise. Had been BUR-LINGTON BEES, 1945–1951. Disbanded after 1955 season.

Burlington Bees
Carolina League (C), 1945–1951; charter franchise. Renamed BUR-GRA PIRATES, 1952.

BUTLER, PA

Butler
POM League (D), 1906; charter franchise. Became PIEDMONT, mid-1906.

Butler Indians
Pennsylvania State Association (D), 1935; new franchise. Renamed BUTLER YANKEES, 1936.

Butler Sailors
Ohio–Pennsylvania League (D), mid-1908; relocated franchise. Had been GIRARD SAILORS, 1908. Became ERIE SAILORS, mid-1908.

Butler Tigers
Middle Atlantic League (D), 1948–1951; renamed franchise. Had been BUTLER YANKEES, 1936–1942; 1946–1947. Disbanded with league after 1951 season.

Butler White Sox
Western Pennsylvania League (D), 1907; charter franchise. Disbanded with league after 1907 season.

Butler Yankees
Pennsylvania State Association (D), 1936–1942; renamed franchise. Had been BUTLER INDIANS, 1935. Suspended operations, 1942; resumed with Middle Atlantic League (D), 1946–1947; charter franchise. Renamed BUTLER TI-GERS, 1948.

BUTTE, MT

Butte
Montana State League, 1892; charter franchise. Disbanded with league after 1892 season.

Butte Copper Kings
Pioneer League (R), 1978–(still in existence as of 5-1-92); new franchise.

Butte Miners
Pacific Northwest League (D), 1902; new franchise. Pacific Na-

tional League (A), 1903; (B), 1904; charter franchise. Disbanded with league after 1904 season.

Butte Miners
Northwestern League (B), 1906–1908; new franchise. Inter-Mountain League (D), 1909; charter franchise. Disbanded with league during 1909 season.

Butte Miners
Union Association (C), 1911; (D), 1912–1914; charter franchise. Disbanded with association during 1914 season.

Butte Miners
Northwestern League (B), 1916–mid-1917; new franchise. Disbanded with league during 1917 season.

Butte Smoke Eaters
Montana State League, 1898–1900; charter franchise. Disbanded with league after 1900 season.

CABORCA, SONORA, MEXICO

Caborca Reds
Mexican Northern League (A), 1969; new franchise. Disbanded with league after 1969 season.

Caborca Tigers
Mexican Rookie League (R), 1968; charter franchise. Disbanded with league after 1968 season.

CADILLAC, MI

Cadillac Chiefs
Michigan State League (D), 1910–1913; charter franchise. Renamed CADILLAC CHIEFTANS, 1914.

Cadillac Chieftans
Michigan State League (D), 1914; renamed franchise. Had been CADILLAC CHIEFS, 1910–1913. Disbanded with league after 1914 season.

CAIRO, IL

Cairo Champions
KITTY League (D), 1903–1904; charter franchise. Renamed CAIRO GIANTS, 1905.

Cairo Dodgers
KITTY League (D) 1949; renamed franchise. Had been CAIRO EGYPTIANS, 1946–1948. Renamed CAIRO EGYPTIANS, 1950.

Cairo Egyptians
Central League, 1897; charter franchise. Disbanded with league after 1897 season.

Cairo Egyptians
KITTY League (D), 1911–1914; new franchise. Disbanded with league after 1914 season.

Cairo Egyptians
KITTY League (D), 1922–1924; charter franchise. Disbanded with league after 1924 season.

Cairo Egyptians
KITTY League (D), 1946–1948; charter franchise. Renamed CAIRO DODGERS, 1949.

Cairo Egyptians
KITTY League (D), 1950; renamed franchise. Had been CAIRO DODGERS, 1949. Disbanded after 1950 season.

Cairo Giants (aka Mud Wallopers and Tadpoles)
KITTY League (D) 1905–1906; charter franchise. Had been CAIRO CHAMPIONS, 1903–1904. Disbanded with league after 1906 season.

Cairo Mud Wallopers
Alternate name for CAIRO GIANTS, 1905–1906.

Cairo Tadpoles
Alternate name for CAIRO GIANTS, 1905–1906.

CALAIS, ME–ST. STEPHENS, NEW BRUNSWICK, CANADA

Calais, ME–St. Stephens Downeasters
New Brunswick–Maine League (D), 1913; charter franchise. Disbanded during 1913 season.

CALDWELL, ID

Caldwell Cubs
Pioneer League (R), 1967–1971; renamed franchise. Had been TREASURE VALLEY CUBS, 1964–1966. Disbanded after 1971 season.

Treasure Valley Cubs
Pioneer League (R), 1964–1966; charter franchise. Renamed CALDWELL CUBS, 1967.

CALGARY, ALBERTA, CANADA

Calgary Bronchos
Western Canada League (C), 1907; charter franchise. Disbanded after 1907 season.

Calgary Bronchos
Western Canada League (C), 1910–1914; new franchise. Disbanded with league after 1914 season.

Calgary Bronchos
Western Canada League (B), 1920–1921; charter franchise. Western International League (B), 1922; charter franchise. Disbanded with league during 1922 season.

Calgary Cannons
Pacific Coast League (AAA), 1985–(still in existence as of 5-1-92); relocated franchise. Had been SALT LAKE CITY ANGELS, 1970–1984.

Calgary Cardinals
Pioneer League ("Summer Class A"), 1977–1978; new franchise. Renamed CALGARY EXPOS, 1979.

Calgary Expos
Pioneer League (R), 1979–1984; renamed franchise. Had been CALGARY CARDINALS, 1977–1978. Became SALT LAKE CITY TRAPPERS, 1985.

Calgary Eyeopeners
Western Canada League (C), 1909; charter franchise. Renamed CALGARY BRONCHOS, 1910.

Calgary Stampeders
Western International League (A), 1953–1954; expansion franchise. Disbanded during 1954 season.

CALUMET, MI

Calumet Aristocrats
Copper Country League (D), 1905; charter franchise. Northern Copper Country League (C), 1906–1907; charter franchise. Disbanded with league after 1907 season.

Calumet Red Jackets
Upper Peninsula League, 1890; charter franchise. Disbanded during 1890 season.

Calumet Red Jackets
Upper Peninsula League, 1891; charter franchise. Disbanded with league after 1891 season.

CAMBRIDGE, MD

Cambridge Canners
Eastern Shore League (D), 1922–mid-1928; charter franchise. Disbanded with league during 1928 season.

Cambridge Cardinals
Eastern Shore League (D), 1937–1941; charter franchise. Disbanded with league after 1928 season.

Cambridge Dodgers
Eastern Shore League (D), 1946–1949; charter franchise. Disbanded with league after 1949 season.

CAMBRIDGE, MA

Cambridge
New England League, 1899; new franchise. Became LOWELL, mid-1899.

Cambridge Cantabs
Northeastern League (A), 1934; charter franchise. Became WAYLAND BIRDS, mid-1934.

CAMBRIDGE, OH

Cambridge
Ohio–West Virginia League, 1897; charter franchise. Became DENISON–URICHSVILLE, mid-1897.

CAMDEN, AR

Camden
Arkansas–Texas League (D), 1905–1906; charter franchise. Disbanded after 1906 season.

CAMDEN, NJ

Camden
Tri-State League (D), 1904; charter franchise. Disbanded after 1904 season.

Camden Merrits
Inter-State Association, 1883; charter franchise. Disbanded with association after 1883 season.

CAMDEN, SC

Camden
South Carolina League (D), 1906; charter franchise. Disbanded after 1906 season.

CAMPECHE, SONORA, MEXICO
(See also CARMEN, MEXICO)

Campeche Alcrames
Mexican League (AAA), 1980; new franchise. Renamed CAMPECHE PIRATAS (Pirates), 1981.

Campeche Camaraneros
Mexican Southeast League (A), 1964–1965; charter franchise. Renamed CAMPECHE PIRATES, 1966.

Campeche Piratas (Pirates)
Mexican League (AAA), 1981– (still in existence as of 5-1-92); renamed franchise. Had been CAMPECHE ALCRAMES, 1980.

Campeche Pirates
Mexican Southeast League (A), 1966–1970; renamed franchise. Had been CAMPECHE CAMARANEROS, 1964–1965. Disbanded with league after 1970 season.

CANANDAIGUA, NY

Canandaigua
New York State League, 1888–1889; charter franchise. Disbanded with league after 1889 season.

Canandaigua Rustlers
New York State League, 1897–1898; charter franchise. Disbanded after 1898 season.

CANANEA, SONORA, MEXICO

Cananea Mineros (aka Miners)
Arizona–Texas League (C), 1954; expansion franchise. Arizona–Mexico League (C), 1955–1957; charter franchise. Disbanded after 1957 season.

Cananea Miners
Alternate name for CANANEA MINEROS, 1954–1957.

Cananea Miners
Mexican Rookie League (R), 1968; charter franchise. Disbanded with league after 1968 season.

CANASOTA, NY

Canasota
Central New York League, 1886; charter franchise. Disbanded with league after 1886 season.

CANISTEO, NY

Canisteo
Western New York League, 1890; charter franchise. Disbanded with league after 1890 season.

CANON CITY, CO

Canon City Swastikas
Rocky Mountain League (D), 1912; charter franchise. Disbanded with league after 1912 season.

CANTON, IL

Canton Canteens
Illinois–Missouri League (D), 1908–1913; charter franchise. Disbanded after 1913 season.

Canton Chinks
Illinois–Missouri League (D), 1909–1911; renamed franchise. Had been CANTON CANTEENS, 1908. Renamed CANTON HIGHLANDERS, 1912.

Canton Chinks
Illinois–Missouri League (D), 1913; charter franchise. Had been CANTON HIGHLANDERS, 1912. Disbanded after 1913 season.

Canton Citizens
MOV League (D), 1952; relocated franchise. Had been VINCENNES VELVETS, 1951–mid-1952. Disbanded after 1952 season.

Canton Highlanders
Illinois–Missouri League (D), 1912; renamed franchise. Had been CANTON CHINKS, 1909–1911. Renamed CANTON CHINKS, 1913.

CANTON, MS

Canton
Delta League (D), 1904; charter franchise. Disbanded after 1904 season.

CANTON, OH

Canton
Tri-State League, 1888–1890; charter franchise. Disbanded with league after 1890 season.

Canton
Central League (C), mid-1904–1907; relocated franchise. Had been FORT WAYNE RAILROADERS, 1904. Disbanded after 1907 season.

Canton
Ohio–Pennsylvania League (D), 1905; charter franchise. Disbanded with league after 1905 season.

Canton
Buckeye League (D), 1915; charter franchise. Disbanded with league after 1915 season.

Canton Deubers
Ohio–Michigan League, 1893; charter franchise. Inter-State League, 1894; charter franchise. Disbanded with league after 1894 season.

Canton Deubers
Ohio–Pennsylvania League (C), 1910–1911; renamed franchise. Had been CANTON WATCHMAKERS, 1908–1909. Disbanded with league after 1911 season.

Canton Statesmen
Central League (B), 1912; new franchise. Inter-State League (B), 1913; charter franchise. Disbanded during 1913 season.

Canton Terriers
Central League (B), 1928–1930; charter franchise. Disbanded with league after 1930 season.

Canton Terriers
Central League (B), mid-1932; relocated franchise. Had been AKRON TYRITES, 1932. Disbanded with league after 1932 season.

Canton Terriers
Middle Atlantic League (C), 1936–1942; new franchise. Disbanded after 1942 season.

Canton Watchmakers
Ohio–Pennsylvania League (C), 1908–1909; new franchise. Renamed CANTON DEUBERS, 1910.

CANTON–AKRON, OH
(See also AKRON, OH)

Canton–Akron Indians
Eastern League (AA), 1989–(still in existence as of 5-1-92); relocated franchise. Had been VERMONT MARINERS, 1987–1988.

CAP DE LA MADELEINE, QUEBEC, CANADA

Cap de la Madeleine Madcaps
Eastern Canada League (B), mid-1922; relocated franchise. Had been VALLEYFIELD, 1922. Disbanded after 1922 season.

CAPE CHARLES, VA

Northampton Red Sox
Eastern Shore League (D), mid-1927–mid-1928; relocated franchise. Had been DOVER SENATORS, 1926–mid-1927. Disbanded with league during 1928 season.

CARACAS, VENEZUELA

Caracas Mets
Inter-American League (AAA), 1979; charter franchise. Disbanded with league during 1979 season.

CARBONDALE, PA

Carbondale Anthracites
Pennsylvania State League, 1895–mid-1896; new franchise. Became POTTSVILLE LAMBS, mid-1896.

Carbondale Blue Sox
North Atlantic League (D), 1947; renamed franchise. Had been CARBONDALE PIONEERS (aka Pioneer Blues), 1946. Renamed CARBONDALE PIONEERS (aka Pioneer Blues), 1948.

Carbondale Pioneer Blues
Alternate name for CARBONDALE PIONEERS, 1946–1950.

Carbondale Pioneers (aka Pioneer Blues)
North Atlantic League (D), 1946; charter franchise. Renamed CARBONDALE BLUE SOX, 1947.

Carbondale Pioneers (aka Pioneer Blues)
North Atlantic League (D), 1948–1950; renamed franchise. Had been CARBONDALE BLUE SOX, 1947. Disbanded with league after 1950 season.

CARBORCA, SONORA, MEXICO

Carborca Vaqueros
Mexican Rookie League (R), 1968; charter franchise. Mexican Northern League (A), 1969; new franchise. Disbanded with league after 1969 season.

CARIBOU– PRESQUE ISLAND, ME

Caribou–Presque Island
Northern Maine League (D), 1909; charter franchise. Disbanded with league after 1909 season.

CARLISLE, PA

Carlisle
Keystone Association, 1884; charter franchise. Cumberland Valley League, 1895–1896; charter franchise. Disanded with league after 1896 season.

CARLSBAD, NM

Carlsbad Potashers
Longhorn League (C), 1953–1955; new franchise. Southwestern League (B), 1956–1957; charter franchise. Sophomore League (D), 1958–1961; charter franchise. Disbanded with league after 1961 season.

CARMEN, CAMPECHE, MEXICO

Carmen Shrimpers
Mexican Southeast League (A), 1967–1970; new franchise. Disbanded with league after 1970 season.

CARRINGTON, ND
(See also NEW ROCKFORD, ND)

Carrington
North Dakota League (D), 1923; charter franchise. Disbanded with league after 1923 season.

CARROLLTON, GA

Carrollton
Georgia State League (D), 1920–1921; charter franchise. Disbanded with league after 1921 season.

Carrollton Champs
Georgia–Alabama League; (D), mid-1929–mid-1930; charter franchise. Disbanded during 1930 season.

Carrollton Frogs
Georgia–Alabama Association (D), mid-1928; charter franchise. Disbanded with association after 1928 season.

Carrollton Hornets
Georgia–Alabama League (D), 1946–1950; charter franchise. Disbanded after 1950 season.

CARTHAGE, MO

Carthage
Southwestern League, 1891; charter franchise. Disbanded with league after 1891 season.

Carthage Browns
Western Association (C), 1941; relocated franchise. Had been ST. JOSEPH SAINTS, 1940. Disbanded after 1941 season.

Carthage Cardinals
Alternate name for CARTHAGE CARDS, 1946–1948.

Carthage Cards (aka Cardinals)
Kansas–Oklahoma–Missouri League (D), 1946–1948; charter franchise. Renamed CARTHAGE CUBS, 1949.

Carthage Cubs
Kansas–Oklahoma–Missouri League (D), 1949–1951; renamed franchise. Had been CARTHAGE CARDS (aka Cardinals), 1946–1948. Disbanded after 1951 season.

Carthage Pirates
Arkansas–Missouri League (D), 1938–1940; expansion franchise. Disbanded with league during 1940 season.

CARUTHERSVILLE, MO

Caruthersville
Northeast Arkansas League (D), 1910; new franchise. Disbanded after 1910 season.

Caruthersville Badgers
Northeast Arkansas League (D), mid-1936; relocated franchise. Had been WEST PLAINS BADGERS, 1936. Renamed CARUTHERSVILLE PILOTS, 1937.

Caruthersville Pilots
Northeast Arkansas League (D), 1937–mid-1940; renamed franchise. Had been CARUTHERSVILLE

BADGERS, mid-1936. Became BATESVILLE PILOTS, mid-1940.

CASSVILLE, MO

Cassville Blues
Arkansas–Missouri League (D), 1936; charter franchise. Disbanded after 1936 season.

Cassville Tigers
Arkansas State League (D), 1935; expansion franchise. Disbanded with league after 1935 season.

CATLETTSBURG, KY

(See ASHLAND, KY)

CATSKILL, NY

Catskill
Hudson River League (D), mid-1903; relocated franchise. Had been OSSINING, 1903. Disbanded after 1903 season.

CAVALIER, ND

Cavalier
Northern League (D), 1902; charter franchise. Disbanded after 1902 season.

CEDAR RAPIDS, IA

Cedar Rapids
Eastern Iowa League, 1895; charter franchise. Disbanded with league after 1895 season.

Cedar Rapids Astros
Midwest League (A), 1973–1974; renamed franchise. Had been CEDAR RAPIDS CARDINALS, 1964–1972. Renamed CEDAR RAPIDS GIANTS, 1975.

Cedar Rapids Braves
Three I League (B), 1958–1961; renamed franchise. Had been CEDAR RAPIDS RAIDERS, 1955–1957. Disbanded after 1962 season.

Cedar Rapids Bunnies
Western Association, 1896–mid-1898; new franchise. Disbanded during 1898 season.

Cedar Rapids Bunnies
Mississippi Valley League (D), 1922–1932; charter franchise. Disbanded after 1932 season.

Cedar Rapids Canaries (aka Pork Packers)
Illinois–Iowa League, 1891; renamed franchise. Had been CEDAR RAPIDS KICKERS, 1890. Disbanded after 1891 season.

Cedar Rapids Cardinals
Midwest League (A), 1964–1972; renamed franchise. Had been CEDAR RAPIDS RED RAIDERS, 1962–1964. Renamed CEDAR RAPIDS ASTROS, 1973.

Cedar Rapids Giants
Midwest League (A), 1975–1979; renamed franchise. Had been CEDAR RAPIDS ASTROS, 1973–1974. Renamed CEDAR RAPIDS REDS, 1980.

Cedar Rapids Indians
Three I League (B), 1950–1954; new franchise. Renamed CEDAR RAPIDS RAIDERS, 1955.

Cedar Rapids Kickers
Illinois–Iowa League, 1890; charter franchise. Renamed CEDAR RAPIDS CANARIES, 1891.

Cedar Rapids Pork Packers
Alternate name for CEDAR RAPIDS CANARIES, 1891.

Cedar Rapids Rabbits
Illinois–Iowa–Indiana League, 1901; (B), 1902–1909; charter franchise. Disbanded after 1909 season.

Cedar Rapids Rabbits
Central Association (D), 1913–mid-1917; charter franchise. Became CLEAR LAKE, mid-1917.

Cedar Rapids Rabbits
Illinois–Iowa–Indiana League (B), 1920–1921; new franchise. Disbanded after 1921 season.

Cedar Rapids Raiders
Western League (A), 1934–1937; new franchise. Three I League (B), 1938–1942; new franchise. Disbanded after 1942 season.

Cedar Rapids Raiders
Three I League (B), 1955–1957; renamed franchise. Had been CEDAR RAPIDS INDIANS, 1950–1954. Renamed CEDAR RAPIDS BRAVES, 1958.

Cedar Rapids Red Raiders
Midwest League (D), 1962; (A), 1963–1964; new franchise. Renamed CEDAR RAPIDS CARDINALS, 1965.

Cedar Rapids Reds
Midwest League (A), 1980–(still in existence as of 5-1-92); renamed franchise. Had been CEDAR RAPIDS GIANTS, 1975–1979.

Cedar Rapids Rockets
Central Association (C), 1949; new franchise. Disbanded with association after 1949 season.

CEDARTOWN, GA

Cedartown
Southeastern League (D), mid-1912; relocated franchise. Had been BESSEMER PIPE MAKERS, 1912. Disbanded during 1912 season.

Cedartown
Georgia State League (D), 1920–1921; charter franchise. Disbanded with league after 1921 season.

Cedartown Braves
Georgia–Alabama League (C), 1930; renamed franchise. Had been CEDARTOWN SEA COWS, 1928–1929. Disbanded with league after 1930 season.

Cedartown Sea Cows

Georgia–Alabama Association (C), 1928; /League 1929; charter franchise. Renamed CEDARTOWN BRAVES, 1930.

CELAYA, QUERETARO, MEXICO

Celaya Cajeteros
Mexican Center League (D), 1960; (C), 1961; charter franchise. Disbanded after 1961 season.

Celaya Cajeteros
Mexican Center League (A), 1975; new franchise. Disbanded after 1975 season.

CELERON, NY
(See CHATAUQUA, NY)

CENTRAL CITY, KY

Central City Reds
KITTY League (D), mid-1954; relocated franchise. Had been JACKSON GENERALS, 1954. Disbanded after 1954 season.

CENTRALIA, IL

Centralia Cubs
Illinois State League (B), 1947–1948; charter franchise. MOV League (D), 1949; charter franchise. Renamed CENTRALIA STERLINGS, 1950.

Centralia Sterlings
MOV League (D), 1950; charter franchise. Had been CENTRALIA CUBS, 1949. Renamed CENTRALIA ZEROS, 1951.

Centralia White Stockings
Eastern Illinois League (D), 1907; charter franchise. Became PARIS COLTS, mid-1907.

Centralia Zeros
MOV League (D), 1951–1952; charter franchise. Had been CENTRALIA STERLINGS, 1950. Disbanded after 1952 season.

CENTRALIA, WA

Centralia Midgets
Southwestern Washington League (D), 1903; charter franchise. Disbanded after 1903 season.

Centralia Pets
Washington State League (D), 1911; new franchise. Became CENTRALIA RAILROADERS, 1912.

Centralia Railroaders
Washington State League (D), 1912; renamed franchise. Had been CENTRALIA PETS, 1911. Disbanded during 1912 season.

CENTRAL OREGON
(See BEND, OR)

CENTREVILLE, MD

Centreville Colts
Eastern Shore League (D), 1937; charter franchise. Renamed QUEEN ANNE COLTS, 1938.

Centreville Orioles
Eastern Shore League (D), 1946; charter franchise. Disbanded after 1946 season.

Centreville Red Sox
Eastern Shore League (D), 1939–1941; renamed franchise. Had been QUEEN ANNE COLTS, 1938. Disbanded with league after 1941 season.

Queen Anne Colts
Eastern Shore League (D), 1938; renamed franchise. Had been CENTREVILLE COLTS, 1937. Renamed CENTREVILLE RED SOX, 1939.

CERRO AZUL, MEXICO

Cerro Azul
Mexican Center League (A), 1978; new franchise. Disbanded after 1978 season.

CHAMBERSBURG, PA

Chambersburg
Keystone Association, 1884; charter franchise. Disbanded with association after 1884 season.

Chambersburg
Cumberland Valley League, 1895–1896; charter franchise. Disbanded with league after 1896 season.

Chambersburg Maroons
Cumberland Valley League, 1895–1896; charter franchise. Disbanded with league after 1896 season.

Chambersburg Maroons
Blue Ridge League (D), 1915–1917; charter franchise. Became CUMBERLAND COLTS, mid-1917.

Chambersburg Maroons
Blue Ridge League (D), 1920–1928; charter franchise. Renamed CHAMBERSBURG YOUNG YANKS.

Chambersburg Young Yanks
Blue Ridge League (D), 1929–1930; renamed franchise. Had been CHAMBERSBURG MAROONS, 1920–1928. Disbanded with league after 1930 season.

CHAMPAIGN, IL

Champaign Clippers
Illinois–Indiana League, 1889; charter franchise. Disbanded with league after 1889 season.

Champaign Twins
Alternate name for CHAMPAIGN VELVETS.

Champaign Velvets (aka Twins)
Illinois–Missouri League (D), 1912–1914; renamed franchise. Had been CHAMPAIGN–URBANA VELVETS (aka Twins), 1911. Disbanded with league after 1914 season.

CHAMPAIGN–URBANA, IL

Champaign–Urbana Twins
Alternate name for CHAMPAIGN–URBANA VELVETS.

Champaign–Urbana Velvets (aka Twins)
Illinois–Missouri League (D), 1911; new franchise. Renamed CHAMPAIGN VELVETS (aka Twins), 1912.

CHANNEL CITIES
(See SANTA BARBARA–VENTURA, CA)

CHANUTE, KS

Chanute
Kansas State League, 1896; new franchise. Disbanded during 1896 season.

Chanute
Kansas State League (D), 1902; charter franchise. Disbanded after 1902 season.

Chanute
OAK League (D), mid-1907; relocated franchise. Had been MUSKOGEE, 1907. Disbanded with league after 1907 season.

Chanute Athletics
Kansas–Oklahoma–Missouri League (D), 1946–1947; charter franchise. Renamed CHANUTE GIANTS, 1948.

Chanute Athletics
Kansas–Oklahoma–Missouri League (D), 1949–1950; renamed franchise. Had been CHANUTE GIANTS, 1948. Disbanded after 1950 season.

Chanute Giants
Kansas–Oklahoma–Missouri League (D), 1948; renamed franchise. Had been CHANUTE ATH-LETICS, 1946–1947. Renamed CHANUTE ATHLETICS, 1949.

Chanute Indians
Missouri Valley League (D), mid-1902; relocated franchise. Had been COFFEYVILLE INDIANS, 1902. Disbanded after 1902 season.

CHAPMAN, KS

Chapman
Central Kansas League (D), mid-1910; new franchise. Had been BELOIT, 1909–mid-1910. Disbanded after 1910 season.

CHARLEROI, PA

Charleroi
Penn State League (D), 1902; charter franchise. Disbanded after 1902 season.

Charleroi
POM League (D), mid-1906–1907; relocated franchise. Had been PIEDMONT, mid-1906. Pennsylvania–West Virginia League (D), 1908–1909; charter franchise. Became PARKERSBURG, mid-1909.

Charleroi
Pennsylvania–West Virginia League (D), 1914; charter franchise. Disbanded with league after 1914 season.

Charleroi Babes
Middle Atlantic League (C), 1927–1928; new franchise. Renamed CHARLEROI GOVERNORS, 1929.

Charleroi Governors
Middle Atlantic League (C), 1929–1931; renamed franchise. Had been CHARLEROI BABES, 1927–1928. Disbanded after 1931 season.

Charleroi Tigers
Pennsylvania State League (D), mid-1934–mid-1936; charter franchise. Disbanded during 1936 season.

CHARLES CITY, IA

Charles City Tractorites
Central Association (D), mid-1917; relocated franchise. Had been DUBUQUE, 1917. Disbanded with association after 1917 season.

CHARLESTON, IL
(See also MATTOON, IL)

Charleston Broom Corn Cutters
KITTY League (D), 1906; new franchise. Eastern Illinois League (D), 1907; charter franchise. Renamed CHARLESTON EVANGELISTS, 1908.

Charleston Evangelists
Eastern Illinois League (D), 1908; renamed franchise. Had been CHARLESTON BROOM CORN CUTTERS, 1907. Disbanded with league after 1908 season.

CHARLESTON, NH

Charleston
Twin State League (D), 1911; charter franchise. Disbanded with league after 1911 season.

CHARLESTON, SC

Charleston
South Atlantic League, 1892; charter franchise. Disbanded with league after 1892 season.

Charleston
South Atlantic League (C), 1911; new franchise. Disbanded after 1911 season.

Charleston Chisox
South Atlantic League (A), 1959; new franchise. Renamed CHARLESTON WHITE SOX, 1960.

Charleston Gulls
South Atlantic Association (C), 1919; charter franchise. Renamed CHARLESTON PALMETTOS, 1920.

Charleston Palmettos
South Atlantic Association (C), 1920; renamed franchise. Had been CHARLESTON GULLS, 1919. Renamed CHARLESTON PALS, 1921.

Charleston Pals
South Atlantic Association (C), 1921–mid-1923; renamed franchise. Had been CHARLESTON PALMETTOS, 1919–1920. Became MACON PEACHES, mid-1923.

Charleston Patriots
Western Carolinas League (A), 1976–1977; renamed franchise. Had been CHARLESTON PIRATES, 1973–1975. Renamed CHARLESTON PIRATES, 1978.

Charleston Pirates
Western Carolinas League (A), 1973–1975; new franchise. Renamed CHARLESTON PATRIOTS, 1976.

Charleston Pirates
Western Carolinas League (A), 1978; renamed franchise. Had been CHARLESTON PATRIOTS, 1976–1977. Disbanded after 1978 season.

Charleston Rainbows
South Atlantic League (A), 1985–(still in existence as of 5-1-92); renamed franchise. Had been CHARLESTON ROYALS, 1980–1984.

Charleston Rebels
South Atlantic League (A), mid-1940–1942; 1946–1953; relocated franchise. Had been SPARTANBURG SPARTANS, 1938–mid-1940. Disbanded after 1953 season.

Charleston Royals
South Atlantic League (A), 1980–1984; charter franchise. Renamed CHARLESTON RAINBOWS, 1985.

Charleston Seagulls
Southern League, 1886–mid-1888; new franchise. Disbanded with league during 1888 season. South-

ern League, 1889; charter franchise. Became ATLANTA, mid-1889.

Charleston Seagulls
Southern League, 1893; new franchise. Disbanded with league during 1893 season. Southern League, 1894; new franchise. Disbanded during 1894 season.

Charleston Seagulls
Southern League, 1898; charter franchise. Disbanded with league during 1898 season.

Charleston Sea Gulls
South Atlantic League (C), 1904–1909; charter franchise. Became KNOXVILLE APPALACHIANS, mid-1909.

Charleston Sea Gulls
South Atlantic League (C), 1913–mid-1917; new franchise. Disbanded with league during 1917 season.

Charleston White Sox
South Atlantic League (A), 1960; renamed franchise. Had been CHARLESTON CHISOX, 1959. Disbanded after 1960 season.

CHARLESTON, VT
(See SPRINGFIELD, VT)

CHARLESTON, WV

Charleston Charlies
International League (AAA), 1971–1983; new franchise. Disbanded after 1983 season.

Charleston Indians
Eastern League (A), 1962; (AA), 1963–1964; new franchise. Disbanded after 1964 season.

Charleston Marlins
International League (AAA), mid-1961; relocated franchise. Had been SAN JUAN MARLINS, 1961.

Charleston Senators
Virginia Valley League (D), 1910; charter franchise. Mountain States League (D), 1911–1912; charter franchise. Disbanded during 1912 season.

Charleston Senators
Ohio State League (D), 1913–1916; new franchise. Disbanded with league after 1916 season.

Charleston Senators
Middle Atlantic League (C), 1931–1942; expansion franchise. Disbanded after 1942 season.

Charleston Senators
Central League (A), 1949–1951; new franchise. American Association (AAA), 1952–1960; new franchise. Disbanded after 1960 season.

Charleston Wheelers
South Atlantic League (A), 1987–(still in existence as of 5-1-92); new franchise.

CHARLOTTE, FL

Charlotte Rangers
Florida State League (A), 1991–(still in existence as of 5-1-92); new franchise.

CHARLOTTE, MI

Charlotte Giants
Michigan State League (D), mid-1926; relocated franchise. Had been FLINT VEHICLES, mid-1926. Disbanded with league after 1926 season.

CHARLOTTE, NC

Charlotte
South Atlantic League, 1892; charter franchise. Disbanded with league after 1892 season.

Charlotte
Virginia–North Carolina League (D), 1905; charter franchise. Dis-

banded with league after 1905 season.

Charlotte Hornets
Virginia–North Carolina League, mid-1901; relocated franchise. Had been PORTSMOUTH, 1901. North Carolina League (D), 1902; charter franchise. Disbanded during 1902 season.

Charlotte Hornets
Carolina Association (D), 1908–1912; charter franchise. North Carolina State League (D), 1913–1917; charter franchise. Disbanded with league after 1917 season.

Charlotte Hornets
South Atlantic Association (C), 1919–1920; (B), 1921–1930; charter franchise. Piedmont League (C), 1931–32; (B), 1933–35; 1937–1942; new franchise. Tri-State League (B), 1946–1953; charter franchise. South Atlantic League (A); new franchise, 1954–1963.

Charlotte Hornets
Southern League (AA), 1964–1970; charter franchise. Dixie Association (C), 1971; charter franchise. Southern League (AA), 1972; charter franchise. Disbanded after 1972 season.

Charlotte Knights
Southern League (AA), 1987–(still in existence as of 5-1-92); renamed franchise. Had been CHARLOTE O'S, 1976–1986.

Charlotte O's
Southern League (AA), 1976–1986; new franchise. Renamed CHARLOTTE KNIGHTS, 1987.

Charlotte Presbyterians
Virginia–North Carolina League, 1900; charter franchise. Disbanded after 1900 season.

Charlotte Twins
Western Carolinas League (A), 1972; new franchise. Disbanded after 1972 season.

CHARLOTTESVILLE, VA

Charlottesville Tuckahoes
Virginia Mountain League (D), 1914; charter franchise. Disbanded with league during 1914 season.

CHATAUQUA–CELERON, NY

Celeron
New York State, 1893; new franchise. Disbanded during 1893 season.

Celeron Acme Colored Giants
Iron and Oil League, 1898; charter franchise. Disbanded with league after 1898 season.

CHATHAM, ONTARIO, CANADA

Chatham Babes
Canadian League, mid-1898; relocated franchise. Had been SAGINAW TIGERS, International League, 1898. Renamed CHATHAM REDS, 1899.

Chahtam Reds
Canadian League, 1899; renamed franchise. Had been CHATHAM BABES, 1898. International League, 1900; charter franchise. Disbanded with league after 1900 season.

CHATTANOOGA, TN

Chattanooga
Southern League, 1889; new franchise. Disbanded with league after 1889 season.

Chattanooga
Southeastern League, 1897; charter franchise. Southern League, 1898; charter franchise. Disbanded after 1898 season.

Chattanooga
Tennessee–Alabama League (D), 1904; charter franchise. Disbanded after 1904 season.

Chattanooga Chatts
Southern League, 1892; charter franchise. Renamed CHATTANOOGA WARRIORS, 1893.

Chattanooga Lookouts
Southern League, 1885–1886; charter franchise. Disbanded after 1886 season.

Chattanooga Lookouts
Southern Association, 1901; (A), 1902; charter franchise. Became MONTGOMERY BLACK SOX, 1903.

Chattanooga Lookouts
South Atlantic League (C), 1909; new franchise. Disbanded after 1910 season.

Chattanooga Lookouts
Southern Association (A), 1910–1935; (A1) 1936–mid-1943; relocated franchise. Had been ARKANSAS (aka Little Rock Travelers) 1901–1909. Became MONTGOMERY REBELS, mid-1943.

Chattanooga Lookouts
Southern Association (A1), 1944–1945; (AA), 1946–1961; new franchise. Disbanded with association after 1961 season.

Chattanooga Lookouts
South Atlantic League (AA), 1963; charter franchise. Southern League (AA), 1964–1965; charter franchise. Disbanded after 1965 season.

Chattanooga Lookouts
Southern League (AA), 1976–(still in existence as of 5-1-92); new franchise.

Chattanooga Warriors
Southern League, 1893; renamed franchise. Had been CHATTA-

NOOGA CHATTS, 1892. Disbanded after 1893 season.

Chattanooga Warriors
Southern League, 1895; new franchise. Became MOBILE, mid-1895.

CHEHALIS, WA

Chehalis Protoges
Washington State League (D), 1910–1911; new franchise. Disbanded with league after 1911 season.

CHERRYVALE, KS

Cherryvale Boosters
Kansas State League (D), mid-1906; relocated franchise. Had been IOLA GRAYS, 1906. Disbanded with league after 1906 season.

CHESTER, PA

Chester
Keystone Association, 1884; charter franchise. Disbanded with association after 1884 season.

Chester
Tri-State League (D), mid-1912; relocated franchise. Had been JOHNSTOWN JOHNS, 1912. Disbanded after 1912 season.

CHESTER, SC

Chester
South Carolina League (D), 1908; new franchise. Disbanded with league after 1908 season.

CHEYENNE, WY

Cheyenne
Rocky Mountain League (D), 1912; charter franchise. Disbanded with league after 1912 season.

Cheyenne Indians
Western League (D), 1941; new franchise. Suspended operations with league after 1941 season, and did not rejoin when league resumed operations, 1947.

CHICAGO, IL

CHICAGO AMERICAN GIANTS
Negro National League, 1920–31; charter franchise. Negro Southern League, 1932; new franchise. Renamed COLE'S AMERICAN GIANTS, 1932.

CHICAGO AMERICAN GIANTS
Negro American League, 1937–1948; 1950; charter franchise. Disbanded with league after 1950 season.

CHICAGO BABES
Alternate name for CHICAGO COLTS, 1894–1897.

CHICAGO BROWNS
Union Association, 1884; charter franchise. Became PITTSBURGH, 1885.

CHICAGO CHIFEDS
Federal League, 1914; charter franchise. Renamed CHICAGO WHALES, 1915.

Chicago Colleens
All-American Girls Professional Baseball League, 1948; new franchise. Disbanded after 1948 season.

CHICAGO COLTS (aka BABES, CUBS and RAINMAKERS)
National League, 1890–1897; renamed franchise. Had been CHICAGO WHITE STOCKINGS, 1876–1889. Renamed CHICAGO ORPHANS, 1898.

CHICAGO CUBS
Alternate name for CHICAGO COLTS, 1894–1897.

CHICAGO CUBS
National League, 1899–(still in existence as of 5-1-92); renamed fran-

chise. Had been CHICAGO ORPHANS, 1898.

CHICAGO FAIRBANKS
League Alliance, 1877; charter franchise. Disbanded with alliance after 1877 season.

CHICAGO GIANTS
Negro National League, 1920–1921; charter franchise. Disbanded after 1921 season.

Chicago Maroons
Western Association, 1888; charter franchise. Disbanded after 1888 season.

CHICAGO ORPHANS
National League, 1898–1901; renamed franchise. Had been CHICAGO COLTS, 1894–1897. Renamed CHICAGO CUBS, 1902.

CHICAGO PIRATES
Players' League, 1890; charter franchise. Disbanded with league, 1890.

CHICAGO RAINMAKERS
Alternate name for CHICAGO COLTS, 1894–1897.

CHICAGO WHALES
Federal League, 1915; renamed franchise. Had been CHICAGO CHIFEDS, 1914. Disbanded with league, 1915.

CHICAGO WHITE SOX
Alternate name for CHICAGO WHITE SOX, 1871.

CHICAGO WHITE SOX (aka UNIQUES)
American League, 1904–(still in existence as of 5-1-92); charter franchise.

CHICAGO WHITE STOCKINGS
National Association, 1871; 1874–1875; charter franchise. National League, 1876–1889; charter franchise. Renamed CHICAGO COLTS, 1890.

CHICAGO WHITE STOCKINGS

American League, 1900–1903; renamed franchise. Renamed CHICAGO WHITE SOX, 1904.

COLE'S AMERICAN GIANTS

Negro National League, 1932; 1934–1936; new franchise. Disbanded after 1936 season.

CHICKASHA, OK

Chickasha Chicks
Western Association (D), 1920–1921; new franchise. Disbanded after 1921 season.

Chickasha Chicks
Alternate name for CHICKASHA TRAVELERS, 1922.

Chickasha Chiefs
Sooner State League (D), 1948–1952; new franchise. Disbanded after 1952 season.

Chickasha Indians
Southwestern Association (A), mid-1904; relocated franchise. Had been SHAWNEE INDIANS, 1904. Became SHAWNEE BROWNS, mid-1904.

Chickasha Orphans
Alternate name for CHICKASHA TRAVELERS, 1922.

Chickasha Travelers (aka Chicks and Orphans)
Oklahoma State League (D), 1922–mid-1923; charter franchise. Disbanded during 1923 season.

CHIHUAHUA, CHIHUAHUA, MEXICO

Chihuahua Dorados (Golden Ones)
Central Mexican League (C), 1956–1957; charter franchise. Arizona–Mexico League (C), 1958; new franchise. Disbanded with league after 1958 season.

Chihuahua Dorados (Golden Ones)
Mexican National League (B), 1946; charter franchise. Disbanded during 1946 season.

Chihuahua Dorados (Golden Ones)
Arizona–Texas League (C), 1952; charter franchise. Disbanded after 1952 season.

Chihuahua Dorados (Golden Ones)
Mexican League (AAA), 1973–1982; new franchise. Disbanded after 1982 season.

CHILLICOTHE, OH

Chillicothe
Tri-State League, 1894; charter franchise. Disbanded with league during 1894 season.

Chillicothe Babes
Ohio State League (D), 1913–mid-1915; new franchise. Had been CHILLICOTHE INFANTS, 1910–1912. Became MAYSVILLE ANGELS, mid-1915.

Chillicothe Babes
Ohio State League (D), mid-1916; relocated franchise. Had been HUNTINGTON BOOSTERS, 1916. Disbanded with league after 1916 season.

Chillicothe Infants
Ohio State League (D), 1910–1912; new franchise. Renamed CHILLICOTHE BABES, 1913.

Chillicothe Logans
Ohio State Association, 1884; charter franchise. Disbanded with association after 1884 season.

CHIPPEWA FALLS, WI
(See EAU CLAIRE, WI)

CINCINNATI, OH

Cincinnati
Federal League, 1913; charter franchise. Disbanded after 1913 season.

CINCINNATI BUCKEYES

Negro American League, 1942; new franchise. Renamed CINCINNATI CLOWNS, 1943.

CINCINNATI CLOWNS

Negro American League, 1943; renamed franchise. Became INDIANAPOLIS–CINCINNATI CLOWNS, 1944.

CINCINNATI CLOWNS

Negro American League, 1945; relocated franchise. Had been INDIANAPOLIS–CINCINNATI CLOWNS, 1944. Became INDIANAPOLIS CLOWNS, 1946.

CINCINNATI CUBAN STARS

Negro National League, 1921; expansion franchise. Renamed CUBAN STARS, 1922.

CINCINNATI KELLYS (aka KILLERS)

National League, 1890–1891; new franchise. Disbanded during 1891 season.

CINCINNATI KILLERS

Name for CINCINNATI KELLYS, 1891.

CINCINNATI OUTLAW REDS

Union Association, 1884; charter franchise. Disbanded with association after 1884 season.

CINCINNATI REDLEGS

National League, 1944–1945; renamed franchise. Renamed CINCINNATI REDS, 1946–1953.

CINCINNATI REDLEGS

National League, 1954–1960; renamed franchise. Renamed CINCINNATI REDS, 1961.

CINCINNATI REDS

Alternate name for CINCINNATI RED STOCKINGS, 1876–1880.

CINCINNATI REDS
National League, 1890–1943; renamed franchise. Renamed CINCINNATI REDLEGS, 1944–1945.

CINCINNATI REDS
National League, 1946–1953; renamed franchise. Had been CINCINNATI REDLEGS, 1944–1945. Renamed CINCINNATI REDLEGS, 1954–1960.

CINCINNATI REDS*
National League, 1961–(still in existence as of 5-1-92); renamed franchise. Had been CINCINNATI REDLEGS, 1954–1960.

CINCINNATI RED STOCKINGS
The first professional baseball club, formed March 15, 1869. Reverted to non-pro after 1870 season.

CINCINNATI RED STOCKINGS
National League, 1876–1880; charter franchise. American Association, 1881–1889. Became CINCINNATI REDS, 1890.

CINCINNATI TIGERS
Negro American League, 1937; charter franchise. Disbanded with league during 1937 season.

CUBAN STARS
Negro National League, 1922; renamed franchise. Had been CINCINNATI CUBAN STARS, 1921. Split into CUBAN STARS EAST and CUBAN STARS WEST, 1923.

CUBAN STARS
East–West League, 1932; charter franchise. Disbanded with league during 1932 season.

CUBAN STARS EAST
Eastern Colored League, 1923–mid-1928; charter franchise. Had been CUBAN STARS, 1922. Disbanded with league during 1928 season. American Negro League, 1929; charter franchise. Disbanded with league after 1929 season.

CUBAN STARS WEST
Negro National League, 1923–1930; renamed franchise. Had been CUBAN STARS, 1922. Disbanded after 1930 season.

CIRCLEVILLE, OH

Circleville
Tri-State League, 1894; charter franchise. Disbanded with league during 1894 season.

CISCO, TX

Cisco Scouts
West Texas League (D), 1920–1921; charter franchise. Disbanded after 1921 season.

CIUDAD MADERO, VERACRUZ, MEXICO

Ciudad Madero Braves
Mexican Center League (A), 1968–1970; new franchise. Disbanded after 1970 season.

CIUDAD MANTE, TAMAULIPAS, MEXICO

Ciudad Mante Alijadores (Smugglers)
Mexican Center League (A), 1969; new franchise. Renamed CIUDAD MANTE CANEROS, 1970.

Ciudad Mante Caneros (Cannons)
Mexican Center League (A), 1970–1972; renamed franchise. Had been CIUDAD MANTE AL-IJADORES, 1969. Renamed CIUDAD MANTE VALLES, 1973.

Ciudad Mante Valles (Valleys)
Mexican Center League (A), 1973–1974; renamed franchise. Had been CIUDAD MANTE CANEROS, 1970–1972. Disbanded after 1974 season.

Ciudad Mante Valles (Valleys)
Mexican Center League (A), 1977; new franchise. Disbanded after 1977 season.

CIUDAD OBREGON, MEXICO

Ciudad Obregon
Mexican Pacific League (A), 1976; charter franchise. Disbanded after 1976 season.

CIUDAD VALLES, MEXICO

Ciudad Valles
Mexican Center League (A), 1974; new franchise. Disbanded after 1974 season.

Ciudad Valles
Mexican Center League (A), 1978; new franchise. Disbanded after 1978 season.

CIUDAD VICTORIA, TAMAULIPAS, MEXICO

Ciudad Victoria
Mexican Center League (A), 1971; new franchise. Disbanded after 1971 season.

Ciudad Victoria
Mexican Center League (A), 1973–1974; new franchise. Disbanded after 1974 season.

---

* The team's seemingly schizophrenic inability to land on the Reds or the Redlegs as its nickname has much to do with the political "Red Scare." During the periods of history when this concern has been in the forefront, the team seems to prefer "Redlegs" instead of the apparent Communist-sympathetic "Reds."

Ciudad Victoria

Mexican Center League (A), 1976–1978; new franchise. Disbanded after 1978 season.

CLARINDA, IA

Clarinda

Iowa State League, 1903; new franchise. Disbanded during 1903 season.

Clarinda Antelopes

MINK League (D) 1910–1911; charter franchise. Disbanded after 1911 season.

CLARKSBURG, WV

Clarksburg

Pennsylvania–West Virginia League (D), 1914; charter franchise. Disbanded with league after 1914 season.

Clarksburg Bees

Western Pennsylvania League (D), 1907; charter franchise. Pennsylvania–West Virginia League (D), 1908–1909; charter franchise. West Virginia League (D), 1910; charter franchise. Disbanded with league after 1910 season.

Clarksburg Cyrians

Alternate name for CLARKSBURG GENERALS.

Clarksburg Generals (aka Cyrians and Ghosts)

Middle Atlantic League (C), mid-1925–1932; charter franchise. Disbanded after 1932 season.

Clarksburg Ghosts

Alternate name for CLARKSBURG GENERALS.

CLARKSDALE, MS

Clarksdale

Delta League (D), 1904; charter franchise. Disbanded after 1904 season.

Clarksdale

Cotton States League (D), 1913; new franchise. Disbanded after 1913 season.

Clarksdale Cubs

Mississippi State League (D), 1921; charter franchise. Cotton States League (D), 1922–mid-1923; charter franchise. Disbanded with league during 1923 season.

Clarksdale Ginners

East Dixie League (C) mid-1934–1935; relocated franchise. Had been BATON ROUGE RED STICKS, 1934. Cotton States League (C), 1936; charter franchise. Renamed CLARKSDALE LITTLE RED SOX, 1937.

Clarksdale Little Red Sox

Cotton States League (C), 1937; renamed franchise. Had been CLARKSDALE GINNERS, 1936. Renamed CLARKSDALE RED SOX, 1938.

Clarksdale Planters

Cotton States League (C), 1947–1951; charter franchise. Disbanded after 1951 season.

Clarksdale Red Sox

Cotton States League (C), 1938–mid-1941; renamed franchise. Had been CLARKSDALE LITTLE RED SOX, 1937. Became MARSHALL TIGERS, mid-1941.

CLARKSTON, WA

(See LEWISTON, ID)

CLARKSVILLE, AR

Clarksville

Arkansas State League, 1924; new franchise. Disbanded during 1924 season.

CLARKSVILLE, TN

Clarksville Billies

KITTY League (D), 1911; renamed franchise. Had been CLARKSVILLE VOLUNTEERS, 1910. Renamed CLARKSVILLE REBELS, 1912.

Clarksville Boosters

KITTY League (D), 1913–1914; renamed franchise. Had been CLARKSVILLE REBELS, 1912. Disbanded with league after 1914 season.

Clarksville Cats

KITTY League (D), 1947–1951; renamed franchise. Had been CLARKSVILLE OWLS, 1946. Disbanded after 1951 season.

Clarksville Grays

KITTY League (D), 1903–1904; charter franchise. Disbanded after 1904 season.

Clarksville Owls

KITTY League (D), 1946; charter franchise. Renamed CLARKSVILLE CATS, 1947.

Clarksville Rebels

KITTY League (D), 1912; renamed franchise. Had been CLARKSVILLE BILLIES, 1911. Renamed CLARKSVILLE BOOSTERS, 1913.

Clarksville Volunteers

KITTY League (D), 1910; charter franchise. Renamed CLARKSVILLE BILLIES, 1911.

Clarksville Volunteers

KITTY League (D), 1916; charter franchise. Disbanded with league after 1916 season.

CLARKSVILLE, TX

Clarksville

Texas League, 1905; new franchise. Disbanded during 1905 season.

CLAY CENTER, KS

Clay Center

Kansas State League (D), 1913; charter franchise. Disbanded after 1913 season.

Clay Center Colts
Central Kansas League (D), 1909–1911; new franchise. Disbanded after 1911 season.

CLAY CENTER, NE

Clay Center
Nebraska State League, 1887; charter franchise. Disbanded with league after 1887 season.

CLAYPOOL, AZ
(See GLOBE, AZ)

CLEAR LAKE, IA

Clear Lake
Iowa State League (D), 1912; new franchise. Disbanded with league after 1912 season.

Clear Lake
Central Association (D), mid-1917; relocated franchise. Had been CEDAR RAPIDS RABBITS, 1913–mid-1917. Disbanded with association after 1917 season.

CLEARWATER, FL

Clearwater Pelicans
Florida State League (D), 1924; relocated franchise. Had been DAYTONA BEACH ISLANDERS, 1920–mid-1924. Disbanded with league during 1924 season.

Clearwater Phillies
Florida State League (A), 1985–(still in existence as of 5-1-92); new franchise.

CLEBURNE, TX

Cleburne Generals
Texas–Oklahoma League (D), 1921–1922; charter franchise. Disbanded with league after 1922 season.

Cleburne Railroaders
Texas League (C), 1906; expansion franchise. Disbanded after 1906 season.

Cleburne Railroaders
Texas–Oklahoma League (D), 1911; charter franchise. South Central League (D), 1912; charter franchise. Disbanded with league after 1912 season.

CLEVELAND, MS

Cleveland Bengals
East Dixie League (C), mid-1935; relocated franchise. Had been COLUMBUS BENGALS, 1935. Disbanded with league after 1935 season.

Cleveland Little A's
Cotton States League (C), 1936; new franchise. Disbanded after 1936 season.

CLEVELAND, OH

Cleveland
Federal League, 1913; charter franchise. Disbanded after 1913 season.

Cleveland Bearcats
American Association (AA), 1914; new franchise. Renamed CLEVELAND SPIDERS, 1915.

CLEVELAND BEARS
Negro American League, mid-1939–1940; new franchise. Disbanded after 1940 season.

CLEVELAND BLUEBIRDS (aka BLUES)
American League, 1901; renamed franchise. Had been CLEVELAND LAKE SHORES, 1900. Renamed CLEVELAND BRONCOS, 1902.

CLEVELAND BLUES
National League, 1879–1884; new franchise. Disbanded after 1884 season.

CLEVELAND BLUES
American Association, 1887–1888; charter franchise. National League, 1889–1898; new franchise. Became ST. LOUIS PERFECTOS, 1899.

CLEVELAND BLUES
Alternate name for CLEVELAND BLUEBIRDS, 1901.

CLEVELAND BRONCOS
American League, 1902; renamed franchise. Had been CLEVELAND BLUEBIRDS, (aka Blues), 1900–1901. Renamed CLEVELAND NAPS, 1903.

CLEVELAND BROWNS
Negro National League, 1924; new franchise. Disbanded after 1924 season.

CLEVELAND BUCKEYES
Negro American League, 1943–1948; new franchise. Disbanded after 1948 season.

CLEVELAND BUCKEYES
Negro American League, 1950; new franchise. Disbanded during 1950 season.

CLEVELAND ELITES
Negro National League, 1926; new franchise. Renamed CLEVELAND HORNETS, 1927.

CLEVELAND FOREST CITY
Western League, 1885; charter franchise. Disbanded during 1885 season.

CLEVELAND GIANTS
Negro National League, mid-1933; new franchise. Renamed CLEVELAND RED SOX, 1934.

CLEVELAND HORNETS
Negro National League, 1927; renamed franchise. Had been CLEVELAND ELITES, 1926. Disbanded after 1927 season.

CLEVELAND INDIANS
American League, 1915–(still in existence as of 5-1-92); renamed franchise. Had been CLEVELAND MOLLY McGUIRES, 1912–1914.

CLEVELAND INFANTS

Players' League, 1890; charter franchise. Disbanded with league, 1890.

Cleveland Lake Shores

American League, 1900; charter franchise. Became CLEVELAND BLUEBIRDS, 1901.

CLEVELAND MOLLY McGUIRES (named after manager Jim McGuire)

American League, 1912–1914; renamed franchise. Had been CLEVELAND NAPS, 1903–1911. Renamed CLEVELAND INDIANS, 1915.

CLEVELAND NAPS (named after manager Napoleon Lajoie)

American League, 1903–1911; renamed franchise. Had been CLEVELAND BRONCOS, 1902. Became CLEVELAND MOLLY McGUIRES, 1912–1914.

CLEVELAND RED SOX

Negro National League, 1934; renamed franchise. Had been CLEVELAND GIANTS, mid-1933. Disbanded after 1934 season.

CLEVELAND SPIDERS

National League, 1889–1899; new franchise. Disbanded after 1899 season.

Cleveland Spiders

American Association (AA), 1915; renamed franchise. Had been CLEVELAND BEARCATS, 1914. Disbanded after 1915 season.

CLEVELAND TATE STARS

Negro National League, 1922; new franchise. Disbanded during 1922 season.

FOREST CITY OF CLEVELAND

National Association, 1871–1872; charter franchise. Disbanded after 1872 season.

CLEVELAND, TN

Cleveland Counts

Appalachian League (D), 1911–mid-1913; charter franchise. Became MORRISTOWN JOBBERS, 1913.

Cleveland Manufacturers

Appalachian League (D), 1921–1922; charter franchise. Disbanded after 1922 season.

CLIFTON FORGE, VA

Clifton Forge Railroaders

Virginia Mountain League (D), 1914; charter franchise. Disbanded with league during 1914 season.

CLINTON, IL

Clinton Champs

Illinois–Missouri League (D), 1910–mid-1912; charter franchise. Became KANKAKEE KANKS, mid-1912.

CLINTON, IA

Clinton

Eastern Iowa League, 1895; charter franchise. Disbanded with league after 1895 season.

Clinton

Iowa State League (D), mid-1906; relocated franchise. Had been BOONE MINERS, 1906. Disbanded after 1906 season.

Clinton C-Sox

Midwest League (D), 1960–1962; (A), 1963–1965; renamed franchise. Had been CLINTON PIRATES, 1956–1959. Renamed CLINTON PILOTS, 1966.

Clinton Cubs

Central Association (C), 1947–1948; charter franchise. Renamed CLINTON STEERS, 1949.

Clinton Dodgers

Midwest League (D), 1977–1979; renamed franchise. Had been CLIN-

TON PILOTS, 1966–1976. Renamed CLINTON GIANTS, 1980.

Clinton Giants

Three I League (B), 1939–1941; renamed franchise. Had been CLINTON OWLS, 1937–1938. Disbanded after 1941 season.

Clinton Giants

Midwest League (A), 1980–(still in existence as of 5-1-92); renamed franchise. Had been CLINTON DODGERS, 1977–1979.

Clinton Infants

Illinois–Iowa–Indiana League (B), 1907–1908; new franchise. Disbanded after 1908 season.

Clinton Owls

Three I League (B), 1937–1938; charter franchise. Renamed CLINTON GIANTS, 1939.

Clinton Pilots

Central Association (D), 1914–1917; new franchise. Disbanded during 1917 season.

Clinton Pilots

Midwest League (D), 1966–1976; renamed franchise. Had been CLINTON C-SOX, 1960–1965. Renamed CLINTON DODGERS, 1977.

Clinton Pirates

MOV League (D), 1954–1955; new franchise. Midwest League (D), 1956–1959; charter franchise. Renamed CLINTON C-SOX, 1960.

Clinton Steers

Central Association (C), 1949; renamed franchise. Had been CLINTON CUBS, 1947–1948. Disbanded after 1949 season.

Clinton Teddies

Northern Association of Baseball (C), 1910; (D), mid-1910; charter franchise. Disbanded with league after 1910 season.

CLINTON, NC

Clinton Blues
Tobacco State League (D), 1946–1948; charter franchise. Renamed CLINTON SAMPSON BLUES, 1949.

Clinton Sampson Blues
Tobacco State League (D), 1949–1950; renamed franchise. Had been CLINTON BLUES, 1946–1948. Disbanded with league after 1950 season.

CLINTON, OK

Clinton Bulldogs
Oklahoma State League (D), mid-1922–1923; charter franchise. Disbanded after 1923 season.

CLOVIS, NM

Clovis
West Texas League (D), 1922; new franchise. Disbanded with league after 1922 season.

Clovis Cubs
Panhandle Pecos Valley League (D), 1923; charter franchise. Disbanded after 1923 season.

Clovis Pioneers
West Texas–New Mexico League (D), 1938–1942; (B), 1946–1955; new franchise. Southwestern League (B), 1956; charter franchise. Renamed CLOVIS REDLEGS, 1957.

Clovis Redlegs
Southwestern League (B), 1957; renamed franchise. Had been CLOVIS PIONEERS, 1938–1942; 1946–1956. Disbanded with league after 1957 season.

COAHUILA, MEXICO

(See also MONELOUA, MEXICO; SALTILLO, MEXICO)

Coahuila Miners
Mexican League (AAA), 1974–1979; new franchise. Disbanded after 1979 season.

COALINGA, CA

Coalinga Savages
San Joaquin Valley League (D), 1910; charter franchise. Disbanded after 1910 season.

COATZACOALCOS, VERACRUZ, MEXICO

Coatzacoalcos Puerto Mexico Portenos
Mexican Southeast League (A), 1966–1970; new franchise. Disbanded after 1970 season.

COBLESKILL, NY

Cobleskill Giants
New York State League, 1890; new franchise. Disbanded with league after 1890 season.

COCOA, FL

Cocoa
Cocoa Rookie League (R), 1964; charter franchise. Disbanded with league after 1964 season.

Cocoa Astros
Florida State League (A), 1965–1971; new franchise. Florida East Coast League (R), 1972; charter franchise. Disbanded with league after 1972 season.

Cocoa Astros
Florida State League (A), 1977; new franchise. Disbanded after 1977 season.

Cocoa Fliers
Florida East Coast League (D), 1941–mid-1942; charter franchise. Disbanded during 1942 season.

Cocoa Indians
Florida State League (D), 1951–1958; new franchise. Disbanded after 1958 season.

COFFEYVILLE, KS

Coffeyville
Kansas State League, 1896; new franchise. Disbanded with league after 1896 season.

Coffeyville Bricks
Kansas State League (D), 1906; new franchise. Oak League (D), 1907; charter franchise. Disbanded with league after 1907 season.

Coffeyville Indians
Missouri Valley League, 1902; new franchise. Became CHANUTE INDIANS, mid-1902.

Coffeyville Refiners
Southwestern Association (D) 1921, (C) 1922–mid-1924; charter franchise. Disbanded during 1924 season.

Coffeyville White Sox
Western Association (D), 1911; new franchise. Disbanded with association during 1911 season.

COLEMAN, TX

Coleman Bearcats
Alternate name for COLEMAN RANGERS.

Coleman Rangers (aka Bearcats)
West Texas League (D), 1928–1929; charter franchise. Disbanded with league after 1929 season.

COLONIAL HEIGHTS–PETERSBURG, VA

Colonial Heights–Petersburg Generals
Virginia League (C), 1951, relocated franchise. Disbanded with league after 1951 season.

Colonial Heights–Petersburg Colts
Piedmont League (B), 1954; new franchise. Disbanded after 1954 season.

COLONIES, NY

(See ALBANY, NY)

COLORADO SPRINGS, CO

Colorado Springs
Colorado State League, 1889; charter franchise. Disbanded with league after 1889 season.

Colorado Springs Millionaires
Western League, 1901; (A), 1902–1904; expansion franchise. Became PUEBLO INDIANS, 1905.

Colorado Springs Millionaires
Rocky Mountain League (D), 1912; charter franchise. Disbanded with league after 1912 season.

Colorado Springs Millionaires
Western League (A), mid-1916; relocated franchise. Had been WICHITA WOLVES, 1909–1916. Disbanded after 1916 season.

Colorado Springs Sky Sox
Western League (A), 1950–1958; expansion franchise. Disbanded with league after 1958 season.

Colorado Springs Sky Sox
Pacific Coast League (AAA), 1988–(still in existence as of 5-1-92); relocated franchise. Had been HAWAII ISLANDERS, 1961–1987.

COLUMBIA, SC

Columbia
South Atlantic League, 1892; charter franchise. Disbanded with league after 1892 season.

Columbia
Southeastern League, 1896; charter franchise. Disbanded after 1896 season.

Columbia Comers
South Atlantic League (C), 1912; renamed franchise. Had been COLUMBIA COMMIES, 1911. Disbanded after 1912 season.

Columbia Comers
South Atlantic League (C), 1914–1917; new franchise. Disbanded with league during 1917 season.

Columbia Comers
South Atlantic Association (C), 1919–1920; (B), 1921–mid-1923; charter franchise. Became GASTONIA COMERS, mid-1923.

Columbia Comers
South Atlantic Association (B), 1925–1930; new franchise. Disbanded with league after 1930 season.

Columbia Commies
South Atlantic League (C), 1911; renamed franchise. Had been COLUMBIA GAMECOCKS, 1905–1910. Renamed COLUMBIA COMERS, 1912.

Columbia Gamecocks
South Atlantic League (C), 1905–1910; renamed franchise. Had been COLUMBIA SKYSCRAPERS, 1904. Renamed COLUMBIA COMMIES, 1911.

Columbia Gems
South Atlantic League (A), 1956; renamed franchise. Had been COLUMBIA REDS, 1938–1942; 1946–1955. Disbanded after 1957 season.

Columbia Mets
South Atlantic League (AA), 1983–(still in existence as of 5-1-92); new franchise.

Columbia Reds
South Atlantic League (A), 1938–1942; 1946–1955; charter franchise. Renamed COLUMBIA GEMS, 1956.

Columbia Reds
South Atlantic League (A), 1960–1961; charter franchise. Disbanded after 1961 season.

Columbia Sandlappers
Piedmont League (B), 1934; new franchise. Became ASHEVILLE TOURISTS, mid-1934.

Columbia Senators
South Atlantic League (B), 1936–1937; charter franchise. Renamed COLUMBIA REDS, 1938.

Columbia Skyscrapers
South Atlantic League (C), 1904; charter franchise. Renamed COLUMBIA GAMECOCKS, 1905.

COLUMBIA, TN

Columbia
Tennessee–Alabama League (D), 1903–1904; charter franchise. Disbanded with league after 1904 season.

Columbia Mules
Alabama–Tennessee League (D), mid-1921; charter franchise. Disbanded with league after 1921 season.

COLUMBUS, GA

Columbus
Southern League, 1885; charter franchise. Disbanded during 1885 season.

Columbus Astros
Southern League (AA), 1970; renamed franchise. Had been COLUMBUS WHITE SOX, 1969. Dixie Association (AA), 1971; charter franchise. Southern League (AA), 1972–1980; charter franchise. Renamed COLUMBUS MUDCATS, 1989.

Columbus Babies
Southern League, 1896; new franchise. Became ASHEVILLE MOONSHINERS, mid-1896.

Columbus Babies
Southeastern League, 1897; new franchise. Disbanded with league after 1897 season.

Columbus Cardinals
South Atlantic League (A), 1946–1955; charter franchise. Renamed COLUMBUS FOXES, 1956.

Columbus Confederate Yankees
Southern League (AA), 1964–1968; charter franchise. Renamed COLUMBUS WHITE SOX, 1969.

Columbus Foxes
South Atlantic League (C), 1909–1917; new franchise. Disbanded during 1917 season.

Columbus Foxes
Southeastern League (B), 1926–1930; charter franchise. Disbanded after 1930 season.

Columbus Foxes
Southeastern League (B), 1932; charter franchise. Disbanded with league during 1932 season.

Columbus Foxes
South Atlantic League (A), 1956–1957; renamed franchise. Had been COLUMBUS CARDINALS, 1946–1955. Alabama–Florida League (D); expansion franchise, 1958. Renamed COLUMBUS PIRATES, 1959.

Columbus Indians
South Atlantic League (A), 1991–(still in existence as of 5-1-92); expansion franchise.

Columbus Mudcats
Southern League (AA), 1989–1990; renamed franchise. Had been COLUMBUS ASTROS, 1970–1988. Became CAROLINA MUDCATS (ZEBULON, NC), 1991.

Columbus Pirates
South Atlantic League (A), 1959; charter franchise. Had been COLUMBUS FOXES, Alabama–Florida League, 1956–1958. Became GASTONIA PIRATES, mid-1959.

Columbus Red Birds
South Atlantic League (B), 1936–1942; charter franchise. Suspended operations with league after 1942 season, and rejoined as COLUMBUS CARDINALS, 1946.

Columbus River Snipes
Georgia State League (D), 1906; charter franchise. Became BRUNSWICK, mid-1906.

Columbus White Sox
Southern League (AA), 1969; renamed franchise. Had been COLUMBUS CONFEDERATE YANKEES, 1964–1968. Renamed COLUMBUS ASTROS, 1970.

COLUMBUS, MS

Columbus Bengals
East Dixie League (C), 1935; expansion franchise. Became CLEVELAND BENGALS, mid-1935.

Columbus Discoverers
Cotton States League (D), 1907–1908; new franchise. Disbanded after 1908 season.

Columbus Joy Riders
Cotton States League (D), mid-1912–1913; relocated franchise. Had been HATTIESBURG TIMBERJACKS, 1912. Disbanded with league after 1913 season.

COLUMBUS, NE

Columbus Discoverers
Nebraska State League (D), 1910–1913; charter franchise. Renamed COLUMBUS PAWNEES, 1914.

Columbus Pawnees
Nebraska State League (D), 1914–1915; renamed franchise. Had been COLUMBUS DISCOVERERS, 1911–1913. Disbanded with league during 1915 season.

COLUMBUS, OH

COLUMBUS BLUEBIRDS
Negro National League, 1933; new franchise. Disbanded during 1933 season.

Columbus Buckeyes
International Association, 1877; charter franchise. Disbanded with association after 1877 season.

Columbus Buckeyes
Ohio State League, 1887; charter franchise. Disbanded with league after 1887 season.

COLUMBUS BUCKEYES
Alternate name for COLUMBUS SENATORS, 1883–1884.

COLUMBUS BUCKEYES
Alternate name for COLUMBUS COLTS, 1889–1891.

COLUMBUS BUCKEYES
Negro National League, 1921; new franchise. Disbanded after 1921 season.

Columbus Clippers
International League (AAA); 1977–(still in existence as of 5-1-92); new franchise.

COLUMBUS COLTS (aka BUCKEYES)
American Association, 1889–1891; new franchise. Disbanded with association after 1891 season.

Columbus Cubs
Inter-State League (B), 1913; charter franchise. Disbanded with league after 1913 season.

Columbus Discoverers
Western Association, 1901; charter franchise. Disbanded with league after 1901 season.

COLUMBUS ELITE GIANTS
Negro National League, 1935; new franchise. Became WASHINGTON ELITE GIANTS, 1936.

Columbus Jets
International League (AAA), 1955–1970; new franchise. Had been COLUMBUS SENATORS, 1902–1954. Disbanded after 1970 season.

Columbus Red Birds
American Association (AA), 1940–1945; (AAA), 1946–1954; renamed franchise. Renamed COLUMBUS JETS, 1955.

Columbus Reds
Western League, 1892; charter franchise. Disbanded after 1892 season.

Columbus Senators
Tri-State League, 1888; charter franchise. Disbanded after 1888 season.

Columbus Senators
Inter-State League, mid-1899–mid-1900; relocated franchise. Had been GRAND RAPIDS FURNITUREMAKERS, 1899. Became ANDERSON, mid-1900.

COLUMBUS SENATORS (aka BUCKEYES)
American Association, 1883–1884; new franchise. Disbanded with league after 1884 season.

Columbus Senators
Western League, 1896–mid-1899; new franchise. Became GRAND RAPIDS FURNITUREMAKERS, mid-1899.

Columbus Senators
American Association (A), 1902–1907; (AA), 1908–1939; charter franchise. Renamed COLUMBUS RED BIRDS, 1940.

Columbus Statesmen
Inter-State League, 1895; new franchise. Disbanded after 1895 season.

CONCORD, NH

Concord Marines
New England League (B), 1902–1905; new franchise. Disbanded after 1905 season.

CONCORD, NC

Concord Nationals
North Carolina State League (D), 1949–1950; renamed franchise.

Had been CONCORD WEAVERS, 1939–1942; 1946–1948. Renamed CONCORD SPORTS, 1951.

Concord Sports
North Carolina State League (D), 1951; renamed franchise. Had been CONCORD NATIONALS, 1949–1950. Disbanded after 1951 season.

Concord Weavers
North Carolina State League (D), 1939–1942; 1945–1948; new franchise. Renamed CONCORD NATIONALS, 1949.

CONCORDIA, KS

Concordia Boosters
Central Kansas League (D), 1910; new franchise. Renamed CONCORDIA TRAVELERS, 1911.

Concordia Travelers
Central Kansas League (D), 1911; renamed franchise. Had been CONCORDIA BOOSTERS, 1910. Disbanded after 1911 season.

CONNELLSVILLE, PA

Connellsville
Penn State League (D), 1903–1905; new franchise. Disbanded after 1905 season.

Connellsville
Ohio–Pennsylvania League (D), 1912; new franchise. Disbanded with league after 1912 season.

Connellsville
Pennsylvania–West Virginia League (D), 1914; charter franchise. Disbanded with league after 1914 season.

Connellsville Cokers
Western Pennsylvania League (D), 1907; charter franchise. Pennsylvania–West Virginia League (D), 1908–1909; charter franchise. Disbanded with league after 1909 season.

CONNERSVILLE, IN

Connersville
Indiana State League, 1896; charter franchise. Disbanded with league after 1896 season.

CONOVER, NC
(See NEWTON, NC)

CONSTABLEVILLE, NY

Constableville
Central New York League, 1886; charter franchise. Disbanded with league after 1886 season.

COOLEEMEE, NC

Cooleemee Cards
North Carolina State League (D), 1940–1941; charter franchise. Had been COOLEEMEE COOLS, 1939. Disbanded after 1941 season.

Cooleemee Cools
North Carolina State League (D), 1939; renamed franchise. Had been COOLEEMEE WEAVERS, 1937–1938. Renamed COOLEEMEE CARDS, 1940.

Cooleemee Weavers
North Carolina State League (D), 1937–1938; charter franchise. Renamed COOLEEMEE COOLS, 1939.

COOS BAY, OR
(See NORTH BEND, OR)

CORDELE, GA
(See also AMERICUS, GA)

Cordele
Georgia State League (D), 1906; charter franchise. Disbanded with league during 1906 season.

Cordele A's
Georgia–Florida League (D), 1950–1954; renamed franchise. Had been CORDELE INDIANS, 1947–1949. Renamed CORDELE ORIOLES, 1955.

Cordele Babies
Empire State League (D), 1913; charter franchise. Disbanded with league after 1913 season.

Cordele Bees
Georgia–Florida League (D), 1939–1940; renamed franchise. Had been CORDELE REDS, 1936–1938. Renamed CORDELE REDS, 1941.

Cordele Indians
Georgia–Florida League (D), 1947–1949; renamed franchise. Had been CORDELE WHITE SOX, 1946. Renamed CORDELE A'S, 1950.

Cordele Orioles
Georgia–Florida League (D), 1955; renamed franchise. Had been CORDELE A'S, 1950–1954. Disbanded after 1955 season.

Cordele Ramblers
Georgia State League (D), 1914; charter franchise. Disbanded after 1914 season.

Cordele Reds
Georgia–Florida League (D), 1936–1938; new franchise. Renamed CORDELE BEES, 1941.

Cordele Reds
Georgia–Florida League (D), 1941–1942; renamed franchise. Had been CORDELE BEES, 1939–1940. Became CORDELE WHITE SOX when league resumed, 1946.

Cordele White Sox
Georgia–Florida League (D), 1946; charter franchise. Renamed CORDELE INDIANS, 1947.

CORDOBA, VERACRUZ, MEXICO

Cordoba Coffeegrowers
Mexican League (AAA), 1972–1979; new franchise. Disbanded after 1979 season.

Cordoba Coffeegrowers
Mexican League (AAA), 1984–1986; new franchise. Disbanded after 1986 season.

Cordoba Coffeegrowers
Mexican League (AAA), 1991– (still in existence as of 5-1-92); new franchise.

CORINTH, MS

Corinth
Alabama–Mississippi League (D), 1936; charter franchise. Disbanded with league during 1936 season.

Corinth Corinthians
Tri-State League (D), 1925–1926; charter franchise. Disbanded with league after 1926 season.

CORNING, NY

Corning Athletics
PONY League (D), 1951–1952; new franchise. Renamed CORNING INDEPENDENTS, 1953.

Corning Cor-Sox
New York–Pennsylvania League (D), 1958–1959; renamed franchise. Had been CORNING RED SOX, 1954–1957. Renamed CORNING RED SOX, 1960.

Corning Independents
PONY League (D), 1953; renamed franchise. Had been CORNING ATHLETICS, 1951–1952. Renamed CORNING RED SOX, 1954.

Corning Red Sox
PONY League (D), 1954–1956; renamed franchise. New York–Pennsylvania League (D), 1957; charter franchise. Had been CORNING INDEPENDENTS, 1953. Renamed CORNING COR-SOX, 1958.

Corning Red Sox
New York–Pennsylvania League (D), 1960; renamed franchise. Had been CORNING COR-SOX, 1958–1959. Disbanded after 1960 season.

Corning Royals
New York–Pennsylvania League (A), 1968–1969; expansion franchise. Disbanded after 1969 season.

CORNWALL, QUEBEC, CANADA
(See also PERTH, ONTARIO, CANADA)

Cornwall Bisons
Canadian–American League (C), 1938; relocated franchise. Had been PERTH-CORNWALL GRAYS, 1937. Renamed CORNWALL MAPLE LEAFS, 1939.

Cornwall Canadians
Border League (C), 1951; new franchise. Disbanded with league during 1951 season.

Cornwall Maple Leafs
Canadian–American League (C), 1939; renamed franchise. Had been CORNWALL BISONS, 1937–1938. Became ONEONTA INDIANS, 1940.

CORONADO, CA

Coronado Arabs
California State League (D), mid-1929; relocated franchise. Had been POMONA, mid-1929. Disbanded with league during 1929 season.

CORPUS CHRISTI, TX

Corpus Christi Aces
Rio Grande Valley League (C), 1949–1950; charter franchise. Gulf Coast League (B), 1951–1953; new franchise. Disbanded with league after 1953 season.

Corpus Christi Clippers
Big State League (B) 1954–1957; new franchise. Disbanded with league after 1957 season.

Corpus Christi Giants
Texas League (AA), 1958–1959; relocated franchise. Had been OKLAHOMA CITY INDIANS, 1933–1957. Became RIO GRANDE VALLEY GIANTS, 1960.

Corpus Christi Pelicans
Southwest Texas League (D), 1910–1911; charter franchise. Disbanded with league after 1911 season.

Corpus Christi Sea Gulls
Gulf States League (A), 1976; charter franchise. Lone Star League (A), 1977; charter franchise. Disbanded after 1977 season.

Corpus Christi Seahawks
Gulf Coast League (D), 1926; charter franchise. Texas Valley League (D), 1927–mid-1928; charter franchise. Disbanded with league during 1928 season.

Corpus Christi Seahawks
Rio Grande Valley League (C), 1931; charter franchise. Disbanded with league after 1931 season.

Corpus Christi Spudders
Texas Valley League (D), 1938; charter franchise. Disbanded with league after 1938 season.

CORSICANA, TX

Corsicana A's
Central Texas Trolley League (D), mid-1914–mid-1915; charter franchise. Disbanded with league during 1915 season.

Corsicana Desperados
North Texas League (D), 1907; new franchise. Disbanded with league after 1907 season.

Corsicana Gumbo Busters
Texas–Oklahoma League (D), 1922; new franchise. Disbanded with league after 1922 season.

Corsicana Oil Citys
Texas League (D), 1902–1904; new franchise. Renamed CORSICANA OILERS, 1905.

Corsicana Oilers
Texas League (D), 1905; renamed franchise. Had been CORSICANA OIL CITYS, 1902–1904. Disbanded during 1905 season.

Corsicana Oilers
Central Texas League (D), mid-1917; relocated franchise. Had been TEMPLE GOVERNORS, 1915–mid-1917. Disbanded with league during 1917 season.

Corsicana Oilers
Texas Association (D), 1923–1926; charter franchise. Lone Star League (D), 1927–1928; charter franchise. Disbanded after 1928 season.

CORTAZAR, MEXICO

Cortazar
Mexican Center League (A), 1975; new franchise. Disbanded after 1975 season.

CORTLAND, NY

Cortland
Central New York League, 1886; charter franchise. Disbanded with league after 1886 season.

Cortland
Empire State League, (C), 1905; charter franchise. Disbanded during 1905 season.

Cortland
Central New York League (C), 1910; charter franchise. Disbanded with league after 1910 season.

Cortland Wagonmakers
New York State League, 1897–mid-1901; charter franchise. Became WAVERLY WAGONMAKERS, mid-1901.

COSHOCTON, OH

Coshocton
Ohio State League, 1898; charter franchise. Disbanded during 1898 season.

Coshocton
Ohio State League (D), 1936; charter franchise. Disbanded during 1936 season.

COUDERSPORT, PA

Coudersport Giants
Inter-State League (D), 1905; charter franchise. Disbanded after 1905 season.

COUNCIL BLUFFS, IA

Council Bluffs
Iowa–South Dakota League (D), 1903; new franchise. Became SHELDON, mid-1903.

Council Bluffs Rails
Western League (A) mid-1935; relocated franchise. Had been OMAHA PACKERS, 1929–mid-1935. Disbanded during 1935 season.

COVINGTON, KY

Covington
Federal League, 1913; charter franchise. Became KANSAS CITY, mid-1913.

COVINGTON, VA

Covington Astros
Appalachian League (R), 1967–1976; renamed franchise. Had been COVINGTON RED SOX, 1966. Disbanded after 1976 season.

Covington Papermakers
Virginia Mountain League (D), 1914; charter franchise. Disbanded with league during 1914 season.

Covington Red Sox
Appalachian League (R), 1966; new franchise. Renamed COVINGTON ASTROS, 1967.

CRAWFORDSVILLE, IN

Crawfordsville Hoosiers
Central Inter-State League, 1888; charter franchise. Became TERRE HAUTE HOOSIERS, mid-1888.

Crawfordsville Orphans
Indiana–Illinois League, mid-1899; relocated franchise. Had been MUNCIE HOOSIERS, 1899. Disband-ed with league after 1899 season.

CRESTON, IA

Creston
Iowa State League, 1904; new franchise. Disbanded after 1904 season.

CRESTVIEW, FL

Crestview Braves
Alabama–Florida League (D), 1954–1956; new franchise. Disbanded after 1956 season.

CRISFIELD, MD

Crisfield Crabbers
Eastern Shore League (D), 1922–1928; charter franchise. Disbanded with league during 1928 season.

Crisfield Crabbers
Eastern Shore League (D), 1937; charter franchise. Became MILFORD GIANTS, 1938.

CROCKETT, TX

Crockett
East Texas League (D), 1916; charter franchise. Disbanded with league after 1916 season.

CROOKSTON, MD

Crookston
Midwest League, 1891; new franchise. Disbanded during 1891 season.

Crookston Crooks
Northern League (D), 1902–1905; charter franchise. Disbanded with league after 1905 season.

Crookston Pirates
Northern League (D), 1933–1941; charter franchise. Disbanded after 1941 season.

CROWLEY, LA

Crowley Millers
Gulf Coast League (C), 1950; charter franchise. Evangeline League, 1951–1957; new franchise. Disbanded with league after 1957 season.

Crowley Rice Birds
Gulf Coast League (D), 1908; new franchise. Disbanded with league after 1908 season.

CULIACAN, MEXICO
(See GUAMUCHIL, MEXICO)

CUMBERLAND, MD

Cumberland
POM League (D), 1906; charter franchise. Disbanded after 1906 season.

Cumberland Colts
Blue Ridge League (D), mid-1917; relocated franchise. Had been CHAMBERSBURG MAROONS, 1915–1917. Disbanded with league during 1918 season.

Cumberland Colts
Middle Atlantic League (C), mid-1925–1932; charter franchise. Disbanded after 1932 season.

Cumberland Rooters
Western Pensylvania League (D), mid-1907; relocated franchise. Had been LATROBE, 1907. Became PIEDMONT, mid-1907.

CUSHING, OK

Cushing
Southwestern League (D), mid-1921; relocated franchise. Had been PARSONS, 1921. Disbanded after 1921 season.

Cushing
Oklahoma State League (D), 1923–1924; new franchise. Disbanded with league after 1924 season.

Cushing Refiners
Southwestern League (D), 1925; new franchise. Disbanded after 1925 season.

CYNTHIANA, KY

Cynthiana Cobblers
Blue Grass League (D), 1923–1924; renamed franchise. Had been CYNTHIANA MERCHANTS, 1922. Disbanded with league after 1924 season.

Cynthiana Merchants
Blue Grass League (D), 1922; charter franchise. Renamed CYNTHIANA COBBLERS, 1923.

DALE CITY–WOODBRIDGE, VA

Prince William Cannons
Carolina League (A), 1989–(still in existence as of 5-1-92); renamed franchise. Had been PRINCE WILLIAM YANKEES, 1987–1988.

Prince William Pirates
Carolina League (A), 1984–1986; relocated franchise. Had been ALEXANDRIA DUKES, 1978–1983. Renamed PRINCE WILLIAM YANKEES, 1987.

Prince William Yankees
Carolina League (A), 1987–1988; renamed franchise. Had been PRINCE WILLIAM PIRATES, 1984–1986. Renamed PRINCE WILLIAM CANNONS, 1989.

DALLAS, TX

Dallas Browns
Texas League, 1884; charter franchise. Disbanded after 1884 season.

Dallas Colts
Alternate name for DALLAS SCRAPPERS, 1898.

Dallas Eagles
Texas League (AA), 1949–1957; renamed franchise. Had been DALLAS REBELS, 1939–1942; 1946–1948. Renamed DALLAS RANGERS, 1958.

Dallas Giants
Texas League (D), 1903–1905; (C), 1906–1910; (B), 1911–1918; renamed franchise. Had been DALLAS STEERS, 1902. Renamed DALLAS MARINES.

Dallas Hams
Texas League, 1888; charter franchise. Renamed DALLAS TIGERS, 1889.

Dallas Marines
Texas League (B), 1919; renamed franchise. Had been DALLAS GIANTS, 1903–1918. Renamed DALLAS SUBMARINES, 1920.

Dallas Navigators
Texas Southern League, 1896; charter franchise. Became DALLAS STEERS, 1897.

Dallas Rangers
Texas League (AA), 1958; renamed franchise. Had been DALLAS EAGLES, 1949–1957. American Association (AAA), 1959, New franchise. Became DALLAS–FORT WORTH RANGERS, 1960.

Dallas Rangers
Pacific Coast League (AAA), 1964; relocated franchise. Had been DALLAS–FORT WORTH RANGERS, 1960–1963. Merged with FORT WORTH CATS to become DALLAS–FORT WORTH SPURS (ARLINGTON, TX), 1965.

Dallas Rebels
Texas League (A1), 1939–1942; (AA), 1946–1948; renamed fran-

chise. Had been DALLAS STEERS, 1928–1938. Renamed DALLAS EAGLES, 1949.

Dallas Scrappers (aka Colts)
Texas League, 1898; renamed franchise. Had been DALLAS STEERS, 1897. Disbanded during 1898 season.

Dallas Steers
Texas League, 1897; renamed franchise. Had been DALLAS NAVIGATORS, 1896. Renamed DALLAS SCRAPPERS (aka Colts), 1898.

Dallas Steers
Texas League (D), 1902; charter franchise. Renamed DALLAS GIANTS, 1903.

Dallas Steers
Texas League (A) 1923–1935; (A1), 1936–1938; renamed franchise. Had been DALLAS SUBMARINES, 1920–1922. Renamed DALLAS REBELS, 1938.

Dallas Submarines
Texas League (B) 1920; (A), 1921–1922; renamed franchise. Had been DALLAS MARINES, 1919. Renamed DALLAS STEERS, 1923.

Dallas Sullivan's Steers
Texas League, 1895; new franchise. Renamed DALLAS NAVIGATORS, 1896.

Dallas Tigers
Texas League, 1889–1890; renamed franchise. Had been DALLAS HAMS, 1888. Disbanded with league after 1890 season.

DALLAS–FORT WORTH, TX
(See also FORT WORTH, TX)

Dallas–Fort Worth
Texas League, 1892; charter franchise. Became WACO, mid-1892.

Dallas–Fort Worth
Southwestern League, mid-1898; relocated franchise. Had been SHERMAN, 1898. Disbanded with league after 1898 season.

Dallas–Fort Worth
Southern League, mid-1899; relocated franchise. Had been MONTGOMERY SENATORS, 1899. Disbanded with league after 1899 season.

Dallas–Fort Worth Rangers
American Association (AAA), 1960–1962; renamed franchise. Had been DALLAS RANGERS, 1959. Pacific Coast League (AAA), 1963; new franchise. Renamed DALLAS RANGERS, 1964.

Dallas–Fort Worth Spurs
Texas League (AA), 1965–1970; relocated franchise. Had been FORT WORTH CATS, 1964. Dixie Association (C), 1971. Disbanded after 1971 season.

DANBURY, CT

Danbury Hatters
Eastern League, 1887; new franchise. Connecticut State League, 1888; charter franchise. Disbanded with league after 1888 season.

Danbury Hatters
Connecticut League, 1898; charter franchise. Disbanded after 1898 season.

Danbury Hatters
New York–New Jersey League (D), 1913; charter franchise. Atlantic League (D), 1914; charter franchise. Disbanded with league after 1914 season.

DANVILLE, IL

Danville
Central Inter-State League, 1888; charter franchise. Indiana–Illinois League, 1889; charter franchise.

Disbanded with league after 1889 season.

Danville Champions
Indiana–Illinois League, 1899; charter franchise. Central League, 1900; charter franchise. Disbanded after 1900 season.

Danville Dans
MOV League (D), 1951–1954; new franchise. Disbanded after 1954 season.

Danville Dodgers
Three I League (B), 1946–1950; charter franchise. Disbanded after 1950 season.

Danville Dodgers
Midwest League (A), 1975–1976; renamed franchise. Had been DAN-VILLE WARRIORS, 1970–1974. Disbanded after 1976 season.

Danville Old Soldiers
KITTY League (D), 1906; new franchise. Disbanded with league after 1906 season.

Danville Speakers
Eastern Illinois League (D), 1908; new franchise. Became STAUNTON, mid-1908.

Danville Speakers
Illinois–Iowa–Indiana League (B), 1910–mid-1914; new franchise. Became MOLINE PLOWBOYS, mid-1914.

Danville Suns
Midwest League (A), 1982; new franchise. Disbanded after 1982 season.

Danville Veterans
Illinois–Iowa–Indiana League (B), 1922–mid-1932; new franchise. Became SPRINGFIELD IL BROWNS, mid-1932.

Danville Warriors
Midwest League (A), 1970–1974; new franchise. Renamed DANVILLE DODGERS, 1975.

DANVILLE, PA

Danville
Pennsylvania State Association, mid-1886; relocated franchise. Had been LANCASTER, 1886. Disbanded after 1886 season.

Danville
Central Pennsylvania League, 1887; charter franchise. Disbanded after 1887 season.

Danville
Pennsylvania State League, 1892–mid-1893; charter franchise. Became READING, mid-1893.

Danville
Central Pennsylvania League, 1896; charter franchise. Disbanded after 1896 season.

Danville
Central Pennsylvania League, 1898; charter franchise. Disbanded after 1898 season.

DANVILLE, VA

Danville Bugs
Alternate name for DANVILLE RED SOX, 1911.

Danville Leafs
Piedmont League (C), 1926; new franchise. Became HIGH POINT POINTERS, mid-1926.

Danville Leafs
Carolina League (C), 1946–1958; charter franchise. Disbanded after 1958 season.

Danville Red Sox (aka Bugs, 1911)
Virginia League (C), 1906–1912; charter franchise. Disbanded during 1912 season.

Danville Tobacconists
Virginia–North Carolina League (D), 1905; charter franchise. Disbanded with league during 1905 season.

Danville Tobacconists
Piedmont League (D), 1920; (C), 1921–1924; new franchise. Disbanded after 1924 season.

Danville Tobacconists
Piedmont League (C), mid-1925; relocated franchise. Had been HIGH POINT POINTERS, 1920–mid-1925. Renamed DANVILLE LEAFS, 1926.

DANVILLE–SCHOOLFIELD, VA

Danville–Schoolfield Leafs
Bi-State League (D), 1934–1942; 1945; charter franchise. Disbanded with league after 1945 season.

DARDANELLE, AR

Dardanelle
Arkansas State League (D), 1924; new franchise. Disbanded during 1924 season.

DARLINGTON, SC

Darlington Fiddlers
South Carolina League (D), 1907; charter franchise. Disbanded after 1907 season.

DAVENPORT, IA

Davenport
Central Inter-State League, 1888–mid-1889; charter franchise. Became MONMOUTH MAPLE CITIES, mid-1889.

Davenport
Western Association, mid-1888; relocated franchise. Had been MINNEAPOLIS MINNIES, 1888.

Davenport Blue Sox
Illinois–Iowa–Indiana League (B), 1913–1916; renamed franchise. Had been DAVENPORT PRODIGALS, 1909–1912. Disbanded after 1916 season.

Davenport Blue Sox
Mississippi Valley League (D), 1929–1933; new franchise. Western League (A), 1934–1937; new franchise. Disbanded with league after 1937 season.

Davenport Brown Stockings
Northwestern League, 1879; charter franchise. Disbanded with league after 1879 season.

Davenport Cubs
Three I League (B), 1946–1947; charter franchise. Renamed DAVENPORT PIRATES, 1948.

Davenport DavSox
Three I League (B), 1957–1958; new franchise. Disbanded after 1958 season.

Davenport Hawkeyes
Illinois–Iowa League, 1891; new franchise. Disbanded after 1891 season.

Davenport Knickerbockers
Illinois–Iowa–Indiana League (B), 1906; renamed franchise. Had been DAVENPORT RIVERRATS, 1901–1905. Disbanded after 1906 season.

Davenport Pirates
Three I League (B), 1948–1949; renamed franchise. Had been DAVENPORT CUBS, 1946–1947. Renamed DAVENPORT QUADS, 1950.

Davenport Prodigals
Illinois–Iowa–Indiana League (B), 1909–1912; new franchise. Renamed DAVENPORT BLUE SOX, 1913.

Davenport Quads
Three I League (B), 1950; renamed franchise. Had been DAVENPORT PIRATES, 1948–1949. Renamed QUAD CITY TIGERS, 1951.

Davenport Riverrats
Illinois–Iowa–Indiana League, 1901 (B), 1902–1905; charter franchise. Renamed DAVENPORT KNICKERBOCKERS, 1906.

DAVENPORT, IA
(In conjunction with Bettendorf, IA–Moline, IL–Rock Island, IL)

Quad Cities Angels
Midwest League (A), 1962–1978; renamed franchise. Had been QUAD CITIES BRAVES, 1960–1961. Renamed QUAD CITIES CUBS, 1979.

Quad Cities Angels
Midwest League (A), 1985–(still in existence as of 5-1-92); renamed franchise. Had been QUAD CITIES CUBS, 1979–1984.

Quad Cities Braves
Midwest League (A), 1960–1961; new franchise. Renamed QUAD CITY ANGELS, 1962.

Quad Cities Pirates
Three I League (B), 1949; renamed franchise. Had been QUAD CITY CUBS, 1946–1948. Renamed QUAD CITY QUADS, 1950.

Quad Cities Quads
Three I League (B), 1950; renamed franchise. Had been DAVENPORT PIRATES, 1948–1949. Renamed QUAD CITIES TIGERS, 1951.

Quad Cities Tigers
Three I League (B), 1951; renamed franchise. Had been QUAD CITIES QUADS, 1950. Disbanded after 1952 season.

Quad City Cubs
Three I League (B), 1946–1948; charter franchise. Renamed QUAD CITIES PIRATES, 1949.

Quad City Cubs
Midwest League (A), 1979–1984; charter franchise. Renamed QUAD CITIES ANGELS, 1985.

DAWSON, NM

Dawson Stags
Rocky Mountain League (D), 1912; charter franchise. Disbanded with league after 1912 season.

DAWSON SPRINGS, KY

Dawson Springs
KITTY League (D), 1916; charter franchise. Disbanded with league during 1916 season.

DAYTON, OH

Dayton Aviators
Central League (D), 1928–1929; 1930; charter franchise. Disbanded with league after 1930 season.

Dayton Ducks
Central League (D), 1932; charter franchise. Middle Atlantic League (C), 1933–1938; expansion franchise. Renamed DAYTON WINGS, 1939.

Dayton Ducks
Middle Atlantic League (C), 1941–1942; renamed franchise. Had been DAYTON WINGS, 1939–1940. Suspended operations after 1942 season, and resumed as DAYTON INDIANS, 1946.

Dayton Gem Citys
Ohio State League, 1884; charter franchise. Disbanded after 1884 season.

Dayton Indians
Ohio State League (D), 1946–1947; charter franchise. Central League (A), 1948–1951; charter franchise. Disbanded with league after 1951 season.

DAYTON MARCOS
Negro National League, 1920; charter franchise. Disbanded after 1920 season.

Dayton Old Soldiers
Inter-State League, 1897–1899; new franchise. Renamed DAYTON VETERANS, 1900.

Dayton Old Soldiers
Western Association, 1901; charter franchise. Disbanded with association after 1901 season.

Dayton Reds
Tri-State League, 1889–1890; charter franchise. Northwestern League, 1891; charter franchise. Inter-State League, 1891; charter franchise. Disbanded with league after 1891 season.

Dayton Veterans
Inter-State League, 1900; renamed franchise. Had been DAYTON OLD SOLDIERS, 1897–1899. Renamed DAYTON OLD SOLDIERS, 1901.

Dayton Veterans
Central League (D), 1903–1917; charter franchise. Disbanded with league after 1917 season.

Dayton Wings
Middle Atlantic League (C), 1939–1940; renamed franchise. Had been DAYTON DUCKS, 1933–1938. Renamed DAYTON DUCKS, 1941.

DAYTONA BEACH, FL

Daytona Beach Admirals
Florida State League (A), 1985–1988; renamed franchise. Had been DAYTONA BEACH ASTROS, 1978–1984. Disbanded after 1988 season.

Daytona Beach Astros
Florida State League (A), 1978–1984; renamed franchise. Had been DAYTON BEACH ISLANDERS, 1977. Renamed DAYTONA BEACH ADMIRALS, 1985.

Daytona Beach Dodgers
Florida State League (D), 1946; charter franchise. Renamed DAYTONA BEACH ISLANDERS, 1947.

Daytona Beach Dodgers
Florida State League (A), 1968–1973; new franchise. Disbanded after 1973 season.

Daytona Beach Explorers
Senior Professional Baseball Association, 1990; relocated franchise. Had been BRADENTON EXPLORERS, 1989–1990. Disbanded with association during 1990–91 season.

Daytona Beach Islanders
Florida State League (D), 1920, mid-1924; (C), 1921–1923; new franchise. Became CLEARWATER PELICANS, mid-1924.

Daytona Beach Islanders
Florida State League (D), 1928; new franchise. Disbanded with league during 1928 season.

Daytona Beach Islanders
Florida State League (D), 1936–1941; charter franchise. Disbanded after 1941 season.

Daytona Beach Islanders
Florida State League (D), 1947–1962; (A), 1963–1966; renamed franchise. Had been DAYTONA BEACH DODGERS, 1946. Disbanded after 1966 season.

Daytona Beach Islanders
Florida State League (A), 1977–1966; new franchise. Renamed DAYTONA BEACH ASTROS, 1978.

DEADWOOD, SD

Deadwood Mets
Black Hills League, 1891–1892; charter franchise. Disbanded with league after 1892 season.

DECATUR, AL

Decatur
Tennessee–Alabama League (D), 1903–1904; charter franchise. Disbanded with league after 1904 season.

Decatur
Alabama–Mississippi League (D), 1936; charter franchise. Disbanded with league during 1936 season.

Decatur Twins
Southeastern League (D), 1911; new franchise. Disbanded after 1911 season.

DECATUR–ALBANY, AL

Decatur–Albany
Alabama–Tennessee League (D), mid-1921; charter franchise. Disbanded with league after 1921 season.

DECATUR, IL

Decatur
Central Inter-State League, 1888; charter franchise. Became LAFAYETTE, mid-1888.

Decatur
Illinois–Indiana League, 1889; charter franchise. Disbanded with league after 1889 season.

Decatur Commies
MOV League (D), 1952–1955; new franchise. Disbanded with league after 1955 season.

Decatur Commies
Alternate name for DECATUR COMMODORES.

Decatur Commodores
Central League, 1900; charter franchise. Illinois–Iowa–Indiana League, 1901; (B), 1902–1909; charter franchise. Northern Association of Baseball, (C), 1910; (D), mid-1910; charter franchise. Became TAYLORVILLE TAYLORED COMMIES, mid-1910.

Decatur Commodores
Northern Association of Baseball, (D), mid-1910; relocated franchise. Had been TAYLORVILLE TAYLORED COMMIES, mid-1910. Disbanded with association after 1910 season.

Decatur Commodores
Illinois–Iowa–Indiana League (B), 1912–1915; renamed franchise.

Had been DECATUR NOMADS, 1911. Disbanded after 1915 season.

Decatur Commodores
Illinois–Iowa–Indiana League (B), 1922–1932; new franchise. Disbanded with league after 1932 season.

Decatur Commodores
Three I League (B), 1935; 1937–1942; 1946–1949; new franchise. Three I League (B), 1950; renamed franchise. Disbanded after 1950 season.

Decatur Commodores
Midwest League (D), 1956–1964; charter franchise. Renamed DECATUR CUBS, 1965.

Decatur Commodores
Midwest League (D), 1967–1974; renamed franchise. Had been DECATUR CUBS, 1965–1966. Disbanded after 1974 season.

Decatur Cubs
Midwest League (D), 1965–1966; renamed franchise. Had been DECATUR COMMODORES, 1956–1964. Renamed DECATUR COMMODORES, 1967.

Decatur Nomads
Illinois–Iowa–Indiana League (B), mid-1911; relocated franchise. Had been SPRINGFIELD SENATORS, 1905–mid-1911. Renamed DECATUR COMMODORES, 1912.

DECATUR, IN

Decatur Admirals
Ohio–Indiana League (D), 1907; charter franchise. Disbanded with league after 1907 season.

DEERFIELD BEACH, FL
(See also POMPANO BEACH, FL)

Deerfield Beach Sun Sox
Florida State League (A), 1966; new franchise. Became WINTER HAVEN WHITE SOX, mid-1966.

DELAND, FL

Deland Red Hats
Florida State League (D), 1933–1941; charter franchise. Had been DELAND REDS, 1936–1938. Florida East Coast League (D), 1942; new franchise. Disbanded during 1942 season. Florida State League (D), 1946–1954; charter franchise. Disbanded after 1954 season.

Deland Reds
Florida State League (D), 1936–1938; charter franchise. Renamed DELAND RED HATS, 1939.

Deland Sun Sox
Florida State League (A), 1970; new franchise. Disbanded with league after 1970 season.

DEL RIO, TX

Del Rio Cowboys
Longhorn League (D), 1948; new franchise. Rio Grande Valley League (C), 1949–1950; charter franchise. Disbanded with league after 1950 season.

Del Rio Indians
Big State League (B), mid-1954; relocated franchise. Had been BRYAN INDIANS, 1954. Disbanded after 1954 season.

DEMOREST, PA

Demorest
Pennsylvania State League, 1887; new franchise. Disbanded during 1887 season.

DENISON, OH

Denison–Urichsville
Ohio–West Virginia League; relocated franchise. Had been CAMBRIDGE, 1897. Disbanded with league after 1897 season.

DENISON, TX

Denison
Texas–Oklahoma League (D), mid-1922; relocated franchise. Had been BONHAM BOOGERS (aka Bingers), 1922. Disbanded with league after 1922 season.

Denison Katydids
Texas–Oklahoma League (D), 1912–1914; new franchise. Disbanded with league after 1914 season.

Denison Railroaders
Western association (D), 1915–1917; new franchise. Disbanded with association after 1917 season.

Denison Tigers
Texas League, 1896; new franchise. Disbanded during 1897 season.

Denison Tigers
Texas League; 1897; new franchise. Became WACO TIGERS, mid-1897.

DENVER, CO

COLORADO ROCKIES
National League; expansion franchise. To begin play in 1993.

Denver
Colorado League, 1885; charter franchise. Disbanded with league after 1885 season.

Denver Bears (aka Grizzlies, 1912)
Western League (A), 1912–1917; renamed franchise. Had been DENVER GRIZZLIES, 1900–1912. Disbanded after 1917 season.

Denver Bears
Western League (A), 1922–1932; new franchise. Disbanded after 1932 season.

Denver Bears
Western League (D), 1941; new franchise. Disbanded with league after 1941 season.

Denver Bears
Western League (A), 1947–1954; charter franchise. American Association (AAA), 1955–1962; new franchise. Pacific Coast League (AAA), 1963–1968; new franchise. American Association (AAA), 1969–1983; charter franchise. Renamed DENVER ZEPHYRS, 1984.

Denver Daisies
Western League, 1887–1888; renamed franchise. Had been DENVER RESERVES, 1886. Disbanded with league after 1888 season.

Denver Grizzlies (aka Mountaineers)
Western Association, 1889–1892; new franchise. Disbanded with association after 1892 season.

Denver Grizzlies
Western Association, 1895; relocated franchise. Had been OMAHA OMAHOGS, 1894–mid-1895. Disbanded during 1895 season.

Denver Grizzlies (aka Bears, 1912)
Western League (A), 1900–1912; charter franchise. Renamed DENVER BEARS, 1912.

Denver Gulfs
Colorado State League, 1898; charter franchise. Disbanded with league after 1898 season.

Denver Mountaineers
Alternate name for DENVER GRIZZLIES, 1889–1891.

Denver Reserves
Western League, 1886; charter franchise. Renamed DENVER DAISIES, 1887.

Denver Solis
Colorado State League, 1889; charter franchise. Disbanded with league after 1889 season.

Denver Zephyrs
American Association (AAA), 1984–(still in existence as of 5-1-92). Had been DENVER BEARS, 1947–1983.

DEQUINCY, LA

DeQuincy Railroaders
Cotton States League (D), mid-1932; relocated franchise. Had been PORT ARTHUR REFINERS, 1932. Disbanded with league during 1932 season.

DERBY, CT

Derby
Connecticut State League, mid-1891; relocated franchise. Had been ANSONIA, 1891. Disbanded with league after 1891 season.

Derby
Naugatuck Valley League, 1898; charter franchise. Became SHELTON, mid-1898.

Derby Angels
Connecticut League, 1897–1898; charter franchise. Renamed DERBY LUSHERS, 1899.

Derby Lushers
Connecticut League, 1899–1901; renamed franchise. Had been DERBY ANGELS, 1897–1898. Disbanded after 1901 season.

DERBY–ANSONIA, CT
(See also ANSONIA, CT)

Derby–Ansonia
Connecticut State League, 1888; charter franchise. Disbanded with league after 1888 season.

DES MOINES, IA

Des Moines Boosters
Western League (A), 1908–1924; renamed franchise. Renamed DES MOINES DEMONS, 1925.

Des Moines Bruins
Western League (A), 1947–1957; charter franchise. Renamed DES MOINES DODGERS, 1958.

Des Moines Champs
Western Association (A), 1906; renamed franchise. Had been DES MOINES UNDERWRITERS, 1905. Renamed DES MOINES CHAMPS II, 1907.

Des Moines Champs II
Western Association (A), 1907; renamed franchise. Had been DES MOINES CHAMPS, 1906. Renamed DES MOINES BOOSTERS, 1908.

Des Moines Colts (aka Hawkeyes, 1890)
Western Association, 1888–mid-1890; charter franchise. Became LINCOLN TREEPLANTERS, mid-1890.

Des Moines Demons
Western League (A), 1925–1937; renamed franchise. Had been DES MOINES BOOSTERS, 1908–1924. Disbanded with league after 1937 season.

Des Moines Demons
Three I League (B), 1959–1961; new franchise. Disbanded with league after 1961 season.

Des Moines Dodgers
Western League (A), 1958; renamed franchise. Had been DES MOINES BRUINS, 1947–1957. Disbanded with league after 1958 season.

Des Moines Hawkeyes
Northwestern League, 1887; new franchise. Disbanded with league after 1887 season.

Des Moines Hawkeyes
Alternate name for DES MOINES COLTS, 1890.

Des Moines Indians
Alternate name for DES MOINES PROHIBITIONISTS, 1894–1896.

Des Moines Midgets
Western Association, 1901; (A), 1902; renamed franchise. Had been DES MOINES PROHIBITIONISTS, 1900. Renamed DES MOINES UNDERTAKERS, 1903.

Des Moines Prohibitionists (aka Indians)
Western Association, 1894–1897; charter franchise. Became OTTUMWA COAL PALACE GIANTS, 1898.

Des Moines Prohibitionists
Western Association, 1900; charter franchise. Renamed DES MOINES MIDGETS, 1901.

Des Moines Prohibitionists
Western Association (A), 1904; renamed franchise. Had been DES MOINES UNDERTAKERS, 1903. Renamed DES MOINES UNDERWRITERS, 1905.

Des Moines Undertakers
Western Association (A), 1903; renamed franchise. Had been DES MOINES MIDGETS, 1900–1902. Renamed DES MOINES PROHIBITIONISTS, 1904.

Des Moines Underwriters
Western Association (A), 1905; renamed franchise. Had been DES MOINES PROHIBITIONISTS, 1904. Renamed DES MOINES CHAMPS, 1906.

Iowa Cubs
American Association (AAA), 1982–(still in existence as of 5-1-92); renamed franchise. Had been IOWA OAKS, 1969–1981.

Iowa Oaks
American Association (AAA), 1969–1981; new franchise. Renamed IOWA CUBS, 1982.

DETROIT, MI

Detroit
Western League, mid-1885; relocated franchise. Had been INDIA-NAPOLIS, 1885. Disbanded during 1885 season.

Detroit Creams
Alternate name for DETROIT TIGERS, 1894.

Detroit Detroits
Northwestern League, 1891; charter franchise. Disbanded with league during 1891 season.

DETROIT STARS
Negro National League, 1920–1931; 1933; charter franchise. Became PHILADELPHIA STARS, 1934.

Detroit Tigers
Western Association, 1892; new franchise. Disbanded with association during 1892 season.

Detroit Tigers (aka Creams, 1894)
Western League, 1894–1899; new franchise. Disbanded with league after 1899 season.

DETROIT TIGERS
American League, 1901–(still in existence as of 5-1-92); renamed franchise. Had been DETROIT WOLVERINES, 1900.

DETROIT WOLVERINES
National League, 1881–1888; new franchise. International Association, 1889–1890; new franchise. Disbanded with league during 1890 season.

DETROIT WOLVERINES
American League, 1900; charter franchise. Renamed DETROIT TIGERS, 1901.

DEVILS LAKE, ND

Devils Lake
Northern League (C), 1902; charter franchise. Disbanded after 1902 season.

DIAZ ORDAS, MEXICO

Diaz Ordas
Mexican League (AAA), 1978; new franchise. Disbanded after 1978 season.

DISTRITO FEDERAL, MEXICO
(See MEXICO CITY, MEXICO)

DOMINION, NOVA SCOTIA, CANADA

Dominion Hawks
Cape Breton Gallery (D), 1937–1938; charter franchise. Disbanded after 1938 season.

DONALSONVILLE, GA

Donalsonville Indians
Alabama–Florida League (D), 1955; new franchise. Renamed DONALSONVILLE SEMINOLES, 1956.

Donalsonville Seminoles
Alabama–Florida League (D), 1956; renamed franchise. Had been DONALSONVILLE INDIANS, 1955. Disbanded after 1956 season.

DONNA–WESLACO, TX

Donna–Weslaco Twins
Rio Grande Valley League (C), 1950; new franchise. Disbanded after 1950 season.

DOTHAN, AL

Dothan
FLAG League (D), 1915; charter franchise. Dixie League (D), mid-1916–mid-1917; charter franchise. Disbanded with league during 1917 season.

Dothan Boll Weevils
Alabama–Florida League (D), 1936; charter franchise. Renamed DOTHAN BROWNS, 1937.

Dothan Browns
Alabama–Florida League (D), 1937–1939; renamed franchise. Had been DOTHAN BOLL WEEVILS, 1936. Alabama State League (D), 1940–1941; charter franchise. Georgia–Florida League (D), 1942; 1946–1950; new franchise. Alabama–Florida League (D), 1951–1952; charter franchise. Renamed DOTHAN REBELS, 1953.

Dothan Cardinals
Alabama–Florida League (D), 1955–1956; renamed franchise. Had been DOTHAN REBELS, 1953–1954. Disbanded after 1956 season.

Dothan Cardinals
Alabama–Florida League (D), 1958–1960; charter franchise. Renamed DOTHAN PHILLIES, 1961.

Dothan Phillies
Alabama–Florida League (D), 1960–1962; charter franchise. Had been DOTHAN CARDINALS, 1958–1960. Disbanded with league after 1962 season.

Dothan Rebels
Alabama–Florida League (D), 1953–1954; renamed franchise. Had been DOTHAN BROWNS, 1937–1942; 1946–1952. Renamed DOTHAN CARDINALS, 1955.

DOUGLAS, AZ
(See also BISBEE, AZ)

Bisbee–Douglas Copper Kings
Arizona–Mexico League (C), 1955–1958; renamed franchise. Had been BISBEE COPPER KINGS, 1949–1954. Disbanded with league after 1958 season.

Douglas Smeltermen
Rio Grande Valley Association (D), 1915; charter franchise. Disbanded with league after 1915 season.

DOUGLAS, GA

Douglas Rebels
Georgia State League (D), 1948; charter franchise. Renamed DOUGLAS TROJANS, 1949.

Douglas Reds
Georgia State League (D), 1956; renamed franchise. Had been DOUGLAS TROJANS, 1949–1955. Disbanded with league after 1956 season.

Douglas Trojans
Georgia State League (D), 1949–1955; renamed franchise. Had been DOUGLAS REBELS, 1948. Renamed DOUGLAS REDS, 1956.

DOVER, DE

Dover Dobbins
Eastern Shore League (D), 1925; renamed franchise. Had been DOVER SENATORS, 1923–1924. Renamed DOVER SENATORS, 1926.

Dover Orioles
Eastern Shore League (D), 1937–1940; charter franchise. Disbanded after 1940 season.

Dover Phillies
Eastern Shore League (D), 1946–1948; charter franchise. Disbanded after 1948 season.

Dover Senators
Eastern Shore League (D), 1923–1924; new franchise. Renamed DOVER DOBBINS, 1925.

Dover Senators
Eastern Shore League (D), 1926–mid-1927; renamed franchise. Became NORTHAMPTON RED SOX, mid-1927.

DOVER–FOXCROFT, ME

Dover–Foxcroft
Maine State League (D), 1909; new franchise. Disbanded during 1909 season.

DOVER, NH

Dover
New England Inter-State League, 1888; charter franchise. Disbanded with league after 1888 season.

Dover
New England League, 1893; new franchise. Disbanded during 1893 season.

Dover
New England League (B), 1902; new franchise. Disbanded with league after 1902 season.

DOWAGIAC, MI

Dowagiac
Indiana–Michigan League (D), 1910; charter franchise. Disbanded with league during 1910 season.

DRAPER, NC
(See LEAKSVILLE, NC)

DRUMMONDVILLE, QUEBEC, CANADA

Drummondville A's
Provincial League (C), 1954; renamed franchise. Had been DRUMMONDVILLE ROYALS, 1953. Disbanded after 1954 season.

Drummondville Cubs
Provincial League (C), 1950–1952; charter franchise. Renamed DRUMMONDVILLE ROYALS, 1953.

Drummondville Royals
Provincial League (C), 1953; renamed franchise. Had been DRUMMONDVILLE CUBS, 1950–1952. Renamed DRUMMONDVILLE A'S, 1954.

Drummondville Tigers
Quebec–Provincial League (B), 1940; charter franchise. Disbanded during 1940 season.

DRUMWRIGHT, OK

Drumwright
Oklahoma State League (D), 1923; new franchise. Became PONCA CITY, mid-1923.

Drumwright Drummers
Western Association (D), 1920–1921; charter franchise. Disbanded after 1921 season.

DUBLIN, GA

Dublin Braves
Georgia–Florida League (D), 1962; charter franchise. Disbanded after 1962 season.

Dublin Green Sox
Georgia State League (D), 1950–1952; renamed franchise. Had been DUBLIN TROJANS, 1949. Renamed DUBLIN IRISH, 1953.

Dublin Irish
Georgia State League (D), 1953–1956; renamed franchise. Had been DUBLIN GREEN SOX, 1950–1952. Disbanded with league after 1956 season.

Dublin Orioles
Georgia–Florida League (D), 1958; new franchise. Disbanded with league after 1958 season.

Dublin Trojans
Georgia State League (D), 1949; new franchise. Renamed DUBLIN GREEN SOX, 1950.

DUBLIN, TX

Dublin, TX
Texas League (D), 1905; new franchise. Disbanded during 1905 season.

DUBOIS, PA

DuBois
Inter-State League (C), mid-1905–1907; relocated franchise. Had been JAMESTOWN HILL CLIMBERS, 1905. Disbanded after 1907 season.

DUBUQUE, IA

Dubuque
Central Inter-State League, 1888; charter franchise. Disbanded after 1888 season.

Dubuque
Western Association, mid-1899; relocated franchise. Had been QUINCY, 1899. Disbanded with league after 1899 season.

Dubuque
Central Association (D), 1917; new franchise. Became CHARLES CITY TRACTORITES, mid-1917.

Dubuque Champs (aka Colts)
East Iowa League, 1895; charter franchise. Disbanded with league after 1895 season.

Dubuque Climbers
Mississippi Valley League (D), 1922–1923; charter franchise. Disbanded with league after 1932 season.

Dubuque Colts
Alternate name for DUBUQUE CHAMPS, 1895.

Dubuque Dubs
Illinois–Iowa–Indiana League (B), 1907–1910; renamed franchise. Had been DUBUQUE SHAMROCKS, 1903–1906. Renamed DUBUQUE HUSTLERS, 1911.

Dubuque Dubs
Illinois–Iowa–Indiana League (B), 1912–1915; renamed franchise. Had been DUBUQUE HUSTLERS, 1911. Became FREEPORT COMEONS, mid-1915.

Dubuque Dubs
Mississippi Valley League (D), 1924; renamed franchise. Had been DUBUQUE CLIMBERS, 1922–1923. Renamed DUBUQUE IRONMEN, 1925.

Dubuque Dubs
Alternate name for DUBUQUE IRONMEN, 1927–1928.

Dubuque Giants
Illinois–Iowa League, 1890; charter franchise. Disbanded after 1890 season.

Dubuque Hustlers
Illinois–Iowa–Indiana League (B), 1911; renamed franchise. Had been DUBUQUE DUBS, 1907–1910. Renamed DUBUQUE DUBS, 1912.

Dubuque Ironmen (aka Dubs, 1927–1928)
Mississippi Valley League (D), 1925–1928; renamed franchise. Had been DUBUQUE CLIMBERS, 1922–1923. Renamed DUBUQUE TIGERS, 1929.

Dubuque Packers
MOV League (D), 1954–1955; new franchise. Midwest League (D), 1956–1962; (A), 1963–1968; charter franchise. Disbanded after 1968 season.

Dubuque Packers
Midwest League (A), 1974–1976; new franchise. Disbanded after 1976 season.

Dubuque Red Stockings
Northwestern League, 1879; charter franchise. Disbanded with league after 1879 season.

Dubuque Shamrocks
Illinois–Iowa–Indiana League (B), 1903–1906; new franchise. Renamed DUBUQUE DUBS, 1907.

Dubuque Tigers
Mississippi Valley League (D), 1929–1932; renamed franchise. Had been DUBUQUE IRONMEN, 1925–1928. Disbanded with league after 1932 season.

Midwest Dodgers
Midwest League (D), mid-1962; relocated franchise. Had been KEOKUK CARDINALS, 1962. Disbanded after 1962 season.

DULUTH, MN

Duluth
Western Association, 1895–1898; new franchise. Disbanded with league during 1898 season.

Duluth
Central International League (C), 1912; charter franchise. Disbanded with league after 1912 season.

Duluth Cardinals
Northern League (D), 1903; new franchise. Disbanded with league after 1905 season.

Duluth Dukes
Northern League (D), 1935–1940, (C), 1941–1942; new franchise. Had been DULUTH WHITE SOX, 1934. Twin Ports League (E), 1943; charter franchise. Disbanded with league during 1943 season.

Duluth Dukes
Northern League (C), 1946–1955; charter franchise. Became DULUTH–SUPERIOR WHITE SOX, 1956.

Duluth Heralds
Twin Ports League (E), 1943; charter franchise. Disbanded with league during 1943 season.

Duluth Jayhawkers
Western Association, mid-1891; relocated franchise. Had been ST. PAUL APOSTLES, 1891. Disbanded with association after 1891 season.

Duluth Marine Iron
Twin Ports League (E), 1943; charter franchise. Disbanded with league during 1943 season.

Duluth White Sox
Northern League (D), 1904–1905; new franchise. Had been DULUTH CARDINALS, 1903. Northern Copper Country League (C), 1906–1907; charter franchise. Northern League (D), 1908; charter franchise. Minnesota–Wisconsin League (D), 1909; (C) 1910–1911; charter franchise. Northern League (C), 1913–1916; charter franchise. Disbanded with league after 1916 season.

Duluth White Sox
Northern League (D), 1934; new franchise. Renamed DULUTH DUKES, 1935.

Duluth Zenith City
Northwestern League, 1886–1887; charter franchise. Disbanded with league after 1887 season.

DULUTH, MN– SUPERIOR, WI
(See also SUPERIOR, WI)

Duluth–Superior Dukes
Northern League (C), 1960–1962; (A), 1963–1970; renamed franchise. Had been DULUTH WHITE SOX, 1956–1959. Disbanded after 1970 season.

Duluth–Superior White Sox
Northern League (C), 1956–1959; renamed franchise. Had been DULUTH DUKES, 1946–1955. Renamed DULUTH–SUPERIOR DUKES, 1960.

DUNCAN, OK

Duncan Cementers
Sooner State League (D), 1947–1948; charter franchise. Renamed DUNCAN UTTMEN, 1949.

Duncan Oilers
Oklahoma State League (D), mid-1922–1924; charter franchise. Disbanded during 1924 season.

Duncan Uttmen
Sooner State League (D), 1949–mid-1950; renamed franchise. Had been DUNCAN CEMENTERS, 1947–1948. Became SHAWNEE HAWKS, mid-1950.

DUNEDIN, FL

Dunedin Blue Jays
Florida State League (A), 1978–1979; new franchise. Disbanded after 1979 season.

Dunedin Blue Jays
Florida State League (A), 1987– (still in existence as of 5-1-92); new franchise.

DUNKIRK, NY

Dunkirk
Iron and Oil League, mid-1898; relocated franchise. Had been OIL CITY, 1898. Disbanded with league after 1898 season.

Dunkirk Dandies
New York–Pennsylvania League, 1890; charter franchise. Disbanded after 1890 season.

DUNN–ERWIN, NC

Dunn–Erwin Twins
Tobacco State League (D), 1946–mid-1950; charter franchise. Became WHITEVILLE TOBACCONISTS, mid-1950.

DURANGO, MEXICO

Durango
Mexican League (AAA), 1976–1979; new franchise. Disbanded after 1979 season.

Durango Alacranes
Central Mexican League (C), 1956; charter franchise. Renamed DURANGO–LAGUNA SCORPIONS, 1957.

Durango Alacranes
Mexican Center League (A), 1966–1967; renamed franchise. Had been DURANGO SCORPIONS, 1965. Disbanded after 1967 season.

Durango Algodoneros
Mexican Center League (A), 1972–1974; new franchise. Disbanded after 1974 season.

Durango Scorpions
Mexican Center League (A), 1965; new franchise. Became DURANGO ALACRANES, 1966.

DURANGO– LAGUNA, MEXICO
(See also GOMEZ PALACIO, MEXICO)

Durango–Laguna Scorpions
Central Mexican League (C), 1957; charter franchise. Had been DURANGO ALACRANES, 1956. Disbanded with league after 1957 season.

DURANT, OK

Durant Chocktaws (aka Hustlers)
Texas–Oklahoma League (D), 1912–1914; renamed franchise. Had been DURANT EDUCATORS, 1911. Disbanded with league after 1914 season.

Durant Educators
Texas–Oklahoma League (D), 1911; charter franchise. Renamed DURANT CHOCKTAWS (aka Hustlers), 1912.

Durant Hustlers
Alternate name for DURANT CHOCKTAWS, 1912.

DURHAM, NC
(See also RALEIGH, NC)

Durham Bulls
North Carolina League (D), 1902; charter franchise. Disbanded during 1902 season.

Durham Bulls
North Carolina State League (D), 1913–1917; charter franchise. Disbanded with league during 1917 season.

Durham Bulls
Piedmont League (D), 1920; (C), 1921–1930, (B), 1931–1933; charter franchise. Became NORFOLK TARS, 1934.

Durham Bulls
Piedmont League (B), 1937–1943; renamed franchise. Had been DURHAM RED BULLS, 1936. Disbanded after 1943 season.

Durham Bulls
Carolina League (C), 1945–1962; (A), 1963–1967; charter franchise. Merged with RALEIGH PIRATES and became RALEIGH-DURHAM METS, 1968.

Durham Bulls
Carolina League (A), 1980–(still in existence as of 5-1-92); new franchise.

Durham Red Bulls
Piedmont League (B), 1936; new franchise. Renamed DURHAM BULLS, 1937.

DYERSBURG, TN

Dyersburg Champions (aka Forked Deers and Tennesseens)
KITTY League (D), 1923; new franchise. Renamed DYERSBURG FORKED DEERS, 1924.

Dyersburg Deers
Tri-State League (D), 1925; charter franchise. Had been DYERSBURG FORKED DEERS, KITTY League, 1923–1924. Disbanded after 1925 season.

Dyersburg Forked Deers (aka Dyersburg Champions, 1923)
KITTY League (D), 1923–1924; new franchise. Became DYERSBURG DEERS, Tri–State League, 1925.

Dyersburg Tennesseens
Alternate name for DYERSBURG CHAMPIONS, 1923.

EAST GRAND FORKS, MN

East Grand Forks Colts
Northern League (D), 1933; 1935; charter franchise. Disbanded after 1935 season.

EASTLAND, TX

Eastland
West Texas League (D), 1920; charter franchise. Disbanded after 1920 season.

EAST LIBERTY, PA

East Liberty Stars
Iron and Oil Association, 1884; new franchise. Disbanded during 1884 season.

EAST LIVERPOOL, OH

East Liverpool
POM League (D), 1906–1907; charter franchise. Disbanded with league after 1907 season.

East Liverpool East End Stars
Ohio State League, 1893; new franchise. Disbanded after 1893 season.

East Liverpool Potters
Ohio–Pennsylvania League (C), 1908–1911; (D), 1912; new franchise. Disbanded with league after 1912 season.

EASTMAN, GA

Eastman Dodgers
Georgia State League (D), 1948–1953; charter franchise. Disbanded after 1953 season.

EASTON, MD

Easton Browns
Eastern Shore League (D), 1937; charter franchise. Renamed EASTON CUBS, 1938.

Easton Cubs
Eastern Shore League (D), 1938–1941; renamed franchise. Had been EASTON BROWNS, 1937. Disbanded with league after 1941 season.

Easton Farmers
Eastern Shore League (D), 1924–1928; new franchise. Disbanded with league during 1928 season.

Easton Yankees
Eastern Shore League (D), 1939–1941; 1946–1949; renamed franchise. Had been EASTON CUBS, 1938. Disbanded with league after 1949 season.

EASTON, PA

Easton
Pennsylvania League, 1879; charter franchise. Disbanded with league after 1879 season.

Easton
Central Pennsylvania League, mid-1888; charter franchise. Had been ASHLAND, 1887–mid-1888. Disbanded with league after 1888 season.

Easton
Atlantic Association, 1889; charter franchise. Eastern League, 1889; charter franchise. Inter-State League, 1889; charter franchise. Disbanded with league after 1889 season.

Easton
Pennsylvania State League, 1893; new franchise. Disbanded after 1893 season.

Easton
Atlantic League (D), 1907–1908; charter franchise. Disbanded with league after 1908 season.

Easton Colts
Pennsylvania State League, mid-1894; relocated franchise. Had been ALLENTOWN COLTS, 1892–mid-1894. Became PHILADELPHIA COLTS, mid-1894.

Easton Gorhams
Pennsylvania State League, 1890; charter franchise. Disbanded with league after 1890 season.

Easton Triple Cities
Pennsylvania State League, 1896; new franchise. Disbanded with league after 1896 season.

EASTON, PA–PHILLIPSBURG, NJ

Easton–Phillipsburg
Pennsylvania State League (D), 1916; new franchise. Disbanded during 1916 season.

EAST SAGINAW, MI

East Saginaw Greys
Saginaw Valley League, 1888; charter franchise. Disbanded with league after 1888 season.

EAU CLAIRE, WI

Eau Claire
Northwestern League, 1886–1887; charter franchise. Disbanded with league after 1887 season.

Eau Claire Bears
Northern League (D), 1934–1940; (C), 1941–1942, 1946–1953; renamed franchise. Had been EAU CLAIRE CARDINALS, 1933. Renamed EAU CLAIRE BRAVES, 1954.

Eau Claire Braves
Northern League (C), 1954–1962; renamed franchise. Disbanded after 1962 season.

Eau Claire Cardinals
Northern League (D), 1933; charter franchise. Renamed EAU CLAIRE BEARS, 1934.

Eau Claire Commissioners
Minnesota–Wisconsin League (D), 1909–1910; 1912; (C), 1911;

charter franchise. Disbanded with league after 1912 season.

Eau Claire Tigers
Wisconsin State League (D), 1907; relocated franchise. Had been EAU CLAIRE ORPHANS, 1906. Disbanded with league after 1907 season.

EAU CLAIRE–CHIPPEWA FALLS, WI

Eau Claire Orphans
Wisconsin State League (D), 1906; charter franchise. Became EAU CLAIRE TIGERS, 1907.

EBANO, SAN LUIS POTOSI, MEXICO
(See also SAN LUIS POTOSI, MEXICO)

Ebano
Mexican Center League (A), 1977; new franchise. Disbanded after 1977 season.

Ebano Oilers
Mexican Center League (A), 1972–1974; renamed franchise. Had been EBANO REDS, 1971. Disbanded after 1974 season.

Ebano Reds
Mexican Center League (A), 1971; new franchise. Renamed EBANO OILERS, 1972.

EDENTON, NC

Edenton Colonials
Virginia League (D), 1951; new franchise. Coastal Plain League (D), 1952; new franchise. Disbanded with league after 1952 season.

EDINBURG, TX

Edinburg Bobcats
Gulf Coast League (D), mid-1926; relocated franchise. Had been VICTORIA ROSEBUDS, 1926. Texas Valley League (D), 1927; charter

franchise. Disbanded after 1927 season.

EDMONTON, ALBERTA, CANADA

Edmonton Eskimos
Western Canada League (D), 1909–1911; charter franchise. Renamed EDMONTON GRAY BIRDS, 1912.

Edmonton Eskimos
Western Canada League (D), 1914; renamed franchise. Had been EDMONTON GRAY BIRDS, 1912–1913. Disbanded with league after 1914 season.

Edmonton Eskimos
Western Canada League (B), 1921; renamed franchise. Had been EDMONTON ESQUIMOS, 1920. Western International League (B), 1922; charter franchise. Disbanded with league during 1922 season.

Edmonton Eskimos
Western International League (A), 1953–1954; expansion franchise. Disbanded with league after 1954 season.

Edmonton Esquimos
Western Canada League (B), 1920; new franchise. Renamed EDMONTON ESKIMOS, 1921.

Edmonton Gray Birds
Western Canada League (D), 1912–1913; renamed franchise. Had been EDMONTON ESKIMOS, 1909–1911. Renamed EDMONTON ESKIMOS, 1914.

Edmonton Grays
Western Canada League (D), 1907; charter franchise. Disbanded with league after 1907 season.

Edmonton Trappers
Pacific Coast League (AAA), 1981–(still in existence as of 5-1-

92); relocated franchise. Had been OGDEN A'S, 1979–1980.

ELBERON, PA

Elberon
Iron and Oil League, mid-1895; relocated franchise. Had been SHARON, 1895. Disbanded with league after 1895 season.

EL CENTRO, CA

El Centro Imperials
Sunset League (C), 1947–1950; charter franchise. Southwest International League (C), 1951; charter franchise. Renamed EL CENTRO IMPS, 1952.

El Centro Imps
Southwest International League (C), 1952; renamed franchise. Had been EL CENTRO IMPERIALS, 1951. Disbanded with league after 1952 season.

EL DORADO, AR

El Dorado
Arkansas State League (D), 1905; new franchise. Disbanded during 1905 season.

El Dorado Lions
Cotton States League (D), 1929–1930; (C), 1931–mid-1932; new franchise. Disbanded with league during 1932 season.

El Dorado Lions
Dixie League (C), 1933; charter franchise. East Dixie League (C), 1934–1935; charter franchise. Cotton States League (C), 1936–1939; charter franchise. Renamed EL DORADO OILERS, 1940.

El Dorado Oilers
Cotton States League (C), 1940–1941; 1947–1955; renamed franchise. Had been EL DORADO LIONS, 1936–1939. Disbanded with league after 1955 season.

EL DORADO, IL

El Dorado
Southern Illinois League (D), 1910; charter franchise. Disbanded with league after 1911 season.

EL DORADO, KS

El Dorado Crushers
Kansas State League (D), 1911; new franchise. Disbanded with league after 1911 season.

ELGIN, IL

Elgin Kittens
National Association of Baseball (D), 1910; charter franchise. Disbanded with league after 1910 season.

Elgin Watchmakers
Bi-State League (WI-IL), (D), 1915; charter franchise. Disbanded with league during 1915 season.

ELIZABETH, NJ

Elizabeth
Central New Jersey League, 1892; charter franchise. Disbanded with league after 1892 season.

ELIZABETH RESOLUTES
National Association, 1873; charter franchise. Disbanded with association after 1873 season.

ELIZABETH CITY, NC

Elizabeth City Albemarles
Virginia League (D), 1950–1951; relocated franchise. Had been LAWRENCEVILLE CARDINALS, 1948–1949. Disbanded with league after 1951 season.

ELIZABETHTON, TN

Elizabethton Betsy Cubs
Alternate name for ELIZABETHTON CUBS, 1946–1947.

Elizabethton Betsy Local
Appalachian League (D), 1949–1950; renamed franchise. Had been ELIZABETHTON BETSY CUBS, 1945–1948. Renamed ELIZABETHTON PHILS, 1951.

Elizabethton Betsy Red Sox
Appalachian League (D), 1937–1942; charter franchise. Disbanded after 1942 season.

Elizabethton Cubs (aka Betsy Cubs, 1946–1947)
Appalachian League (D), 1945–1948; new franchise. Renamed ELIZABETHTON BETSY LOCAL, 1949.

Elizabethton Phils
Appalachian League (D), 1951; renamed franchise. Had been ELIZABETHTON BETSY LOCAL, 1949–1950. Disbanded after 1951 season.

Elizabethton Twins
Appalachian League (R), 1974– (still in existence as of 5-1-92); new franchise.

ELKHART, IN

Elkhart
Indiana State League, 1888; charter franchise. Disbanded with league after 1888 season.

Elhart
Indiana State League, 1890; charter franchise. Disbanded with league after 1890 season.

Elhart
Indiana–Michigan League (D), 1910; charter franchise. Disbanded with league after 1910 season.

ELKIN, NC

Elkin Blanketeers
Blue Ridge League (D), 1949–1950; new franchise. Disbanded with league after 1950 season.

Elkin Blanketeers
North Carolina State League (D), mid-1951–1952; relocated franchise. Had been LANDIS SPINNERS, 1949–mid-1951. Disbanded with league after 1952 season.

ELLSWORTH, KS

Ellsworth
Kansas State League (D), 1905; charter franchise. Disbanded after 1905 season.

Ellsworth Blues
Central Kansas League (D), 1910; renamed franchise. Had been ELLSWORTH WORTHIES, 1908–1909. Disbanded after 1910 season.

Ellsworth Worthies
Central Kansas League (D), 1908–1909; charter franchise. Renamed ELLSWORTH BLUES, 1910.

ELMHURST, CA

Elmhurst
Central California Baseball League (D), mid-1910–mid-1911; relocated franchise. Had been PETALUMA, 1910. Became OAKLAND EMERY ARMS, mid-1911.

ELMIRA, NY

Elmira
New York State League, 1885; charter franchise. Disbanded with league after 1885 season.

Elmira
New York State League, 1889; new franchise. Disbanded with league after 1889 season.

Elmira
Atlantic League, 1900; new franchise. Disbanded during 1900 season.

Elmira
New York State League, mid-1900; relocated franchise. Had been OS-WEGO STARCHMAKERS, 1900. Disbanded after 1900 season.

Elmira Babies
Central League, 1888; charter franchise. Disbanded with league after 1888 season.

Elmira Colonels
New York State League (B), mid-1908–1917; relocated franchise. Had been JOHNSTOWN–AMSTERDAM–GLOVERSVILLE JAGS, 1905–mid-1908. Disbanded with league after 1917 season.

Elmira Colonels
New York–Pennsylvania League (B), 1923–1937; charter franchise. Renamed ELMIRA RED BIRDS, 1932.

Elmira Dodgers
Eastern League (A), 1950–1955; charter franchise. Disbanded after 1955 season.

Elmira Gladiators
New York–Pennsylvania League, 1891; new franchise. Eastern League, 1892; charter franchise. Disbanded after 1892 season.

Elmira Maple Cities
New York State League, 1895; new franchise. Disbanded after 1895 season.

Elmira Pioneer Red Sox
New York–Pennsylvania League (A), 1977–1980; renamed franchise. Had been ELMIRA PIONEERS, 1976. Renamed ELMIRA PIONEERS, 1981.

Elmira Pioneers
New York–Pennsylvania League (B), 1935–1937; renamed franchise. Had been ELMIRA RED WINGS, 1933–1934. Eastern League (A), 1938–1949; charter franchise. Renamed ELMIRA DODGERS, 1950.

Elmira Pioneers
New York–Pennsylvania League (D), 1957–1961; new franchise.

Eastern League (A), 1962; (AA), 1963–1970; new franchise. Renamed ELMIRA ROYALS, 1971.

Elmira Pioneers
New York–Pennsylvania League (A), 1972; renamed franchise. Had been ELMIRA ROYALS, 1971. Renamed ELMIRA RED SOX, 1973.

Elmira Pioneers
New York–Pennsylvania League (A), 1976; renamed franchise. Had been ELMIRA RED SOX, 1973–1975. Renamed ELMIRA PIONEER RED SOX, 1977.

Elmira Pioneers
New York–Pennsylvania League (A), 1981–1982; renamed franchise. Had been ELMIRA PIONEER RED SOX, 1977–1980. Renamed ELMIRA SUNS, 1983.

Elmira Pioneers
New York–Pennsylvania League (A), 1989–(still in existence as of 5-1-92); renamed franchise. Had been ELMIRA SUNS, 1983–1988.

Elmira Red Birds
New York–Pennsylvania League (B), 1932; renamed franchise. Had been ELMIRA COLONELS, 1923–1931. Renamed ELMIRA RED WINGS, 1933.

Elmira Red Sox
New York–Pennsylvania League (A), 1973–1975; renamed franchise. Had been ELMIRA PIONEERS, 1972. Renamed ELMIRA PIONEERS, 1976.

Elmira Red Wings
New York–Pennsylvania League (B), 1933–1934; renamed franchise. Had been ELMIRA RED BIRDS, 1932.

Elmira Royals
Eastern League (AA), 1971; renamed franchise. Had been ELMIRA PIONEERS, 1957–1970. Renamed ELMIRA PIONEERS, 1972.

Elmira Suns
New York–Pennsylvania League (A), 1983–1988; renamed franchise. Had been ELMIRA PIONEERS, 1981–1982. Renamed ELMIRA PIONEERS, 1989.

ELON, NC
(See BURLINGTON, NC)

EL PASO, TX

El Paso Cowboys
Alternate name for EL PASO TEXANS, 1930.

El Paso Diablos
Texas League (AA), 1974–(still in existence as of 5-1-92); renamed franchise. Had been EL PASO SUN KINGS, 1972.

El Paso Longhorns
Arizona State League (D), 1930; expansion franchise. Became EL PASO TEXANS, 1931.

El Paso Mackmen
Rio Grande Valley Association (D), 1915; charter franchise. Disbanded with association after 1915 season.

El Paso Sun Dodgers
Texas League (AA), 1972; new franchise. Renamed EL PASO SUN KINGS, 1973.

El Paso Sun Kings
Sophomore League (D), 1961; new franchise. Texas League (AA), 1962–1970; new franchise. Became SHREVEPORT CAPTAINS, 1971.

El Paso Sun Kings
Texas League (AA), 1973; renamed franchise. Renamed EL PASO DIABLOS, 1974.

El Paso Texans (aka Cowboys, 1930)
Arizona–Texas League (D), 1931–1932; charter franchise. Had been

EL PASO LONGHORNS, 1930. Disbanded with league during 1932 season.

El Paso Texans
Arizona–Texas League (D), 1937–1939; (C), 1940–1941; charter franchise. Mexican National League (B); 1946; charter franchise. Suspended operations during 1946 season. Arizona–Texas League (C), 1947–1950; charter franchise. Southwest International League (C), 1951; charter franchise. Arizona–Texas League (C), 1952–1954; charter franchise. West Texas–New Mexico League (B), 1955; new franchise. Southwestern League (D), 1956–1957; charter franchise. Disbanded with league after 1957 season.

EL RENO, OK

El Reno Browns
Oklahoma State League (D), mid-1904; relocated franchise. Had been SHAWNEE BROWNS, mid-1904. Became SHAWNEE SEMINOLES, mid-1904.

El Reno Packers
Western Association (C), mid-1909–1910; relocated franchise. Had been JOPLIN MINERS, 1905–mid-1909. Disbanded during 1910 season.

El Reno Railroaders
Oklahoma State League (D), 1922–1923; charter franchise. Disbanded after 1923 season.

ELWOOD, IN

Elwood
Indiana State League, 1896; charter franchise. Disbanded with league after 1896 season.

Elwood
Indiana State League, 1900; charter franchise. Disbanded with league after 1900 season.

EMMETSBURG, IA

Emmetsburg
Iowa State League (D), 1912; charter franchise. Disbanded after 1912 season.

EMPALME, SONORA, MEXICO

Empalme Railmen
Mexican Rookie League (R), 1968; charter franchise. Disbanded with league after 1968 season.

EMPORIA, KS

Emporia
Western League, 1887; new franchise. Kansas State League, 1887; charter franchise. Disbanded with league after 1887 season.

Emporia
Kansas State League (D), 1905; charter franchise. Disbanded after 1905 season.

Emporia Bidwells
Kansas State League (D), 1914; new franchise. Disbanded with league after 1914 season.

Emporia Maroons
Kansas State League, 1895–1896; charter franchise. Disbanded with league after 1897 season.

Emporia Traders
Southwestern League (D), 1924; charter franchise. Disbanded after 1924 season.

EMPORIA, VA

Emporia Nationals
Virginia League (D), 1950; renamed franchise. Had been EMPORIA NATS, 1948–1949. Renamed EMPORIA REBELS, 1951.

Emporia Nats
Virginia League (D), 1948–1949; new franchise. Renamed EMPORIA NATIONALS, 1950.

Emporia Rebels
Virginia League (D), 1951; renamed franchise. Had been EMPORIA NATIONALS, 1950. Disbanded with league after 1951 season.

ENDICOTT, NY
(See BINGHAMTON, NY)

ENID, OK

Enid
Oklahoma State League (D), mid-1912; relocated franchise. Had been ANADARKO, 1912. Disbanded with league after 1912 season.

Enid Boosters
Southwestern League (D), 1924–mid-1925; charter franchise. Became SHAWNEE BRAVES, mid-1925.

Enid Boosters
Southwestern League (D), 1926; new franchise. Disbanded with league after 1926 season.

Enid Buffaloes
Western Association (C), 1951; renamed franchise. Had been ENID GIANTS, 1950. Disbanded after 1951 season.

Enid Evangelists
Southwestern League (B), 1904; charter franchise. Disbanded with league after 1904 season.

Enid Giants
Western Association (C), 1950; new franchise. Renamed ENID BUFFALOES, 1951.

Enid Harvesters
Western Association (D), 1920–1921; (C), 1922–1923; charter franchise. Disbanded after 1923 season.

Enid Railroaders
Western Association (C), 1908–1910; new franchise. Disbanded after 1910 season.

ENNIS, TX

Ennis Tigers
Central Texas Trolley League (D), 1914–1915; charter franchise. Central Texas League (D), 1916–1917. Disbanded with league after 1917 season.

ENSENADA, BAJA CALIFORNIA, MEXICO
(See also RIVERSIDE, CA)

Ensenada Tigres
Mexican Northern League (A), 1968–1969; charter franchise. Disbanded after 1969 season.

Ensenada Tigres
Mexican League (AAA), 1971; new franchise. Disbanded after 1971 season.

ENTERPRISE, AL

Enterprise Boll Weevils
Alabama State League (D), 1947–1950; new franchise. Alabama–Florida League (D), 1951–mid-1952; charter franchise. Became GRACEVILLE BOLL WEEVILS, mid-1952.

Enterprise Browns
Alabama–Florida League (D), 1936; charter franchise. Disbanded after 1936 season.

ENTERPRISE, KS

Enterprise
Kansas State League (D), 1907; new franchise. Disbanded during 1907 season.

EPPING, NH

Epping
New Hampshire League (D), 1907; charter franchise. Disbanded with league after 1907 season.

ERIE, PA

Erie
League Alliance, 1877; charter franchise. Disbanded with league after 1877 season.

Erie
New York–Pennsylvania League, 1890–1891; charter franchise. Disbanded with league after 1891 season.

Erie Blackbirds
Eastern League, 1893–1894; charter franchise. Disbanded with league after 1894 season.

Erie Brewers
New York–Pennsylvania League (D), 1961; renamed franchise. Had been ERIE SENATORS, 1960. Renamed ERIE SAILORS, 1962.

Erie Cardinals
New York–Pennsylvania League (A), 1981–1987; new franchise. Renamed ERIE ORIOLES, 1988.

Erie Fishermen
Inter-State League (D), 1905–1908; charter franchise. Disbanded with league after 1908 season.

Erie Olympics
Inter-State League, 1885; charter franchise. Disbanded with league after 1885 season.

Erie Orioles
New York–Pennsylvania League (A), 1988–1989; renamed franchise. Had been ERIE CARDINALS, 1981–1987. Renamed ERIE SAILORS, 1990.

Erie Sailors
Ohio–Pennsylvania League (D), mid-1908–1911; relocated franchise. Had been BUTLER SAILORS, mid-1908. Central League (D), 1912; new franchise. Inter-State League (B), 1913; charter franchise. Disbanded after 1913 season.

Erie Sailors
Central League (D), 1915; new franchise. Disbanded after 1915 season.

Erie Sailors
Central League (D), 1928–1930; charter franchise. Disbanded with league after 1930 season.

Erie Sailors
Central League (D), 1932; charter franchise. Disbanded with league after 1932 season.

Erie Sailors
Middle Atlantic League (D), 1938–1939; new franchise. Disbanded after 1939 season.

Erie Sailors
Middle Atlantic League (C), 1941–1942; 1946–1951; expansion franchise. Disbanded with league after 1951 season.

Erie Sailors
PONY League (D), 1944–1945; expansion franchise. Became HAMILTON CARDINALS, 1946.

Erie Sailors
PONY League (D), 1954–1956; new franchise. New York–Pennsylvania League (D), 1957–1959; charter franchise. Renamed ERIE SENATORS, 1960.

Erie Sailors
New York–Pennsylvania League (D), 1962; (A), 1963; renamed franchise. Had been ERIE BREWERS, 1961. Disbanded after 1963 season.

Erie Sailors
New York–Pennsylvania League (A), 1990–(still in existence as of 5-1-92); renamed franchise. Had been ERIE ORIOLES, 1988–1989.

Erie Savages
Inter-State League (D), 1916; new franchise. Disbanded with league after 1916 season.

Erie Senators
New York–Pennsylvania League (D), 1960; renamed franchise. Had been ERIE SAILORS, 1957–1959. Renamed ERIE BREWERS, 1961.

Erie Tigers
New York–Pennsylvania League (A), 1967; new franchise. Disbanded after 1967 season.

Erie Yankees
Canadian League (C), 1914; (B), mid-1914; new franchise. Disbanded after 1914 season.

ERWIN, NC
(See DUNN, NC)

ERWIN, TN

Erwin Aces
Appalachian League (D), 1943; new franchise. Renamed ERWIN CUBS, mid-1943.

Erwin Cubs
Appalachian League (D), mid-1943–1944; renamed franchise. Had been ERWIN ACES, 1943. Disbanded after 1944 season.

Erwin Mountaineers
Appalachian League (D), 1940; expansion franchise. Disbanded after 1940 season.

ESPERANZA, MEXICO
(See TORREON LAGUNA, MEXICO)

ESTHERVILLE, IA

Estherville
Iowa State League (D), 1912; new franchise. Disbanded during 1912 season.

EUFAULA, AL

Eufaula
Dixie League (D), 1916–1917; charter franchise. Disbanded with league after 1916 season.

Eufaula Millers
Alabama–Florida League (D), 1952–1953; new franchise. Disbanded after 1953 season.

EUFAULA, OK

Eufaula
Oklahoma State League (D), 1912; charter franchise. Disbanded with league after 1912 season.

EUGENE, OR

Eugene Blues
Oregon State League (D), 1904; charter franchise. Disbanded with league after 1904 season.

Eugene Emeralds
Northwest League (B), 1955–1962; (A), 1963–1968; charter franchise. Pacific Coast League (AAA), 1969–1973; new franchise. Became SACRAMENTO SOLONS, 1974.

Eugene Emeralds
Northwest League (A), 1974–(still in existence as of 5-1-92); new franchise.

Eugene Larks
Far West League (D), 1950–1951; new franchise. Disbanded with league after 1951 season.

EUREKA, KS

Eureka Oilers
Southwestern League (D), 1924; charter franchise. Disbanded after 1924 season.

Eureka Oilers
Southwestern League (D), 1926; new franchise. Became PONCA CITY PONCANS, mid-1926.

EVANSVILLE, IN

Evansville
League Alliance, 1877; charter franchise. Disbanded with alliance after 1877 season.

Evansville
Northwest League, mid-1884; relocated franchise. Had been BAY CITY, 1884. Disbanded with league after 1884 season.

Evansville
Central Inter-State League, 1889; new franchise. Western Inter-State League, 1890; charter franchise. Northwestern League, 1891; charter franchise. Illinois–Iowa League, 1892; new franchise. Disbanded with league after 1892 season.

Evansville
Central League, 1897; charter franchise. Disbanded with league after 1897 season.

Evansville Bees (aka Braves, 1940)
Three I League (B), 1938–1942; 1946–1956; new franchise. Renamed EVANSVILLE BRAVES, 1957.

Evansville Blackbirds
Southern League, 1895; new franchise. Disbanded with league after 1895 season.

Evansville Black Sox
Alternate name for EVANSVILLE EVAS, 1921.

Evansville Braves
Alternate name for EVANSVILLE BEES, 1940.

Evansville Braves
Three I League (B), 1957; renamed franchise. Had been EVANSVILLE BEES, 1938–1942; 1946–1956. Disbanded after 1957 season.

Evansville Evas
Central League (D), 1915–1917; renamed franchise. Had been EVANSVILLE RIVERRATS, 1913–1914. Disbanded with league after 1917 season.

Evansville Evas (aka Black Sox, 1921, and Little Evas, 1922–1924)
Illinois–Iowa–Indiana League (B), 1919–1924; charter franchise. Re-

named EVANSVILLE POCKETEERS, 1925.

Evansville Hubs
Illinois–Iowa–Indiana League (B), 1926–1931; renamed franchise. Had been EVANSVILLE POCKETEERS, 1925. Disbanded after 1931 season.

Evansville Little Evas
Alternate name for Evansville Evas, 1922–1924.

Evansville Pocketeers
Illinois–Iowa–Indiana League (B), 1925; renamed franchise. Had been EVANSVILLE EVAS, 1919–1924. Renamed EVANSVILLE HUBS, 1926.

Evansville Riverrats
Illinois–Iowa–Indiana League, 1901; (B), 1902; charter franchise. Central League (D), 1903–1910; charter franchise. Renamed EVANSVILLE STRIKERS, 1911.

Evansville Riverrats
Central League (D), 1913–1914; renamed franchise. Had been EVANSVILLE YANKEES, 1912. Renamed EVANSVILLE EVAS, 1915.

Evansville Strikers
Central League (D), 1911; renamed franchise. Had been EVANSVILLE RIVERRATS, 1903–1910. Became SOUTH BEND BUX, mid-1911.

Evansville Triplets
American Association (AAA), 1970–1984; new franchise. Disbanded after 1984 season.

Evansville White Sox
Southern League (AA), 1966–1968; new franchise. Disbanded after 1968 season.

Evansville Yankees
KITTY League (D), 1912; new franchise. Had been EVANSVILLE STRIKERS, 1911. Disbanded after 1912 season.

EVART, MI

Evart
Northern Michigan League, 1887; charter franchise. Disbanded during 1887 season.

EVERETT, WA

Everett Giants
Northwest League (A), 1984–(still in existence as of 5-1-92); new franchise.

Everett Smokestackers
Northwestern League (B), 1905; charter franchise. Disbanded after 1905 season.

EVERGREEN, AL

Evergreen Greenies
Alabama–Florida League (D), mid-1937–1938; relocated franchise. Had been OZARK CARDINALS, 1936–mid-1937. Disbanded after 1938 season.

FAIRBURY, NE

Fairbury
Nebraska State League (D), 1922–1923; charter franchise. Disbanded with league after 1923 season.

Fairbury Jeffersons
Nebraska State League (D), 1928–1930; charter franchise. Disbanded after 1930 season.

Fairbury Jeffs
Nebraska State League (D), 1936–1937; new franchise. Disbanded after 1937 season.

Fairbury Shaners
Nebraska State League (D), 1915; new franchise. Disbanded with league during 1915 season.

FAIRFAX, GA
(See LANNETT, GA)

FAIRMOUNT, WV

Fairmount
Ohio–Pennsylvania League (D), mid-1912; relocated franchise. Had been SALEM, 1912.

Fairmount
Pennsylvania–West Virginia League (D), 1914; charter franchise. Disbanded with league after 1914 season.

Fairmount Black Diamonds
Middle Atlantic League (D), 1926–1931; renamed franchise. Had been FAIRMOUNT MAROONS, 1925.

Fairmount Champions
Western Pennsylvania League (D), 1907; charter franchise. Pennsylvania–West Virginia League (D), 1908–1909; charter franchise. West Virginia League (D), 1910; charter franchise. Disbanded with league after 1910 season.

Fairmount Maroons
Middle Atlantic League (D), mid-1925; charter franchise. Renamed FAIRMOUNT BLACK DIAMONDS, 1926.

FALL RIVER, MA

Fall River
New England League, 1877; charter franchise. Disbanded with league after 1877 season.

Fall River
New England League (B), 1902–1910; new franchise. Named FALL RIVER BRINIES, 1911.

Fall River
Colonial League (C), 1914–1915; charter franchise. Disbanded with league after 1915 season.

Fall River Adopted Sons
New England League (B), 1913; renamed franchise. Had been FALL RIVER BRINIES, 1911–1912. Disbanded after 1913 season.

Fall River Brinies
New England League (B), 1911–1912; Named franchise. Renamed FALL RIVER ADOPTED SONS, 1913.

Fall River Indians
New England League, 1894; 1896–1898; new franchise. Disbanded with league after 1898 season.

Fall River Indians
New England League (B), 1946–1949; charter franchise. Disbanded with league after 1949 season.

FALLS CITY, NE

Falls City Colts
MINK League (D), 1910–1913; charter franchise. Disbanded with league after 1913 season.

FARGO, ND

Fargo
Dakota League, 1887; new franchise. Disbanded during 1887 season.

Fargo
Dakota League, 1891; new franchise. Disbanded during 1891 season.

Fargo
Northern League (D), 1902–1905; charter franchise. Northern Copper County League (C), 1906; charter franchise. Disbanded after 1906 season.

Fargo
Northern League (D), 1908; charter franchise. Disbanded after 1908 season.

Fargo Twins
Northern League (D), 1933–1940; (C), 1941–1942; charter franchise. Suspended operations after 1942 season. Resumed operations as FARGO–MOREHEAD TWINS, 1946.

FARGO, ND– MOREHEAD, MN

Fargo–Morehead A's
Dakota League (D); 1922; new franchise. Disbanded after 1922 season.

Fargo–Morehead Graingrowers
Northern League (C), 1913–1917; charter franchise. Renamed FARGO–MOREHEAD TWINS, 1917.

Fargo–Morehead Twins
Northern League (C), 1917; renamed franchise. Had been FARGO–MOREHEAD GRAINGROWERS, 1913–1916. Disbanded during 1917 season.

Fargo–Morehead Twins
Northern League (C) 1946–1960; renamed franchise. Had been FARGO TWINS, 1933–1942. Disbanded after 1960 season.

FARNHAM, QUEBEC, CANADA

Farnham Pirates
Provincial League (C), 1950–1951; charter franchise. Disbanded after 1951 season.

FAYETTEVILLE, AR

Fayetteville Angels
Arkansas–Missouri League (D), 1937–1940; renamed franchise. Had been FAYETTEVILLE BEARS, 1934–1937. Disbanded during 1940 season.

Fayetteville Bears
Arkansas State League (D), 1935; renamed franchise. Had been FAYETTEVILLE EDUCATORS, 1934. Arkansas–Missouri League (D), 1936; charter franchice. Renamed FAYETTEVILLE ANGELS, 1937.

Fayetteville Educators
Arkansas State League (D), 1934; charter franchise. Renamed FAYETTEVILLE BEARS, 1935.

FAYETTEVILLE, NC

Fayetteville A's
Alternate name for FAYETTEVILLE ATHLETICS.

Fayetteville Athletics (aka A's)
Carolina League (B), 1950–1952; relocated franchise. Had been MARTINSVILLE ATHLETICS, 1945–1949. Renamed FAYETTEVILLE HIGHLANDERS, 1953.

Fayetteville Cubs
Coastal Plain League (D), 1946; new franchise. Tri–State League (B), 1947–1948; new franchise. Became FAYETTEVILLE SCOTTIES, 1949.

Fayetteville Generals
South Atlantic League (A), 1987– (still in existence as of 5-1-92); new franchise.

Fayetteville Highlanders
Eastern Carolina Association (D), 1909–1910/League (D), 1911; new franchise. Disbanded with league after 1911 season.

Fayetteville Highlanders
East Carolina League (D), 1928–1929; charter franchise. Disbanded with league after 1929 season.

Fayetteville Highlanders
Carolina League (B), 1953–1956; renamed franchise. Had been FAYETTEVILLE A'S, 1951–1952. Disbanded after 1956 season.

Fayetteville Scotties
Tobacco State League (D), 1949; new franchise. Disbanded after 1949 season.

FEDERALSBURG, MD

Federalsburg A's
Eastern Shore League (D), 1946–1948; charter franchise. Renamed FEDERALSBURG FEDS, 1949.

Federalsburg Feds
Eastern Shore League (D), 1949; renamed franchise. Had been FEDERALSBURG A'S, 1946–1948. Disbanded with league after 1949 season.

Federalsburg Little A's
Eastern Shore League (D), 1937–1941; charter franchise. Disbanded with league after 1941 season.

FERGUS FALLS, ND

Fergus Falls
Dakota League, 1887; new franchise. Disbanded during 1887 season.

Fergus Falls
Dakota League, 1891; new franchise. Disbanded during 1891 season.

FIELDALE, VA

Fieldale Towlers
Bi-State League (NC–VA), (D), 1935–1937; renamed franchise. Had been FIELDALE VIRGINIANS, 1934. Disbanded after 1937 season.

Fieldale Virginians
Bi-State League (NC–VA), (D), 1934; charter franchise. Renamed FIELDALE TOWLERS, 1935.

FINDLAY, OH

Findlay Browns
Ohio State League (D), 1937–1938; new franchise. Renamed FINDLAY OILERS, 1939.

Findlay Browns
Ohio State League (D), 1941; renamed franchise. Had been FINDLAY OILERS, 1939–1940. Disbanded with league after 1941 season.

Findlay Natural Gassers
Inter-State League, 1895; new franchise. Disbanded after 1895 season.

Findlay Oilers
Ohio State League (D), 1939–1940; renamed franchise. Had been FINDLAY BROWNS, 1937–1938. Renamed FINDLAY BROWNS, 1941.

FITCHBURG, MA

Fitchburg
New England League, 1899; charter franchise. Became LAWRENCE, mid-1899.

Fitchburg
Eastern League (A), mid-1922; relocated franchise. Had been WORCESTER BOOSTERS, 1918–mid-1922.

Fitchburg Burghers
New England League (B), 1914; new franchise. Became MANCHESTER TEXTILES, mid-1914.

Fitchburg Burghers
New England League (B), 1915; new franchise. Disbanded with league after 1915 season.

Fitchburg Foxes
New England League (B), 1919; charter franchise. Disbanded with league after 1919 season.

Fitchburg Trilbies
New England League, 1895; new franchise. Disbanded after 1895 season.

Fitchburg Wanderers
New England League (B), mid-1929; relocated franchise. Had been HAVERHILL HILLIES, 1929. Became GLOUCESTER HILLIES, mid-1929.

FITZGERALD, GA

Fitzgerald A's
Georgia–Florida League (D), 1956; new franchise. Renamed FITZGERALD ORIOLES, 1957.

Fitzgerald Orioles
Georgia–Florida League (D), 1957; renamed franchise. Had been FITZ-GERALD A'S, 1956. Disbanded after 1957 season.

Fitzgerald Pioneers
Georgia State League (D), 1948–1952; charter franchise. Georgia–Florida League (D), 1953–1954; new franchise. Disbanded after 1954 season.

Fitzgerald Red Legs
Georgia–Florida League (D), 1954; renamed franchise. Had been FITZ-GERALD PIONEERS, 1948–1953. Disbanded after 1954 season.

FLANDREAU, SD

Flandreau
Iowa–South Dakota League (D), 1902; charter franchise. Disbanded after 1902 season.

FLINT, MI

Flint
Michigan State League, mid-1897; relocated franchise. Had been KALAMAZOO KAZOOS, 1897. Disbanded with league after 1897 season.

Flint
Michigan State League (D), 1902; charter franchise. Disbanded with league during 1902 season.

Flint Arrows
Central League (D), 1948–1951; charter franchise. Disbanded with league after 1951 season.

Flint Flyers
Michigan State League, 1889–1890; relocated franchise. Had been KALAMAZOO KAZOOS, 1887–mid-1889. Disbanded during 1890 season.

Flint Gems
Michigan State League (D), 1940; charter franchise. Renamed FLINT INDIANS, 1941.

Flint Halligans
Michigan–Ontario League (B), 1919–1920; charter franchise. Became FLINT VEHICLES, 1921.

Flint Indians
Michigan State League (D), 1941; renamed franchise. Had been FLINT GEMS, 1940. Disbanded with league after 1941 season.

Flint Vehicles
Inter-State Association (D), 1906; new franchise. Became MARION (IN), mid-1906.

Flint Vehicles
Southern Michigan League (D), 1907–1910; (C), 1911–1915; new franchise. Disbanded with league during 1915 season.

Flint Vehicles
Michigan–Ontario League (B), 1921–mid-1926; renamed franchise. Had been FLINT HALLIGANS, 1919–1920. Michigan State League (D), mid-1926; charter franchise. Became CHARLOTTE GIANTS, mid-1926.

FLORENCE, SC

Florence
South Carolina League (D), 1907; charter franchise. Disbanded during 1907 season.

Florence Blue Jays
South Atlantic League (A), 1981–1988; new franchise. Disbanded after 1988 season.

Florence Pee Deans
Palmetto League (D), 1931; charter franchise. Disbanded with league after 1931 season.

Florence Steelers
Tri–State League (B), 1948–1950; new franchise. Disbanded after 1950 season.

FLORENCE–SHEFFIELD–TUSCUMBIA, AL
(See also SHEFFIELD, AL)

Tri-City
Alabama–Tennessee League (D),
1921; charter franchise. Disbanded
with league after 1921 season.

FOLLANSBEE, WV

Follansbee
Ohio–Pennsylvania League (D),
mid-1912; relocated franchise. Had
been STEUBENVILLE STUBS, 1911–
mid-1912. Disbanded with league
after 1912 season.

FOND DU LAC, WI

Fond du Lac Cubs
Wisconsin–Illinois League (D),
1908; renamed franchise. Had been
FOND DU LAC WEBFOOTERS (aka
Fondies), 1907. Renamed FOND DU
LAC GIANTS, 1909.

Fond du Lac Fondies
Alternate name for FOND DU LAC
WEBFOOTERS, 1907.

Fond du Lac Giants
Wisconsin–Illinois League (D), 1909–
1910; renamed franchise. Had been
FOND DU LAC CUBS, 1908. Renamed
FOND DU LAC MUDHENS, 1911.

Fond du Lac Molls
Wisconsin–Illinois League (C),
mid-1913; renamed franchise.
Had been MILWAUKEE CREAMS,
1913. Disbanded after 1913 season.

Fond du Lac Mudhens
Wisconsin–Illinois League (C),
1911; renamed franchise. Had
been FOND DU LAC GIANTS, 1909–
1910. Disbanded after 1911 season.

Fond du Lac Panthers
Wisconsin State League (D),
1940–1942; 1946–1953; charter
franchise. Disbanded with league
after 1953 season.

Fond du Lac Webfeet
Wisconsin State League, 1891;
charter franchise. Disbanded with
league after 1891 season.

**Fond du Lac Webfooters (aka
Fondies)**
Wisconsin–Illinois League (D),
1907; new franchise. Renamed
FOND DU LAC CUBS, 1908.

FOREST CITY, NC

Forest City Owls
Western Carolinas League (D),
1948; charter franchise. Became
FOREST CITY–SPINDALE OWLS,
1949.

FOREST CITY–SPINDALE, NC

Forest City–Spindale Owls
Western Carolina League (D),
1949–1951; renamed franchise.
Had been FOREST CITY OWLS, 1948.
Became RUTHERFORD COUNTY
OWLS, 1952.

Rutherford County Owls
Western Carolina League (D),
1952; new franchise. Tar Heel
League (D), 1953–1954; charter
franchise. Disbanded with league
after 1954 season.

Rutherford County Owls
Western Carolinas League (D),
1960; charter franchise. Disbanded
after 1960 season.

FORT COLLINS, CO

Fort Collins
Colorado State League, 1898; charter franchise. Disbanded during
1898 season.

FORT DODGE, IA

Fort Dodge
Iowa State League (D), 1912; charter franchise. Disbanded with
league after 1912 season.

Fort Dodge Dodgers
Central Association (D), 1916–
1917; new franchise. Disbanded
with league after 1917 season.

Fort Dodge Gypsumeaters
Iowa State League (D), 1904–
1906; charter franchise. Renamed
FORT DODGE GYPSUMITES, 1905.

Fort Dodge Gypsumites
Iowa State League (D), 1905–
1906; renamed franchise. Had been
FORT DODGE GYPSUMEATERS, 1904.
Disbanded after 1906 season.

FORT LAUDERDALE, FL

Fort Lauderdale Braves
Florida International League (B),
1947–1952; new franchise. Became KEY WEST CONCHS, mid-
1952.

Fort Lauderdale Lions
Florida International League (B),
1953; new franchise. Disbanded
after 1953 season.

Fort Lauderdale Tarpons
Florida State League (D), 1928;
new franchise. Became ST. PETERS-
BURG SAINTS, mid-1928.

Fort Lauderdale Tarpons
Florida East Coast League (D),
1940–mid-1942; charter franchise.
Disbanded during 1942 season.

Fort Lauderdale Yankees
Florida State League (D), 1962;
(A), 1963–(still in existence as of
5-1-92); new franchise.

FORT MYERS, FL

Fort Myers Palms
Florida State League (D), 1926–
mid-1927; charter franchise. Became MIAMI HUSTLERS, mid-1927.

Fort Myers Royals
Florida State League (A), 1978–
1987; new franchise. Disbanded
after 1987 season.

Fort Myers Sun Sox
Senior Professional Baseball Association, 1989–90; charter franchise. Suspended operations with league during 1990–91 season.

FORT PIERCE, FL

Fort Pierce Bombers
Florida East Coast League (D), 1940–mid-1942; charter franchise. Disbanded with league during 1942 season.

FORT SCOTT, KS

Fort Scott
Southeast Kansas League (D), 1911; charter franchise. Disbanded with league after 1911 season.

Fort Scott Giants
Missouri Valley Association (D), 1904; renamed franchise. Had been FORT SCOTT JAYHAWKERS, 1902–1903. Renamed FORT SCOTT HAY DIGGERS, 1905.

Fort Scott Hay Diggers
Missouri Valley Association (D), 1905; renamed franchise. Had been FORT SCOTT GIANTS, 1904. Disbanded with league after 1905 season.

Fort Scott Jayhawkers
Missouri Valley Association (D), 1902–1903; charter franchise. Renamed FORT SCOTT GIANTS, 1904.

Fort Scott Kickers
Southwestern League, 1891; charter franchise. Disbanded with league after 1891 season.

Fort Scott Scotties
Kansas State League (D), 1906; new franchise. Disbanded with league after 1906 season.

FORT SMITH, AR

Fort Smith
Missouri Valley League (D), mid-1905; relocated franchise. Had been SOUTH MCALESTER COAL MINERS (aka Giants), 1905.

Fort Smith
South Central League (D), 1906; charter franchise. Disbanded with league after 1906 season.

Fort Smith
OAK League (D), 1907; charter franchise. Disbanded with league after 1907 season.

Fort Smith
Arkansas League (D), 1909; new franchise. Disbanded with league after 1909 season.

Fort Smith
Western Association (D), 1911; new franchise. Disbanded with league during 1911 season.

Fort Smith Electrics
Alternate name for FORT SMITH INDIANS, 1897.

Fort Smith Giants
Western Association (C), 1938–1942, 1946–1949; new franchise. Disbanded after 1949 season.

Fort Smith Indians (aka Electrics)
Arkansas League, 1897; charter franchise. Disbanded with league after 1897 season.

Fort Smith Indians
Southwestern League, 1887; charter franchise. Disbanded with league after 1887 season.

Fort Smith Indians
Western Association (C), 1951–1952; new franchise. Became FORT SMITH–VAN BUREN INDIANS, 1953.

Fort Smith Twins
Western Association (D), 1916–1917; charter franchise. Disbanded after 1917 season.

Fort Smith Twins
Western Association (D), 1920–1921; (C), 1922–1926; (B), 1927; (C), mid-1927–mid-1932; charter franchise. Became MUSKOGEE NIGHTHAWKS, mid-1932.

FORT SMITH– VAN BUREN, AR

Fort Smith–Van Buren Indians
Western Association (C), 1953; renamed franchise. Had been FORT SMITH INDIANS, 1951–1952. Disbanded after 1953 season.

Fort Smith–Van Buren Twins
Western Association (D), 1914–1917; charter franchise. Disbanded with league after 1917 season.

FORT WALTON BEACH, FL

Fort Walton Beach Jets
Alabama–Florida League (D), 1953–1962; new franchise. Disbanded with league after 1962 season.

FORT WAYNE, IN

Fort Wayne
Indiana State League, 1888; charter franchise. Disbanded with league after 1888 season.

Fort Wayne
Indiana State League, 1890; charter franchise. Disbanded with league after 1890 season.

Fort Wayne
Western League, mid-1892; relocated franchise. Had been ST. PAUL APOSTLES, 1892. Disbanded after 1892 season.

Fort Wayne
Inter-State Association (D), 1906; charter franchise. Disbanded with league after 1906 season.

Fort Wayne Billikens
Central League (B), 1908–1910; new franchise. Renamed FORT WAYNE BRAKIES, 1911.

Fort Wayne Brakies
Central League (B), 1911; renamed franchise. Had been FORT WAYNE

BILLIKENS, 1908–1910. Renamed FORT WAYNE RAILROADERS, 1912.

Fort Wayne Champs
Central League (B), 1913; renamed franchise. Had been FORT WAYNE RAILROADERS, 1912. Renamed FORT WAYNE RAILROADERS, 1914.

Fort Wayne Chiefs
Central League (D), 1917; new franchise. Disbanded with league after 1917 season.

Fort Wayne Chiefs
Central League (D), 1928–1930; charter franchise. Disbanded with league after 1930 season.

Fort Wayne Chiefs
Central League (D), 1932; charter franchise. Disbanded after 1932 season.

Fort Wayne Chiefs
Central League (B), 1934; charter franchise. Three I League (B), 1935; charter franchise. Disbanded with league after 1935 season.

Fort Wayne Cubs
Central League (B), 1915; renamed franchise. Had been FORT WAYNE RAILROADERS, 1914. Disbanded after 1915 season.

Fort Wayne Daisies
All-American Girls' Baseball League, 1954; new franchise. Disbanded with league after 1954 season.

Fort Wayne Farmers
Inter-State League, 1896; charter franchise. Disbanded with league after 1896 season.

Fort Wayne Generals
Central League (D), 1948; charter franchise. Disbanded after 1948 season.

Fort Wayne Hoosiers
Northwestern League, 1883–1884; charter franchise. Disbanded with league after 1884 season.

Fort Wayne Hoosiers
Alternate name for FORT WAYNE INDIANS, 1899.

Fort Wayne Indians (aka Hoosiers, 1899)
Inter-State League, 1898–1900; new franchise. Disbanded with league after 1900 season.

Fort Wayne Jewels
Western Inter-State League, 1895; charter franchise. Disbanded with league after 1895 season.

FORT WAYNE KEKIONGAS
National Association, 1871; charter franchise. Disbanded during 1871 season.

Fort Wayne Railroaders
Western Association, 1901; charter franchise. Disbanded with league after 1901 season.

Fort Wayne Railroaders
Central League (D), 1903–1904; charter franchise. Became CANTON, mid-1904.

Fort Wayne Railroaders
Central League (B), 1912; renamed franchise. Had been FORT WAYNE BRAKIES, 1911. Renamed FORT WAYNE CHAMPS, 1913.

Fort Wayne Railroaders
Central League (B), 1914; renamed franchise. Had been FORT WAYNE CHAMPS, 1913. Renamed FORT WAYNE CUBS, 1915.

Fort Wayne Warriors
Northwestern League, 1891; charter franchise. Disbanded with league after 1891 season.

FORT WILLIAM, ONTARIO, CANADA

Fort William Canadians
Northern League (C), 1914–1915; new franchise. Became FORT WILLIAM–PORT ARTHUR CANADIANS, 1916.

FORT WILLIAM–PORT ARTHUR, ONTARIO, CANADA

Fort William–Port Arthur Canadians
Northern League (C), 1916; relocated franchise. Had been FORT WILLIAM CANADIANS, 1914–1915. Disbanded during 1916 season.

FORT WORTH, TX
(See also DALLAS, TX)

Fort Worth
North Texas League (D), 1903–1904; charter franchise. Disbanded after 1904 season.

Fort Worth
Dixie Association (D), 1971; charter franchise. Disbanded with league after 1971 season.

Fort Worth Cats
Texas League (A), 1933–1935; (A1), 1936–1942; (AA), 1946–1958; renamed franchise. Had been FORT WORTH PANTHERS, 1902–1932. American Association (AAA), 1959; new franchise. Became DALLAS–FORT WORTH RANGERS, 1960.

Fort Worth Cats
Texas League (AA), 1964; new franchise. Became DALLAS–FORT WORTH SPURS, 1965.

Fort Worth Jackrabbits
Alternate name for FORT WORTH PANTHERS, 1889.

Fort Worth Panthers (aka Jackrabbits, 1889)
Texas League, 1888–1890; 1892; charter franchise. Disbanded during 1892 season.

Fort Worth Panthers
Texas Southern League, 1895; charter franchise. League reconfigured as Texas League, 1896–1898.

Fort Worth Panthers
Texas League (D), 1902–1905; (C), 1906–1910; (B), 1911–1920; (A),

1921–1932; new franchise. Re-named FORT WORTH CATS, 1933.

Fort Worth Rangers
Pacific Coast League (AAA), 1963; new franchise. Disbanded after 1963 season.

FOSTORIA, OH

Fostoria Cardinals
Ohio State League (D), 1936; charter franchise. Renamed FOSTORIA RED BIRDS, 1937.

Fostoria Red Birds
Ohio State League (D), 1936–1941; renamed franchise. Had been FOSTORIA CARDINALS, 1936. Disbanded with league after 1941 season.

FOXCROFT, ME
(See DOVER, ME)

FRANKFORT, IN

Frankfort
Indiana State League, 1888; charter franchise. Disbanded with league after 1888 season.

FRANKFORT, KY

Frankfort
Inter-State League, 1885; charter franchise. Disbanded during 1885 season.

Frankfort Lawmakers
Blue Grass League (D), 1912; renamed franchise. Had been FRANKFORT STATESMEN, 1908–1911. Disbanded with league after 1912 season.

Frankfort Old Taylors
Ohio State League (D), 1915–1916; new franchise. Disbanded during 1916 season.

Frankfort Statesmen
Blue Grass League (D), 1908–1911; charter franchise. Renamed FRANKFORT LAWMAKERS, 1912.

FRANKLIN, NH

Franklin
New Hampshire League, 1907; new franchise. Disbanded during 1907 season.

FRANKLIN, PA

Franklin Braves
Iron and Oil Association, 1884; charter franchise. Disbanded with association after 1884 season.

Franklin Millionaires
Inter-State League (D), 1908; charter franchise. Disbanded with league after 1908 season.

FRANKLIN, VA

Franklin Cubs
Virginia League (D), 1948; new franchise. Renamed FRANKLIN KIL-DEES, 1949.

Franklin Kildees
Virginia League (D), 1949–1951; renamed franchise. Had been FRANKLIN CUBS, 1948. Disbanded with league after 1951 season.

FREDERICK, MD

Frederick Hustlers
Blue Ridge League (D), 1915–1917; charter franchise. Disbanded with league during 1917 season.

Frederick Hustlers
Blue Ridge League (D), 1920–1928; charter franchise. Renamed FREDERICK WARRIORS, 1929.

Frederick Keys
Carolina League (A), 1989–(still in existence as of 5-1-92); new franchise.

Frederick Warriors
Blue Ridge League (D), 1929–1930; charter franchise. Had been FREDERICK HUSTLERS, 1920–1928. Disbanded with league after 1930 season.

FREDERICTON, NEW BRUNSWICK, CANADA

Fredericton
New Brunswick League, 1890; charter franchise. Disbanded with league after 1890 season.

Fredericton Pets
New Brunswick–Maine League (D), 1913; charter franchise. Disbanded during 1913 season.

FREEPORT, IL

Freeport Comeons
Illinois-Iowa-Indiana League (B), mid-1915; relocated franchise. Had been DUBUQUE HUSTLERS, 1911–mid-1915. Disbanded after 1915 season.

Freeport Pretzels
Wisconsin State Association (D), 1905/League (D), 1906; charter franchise. Wisconsin–Illinois League (D), 1907–1909; charter franchise. Northern Association of Baseball (C), 1910; (D), mid-1910; charter franchise. Disbanded with league after 1910 season.

Freeport Pretzels
Wisconsin–Illinois League (D), 1914; new franchise. Bi-State League (WI–IL), (D), 1915; charter franchise. Disbanded with league during 1915 season.

FREMONT, NE

Fremont Freaks
Nebraska State League, 1892; charter franchise. Disbanded with league after 1892 season.

Fremont Pathfinders
Nebraska State League (D), 1910–1913; charter franchise. Disbanded after 1913 season.

FREMONT, NH

Fremont
Southern New Hamsphire League (D), 1907; charter franchise. Disbanded with league after 1907 season.

FREMONT, OH

Fremont Green Sox
Ohio State League (D), mid-1938–1941; renamed franchise. Had been FREMONT REDS, 1936–mid-1938. Disbanded with league after 1941 season.

Fremont Reds
Ohio State League (D), 1936–mid-1938; charter franchise. Renamed FREMONT GREEN SOX, mid-1938.

FRESNILLO, ZACATECAS, MEXICO

(See also ZACATECAS, MEXICO)

Fresnillo Charros (Gamers)
Mexican Center League (A), 1964; new franchise. Renamed FRESNILLO MINEROS, 1965.

Fresnillo Mineros (Miners)
Mexican Center League (C), 1956; new franchise. Renamed FRESNILLO ROJOS (Reds), 1957.

Fresnillo Mineros (Miners)
Mexican Center League (A), 1965–1966; renamed franchise. Had been FRESNILLO CHARROS, 1964. Renamed FRESNILLO TUZOS, 1967.

Fresnillo Rojos (Reds)
Mexican Center League (C), 1957; renamed franchise. Had been FRESNILLO MINEROS, 1956. Disbanded after 1957 season.

Fresnillo Rojos (Reds)
Mexican Center League (A), 1962; new franchise. Disbanded after 1962 season.

Fresnillo Tuzos (Gophers)
Mexican Center League (A), 1967–1968; renamed franchise. Had been FRESNILLO MINEROS, 1964–1965. Disbanded after 1968 season.

Fresnillo Tuzos (Gophers)
Mexican Center League (A), 1976–1978; new franchise. Disbanded after 1978 season.

FRESNO, CA

Fresno Cardinals
California State League (C), 1941–1942; 1946–1956; charter franchise. Renamed FRESNO SUN SOX, 1957.

Fresno Giants
California League (C), 1958–1962; (A), 1963–1987; renamed franchise. Had been FRESNO SUN SOX, 1957. Renamed FRESNO SUNS, 1988.

Fresno Packers
California State League (D), 1913–1914; charter franchise. Disbanded with league during 1914 season.

Fresno Raisineaters
Pacific Coast League (A), 1906; relocated franchise. Had been SACRAMENTO SACTS, 1905. California State League (B), 1907–1909; new franchise. Disbanded after 1909 season.

Fresno Suns
California League (A), 1988; renamed franchise. Had been FRESNO GIANTS, 1958–1962 . Became SALINAS SPURS, 1989.

Fresno Sun Sox
California State League (C), 1957; renamed franchise. Had been FRESNO CARDINALS, 1941–1942, 1946–1956. Renamed FRESNO GIANTS, 1958.

Fresno Tigers
California State League, 1898; charter franchise. Became WATSONVILLE INFANTS, mid-1898.

Fresno Tigers
California Baseball League (B), 1910; charter franchise. Disbanded after 1910 season.

FROSTBURG, MD

Frostburg Demons
Potomac League (D), 1916; charter franchise. Disbanded with league after 1916 season.

FRUITVALE, CA

Fruitvale
Central California Baseball League (D), mid-1910; relocated franchise. Had been ST. HELENA, 1910. Became ALAMEDA, mid-1910.

Fruitvale
Central California Baseball League (D), mid-1910; relocated franchise. Had been HAYWARD CUBS, 1910.

Fruitvale
Central California Baseball League (D), 1911; new franchise. Became OAKLAND MONDAY MODELS, mid-1911.

FULTON, KY

Fulton Bulldogs
KITTY League (D), 1946; charter franchise. Renamed FULTON CHICKS, 1947.

Fulton Chicks
KITTY League (D), 1947–mid-1948; renamed franchise. Had been FULTON BULLDOGS, 1946. Renamed FULTON RAILROADERS, mid-1948.

Fulton Colonels
KITTY League (D), 1910–1912; charter franchise. Disbanded after 1912 season.

Fulton Eagles
KITTY League (D), 1936–1938; new franchise. Renamed FULTON TIGERS, 1939.

Fulton Lookouts
KITTY League (D), 1951–1955; renamed franchise. Had been FULTON RAILROADERS, mid-1948–1950. Disbanded with league after 1955 season.

Fulton Railroaders
KITTY League (D), 1922–1924; charter franchise. Disbanded after 1924 season.

Fulton Railroaders
KITTY League (D), mid-1948–1950; renamed franchise. Had been FULTON CHICKS, 1947–mid-1948. Renamed FULTON LOOKOUTS, 1951.

Fulton Tigers
KITTY League (D), 1939–1942; renamed franchise. Had been FULTON EAGLES, 1936–1938. Disbanded during 1942 season.

FULTON, NY

Fulton
Empire State League (NY), (C), 1905–1907; charter franchise. Disbanded with league after 1907 season.

FUQUAY SPRINGS, NC
(See ANGIER, NC)

GADSDEN, AL
(See also ALABAMA CITY, AL)

Gadsden
Alabama–Mississippi League (D), 1936; charter franchise. Disbanded with league during 1936 season.

Gadsden Chiefs
Southeastern League (B), 1949; renamed franchise. Had been GADSDEN PILOTS, 1938–1941; 1946–1948. Renamed GADSDEN PILOTS, 1950.

Gadsden Eagles (aka Fliers)
Georgia–Alabama Association (C), mid-1928; charter franchise.

Disbanded with association after 1928 season.

Gadsden Fliers
Alternate name for Gadsden Eagles, 1928.

Gadsden Pilots
Southeastern League (B), 1938–1941; 1946–1948; expansion franchise. Became GADSDEN CHIEFS, 1949.

Gadsden Pilots
Southeastern League (B), 1950; renamed franchise. Had been GADSDEN CHIEFS, 1949. Disbanded with league after 1950 season.

Gadsden Steel Makers
Southeastern League (D), 1910–1912; charter franchise. Georgia–Alabama League (D), 1913–1914; charter franchise. Disbanded after 1914 season.

GAINESVILLE, FL

Gainesville G Men
Florida State League (D), 1936–1941; 1946–1952; charter franchise. Disbanded during 1952 season.

Gainesville G–Men
Florida State League (D), 1955–1958; new franchise. Disbanded after 1958 season.

Gainesville Sharks
FLAG League (D), mid-1915; charter franchise. Had been AMERICUS MUCKALEES, Georgia State League, 1914–mid-1915. Disbanded with league after 1915 season.

GAINESVILLE, TX

Gainesville Blue Ribbons
Texas–Oklahoma League (D), 1911; charter franchise. Disbanded during 1911 season.

Gainesville Owls
Big State League (B) 1947–1951; charter franchise. Became LONGVIEW CHEROKEES, 1952.

Gainesville Owls
Sooner State League (D), 1953–mid-1955; new franchise. Became PONCA CITY CUBS, mid-1955.

GALAX, VA

Galax Leafs
Blue Ridge League (D), 1946–1950; charter franchise. Disbanded with league after 1950 season.

GALESBURG, IL

Galesburg
Western Inter-State League, 1890; charter franchise. Became INDIANPOLIS, mid-1890.

Galesburg
Illinois–Iowa League, mid-1890; relocated franchise. Had been STERLING RAG CHEWERS, 1890. Became BURLINGTON, mid-1890.

Galesburg
Indiana State League, 1895; new franchise. Disbanded during 1895 season.

Galesburg
Illinois–Missouri League (D), 1908–1909; charter franchise. Disbanded after 1909 season.

Galesburg
Central Association (B), mid-1914; relocated franchise. Had been ROCK ISLAND ISLANDERS, mid-1914. Disbanded after 1914 season.

Galesburg Pavers
Central Association (B), 1910–1912; new franchise. Disbanded after 1912 season.

GALLIPOLIS, OH
(See POINT PLEASANT, OH)

GALT, ONTARIO, CANADA

Galt
Canadian League, 1896; new franchise. Disbanded after 1896 season.

Galt
Canadian League, 1914; new franchise. Disbanded after 1914 season.

GALVESTON, TX

Galveston Buccaneers (aka Pirates)
Texas League (A), 1931–1935; (A1), 1936–1937; relocated franchise. Had been WACO Cubs, 1925–1930. Became SHREVEPORT SPORTS, 1938.

Galveston Giants
Texas League, 1888; charter franchise. Named GALVESTON SANDCRABS, 1889.

Galveston Pirates
Alternate name for GALVESTON BUCCANEERS.

Galveston Pirates
Texas League (B), mid-1912–1917; renamed franchise. Had been GALVESTON SANDCRABS, 1907–mid-1912. Disbanded during 1917 season.

Galveston Pirates
Texas League (B), 1919–1921; expansion franchise. Renamed GALVESTON SAND CRABS, 1922.

Galveston Sandcrabs
Texas Southern League, 1895–1899; charter franchise. League reconfigured as Texas League, 1896–1899. Disbanded after 1899 season.

Galveston Sandcrabs
Texas League, 1889–1890; 1892; renamed franchise. Had been GALVESTON GIANTS, 1888. Disbanded with league after 1892 season.

Galveston Sandcrabs
South Texas League (D), 1903–1906; relocated franchise. Had been PARIS EISENFELDER'S HOMESEEKERS, 1902. Texas League (C), 1907–1910; (B), 1911–mid-1912; expansion franchise. Renamed GALVESTON PIRATES, mid-1912.

Galveston Sand Crabs
Texas League (A), 1922–1924; renamed franchise. Had been GALVESTON PIRATES, 1919–1921. Became WACO CUBS, 1925.

Galveston White Caps
Gulf Coast League (D), 1950–1953; charter franchise. Big State League (B), 1954–1955; new franchise. Disbanded during 1955 season.

GARY, IN

Gary Sand Fleas
Indiana–Michigan League (D), 1910; charter franchise. Disbanded with league after 1910 season.

GASTONIA, NC

Gastonia Browns
Western Carolina League (D), 1950; new franchise. Disbanded after 1950 season.

Gastonia Cardinals
North Carolina State League (D), 1938; new franchise. Tar Heel League (D), 1939–1940; charter franchise. Disbanded with league after 1940 season.

Gastonia Cardinals
South Atlantic League (A), 1977–1982; new franchise. Renamed GASTONIA EXPOS, 1983.

Gastonia Comers
South Atlantic League (B), mid-1923; relocated franchise. Had been COLUMBIA COMERS, 1919–mid-1923. Disbanded after 1923 season.

Gastonia Expos
South Atlantic League (A), 1983–1984; renamed franchise. Had been GASTONIA CARDINALS, 1977–1982. Renamed GASTONIA JETS, 1985.

Gastonia Jets
South Atlantic League (A), 1985; renamed franchise. Had been GASTONIA EXPOS, 1983–1984. Renamed GASTONIA TIGERS, 1986.

Gastonia Pirates
South Atlantic League (A), mid-1959; relocated franchise. Had been COLUMBUS PIRATES, 1959. Disbanded after 1959 season.

Gastonia Pirates
Western Carolinas League (A), 1963–1972; new franchise. Renamed GASTONIA RANGERS, 1973.

Gastonia Rangers
Western Carolinas League (A), 1973–1974; renamed franchise. Had been GASTONIA PIRATES, 1963–1973. Disbanded after 1974 season.

Gastonia Rangers
South Atlantic League (A), 1987–(still in existence as of 5-1-92); renamed franchise. Had been GASTONIA TIGERS, 1986.

Gastonia Rippers
Western Carolinas League (D), 1960; charter franchise. Disbanded after 1960 season.

Gastonia Rockets
Tri-State League (B), 1952–1953; new franchise. Disbanded after 1953 season.

Gastonia Tigers
South Atlantic League (A), 1986; renamed franchise. Had been GASTONIA JETS, 1985. Renamed GASTONIA RANGERS, 1987.

GENEVA, AL

Geneva Red Birds
Alabama State League (D), 1946–1950; charter franchise. Disbanded with league after 1950 season.

GENEVA, IL

Kane County Cougars
Midwest League (A), 1991–(still in existence as of 5-1-92); relocated franchise. Had been WAUSAU TIMBERS, 1979–1990.

GENEVA, NY

Geneva
New York State League, mid-1897; relocated franchise. Had been BATAVIA REDS, 1897. Disbanded after 1897 season.

Geneva
Empire State League (NY), (C), 1905–1907; charter franchise. Disbanded with league after 1907 season.

Geneva
Central New York League (C), 1910; charter franchise. Disbanded with league after 1910 season.

Geneva Cubs
New York–Pennsylvania League (A), 1977–(still in existence as of 5-1-92); new franchise.

Geneva Rangers
New York–Pennsylvania League (A), 1972; renamed franchise. Had been GENEVA SENATORS, 1963–1971. Renamed GENEVA TWINS, 1973.

Geneva Red Birds
Border League (C), 1947; new franchise. Renamed GENEVA ROBINS, 1948.

Geneva Redlegs
New York–Pennsylvania League (D), 1958–1962; new franchise.

Renamed GENEVA SENATORS, 1963.

Geneva Robins
Border League (C), 1948–1951; renamed franchise. Had been GENEVA REDBIRDS, 1947. Disbanded during 1951 season.

Geneva Senators
New York–Pennsylvania League (A), 1963–1971; renamed franchise. Had been GENEVA REDLEGS, 1958–1962. Renamed GENEVA RANGERS, 1972.

Geneva Twins
New York–Pennsylvania League (A), 1973; renamed franchise. Had been GENEVA RANGERS, 1972. Disbanded after 1973 season.

GEORGETOWN, TX

Georgetown Collegians (aka Pedagogues)
Middle Texas League (D), mid-1914; charter franchise. Disbanded during 1914 season.

Georgetown Pedagogues
Alternate name for GEORGETOWN COLLEGIANS.

GETTSYBURG, PA

Gettsyburg Patriots
Blue Ridge League (D), 1915; charter franchise. Renamed GETTSYBURG PONIES, 1916.

Gettsyburg Ponies
Blue Ridge League (D), 1916–1917; renamed franchise. Had been GETTSYBURG PATRIOTS, 1915. Disbanded after 1917 season.

GILLETTE, CO

Gillette
Colorado State League, 1896; new franchise. Disbanded during 1896 season.

GIRARD, PA

Girard Sailors
Ohio–Pennsylvania League (D), 1908; new franchise. Became BUTLER SAILORS, mid-1908.

GLACE BAY, NOVA SCOTIA, CANADA

Glace Bay Miners
Cape Breton Colliery League (D), 1937–1938, (C), 1939; charter franchise. Disbanded with league after 1939 season.

GLADEWATER, TX

Gladewater Bears
West Dixie League (C), mid-1935; relocated franchise. Had been SHREVEPORT SPORTS, 1935. East Texas League (C), 1936; charter franchise. Disbanded after 1936 season.

Gladewater Bears
Lone Star League (C), 1948; new franchise. East Texas League (C), 1949–1950; charter franchise. Disbanded with league after 1950 season.

GLENS FALLS, NY

Glens Falls White Sox
Eastern League (AA); 1980–1985; new franchise. Renamed GLENS FALLS TIGERS, 1986.

Glens Falls White Sox
Eastern League (AA), 1986–1988; renamed franchise. Had been GLENS FALLS WHITE SOX, 1980–1985. Disbanded after 1988 season.

GLENS FALLS– SARATOGA SPRINGS, NY

(See also SARATOGA SPRINGS, NY)

Tri-County
Hudson River League (D), 1906; new franchise. Disbanded after 1906 season.

GLENWOOD, CO

Glenwood
Colorado State League, 1898; charter franchise. Disbanded during 1898 season.

GLOBE, AZ

Globe Bears
Arizona State League (D), 1928–1930; charter franchise. Arizona–Texas League (D), 1931; charter franchise. Disbanded after 1931 season.

GLOBE–CLAYPOOL– MIAMI, AZ
(See also MIAMI, AZ)

Globe–Miami Apaches
Alternate name for GLOBE–MIAMI BROWNS, 1947–1950.

Globe–Miami Browns (aka Apaches)
Arizona–Texas League (C), 1947–1950; charter franchise. Disbanded with league after 1950 season.

Globe–Miami Miners
Arizona–Mexico League (C), 1955; charter franchise. Disbanded after 1955 season.

GLOUCESTER, MA

Gloucester
New England League (B), 1930; new franchise. Disbanded with league after 1930 season.

Gloucester Hillies
New England League (B), 1929; relocated franchise. Had been FITCHBURG WANDERERS, mid-1929. Disbanded with league after 1929 season.

GLOVERSVILLE, NY
(See also AMSTERDAM, NY; JOHNSTOWN, NY)

Gloversville Glovers
Canadian–American League (C), mid-1937; renamed franchise. Had been BROCKVILLE BLUES, 1937. Renamed GLOVERSVILLE–JOHNSTOWN GLOVERS, 1938.

Gloversville Mitten Makers
New York State League, 1895; new franchise. Disbanded after 1895 season.

GLOVERSVILLE– JOHNSTOWN, NY
(See also AMSTERDAM,NY; JOHNSTOWN, NY)

Gloversville–Johnstown
New York State League, 1890; new franchise. Disbanded with league after 1890 season.

Gloversville–Johnstown Glovers
Canadian–American League (C), 1938–1942; 1946–1951; renamed franchise. Had been GLOVERSVILLE GLOVERS, mid-1937. Disbanded with league after 1951 season.

GOLD COAST, FL

Gold Coast Suns
Senior Professional Baseball Association, 1989–90; charter franchise. Disbanded after 1989–1990 season.

GOLDSBORO, NC

Goldsboro Cardinals
Coastal Plain League (D), 1950–1951; renamed franchise. Had been GOLDSBORO GOLDBUGS, 1937–1941; 1946–1949. Renamed GOLDSBORO JETS, 1952.

Goldsboro Giants
Eastern Carolina League (D), 1908–1909/Association (D), 1910; charter franchise. Disbanded with association after 1910 season.

Goldsboro Goldbugs
Eastern Carolina League (D), 1929; renamed franchise. Had been GOLDSBORO MANUFACTURERS, 1928. Disbanded with league after 1929 season.

Goldsboro Goldbugs
Coastal Plain League (D), 1937–1941; 1946–1949; expansion franchise. Renamed GOLDSBORO CARDINALS, 1946.

Goldsboro Jets
Coastal Plain League (D), 1952; renamed franchise. Had been GOLDSBORO CARDINALS, 1950–1951. Disbanded with league after 1952 season.

Goldsboro Manufacturers
Eastern Carolina League (D), 1928; charter franchise. Renamed GOLDSBORO GOLDBUGS, 1929.

GORMAN, TX

Gorman
West Texas League (D), 1920; charter franchise. Became SWEETWATER SWATTERS, mid-1920.

GOMEZ PALACIO, DURANGO, UNION LAGUNA, TORREON, MEXICO
(See also DURANGO, MEXICO; UNION LAGUNA, MEXICO; TORREON, MEXICO)

Gomez Palacio
La Laguna League (R), 1985–1986; new franchise. Disbanded after 1986 season.

Gomez Palacio Cotton Growers
Mexican League (AAA), 1970–1974; new franchise. Disbanded after 1974 season.

GRACEVILLE, FL

Graceville Boll Weevils
Alabama–Florida League (D), mid-1952; relocated franchise. Had been ENTERPRISE BOLL WEEVILS, 1947–mid-1952. Renamed GRACEVILLE OILERS, 1953.

Graceville Oilers

Alabama–Florida League (D), 1953–1958; renamed franchise. Had been GRACEVILLE BOLL WEE-VILS, mid-1952. Disbanded after 1958 season.

GRAFTON, WV

Grafton

Pennsylvania–West Virginia League (D), mid-1908–1909; relocated franchise. Had been SCOTTDALE GIANTS, 1907–mid-1908. West Virginia League (D), 1910; charter franchise. Disbanded with league after 1910 season.

GRAHAM, NC

(See BURLINGTON, NC)

GRAHAM, TX

Graham Hijackers

Texas–Oklahoma League (D), 1921; charter franchise. Became MINERAL WELLS, mid-1921.

GRANBY, QUEBEC, CANADA

Granby Phillies

Provincial League (C), 1952–1953; renamed franchise. Had been GRANBY RED SOX, 1950–1951. Disbanded after 1953 season.

Granby Red Socks

Quebec Provincial League (B), 1940; charter franchise. Disbanded after 1940 season.

Granby Red Sox

Border League (C), 1946; charter franchise. Disbanded after 1946 season.

Granby Red Sox

Provincial League (C), 1950–1951; charter franchise. Renamed GRANBY PHILLIES, 1952.

GRAND FORKS, ND

Grand Forks

Central International League (C), 1912; charter franchise. Disbanded with league after 1912 season.

Grand Forks

Northern League (D), 1933–1935; charter franchise. Disbanded after 1935 season.

Grand Forks Chiefs

Northern League (D), 1938–1940; (C), 1941–1942; 1946–1962; (A), 1963; new franchise. Had been GRAND FORKS DODGERS, 1964.

Grand Forks Dodgers

Northern League (A), 1964; renamed franchise. Had been GRAND FORKS CHIEFS, 1938–1942; 1946–1962. Disbanded after 1964 season.

Grand Forks Flickertails

Northern League (C), 1913–1915; charter franchise. Disbanded after 1915 season.

Grand Forks Forkers

Northern League (D), 1902–1905; charter franchise. Northern Copper County League (C), 1906–1907; charter franchise. Disbanded with league after 1907 season.

GRAND ISLAND, NE

Grand Island Athletics

Nebraska State League (D), 1956–1959; charter franchise. Disbanded with league after 1959 season.

Grand Island Cardinals

Nebraska State League (D), 1938; renamed franchise. Had been GRAND ISLAND RED BIRDS, 1937. Disbanded with league after 1938 season.

Grand Island Champions

Nebraska State League (D), 1915; renamed franchise. Had been GRAND ISLAND ISLANDERS, 1914.

Disbanded with league after 1915 season.

Grand Island Champions

Nebraska State League (D), 1922–1923; charter franchise. Tri-State League (D), 1924; charter franchise. Disbanded with league after 1924 season.

Grand Island Champions

Nebraska State League (D), 1928–1931; charter franchise. Renamed GRAND ISLAND ISLANDERS, 1932.

Grand Island Collegians

Nebraska State League (D), 1911–1913; charter franchise. Renamed GRAND ISLAND ISLANDERS, 1914.

Grand Island Islanders

Nebraska State League (D), 1914; renamed franchise. Renamed GRAND ISLAND CHAMPIONS, 1915.

Grand Island Islanders

Nebraska State League (D), 1932; renamed franchise. Had been GRAND ISLAND CHAMPIONS, 1928–1931. Disbanded after 1932 season.

Grand Island Red Birds

Nebraska State League (D), 1937; new franchise. Renamed GRAND IS-LAND CARDINALS, 1938.

Grand Island Sugar City

Nebraska State League, 1892; charter franchise. Disbanded after 1892 season.

GRAND RAPIDS, MI

Grand Rapids

Northwestern League, 1883–1884; charter franchise. Disbanded during 1884 season.

Grand Rapids

Michigan State League, 1889–1890; charter franchise. Disbanded during 1890 season.

Grand Rapids

International League, mid-1890; relocated franchise. Had been

MONTREAL, mid-1890. Became QUEBEC, mid-1890.

Grand Rapids
Northwestern League, 1891; charter franchise. Disbanded during 1891 season.

Grand Rapids
Michigan State League, 1893; charter franchise. Disbanded after 1893 season.

Grand Rapids
Western Association, mid-1901; relocated franchise. Had been LOUISVILLE COLONELS, 1901. Disbanded with league after 1901 season.

Grand Rapids
Michigan State League (D), 1902; charter franchise. Disbanded during 1902 season.

Grand Rapids
Central League (B), 1934; charter franchise. Disbanded with league during 1934 season.

Grand Rapids Billbobs
Central League (B), 1922; renamed franchise. Had been GRAND RAPIDS JOSHERS, mid-1920–1921. Michigan–Ontario League (B), 1923; new franchise. Renamed GRAND RAPIDS HOMONERS, 1924.

Grand Rapids Bill-Eds
Central League (B), 1913; renamed franchise. Had been GRAND RAPIDS BLACK SOX, 1912. Renamed GRAND RAPIDS CHAMPS, 1914.

Grand Rapids Blackbirds
Western League, 1895; renamed franchise. Had been GRAND RAPIDS RUSTLERS, 1894. Renamed GRAND RAPIDS GOLDBUGS, mid-1895.

Grand Rapids Black Sox
Central League (B), 1912; renamed franchise. Had been GRAND RAPIDS GRADS, mid-1911. Renamed GRAND RAPIDS BILL-EDS, 1913.

Grand Rapids Black Sox
Central League (B), 1915–1916; renamed franchise. Had been GRAND RAPIDS CHAMPS, 1914. Became BATTLE CREEK BLACK SOX, mid-1916, but returned as Grand Rapids Black Sox after one week. Disbanded after 1916 season.

Grand Rapids Black Sox
Central League (C), 1926; charter franchise. Michigan State League (D), mid-1926; charter franchise. Disbanded with league after 1926 season.

Grand Rapids Bobolinks
Western League, mid-1897; renamed franchise. Had been GRAND RAPIDS GOLDBUGS, 1895–mid-1897. Disbanded after 1897 season.

Grand Rapids Boers
International League, 1900; charter franchise. Disbanded during 1900 season.

Grand Rapids Cabinetmakers
Inter-State League, 1898; new franchise. Renamed GRAND RAPIDS FURNITUREMAKERS, 1899.

Grand Rapids Champs
Central League (B), 1914; renamed franchise. Had been GRAND RAPIDS BILL-EDS, 1913. Renamed GRAND RAPIDS BLACK SOX, 1915.

Grand Rapids Chicks
All-American Girls Professional Baseball League, 1945; relocated franchise. Had been MILWAUKEE CHICKS, 1944. Disbanded with league after 1954 season.

Grand Rapids Colts
Michigan State League (C), 1941; renamed franchise. Had been GRAND RAPIDS DODGERS, 1940. Disbanded with league after 1941 season.

Grand Rapids Dodgers
Michigan State League (C), 1940; charter franchise. Renamed GRAND RAPIDS COLTS, 1941.

Grand Rapids Furnituremakers
Inter-State League, 1899; new franchise. Had been GRAND RAPIDS CABINETMAKERS, 1898. Became COLUMBUS SENATORS, mid-1899.

Grand Rapids Furnituremakers
Western League, mid-1899; relocated franchise. Had been COLUMBUS SENATORS, 1899.

Grand Rapids Goldbugs
Western League, mid-1895–mid-1897; renamed franchise. Had been GRAND RAPIDS BLACKBIRDS, 1895. Renamed GRAND RAPIDS BOBOLINKS, mid-1897.

Grand Rapids Grads
Central League (B), mid-1911–1917; relocated franchise. Had been SOUTH BEND BUX, mid-1911. Disbanded with league after 1917 season.

Grand Rapids Homoners
Michigan–Ontario League (B), 1924; renamed franchise. Had been GRAND RAPIDS BILLBOBS, 1922–1923. Disbanded after 1924 season.

Grand Rapids Jets
Central League (A), 1948–1951; charter franchise. Disbanded after 1951 season.

Grand Rapids Joshers
Central League (B), mid-1920–1921; charter franchise. Renamed GRAND RAPIDS BILLBOBS, 1922.

Grand Rapids Orphans
Central League (D), mid-1903–1906; relocated franchise. Had been ANDERSON, 1903. Renamed GRAND RAPIDS WOLVERINES, 1907.

Grand Rapids Raiders (aka Furnituremakers)
Central League (D), 1910–mid-1911; renamed franchise. Had been GRAND RAPIDS WOLVERINES, 1907–1909. Became NEWARK SKEETERS, mid-1911.

Grand Rapids Rustlers
Western League, 1894; new franchise. Renamed GRAND RAPIDS BLACKBIRDS, 1895.

Grand Rapids Wolverines
Central League (D), 1907–1909; renamed franchise. Had been GRAND RAPIDS ORPHANS, 1903–1906. Renamed GRAND RAPIDS RAIDERS, 1910.

Grand Rapids Woodworkers
Western Association, 1901; charter franchise. Became WHEELING STOGIES, mid-1901.

GRANITE FALLS, NC

Granite Falls Graniteers
Western Carolina League (D), 1951; new franchise. Disbanded after 1951 season.

GRAY'S HARBOR, WA
(See ABERDEEN, WA)

GREAT BEND, KS

Great Bend Benders
Kansas State League (D), 1909–1910; charter franchise. Renamed GREAT BEND MILLERS, 1911.

Great Bend Big Benders
Kansas State League (D), 1905; charter franchise. Disbanded after 1905 season.

Great Bend Millers
Kansas State League (D), 1911; charter franchise. Had been GREAT BEND BENDERS, 1909–1910. Central Kansas League (D), 1912; new franchise. Kansas State League (D), 1913–1914; charter franchise. Disbanded with league after 1914 season.

GREATER MIAMI, FL

Greater Miami Flamingos
Florida International League (B), mid-1954; relocated franchise. Had been MIAMI BEACH FLAMINGOS, 1954. Disbanded with league after 1954 season.

GREAT FALLS, MT

Great Falls
Montana State League, 1892; charter franchise. Disbanded with league during 1892 season.

Great Falls
Union Association (C), 1911–1912; (D), 1913; charter franchise. Disbanded after 1913 season.

Great Falls Dodgers
Pioneer League (R), 1984–(still in existence as of 5-1-92); renamed franchise. Had been GREAT FALLS GIANTS, 1969–1983.

Great Falls Electrics
Northwestern League (B), 1916–mid-1917; new franchise. Disbanded with league during 1917 season.

Great Falls Electrics
Pioneer League (C), 1948; new franchise. Renamed GREAT FALLS SELECTRICS, 1949.

Great Falls Electrics
Pioneer League (C), 1951–1962; (A), 1963; renamed franchise. Had been GREAT FALLS SELECTRICS, 1949–1950. Disbanded after 1963 season.

Great Falls Giants
Pioneer League (R), 1969–1976; ("Summer Class A") 1977–1978; (R), 1979–1983; new franchise. Renamed GREAT FALLS DODGERS, 1984.

Great Falls Indians
Montana State League, 1900; new franchise. Disbanded with league after 1900 season.

Great Falls Selectrics
Pioneer League (C), 1949–1950; renamed franchise. Had been GREAT FALLS ELECTRICS, 1948. Renamed GREAT FALLS ELECTRICS, 1951.

GREEN BAY, WI

Green Bay Bays
Wisconsin–Illinois League (D), 1909–1914; renamed franchise. Had been GREEN BAY TIGERS, 1908. Disbanded with league after 1914 season.

Green Bay Blue Jays
Wisconsin State League (D) 1940–1942; 1946–1953; charter franchise. Disbanded with league after 1953 season.

Green Bay Blue Jays
Three I League (B), 1958–1959; new franchise. Renamed GREEN BAY DODGERS, 1960.

Green Bay Colts
Wisconsin State League (D), 1905–1906; charter franchise. Disbanded with league after 1906 season.

Green Bay Dodgers
Three I League (B), 1960; renamed franchise. Had been GREEN BAY BLUE JAYS, 1958–1959. Disbanded after 1960 season.

Green Bay Duck Wallopers
Wisconsin State League, 1891; charter franchise. Disbanded with league after 1891 season.

Green Bay Green Bays
Michigan–Wisconsin League, 1892; charter franchise. Disbanded with league after 1892 season.

Green Bay Orphans
Wisconsin–Illinois League (D), 1907; charter franchise. Renamed GREEN BAY TIGERS, 1908.

Green Bay Tigers
Wisconsin–Illinois League (D), 1908; renamed franchise. Had been

GREEN BAY ORPHANS, 1907. Renamed GREEN BAY BAYS, 1909.

GREENEVILLE, TN

Greeneville Burley Cubs
Appalachian League (D), 1921–1925; charter franchise. Disbanded with league during 1925 season.

Greeneville Burley Cubs
Appalachian League (D), 1937–1942; expansion franchise. Disbanded during 1942 season.

GREENPOINT, NY

Greenpoint Eckfords
New York League, 1870–1872; charter franchise. Disbanded during 1872 season.

GREENSBORO, NC

Greensboro
Virginia–North Carolina League (D), 1905; charter franchise. Disbanded with league after 1905 seaon.

Greensboro
Western Carolinas League (A), 1979; new franchise. Disbanded after 1979 season.

Greensboro Champs
Carolina Association (D), 1908–1910; charter franchise. Renamed GREENSBORO PATRIOTS, 1911.

Greensboro Farmers
North Carolina League (D), 1902; charter franchise. Disbanded during 1902 season.

Greensboro Hornets
South Atlantic League (A), 1980–(still in existence as of 5-1-92); charter franchise.

Greensboro Patriots
Carolina Association (D), 1911–1912; renamed franchise. Had been GREENSBORO CHAMPS, 1908–1910. North Carolina Association, (D),

1913–1915/State League (D), 1916–1917; charter franchise. Disbanded with league after 1917 season.

Greensboro Patriots
Piedmont League (D), 1920; (C), 1921–1932; (B), 1933–1934; charter franchise. Became ASHEVILLE TOURISTS, 1935.

Greensboro Patriots
Carolina League (C), 1945–1951; charter franchise. Renamed GREENSBORO PIRATES, 1952.

Greensboro Patriots
Carolina League (C), 1955–1957; renamed franchise. Had been GREENSBORO PIRATES, 1952–1954. Renamed GREENSBORO YANKEES, 1958.

Greensboro Pirates
Carolina League (C), 1952–1954; renamed franchise. Had been GREENSBORO PATRIOTS, 1945–1951. Renamed GREENSBORO PATRIOTS, 1955

Greensboro Red Sox
Piedmont League (B), 1941; new franchise. Disbanded after 1941 season.

Greensboro Red Sox
Piedmont League (B), 1942; relocated franchise. Had been ROCKY MOUNT LEAFS, 1941. Became ROANOKE–SALEM RED SOX, 1943.

Greensboro Yankees
Carolina League (C), 1958–1962; (A), 1963–1968; renamed franchise. Had been GREENSBORO PATRIOTS, 1955–1957. Disbanded after 1968 season.

GREENSBURG, PA

Greensburg Green Sox
Pennsylvania State Association (D), 1937–1938; renamed franchise. Had been GREENSBURG RED

WINGS, 1934–1936. Renamed GREENSBURG CARDINALS, 1939.

Greensburg Red Sox
Western Pennsylvania League (D), 1907; charter franchise. Disbanded with league after 1907 season.

Greensburg Red Wings
Pennsylvania State Association (D), 1935–1936; renamed franchise. Renamed GREENSBURG GREEN SOX, 1937.

Greensburg Senators
Pennsylvania State Association (D), 1939; renamed franchise. Had been GREENSBURG GREEN SOX, 1938. Disbanded after 1939 season.

Greensburg Trojans
Pennsylvania State Association (D), mid-1934; charter franchise. Renamed GREENSBURG RED WINGS, 1935.

GREENVILLE, AL

Greenville Lions
Alabama–Florida League (D), 1939; new franchise. Alabama State League (D), 1940–1941; 1946–1948; charter franchise. Renamed GREENVILLE PIRATES, 1949.

Greenville Pirates
Alabama State League (D), 1949–1950; renamed franchise. Had been GREENVILLE LIONS, 1940–1941; 1946–1948. Disbanded with league after 1950 season.

GREENVILLE, MI

Greenville
Northern Michigan League, 1887; charter franchise. Disbanded with league after 1887 season.

Greenville
Michigan State League, 1889; charter franchise. Disbanded after 1889 season.

GREENVILLE, MS

Greenville
Mississippi League, 1894; new franchise. Disbanded during 1894 season.

Greenville
Cotton States League (D), 1902–1905; charter franchise. Disbanded after 1905 season.

Greenville Bucks
Cotton States League (D), 1922; new franchise. Renamed GREENVILLE SWAMP ANGELS, 1923.

Greenville Bucks
Cotton States League (C), 1936–1938; charter franchise. Renamed GREENVILLE BUCKSHOTS, 1939.

Greenville Bucks
Cotton States League (C), 1947–1953; charter franchise. Renamed GREENVILLE TIGERS, 1954.

Greenville Bucks
Cotton States League (C), 1955; renamed franchise. Had been GREENVILLE TIGERS, 1954. Disbanded with league after 1955 season.

Greenville Buckshots
East Dixie League (C), 1934–1935; charter franchise. Disbanded with league after 1935 season.

Greenville Buckshots
Cotton States League (C), 1939–1941; renamed franchise. Had been GREENVILLE BUCKS, 1934–1935. Resumed as GREENVILLE BUCKS, 1947.

Greenville Swamp Angels
Cotton States League (D), 1923; renamed franchise. Had been GREENVILLE BUCKS, 1922. Disbanded after 1923 season.

Greenville Tigers
Cotton States League (C), 1954; renamed franchise. Had been GREENVILLE BUCKS, 1947–1953.

Renamed GREENVILLE BUCKS, 1955.

GREENVILLE, NC

Greenville Greenies (aka The Greenies)
Coastal Plain League (D), 1937–1941; 1946–1949; charter franchise. Renamed GREENVILLE ROBINS, 1950.

Greenville Robins
Coastal Plain League (D), 1950–1951; renamed franchise. Had been GREENVILLE GREENIES, 1937–1941; 1946–1949. Disbanded after 1951 season.

Greenville Tobacconists
Eastern Carolina League (D), 1928–1929; charter franchise. Disbanded with league after 1929 season.

GREENVILLE, SC

Greenville Braves
Western Carolinas League (A), 1963–1964; new franchise. Renamed GREENVILLE METS, 1965.

Greenville Braves
Southern League (AA), 1984–(still in existence as of 5-1-92); new franchise.

Greenville Edistoes
South Carolina League (D), 1907; charter franchise. Disbanded during 1907 season.

Greenville Mets
Western Carolinas League (A), 1965–1966; new franchise. Had been GREENVILLE BRAVES, 1963–1964. Renamed GREENVILLE RED SOX, 1967.

Greenville Rangers
Western Carolinas League (A), 1972; renamed franchise. Had been GREENVILLE RED SOX, 1967–1971. Disbanded after 1972 season.

Greenville Red Sox
Western Carolinas League (A), 1967–1971; renamed franchise. Had been GREENVILLE METS, 1965–1966. Renamed GREENVILLE RANGERS, 1972.

Greenville Spinners
Carolina Association (D), 1908–1912; charter franchise. Disbanded with league after 1912 season.

Greenville Spinners
South Atlantic Association (C), 1919–1920/League (B), 1921–1930; charter franchise. Disbanded with league after 1930 season.

Greenville Spinners
Palmetto League (D), 1931; charter franchise. Disbanded with league during 1931 season.

Greenville Spinners
South Atlantic League (A), 1938–1942; 1946–1950; new franchise. Tri-State League (B), 1951–1952; 1954–1955; new franchise. Disbanded with league after 1955 season.

Greenville Spinners
South Atlantic League (A), 1961–1962; new franchise. Renamed GREENVILLE BRAVES, 1963.

GREENVILLE, TX

Greenville Highlanders
Texas–Oklahoma League (D), 1912; new franchise. Disbanded after 1912 season.

Greenville Hunters
East Texas League (D), 1924–1926; renamed franchise. Had been GREENVILLE STAPLERS, 1923. Disbanded with league after 1926 season.

Greenville Hunters
Texas League (C), 1906; new franchise. North Texas League (D),

1907; new franchise. Disbanded with league after 1907 season.

Greenville Majors
East Texas League (C), 1946; charter franchise. Big State League (B), 1947–1950; 1953; charter franchise. Disbanded after 1953 season.

Greenville Majors
Big State League (B), 1955; new franchise. Became BRYAN MAJORS, mid-1955.

Greenville Majors
Sooner State League (D), 1957; new franchise. Disbanded with league after 1957 season.

Greenville Midlands
Texas League, 1905–1906; new franchise. Disbanded after 1906 season.

Greenville Staplers
East Texas League (D), 1923; charter franchise. Renamed GREENVILLE HUNTERS, 1924.

Greenville Togs
Texas–Oklahoma League (D), 1922; new franchise. Disbanded with league after 1922 season.

GREENWOOD, MS

Greenwood Chiefs (aka Indian Chiefs)
East Dixie League (C), mid-1934–1935; relocated franchise. Had been SHREVEPORT SPORTS, 1934. Disbanded with league after 1935 season.

Greenwood Choctaws
Cotton States League (C), 1940; renamed franchise. Had been GREENWOOD CRACKERS, 1939. Disbanded after 1940 season.

Greenwood Crackers
Cotton States League (C), 1939; renamed franchise. Had been GREENWOOD DODGERS, 1938. Re-

named GREENWOOD CHOCTAWS, 1940.

Greenwood Dodgers
Cotton States League (C), 1938; renamed franchise. Had been GREENWOOD GIANTS, 1937. Renamed GREENWOOD CRACKERS, 1939.

Greenwood Dodgers
Cotton States League (C), 1947–1952; charter franchise. Disbanded after 1952 season.

Greenwood Giants
Cotton States League (C), 1937; renamed franchise. Had been GREENWOOD LITTLE GIANTS, 1936. Renamed GREENWOOD DODGERS, 1938.

Greenwood Indian Chiefs
Alternate name for GREENWOOD CHIEFS, 1934.

Greenwood Indians
Mississipi State League (D), 1921; charter franchise. Cotton States League (D), 1922–1923; new franchise. Disbanded during 1923 season.

Greenwood Little Giants
Cotton States League (C), 1936; charter franchise. Renamed GREENWOOD GIANTS, 1937.

Greenwood Scouts
Cotton States League (D), 1910–1912; new franchise. Disbanded after 1912 season.

GREENWOOD, SC

Greenwood Braves
Western Carolinas League (A), 1968–1979; new franchise. Disbanded with league after 1979 season.

Greenwood Pirates
South Atlantic League (A), 1981–1983; new franchise. Disbanded after 1983 season.

Greenwood Tigers
Tri-State League (B), 1951; new franchise. Disbanded after 1951 season.

GRIFFIN, GA

Griffin
Georgia State League (D), 1920–1921; charter franchise. Disbanded with league after 1921 season.

Griffin Griffs
Georgia–Alabama League (C), 1917; renamed franchise. Had been GRIFFIN LIGHTFOOTS, 1915–1916. Disbanded with league during 1917 season.

Griffin Lightfoots
Georgia–Alabama League (C), 1915–1916; new franchise. Renamed GRIFFIN GRIFFS, 1917.

Griffin Pimientos
Georgia–Alabama League (C), 1947–1949; expansion franchise. Renamed GRIFFIN TIGERS, 1950.

Griffin Pimientos
Georgia–Alabama League (C), 1951; renamed franchise. Disbanded with league after 1951 season.

Griffin Tigers
Georgia–Alabama League (C), 1950; renamed franchise. Had been GRIFFIN PIMIENTOS, 1947–1949. Renamed GRIFFIN PIMIENTOS, 1951.

GUADALAJARA, JALISCO, MEXICO

Guadalajara Charros (Chapmen)
Mexican League (AA), 1964–1972; new franchise. Renamed JALISCO CHARROS, 1973.

Jalisco Charros (Chapmen)
Mexican League (AA), 1973–1975; renamed franchise. Had been

GUADALAJARA CHARROS, 1964–1972. Disbanded after 1975 season.

Jalisco Charros (Chapmen)
Mexican Center League (AA), 1977; new franchise. Disbanded after 1977 season.

Jalisco Charros (Chapmen)
Mexican League (AAA), 1988; new franchise. Disbanded after 1988 season.

Jalisco Charros (Chapmen)
Mexican League (AAA), 1991–(still in existence as of 5-1-92); new franchise. Disbanded after 1988 season.

GUADALUPE, MEXICO

Guadalupe
Mexican Center League (A), 1978; new franchise. Disbanded after 1978 season.

GUAMUCHIL–CULIACAN, MEXICO

Guamuchil–Culiacan
Mexican Pacific League (AAA), 1976; new franchise. Disbanded after 1976 season.

GUANAJUATO, GUANAJUATO, MEXICO
(See also LEON, MEXICO; SALAMANCA, MEXICO)

Guanajuato Tuzos (Gophers)
Mexican Center League (A), 1960–1967; new franchise. Disbanded after 1967 season.

Guanajuato Tuzos (Gophers)
Mexican Center League (A), 1975–1976; new franchise. Disbanded after 1976 season.

Guanajuato Tuzos (Gophers)
Mexican Center League (A), 1978; new franchise. Disbanded after 1978 season.

GUASAVE, MEXICO

Guasave Algodoneros
Mexican Pacific League (AAA), 1976; new franchise. Disbanded after 1976 season.

GUAYMAS, MEXICO

Guaymas Marineros (aka Ostineros)
Mexican Pacific League (AAA), 1976; charter franchise. Disbanded after 1976 season.

GUELPH, ONTARIO, CANADA

Guelph Biltmores
Canadian League (C), 1905; charter franchise. Disbanded with league after 1905 season.

Guelph Biltmores
Ontario League (D), 1930; charter franchise. Disbanded during 1930 season.

Guelph Maple Leafs
International Association, 1877; charter franchise. Disbanded after 1877 season.

Guelph Maple Leafs
Ontario League, 1884; charter franchise. Canadian League, 1885; charter franchise. Disbanded after 1885 season.

Guelph Maple Leafs
Canadian League, 1896–1897; charter franchise. Disbanded after 1897 season.

Guelph Maple Leafs
Canadian League, 1899; new franchise. Disbanded with league after 1899 season.

Guelph Maple Leafs
Canadian League (C), 1911; (D), mid-1911; (C), 1912–1913; (B), 1915; charter franchise. Disbanded with league after 1915 season.

GULF COAST
(Playing in the Sarasota areas of Florida)

Gulf Coast Astros
Gulf Coast League (R), 1988–(still in existence as of 5-1-92); relocated franchise. Had been SARASOTA ASTROS, 1987.

Gulf Coast Blue Jays
Gulf Coast League (R), 1990–(still in existence as of 5-1-92); new franchise.

Gulf Coast Braves
Gulf Coast League (R), 1988–(still in existence as of 5-1-92); new franchise.

Gulf Coast Dodgers
Gulf Coast League (R), 1988–(still in existence as of 5-1-92); relocated franchise. Had been SARASOTA DODGERS, 1987.

Gulf Coast Expos
Gulf Coast League (R), 1988–(still in existence as of 5-1-92); new franchise.

Gulf Coast Indians
Gulf Coast League (R), 1988–(still in existence as of 5-1-92); new franchise.

Gulf Coast Mets
Gulf Coast League (R), 1988–(still in existence as of 5-1-92); new franchise.

Gulf Coast Orioles
Gulf Coast League (R), 1990–(still in existence as of 5-1-92); new franchise.

Gulf Coast Pirates
Gulf Coast League (R), 1988–(still in existence as of 5-1-92); new franchise.

Gulf Coast Rangers
Gulf Coast League (R), 1988–(still in existence as of 5-1-92); new franchise.

Gulf Coast Reds
Gulf Coast League (R), 1988–1990; relocated franchise. Had been SARASOTA REDS, 1987. Disbanded after 1990 season.

Gulf Coast Red Sox
Gulf Coast League (R), 1990–(still in existence as of 5-1-92); new franchise.

Gulf Coast Royals
Gulf Coast League (R), 1988–(still in existence as of 5-1-92); relocated franchise. Had been SARASOTA ROYALS, 1987.

Gulf Coast Twins
Gulf Coast League (R), 1990–(still in existence as of 5-1-92); new franchise.

Gulf Coast White Sox
Gulf Coast League (R), 1988–(still in existence as of 5-1-92); relocated franchise. Had been SARASOTA WHITE SOX, 1987.

Gulf Coast Yankees
Gulf Coast League (R), 1988–(still in existence as of 5-1-92); relocated franchise. Had been SARASOTA YANKEES, 1987.

GULFPORT, MS

Gulfport Crabs
Cotton States League (D), 1906–1907; new franchise. Became GULFPORT–BILOXI CRABS, 1908.

Gulfport Tarpons
Cotton States League (D), 1926–1928; new franchise. Disbanded after 1928 season.

GULFPORT–BILOXI, MS

Gulfport–Biloxi Crabs
Cotton States League (D), 1908; renamed franchise. Had been GULFPORT CRABS, 1906–1907. Disbanded after 1908 season.

GUTHRIE, OK

Guthrie
Oklahoma State League (D), 1912; charter franchise. Disbanded with league during 1912 season.

Guthrie
Western Association (D), mid-1914; relocated franchise. Had been JOPLIN, 1914. Became HENRYETTA BOOSTERS, mid-1914.

Guthrie
Oklahoma State League (D), mid-1922–mid-1924; charter franchise. Became MCALESTER, mid-1924.

Guthrie Legislators
Western Association (C), 1909; new franchise. Renamed GUTHRIE SENATORS, 1910.

Guthrie Senators
Southwestern League (B), 1904; charter franchise. Western Association (D), 1905; charter franchise. South Central League (D), 1906; charter franchise. Disbanded with league after 1906 season.

Guthrie Senators
Western Association (C), 1910; renamed franchise. Became TULSA OILERS, mid-1910.

HAGERSTOWN, MD

Hagerstown
Cumberland Valley League, 1896; charter franchise. Disbanded with league after 1896 season.

Hagerstown Blues
Blue Ridge League (D), 1915; charter franchise. Renamed HAGERSTOWN HUBS, 1916.

Hagerstown Braves
Inter-State League (B), 1950–1951; renamed franchise. Had been HAGERSTOWN OWLS, 1941–1949. Piedmont League (B), 1953; expansion franchise. Renamed HAGERSTOWN PACKETS, 1954–1955.

Hagerstown Champs
Blue Ridge League (D), 1920–1922; new franchise. Renamed HAGERSTOWN TERRIERS, 1923.

Hagerstown Hubs
Blue Ridge League (D), 1916; renamed franchise. Had been HAGERSTOWN BLUES, 1915. Renamed HAGERSTOWN TERRIERS, 1917.

Hagerstown Hubs
Blue Ridge League (D), 1924–1931; renamed franchise. Had been HAGERSTOWN TERRIERS, 1923. Middle Atlantic League (C), 1931; expansion franchise. Became PARLERSBIRG PARKERS, mid-1931.

Hagerstown Owls
Inter-State League (B), 1941–1949; relocated franchise. Had been SUNBURY INDIANS, 1940. Renamed HAGERSTOWN BRAVES, 1950.

Hagerstown Packets
Piedmont League (B), 1954–1955; renamed franchise. Had been HAGERSTOWN BRAVES, 1950–1953. Disbanded with league after 1955 season.

Hagerstown Suns
Carolina League (A), 1981–1988; new franchise. Eastern League (AA), 1989–(still in existence as of 5-1-92); new franchise.

Hagerstown Terriers
Blue Ridge League (D), 1917; charter franchise. Had been HAGERSTOWN HUBS, 1916. Disbanded after 1917 season.

Hagerstown Terriers
Blue Ridge League (D), 1923; renamed franchise. Had been HAGERSTOWN CHAMPS, 1920–1922. Renamed HAGERSTOWN HUBS, 1924.

HAINES CITY, FL
(See BASEBALL CITY, FL)

HALIFAX, VA

(See SOUTH BOSTON, VA)

HAMILTON, OH

Hamilton
Ohio State Association, 1884; charter franchise. Disbanded with league after 1884 season.

Hamilton
Tri–State League, 1889; charter franchise. Disbanded with league after 1889 season.

Hamilton Maroons
Ohio State League (C), 1911; (D), 1913; charter franchise. Disbanded after 1913 season.

HAMILTON, ONTARIO, CANADA

Hamilton Blackbirds
International League, 1890; renamed franchise. Had been HAMILTON HAMS, 1886–1889. Became MONTREAL, mid-1890.

Hamilton Blackbirds
Alternate name for HAMILTON HAMS, 1897.

Hamilton Cardinals (aka Cards, 1947–1949; 1952–1956)
PONY League (D), 1946–1956; relocated franchise. Had been ERIE SAILORS, 1944–1945. Disbanded during 1956 season.

Hamilton Cards
Alternate name for HAMILTON CARDINALS, 1947–1949; 1952–1956.

Hamilton Clippers
Canadian League, 1885; charter franchise. Disbanded with league during 1885 season.

Hamilton Clippers
International League, 1886; charter franchise. Renamed HAMILTON HAMS, 1887.

Hamilton Clippers
Michigan–Ontario League (B), 1924–mid-1925; renamed franchise. Had been HAMILTON TIGERS, 1919–1923. Disbanded with league during 1925 season.

Hamilton Hams
International League, 1887/Association, 1888–1889; renamed franchise. Renamed HAMILTON BLACKBIRDS, 1890.

Hamilton Hams (aka Blackbirds, 1897)
Canadian League, 1896–1899; charter franchise. International League, 1900; charter franchise. Disbanded with league after 1900 season.

Hamilton Hams
International League (D), 1908; charter franchise. Disbanded with league after 1908 season.

Hamilton Hams
Canadian League (B), mid-1914–1915; renamed franchise. Had been HAMILTON KOLTS, 1911–mid-1914. Disbanded with league after 1915 season.

Hamiltoon Kolts
Canadian League (C), 1911; (D), mid-1911; (C), 1912–mid-1914; charter franchise. Renamed HAMILTON HAMS, mid-1914.

Hamilton Primroses
Canadian League, 1885; charter franchise. Disbanded with league during 1885 season.

Hamilton Redbirds
New York–Pennsylvania League (A), 1988–(still in existence as of 5-1-92); new franchise.

Hamilton Red Wings
PONY League (D), 1939–1942; charter franchise. Disbanded after 1942 season.

Hamilton Tigers
International League (AA), mid-1918; relocated franchise. Had been SYRACUSE STARS, 1894–mid-1918. Disbanded after 1918 season.

Hamilton Tigers
Michigan–Ontario League (B), 1919–1923; charter franchise. Renamed HAMILTON CLIPPERS, 1924.

Hamilton Tigers
Ontario League (D), 1930; charter franchise. Disbanded during 1930 season.

HAMLIN, TX

Hamlin Pipers
West Texas League (D), 1928; charter franchise. Disbanded after 1928 season.

HAMMOND, IN

Hammond
Western Inter-State League, 1895; charter franchise. Disbanded with league during 1895 season.

HAMMOND, LA

Hammond Berries
Evangeline League (C), 1946–1951; charter franchise. Disbanded after 1951 season.

HAMPTON, VA

(See also NEWPORT NEWS, VA)

Hampton
Virginia League, mid-1896; relocated franchise. Had been PETERSBURG FARMERS, 1895–mid-1896. Disbanded with league after 1896 season.

Hampton
Southeast Virginia League, 1897; charter franchise. Disbanded with league during 1897 season.

Hampton

Virginia League, 1900; charter franchise. Disbanded with league after 1900 season.

HAMPTON–
NEWPORT NEWS, VA
(See also NEWPORT NEWS, VA)

Hampton–Newport News

Virginia League, 1894; charter franchise. Disbanded after 1894 season.

Hampton–Newport News Shipbuilders

Virginia–North Carolinas League, 1901; charter franchise. Disbanded with league after 1901 season.

Peninsula Astros

Carolina League (A), 1969–1970; renamed franchise. Had been PEN-INSULA GRAYS, 1964–1968. Renamed PENINSULA PILOTS, 1971.

Peninsula Grays

Carolina League (A), 1964–1968; renamed franchise. Had been PEN-INSULA SENATORS, 1963. Renamed PENINSULA ASTROS, 1969.

Peninsula Pennants

Carolina League (A), 1974; new franchise. Had been PENINSULA WHIPS, 1973. Disbanded after 1974 season.

Peninsula Pilots

Carolina League (A), 1971; renamed franchise. Had been PENIN-SULA ASTROS, 1969–1970. Became PENINSULA WHIPS, 1972.

Peninsula Pilots

Carolina League (A), 1976–1978; new franchise. Western Carolinas League (A), 1979–1985; new franchise. Renamed PENINSULA WHITE SOX, 1986.

Peninsula Pilots

Carolina League (A), 1989–(still in existence as of 5-1-92); renamed franchise.

Peninsula Senators

Carolina League (A), 1963; charter franchise. Renamed PENINSULA GRAYS, 1964.

Peninsula Whips

International League (AAA), 1972–1973; new franchise. Had been PENINSULA PILOTS, 1971. Renamed PENINSULA PENNANTS, 1974.

Peninsula White Sox

Carolina League (A), 1986–1987; renamed franchise. Had been PEN-INSULA PILOTS, 1976–1985. Disbanded after 1987 season.

Virginia

Carolina League (A), 1988; renamed franchise. Had been PENIN-SULA WHITE SOX, 1986–1987. Renamed PENINSULA PILOTS, 1989.

HANCOCK, MI

Hancock

Upper Peninsula League, 1890; charter franchise. Disbanded after 1890 season.

Hancock

Copper County–Soo League (D), 1905; charter franchise. Disbanded with league during 1905 season.

Hancock

Northern Copper County League (C), 1906; charter franchise. Disbanded during 1906 season.

HANNIBAL, MO

Hannibal Bears

MOV League (D), 1953; renamed franchise. Had been HANNIBAL STAGS, 1952. Renamed HANNIBAL CARDINALS, 1954.

Hannibal Cannibals

Illinois–Missouri (D), 1908; charter franchise. Central Association (D), 1909–1912; new franchise. Disbanded after 1912 season.

Hannibal Cardinals

MOV League (D), 1954; renamed franchise. Had been HANNIBAL BEARS, 1953. Renamed HANNIBAL PEPSIES, 1955.

Hannibal Mules

Illinois–Iowa–Indiana League (B), 1916–1917; new franchise. Disbanded with league during 1917 season.

Hannibal Pepsies

MOV League (D), 1955; renamed franchise. Had been HANNIBAL CARDINALS, 1954. Disbanded with league after 1955 season.

Hannibal Pilots

Central Association (C), 1947–1948; charter franchise. Disbanded after 1948 season.

Hannibal Stags

MOV League (D), 1952; new franchise. Renamed HANNIBAL BEARS, 1953.

HANOVER, PA

Hanover

Cumberland Valley League, 1896; charter franchise. Disbanded with league after 1896 season.

Hanover Hornets

Blue Ridge League (D), 1915–1916; charter franchise. Renamed HANOVER RAIDERS, 1917.

Hanover Raiders

Blue Ridge League (D), 1917; renamed franchise. Had been HANO-VER HORNETS. Disbanded after 1917 season.

Hanover Raiders

Blue Ridge League (D), 1920–1929; charter franchise. Disbanded after 1929 season.

HARLAN, KY

Harlan Red Sox

Appalachian League (R), 1965; new franchise. Disbanded after 1965 season.

Harlan Smokies
Mountain States League (D), 1948–1954; charter franchise. Disbanded with league after 1954 season.

Harlan Smokies
Appalachian League (D), 1961–1962; new franchise. Renamed HARLAN YANKEES, 1963.

Harlan Yankees
Appalachian League (R), 1963; renamed franchise. Had been HARLAN SMOKIES, 1961–1962. Disbanded after 1963 season.

HARLINGEN, TX

Harlingen Capitals
Rio Grande Valley League (C), 1950; new franchise. Gulf Coast League (D), 1951–1953; new franchise. Big State League (B), 1954–1955; new franchise. Disbanded after 1955 season.

Harlingen Hubs
Texas Valley League (D), 1938; charter franchise. Disbanded with league after 1938 season.

Rio Grande Valley Giants
Texas League (AA), 1960–mid-1961; relocated franchise. Had been CORPUS CHRISTI GIANTS, 1958–1959. Became VICTORIA GIANTS, mid-1961.

Rio Grande Valley Whitewings
Gulf States League (R), 1976; charter franchise. Lone Star League (A), 1977; charter franchise. Disbanded with league after 1977 season.

HARLINGEN– SAN BENITO, TX

Harlingen–San Benito Ladds
Rio Grande Valley League (C), 1931; charter franchise. Disbanded with league after 1931 season.

HARRIMAN, TN

Harriman Boosters
Appalachian League (D), 1914; relocated franchise. Had planned to play as PINEVILLE, 1914. Disbanded with league during 1914 season.

HARRISBURG, IL

Harrisburg Coal Miners
KITTY League (D), 1913; new franchise. Disbanded after 1913 season.

Harrisburg Merchants
Southern Illinois League (D), 1910; charter franchise. KITTY League (D), 1910–mid-1911; charter franchise. Became JACKSON, mid-1911.

HARRISBURG, PA

Harrisburg
Inter-State Association, 1883; charter franchise. Disbanded with association after 1883 season.

Harrisburg
Eastern Inter-State League, 1889; charter franchise. Disbanded with league during 1889 season.

Harrisburg
Atlantic League, mid-1900; relocated franchise. Had been PHILADELPHIA, 1900. Disbanded with league after 1900 season.

HARRISBURG GIANTS
Eastern Colored League, 1924–1927; new franchise. Disbanded after 1927 season.

Harrisburg Hustlers
Pennsylvania State League, 1893–1894; new franchise. Renamed HARRISBURG SENATORS, 1895.

Harrisburg Islanders
New York State League (B), mid-1916–mid-1917; relocated franchise. Had been TROY TROJANS,

1900–mid-1916. Disbanded during 1917 season.

Harrisburg Olympics
Eastern League, 1884; charter franchise. Became YORK, mid-1884.

Harrisburg Ponies
Middle States League, 1889; charter franchise. Pennsylvania State League, 1890; charter franchise. Disbanded with league during 1890 season.

Harrisburg Ponies
Pennsylvania State League, 1892; charter franchise. Became SCRANTON INDIANS, mid-1892.

Harrisburg Ponies
Atlantic Association, mid-1890; relocated franchise. Had been JERSEY CITY JERSEYS, 1889–mid-1890. Disbanded with association after 1890 season.

Harrisburg Ponies
Alternate name for HARRISBURG SENATORS, 1911.

Harrisburg Senators
Pennsylvania State League, 1895; renamed franchise. Had been HARRISBURG HUSTLERS, 1893–1894. Disbanded after 1895 season.

Harrisburg Senators (aka Ponies, 1911)
Tri-State League (D), 1904–1914; charter franchise. International League (AA), mid-1915; relocated franchise. Had been NEWARK INDIANS, 1908–mid-1915. Disbanded after 1915 season.

Harrisburg Senators
New York–Pennsylvania League (B), mid-1924–1932, (A), 1933–1935; new franchise. Disbanded after 1935 season.

Harrisburg Senators
Inter-State League (B), 1940–1942; expansion franchise. Became YORK WHITE ROSES, 1943.

Harrisburg Senators
Inter-State League (B), 1946–1952; charter franchise. Disbanded with league, 1952.

Harrisburg Senators
Eastern League (AA), 1987–(still in existence as of 5-1-92); new franchise.

HARRISBURG, PA– ST. LOUIS, MO
(See also ST. LOUIS, MO)

HARRISBURG–ST. LOUIS STARS
Negro National League, 1943; new franchise. Disbanded during 1943 season.

HARRISONBURG, VA

Harrisonburg
Virginia Mountain League (D), mid-1914; relocated franchise. Had been STAUNTON, 1914. Disbanded during 1914 season.

Harrisonburg Turks
Virginia League (D), 1939–1941; charter franchise. Disbanded after 1941 season.

HARTFORD, CT

HARTFORD
International Association, 1878; charter franchise. Disbanded after 1878 season.

Hartford
Connecticut League, 1884; charter franchise. Southern New England League, 1885; charter franchise. Eastern League, 1886–1887; new franchise. Disbanded after 1887 season.

Hartford
Atlantic Association, 1889–1890; charter franchise. Disbanded with association after 1890 season.

Hartford
Atlantic League, 1896–1898; charter franchise. Disbanded with league after 1898 season.

Hartford Bees
Eastern League (A), 1939–1947; renamed franchise. Had been HARTFORD LAURELS, 1938. Renamed HARTFORD CHIEFS, 1948.

Hartford Bluebirds
Atlantic League, 1896–1897; charter franchise. Renamed HARTFORD CO-OPERATIVES, 1898.

Hartford Chiefs
Eastern League (A), 1948–1952; renamed franchise. Had been HARTFORD BEES, 1939–1947. Disbanded after 1952 season.

Hartford Co-operatives
Atlantic League, 1898; renamed franchise. Had been HARTFORD BLUEBIRDS, 1896–1897. Disbanded after 1898 season.

HARTFORD DARK BLUES
National Association, 1874–1875; new franchise. National League, 1876–1877; charter franchise. Disbanded after 1877 season.

Hartford Indians
Eastern League, 1899–1900; charter franchise. Renamed HARTFORD WOODEN NUTMEGS, 1901.

Hartford Laurels
Eastern League (A), 1938; charter franchise. Had been SCRANTON MINERS, 1933–1937. Renamed HARTFORD BEES, 1939.

Hartford Senators
Connecticut League (D), 1902; 1904–1912/Valley League (B), 1903; charter franchise. Eastern Association (B), 1913–1914; charter franchise. Disbanded with league after 1914 season.

Hartford Senators
Eastern League (B), 1916–1918; (A), 1919–mid-1930, 1931–1932; charter franchise. Disbanded with league after 1932 season.

Hartford Senators
Northeastern League (A), 1934; charter franchise. Disbanded with league after 1934 season.

Hartford Wooden Nutmegs
Eastern League, 1901; renamed franchise. Had been HARTFORD INDIANS, 1899–1900. Disbanded after 1901 season.

HASTINGS, NE

Hastings
Western League, 1887; new franchise. Disbanded after 1887 season.

Hastings
Western League, mid-1889; relocated franchise. Had been LEAVENWORTH MAROONS, 1886–mid-1889. Disbanded after 1889 season.

Hastings Brickmakers
Nebraska State League (D), 1910; charter franchise. Became HASTINGS THIRD CITYS, 1911.

Hastings Cubs
Nebraska State League (D), 1922–1923; charter franchise. Tri-State League (D), 1924; charter franchise. Disbanded with league after 1924 season.

Hastings Giants
Nebraska State League (D), 1956–1959; charter franchise. Disbanded with league after 1959 season.

Hastings Hustlers
Nebraska State League, 1892; charter franchise. Disbanded with league after 1892 season.

Hastings Reds
Western League, 1887; expansion franchise. Disbanded after 1887 season.

Hastings Reds

Nebraska State League (D), 1914–1915; renamed franchise. Had been HASTINGS THIRD CITYS, 1911–1913. Disbanded with league after 1915 season.

Hastings Third Citys

Nebraska State League (D), 1911–1913; renamed franchise. Had been HASTINGS BRICKMAKERS, 1910. Renamed HASTINGS REDS, 1914.

HATTIESBURG, MS

Hattiesburg

Delta League (D), 1904; charter franchise. Cotton States League (D), 1905; new franchise. Disbanded after 1905 season.

Hattiesburg Hubmen

Cotton States League (D), 1923–mid-1925; expansion franchise. Renamed HATTIESBURG PINE-TOPPERS, mid-1925.

Hattiesburg Pinetoppers

Cotton States League (D), mid-1925–mid-1929; renamed franchise. Had been HATTIESBURG HUBMEN, 1923–mid-1925. Became BATON ROUGE, mid-1928.

Hattiesburg Timberjacks

Cotton States League (D), 1912; renamed franchise. Had been HATTIESBURG WOODPECKERS, 1910–1911. Became COLUMBUS JOY RIDERS, mid-1912.

Hattiesburg Woodpeckers

Cotton States League (D), 1910–1911; new franchise. Renamed HATTIESBURG TIMBERJACKS, 1912.

HAVANA, CUBA

Havana Cubans

Florida International League (C), 1946–1948; (B), 1949–1953; charter franchise. Became HAVANA SUGAR KINGS, 1954.

Havana Sugar Kings

International League (AAA), 1954–mid-1960; new franchise. Became JERSEY CITY REDS, mid-1960.

HAVANA, IL

Havana

Illinois–Missouri League (D), 1908; charter franchise. Disbanded after 1908 season.

HAVERHILL, MA

Haverhill

Eastern New England League, 1885; charter franchise. Disbanded with league after 1885 season.

Haverhill

New England Inter-State League, 1888; charter franchise. Disbanded with league after 1888 season.

Haverhill

New England League, 1894; charter franchise. Disbanded with league after 1884 season.

Haverhill Blues

New England League, mid-1887; relocated franchise. Had been BOSTON BLUES, 1886–mid-1887. Disbanded after 1887 season.

Haverhill Colts

New England League, 1886; charter franchise. Disbanded after 1886 season.

Haverhill Duffers

New England Association, mid-1895; relocated franchise. Had been SALEM, 1895. Disbanded with association after 1895 season.

Haverhill Hillies

New England League (B), 1926–mid-1929; charter franchise. Became FITCHBURG WANDERERS, mid-1929.

Haverhill Hustlers

New England League, 1901; (B), 1902–1912; 1914; charter franchise. Disbanded after 1914 season.

Haverhill Orphans

New England League (B), 1919; charter franchise. Disbanded with league after 1919 season.

HAVERSTRAW, NY

Haverstraw

Hudson River League, 1888; charter franchise. Disbanded with league after 1888 season.

HAYWARD, CA

Hayward Cubs

Central California Baseball League (D), 1910–1911; relocated franchise. Had been SAN RAFAEL, 1910. Became FRUITVALE, mid-1910.

HAZARD, KY

Hazard Bombers

Mountain States League (D), mid-1948–1952; relocated franchise. Had been OAK RIDGE BOMBERS, 1948. Disbanded after 1952 season.

HAZLEHURST–BAXLEY, GA

(See also BAXLEY, GA)

Hazlehurst–Baxley Cardinals

Georgia State League (D), 1952–1956; renamed franchise. Had been HAZLEHURST–BAXLEY RED SOX, 1951. Disbanded with league after 1956 season.

Hazlehurst–Baxley Red Socks

Georgia State League (D), 1949–1950; relocated franchise. Had been BAXLEY RED SOX, 1948. Renamed HAZLEHURST–BAXLEY RED SOX, 1951.

Hazlehurst–Baxley Red Sox

Georgia State League (D), 1951; renamed franchise. Had been

HAZLEHURST–BAXLEY RED SOCKS, 1949–1950. Renamed HAZLEHURST–BAXLEY CARDINALS, 1952.

HAZLETON, PA

Hazleton
Central Pennsylvania League, 1887–1888; charter franchise. Middle States League, 1889; charter franchise. Disbanded with league after 1889 season.

Hazleton Dodgers
North Atlantic League (D), 1950; renamed franchise. Had been HAZLETON MOUNTAINEERS, 1949. Disbanded with league after 1950 season.

Hazleton Mountaineers
Anthracite League (D), 1928; charter franchise. Disbanded with league during 1928 season.

Hazleton Mountaineers
New York–Pennsylvania League (B), mid-1929–1932; 1934–1936; relocated franchise. Had been SYRACUSE STARS, 1928–mid-1929. Became HAZLETON RED SOX, 1937.

Hazleton Mountaineers
Inter-State League (C), 1939–mid-1940; charter franchise. Became LANCASTER RED ROSES, mid-1940.

Hazleton Mountaineers
North Atlantic League (D), 1949; new franchise. Renamed HAZLETON DODGERS, 1950.

Hazleton Pugilists
Central League, mid-1888; charter franchise. Had been BINGHAMTON BINGOS, 1888.

Hazleton Quay-kers
Pennsylvania State League, 1894–1896; new franchise. Disbanded with league after 1896 season.

Hazleton Red Sox
New York–Pennsylvania League (B), 1937; renamed franchise. Eastern League (A), 1938; charter franchise. Became SCRANTON RED SOX, 1939.

HEADLAND, AL

Headland Dixie Runners
Alabama State League (D) 1950; new franchise. Alabama–Florida League (D), 1951–1952; charter franchise. Disbanded after 1952 season.

HEALDSBURG, CA

Healdsburg
Central California Baseball League (D), 1910; charter franchise. Became SAN LEANDRO, mid-1910.

HELENA, AR

Helena
Arkansas State League (D), 1908–1909; charter franchise. Disbanded with league after 1909 season.

Helena
Northeast Arkansas League (D), 1911; new franchise. Disbanded with league during 1911 season.

Helena Seaporters
East Dixie League (C), 1935; expansion franchise. Cotton States League (C), 1936–1941; 1947–1949; charter franchise. Disbanded after 1949 season.

HELENA, MT

Helena
Montana State League, 1892; charter franchise. Disbanded with league after 1892 season.

Helena
Inter-Mountain League (D), 1909; charter franchise. Disbanded with league during 1909 season.

Helena Brewers
Pioneer League (R), 1987–(still in existence as of 5-1-92); renamed franchise. Had been HELENA GOLD SOX, 1984–1986.

Helena Gold Sox
Pioneer League (R), 1984–1986; renamed franchise. Had been HELENA PHILLIES, 1978–1983. Renamed HELENA BREWERS, 1987.

Helena Phillies
Pioneer League (R), 1978–1983; new franchise. Renamed HELENA GOLD SOX, 1984.

Helena Senators
Montana State League, 1900; new franchise. Disbanded with league after 1900 season.

Helena Senators
Pacific Northwest League (C), 1902; new franchise. Pacific National League (C), 1903; charter franchise. Disbanded during 1903 season.

Helena Senators
Union Association (D), 1911–1914; charter franchise. Disbanded with league after 1914 season.

HENDERSON, KY

Henderson
Kentucky–Indiana League, 1896–1897; charter franchise. Disbanded with league during 1897 season.

Henderson
KITTY League (D), 1916; charter franchise. Disbanded with league after 1916 season.

Henderson Blue Birds
KITTY League (D), 1903–1904; charter franchise. Renamed HENDERSON HENS, 1905.

Henderson Hens
KITTY League (D), 1905; charter franchise. Had been HENDERSON BLUE BIRDS, 1903–1904. Disbanded after 1905 season.

Henderson Hens
KITTY League (D), mid-1911–1914; relocated franchise. Had been MCLEANSBORO MINERS, 1911. Disbanded with league after 1914 season.

HENDERSON, NC

Henderson Bunnies
Piedmont League (C), 1929; new franchise. Renamed HENDERSON GAMECOCKS, 1930.

Henderson Gamecocks
Piedmont League (C), 1930–1931; renamed franchise. Had been HENDERSON BUNNIES, 1929. Disbanded after 1931 season.

HENDERSON, TX

Henderson Oilers
East Texas League (D), 1931; charter franchise. Disbanded with league during 1931 season.

Henderson Oilers
Dixie League (D), 1933; charter franchise. West Dixie League (D), 1934–1935. East Texas League (C), 1936–1940; 1946; charter franchise. Lone Star League (C), 1947–1948; charter franchise. East Texas League (C), 1949–1950; charter franchise. Disbanded with league after 1950 season.

HENDERSONVILLE, NC

Hendersonville Skylarks
Western Carolina League (D), 1948–1949; charter franchise. Disbanded after 1949 season.

HENRYETTA, OK

Henryetta Boosters
Western Association (D), mid-1914; relocated franchise. Had been GUTHRIE, mid-1914. Disbanded after 1914 season.

Henryetta Hens
Western Association (D), 1920–1921, (C), 1922–1923; charter franchise. Disbanded during 1923 season.

HERALDSBURG, CA

Heraldsburg
Central California Baseball League (D), 1911; charter franchise. Disbanded after 1911 season.

HERMOSILLO, MEXICO

Hermosillo Orangepickers
Mexican Pacific League (AAA), 1976; charter franchise. Disbanded with league after 1976 season.

HERRIN, IL

Herrin
Southern Illinois (D), 1910; charter franchise. Disbanded with league during 1910 season.

HERTFORD, NC

Hertford
Carolina Coast League (D), 1909; charter franchise. Disbanded with league after 1909 season.

HIAWATHA, KS

Hiawatha
Eastern Kansas League (D), 1910–1911; charter franchise. MINK League (D), 1912; new franchise. Disbanded after 1912 season.

HICKORY, NC

Hickory Rebels
Tar Heel League (D), 1939–1940; charter franchise. North Carolina State League (D), 1942; 1945–1951; new franchise. Western Carolina League (D), 1952; new franchise. Tar Heel League (D), 1953–1954; charter franchise. Disbanded with league after 1954 season.

Hickory Rebels
Western Carolina League (D), 1960; charter franchise. Disbanded after 1960 season.

HIGH POINT, NC
(See also THOMASVILLE, NC)

High Point Furniture Makers
Piedmont League (D), 1920; (C), 1921–1922; charter franchise. Renamed HIGH POINT POINTERS, 1923.

High Point Pointers
Piedmont League (C), 1923–mid-1925; renamed franchise. Had been HIGH POINT FURNITURE MAKERS, 1920–1922. Became DANVILLE TOBACCONISTS, mid-1925.

High Point Pointers
Piedmont League (C), mid-1926–1931; (B), 1932; relocated franchise. Had been DANVILLE LEAFS, 1926. Disbanded during 1932 season.

High Point Pointers
Piedmont League (B), mid-1932; relocated franchise. Had been WINSTON-SALEM TWINS, 1920–mid-1932. Disbanded after 1932 season.

HILLSBORO, TX

Hillsboro
Central Texas Trolley League (D), mid-1914; charter franchise. Disbanded after 1914 season.

HILLDALE, PA

HILLDALE
Eastern Colored League, 1923–1927; charter franchise. Disbanded after 1927 season. American Negro League, 1929; charter franchise. Disbanded after 1929 season. East–West League, 1932; charter fran-

chise. Disbanded with league after 1932 season.

HOBBS, NM

Hobbs Boosters
West Texas–New Mexico League (D), 1938; renamed franchise. Had been HOBBS DRILLERS, 1937. Disbanded after 1938 season.

Hobbs Cardinals
Sophomore League (D), 1958–1959; charter franchise. Renamed HOBBS PIRATES, 1960.

Hobbs Drillers
West Texas–New Mexico League (D), 1937; charter franchise. Renamed HOBBS BOOSTERS, 1938.

Hobbs Pirates
Sophomore League (D), 1960–1961; renamed franchise. Had been HOBBS CARDINALS, 1958–1959. Disbanded with league after 1961 season.

Hobbs Sports
Longhorn League (C), 1955; new franchise. Southwestern League (B), 1956–1957; charter franchise. Disbanded with league after 1957 season.

HOBOKEN, NJ

Hoboken
Inter-State League, 1886; new franchise. Disbanded with league after 1886 season.

Hoboken Cuban Giants
Middle States League, mid-1889; relocated franchise. Had been TRENTON CUBAN GIANTS, 1889. Disbanded with league during 1889 season.

HOISINGTON, KS

Hoisington
Kansas State League (D), mid-1905; relocated franchise. Had

been KINGMAN, 1905. Disbanded after 1905 season.

HOLDENVILLE, OK

Holdenville Villies
Oklahoma State League (D), 1912; charter franchise. Disbanded with league during 1912 season.

HOLDREGE, NE

Holdrege White Sox
Nebraska State League (D), 1956–1959; charter franchise. Disbanded with league after 1959 season.

HOLLAND, MI

Holland Wooden Shoes
Michigan State League (D), 1910–1911; charter franchise. Disbanded after 1911 season.

HOLLYWOOD, CA

Hollywood Sheiks
Alternate name for HOLLYWOOD STARS.

Hollywood Stars (aka Sheiks and Twinks)
Pacific Coast League (AAA), 1926–1935; relocated franchise. Had been SALT LAKE CITY BEES, 1915–1925. Became SAN DIEGO PADRES, 1936.

Hollywood Stars
Pacific Coast League (AA), 1938–1945; (AAA), 1946–1957; relocated franchise. Had been MISSION OF SAN FRANCISCO, 1926–1937. Became SALT LAKE CITY BEES, 1958.

Hollywood Twinks
Alternate name for HOLLYWOOD STARS.

HOLLYWOOD, FL

Hollywood Chiefs
Florida East Coast League (D), 1940; charter franchise. Disbanded after 1940 season.

HOLTON, KS

Holton
Eastern Kansas League (D), 1910; charter franchise. Became BLUE RAPIDS CHAMPIONS, mid-1910.

HOLTON–WHITING, KS

Holton–Whiting
Kansas State League, 1895; charter franchise. Disbanded after 1895 season.

HOLYOKE, MA

HOLYOKE
International Association, 1878; charter franchise. National Association, 1879; charter franchise. Disbanded with league after 1879 season.

Holyoke
Massachusetts State Association, 1884; charter franchise. Disbanded with league during 1884 season.

Holyoke Millers
Eastern League (AA), 1977–1982; new franchise. Disbanded after 1982 season.

Holyoke Papermakers
Connecticut League (B), 1907–1912; renamed franchise. Had been HOLYOKE PAPERWEIGHTS, 1903–1906. Eastern Association (B), 1913; charter franchise. Became MERIDEN, mid-1913.

Holyoke Paperweights
Connecticut League (B), mid-1903–1906; relocated franchise. Had been WATERBURY, 1903. Renamed HOLYOKE PAPERMAKERS, 1907.

HOMESTEAD, PA

HOMESTEAD GRAYS
American Negro League, 1929; charter franchise. Disbanded dur-

ing 1929 season. East–West League, 1932; charter franchise. Disbanded during 1932 season. Negro National League, 1935–1948; new franchise. Disbanded after 1948 season.

Homestead Steel Workers
Ohio–Pennsylvania League (D), 1905; charter franchise. Disbanded after 1905 season.

HONOLULU, HI
Hawaii Islanders
Pacific Coast League (AAA), 1961–1987; relocated franchise. Had been SACRAMENTO SOLONS, 1918–1960. Became COLORADO SPRINGS SKY SOX, 1988.

HOISINTON, KS
Hoisinton
Kansas State League (D), mid-1905; relocated franchise. Had been KINGMAN, 1905.

HOPE, AR
Hope
Arkansas–Texas League (D), 1905; charter franchise. Disbanded after 1905 season.

HOPEWELL, VA
Hopewell Blue Sox
Virginia League (D), 1949–1950; relocated franchise. Had been BLACKSTONE BARRISTERS. Disbanded after 1950 season.

Hopewell Powder Puffs
Virginia League (C), 1916; new franchise. Became ROANOKE, mid-1916.

HOPKINSVILLE, KY
Hopkinsville Browns
KITTY League (D), 1903–1904; charter franchise. Renamed HOPKINSVILLE HOPPERS, 1905.

Hopkinsville Hoppers
KITTY League (D), 1905; renamed franchise. Had been HOPKINSVILLE BROWNS, 1903–1904. Disbanded after 1905 season.

Hopkinsville Hoppers
KITTY League (D), 1910–1914; charter franchise. Disbanded with league after 1914 season.

Hopkinsville Hoppers
KITTY League (D), mid-1916; charter franchise. Disbanded with league after 1916 season.

Hopkinsville Hoppers
KITTY League (D), 1922–1924; charter franchise. Disbanded with league after 1924 season.

Hopkinsville Hoppers
KITTY League (D), mid-1935–1942; 1946–1954; charter franchise. Disbanded after 1954 season.

HOQUIAM, WA
Hoquiam
Washington State League (D), 1910; charter franchise. Disbanded after 1910 season.

Hoquiam Cougars
Washington State League (D), 1912; new franchise. Disbanded with league after 1912 season.

Hoquiam Perfect Gentlemen
Southwest Washington League (D), 1903–1905; charter franchise. Disbanded after 1905 season.

HORNELL (HORNELLSVILLE), NY
Hornell
Western New York League, 1890; charter franchise. Disbanded with league after 1890 season.

Hornell
Inter-State League (D), 1906; new franchise. Became PATTON, mid-1906.

Hornell Dodgers
PONY League (D), 1950–1956; renamed franchise. Had been HORNELL MAPLE LEAFS, 1948–1949. Disbanded after 1956 season.

Hornell Green Sox
Inter-State League (D), mid-1914; charter franchise. Renamed HORNELL MAPLES, 1915.

HORNELLSVILLE HORNELLS
International Association, 1878; charter franchise. Disbanded after 1878 season.

Hornell Maple Leafs
PONY League (D), 1948–1949; renamed franchise. Had been HORNELL MAPLES, 1942–1947. Renamed HORNELL DODGERS, 1950.

Hornell Maples
Inter-State League (D), 1915; renamed franchise. Had been HORNELL GREEN SOX, mid-1914. Disbanded after 1915 season.

Hornell Maples
PONY League (D), 1942–1947; expansion franchise. Renamed HORNELL MAPLE LEAFS, 1948.

Hornell Redlegs
New York–Pennsylvania League (D), mid-1957; relocated franchise. Had been BRADFORD BEAGLES, 1957. Disbanded after 1957 season.

HORNELLSVILLE, NY
(See HORNELL, NY)

HORTON, KS
Horton
Eastern Kansas League (D), 1910–mid-1911; charter franchise. Disbanded with league during 1911 season.

HOT SPRINGS, AR

Hot Springs
Arkansas State League, 1897; charter franchise. Disbanded with league during 1897 season.

Hot Springs
Arkansas–Texas League (D), 1906; new franchise. Disbanded after 1906 season.

Hot Springs
Arkansas States League (D), 1908–1909; charter franchise. Disbanded with league after 1909 season.

Hot Springs Bathers
Cotton States League (C), 1938–1941; 1947–1955; new franchise. Disbanded with league after 1955 season.

Hot Springs Blues (aka Sluggers)
Southwestern League, 1887; charter franchise. Disbanded with league after 1887 season.

Hot Springs Sluggers
Alternate name for HOT SPRINGS BLUES, 1887.

HOUGHTON, MI

Houghton
Upper Peninsula League, 1890–1891; charter franchise. Disbanded with league after 1891 season.

Houghton
Upper Peninsula League, 1895; charter franchise. Disbanded with league after 1895 season.

Houghton
Northern Copper County League (C), 1906–1907; charter franchise. Disbanded with league after 1907 season.

HOULTON, ME

Houlton
Northern Maine League (D), 1909; charter franchise. Disbanded with league during 1909 season.

HOUMA, LA

Houma Buccaneers
Evangeline League (D), 1940; new franchise. Became NATCHEZ PILGRIMS, mid-1940.

Houma Indians
Evangeline League (C), 1946–1952; charter franchise. Disbanded after 1952 season.

HOUSTON, TX

HOUSTON ASTROS
National League, 1965–(still in existence as of 5-1-92); Renamed FRANCHISE. Had been HOUSTON COLT '45S, 1962–1964.

Houston Babies (aka Red Stockings)
Texas League, 1888; charter franchise. Disbanded during 1888 season.

Houston Buffaloes (aka Buffs)
Texas Association, 1897–1899 (aka Houston Gladiators). Disbanded after 1899 season.

Houston Buffaloes (aka Buffs)
South Texas League (D); 1905; renamed franchise. Had been HOUSTON WANDERERS, 1904. Texas League (C), 1907–1910; (B), 1911–1920; (A), 1921–1935; (A1), 1936–1942; (AA), 1946–1958; new franchise. American Association (AAA), 1959–1961; new franchise. Disbanded after 1961 season.

Houston Buffs
Alternate name for HOUSTON BUFFALOES.

Houston Colt '45s
National League, 1962–1964; expansion franchise. Renamed HOUSTON ASTROS, 1965.

HOUSTON COLTS
Texas League, 1892; charter franchise. Disbanded with league after 1892 season.

HOUSTON EAGLES
Negro American League, 1950; new franchise. Disbanded during 1950 season.

Houston Gladiators
Alternate name for HOUSTON BUFFALOES, 1897.

Houston Magnolias
Texas Southern Association, 1895–1896; charter franchise. Disbanded with association after 1896 season.

Houston Moore's Marvels (named after catcher–manager Wade Moore)
South Texas League (D); 1903; charter franchise. Renamed HOUSTON WANDERERS, 1904.

Houston Mud Cats
Texas League, 1889–1890; new franchise. Disbanded during 1889 season.

Houston Wanderers
South Texas League (D); 1904; renamed franchise. Had been HOUSTON MOORE'S MARVELS, 1903. Renamed HOUSTON BUFFALOES, 1905.

Houston Red Stockings
Alternate name for HOUSTON BABIES, 1888.

HUDSON, NY

Hudson
Hudson River League, 1885; charter franchise. Disbanded during 1885 season.

Hudson Marines
Hudson River League (D), 1903; (C), 1904–1907; charter franchise. Disbanded with league after 1907 season.

HUGO, OK

Hugo
Texas–Oklahoma League (D), mid-1913–1914; relocated fran-

chise. Had been WICHITA FALLS OILERs (aka Drillers), 1912–mid-1913. Disbanded during 1914 season.

HULL, ONTARIO, CANADA

(See OTTAWA, ONTARIO, CANADA)

HUMBOLDT, NE

Humboldt Infants
MINK League (D), mid-1911–1912; relocated franchise. Had been MARYVILLE COMETS, 1910–mid-1911. Disbanded with league after 1912 season.

HUNTINGTON, IN

Huntington Indians
Northern State League of Indiana (D), 1911; renamed franchise. Had been HUNTINGTON JOHNNIES, 1909–1910. Disbanded with league during 1911 season.

Huntington Johnnies
Northern State League of Indiana (D), 1909–1910; charter franchise. Renamed HUNTINGTON INDIANS, 1911.

Huntington Miamis
Indiana–Ohio League (D), 1908; new franchise. Disbanded with league after 1908 season.

HUNTINGTON, WV

Huntington
Tri-State League, 1894; charter franchise. Disbanded with league during 1894 season.

Huntington
Virginia Valley League (D), 1910; charter franchise. Disbanded with league after 1910 season.

Huntington Aces
Mountain States League (D), 1940–1941; renamed franchise.

Had been HUNTINGTON BEES, 1938. Renamed HUNTINGTON JEWELS, 1942.

Huntington Bees
Mountain States League (D), 1938; new franchise. Renamed HUNTINGTON BOOSTERS, 1939.

Huntington Blue Sox
Mountain State League (D), 1911–1912; charter franchise. Ohio State League (D), 1913–1914; new franchise. Disbanded after 1914 season.

Huntington Boosters
Ohio State League (D), 1916; new franchise. Became CHILLICOTHE BABES, mid-1916.

Huntington Boosters
Middle Atlantic League (C), 1931; expansion franchise. Renamed HUNTINGTON RED BIRDS, 1932.

Huntington Boosters
Mountain States League (D), 1937; renamed franchise. Had been HUNTINGTON RED BIRDS, 1934–1936. Disbanded during 1937 season.

Huntington Boosters
Mountain States League (D), 1939; renamed franchise. Had been HUNTINGTON BEES, 1938. Renamed HUNTINGTON ACES, 1940.

Huntington Cubs
Appalachian League (R), 1990–(still in existence as of 5-1-92); new franchise.

Huntington Jewels
Mountain States League (C), 1942; renamed franchise. Had been HUNTINGTON RED BIRDS, 1937–1941. Disbanded with league after 1942 season.

Huntington Red Birds
Middle Atlantic League (D), 1932; 1934–1936; renamed franchise. Had been HUNTINGTON BOOSTERS,

1931. Renamed HUNTINGTON BOOSTERS, 1937.

HUNTSVILLE, AL

Huntsville
Tennessee–Alabama League (D), 1903–1904; charter franchise. Disbanded with league after 1904 season.

Huntsville
Alabama–Mississippi League (D), 1936; charter franchise. Disbanded with league during 1936 season.

Huntsville Mountaineers
Southeastern League (D), 1912; renamed franchise. Had been HUNTSVILLE WESTERNERS, 1911. Became TALLADEGA INDIANS, mid-1912.

Huntsville Springers
Georgia–Alabama League (C), 1930; new franchise. Disbanded with league after 1930 season.

Huntsville Stars
Southern League (AA), 1985–(still in existence as of 5-1-92); relocated franchise. Had been NASHVILLE SOUNDS, 1978–1984.

Huntsville Westerners
Southeastern League (D), 1911; charter franchise. Renamed HUNTSVILLE MOUNTAINEERS, 1912.

HUNTSVILLE, AR

Huntsville Red Birds
Arkansas State League (D), 1935; expansion franchise. Disbanded with league after 1935 season.

HURON, SD

Huron
South Dakota League (D), 1920; charter franchise. Dakota League (D), 1921; charter franchise. Disbanded after 1921 season.

Huron Cubs
Northern League (A), 1969–1970; renamed franchise. Had been HURON PHILLIES, 1965–1968. Disbanded after 1970 season.

Huron Phillies
Northern League (A), 1965–1968; new franchise. Renamed HURON CUBS, 1969.

HUTCHINSON, KS

Hutchinson
Western Association, 1897; new franchise. Kansas State League, 1898; charter franchise. Disbanded with league after 1898 season.

Hutchinson Blues
Alternate name for HUTCHINSON GIANTS, 1887.

Hutchinson Cubs
Western Association (C), 1946–1948; charter franchise. Renamed HUTCHINSON ELKS, 1949.

Hutchinson Elks
Western Association (C), 1949–1954; renamed franchise. Had been HUTCHINSON CUBS, 1946–1948. Disbanded with league after 1954 season.

Hutchinson Giants (aka Blues)
Kansas State League, 1887; charter franchise. Disbanded with league during 1887 season.

Hutchinson Larks
Western Association (C), 1934–1938; new franchise. Renamed HUTCHINSON PIRATES, 1939.

Hutchinson Packers
Kansas State League (D), 1914; new franchise. Disbanded with league after 1914 season.

Hutchinson Pirates
Western Association (C), 1939–1942; renamed franchise. Had been HUTCHINSON LARKS, 1934–1938. Suspended operations after 1942

season, and resumed as HUTCHINSON CUBS, 1946.

Hutchinson Salt Miners
Western League (A), 1905; new franchise. Disbanded after 1905 season.

Hutchinson Salt Packers
Western Association (C), mid-1908; renamed franchise. Had been HUTCHINSON WHITE SOX, mid-1906–mid-1908. Kansas State League (D), 1909–1911; charter franchise. Disbanded with league after 1911 season.

Hutchinson Salt Packers
Western Association (D), mid-1917; relocated franchise. Had been OKLAHOMA CITY BOOSTERS, 1914–mid-1917. Disbanded after 1917 season.

Hutchinson Wheatshockers
Western League (A), mid-1917–mid-1918; relocated franchise. Had been ST. JOSEPH DRUMMERS, 1910–mid-1917. Became OKLAHOMA CITY INDIANS, mid-1918.

Hutchinson Wheatshockers
Western League (A), mid-1918; relocated franchise. Had been TOPEKA KAW-NEES, 1918. Disbanded with league after 1918 season.

Hutchinson Wheatshockers
Southwestern League (C), 1922–1923; new franchise. Western Association (C), 1924; new franchise. Disbanded after 1924 season.

Hutchinson Wheatshockers
Western Association (C), mid-1932; relocated franchise. Had been MUSKOGEE NIGHTHAWKS, 1932. Western League (A), 1933; new franchise. Merged to become BARTLESVILLE BRONCOS, mid-1932.

Hutchinson Wheatshockers
Western Association (C), mid-1932; relocated franchise. Had been INDEPENDENCE PRODUCERS, mid-1932. Disbanded with league after 1932 season.

Hutchinson White Sox
Western Association (C), mid-1906–mid-1908; relocated franchise. Had been ST. JOSEPH, 1906. Renamed HUTCHINSON SALT-PACKERS, mid-1908.

IDAHO FALLS, ID

Idaho Falls A's
Pioneer League (C), 1982–1985; renamed franchise. Had been IDAHO FALLS ANGELS, 1964–1981. Renamed IDAHO FALLS BRAVES, 1986.

Idaho Falls Angels
Pioneer League (R), 1964–1976; ("Summer Class A") 1977–1978; (R), 1981; renamed franchise. Had been IDAHO FALLS YANKEES, 1962–1963. Renamed IDAHO FALLS A'S, 1982.

Idaho Falls Braves
Pioneer League (R), 1986–(still in existence as of 5-1-92); renamed franchise. Had been IDAHO FALLS A'S, 1982–1985.

Idaho Falls Russets
Pioneer League (C), 1940–1942; 1946–1961; new franchise. Renamed IDAHO FALLS YANKEES, 1962.

Idaho Falls Spuds
Utah–Idaho League (D), 1926–1928; charter franchise. Disbanded during 1928 season.

Idaho Falls Yankees
Pioneer League (C), 1962; (A), 1963; renamed franchise. Had been IDAHO FALLS RUSSETS, 1940–1942; 1946–1961. Renamed IDAHO FALLS ANGELS, 1964.

ILION, NY

Ilion Typewriters
New York State League, 1901; (B), 1902–1904; charter franchise. Empire State League (NY), (C), 1905; charter franchise. Disbanded after 1905 season.

INDEPENDENCE, KS

Independence
Kansas State League, 1896; new franchise. Disbanded with league after 1896 season.

Independence
Western Association (C), 1911; new franchise. Disbanded during 1911 season.

Independence Browns
KOM League (D), 1952; new franchise. Disbanded with league after 1952 season.

Independence Coyotes (aka Oilers)
Kansas State League (D), 1905–1906; charter franchise. OAK League (D), 1907; charter franchise. Oklahoma–Kansas League (D), 1908; charter franchise. Disbanded with league after 1908 season.

Independence Oilers
Alternate name for Independence Coyotes, 1905–1908.

Independence Producers
Southwestern League (D), 1921; (C), 1922–1923; (D), 1924; charter franchise. Disbanded during 1924 season.

Independence Producers
Western Association (C), 1925; new franchise. Disbanded after 1925 season.

Independence Producers
Western Association (C), 1928–mid-1932; new franchise. Became JOPLIN MINERS, mid-1932.

Independence Producers
Western Association (C), mid-1932; Relocated franchise. Had been JOPLIN MINERS, mid-1932. Became HUTCHINSON WHEATSHOCKERS, mid-1932.

Independence Yankees
KOM League (D), 1947–1950; new franchise. Disbanded after 1950 season.

INDIANAPOLIS, IN

Indianapolis
Western Inter-State League, mid-1890; relocated franchise. Had been GALESBURG, 1890. Disbanded after 1890 season.

INDIANAPOLIS ABC'S
Negro National League, 1920–1923; 1925–1926; charter franchise. Disbanded after 1926 season. Negro Southern League, 1932; charter franchise. Disbanded with league after 1932 season.

INDIANAPOLIS ABC'S
Negro American League, 1938–mid-1939; new franchise. Disbanded during 1939 season.

INDIANAPOLIS ATHLETICS
Negro American League, 1937; charter franchise. Disbanded after 1937 season.

Indianapolis Capital Citys
Keystone Association, 1877; charter franchise. Disbanded after 1877 season.

INDIANAPOLIS–CINCINNATI CLOWNS
Negro American League, 1944; relocated franchise. Had been CINCINNATI CLOWNS, 1943. Became CINCINNATI CLOWNS, 1945.

INDIANAPOLIS CLOWNS
Negro American League, 1946–1950; relocated franchise. Had been CINCINNATI CLOWNS, 1945. Disbanded with league after 1950 season.

INDIANAPOLIS CRAWFORDS
Negro American League, 1940; relocated franchise. Had been TOLEDO CRAWFORDS, mid-1939. Disbanded after 1940 season.

INDIANAPOLIS HOOFEDS
Alternate name for FEDERAL LEAGUE TEAM, 1915.

INDIANAPOLIS HOOSIERFEDS
Alternate name for FEDERAL LEAGUE TEAM, 1915.

INDIANAPOLIS HOOSIERS
National League, 1878; new franchise. Disbanded after 1878 season.

INDIANAPOLIS HOOSIERS
American Association, 1884; charter franchise. Disbanded with league after 1884 season.

Indianapolis Hoosiers
Western League, 1885; charter franchise. Became DETROIT, mid-1885.

INDIANAPOLIS HOOSIERS
National League, 1887–1889; new franchise. Disbanded after 1889 season.

Indianapolis Hoosiers
Western League, 1892; expansion franchise. Disbanded with league during 1892 season.

Indianapolis Hoosiers
Western League, 1894–1899; new franchise. American League, 1900; charter franchise. Western Association, 1901; charter franchise. Became MATTHEWS, mid-1901. Disbanded with league after 1899 season.

Indianapolis Hoosiers
Federal League, 1913; charter franchise. Assumed Major-League sta-

tus, 1914. Became NEWARK PEPPERS, 1915.

Indianapolis Indians
American Association (AAA), 1903–1907; (AA), 1908–1945; (AAA), 1946–1962; charter franchise. International League (AAA), 1963; new franchise. Pacific Coast League (AAA), 1964–1968; new franchise. American Association (AAA), 1969–(still in existence as of 5-1-92); charter franchise.

INGERSOLL, ONTARIO, CANADA

Ingersoll
Canadian League (C), 1905; charter franchise. Disbanded with league after 1905 season.

IOLA, KS

Iola Cubs
Kansas–Oklahoma–Missouri League (D), 1946–1947; charter franchise. Renamed IOLA INDIANS, 1948.

Iola Gasbags
Missouri Valley League (D), 1902–1904; charter franchise. Disbanded with league after 1904 season.

Iola Grays
Kansas State League (D), 1905–mid-1906; charter franchise. Became CHERRYVALE BOOSTERS, mid-1906.

Iola Indians
Kansas–Oklahoma–Missouri League (D), 1948–1952; renamed franchise. Had been IOLA CUBS, 1946–1947. Disbanded with league after 1952 season.

Iola Indians
Western Association (C), 1954; new franchise. Disbanded with league after 1954 season.

IONIA, MI

Ionia
Northern Michigan League, 1887; charter franchise. Disbanded with league during 1887 season.

Ionia Mayors
Central League (D), mid-1921–1922; Relocated franchise. Had been JACKSON, 1921. Disbanded with league after 1922 season.

IRONTON, OH

Ironton Nailers
Ohio State League (D), 1915; renamed franchise. Had been IRONTON ORPHANS, 1911–1914. Disbanded after 1915 season.

Ironton Orphans
Ohio State League (D), mid-1912–1914; relocated franchise. Had been MARION DIGGERS, 1908–mid-1912. Renamed IRONTON NAILERS, 1915.

ISHPEMING, MI

Ishpeming
Upper Peninsula League, 1891; charter franchise. Disbanded during 1891 season.

Ishpeming
Upper Peninsula League, 1895; charter franchise. Disbanded during 1895 season.

ISHPEMING–NEGAUNEE, MI
(See also NEGAUNEE, MI)

Ishpeming–Negaunee Unions
Michigan–Wisconsin League, 1892; charter franchise. Disbanded during 1892 season.

JACKSON, MI

Jackson
Michigan State League, 1897; charter franchise. Disbanded after 1897 season.

Jackson
Central League (D), 1921; new franchise. Became IONIA MAYORS, mid-1921.

Jackson
Michigan State League (D), mid-1902; relocated franchise. Had been SAGINAW, 1902. Disbanded with league during 1902 season.

Jackson Chiefs
Southern Michigan League (D), 1914; renamed franchise. Had been JACKSON CONVICTS (aka Yeggs, 1906–1913. Renamed JACKSON VETS, 1915.

Jackson Convicts (aka Yeggs, 1912)
Southern Michigan League (D), 1906–1907; charter franchise. Disbanded during 1907 season.

Jackson Convicts
Southern Michigan League (D), 1908–1910; (C), mid-1912/League (C), 1911, 1913. Renamed JACKSON CHIEFS, 1914.

Jackson Jaxons
Tri-State League, 1888; charter franchise. Michigan State League, 1889; charter franchise. Disbanded after 1889 season.

Jackson Jaxons
Michigan State League, mid-1895; relocated franchise. Had been BATTLE CREEK, 1895. Disbanded with league after 1895 season.

Jackson Vets
Southern Michigan League (D), 1915; renamed franchise. Had been JACKSON CHIEFS, 1914. Disbanded with league during 1915 season.

Jackson Wolverines
Inter-State League, 1896; charter franchise. Michigan State League, 1897; charter franchise. Disbanded during 1897 season.

Jackson Yeggs
Alternate name for JACKSON CON-VICTS, 1912.

JACKSON, MS

Jackson Drummers
Cotton States League (D), 1911; renamed franchise. Had been JACK-SON SENATORS, 1910. Renamed JACKSON LAWMAKERS, 1912.

Jackson Generals
Texas League (AA), 1991–(still in existence as of 5-1-92); renamed franchise. Had been JACK-SON METS, 1975–1990.

Jackson Lawmakers
Cotton States League (D), 1912–1914; renamed franchise. Had been JACKSON DRUMMERS, 1911. Disbanded with league during 1914 season.

Jackson Mets
Texas League (AA), 1975–1990; renamed franchise. Renamed JACK-SON GENERALS, 1991.

Jackson Mississippians
Southeastern League (B), 1932; new franchise. Dixie League (C), 1933; charter franchise. East Dixie League (C), 1934–1935; charter franchise. Cotton States League (C), 1936; charter franchise. Southeastern League (B), 1937–1942; 1946–1950; charter franchise. Disbanded with league after 1950 season.

Jackson Red Sox
Cotton States League (D), 1922–1931; charter franchise. Disbanded after 1931 season.

Jackson Senators
Delta League (D), 1904; charter franchise. Disbanded after 1904 season.

Jackson Senators
Cotton States League (D), 1905–1908; new franchise. Disbanded after 1908 season.

Jackson Senators
Cotton States League (D), 1910; charter franchise. Renamed JACK-SON DRUMMERS, 1911.

Jackson Senators
Cotton States League (D), mid-1932; relocated franchise. Had been VICKSBURG HILL BILLIES, 1922–mid-1932. Disbanded with league after 1932 season.

Jackson Senators
Cotton States League (C), 1953; new franchise. Disbanded after 1953 season.

Jackson Senators
Mississippi State League (D), 1921; charter franchise. Disbanded with league after 1921 season.

JACKSON, OH

Jackson
Tri-State League, 1894; charter franchise. Disbanded with league after 1894 season.

JACKSON, TN

Jackson
KITTY League (D), 1903; charter franchise. Disbanded after 1903 season.

Jackson
KITTY League (D), 1911; relocated franchise. Had been HARRIS-BURG MERCHANTS, 1910–1911. Disbanded after 1911 season.

Jackson Blue Jays
KITTY League (D), 1924; new franchise. Disbanded with league after 1924 season.

Jackson Generals
KITTY League (D), mid-1935–1942; charter franchise. Disbanded during 1942 season.

Jackson Generals
KITTY League (D), 1950–1954; new franchise. Became CENTRAL CITY REDS, mid-1954.

Jackson Giants
Tri-State League (D), 1925; charter franchise. Renamed JACKSON JAYS, 1926.

Jackson Jays
Tri-State League (D), 1926; renamed franchise. Had been JACK-SON GIANTS, 1925. Disbanded with league after 1926 season.

Jackson Mets
Texas League (AA), 1975–1986; relocated franchise. Had been VIC-TORIA TOROS, 1974.

JACKSONVILLE, FL

Jacksonville
Florida State League, 1892; charter franchise. Disbanded with league after 1892 season.

Jacksonville Braves
South Atlantic League (A), 1953–1960; renamed franchise. Had been JACKSONVILLE TARS, 1946–1952. Renamed JACKSONVILLE JETS, 1961.

Jacksonville Jets
South Atlantic League (A), 1961; renamed franchise. Had been JACK-SONVILLE BRAVES, 1953–1960. Disbanded after 1961 season.

Jacksonville Expos
Southern League (AA), 1985–1996; renamed franchise. Had been JACKSONVILLE SUNS, 1970–1984. Renamed JACKSONVILLE SUNS, 1991.

Jacksonville Indians
Florida State League (C), 1922; renamed franchise. Had been JACK-SONVILLE SCOUTS, 1921. Disbanded after 1922 season.

Jacksonville Jays
South Atlantic League (C), 1904–1910; charter franchise. Renamed JACKSONVILLE TARPONS, 1911.

Jacksonville Mets
International League (AAA), 1968; new franchise. Had been JACKSONVILLE SUNS, 1962–1967. Disbanded after 1968 season.

JACKSONVILLE RED CAPS
Negro American League, 1938; 1941; new franchise. Disbanded after 1941 season.

Jacksonville Roses
South Atlantic League (C), 1917; renamed franchise. Had been JACKSONVILLE TARPONS, 1911–1916. Disbanded with league during 1917 season.

Jacksonville Scouts
Florida State League (C), 1921; new franchise. Renamed JACKSONVILLE INDIANS, 1922.

Jacksonville Suns
International League (AAA), 1962–1967; new franchise. Renamed JACKSONVILLE METS, 1968.

Jacksonville Suns
Southern League (AA), 1970; new franchise. Dixie Association (C), 1971; charter franchise. Southern League (AA), 1972–1985; charter franchise. Renamed JACKSONVILLE EXPOS, 1986.

Jacksonville Suns
Southern League (AA), 1991– (still in existence as of 5-1-92); renamed franchise. Had been JACKSONVILLE EXPOS, 1986–1990.

Jacksonville Tarpons
South Atlantic League (C), 1911–1916; renamed franchise. Had been JACKSONVILLE JAYS, 1904–1910. Renamed JACKSONVILLE ROSES, 1917.

Jacksonville Tars
Southeastern League (D), 1926–1930; charter franchise. Disbanded with league after 1930 season.

Jacksonville Tars
South Atlantic League (A), 1936–1942; 1946–1952; charter franchise. Renamed JACKSONVILLE BRAVES, 1953.

JACKSONVILLE, IL

Jacksonville
Illinois–Iowa League, 1892; new franchise. Disbanded with league after 1892 season.

Jacksonville Braves (aka Lunatics)
KITTY League (D), 1906; new franchise. Iowa State League (D), 1907; new franchise. Central Association (D), 1908–1909; charter franchise.

Jacksonville Jacks
Western Association, 1894–mid-1895; charter franchise. Became SPRINGFIELD, mid-1895.

Jacksonville Jacks
Illinois–Missouri League (D), mid-1910; relocated franchise. Had been BEARDSTOWN, 1909–mid-1910. Northern Association (C), mid-1910; (D), mid-1910; charter franchise. Disbanded with league after 1910 season.

Jacksonville Lunatics
Alternate name for JACKSONVILLE BRAVES, 1906–1908.

Jacksonville Reds
Central League, mid-1900; relocated franchise. Had been SPRINGFIELD, 1900. Disbanded with league after 1900 season.

JACKSONVILLE, TX

Jacksonville
East Texas League (D), mid-1916; relocated franchise. Had been KEMP, 1916. Disbanded with league after 1916 season.

Jacksonville Jax
West Dixie League (C), 1934–1935; charter franchise. East Texas League (C), 1936–1940; 1946; charter franchise. Lone Star League (C); 1947; charter franchise. Disbanded after 1947 season.

Jacksonville Jax
Gulf Coast League (D), 1950; charter franchise. Disbanded after 1950 season.

JACKSONVILLE BEACH, FL

Jacksonville Beach Sea Birds
Florida State League (D), 1952–1954; new franchise. Disbanded after 1954 season.

JALAPA, MEXICO

Jalapa Ocampo
Mexican League (AAA), 1991– (still in existence as of 5-1-92); new franchise.

JALISCO, MEXICO
(See GUADALAJARA, MEXICO)

JAMESTOWN, NY

Jamestown
New York–Pennsylvania League, 1890–1891; charter franchise. Disbanded with league after 1891 season.

Jamestown Braves
New York–Pennsylvania League (A), 1967–1969; renamed franchise. Had been JAMESTOWN DODGERS, 1966. Renamed JAMESTOWN FALCONS, 1970.

Jamestown Dodgers
New York–Pennsylvania League (A), 1966; renamed franchise. Had been JAMESTOWN TIGERS, 1961–1965. Renamed JAMESTOWN BRAVES, 1967.

Jamestown Expos
New York–Pennsylvania League (A), 1977–(still in existence as of 5-1-92); new franchise.

Jamestown Falcons
New York–Pennsylvania League (A), 1970–1973; renamed franchise. Had been JAMESTOWN BRAVES, 1967–1969. Disbanded after 1973 season.

Jamestown Falcons (aka Jockeys and Ponies)
PONY League (D), 1939; charter franchise. Merged to become NIAGARA FALLS–JAMESTOWN FALCONS, 1940. Renamed JAMESTOWN FALCONS, 1941–1956; charter franchise. New York–Pennsylvania League (D), 1957; new franchise. Disbanded during 1957 season.

Jamestown Giants
Inter-State League (D), mid-1914; charter franchise. Renamed JAMESTOWN RABBITS, 1915.

Jamestown Hill Climbers
Inter-State League (D), 1905; charter franchise. Became DUBOIS, mid-1905.

Jamestown Jockeys
Alternate name for JAMESTOWN FALCONS, 1939.

Jamestown Oseejays
Inter-State League (D), mid-1906; relocated franchise. Had been OIL CITY OSEEJAYS, 1906. Disbanded with league after 1906 season.

Jamestown Ponies
Alternate name for JAMESTOWN FALCONS, 1939.

Jamestown Rabbits
Inter-State League (D), 1915; renamed franchise. Had been JAMESTOWN GIANTS, mid-1914.

Jamestown Tigers
New York–Pennsylvania League (D), 1961–1962; (A), 1963–1965;

new franchise. Renamed JAMESTOWN DODGERS, 1966.

JAMESTOWN, ND

Jamestown Jimkotans
Dakota League (D), 1922; new franchise. North Dakota League (D), 1923; charter franchise. Disbanded with league after 1923 season.

Jamestown Jimmies
Northern League (D), 1936–1937; new franchise. Disbanded after 1937 season.

JANESVILLE, WI

Janesville
Keystone Association, 1877; charter franchise. Disbanded with alliance after 1877 season.

Janesville Bears
Wisconsin State League (D), 1946–1953; charter franchise. Disbanded with league after 1953 season.

Janesville Cubs
Wisconsin State League (D), 1941–1942; new franchise. Suspended operations after 1942 season, and resumed as JANESVILLE BEARS, 1946.

JEANERETTE, LA

Jeanerette Blues
Evangeline League (D), mid-1934–1939; relocated franchise. Had been LAKE CHARLES EXPORTERS, 1934. Disbanded after 1939 season.

JEANETTE, PA

Jeanette Jays
Middle Atlantic League (C), 1926–mid-1931; expansion franchise. Became ALTOONA ENGINEERS, mid-1931.

Jeanette Little Bisons
Pennsylvania State Association (D), 1937; renamed franchise. Had been JEANETTE LITTLE PIRATES, 1936. Disbanded during 1937 season.

Jeanette Little Pirates
Pennsylvania State Association (D), 1936; new franchise. Renamed JEANETTE LITTLE BISONS, 1937.

Jeanette Reds
Pennsylvania State Association (D), mid-1934; charter franchise. Disbanded after 1934 season.

JEFFERSON CITY, MO

Jefferson City Capitolites
Alternate name for JEFFERSON CITY CONVICTS, 1902.

Jefferson City Convicts (aka Capitolites)
Missouri Valley League (D), 1902; charter franchise. Disbanded after 1902 season.

Jefferson City Senators
Missouri State League (D), 1911; charter franchise. Disbanded during 1911 season.

JENKINS, KY

Jenkins Cavaliers
Mountain States League (D), 1948–1951; charter franchise. Disbanded after 1951 season.

JERSEY CITY, NJ

Jersey City
Atlantic League, 1900; charter franchise. Disbanded with league after 1900 season.

Jersey City Colts
Alternate name for JERSEY CITY SKEETERS, 1922–1924.

Jersey City Giants
International League (AA), 1937–1945; (AAA), 1946; new fran-

chise. Renamed JERSEY CITY LITTLE GIANTS, 1947.

Jersey City Indians
Eastern League (A), 1977–1978; new franchise. Disbanded after 1978 season.

Jersey City Jerseys
Eastern League, mid-1885–1886; relocated franchise. Had been TRENTON, 1885. Disbanded after 1886 season.

Jersey City Jerseys
Atlantic Association, 1889–mid-1890; charter franchise. Became HARRISBURG PONIES, mid-1890.

Jersey City Jerseys
International League (AAA), 1961; renamed franchise. Had been JERSEY CITY REDS, 1960. Became ATLANTA CRACKERS, 1962.

Jersey City Little Giants
International League (AAA), 1947–1950; renamed franchise. Had been JERSEY CITY GIANTS, 1937–1946. Became OTTOWA GIANTS, 1950.

Jersey City Moran's Colts
Alternate name for JERSEY CITY SKEETERS.

Jersey City Reds
International League (AAA), mid-1960; relocated franchise. Had been HAVANA SUGAR KINGS, 1954–mid-1960. Became JERSEY CITY JERSEYS, 1961.

Jersey City Skeeters
International League, 1887; new franchise. Central League, 1888; charter franchise. Disbanded with league after 1888 season.

Jersey City Skeeters
Eastern League (A), 1902–1907; (AA), 1908–1911; new franchise. International League (AA), 1912–1915; charter franchise. Disbanded after 1915 season.

Jersey City Skeeters (aka Colts and Moran's Colts)
(New) International League (AA), 1918–1933; charter franchise. Disbanded after 1933 season.

JESUP, GA

Jesup Bees
Georgia State League (D), 1950–1953; new franchise. Disbanded after 1953 season.

JOHNSONBURG, PA

Johnsonburg
Inter-State League (D), 1916; new franchise. Disbanded with league after 1916 season.

JOHNSON CITY, NY
(See BINGHAMTON, NY)

JOHNSON CITY, TN

Johnson City Cardinals
Alternate name for JOHNSON CITY SOLDIERS, 1937–1938.

Johnson City Cardinals
Appalachian League (D), 1939–1955; renamed franchise. Had been JOHNSON CITY SOLDIERS, 1937–1938. Disbanded with league after 1955 season.

Johnson City Cardinals
Appalachian League (D), 1961; renamed franchise. Had been JOHNSON CITY PHILLIES, 1957–1960. Disbanded after 1961 season.

Johnson City Cardinals
Appalachian League (R), 1975–(still in existence as of 5-1-92); renamed franchise. Had been JOHNSON CITY YANKEES, 1964–1974.

Johnson City Phillies
Appalachian League (D), 1957–1961; charter franchise. Disbanded after 1961 season.

Johnson City Soldiers
Southeastern League (D), 1910; charter franchise. Appalachian League (D), 1911–1913; charter franchise. Disbanded after 1913 season.

Johnson City Soldiers
Appalachian League (D), 1920–1924; charter franchise. Disbanded after 1924 season.

Johnson City Soldiers
Appalachian League (D), 1937–1938; charter franchise. Renamed JOHNSON CITY CARDINALS, 1939.

Johnson City Yankees
Appalachian League (R), 1964–1974; new franchise. Renamed JOHNSON CITY CARDINALS, 1975.

JOHNSTOWN–AMSTERDAM–GLOVERSVILLE, NY
(See also AMSTERDAM, NY; GLOVERSVILLE, NY)

Johnstown–Amsterdam–Gloversville Jags
New York State League (B), 1902; new franchise. Renamed JOHNSTOWN–AMSTERDAM–GLOVERSVILLE HYPHENS, 1903.

Johnstown–Amsterdam–Gloversville Hyphens
New York State League (B), 1903–1904; renamed franchise. Had been JOHNSTOWN–AMSTERDAM–GLOVERSVILLE JAGS, 1902. Renamed JOHNSTOWN–AMSTERDAM–GLOVERSVILLE JAGS, 1905.

Johnstown–Amsterdam–Gloversville Jags
New York State League (B), 1905–mid-1908; renamed franchise. Had been JOHNSTOWN–AMSTERDAM–GLOVERSVILLE HYPHENS, 1903–1904. Became ELMIRA COLONELS, mid-1908.

JOHNSTOWN, NY

Johnstown Buckskins
New York State League, 1894–1895; charter franchise. Disbanded with league after 1895 season.

Johnstown Foundlings
New York State League, 1898; new franchise. Disbanded after 1898 season.

Johnstown Johnnies
New York State League (B), 1902–1908; new franchise. Eastern League (AA), 1909; new franchise. Disbanded after 1909 season.

JOHNSTOWN–GLOVERSVILLE, NY
(See GLOVERSVILLE, NY)

Johnstown–Gloversville Jays
New York State League, 1890; new franchise. Disbanded after 1890 season.

JOHNSTOWN, PA

Johnstown
Iron & Oil Association, mid-1884; relocated franchise. Had been NEW BRIGHTON, 1884. Disbanded with association after 1884 season.

Johnstown
Mountain League, 1887; charter franchise. Disbanded with league after 1887 season.

Johnstown
Pennsylvania State League, 1892–1893; charter franchise. Disbanded after 1893 season.

Johnstown Jawns
Tri-State League (D), 1909; renamed franchise. Renamed JOHNSTOWN JOHNS, 1910.

Johnstown Johnnies
Tri-State League (D), 1905–1908; new franchise. Renamed JOHNSTOWN JAWNS, 1909.

Johnstown Johnnies
Middle Atlantic League (C), 1925–1938; charter franchise. Pennsylvania State Association (D), 1939–1942; new franchise. Middle Atlantic League (D), 1946–1950; charter franchise. Disbanded after 1950 season.

Johnstown Johnnies
Eastern League (A), mid-1955–1956; relocated franchise. Had been WILKES-BARRE BARONS, 1953–mid-1955. Disbanded after 1955 season.

Johnstown Johns
Tri-State League (D), 1910–mid-1912; renamed franchise. Became CHESTER, mid-1912.

Johnstown Red Sox
Eastern League (A), 1961; new franchise. Disbanded after 1961 season.

JOLIET, IL

Joliet
Western–Inter-State League, 1895; charter franchise. Disbanded with league after 1895 season.

Joliet Convicts
Illinois–Iowa League, 1890–1891; charter franchise. Renamed JOLIET STONE CITYS, 1892.

Joliet Jolly-ites
Northern Association of Baseball (C), 1910; (D), mid-1910; charter franchise. Became STERLING INFANTS, mid-1910.

Joliet Standards
Illinois–Iowa–Indiana League (D), 1903; new franchise. Became SPRINGFIELD FOOT TRACKERS, mid-1903.

Joliet Stone Citys
Illinois–Iowa League, 1892; renamed franchise. Had been JOLIET CONVICTS, 1890–1891. Disbanded with league after 1892 season.

JONESBORO, AR

Jonesboro
Arkansas State League (D), 1909; new franchise. Northeast Arkansas League (D), 1909–1911; charter franchise. Disbanded with league after 1911 season.

Jonesboro Buffaloes
Tri-State League (D), 1925–1926; charter franchise. Disbanded with league after 1926 season.

Jonesboro Giants
Northeast Arkansas League (D), 1936–1938; charter franchise. Renamed JONESBORO WHITE SOX, 1939.

Jonesboro White Sox
Northeast Arkansas League (D), 1939–1941; renamed franchise. Disbanded with league after 1941 season.

JOPLIN, MO

Joplin
Southwestern League, 1887; charter franchise. Disbanded with league after 1887 season.

Joplin
Southwestern League, 1891; charter franchise. Disbanded with league after 1891 season.

Joplin
Western Association (D), 1914; charter franchise. Became GUTHRIE, mid-1914.

Joplin Cardinals
Western League (A), 1954; renamed franchise. Had been JOPLIN MINERS, mid-1927–1932; 1934–1942; 1946–1953. Disbanded after 1954 season.

Joplin Miners
Missouri Valley League (D), 1902–1904; charter franchise. Western

Association (D), 1905; (C), 1906–mid-1909; charter franchise. Became EL RENO PACKERS, mid-1909.

Joplin Miners
Western Association (C), 1910–1911; new franchise. Disbanded with league during 1911 season.

Joplin Miners
Western League (A), 1917–1921/Association, 1922–mid-1924; new franchise. Became BARTLESVILLE BOOSTERS, mid-1924.

Joplin Miners
Western Association (C), mid-1927–mid-1932; new franchise. Renamed TOPEKA JAYHAWKS, mid-1932.

Joplin Miners
Western Association (C), mid-1932; relocated franchise. Had been INDEPENDENCE PRODUCERS, 1932. Became INDEPENDENCE PRODUCERS, mid-1932.

Joplin Miners
Western League (A), 1933/Association (A), 1934–1942; 1946–1953; relocated franchise. Had been ST. JOSEPH SAINTS, 1918–mid-1927.

Joplin Ozarks
Western Association (A), mid-1926; relocated franchise. Had been ARDMORE BOOMERS, 1925–mid-1926. Became TOPEKA JAYHAWKS, 1927.

JUAREZ, MEXICO

Juarez Indians
Mexican League (AAA), 1977–1984; renamed franchise. Had been JUAREZ INDIOS, 1973–1976. Disbanded after 1984 season.

Juarez Indios
Mexican National League (B), 1946; charter franchise. Disbanded during 1946 season. Arizona–

Texas League (C), 1947; charter franchise. Became MESA ORPHANS, mid-1947.

Juarez Indios
Arizona–Texas League (C), 1948–1950; new franchise. Southwest International League (C), 1951; charter franchise. Arizona–Texas League (C), 1952–1954; charter franchise. Disbanded with league after 1954 season.

Juarez Indios
Central Mexican League (C), 1956–1957; charter franchise. Arizona–Mexico League (C), 1958; new franchise. Disbanded with league after 1958 season.

Juarez Indios
Mexican League (AAA), 1973–1976; new franchise. Renamed JUAREZ INDIANS, 1977.

JUNCTION CITY, KS

Junction City
Kansas State League, 1896–1897; charter franchise. Disbanded after 1897 season.

Junction City
Kansas State League, mid-1898; relocated franchise. Had been SALINA, 1898. Became SALINA, mid-1898.

Junction City Soldiers
Central Kansas League (D), 1909–1912; new franchise. Kansas State League (D), 1913; charter franchise. Disbanded after 1913 season.

KALAMAZOO, MI

Kalamazoo Celery Champs
Southern Michigan League (C), 1912; (D), mid-1912; renamed franchise. Had been KALAMAZOO CELERY EATERS, 1911. Renamed KALAMAZOO KAZOOS, 1913.

Kalamazoo Celery Eaters
Southern Michigan League (C), 1911; renamed franchise. Had been KALAMAZOO KAZOOS, 1906–1910. Renamed KALAMAZOO CELERY CHAMPS, 1912.

Kalamazoo Celery Pickers
Central League (D), 1920–1922; charter franchise. Michigan–Ontario League (B), 1923; new franchise. Renamed KALAMAZOO KAZOOS, 1924.

Kalamazoo Kazoos
Michigan–Ontario League (B), 1924; renamed franchise. Had been KALAMAZOO CELERY PICKERS, 1923.

Kalamazoo Kazoos
Ohio State League, 1887; charter franchise. Tri-State League, 1888; charter franchise. Disbanded during 1888 season.

Kalamazoo Kazoos
Michigan State League, 1889; charter franchise. Became FLINT FLYERS, mid-1889.

Kalamazoo Kazoos
Michigan State League, 1897; charter franchise. Became FLINT, mid-1897.

Kalamazoo Kazoos
Southern Michigan Association (1909)/League (1908; 1910–1914) (C), 1908–1910; renamed franchise. Had been KALAMAZOO WHITE SOX, 1906–1908. Renamed KALAMAZOO CELERY EATERS, 1911.

Kalamazoo Kazoos
Southern Michigan League (D), 1913–1914; renamed franchise. Had been KALAMAZOO CELERY CHAMPS, 1912. Disbanded after 1914 season.

Kalamazoo Kazoos
Central League (C), 1926; charter franchise. Michigan State League

(B), mid-1926; charter franchise. Disbanded with league after 1926 season.

Kalamazoo Kazoos
Michigan State League, 1894–1895; new franchise. Disbanded with league after 1895 season.

Kalamazoo Lassies
All-American Girls Professional Baseball League, 1951–1954; relocated franchise. Had been MUSKEGON LASSIES, 1946–1950. Disbanded with league after 1954 season.

Kalamazoo White Sox
Southern Michigan Association (1906–1907)/League (1908) (D), 1906–1907; (C), 1908; charter franchise. Renamed KALAMAZOO KAZOOS, 1909.

KANE, PA

Kane Mountaineers
Inter-State League (D), 1905–1906; charter franchise. Disbanded with league after 1906 season.

KANKAKEE, IL

Kankakee Kanks
Illinois–Missouri League (D), mid-1912–1914; relocated franchise. Had been CLINTON CHAMPS, 1911–mid-1912. Disbanded with league after 1914 season.

Kankakee Kays
Northern Association of Baseball (C), 1910; (D), mid-1910; charter franchise. Disbanded with league after 1910 season.

KANNAPOLIS, NC

Kannapolis Towerlers
North Carolina State League (D), 1939–1941; new franchise. Disbanded after 1941 season.

KANSAS CITY, MO

KANSAS CITY A'S
American League, 1962–1967; renamed franchise. Had been KANSAS CITY ATHLETICS, 1955–1961. Became OAKLAND A'S, 1968.

KANSAS CITY ATHLETICS
American League, 1955–1961; relocated franchise. Had been PHILADELPHIA ATHLETICS, 1901–1954. Became KANSAS CITY A'S, 1962.

Kansas City Blues
Western Association, 1888; charter franchise. Disbanded after 1888 season.

Kansas City Blues
Western Association, 1890–1891; new franchise. Western League, 1892–1899; charter franchise. Disbanded with league after 1899 season.

Kansas City Blues
American Association (A), 1904–1907; (AA), 1908–1945; (AAA), 1946–1954; renamed franchise. Had been KANSAS CITY COWBOYS, 1901–1903. Disbanded after 1954 season.

Kansas City Cowboys
Western League, 1885; charter franchise. Became MEMPHIS BROWNS, 1885.

KANSAS CITY COWBOYS
Western League, 1887; expansion franchise. American Association, 1888–1889; new franchise. Disbanded after 1889 season.

KANSAS CITY COWBOYS
National League, 1886; charter franchise. Disbanded after 1886 season.

KANSAS CITY COWBOYS (aka UNIONS)
Union Association, 1884; charter franchise. Disbanded with league after 1884 season.

KANSAS CITY COWBOYS
American League, 1900; charter franchise. Western League 1901, (A), 1902–1903; expansion franchise. Renamed KANSAS CITY BLUES, 1904.

KANSAS CITY MONARCHS
Negro National League, 1920–1927; 1929–1930; charter franchise. Disbanded after 1930 season. Negro American League, 1937–1948; charter franchise. Disbanded with league after 1948 season.

KANSAS CITY PACKERS
Federal League, 1914–1915; charter franchise. Disbanded with league after 1915 season.

KANSAS CITY ROYALS
American League, 1969–(still in existence as of 5-1-92); expansion franchise.

KANSAS CITY UNIONS
Alternate name for KANSAS CITY COWBOYS, 1884.

KAUFMAN, TX

Kaufman
Central Texas Trolley League (D), mid-1915; new franchise. Disbanded with league during 1915 season.

KEARNEY, NE

Kearney Buffaloes
Nebraska State League (D), 1915; charter franchise. Had been KEARNEY KAPITALISTS, 1912–1914. Disbanded with league after 1915 season.

Kearney Kapitalists
Nebraska State League (D), 1912–1914; charter franchise. Renamed KEARNEY BUFFALOES, 1915.

Kearney Lambs
Nebraska State League, mid-1892; relocated franchise. Had been LIN-

COLN SENATORS, 1892. Disbanded with league after 1892 season.

Kearney Yankees
Nebraska State League (D), 1956–1959; charter franchise. Disbanded with league after 1959 season.

KEENE, NH

Keene Champs
Twin States League (D), 1911; charter franchise. Disbanded with league after 1911 season.

KELSO, WA

Kelso
Washington State League, 1897; charter franchise. Disbanded with league after 1897 season.

KEMP, TX

Kemp
East Texas League (D), 1916; charter franchise. Became JACKSONVILLE, mid-1916.

KENNEWICK–RICHLAND–PASCO, WA

Tri-City Angels
Northwest League (A), 1964; renamed franchise. Had been TRI-CITY BRAVES, 1962–1963. Renamed TRI-CITY ATOMS, 1965.

Tri-City A's
Northwest League (A), 1969; renamed franchise. Had been TRI-CITY ATOMS, 1965–1968. Renamed TRI-CITY PADRES, 1970.

Tri-City Atoms
Northwest League (B), 1961; renamed franchise. Had been TRI-CITY BRAVES, 1950–1960. Renamed TRI-CITY BRAVES, 1962.

Tri-City Atoms
Northwest League (A), 1965–1968; renamed franchise.

Had been TRI-CITY ANGELS, 1964. Renamed TRI-CITY A'S, 1969.

Tri-City Braves
Western International League (B), 1950–1951; (A), 1952–1954; new franchise. Northwest League (B), 1955–1960; charter franchise. Renamed TRI-CITY ATOMS, 1961.

Tri-City Braves
Northwest League (B), 1962; (A), 1963; renamed franchise. Had been TRI-CITY ATOMS, 1961. Renamed TRI-CITY ANGELS, 1964.

Tri-City Imperials
Northwest League (A), 1973; renamed franchise. Had been TRI-CITY PADRES, 1970–1972. Renamed TRI-CITIES PORTS, 1974.

Tri-City Padres
Northwest League (A), 1970–1972; renamed franchise. Had been TRI-CITY A'S, 1969. Renamed TRI-CITY IMPERIALS, 1973.

Tri-Cities Ports
Northwest League, 1974; renamed franchise. Had been TRI-CITY IMPERIALS, 1973. Disbanded after 1974 season.

Tri-City Triplets
Northwest League (A), 1983–1986; new franchise. Disbanded after 1896 season.

KENOSHA, WI

Kenosha Comets
All-American Girls Professional Baseball League, 1943–1951; charter franchise. Disbanded after 1951 season.

Kenosha Twins
Midwest League (A), 1984–(still in existence as of 5-1-92); new franchise.

KENT, OH

Kent Kenties
Ohio State League, 1895–1896; charter franchise. Disbanded with league after 1896 season.

Kent Kings
Ohio–Pennsylvania League (D), 1905; charter franchise. Disbanded after 1905 season.

KEOKUK, IA

Keokuk Cardinals
Midwest League (D), 1958–1962; new franchise. Became MIDWEST DODGERS, 1963.

Keokuk Indians
Iowa State League (D), 1904–1907; charter franchise. Central Association (D), 1908–1915; charter franchise. Disbanded after 1915 season.

Keokuk Indians
Mississippi Valley League (D), 1929–1932; (B), 1933; new franchise. Disbanded with league after 1933 season.

Keokuk Indians
Western League (A), 1935; new franchise. Disbanded after 1935 season.

Keokuk Keokuks
Western League, mid-1885; relocated franchise. Had been OMAHA OMAHOGS, 1885. Disbanded during 1885 season.

Keokuk Kernals
Three I League (B), 1952–1957; expansion franchise. Disbanded after 1957 season.

Keokuk Pirates
Central Association (C), 1947–1949; charter franchise. Disbanded with league after 1949 season.

WESTERN OF KEOKUK
National Association, 1875; expansion franchise. Disbanded during 1875 season.

KEWANEE, IL

Kewanee A's
Central Association (C), mid-1948–1949; relocated franchise. Had been MOLINE A'S, 1947–mid-1948. Disbanded with league after 1949 season.

Kewanee Boilermakers
Central Association (D), 1908–1913; charter franchise. Disbanded after 1913 season.

KEY WEST, FL

Key West Conchs
Florida International League (B), mid-1952–1953; relocated franchise. Had been FORT LAUDERDALE BRAVES, 1947–1952. Disbanded after 1953 season.

Key West Conchs
Florida State League (A), 1972–1974; renamed franchise. Had been KEY WEST SUN CAPS, 1971. Renamed KEY WEST CUBS, 1975.

Key West Cubs
Florida State League (A), 1975–1976; renamed franchise. Had been KEY WEST CONCHS, 1972–1974. Disbanded after 1976 season.

Key West Padres
Florida State League (A), 1969–1970; new franchise. Became KEY WEST SUN CAPS, 1971.

Key West Sun Caps
Florida State League (A), 1971; renamed franchise. Had been KEY WEST PADRES, 1969–1970. Renamed KEY WEST CONCHS, 1972.

KILGORE, TX

Kilgore Boomers
East Texas League (C), 1939–1940; renamed franchise. Had been KILGORE RANGERS, 1937–1938. Disbanded with league after 1940 season.

Kilgore Braves
East Texas League (C), 1936–1940; charter franchise. Renamed KILGORE RANGERS, 1937.

Kilgore Drillers
Lone Star League (C), 1947–1948; charter franchise. East Texas League (C), 1949–1950; charter franchise. Disbanded with league after 1950 season.

Kilgore Gushers
East Texas League (D), 1931; charter franchise. Disbanded with league during 1931 season.

Kilgore Rangers
East Texas League (C), 1937–1938; renamed franchise. Had been KILGORE BRAVES, 1936. Renamed KILGORE BOOMERS, 1939.

KINGMAN, KS

Kingman
Kansas State League (D), 1905; charter franchise. Became HOISINTON, mid-1905.

KINGSPORT, TN

Kingsport Braves
Appalachian League (R), 1974–1979; renamed franchise. Had been KINGSPORT ROYALS, 1969–1973. Renamed KINGSPORT METS, 1980.

Kingsport Cherokees
Appalachian League (D), 1938–1941; expansion franchise. Renamed KINGSPORT DODGERS, 1942.

Kingsport Cherokees (aka White Sox, 1948)
Appalachian League (D), 1943–1952; renamed franchise. Had been KINGSPORT DODGERS, 1942. Mountain States League (D), 1953–1954; new franchise. Appalachian League (D), 1955; new franchise. Disbanded with league after 1955 season.

Kingsport Dodgers
Appalachian League (D), 1942; renamed franchise. Had been KINGSPORT CHEROKEES, 1938–1941. Renamed KINGSPORT CHEROKEES, 1943.

Kingsport Indians
Appalachian League (D) 1921–1925; charter franchise. Disbanded with league during 1925 season.

Kingsport Mets
Appalachian League (R), 1980–(still in existence as of 5-1-92); renamed franchise. Had been KINGSPORT BRAVES, 1974–1979.

Kingsport Orioles
Appalachian League (D), 1957; charter franchise. Disbanded after 1957 season.

Kingsport Pirates
Appalachian League (D), 1960–1962, (R), 1963; new franchise. Disbanded after 1963 season.

Kingsport Royals
Appalachian League (R), 1969–1973; new franchise. Renamed KINGSPORT BRAVES, 1974.

Kingsport White Sox
Alternate name for KINGSPORT CHEROKEES, 1948.

KINGSTON, NH

Kingston
Southern New Hampshire (D), 1907; charter franchise. Disbanded with league after 1907 season.

KINGSTON, NY

Kingston
Hudson River League, 1886; charter franchise. Disbanded with league after 1886 season.

Kingston
Hudson River League, 1888; charter franchise. Disbanded with league after 1888 season.

Kingston Colonial Colts
Eastern Association (B), 1909; new franchise. Disbanded after 1909 season.

Kingston Colonials
Hudson River League (D), 1903–1905; charter franchise. Hudson River League (D), 1906; new franchise. Disbanded after 1906 season.

Kingston Colonials
New York–New Jersey League (D), 1913; charter franchise. Disbanded with league after 1913 season.

Kingston Colonials
Colonial League (B), mid-1948–mid-1950; Relocated franchise. Had been NEW BRUNSWICK HUBS, 1948. Disbanded with league during 1950 season. Canadian–American League (C), 1951; new franchise. Disbanded with league after 1951 season.

Kingston Dodgers (aka Ponies)
North Atlantic League (D), 1947; new franchise. Disbanded after 1947 season.

Kingston Ponies
Alternate name for KINGSTON DODGERS, 1947.

KINGSTON, ONTARIO, CANADA

Kingston
Eastern International League, 1888; charter franchise. Disbanded with league after 1888 season.

Kingston Ponies
Border League (C), 1946–1951; charter franchise. Disbanded with league during 1951 season.

KINGSVILLE, TX

Kingsville Jerseys
Gulf Coast League (D), 1926; charter franchise. Became MISSION GRAPEFRUITERS, mid-1926.

KINSTON, NC

Kinston
Eastern Carolina League (D), 1908; charter franchise. Disbanded after 1908 season.

Kinston Blue Jays
Carolina League (A), 1979; renamed franchise. Renamed KINSTON EAGLES, 1980.

Kinston Blue Jays
Carolina League (A), 1982–1985; renamed franchise. Renamed KINSTON EAGLES, 1986.

Kinston Eagles
Virginia League (B), 1925–1927; new franchise. Eastern Carolina League (D), 1928–1929; charter franchise. Disbanded with league after 1929 season.

Kinston Eagles
Coastal Plains League (D), 1937–1941; 1946–1952; charter franchise. Disbanded with league after 1952 season.

Kinston Eagles
Carolina League (B), 1956–mid-1957; new franchise. Became WILSON TOBS, mid-1957.

Kinston Eagles
Carolina League (B), 1962; (A), 1963–1968; new franchise. Renamed KINSTON YANKEES, 1969.

Kinston Eagles
Carolina League (A), 1970–1973; renamed franchise. Had been KINSTON YANKEES, 1969. Renamed KINSTON EXPOS, 1974.

Kinston Eagles
Carolina League (A), 1978; new franchise. Renamed KINSTON BLUE JAYS, 1979.

Kinston Eagles
Carolina League (A), 1980–1981; renamed franchise. Had been KINSTON BLUE JAYS, 1979. Renamed KINSTON BLUE JAYS, 1982.

Kinston Eagles
Carolina League (A), 1986; renamed franchise. Had been KINSTON BLUE JAYS, 1982–1985. Renamed KINSTON INDIANS, 1987.

Kinston Expos
Carolina League (A), 1974; renamed franchise. Had been KINSTON EAGLES, 1970–1973. Disbanded after 1974 season.

Kinston Indians
Carolina League (A), 1987–(still in existence as of 5-1-92); renamed franchise. Had been KINSTON EAGLES, 1986.

Kinston Yankees
Carolina League (A), 1969; renamed franchise. Had been KINSTON EAGLES, 1962–1968. Renamed KINSTON EAGLES, 1970.

KIRKSVILLE, MO

Kirksville Osteopaths
Missouri State League (D), 1911; charter franchise. Disbanded with league during 1911 season.

KISSIMEE, FL

Osceola Astros
Southern League (AA), 1985–(still in existence as of 5-1-92); new franchise.

KITCHNER, ONTARIO, CANADA

Kitchner Beavers
Michigan–Ontario League (B), 1919–1921; charter franchise. Renamed KITCHNER TERRIERS, 1922.

Kitchner Colts
Michigan–Ontario League (B), 1925; new franchise. Disbanded with league after 1925 season.

Kitchner Terriers
Michigan–Ontario League (B), 1922; renamed franchise. Had

Been KITCHNER BEAVERS, 1919–1921. Disbanded after 1922 season.

KITTANNING, PA

Kittanning Infants
Pennsylvania State League (D), 1907; new franchise. Disbanded with league after 1907 season.

KLAMATH FALLS, OR

Klamath Falls Gems
Far West League (D), 1948–1951; charter franchise. Disbanded with league after 1951 season.

KNOXVILLE, TX

Knoxville
Tennessee–Alabama League (D), 1904; charter franchise. Disbanded with league after 1904 season.

Knoxville Appalachians
South Atlantic League (C), 1909; Relocated franchise. Had been CHARLESTON SEA GULLS, 1904–mid-1909. Southeastern League (D), 1910; charter franchise. Appalachian League (D), 1911; charter franchise. Renamed KNOXVILLE REDS, mid-1911.

Knoxville Blue Jays
Southern League (AA), 1980– (still in existence as of 5-1-92); renamed franchise. Had been KNOXVILLE KNOX SOX, 1974–1979.

Knoxville Indians
Southeastern League, 1896–1897; charter franchise. Disbanded with league after 1897 season.

Knoxville Knox Sox
Southern League (AA), 1974–1979; renamed franchise. Had been KNOXVILLE SOX, 1973. Renamed KNOXVILLE BLUE JAYS, 1980.

Knoxville Pioneers
Appalachian League (D), 1921–1924; charter franchise. Disbanded after 1924 season.

Knoxville Reds
Appalachian League (D), mid-1911–1914; renamed franchise. Had been KNOXVILLE APPALACHIANS, 1909–1911. Disbanded with league during 1914 season.

Knoxville Smokies
South Atlantic Association (B), 1925–1929; new franchise. Disbanded after 1929 season.

Knoxville Smokies
Southern Association (A), mid-1931–1934; (A1), 1935–mid-1944; relocated franchise. Had been MOBILE MARINES, 1931. Became MOBILE BEARS, mid-1944.

Knoxville Smokies
Tri-State League (B), 1946–1952; charter franchise. Mountain States League (D), 1953; expansion franchise. Tri-State League (B), 1954; new franchise. Disbanded after 1954 season.

Knoxville Smokies
South Atlantic League (A), mid-1956–1963; relocated franchise. Had been MONTGOMERY REBELS, 1954–mid-1956. Southern League (AA), 1964–1967; charter franchise. Disbanded after 1967 season.

Knoxville Sox
Southern League (AA), 1973; renamed franchise. Had been KNOXVILLE WHITE SOX, 1972. Renamed KNOXVILLE KNOX SOX, 1974.

Knoxville White Sox
Southern League (AA), 1972; new franchise. Renamed KNOXVILLE SOX, 1973.

KOKOMO, IN

Kokomo
Indiana State League, 1890; charter franchise. Disbanded with league after 1890 season.

Kokomo
Indiana–Illinois State League, mid-1899; relocated franchise. Had been ANDERSON, 1899. Became MATTOON BROOM CORN RAISERS, mid-1899.

Kokomo
Indiana State League, 1900; charter franchise. Disbanded with league after 1900 season.

Kokomo Combines
Ohio–Indiana League (D), 1907; charter franchise. Disbanded with league after 1907 season.

Kokomo Dodgers
Midwest League (D), 1956–1961; charter franchise. Disbanded after 1961 season.

Kokomo Giants
MOV League (D), 1955; new franchise. Disbanded with league after 1955 season.

Kokomo Wildcats
Northern Indiana State League (D), 1909; charter franchise. Disbanded after 1909 season.

LaBARRA, MEXICO

LaBarra Portros
Mexican Center League (A), 1978; new franchise. Disbanded after 1978 season.

LACONIA, NH

Laconia
New Hampshire State (D), 1907; charter franchise. Became PLATTSBURGH BREWERS, mid-1907.

LaCrosse, WI

LaCrosse
Northwestern League, 1887; new franchise. Disbanded with league after 1887 season.

LaCrosse
Central Association (D), 1917; new franchise. Disbanded during 1917 season.

LaCrosse Badgers
Wisconsin State League (D), 1907; renamed franchise. Disbanded with league after 1907 season.

LaCrosse Blackhawks
Wisconsin State League (D), 1940–1942; charter franchise. Suspended operations with league after 1942 season, and did not rejoin when league resumed in 1946.

LaCrosse Colts
Northern League (C), mid-1913; relocated franchise. Had been ST. PAUL, mid-1913. Disbanded after 1913 season.

LaCrosse Outcasts
Minnesota–Wisconsin League (C), 1909; (D), 1910; (C), 1911; (D), 1912; charter franchise. Disbanded with league after 1912 season.

LaCrosse Pinks
Wisconsin State Association (D), 1905/League (D), 1906; charter franchise. Renamed LACROSSE BADGERS, 1907.

LaCrosse Pinks
Wisconsin–Illinois League (D), 1908; charter franchise. Had been LACROSSE BADGERS, 1907. Disbanded after 1908 season.

LAFAYETTE, IN

Lafayette
Central Inter-State League, mid-1888; relocated franchise. Had been DECATUR, 1888. Indiana State League, 1888; charter franchise. Became SOUTH BEND, mid-1888.

Lafayette
Illinois–Indiana League, 1889; charter franchise. Disbanded with league after 1889 season.

Lafayette
Western Indiana State League, 1890; charter franchise. Became ANDERSON, mid-1890.

Lafayette
Western Inter-State League, 1895; charter franchise. Became ANDERSON, mid-1895.

Lafayette Chiefs
MOV League (D), 1955; new franchise. Disbanded with league after 1955 season.

Lafayette Farmers
Northern State League of Indiana (D), 1910–1911; renamed franchise. Had been LAFAYETTE WETS, 1909. Disbanded with league after 1911 season.

Lafayette Red Sox
Midwest League (D), 1956–1957; charter franchise. Disbanded after 1957 season.

Lafayette Wets
Northern State of Indiana League (D), 1909; charter franchise. Renamed LAFAYETTE FARMERS, 1910.

LAFAYETTE, LA

Lafayette Brahman Bulls
Evangeline League (C), 1948–1949; new franchise. Renamed LAFAYETTE BULLS, 1950.

Lafayette Browns
Gulf Coast League (D), 1907; charter franchise. Disbanded after 1907 season.

Lafayette Bulls
Evangeline League (C), 1950–1953; renamed franchise. Had been LAFAYETTE BRAHMAN BULLS, 1948–1949. Renamed LAFAYETTE OILERS, 1954.

Lafayette Drillers
Texas League (AA), 1975–1976; relocated franchise. Had been AMARILLO GIANTS, 1971–1974. Became TULSA DRILLERS, 1977.

Lafayette Hubs
Louisiana State League (D), 1920; charter franchise. Disbanded with league after 1920 season.

Lafayette Oilers
Evangeline League (C), 1954–1957; renamed franchise, 1954. Disbanded with league after 1957 season.

Lafayette White Sox
Evangeline League (D), 1934–1942; charter franchise. Suspended operations with league after 1942 season, and did not rejoin when league resumed in 1946.

LAFERIA, TX

LaFeria Nighthawkes
Rio Grande Valley League (C), 1931; charter franchise. Disbanded with league in 1931 season.

LAGOON, UT

Lagoon
Inter-Mountain League, 1901; charter franchise. Disbanded with league during 1901 season.

LAGOS DE MORENO, MEXICO

Lagos de Moreno Caporales (Chiefs)
Mexican Center League (A), 1975–1977; new franchise. Disbanded after 1977 season.

LaGrande, OR

LaGrande
Pacific Inter-State League, 1891; charter franchise. Disbanded with league after 1891 season.

LaGrande
Inland Empire League (D), 1908; charter franchise. Disbanded with league after 1908 season.

LaGrande Spuds
Western Tri-State League (D), 1912–mid-1913; charter franchise. Became BAKER GOLDDIGGERS (aka Miners), mid-1913.

LaGrange, GA

LaGrange
Georgia State League (D), 1920–1921; charter franchise. Disbanded with league during 1921 season.

LaGrange Grangers
Georgia–Alabama League (C), 1916–1917; renamed franchise. Had been LAGRANGE TERRAPINS, 1913–1915. Disbanded with league after 1917 season.

LaGrange Rebels
Alternate name for LAGRANGE TROUPERS.

LaGrange Terrapins
Georgia–Alabama League (C), 1913–1915; charter franchise. Renamed LAGRANGE GRANGERS, 1916.

LaGrange Troupers (aka Rebels)
Georgia–Alabama League (D), 1946–1951; charter franchise. Disbanded with league after 1951 season.

Laguna, Mexico
(See DURANGO, MEXICO)

Lake Charles, LA

Lake Charles Creoles
South Texas League (D), 1906; expansion franchise. Gulf Coast League (D), 1907–1908; charter franchise. Disbanded with league after 1908 season.

Lake Charles Exporters
Evangeline League (D), 1934; charter franchise.

Lake Charles Giants
Evangeline League (C), 1956–1957; renamed franchise. Had been LAKE CHARLES LAKERS, 1950–1953. Disbanded with league after 1957 season.

Lake Charles Lakers
Gulf Coast League (C), 1950; (B), 1951–1953; charter franchise. Evangeline League (C), 1954–1955; expansion franchise. Renamed LAKE CHARLES GIANTS, 1956.

Lake Charles Newporters
Cotton States League (D), 1929–1930; relocated franchise. Had been MERIDIAN METROS, 1927–1929. Disbanded during 1930 season.

Lake Charles Skippers
Evangeline League (D), 1935–1942; new franchise. Disbanded after 1942 season.

Lakeland, FL

Lakeland Giants
Florida State League (D), 1962; new franchise. Renamed LAKELAND TIGERS, 1963.

Lakeland Highlanders
Florida State League (D), 1919–1920; (C), 1921–mid-1924; charter franchise. Disbanded with league during 1924 season. Florida State League (C), 1925–1926; charter franchise. Disbanded with league after 1926 season.

Lakeland Indians
Florida State League (D), 1960; new franchise. Disbanded after 1960 season.

Lakeland Patriots
Florida International League (B), 1951; renamed franchise. Had been LAKELAND PILOTS, 1946–1950. Renamed LAKELAND PILOTS, 1952.

Lakeland Pilots
Florida International League (C), 1946–1948; (B), 1949–1950; charter franchise. Renamed LAKELAND PATRIOTS, 1951.

Lakeland Pilots
Florida International League (B), 1952; renamed franchise. Had been LAKELAND PATRIOTS, 1951. Disbanded after 1952 season.

Lakeland Pilots
Florida State League (D), mid-1953–1955; relocated franchise. Had been PALATKA AZALEAS, 1946–mid-1953. Disbanded after 1955 season.

Lakeland Tigers
Florida State League (A), 1963–1964; renamed franchise. Had been LAKELAND GIANTS, 1962. Disbanded after 1964 season.

Lakeland Tigers
Florida State League (A), 1967– (still in existence as of 5-1-92); new franchise.

Lake Linden, MI

Lake Linden Lakes
Copper County–Soo League (D), 1905; charter franchise. Disbanded with league during 1905 season.

Lake Linden Lakes
Northern Copper County League (C), 1906–1907; charter franchise. Disbanded with league after 1907 season.

La Marque, TX
(See TEXAS CITY, TX)

LAMESA, TX

Lamesa Dodgers
West Texas–New Mexico League (D), 1942; renamed franchise. Had been LAMESA LOBOS, 1939–1941. Disbanded during 1942 season.

Lamesa Indians
Southwestern League (D), mid-1957; Relocated franchise. Had been MIDLAND INDIANS, 1947–1957. Disbanded with league after 1957 season.

Lamesa Loboes
West Texas–New Mexico League (D), 1939–1941; new franchise. Renamed LAMESA DODGERS, 1942.

Lamesa Lobos
West Texas–New Mexico League (C), 1946–1952; charter franchise. Became PLAINVIEW PONIES, 1953.

Lamesa Lobos
Longhorn League (C), 1953; new franchise. Became BALLINGER-WINTERS EAGLES, mid-1953.

LAMPASSAS, TX

Lampassas
Middle Texas League (D), 1914; charter franchise. Disbanded during 1914 season.

LANCASTER, OH

Lancaster Lanks
Ohio–Pennsylvania League (D), 1905–1907; charter franchise. Ohio State League (D), 1908–1910, (C), 1911; charter franchise. Disbanded after 1911 season.

LANCASTER, PA

Lancaster
Pennsylvania State Association, 1886; charter franchise. Became DANVILLE, mid-1886.

Lancaster
Middle States League, 1889; new franchise. Disbanded during 1889 season.

Lancaster
Pennsylvania State League, 1890; charter franchise. Became ALLENTOWN, mid-1890.

Lancaster
Pennsylvania State League (D), 1902; charter franchise. Disbanded with league after 1902 season.

Lancaster Chicks
Pennsylvania State League, mid-1894–1896; relocated franchise. Had been ALTOONA, 1892–1894. Disbanded with league after 1896 season.

Lancaster Ironsides
Eastern League, mid-1884–mid-1885; relocated franchise. Had been BALTIMORE MONUMENTALS, 1884. Became BRIDGEPORT GIANTS, mid-1885.

Lancaster Maroons
Atlantic League, mid-1896–1899; relocated franchise. Had been NEW HAVEN STUDENTS, 1896. Disbanded after 1899 season.

Lancaster Red Roses
Tri-State League (D), 1907–mid-1912; charter franchise. Became ATLANTIC CITY, mid-1912.

Lancaster Red Roses
Tri-State League (D), mid-1914; relocated franchise. Had been YORK WHITE ROSES, 1909–mid-1914. Disbanded with league after 1914 season.

Lancaster Red Roses
Inter-State League, 1940–1952; relocated franchise. Had been HAZLETON MOUNTAINEERS, 1939–1940. Disbanded with league after 1952 season.

Lancaster Red Roses
Piedmont League (B), 1954–1955; new franchise. Disbanded with league after 1955 season.

Lancaster Red Roses
Eastern League (A), 1958–1961; new franchise. Disbanded after 1961 season.

Lancaster Red Sox
Inter-State League (D), 1932; charter franchise. Disbanded with league after 1932 season.

LANDIS, NC

Landis Dodgers
North Carolina State League (D), 1940; renamed franchise. Had been LANDIS SENS, 1937–1939. Renamed LANDIS SENATORS, 1941.

Landis Millers
North Carolina State League (D), 1942; 1945–1947; renamed franchise. Had been LANDIS SENATORS, 1941. Disbanded after 1947 season.

Landis Senators
North Carolina State League (D), 1941; renamed franchise. Had been LANDIS DODGERS, 1940. Renamed LANDIS MILLERS, 1942.

Landis Sens
North Carolina State League (D), 1937–1939; charter franchise. Renamed LANDIS DODGERS, 1940

Landis Spinners
North Carolina State League (D), 1949–mid-1951; new franchise. Became ELKIN BLANKETEERS, mid-1951.

LANGDALE, GA
(See LANNETT, GA)

LANNETT, AL

Lannett Rebels
Georgia–Alabama League (C), 1951; relocated franchise. Had been VALLEY REBELS, 1946–1950. Disbanded with league after 1951 season.

LANNETT–LANGDALE– FAIRFAX–SHAWMUT, AL– WEST POINT, GA

Valley Rebels
Georgia–Alabama League (C), 1946–1950; charter franchise. Became LANNETT REBELS, 1951.

LANSDALE, PA

Lansdale Dukes
North Atlantic League (D), 1948; charter franchise. Disbanded after 1948 season.

LANSING, MI

Lansing
Michigan State League, 1890; charter franchise. Disbanded with league during 1890 season.

Lansing
Michigan State League, 1897; charter franchise. Disbanded during 1897 season.

Lansing
Michigan State League (D), 1902; charter franchise. Disbanded with league during 1902 season.

Lansing
Michigan State League (D), 1926; charter franchise. Disbanded with league after 1926 season.

Lansing Lancers
Michigan State League (C), 1940; charter franchise. Renamed LANSING SENATORS, 1941.

Lansing Senators
Southern Michigan League (D), 1907, 1909–1910, (C), 1911–mid-1912; (D), mid-1912–mid-1914/Association (D), 1908; new franchise. Became MOUNT CLEMENS BATHERS, mid-1914.

Lansing Senators
Central League (D), 1921–1922; new franchise. Disbanded with league after 1922 season.

Lansing Senators
Michigan State League (C), 1941; renamed franchise. Had been LANSING LANCERS, 1940. Disbanded with league after 1941 season.

Lansing Senators
Michigan State League, 1895; new franchise. Disbanded with league after 1895 season.

LAREDO, TX

Laredo Apaches
Rio Grande Valley League (D), 1949–1950; charter franchise. Gulf Coast League (B), 1951–1953; charter franchise. Disbanded with league after 1953 season.

Laredo Bermudas
Southwest Texas League (D), 1910–1911; charter franchise. Disbanded with league after 1911 season.

Laredo Oilers
Gulf Coast League (D), mid-1926; charter franchise. Had been BEEVILLE BEES, 1926. Texas Valley League (D), 1927; charter franchise. Disbanded after 1927 season.

LARNED, KS

Larned Wheat Kings
Kansas State League (D), mid-1909–1911; relocated franchise. Had been TWIN CITIES, 1909. Disbanded with league after 1911 season.

LaSALLE, IL

LaSalle Blue Sox
Illinois–Missouri League (D), 1914; new franchise. Disbanded with league after 1914 season.

LAS CHOAPAS, VERACRUZ, MEXICO

Las Choapas Reds
Mexican Southeast League (A), mid-1967–mid-1969; relocated franchise. Had been VILLAHERMOSA PLATANEROS, 1966–mid-1967. Became MINATITLAN REDS, mid-1969.

LAS CRUCES, NM

Las Cruces Farmers
Rio Grande Valley Association, 1915; charter franchise. Disbanded with league after 1915 season.

LAS VEGAS, NV

Las Vegas Pirates
California League (C), mid-1958; relocated franchise. Had been SAN JOSE PIRATES, 1958. Disbanded after 1958 season.

Las Vegas Stars
Pacific Coast League (AAA), 1983–(still in existence as of 5-1-92); relocated franchise. Had been SPOKANE INDIANS, 1958–1982.

Las Vegas Wranglers
Sunset League (C), 1947–1950; charter franchise. Southwest International League, 1951–1952; charter franchise. Disbanded after 1952 season.

Las Vegas Wranglers
Arizona–Mexico League (C), 1957; new franchise. Disbanded after 1957 season.

LATROBE, PA

Latrobe
Eastern State League, 1889; charter franchise. Disbanded during 1889 season.

Latrobe
Western Pennsylvania League (D), 1907; charter franchise. Became CUMBERLAND ROOTERS, mid-1907.

LAUREL, DE

Laurel Blue Hens
Eastern Shore League (D), 1922–1923; charter franchise. Disbanded after 1923 season.

LAUREL, MS

Laurel Baby Cardinals
Cotton States League (D), 1929; renamed franchise. Had been LAUREL JUNIOR CARDINALS, 1928. Disbanded after 1929 season.

Laurel Junior Cardinals
Cotton States League (D), 1928; renamed franchise. Had been LAUREL LUMBERJACKS, 1923–1927. Renamed LAUREL BABY CARDINALS, 1929.

Laurel Lumberjacks
Cotton States League (D), 1923–1927; expansion franchise. Renamed LAUREL JUNIOR CARDINALS, 1928.

LAURINBURG, NC
(See RED SPRINGS, NC)

LAWRENCE, KS

Lawrence Collegians (aka Farmers)
Southwestern League, 1893; charter franchise. Disbanded with league after 1893 season.

Lawrence Farmers
Alternate name for LAWRENCE COLLEGIANS.

Lawrence Orioles
Kansas–Missouri League, 1892; charter franchise. Disbanded with league after 1892 season.

LAWRENCE, MA

Lawrence
Massachusetts State Association, 1884; charter franchise. Eastern New England League, 1885; charter franchise. New England League, 1886–mid-1887; charter franchise. Became SALEM FAIRIES, mid-1887.

Lawrence
New England Inter-State League, 1888; charter franchise. Disbanded with league after 1888 season.

Lawrence
New England League, mid-1892; relocated franchise. Had been MANCHESTER, 1891–mid-1892. Disbanded with league during 1892 season.

Lawrence
New England League, mid-1899; relocated franchise. Had been FITCHBURG, 1899. Disbanded with league after 1899 season.

Lawrence
New England League (B), mid-1905–1910; relocated franchise. Had been MANCHESTER, 1901–mid-1905. Renamed LAWRENCE BARRISTERS, 1911.

Lawrence
New England League (B), 1919; charter franchise. Disbanded with league during 1919 season.

Lawrence
New England League (B), mid-1933; relocated franchise. Had been ATTLEBORO, 1933. Became WOONSOCKET, mid-1933.

Lawrence Barristers
New England League (B), 1911–1915; renamed franchise. Had been LAWRENCE COLTS, 1902–1910. Eastern League (B), 1916–1917; charter franchise. Disbanded after 1917 season.

Lawrence Colts
New England League (B), 1902–1904; new franchise. Disbanded after 1904 season.

Lawrence Indians
New England Association, 1895; charter franchise. Disbanded with association after 1895 season.

Lawrence Merry Macks
New England League (B), 1926–1928; charter franchise. Disbanded after 1928 season.

Lawrence Millionaires
New England League (B), 1946; charter franchise. Renamed LAWRENCE ORPHANS, 1947.

Lawrence Orphans
New England League (B), 1947; charter franchise. Had been LAWRENCE MILLIONAIRES, 1946. Became LOWELL ORPHANS, mid-1947.

LAWRENCEBURG, KY

Lawrenceburg
Blue Grass League (D), 1908; charter franchise. Disbanded after 1908 season.

LAWRENCEVILLE, VA

Lawrenceville Cardinals
Virginia League (D), 1948; new franchise. Renamed LAWRENCEVILLE ROBINS, 1949.

Lawrenceville Robins
Virginia League (D), 1949; renamed franchise. Had been LAWRENCEVILLE CARDINALS, 1948. Became ELIZABETH CITY ALBEMARLES, 1950.

LAWTON, OK

Lawton Braves
Sooner State League (D), 1954–1957; renamed franchise. Had been LAWTON REDS, 1952–1953. Disbanded with league after 1957 season.

Lawton Giants
Sooner State League (D), 1947–1951; charter franchise. Renamed LAWTON REDS, 1952.

Lawton Medicine Men
Texas–Oklahoma League (D), 1911; charter franchise. Disbanded during 1911 season.

Lawton Reds
Sooner State League (D), 1952–1953; renamed franchise. Had been LAWTON GIANTS, 1947–1951. Renamed LAWTON BRAVES, 1954.

LEAD, SD

Lead Grays
Black Hills League, 1891–1892; charter franchise. Disbanded with league after 1892 season.

LEADVILLE, CO

Leadville
Colorado League, 1885; charter franchise. Disbanded with league after 1885 season.

Leadville Angels
Colorado State League, 1896; new franchise. Disbanded with league during 1896 season.

Leadville Blues
Western League, 1886; new franchise. Disbanded during 1886 season.

Leadville Blues
Colorado State League, 1889; charter franchise. Disbanded with league after 1889 season.

LEAKSVILLE, NC

Leaksville Triplets
Blue Ridge League (D), 1948; new franchise. Became ABINGDON, mid-1948.

LEAKSVILLE–SPRAY–DRAPER, NC

Tri-City Triplets
Bi-State League (NC–VA), (D), 1934–1942; charter franchise. Disbanded with league after 1942 season.

Tri-City Triplets (or Trips)
Carolina League (C), 1945–1947; charter franchise. Became LEAKSVILLE, 1948.

LEAVENWORTH, KS

Leavenworth Braves
Western Association (C), 1946–1949; charter franchise. Disbanded after 1949 season.

Leavenworth Convicts
Western Association (C), 1907; renamed franchise. Had been LEAVENWORTH OLD SOLDIERS, 1906. Disbanded after 1907 season.

Leavenworth Maroons
Western League, 1886–mid-1889; new franchise. Became HASTINGS, mid-1889.

Leavenworth Old Soldiers
Western Association (C), 1906; renamed franchise. Had been LEAVENWORTH ORIOLES, 1904–1905. Renamed LEAVENWORTH CONVICTS, 1907.

Leavenworth Orioles
Missouri Valley League (D), 1904; new franchise. Western Association (D), 1905; charter franchise. Renamed LEAVENWORTH OLD SOLDIERS, 1906.

Leavenworth Reds
Kansas State League, 1895; charter franchise. Disbanded during 1895 season.

Leavenworth Woodpeckers
Western League, 1886–1887; charter franchise. Disbanded during 1887 season.

LEBANON, PA

Lebanon
Eastern Inter-States League, 1889; charter franchise. Middle States League, 1889; charter franchise. Pennsylvania State League, 1890;

charter franchise. Disbanded with league during 1890 season.

Lebanon
Atlantic Association, 1890; relocated franchise. Had been WORCESTER, 1889–mid-1890. Disbanded with association after 1890 season.

Lebanon
Schuykill Valley League, 1896; charter franchise. Disbanded with league during 1896 season.

Lebanon
Pennsylvania State League (D), 1902; charter franchise. Disbanded with league after 1902 season.

Lebanon
Tri-State League (D), 1904; charter franchise. Disbanded after 1904 season.

Lebanon
Pennsylvania State League (D), 1916; charter franchise. Became MOUNT CARMEL, mid-1916.

Lebanon
Keystone League (D), 1935; charter franchise. Disbanded with league after 1935 season.

Lebanon Cedars
Eastern Association, 1891; charter franchise. Disbanded with association during 1891 season.

Lebanon Chix
North Atlantic League (D), 1949–1950; new franchise. Disbanded with league after 1950 season.

Lebanon Pretzel Eaters
Pennsylvania State League, 1892; charter franchise. Disbanded with league during 1892 season.

LEESBURG, FL

Leesburg Anglers
Florida State League (D), 1939–1941; renamed franchise. Had been LEESBURG GONDOLIERS, 1936–1938. Suspended operations after

1941 season, and resumed as LEESBURG ANGLERS, 1946.

Leesburg Athletics
Florida State League (A), 1965–1968; new franchise. Disbanded after 1968 season.

Leesburg Braves
Florida State League (D), 1954–1957; renamed franchise. Had been LEESBURG LAKERS, 1953. Disbanded after 1957 season.

Leesburg Dodgers
Florida State League (D), 1949; renamed franchise. Had been LEESBURG PIRATES, 1947–1948. Renamed LEESBURG PACKERS, 1950.

Leesburg Gondoliers (aka Anglers)
Florida State League (D), 1936–1938; charter franchise. Renamed LEESBURG ANGLERS, 1939.

Leesburg Lakers
Florida State League (D), 1953; renamed franchise. Had been LEESBURG PACKERS, 1950–1952. Renamed LEESBURG BRAVES, 1954.

Leesburg Orioles
Florida State League (D), 1960–1961; new franchise. Disbanded after 1961 season.

Leesburg Packers
Florida State League (D), 1946; charter franchise. Renamed LEESBURG PIRATES, 1947.

Leesburg Packers
Florida State League (D), 1950–1952; renamed franchise. Had been LEESBURG DODGERS, 1949. Renamed LEESBURG LAKERS, 1953.

Leesburg Pirates
Florida State League (D), 1947–1948; renamed franchise. Had been LEESBURG ANGLERS, 1946. Renamed LEESBURG DODGERS, 1949.

LEESVILLE, LA

Leesville Angels
Gulf Coast League (D), mid-1950; relocated franchise. Had been LUFKIN ANGELS, 1950. Disbanded after 1950 season.

LeMARS, IA

LeMars
Iowa–South Dakota League (D), 1902–1903; charter franchise. Disbanded with league after 1903 season.

LENOIR, NC

Lenoir Indians
Tar Heel League (D), 1939; charter franchise. Renamed LENOIR REDS, 1940.

Lenoir Reds
Tar Heel League (D), 1940; renamed franchise. Had been LENOIR INDIANS, 1939. Disbanded with league after 1940 season.

Lenoir Red Sox
Blue Ridge League (D), mid-1946–1947; relocated franchise. Had been SALEM FRIENDS, 1946. Western Carolinas League (D), 1948–1951; charter franchise. Disbanded after 1951 season.

LEON, GUANAJUATO, MEXICO
(See also GUANAJUATO, MEXICO)

Leon Aguiluchos
Mexican League (AAA), 1970–1971; renamed franchise. Had been LEON EAGLES, 1968–1969. Disbanded after 1971 season.

Leon Bravos (Braves)
Mexican League (AAA), 1983–(still in existence as of 5-1-92); new franchise.

Leon Broncos
Mexican Center League (A), 1964; renamed franchise. Had been LEON DIABLOS VERDES, 1963. Renamed LEON DIABLOS VERDES, 1965.

Leon Cachorros
Alternate name for LEON EAGLES, 1979–1980.

Leon Diablos Verdes
Mexican Center League (A), 1963; renamed franchise. Had been LEON SHOEMAKERS, 1962. Renamed LEON BRONCOS, 1964.

Leon Diablos Verdes
Mexican Center League (A), 1965–1967; renamed franchise. Had been LEON BRONCOS, 1964. Disbanded after 1967 season.

Leon Eagles
Mexican Center League (C), 1961; renamed franchise. Had been LEON RED DEVILS, 1960. Renamed LEON SHOEMAKERS, 1962.

Leon Eagles (aka Cachorros)
Mexican Center League (A), 1979–1980; new franchise. Disbanded after 1980 season. Renamed LEON AGUILUCHOS, 1970.

Leon Lechugueros
Mexican Center League (A), 1975; new franchise. Disbanded with league after 1975 season.

Leon Red Devils
Mexican Center League (D), 1960; charter franchise. Renamed LEON EAGLES, 1961.

Leon Shoemakers
Mexican Center League (C), 1962; renamed franchise. Had been LEON EAGLES, 1961. Renamed LEON DIABLOS VERDES, 1963.

LETHBRIDGE, ALBERTA, CANADA

Lethbridge
Western Canada League (D), 1907; charter franchise. Disbanded with league after 1907 season.

Lethbridge Dodgers
Pioneer League ("Summer Class A"), 1977–1978; (R), 1979–1983; new franchise. Had been LETHBRIDGE EXPOS, 1975–1976. Disbanded after 1983 season.

Lethbridge Expos
Pioneer League (R), 1975–1976; new franchise. Renamed LETHBRIDGE DODGERS, 1977.

Lethbridge Miners
Western Canada League (D), 1909–1911; charter franchise. Disbanded after 1911 season.

LEWISTON, ID

Lewiston Broncs
Pioneer League (R), 1971–1974; relocated franchise. Had been LEWIS–CLARK BRONCS, 1969–1970. Disbanded after 1974 season.

Lewiston Broncs
Western International League (A), 1952–1954; new franchise. Northwest League (B), 1955–1962; (A), 1963–1968; charter franchise. Became LEWIS–CLARK BRONCS, 1969.

Lewiston Indians
Western International League (B), 1937; charter franchise. Disbanded after 1937 season.

Lewiston Indians
Pioneer League (C), 1939; charter franchise. Disbanded after 1939 season.

LEWISTON, ID– CLARKSTON, WA

Lewis–Clark Broncs
Northwest League (A), 1969–1970; relocated franchise. Had been LEWIS-TON BRONCS, 1952–1968. Became LEWISTON BRONCS, 1971.

LEWISTON, ME

Lewiston
New England League, 1891–1896; charter franchise. Maine State League, 1897; charter franchise. Disbanded with league after 1897 season.

Lewiston
New England League, 1901; charter franchise. Disbanded after 1901 season.

Lewiston
Atlantic Association (D), 1908; charter franchise. Disbanded with league after 1908 season.

Lewiston Cupids
New England League (B), 1914–1915; new franchise. Disbanded with league after 1915 season.

LEWISTON– AUBURN, ME

Lewiston–Auburn Twins
New England League (B), 1919; charter franchise. Disbanded with league after 1919 season.

Lewiston–Auburn Twins
New England League (B), 1926– mid-1930; charter franchise. Disbanded with league during 1930 season.

LEWISTON, PA

Lewiston Independents
Pennsylvania State Association, 1886; charter franchise. Disbanded during 1886 season.

LEXINGTON, KY

Lexington
Inter-State League, 1885; charter franchise. Disbanded with league during 1885 season.

Lexington
Ohio State League (D), 1913– 1916; new franchise. Disbanded with league after 1916 season.

Lexington Colts
Blue Grass League (D), 1908– 1912; charter franchise. Disbanded with league after 1912 season.

Lexington Reds
Blue Grass League (D), 1922– 1923; charter franchise. Renamed LEXINGTON STUDEBAKERS, 1924.

Lexington Studebakers
Blue Grass League (D), 1924; renamed franchise. Had been LEX-INGTON REDS, 1922–1923. Disbanded with league after 1924 season.

LEXINGTON, NE

Lexington Red Sox
Nebraska State League (D), 1956– 1958; charter franchise. Disbanded after 1958 season.

LEXINGTON, NC

Lexington A's
North Carolina State League (D), 1945–1948; charter franchise. Renamed LEXINGTON INDIANS, 1949.

Lexington A's
North Carolina State League (D), 1950; renamed franchise. Had been LEXINGTON INDIANS, 1949. Renamed LEXINGTON INDIANS, 1951.

Lexington Giants
Western Carolinas League (A), 1963–1966; charter franchise. Renamed LEXINGTON RED SOX, 1967.

Lexington Indians
North Carolina State League (D), 1937–1942; charter franchise. Suspended operations with league after 1942 season, and resumed as LEXINGTON A'S, 1945.

Lexington Indians
North Carolina State League (D), 1949; renamed franchise. Had been LEXINGTON A'S, 1945–1948. Renamed LEXINGTON A'S, 1950.

Lexington Indians
North Carolina State League (D), 1951–1952; renamed franchise. Had been LEXINGTON A'S, 1950. Tar Heel League (D), 1953; charter franchise. Disbanded after 1953 season.

Lexington Indians
Western Carolinas League (D), 1960–1961; charter franchise. Disbanded after 1961 season.

Lexington Red Sox
Western Carolinas League (A), 1967; charter franchise. Disbanded after 1967 season.

LEXINGTON, TN

Lexington Colts
Mountain States League (D), 1954; new franchise. Disbanded with league after 1954 season.

Lexington Giants
KITTY League (D), mid-1935–1938; charter franchise. Disbanded after 1938 season.

LIGONIER, IN

Ligonier
Indiana–Michigan League (D), 1910; charter franchise. Disbanded with league after 1910 season.

LIMA, OH

Lima
Ohio State League, 1896; charter franchise. Disbanded with league after 1896 season.

Lima
Inter-State Association (C), 1906; charter franchise. Disbanded with league after 1906 season.

Lima
Buckeye League (D), 1915; charter franchise. Disbanded with league after 1915 season.

Lima Bean Eaters
Tri-State League, 1888; charter franchise. Disbanded after 1888 season

Lima Buckeyes
Central League (B), 1934; charter franchise. Disbanded with league after 1934 season.

Lima Chiefs
Ohio–Indiana League (D), 1949; renamed franchise. Had been LIMA TERRIERS, 1946–1948. Renamed LIMA PHILLIES, 1950.

Lima Cigarmakers
Ohio State League (D), 1908–1910; (C), 1910; (D), 1911–1912; charter franchise. Disbanded after 1912 season.

Lima Farmers
Eastern Inter-State League, mid-1895; relocated franchise. Had been AKRON AKRONS, mid-1895. Disbanded during 1895 season.

Lima Pandas
Ohio State League (D), 1939–1941; new franchise. Suspended operations after 1941 season, and resumed as LIMA TERRIERS, 1946.

Lima Phillies
Ohio–Indiana League (D), 1950–1951; renamed franchise. Had been LIMA CHIEFS, 1949. Disbanded with league after 1951 season.

Lima Red Birds
Ohio State League (D), 1944; charter franchise. Renamed LIMA TERRIERS, 1946.

Lima Reds
Ohio State League (D), 1945; renamed franchise. Had been LIMA RED BIRDS, 1944. Renamed LIMA TERRIERS, 1946.

Lima Terriers
Ohio State League (D), 1946–1947; renamed franchise. Had been LIMA REDS, 1945. Ohio–Indiana League (D), 1948; charter franchise. Renamed LIMA CHIEFS, 1949.

LINCOLN GIANTS
Eastern Colored League, 1923–1926; 1928; charter franchise. Disbanded with league during 1928 season. American Negro League, 1929; charter franchise. Disbanded with league after 1929 season.

LINCOLN, IL

Lincoln Abes (aka Blackhawks, Babes and Champs)
Illinois–Missouri League (D), 1910–1914; new franchise. Disbanded with league after 1914 season.

Lincoln Babes
Alternate name for LINCOLN ABES.

Lincoln Blackhawks
Alternate name for LINCOLN ABES.

Lincoln Champs
Alternate name for LINCOLN ABES.

LINCOLN, NE

Lincoln A's
Alternate name for LINCOLN ATHLETICS.

Lincoln Athletics (aka A's)
Western League (A), 1947–1952; charter franchise. Renamed LINCOLN CHIEFS, 1953.

Lincoln Browns
Nebraska State League (D), 1928; charter franchise. Renamed LINCOLN LINKS, 1929.

Lincoln Chiefs
Western League (A), 1953–1958; renamed franchise. Three I League (B), 1959–1961; new franchise.

Disbanded with league after 1961 season.

Lincoln Cornhuskers
Alternate name for LINCOLN DUCK-LINGS, 1907.

Lincoln Ducklings
Western League (A), 1906; new franchise. Renamed LINCOLN TREEPLANTERS, 1907.

Lincoln Links
Western League (A), 1917; renamed franchise. Had been LIN-COLN TIGERS, 1914–1916. Disbanded after 1917 season.

Lincoln Links
Nebraska State League (D), 1922–1923; charter franchise. Western League (A), 1924–1927; new franchise. Disbanded after 1927 season.

Lincoln Links
Nebraska State League (D), 1929–1935; renamed franchise. Had been LINCOLN BROWNS, 1928. Renamed LINCOLN RED LINKS, 1936.

Lincoln Links
Nebraska State League (D), 1938; new franchise. Western League (D), 1939; charter franchise. Disbanded after 1939 season.

Lincoln Missing Links
Western Association, 1895; renamed franchise. Had been LIN-COLN TREEPLANTERS, 1894. Disbanded after 1895 season.

Lincoln Railsplitters
Western League (A), 1908–1913; renamed franchise. Had been LIN-COLN TREEPLANTERS, 1907. Renamed LINCOLN TIGERS, 1914.

Lincoln Red Links
Nebraska State League (D), 1936; renamed franchise. Had been LIN-COLN LINKS, 1929–1935. Disbanded after 1936 season.

Lincoln Senators
Nebraska State League, 1892; charter franchise. Became KEARNEY LAMBS, mid-1892.

Lincoln Sterlings
Alternate name for the LINCOLN DUCKLINGS, 1907.

Lincoln Tigers
Western League (A), 1914–1916; renamed franchise. Had been LIN-COLN GREENBACKERS, 1908–1913. Renamed LINCOLN LINKS, 1917.

Lincoln Treeplanters
Western League, 1886–mid-1888; charter franchise. Became NEW-TON, mid-1888.

Lincoln Treeplanters
Western Association, mid-1890; relocated franchise. Had been DES MOINES COLTS, 1888–1890. Disbanded after 1890 season.

Lincoln Treeplanters
Western Association, 1894; charter franchise. Renamed LINCOLN MISSING LINKS, 1895.

Lincoln Treeplanters
Western League (A), 1907; renamed franchise. Had been LIN-COLN DUCKLINGS, 1906. Renamed LINCOLN RAILSPLITTERS, 1908.

LINCOLNTON, NC

Lincolnton Cardinals (aka Cards, 1950–1953)
Western Carolina League (D), 1948–1952; charter franchise. Tar Heel League (D), 1953; charter franchise. Became STATESVILLE SPORTS, mid-1953.

LINDALE, GA
(See also ROME, GA)

Lindale
Georgia–Alabama League (C), 1917; new franchise. Disbanded with league after 1917 season.

Lindale
Georgia State League (D), 1920–1921; charter franchise. Disbanded with league after 1921 season.

Lindale Collegians
Georgia–Alabama League (C), 1929; charter franchise. Renamed LINDALE PEPPERELLS, 1930.

Lindale Dragons
Georgia–Alabama Association (C), 1928; charter franchise. Became LINDALE COLLEGIANS, Georgia–Alabama League, 1929.

Lindale Pepperells
Georgia–Alabama League (C), 1930; renamed franchise. Had been LINDALE COLLEGIANS, 1929. Disbanded with league after 1930 season.

LINTON, IN

Linton
Eastern Illinois League (D), mid-1908; relocated franchise. Had been PANA COAL MINERS, 1907–mid-1908. Disbanded with league after 1908 season.

LITTLE FALLS, MN
(See also BRAINERD, MN)

Little Falls
Northern League (D), 1933; charter franchise. Disbanded during 1933 season.

LITTLE FALLS, NY

Little Falls Mets
New York–Pennsylvania League (A), 1977–1988; new franchise. Disbanded after 1988 season.

LITTLE RIVER, KS

Little River
Central Kansas League, 1908; new franchise. Disbanded after 1908 season.

LITTLE ROCK, AR

Arkansas (aka Little Rock) Travelers
Southern Association, 1901; (A), 1902–1909; charter franchise. Became CHATTANOOGA LOOKOUTS, 1910.

Arkansas (aka Little Rock) Travelers
Southern Association (A), 1915–1934; (A1), 1935–1945; (AA), 1946–1958; 1960–61; relocated franchise. Had been MONTGOMERY BLACK SOX, 1903–1915. Had also represented Montgomery, mid-1956. Disbanded with league after 1961 season.

Arkansas Travelers
International League (AAA), 1963; new franchise. Pacific Coast League (AAA), 1964–1968; expansion franchise. Texas League (AA), 1969–1970; new franchise. Dixie Association (C), 1971; charter franchise. Texas League (AA), 1972–(still in existence as of 5-1-92); charter franchise.

Little Rock
Southwestern League, 1898; charter franchise. Disbanded with league during 1898 season.

Little Rock Giants
Southwestern League, 1887; charter franchise. Disbanded with league during 1887 season.

Little Rock Rose Buds (aka Travelers)
Southern League, 1895; new franchise. Disbanded with league during 1895 season.

Little Rock Senators
Arkansas State League, 1897; charter franchise. Disbanded with league during 1897 season.

LITTLE ROCK–MONTGOMERY, AR

Akansas Travelers
Southern Association (AA), mid-1956; relocated franchise. Returned to solely representing Little Rock, 1957.

LIVINGSTON, MT

Livingston
Inter-Mountain League (D), 1909; relocated franchise. Had been SALT LAKE CITY, 1909. Disbanded with league during 1909 season.

LIVINGSTON, NY

Livingston
Keystone Association, 1877; charter franchise. Disbanded after 1877 season.

LOCK HAVEN, PA

Lock Haven
Southern New England League, mid-1885; relocated franchise. Had been BRIDGEPORT, 1885. Disbanded with league during 1885 season.

Lock Haven
Central Pennsylvania League, mid-1897–1898; relocated franchise. Had been SHAMOKIN, 1896–mid-1897. Disbanded with league after 1898 season.

LOCKPORT, NY

Lockport Cubs
PONY League (D), 1943–1944; renamed franchise. Had been LOCKPORT WHITE SOX, 1942. Renamed LOCKPORT WHITE SOCKS, 1945.

Lockport Locks
Middle Atlantic League (C), 1951; new franchise. Disbanded with league after 1951 season.

Lockport Reds
PONY League (D), 1946–1950; renamed franchise. Had been LOCK-PORT WHITE SOCKS, 1945. Became LOCKPORT LOCKS, 1951.

Lockport White Socks
PONY League (D), 1945; renamed franchise. Had been LOCKPORT CUBS, 1943–1944. Renamed LOCKPORT REDS, 1946.

Lockport White Sox
PONY League (D), 1942; new franchise. Renamed LOCKPORT CUBS, 1943.

LODI, CA

Lodi Crushers
California League (A), 1966–1969; new franchise. Renamed LODI PADRES, 1970.

Lodi Crushers
California League (A), 1984; renamed franchise. Had been LODI DODGERS, 1976–1983. Disbanded after 1984 season.

Lodi Dodgers
California League (A), 1976–1983; renamed franchise. Had been LODI ORIOLES, 1974–1975. Renamed LODI CRUSHERS, 1984.

Lodi Lions
California League (A), 1973; renamed franchise. Had been LODI ORIONS, 1972. Renamed LODI ORIOLES, 1974.

Lodi Orioles
California League (A), 1974–1975; renamed franchise. Had been LODI LIONS, 1973. Renamed LODI DODGERS, 1976.

Lodi Orions
California League (A), 1972; renamed franchise. Had been LODI PIRATES, 1971. Renamed LODI LIONS, 1973.

Lodi Padres
California League (A), 1970; renamed franchise. Had been LODI

CRUSHERS, 1966–1969. Renamed
LODI PIRATES, 1971.

Lodi Pirates
California League (A), 1971; renamed franchise. Had been LODI PADRES, 1970. Renamed LODI ORIONS, 1972.

LOGAN, UT

Logan
Utah League, 1901; charter franchise. Disbanded with league after 1901 season.

Logan Collegians
Utah–Idaho League (D), 1926–1927; charter franchise. Disbanded after 1927 season.

LOGAN, WV

Logan Indians
Mountain State League (D), 1937–1941; (C), 1942; charter franchise. Disbanded with league after 1942 season.

LOGANSPORT, IN

Logansport
Indiana State League, mid-1890; relocated franchise. Had been MARION, 1890. Disbanded with league during 1890 season.

Logansport Oilers
Indiana State League, 1888; charter franchise. Disbanded with league during 1888 season.

Logansport Whitecaps
Northern State League of Indiana (D), 1911; charter franchise. Became ANDERSON, mid-1911. Disbanded during 1911 season.

LONACOMING, MD

Lonacoming Giants
Potomac League (D), 1916; charter franchise. Disbanded with league after 1916 season.

LONDON, ONTARIO, CANADA

London
International League, 1900; charter franchise. Disbanded with league after 1900 season.

London Alerts
Canadian League, 1896–1897; charter franchise. Renamed LONDON TECUMSEHS, 1898.

London Cockneys
International League (D), 1908; charter franchise. Disbanded with league after 1908 season.

London Cockneys
Canadian League (C), 1911, (D), mid-1911; charter franchise. Renamed LONDON TECUMSEHS, 1911.

London Indians
Michigan–Ontario League (B), 1925; renamed franchise. Had been LONDON TECUMSEHS, 1919–1924. Disbanded with league after 1925 season.

London Pirates
PONY League (D), 1940–1941; new franchise. Disbanded after 1941 season.

London Tecumsehs
International Association, 1877–78; charter franchise. Disbanded with association after 1878 season.

London Tecumsehs
International Association, 1888–1989/League, 1890; charter franchise. Disbanded with league after 1890 season.

London Tecumsehs
Canadian League, 1898–1900; renamed franchise. Had been LONDON ALERTS, 1896–1897. Disbanded after 1900 season.

London Tecumsehs
Canadian League (C), 1912–mid-1914; (B), mid-1914–1915; renamed franchise. Had been

LONDON COCKNEYS, 1911. Disbanded with league after 1915 season.

London Tecumsehs
Michigan–Ontario League (B), 1919–1924; charter franchise. Renamed LONDON INDIANS, 1925.

London Tecumsehs
Ontario League (D), 1930; charter franchise. Disbanded with league during 1930 season.

London Tigers
Eastern League (AA), 1989–(still in existence as of 5-1-92); new franchise.

LONG BEACH, CA

Long Beach
Southern California League (D), 1913; charter franchise. Disbanded with league after 1913 season.

Long Beach Clothiers
Soutern California League (D), 1910; charter franchise. Disbanded with league after 1910 season.

LONG BRANCH, NJ

Long Branch Cubans
New York–New Jersey League (D), 1913; charter franchise. Disbanded with league after 1913 season.

Long Branch Cubans
Atlantic League (D), mid-1914; relocated franchise. Had been NEWARK CUBANS, 1914. Disbanded with league after 1914 season.

LONGVIEW, TX

Longview Browns
Texas League (A), 1932; relocated franchise. Had been WICHITA FALLS SPUDDERS, 1920–mid-1932. Became SAN ANTONIO MISSIONS, 1933.

Longview Cannibals
South Central League (D), 1912; charter franchise. Disbanded with league after 1912 season.

Longview Cannibals (aka Long Cats, 1925)

East Texas League (D), 1923–1926; charter franchise. Merged with MOUNT PLEASANT CATS, 1926. Lone Star League (D), 1927; charter franchise. Disbanded during 1927 season.

Longview Cannibals

East Texas League (D), 1931; charter franchise. Disbanded with league during 1931 season.

Longview Cannibals

Dixie League (D), 1933; charter franchise. West Dixie League (C), 1934–1935; charter franchise. East Texas League (C), 1936–1939; charter franchise. Renamed LONGVIEW TEXANS, 1940.

Longview Cherokees

Big State League (B), 1952–1953; relocated franchise. Had been GAINESVILLE OWLS, 1947–1951. Disbanded after 1953 season.

Longview Long Cats

Alternate name for LONGVIEW CANNIBALS, 1925.

Longview Pirates

Big State League (B), 1953; relocated franchise. Had been WACO PIRATES, 1948–mid-1953. Disbanded after 1953 season.

Longview Texans

East Texas League (C), 1940; renamed franchise. Had been LONGVIEW CANNIBALS, 1933–1939. Disbanded with league after 1940 season.

Longview Texans

Lone Star League (C), 1947–1948; charter franchise. East Texas League (C), 1949–1950; charter franchise. Disbanded with league after 1950 season.

LOS ANGELES, CA

Los Angeles

California League, 1901; (B), 1902; charter franchise. Pacific National League (A), 1903; charter franchise. Disbanded during 1903 season.

Los Angeles Angels

California League, 1893; renamed franchise. Had been LOS ANGELES GIANTS, 1892. Disbanded after 1893 season.

Los Angeles Angels

Pacific Coast League (A), 1903–1907; (AA), 1908–1945; (AAA), 1946–1951; (O), 1952–1957; charter franchise. Became SPOKANE INDIANS, 1958.

LOS ANGELES ANGELS

American League, 1961–1964; expansion franchise. Renamed CALIFORNIA ANGELS, 1965.

LOS ANGELES DODGERS

National League, 1958–(still in existence as of 5-1-92); relocated franchise. Had been BROOKLYN DODGERS, 1932–1957.

Los Angeles Giants

California League, 1892; new franchise. Renamed LOS ANGELES ANGELS, 1893.

Los Angeles Maires

Southern California Trolley League (D), 1910; charter franchise. Disbanded with league after 1910 season.

Los Angeles McCormicks

Southern California Trolley League (D), 1910; charter franchise. Disbanded with league after 1910 season.

LOS MOCHES, MEXICO

Los Moches Caneros

Mexican Pacific League (AAA), 1976; new franchise. Disbanded after 1976 season.

LOUISVILLE, CO

Louisville

Colorado State League, 1898; charter franchise. Disbanded during 1898 season.

LOUISVILLE, KY

LOUISVILLE BLACK CAPS

Negro Southern League, 1932; charter franchise. Disbanded after 1932 season.

LOUISVILLE COLONELS

American Association, 1885–1891; renamed franchise. Had been LOUISVILLE ECLIPSE, 1882–1891. National League, 1892–1899; new franchise. Disbanded after 1899 season.

Louisville Colonels

Western Association, 1901; charter franchise. Became GRAND RAPIDS, mid-1901.

Louisville Colonels

American Association (A), 1902–1907; (AA), 1908–1945; (AAA), 1946–1962; charter franchise. Disbanded with association after 1962 season.

Louisville Colonels

International League (AAA), 1968–1972; new franchise. Disbanded after 1972 season.

LOUISVILLE ECLIPSE

American Association, 1882–1884; charter franchise. Renamed LOUISVILLE COLONELS, 1885.

LOUISVILLE GRAYS

National League, 1876–1877; charter franchise. Disbanded after 1877 season.

Louisville Redbirds

American Association, (AAA), 1982–(still in existence as of 5-1-92); new franchise.

LOWELL, MA

Lowell
Keystone Association, 1877; charter franchise. New England League, 1877–1878; charter franchise. Disbanded with league after 1878 season.

Lowell
Atlantic Association, 1889; charter franchise. Disbanded during 1889 season.

Lowell
New England League, 1891–1892; charter franchise. Disbanded with league during 1892 season.

Lowell
New England Association, 1895; charter franchise. Disbanded with association during 1895 season.

Lowell
New England League, mid-1899; relocated franchise. Had been CAMBRIDGE, 1899. Disbanded during 1899 season.

Lowell
New England League (B), 1919; charter franchise. Disbanded with league after 1919 season.

Lowell Bingling Pans
New England League (B), 1911; renamed franchise. Had been LOWELL TIGERS, 1906–1910. Renamed LOWELL GRAYS, 1912.

Lowell Chippies
New England League, 1888; renamed franchise. Had been LOWELL MAGICIANS, 1887. Disbanded with league during 1888 season.

Lowell Grays
New England League, (B), 1912–1915; renamed franchise. Eastern League (B), 1916; charter franchise. Disbanded after 1916 season.

Lowell Highwaymen
New England League (B), 1926; charter franchise. Became SALEM, mid-1926.

Lowell Hustlers
Northeastern League (A), mid-1934; charter franchise. Disbanded with league after 1934 season.

Lowell Lauriers
New England League (B), 1933; charter franchise. Disbanded with league during 1933 season.

Lowell Magicians
New England League, 1887; new franchise. Renamed LOWELL CHIPPIES, 1888.

Lowell Millers
New England League (B), 1929; new franchise. Became NASHUA MILLIONAIRES, mid-1929.

Lowell Orphans
New England League (B), mid-1947; relocated franchise. Had been LAWRENCE ORPHANS, 1947. Disbanded after 1947 season.

Lowell Tigers
New England League, 1901; (B), 1902–mid-1905; charter franchise. Became TAUNTON, mid-1905.

Lowell Tigers
New England League (B), 1906–1910; new franchise. Renamed LOWELL BINGLING PANS, 1911.

LOWVILLE, NY

Lowville
Central New York League, 1886; charter franchise. Disbanded with league after 1886 season.

LUBBOCK, TX

Lubbock Bobcats
West Texas League (D), 1928; charter franchise. Disbanded after 1928 season.

Lubbock Hubbers
West Texas League (D), 1922; new franchise. Panhandle Pecos Valley League (D), 1923; charter franchise. Disbanded with league after 1923 season.

Lubbock Hubbers
West Texas–New Mexico League (D), 1938–1942; (C), 1946–1955; new franchise. Big State League (B), 1956; new franchise. Became TEXAS CITY HUBBERS, mid-1956.

LUDINGTON, MI

Ludington Mariners
Michigan State League (D), 1912–1914; new franchise. Disbanded with league after 1914 season.

Ludington Mariners
Central League (D), 1920–1922; charter franchise. Disbanded with league after 1922 season.

Ludington Tars
Central League (C), 1926; charter franchise. Michigan State League (B), mid-1926; charter franchise. Disbanded with league during 1926 season.

LUDLOW, KY

Ludlow
Keystone Association, 1877; charter franchise. Disbanded with league after 1877 season.

LUFKIN, TX

Lufkin Angels
Gulf Coast League (B), 1950; charter franchise. Became LEESVILLE ANGELS, mid-1950.

Lufkin Foresters
East Texas League (C), 1946; charter franchise. Lone Star League (C), 1947–1948; charter franchise. Disbanded with league after 1948 season.

Lufkin Lumbermen
West Dixie League (D), mid-1934; relocated franchise. Had been PARIS PIRATES, 1934. Disbanded after 1934 season.

LUMBERTON, NC

Lumberton Auctioneers
Tobacco State League (D), 1949–1950; renamed franchise. Had been LUMBERTON CUBS, 1947–1948. Disbanded with league after 1950 season.

Lumberton Cubs
Tobacco State League (D), 1947–1948; new franchise. Renamed LUMBERTON AUCTIONEERS, 1949.

LYNCHBURG, VA

Lynchburg Cardinals
Piedmont League (B), 1943–1955; new franchise. Had been ASHEVILLE TOURISTS, mid-1934–1942. Disbanded with league after 1955 season.

Lynchburg Grays
Virginia League (D), 1939; charter franchise. Renamed LYNCHBURG SENATORS, 1940.

Lynchburg Hill Climbers
Virginia League, 1894–mid-1896; charter franchise. Disbanded during 1896 season.

Lynchburg Lyn-Sox
Carolina League (A), 1966–1969; new franchise. Renamed LYNCHBURG TWINS, 1970.

Lynchburg Mets
Carolina League (A), 1976–1987; renamed franchise. Had been LYNCHBURG RANGERS, 1975. Renamed LYNCHBURG RED SOX, 1988.

Lynchburg Rangers
Carolina League (A), 1975; renamed franchise. Had been LYNCHBURG TWINS, 1966–1974. Renamed LYNCHBURG METS, 1976.

Lynchburg Red Sox
Carolina League (A), 1988–(still in existence as of 5-1-92); renamed franchise. Had been LYNCHBURG METS, 1976–1987.

Lynchburg Senators
Virginia League (D), 1940–1942; renamed franchise. Had been LYNCHBURG GRAYS, 1939. Disbanded after 1942 season.

Lynchburg Senators
Appalachian League (D), 1959; new franchise. Disbanded after 1959 season.

Lynchburg Shoemakers
Virginia League (C), 1906–1912; charter franchise. Disbanded during 1912 season.

Lynchburg Shoemakers
Virginia League (C), 1917; new franchise. Disbanded with league during 1917 season.

Lynchburg Twins
Carolina League (A), 1970–1974; renamed franchise. Had been LYNCHBURG LYN-SOX, 1966–1969. Renamed LYNCHBURG RANGERS, 1975.

Lynchburg White Sox
South Atlantic League (AA), mid-1962–1963; relocated franchise. Had been SAVANNAH WHITE SOX, 1962. Southern League (AA), 1964–1965; charter franchise. Disbanded after 1965 season.

LYNN, MA

Lynn
New England League, 1891; charter franchise. Disbanded during 1891 season.

Lynn
New England League, mid-1901; relocated franchise. Had been AUGUSTA, 1901. Disbanded after 1901 season.

Lynn Fighters
New England League (B), 1914; renamed franchise. Had been LYNN SHOEMAKERS, 1913. Renamed LYNN PIRATES, 1915.

Lynn Leonardites
New England League (B), 1911–1912; renamed franchise. Had been LYNN SHOEMAKERS, 1905–1910. Renamed LYNN SHOEMAKERS, 1913.

Lynn Lions
New England League, 1888; renamed franchise. Had been LYNN YANKS, 1886–1887. Disbanded with league during 1888 season.

Lynn Live Oaks
International Association, 1877; charter franchise. New England League, 1877; charter franchise. Disbanded with league after 1877 season.

Lynn Ocean Parkers
Alternate name for LYNN PIPERS, 1916.

Lynn Papooses
New England League (B), 1926–1930; charter franchise. Disbanded with league after 1930 season.

Lynn Pipers (aka Ocean Parkers)
Eastern League (B), 1916; charter franchise. Disbanded after 1916 season.

Lynn Pirates
New England League (B), 1915; renamed franchise. Had been LYNN FIGHTERS, 1914. Disbanded with league after 1915 season.

Lynn Red Sox
New England League (B), 1946–1948; charter franchise. Renamed LYNN TIGERS, 1949.

Lynn Sailors
Eastern League (AA), 1980–1983; new franchise. Disbanded after 1983 season.

Lynn Shoemakers
New England League (B), 1905–1910; charter franchise. Renamed LYNN LEONARDITES, 1911.

Lynn Shoemakers
New England League (B), 1913; renamed franchise. Had been LYNN LEONARDITES, 1911–1912. Renamed LYNN FIGHTERS, 1914.

Lynn Tigers
New England League (B), 1949; renamed franchise. Had been LYNN RED SOX, 1946–1948. Disbanded with league after 1949 season.

Lynn Yanks
New England League, mid-1886–1887; relocated franchise. Had been NEWBURYPORT CLAMDIGGERS, 1886. Renamed LYNN LIONS, 1888.

LYONS, GA
(See VIDALIA, GA)

LYONS, KS

Lyons Lions
Kansas State League (D), 1909–1911; charter franchise. Central Kansas League (D), 1912; new franchise. Kansas State League (D), 1913; new franchise. Disbanded after 1913 season.

LYONS, NY

Lyons
New York State League, 1897–1898; charter franchise. Disbanded after 1898 season.

Lyons
Empire State League, (C), 1905; charter franchise. Disbanded during 1905 season.

Lyons
Empire State League, (C), 1907–1908; charter franchise. Disbanded during 1908 season.

MACOMB, IL

Macomb
Illinois–Missouri League (D), 1908–1910; charter franchise. Disbanded after 1910 season.

MACON, GA

Macon
Southern League, 1885–1886; charter franchise. Disbanded after 1886 season.

Macon
Southern League, 1898; charter franchise. Disbanded with league during 1898 season.

Macon Braves
South Atlantic League (A), 1991–(still in existence as of 5-1-92); relocated franchise. Had been SUMTER FLYERS, 1985–1990.

Macon Brigands
Alternate name for MACON PEACHES, 1905.

Macon Central City
Southern League, 1892–1893; charter franchise. Disbanded with league during 1893 season.

Macon Dodgers
South Atlantic League (A), 1956–1960; renamed franchise. Had been MACON PEACHES, 1936–1942; 1946–1956. Renamed MACON PEACHES, 1961.

Macon Highlanders
Alternate name for MACON PEACHES, 1904.

Macon Hornets
Southern League, 1894; renamed franchise. Disbanded during 1894 season.

Macon Peaches (aka Highlanders, 1904; Brigands, 1905)
South Atlantic League (D), 1904–1916; charter franchise. Renamed MACON TIGERS, 1917.

Macon Peaches
South Atlantic Association (B), mid-1923–1930; relocated franchise. Had been CHARLESTON PALS, 1921–mid-1923. Disbanded with league after 1930 season.

Macon Peaches
Southeastern League (B), 1932; charter franchise. Disbanded with league during 1932 season.

Macon Peaches
South Atlantic League (A), 1936–1942; 1946–1956; charter franchise. Renamed MACON DODGERS, 1956.

Macon Peaches
South Atlantic League (A), 1961; renamed franchise. Had been MACON DODGERS, 1956–1960. South Atlantic League (A), 1962; (AA), 1963; new franchise. Southern League (AA), 1964–1967; charter franchise. Disbanded after 1967 season.

Macon Peaches
South Atlantic League (A), 1980–1983; charter franchise. Renamed MACON PIRATES, 1984.

Macon Pirates
South Atlantic League (A), 1984–1987; renamed franchise. Had been MACON PEACHES, 1980–1983. Disbanded after 1987 season.

Macon Tigers
South Atlantic League (D), 1917; renamed franchise. Had been MACON PEACHES, 1904–1916. Disbanded during 1917 season.

MACON, MO

Macon
Missouri State League (D), 1911; charter franchise. Disbanded with league during 1911 season.

MADERA, MEXICO
(See TAMPICO, MEXICO)

MADERA, VERACRUZ, MEXICO
(See also VERACRUZ, MEXICO)

Madera Braves
Mexican Center League (A), 1968–1970; new franchise. Disbanded after 1970 season.

MADISON, SD

Madison
South Dakota League (D), 1920; charter franchise. Dakota League (D), 1921; charter franchise. Disbanded after 1921 season.

MADISON, WI

Madison Blues
Three I League (B), 1940–1942; new franchise. Suspended operations with league after 1942 season.

Madison Muskies
Midwest League (A), 1982–(still in existence as of 5-1-92); new franchise.

Madison Senators
Wisconsin–Illinois League (D), 1905–1914; charter franchise. Disbanded with league after 1914 season.

MADISONVILLE, KY

Madisonville
Kentucky–Indiana League, 1896; charter franchise. Disbanded with league during 1896 season.

Madisonville
KITTY League (D), 1910; charter franchise. Disbanded after 1910 season.

Madisonville
KITTY League (D), 1916; charter franchise. Disbanded with league during 1916 season.

Madisonville Miners
KITTY League (D), 1922; charter franchise. Disbanded with league during 1922 season.

Madisonville Miners
KITTY League (D), 1946–1955; charter franchise. Disbanded with league after 1955 season.

MAHANOY CITY, PA

(See also SHENANDOAH, PA)

Mahanoy City
Central Pennsylvania League, 1887–1888; charter franchise. Disbanded with league during 1888 season.

Mahanoy City
Anthracite League (D), 1928; charter franchise. Disbanded with league during 1928 season.

Mahanoy City Bluebirds
North Atlantic League (D), 1946–1947; charter franchise. Renamed MAHANOY CITY BREWERS, 1948

Mahanoy City Brewers
North Atlantic League (D), 1948–1950; renamed franchise. Had been MAHANOY CITY BLUEBIRDS, 1946–1947. Disbanded with league after 1950 season.

MALDEN, MA

Malden Rosebuds
Northeastern League (A), mid-1934; relocated franchise. Had been WORCESTER, mid-1934. Became WORCESTER, mid-1934.

MALONE, NY

Malone
Northeastern League, 1887; charter franchise. Disbanded with league during 1887 season.

MANCHESTER, NH

Manchester
New England League, 1877–1878; charter franchise. Disbanded with league during 1878 season.

Manchester
New England League, 1892; new franchise. Became LAWRENCE, mid-1892.

Manchester
New England League, 1899; new franchise. Disbanded with league after 1899 season.

Manchester
New England League, 1901; (B), 1902–1904; charter franchise. Disbanded after 1904 season.

Manchester
New England League (B), 1905; new franchise. Became LAWRENCE, mid-1905.

Manchester Amskoegs
New England League, 1891–1892; charter franchise. Disbanded with league after 1892 season.

Manchester Blue Sox
New England League (B), 1926–1930; charter franchise. Disbanded with league during 1930 season.

Manchester Indians
Northeastern League (A), 1934; charter franchise. Disbanded with league after 1934 season.

Manchester Manchesters
National Association, 1877–1880; charter franchise. Disbanded with association during 1880 season.

Manchester Maroons
New Hampshire State League, 1886; charter franchise. New England League, 1887–1888; new franchise. Disbanded with league during 1888 season.

Manchester Textiles
New England League (B), mid-1914–1915; relocated franchise. Had been FITCHBURG BURGHERS, 1914. Disbanded with league after 1915 season.

Manchester Yankees
New England League (B), 1949; renamed franchise. Had been MANCHESTER YOUNG GIANTS, 1946–1948.

Manchester Yankees
Eastern League (AA), 1969–1971; new franchise. Disbanded after 1971 season.

Manchester Young Giants
New England League (B), 1946–1948; charter franchise. Renamed MANCHESTER YANKEES, 1949.

MANCHESTER, OH

Manchester
Tri-State League, 1894; charter franchise. Disbanded with league during 1894 season.

MANDAN, ND

(See BISMARK, ND)

MANHATTAN, KS

Manhattan Elks
Central Kansas League (D), 1909–1912; new franchise. Kansas State League (D), 1913; charter franchise. Disbanded after 1913 season.

MANISTEE, MI

Manistee
Michigan State League, 1890; new franchise. Disbanded with league during 1890 season.

Manistee
Michigan State League, 1893–1894; charter franchise. Disbanded after 1894 season.

Manistee Champs
Michigan State League (D), 1912–1914; renamed franchise. Had been MANISTEE COLTS, 1911. Became BELDING CHAMPS, mid-1914.

Manistee Colts
Michigan State League (D), 1911; charter franchise. Renamed MANISTEE CHAMPS, 1912.

MANKATO, MN

Mankato Mets
Northern League (A), 1967–1968; new franchise. Disbanded after 1968 season.

MANNINGTON, WV

Mannington
West Virginia League (D), 1910; charter franchise. Disbanded with league after 1910 season.

MANSFIELD, OH

Mansfield
Ohio State League, 1887; charter franchise. Tri-State League, 1888–1890; charter franchise. Disbanded with league during 1890 season.

Mansfield Braves
Ohio State League (D), 1939–1941; new franchise. Disbanded with league after 1941 season.

Mansfield Brownies
Ohio–Pennsylvania League (C), 1911; renamed franchise. Had been MANSFIELD REFORMERS, 1910. Ohio State League (D), 1912; new franchise. Disbanded after 1912 season.

Mansfield Electricians
Ohio–Michigan League, 1893; charter franchise. Disbanded with league after 1893 season.

Mansfield Giants
Ohio–Pennsylvania League (D), 1906; new franchise. Renamed MANSFIELD PIONEERS, 1907.

Mansfield Haymakers
Inter-State League, 1899–1900; renamed franchise. Had been MANSFIELD QUAKERS, 1897–1898. Disbanded with league during 1900 season.

Mansfield Kids
Western Inter-State League, 1895; charter franchise. Disbanded with league after 1895 season.

Mansfield Pioneers
Ohio–Pennsylvania League (D), 1907; renamed franchise. Had been MANSFIELD GIANTS, 1906. Ohio State League (D), 1908–1909; charter franchise. Disbanded with league after 1909 season.

Mansfield Quakers
Inter-State League, 1897–1898; new franchise. Renamed MANSFIELD HAYMAKERS, 1899.

Mansfield Red Sox
Ohio State League (D), 1937; renamed franchise. Had been MANSFIELD TIGERS, 1936. Disbanded after 1937 season.

Mansfield Reformers
Ohio–Pennsylvania League (C), 1910; new franchise. Renamed MANSFIELD BROWNIES, 1911.

Mansfield Tigers
Ohio State League (D), 1936; charter franchise. Renamed MANSFIELD RED SOX, 1937.

MARACAIBO, VENEZUELA

Maracaibo Oilers
Inter-American League (AAA), 1979; charter franchise. Disbanded with league during 1979 season.

MARIANNA, AR

Marianna
Northeast Arkansas League (D) 1909; charter franchise. Disbanded after 1909 season.

MARIETTA, OH

Marietta
Inter-State League, 1897; new franchise. Disbanded after 1897 season.

MARINETTE, WI

Marinette Indians
Upper Peninsula League, 1890; charter franchise. Disbanded after 1890 season.

Marinette Log Rollers
Wisconsin State League, 1891; charter franchise. Disbanded with league after 1891 season.

Marinette Lumber Shovers
Wisconsin–Michigan League, 1892; charter franchise. Disbanded with league after 1892 season.

MARINETTE, WI–MENOMINEE, MI
(See also MENOMINEE, MI)

Twin Cities Molls (aka Twins)
Wisconsin–Illinois League (C), 1914; new franchise. Disbanded with league after 1914 season.

Twin Cities Twins
Alternate name for TWIN CITIES MOLLS.

MARION, IL

Marion Indians
Illinois State League (B), 1947–1948; charter franchise. Disbanded with league after 1948 season.

MARION, IN

Marion
Indiana State League, 1888; charter franchise. Disbanded with league after 1888 season.

Marion
Indiana State League, 1890; charter franchise. Became LOGANSPORT, mid-1890.

Marion
Inter-State Association (D), mid-1906; relocated franchise. Had been FLINT VEHICLES, 1906. Disbanded with league after 1906 season.

Marion Boosters
Northern Indiana State League (D), 1909; charter franchise. Disbanded after 1909 season.

Marion Boosters
Northern State League of Indiana (D), 1911; charter franchise. Disbanded with league during 1911 season.

Marion Glass Blowers
Inter-State League, 1900–1901; charter franchise. Disbanded with league after 1900 season.

Marion Oilworkers
Central League (B), 1903–mid-1904; new franchise. Became PEORIA DISTILLERS, mid-1904.

Marion Oilworkers
Central League (B), mid-1904; new franchise. Had been PEORIA DISTILLERS, mid-1904. Disbanded after 1904 season.

MARION, NC

Marion Marauders
Western Carolina League (D), 1948–1952; charter franchise. Tar Heel League (D), 1953–1954; charter franchise. Disbanded with league after 1954 season.

MARION, OH

Marion
Western Association, 1901; charter franchise. Disbanded with league after 1901 season.

Marion
Inter-State League (B), mid-1902; relocated franchise. Had been YOUNGSTOWN, 1902. Central League (D), 1903–1904; charter franchise. Disbanded after 1904 season.

Marion
Buckeye League (D), 1915; charter franchise. Disbanded with league after 1915 season.

Marion Cardinals
Ohio State League (D), 1945–1946; renamed franchise. Had been MARION DIGGERS, 1944. Renamed MARION CUBS, 1947.

Marion Cubs
Ohio State League (D), 1947; renamed franchise. Had been MARION CARDINALS, 1945–1946. Ohio–Indiana League (D), 1948; charter franchise. Renamed MARION RED SOX, 1949.

Marion Diggers
Ohio State League (D), 1908–1910; (C), 1911; (D), mid-1912; charter franchise. Became IRONTON ORPHANS, mid-1912.

Marion Diggers
Ohio State League (D), 1944; charter franchise. Renamed MARION CARDINALS, 1945.

Marion Moguls
Inter-State Association (D), 1906; relocated franchise. Had been ZANESVILLE MOGULS, 1905–mid-1906. Disbanded after 1906 season.

Marion Presidents
Ohio State League (D), mid-1937; relocated franchise. Had been SANDUSKY SAILORS, 1936–mid-1937. Disbanded after 1937 season.

Marion Red Sox
Ohio–Indiana League (D), 1949; renamed franchise. Had been MARION CUBS, 1947–1948. Disbanded with league after 1951 season.

Marion Swamp Foxes
Alternate name for MARION MOGULS.

Zanesville Swamp Foxes
Ohio–Pennsylvania League (C), 1907; new franchise. Disbanded after 1907 season.

MARION, VA

Marion A's
Appalachian League (D), mid-1955; relocated franchise. Had been WELCH MINERS, 1946–mid-

1955. Disbanded with league after 1955 season.

Marion Mets
Appalachian League (R), 1965–1976; new franchise. Disbanded after 1976 season.

MARLIN, TX

Marlin
Central Texas League (D), 1916; charter franchise. Disbanded during 1916 season.

Marlin
Central Texas League (D), 1917; new franchise. Disbanded with league during 1917 season.

Marlin Bathers
Texas Association (D), 1923–mid-1925; charter franchise. Became PALESTINE PALS, mid-1925.

MARQUETTE, MI

Marquette
Upper Peninsula League, 1891–1892; charter franchise. Disbanded with league during 1892 season.

Marquette
Upper Peninsula League, 1895; charter franchise. Disbanded with league during 1895 season.

Marquette Kittens
Michigan–Wisconsin League, 1892; charter franchise. Disbanded during 1892 season.

MARSHALL, TX

Marshall
South Central League (D), 1912; charter franchise. Disbanded with league after 1912 season.

Marshall Browns
East Texas League (C), 1949–1950; charter franchise. Disbanded with league after 1950 season.

Marshall Comets
Lone Star League (D), 1947; charter franchise. Renamed MARSHALL COMETS, 1948.

Marshall Indians
East Texas League (D), 1923–mid-1926; charter franchise. Renamed MARSHALL SNAPPERS, mid-1926.

Marshall Indians
Lone Star League (D), 1927; charter franchise. Disbanded during 1927 season.

Marshall Orphans
East Texas League (C), 1936; charter franchise. Renamed MARSHALL TIGERS, 1937.

Marshall Snappers
East Texas League (D), mid-1926; renamed franchise. Had been MARSHALL INDIANS, 1923–mid-1926. Disbanded with league after 1926 season.

Marshall Tigers
East Texas League (C), 1937–1940; renamed franchise. Had been MARSHALL ORPHANS, 1936. Disbanded after 1940 season.

Marshall Tigers
Cotton States League (C), 1941; renamed franchise. Had been CLARKSDALE RED SOX, mid-1938–1941.

Marshall Tigers
Lone Star League (D), 1948; renamed franchise. Had been MARSHALL COMETS, 1947. Disbanded with league after 1948 season.

MARSHALLTOWN, IA

Marshalltown Ansons
Central Association (D), 1914–1917; new franchise. Disbanded with league after 1917 season.

Marshalltown Ansons
Mississippi Valley League (D), 1922–1928; charter franchise. Disbanded after 1928 season.

Marshalltown Brownies
Iowa State League (D), 1906; renamed franchise. Had been MARSHALLTOWN GRAYS, 1904–1905. Renamed MARSHALLTOWN SNAPPERS, 1907.

Marshalltown Grays
Iowa State League (D), 1904–1905; charter franchise. Renamed MARSHALLTOWN BROWNIES, 1906.

Marshalltown Snappers
Iowa State League (D), 1907; renamed franchise. Had been MARSHALLTOWN BROWNS, 1906. Disbanded with league after 1907 season.

MARTINSBURG, WV

Martinsburg Blue Sox
Blue Ridge League (D), 1916–1917; renamed franchise. Had been MARTINSBURG CHAMPS, 1915. Renamed MARTINSBURG MOUNTAINEERS, 1918.

Martinsburg Blue Sox (aka Champs, 1924)
Blue Ridge League (D), 1922–1930; renamed franchise. Had been MARTINSBURG CHAMPS, 1915. Disbanded with league after 1930 season.

Martinsburg Champs
Blue Ridge League (D), 1915; charter franchise. Renamed MARTINSBURG BLUE SOX, 1916.

Martinsburg Champs
Alternate name for MARTINSBURG BLUE SOX, 1924.

Martinsburg Mountaineers
Blue Ridge League (D), 1918; renamed franchise. Had been MARTINSBURG BLUE SOX, 1916–1917. Disbanded with league after 1918 season.

Martinsburg Mountaineers
Blue Ridge League (D), 1920–1921; charter franchise. Renamed MARTINSBURG BLUE SOX, 1922.

MARTINSVILLE, VA

Martinsville Athletics
Carolina League (C), 1945–1949; charter franchise. Became FAY-ETTEVILLE ATHLETICS, 1950.

Martinsville Manufacturers
Bi-State League (NC–VA), (D), 1934–1941; charter franchise. Disbanded with league after 1941 season.

Martinsville Phillies
Appalachian League (R), 1988– (still in existence as of 5-1-92); new franchise.

MARYSVILLE, CA

Marysville Braves
Far West League (D), 1948–1949; charter franchise. Renamed MARYSVILLE PEACHES, 1950.

Marysville Peaches
Far West League (D), 1950; re-named franchise. Had been MARYS-VILLE BRAVES, 1948–1949. Disbanded after 1950 season.

MARYSVILLE, KS

Marysville
Eastern Kansas League (D), 1910; charter franchise. Disbanded after 1910 season.

MARYVILLE, MO

Maryville Comets
MINK League (D), 1910–mid-1911; charter franchise. Became HUMBOLDT INFANTS, mid-1911.

MARYVILLE, TN

Maryville Canners
Appalachian League (D), mid-1940; relocated franchise. Had been NEWPORT CANNERS, 1940. Became NEWPORT CANNERS, mid-1940.

MARYVILLE–ALCOA, TN

Maryville–Alcoa Twins
Mountain States League (D), 1953; (C), 1954; new franchise. Became MORRISTOWN TWINS, mid-1954.

MASON CITY, IA

Mason City
Iowa State League (D), 1911–1912; charter franchise. Disbanded with league after 1912 season.

Mason City Claydiggers
Central Association (D), 1915–1917; new franchise. Disbanded with league after 1917 season.

MASPETH, NY

Long Island A's
Eastern Association, 1886; charter franchise. Disbanded with league after 1886 season.

MASSILLON, OH

Massillon
Ohio State League, 1898; charter franchise. Disbanded with league during 1898 season.

Massillon Farmers
Ohio–Pennsylvania League (D), 1905; charter franchise. Disbanded after 1905 season.

MATAMOROS, MEXICO

Matamoros
Mexican Center League (A), 1978; new franchise. Disbanded after 1978 season.

Matamoros Castro (Gamers)
La Laguna Rookie League (R), 1990– (still in existence as of 5-1-92); new franchise.

Matamoros Esparza (Merry Men)
La Laguna Rookie League (R), 1990– (still in existence as of 5-1-92); new franchise.

Matamoros Industrias (Manufacturers)
La Laguna Rookie League (R), 1990– (still in existence as of 5-1-92); new franchise.

Matamoros Perforadores (Drillers)
La Laguna Rookie League (R), 1990– (still in existence as of 5-1-92); new franchise.

MATTHEWS, IN

Matthews
Western Association, mid-1901; relocated franchise. Had been INDI-ANAPOLIS HOOSIERS, 1901. Disbanded with league after 1901 season.

MATTOON, IL

Mattoon Athletics
Midwest League (D), 1957; re-named franchise. Had been MAT-TOON PHILLIES, 1953–1956. Disbanded after 1957 season.

Mattoon Broom Corn Raisers
Indiana–Illinois League, mid-1899; relocated franchise. Had been KOKOMO, 1899. Disbanded with league after 1899 season.

Mattoon Comers
Alternate name for MATTOON GIANTS.

Mattoon Giants (aka Comers)
Eastern Illinois League (D), 1907–1908; charter franchise. Disbanded with league after 1908 season.

Mattoon Indians
Illinois State League (B), 1947–1948; charter franchise. MOV League (D), 1949–1952; charter franchise. Renamed MATTOON PHILLIES, 1953.

Mattoon Phillies
MOV League (D), 1953–1955; re-named franchise. Midwest League

(D), 1956; charter franchise. Renamed MATTOON ATHLETICS, 1957.

MATTOON–CHARLESTON, IL
(See also CHARLESTON, IL)

Mattoon–Charleston Hyphens (aka Birdies)
KITTY League (D), 1906; new franchise. Disbanded with league after 1906 season.

MAUD, OK

Maud Chiefs
Western Association (C), 1929; new franchise. Disbanded during 1929 season.

MAYFIELD, KY

Mayfield Browns
KITTY League (D), 1939–1941; renamed franchise. Had been MAYFIELD CLOTHIERS, 1937–1938. Disbanded after 1941 season.

Mayfield Cardinals
KITTY League (D), 1936; new franchise. Renamed MAYFIELD CLOTHIERS, 1937.

Mayfield Clothiers
KITTY League (D), 1937–1938; renamed franchise. Had been MAYFIELD CARDINALS, 1936. Renamed MAYFIELD BROWNS, 1939.

Mayfield Clothiers
KITTY League (D), 1946–1955; charter franchise. Disbanded with league after 1955 season.

Mayfield Pantsmakers
KITTY League (D), 1922–1924; charter franchise. Disbanded with league after 1924 season.

MAYODAN, NC

Mayodan Millers
Bi-State League (D), 1939; renamed franchise. Had been MAY-ODAN SENATORS, 1937–1938. Renamed MAYODAN SENATORS, 1940.

Mayodan Mills
Bi-State League (D), 1935; renamed franchise. Had been MAYDOAN SENATORS, 1934. Renamed MAYODAN ORPHANS, 1936.

Mayodan Orphans
Bi-State League (D), 1936; renamed franchise. Had been MAYODAN MILLS, 1935. Renamed MAYODAN SENATORS, 1937.

Mayodan Senators
Bi-State League (NC–VA), (D), 1934; charter franchise. Renamed MAYDOAN MILLS, 1935.

Mayodan Senators
Bi-State League (D), 1937–1938; renamed franchise. Had been MAYODAN ORPHANS, 1936. Renamed MAYODAN MILLERS, 1939.

Mayodan Senators
Bi-State League (D), 1940–1941; renamed franchise. Had been MAYODAN MILLERS, 1939. Disbanded after 1941 season.

MAYSVILLE, KY

Maysville
Tri-State League, 1894; charter franchise. Disbanded with league during 1894 season.

Maysville
Ohio State League (D), 1913–1914; new franchise. Disbanded after 1914 season.

Maysville Angels
Ohio State League (D), mid-1915; relocated franchise. Had been CHILLICOTHE BABES, 1913–mid-1915. Renamed MAYSVILLE BURLEY CUBS, 1916.

Maysville Burley Cubs
Ohio State League (D), 1916; renamed franchise. Had been MAYS-VILLE ANGELS, 1913–1915. Disbanded with league after 1916 season.

Maysville Cardinals
Blue Grass League (D), 1922–1923; charter franchise. Disbanded after 1923 season.

Maysville Rivermen
Blue Grass League (D), mid-1910–1912; relocated franchise. Had been SHELBYVILLE, 1908–1910. Disbanded with league after 1912 season.

MAZATLAN, MEXICO

Mazatlan
Mexican Pacific League (AAA), 1976; charter franchise. Disbanded with league after 1976 season.

MCALESTER, OK

McAlester
Oklahoma State League (D), mid-1924; relocated franchise. Had been GUTHRIE, 1922–mid-1924. Disbanded with league after 1936 season.

McAlester
Oklahoma State League (D), 1936; charter franchise. Disbanded with league after 1936 season.

McAlester Diggers
OAK League (D), 1907; charter franchise. Became MCALESTER SIGHS, 1908.

McAlester Diggers
Western Association (C), 1923; renamed franchise. Had been MCALESTER MINERS, 1922. Disbanded after 1923 season.

McAlester Miners
Oklahoma State League (D), 1912; charter franchise. Disbanded with league during 1912 season.

McAlester Miners
Western Association (D), 1914–1917; charter franchise. Disbanded with league after 1917 season.

McAlester Miners
Western Association (C), 1922; charter franchise. Became MCALESTER DIGGERS, 1923.

McAlester Miners
Western Association (C), 1926; new franchise. Disbanded after 1926 season.

McAlester Rockets
Sooner State League (D), 1947–1956; charter franchise. Disbanded after 1956 season.

McAlester Sighs
Oak League, 1908; renamed franchise. Had been MCALESTER DIGGERS, 1907. Disbanded with league after 1908 season.

MCALLEN, TX

McAllen
Texas Valley League (D), 1928; new franchise. Disbanded with league during 1928 season.

McAllen Dusters
Lone Star League (A), 1977; charter franchise. Disbanded with league after 1977 season.

McAllen Giants (aka Palms)
Rio Grande Valley League (C), 1949–1950; charter franchise. Disbanded with league after 1950 season.

McAllen Packers
Texas Valley League (D), 1938; charter franchise. Disbanded with league after 1938 season.

McAllen Palms
Rio Grande Valley League (D), 1931; charter franchise. Disbanded with league after 1931 season.

McAllen Palms
Alternate name for MCALLEN GIANTS, 1949–1950.

MCCOOK, NE

McCook Braves
Nebraska State League (D), 1956–1959; charter franchise. Disbanded with league after 1959 season.

McCook Generals
Nebraska State League (D), 1928–mid-1932; charter franchise. Disbanded during 1932 season.

MCKEESPORT, PA

McKeesport
Tri-State League, 1890; new franchise. Disbanded with league during 1890 season.

McKeesport
Ohio–Pennsylvania League (D), 1912; new franchise. Became SALEM, mid-1912.

McKeesport
Pennsylvania–West Virginia League (D), 1914; charter franchise. Disbanded with league after 1914 season.

McKeesport Colts
Ohio–Pennsylvania League (D), 1905; charter franchise. Disbanded after 1905 season.

McKeesport Little Braves
Pennsylvania State Association (D), 1939–mid-1940; charter franchise. Became OIL CITY OILERS, mid-1940.

McKeesport Tubers
POM League (D), 1907; new franchise. Ohio–Pennsylvania League (D), 1908–1910; new franchise. Disbanded with league after 1910 season.

McKeesport Tubers
Pennsylvania State Association (D), 1934–1938; charter franchise. Renamed MCKEESPORT LITTLE BRAVES, 1939.

MCKINNEY, TX

McKinney
Texas–Oklahoma League (D), 1912; new franchise. Disbanded after 1912 season.

MCLEANSBORO, IL

McLeansboro Merchants
Southern Illinois League (D), 1910; charter franchise. Became MCLEANSBORO MINERS, mid-1910.

McLeansboro Miners
KITTY League (D), mid-1910–mid-1911; renamed franchise. Had been MCLEANSBORO MERCHANTS, 1910. Became HENDERSON HENS, mid-1911.

MCPHERSON, KS

McPherson Merry Macks
Kansas State League (D), 1909–1911; charter franchise. Disbanded after 1911 season.

MEADVILLE, PA

Meadville
New York–Pennsylvania League, 1890–1891; charter franchise. Disbanded with league after 1891 season.

Meadville
Iron & Oil League, 1898; charter franchise. Disbanded with league during 1898 season.

MEDFORD OR

Medford Athletics
Northwest League (A), 1979–1987; new franchise. Renamed SOUTHERN OREGON ATHLETICS, 1988.

Medford Dodgers
Northwest League (D), 1969–1971; new franchise. Disbanded with league after 1971 season.

Medford Giants

Northwest League (D), 1967–1968; new franchise. Disbanded after 1968 season.

Medford Nuggets

Far West League (D), 1948–1949; charter franchise. Renamed MEDFORD ROGUES, 1950.

Medford Rogues

Far West League (D), 1950–1951; charter franchise. Had been MEDFORD NUGGETS, 1948–1949. Disbanded with league after 1951 season.

Southern Oregon Athletics

Northwest League (A), 1988–(still in existence as of 5-1-92); renamed franchise. Had been MEDFORD ATHLETICS, 1979–1987.

MEDICINE HAT, ALBERTA, CANADA

Medicine Hat A's

Pioneer League ("Summer Class A"), 1977; new franchise. Renamed MEDICINE HAT BLUE JAYS, 1978.

Medicine Hat Blue Jays

Pioneer League ("Summer Class A"), 1978–(still in existence as of 5-1-92); renamed franchise. Had been MEDICINE HAT A'S, 1977.

Medicine Hat Hatters

Western Canada League (C), 1907; charter franchise. Disbanded with league after 1907 season.

Medicine Hat Hatters

Western Canada League (D), 1913–1914; new franchise. Disbanded with league after 1914 season.

Medicine Hat Mad Hatters

Western Canada League (D), 1909–mid-1910; charter franchise. Became SASKATOON BERRY PICKERS, mid-1910.

MELBOURNE, FL

Melbourne Twins

Florida East Coast League (R), 1972; charter franchise. Disbanded with league after 1972 season.

MEMPHIS, TN

Memphis Blues

Texas League (AA), 1968–1970; expansion franchise. Dixie Association (C), 1971; charter franchise. Texas League (AA), 1972–1973; charter franchise. Became VICTORIA TOROS, 1974.

Memphis Blues

International League (AAA), 1975–1976; new franchise. Disbanded after 1976 season.

Memphis Browns

Western League, mid-1885; relocated franchise. Had been KANSAS CITY COWBOYS, 1885.

Memphis Chickasaws (aka Chicks)

Southern Association (A), 1912–1934; (A1), 1935–1945; (AA), 1946–1960; renamed franchise. Had been MEMPHIS TURTLES, 1909–1910. Disbanded after 1960 season.

Memphis Chicks

Alternate name for MEMPHIS CHICKASAWS.

Memphis Chicks

Southern League (AA), 1978–(still in existence as of 5-1-92); new franchise.

Memphis Egyptians

Southern Association, 1901; (A), 1902–1908; charter franchise. Renamed MEMPHIS TURTLES, 1909.

Memphis Fever Germs

Alternate name for MEMPHIS GIANTS, 1893.

Memphis Giants (aka Fever Germs, 1893; Lambs, 1895)

Southern League, 1892–1895; charter franchise. Disbanded with league after 1895 season.

Memphis Grays

Southern League, mid-1885–1886; relocated franchise. Had been KANSAS CITY COWBOYS, 1885. Renamed MEMPHIS REDS, 1887.

Memphis Lambs

Alternate name for MEMPHIS GIANTS, 1895.

Memphis Reds

Southern League, 1887–mid-1889; renamed franchise. Had been MEMPHIS GRAYS, mid-1885–1886. Disbanded during 1889 season.

MEMPHIS RED SOX

Negro National League, 1924–1925; 1927; 1929–1930; new franchise. Disbanded after 1930 season. Negro Southern League, 1932; charter franchise. Disbanded with league after 1932 season. Negro American League, 1937–1940; 1943–1950; charter franchise. Disbanded with league during 1950 season.

Memphis Red Stockings

Keystone Association, 1877; charter franchise. Disbanded with association after 1877 season.

Memphis Turtles

Southern Association (A), 1909–1910; renamed franchise. Had been MEMPHIS EPYPTIANS, 1901–1908. Renamed MEMPHIS CHICKASAWS, 1912.

MENOMINEE, MI
(See MASINETTE, WI)

Menominee Wolverines

Michigan–Wisconsin League, 1892; charter franchise. Disbanded with league after 1892 season.

MERCED, CA

Merced
California Baseball League (B), mid-1910; relocated franchise. Had been OAKLAND BASCHES, mid-1910. Disbanded with league after 1910 season.

Merced Bears
California League (C), 1941; charter franchise. Disbanded after 1941 season.

MERIDA, YUCATAN, MEXICO

(See also YUCATAN, MEXICO)

Yucatan Lions
Mexican League (AA), 1955–1958; charter franchise. Disbanded after 1958 season.

Yucatan Lions
Mexican League (AAA), 1970–1974; new franchise. Disbanded after 1974 season.

Yucatan Lions
Mexican League (AAA), 1979–(still in existence as of 5-1-92); new franchise.

Yucatan Venados (Deer)
Mexican Southeast League (A), 1964–1969; charter franchise. Disbanded after 1969 season.

MERIDEN, CT

Meriden
Connecticut League, 1884; charter franchise. Southern New England League, 1885; charter franchise. Eastern League, 1886; new franchise. Disbanded after 1886 season.

Meriden
Connecticut State League, 1888; charter franchise. Disbanded with league after 1888 season.

Meriden
Connecticut State League, 1891; charter franchise. Disbanded with league after 1891 season.

Meriden
Connecticut State League (B), 1908; new franchise. Disbanded after 1908 season.

Meriden
Eastern Association (B), mid-1913; relocated franchise. Had been HOLYOKE PAPERMAKERS, 1913. Disbanded after 1913 season.

Meriden Bulldogs
Connecticut State League, 1897/Connecticut League, 1898; charter franchise. Renamed MERIDEN SILVERITES, 1899.

Meriden Doublins
Connecticut Association (D), mid-1910; relocated franchise. Had been NORWICH BONBONS, 1910. Disbanded with association after 1910 season.

Meriden Silverites
Connecticut League, 1899–1901; (B), 1902–1905; renamed franchise. Had been MERIDEN BULLDOGS, 1897–1898. Disbanded after 1905 season.

MERIDIAN, MS

Meridian Bears
Southeastern League (B), 1940; renamed franchise. Had been MERIDIAN SCRAPPERS, 1937–1939. Renamed MERIDIAN EAGLES, 1941.

Meridian Eagles
Southeastern League (B), 1941–1942; renamed franchise. Had been MERIDIAN BEARS, 1940. Suspended operations with league after 1942 season, and did not rejoin when league resumed in 1946.

Meridian Metropolitans
Cotton States League (D), 1910–1913; charter franchise. Disbanded with league after 1913 season.

Meridian Metros
Cotton States League (D), 1927–mid-1929; renamed franchise. Had been MERIDIAN METROS, 1925–1926. Became LAKE CHARLES NEWPORTERS, mid-1929.

Meridian Mets
Mississippi State League (D), 1921; charter franchise. Cotton States League (D), 1922–1923; charter franchise. Disbanded with league after 1923 season.

Meridian Mets
Cotton States League (D), 1925–1926; expansion franchise. Renamed MERIDIAN METROS, 1927.

Meridian Millers
Southeastern League (B), 1949–1950; renamed franchise. Had been MERIDIAN PEPS, 1946–1948. Disbanded with league after 1950 season.

Meridian Millers
Cotton States League (C), 1952–1954; new franchise. Disbanded after 1954 season.

Meridian Millers
Cotton States League (C), mid-1955; relocated franchise. Had been PINE BLUFF JUDGES, 1950–mid-1955. Disbanded with league after 1955 season.

Meridian Peps
Southeastern League (B), 1946–1948; charter franchise. Renamed MERIDIAN MILLERS, 1949.

Meridian Ribboners (aka White Ribbons)
Cotton States League (D), 1905–1908; new franchise. Disbanded with league after 1908 season.

Meridian Scrappers
Southeastern League (B), 1937–1939; charter franchise. Renamed MERIDIAN BEARS, 1940.

Meridian White Ribbons
Alternate name for MERIDIAN RIBBONERS.

MESA, AZ

Mesa Jewels
Arizona State League (D), 1929; expansion franchise. Disbanded after 1929 season.

Mesa Orphans
Arizona-Texas League (C), mid-1947; relocated franchise. Had been JUAREZ INDIOS, 1947. Disbanded after 1947 season.

MEXIA, TX

Mexia Gassers
Central Texas Trolley League (D), 1915; new franchise. Central Texas League, 1916–1917; charter franchise. Disbanded with league during 1917 season.

Mexia Gushers
Texas–Oklahoma League (D), 1922; new franchise. Texas Association (D), 1923–1926; charter franchise. Lone Star League (D), 1927–1928; charter franchise. Disbanded with league after 1928 season.

MEXICALI, BAJA CALIFORNIA, MEXICO

Mexicali Aguilas (aka Eagles)
Mexican Northern League (A), 1968–1969; charter franchise. Disbanded with league after 1969 season.

Mexicali Aguilas (aka Eagles)
Mexican Pacific League (A), 1971; charter franchise. Disbanded after 1971 season.

Mexicali Aguilas (aka Eagles)
Sunset League (C), 1948–1949; new franchise. Renamed MEXICALI EAGLES, 1950.

Mexicali Eagles
Alternate name for MEXICALI AGUILAS, 1948–1949.

Mexicali Eagles
Sunset League (C), 1950; renamed franchise. Had been MEXICALI AGUILAS, 1948–1949. Southwest International League (C), 1951–1952; charter franchise. Arizona–Texas League (C), 1953–1954; new franchise. Arizona–Mexico League; 1955–1958; charter franchise. Disbanded with league after 1958 season.

MEXICO CITY, DISTRITO FEDERAL, MEXICO

Mexico City Aztecas (Aztecs)
Mexican National League (B), 1946; charter franchise. Disbanded during 1946 season.

Mexico City Diablos Rojos (Red Devils) (aka Rojos/Reds)
Mexican League (AA), 1955–1966; (AAA), 1967–(still in existence as of 5-1-92); charter franchise.

Mexico City Rojos (Reds)
Alternate name for MEXICO CITY DIABLOS ROJOS.

Mexico City Tigres (Tigers)
Mexican League (AAA), 1955–(still in existence as of 5-1-92); new franchise.

MIAMI, AZ
(See also GLOBE, AZ)

Miami Miners
Arizona State League (D), 1928–1930; charter franchise. Disbanded with league after 1930 season.

MIAMI, FL

FLORIDA MARLINS
National League; expansion franchise. To begin play, 1993.

Florida Tropics
Senior Professional Baseball Association, 1989–mid-1990; charter franchise. Disbanded during 1990–1991 season.

Greater Miami Flamingos
Florida International League (B), mid-1954; relocated franchise. Had been MIAMI BEACH FLAMINGOS, 1954. Disbanded with league after 1954 season.

Miami Amigos
Inter-American League (AAA), 1979; charter franchise. Disbanded with league during 1979 season.

Miami Hustlers
Florida State League (D), mid-1927–1928; relocated franchise. Has been FORT MYERS PALMS, 1926–mid-1927. Disbanded with league during 1928 season.

Miami Marlins
International League (AAA), 1956–1960; new franchise. Disbanded after 1960 season.

Miami Marlins
Florida State League (D), 1962; (A), 1963–1970; new franchise. Renamed MIAMI ORIOLES, 1971.

Miami Marlins
Florida State League (A), 1982–1987; renamed franchise. Had been MIAMI ORIOLES, 1971–1981. Renamed MIAMI MIRACLE, 1988.

Miami Miracle
Florida State League (A), 1988–(still in existence as of 5-1-92); renamed franchise. Had been MIAMI MARLINS, 1982–1987.

Miami Orioles
Florida State League (A), 1971–1981; renamed franchise. Had been MIAMI MARLINS, 1962–1970. Renamed MIAMI MARLINS, 1982.

Miami Seminoles
Florida East Coast League (D), 1942; renamed franchise. Had been MIAMI WAHOOS, 1940–1941. Dis-

banded with league during 1942 season.

Miami Sun Sox
Florida International League (C), 1946; charter franchise. Renamed MIAMI TOURISTS, 1947.

Miami Sun Sox
Florida International League (C), 1949–1954; renamed franchise. Had been MIAMI TOURISTS, 1947–1948. Disbanded during 1954 season.

Miami Tourists
Florida International League (C), 1947–1948; renamed franchise. Had been MIAMI SUN SOX, 1946. Renamed MIAMI SUN SOX, 1949.

Miami Wahoos
Florida East Coast League (D), 1940–1941; charter franchise. Renamed MIAMI SEMINOLES, 1942.

MIAMI, OK

Miami Blues
Kansas–Oklahoma–Missouri League (D), 1946; charter franchise. Renamed MIAMI OWLS, 1947.

Miami Eagles
Kansas–Oklahoma–Missouri League (D), 1950–1952; renamed franchise. Had been MIAMI OWLS, 1947–1949. Disbanded with league after 1952 season.

Miami Indians
Southwestern League (D), 1921; charter franchise. Disbanded after 1921 season.

Miami Owls
Kansas–Oklahoma–Missouri League (D), 1947–1949; charter franchise. Had been MIAMI BLUES, 1946. Became MIAMI EAGLES, 1950.

MIAMI BEACH, FL

Miami Beach Flamingos
Florida East Coast League (D), 1941–mid-1942; renamed fran-

chise. Disbanded with league during 1942 season.

Miami Beach Flamingos
Florida International League (B), 1946–1952; charter franchise. Disbanded after 1952 season.

Miami Beach Flamingos
Florida International League (B), 1954; new franchise. Became GREATER MIAMI FLAMINGOS, mid-1954.

Miami Beach Tigers
Florida East Coast League (D), 1940; charter franchise. Renamed MIAMI BEACH FLAMINGOS, 1941.

MICHIGAN CITY, IN

Michigan City White Caps
Midwest League (D), 1956–1959; charter franchise. Disbanded after 1959 season.

MIDDLEPORT–POMEROY, OH

Middleport–Pomeroy
Mountain States League (D), mid-1911–mid-1912; relocated franchise. Had been POINT PLEASANT–GALLIPOLIS, 1911. Became MONTGOMERY MINERS, mid-1912.

MIDDLESBORO, KY

Middlesboro Athletics
Mountain States League (D), 1949–1954; new franchise. Disbanded with league after 1954 season.

Middlesboro Colonels
Appalachian League (D), 1913–1914; relocated franchise. Had been ASHEVILLE MOUNTAINEERS, 1911–1912. Disbanded with league during 1914 season.

Middlesboro Cubsox
Appalachian League (R), 1963; renamed franchise. Had been MID-

DLESBORO SENATORS, 1961–1962. Disbanded after 1963 season.

Middlesboro Senators
Appalachian League (D), 1961–1962; new franchise. Renamed MIDDLESBORO CUBSOX, 1963.

MIDDLETOWN, CT

Middletown Jewels
Connecticut Association (D), 1910; charter franchise. Disbanded with league after 1910 season.

MIDDLETOWN MANSFIELDS
National Association, 1872; charter franchise. Disbanded during 1872 season.

MIDDLETOWN, NY

Middletown
Eastern League (AA), 1909; new franchise. Disbanded after 1909 season.

Middletown Middies
New York–New Jersey League (D), 1913; charter franchise. Atlantic League (D), 1914; charter franchise. Disbanded with league after 1914 season.

MIDDLETOWN, OH

Middletown Red Sox
Ohio State League (D), 1944; charter franchise. Renamed MIDDLETOWN ROCKETS, 1945.

Middletown Rockets
Ohio State League (D), 1945–1946; renamed franchise. Had been MIDDLETOWN REDS, 1944. Disbanded after 1946 season.

MIDLAND, TX

Midland Angels
Texas League (AA), 1986–(still in existence as of 5-1-92); renamed

franchise. Had been MIDLAND CUBS, 1972–1985.

Midland Braves
Sophomore League (D), 1958–1959; charter franchise. Disbanded after 1959 season.

Midland Cardinals
West Texas–New Mexico League (D), 1937–1938; charter franchise. Renamed MIDLAND COWBOYS, 1939.

Midland Colts
West Texas League (D), 1928–1929; charter franchise. Disbanded with league after 1929 season.

Midland Cowboys
West Texas–New Mexico League (D), 1939–1940; renamed franchise. Had been MIDLAND CARDINALS, 1937–1938. Disbanded after 1940 season.

Midland Cubs
Texas League (AA), 1972–1985; expansion franchise. Renamed MIDLAND ANGELS, 1986.

Midland Indians
Longhorn League (D), 1947–1950; (C), 1951–1955; charter franchise. Southwestern League (B), 1956–mid-1957; charter franchise. Became LAMESA INDIANS, mid-1957.

MIGUEL ALEMAN, VERACRUZ, MEXICO

Miguel Aleman
Mexican Center League (A), 1978; new franchise. Disbanded after 1978 season.

MILAN–TRENTON, TN
(See also TRENTON, TN)

Milan–Trenton Twins
KITTY League (D), mid-1923; relocated franchise. Had been SPRINGFIELD BLANKETMAKERS, 1923. Disbanded after 1923 season.

MILFORD, DE

Milford Giants
Eastern Shore League (D), 1938–1941; relocated franchise. Had been CRISFIELD CRABBERS, 1937. Disbanded with league after 1941 season.

Milford Red Sox
Eastern Shore League (D), 1946–1948; charter franchise. Disbanded after 1948 season.

Milford Sandpipers
Eastern Shore League (D), 1923; expansion franchise. Disbanded during 1923 season.

MILLER, SD

Miller
South Dakota League (D), 1920; charter franchise. Disbanded after 1920 season.

MILLINOCKET, ME

Millinocket
Northern Maine League (D), 1902; charter franchise. Disbanded with league after 1902 season.

Millinocket Papermakers
Northern Maine League (D), 1909; charter franchise. Disbanded with league after 1909 season.

MILLVILLE, NJ

Millville
New Jersey State League, 1897; charter franchise. Disbanded during 1897 season.

MILTON, PA

Milton
Central Pennsylvania League, 1887–1888; charter franchise. Disbanded with league during 1888 season.

MILWAUKEE, WI

Milwaukee
Northwestern League, 1884; new franchise. Disbanded with league after 1884 season.

MILWAUKEE BEARS
Negro National League, 1923; new franchise. Disbanded during 1923 season.

MILWAUKEE BRAVES
National League, 1953–1965; relocated franchise. Had been BOSTON BRAVES, 1941–1952. Became ATLANTA BRAVES, 1966.

MILWAUKEE BREWERS
National League, 1878; new franchise. Disbanded during 1878 season.

MILWAUKEE BREWERS (aka GRAYS or CREAM CITY)
Union Association, 1884; charter franchise. Disbanded during 1884 season.

Milwaukee Brewers
Western Association, 1888; charter franchise. Renamed MILWAUKEE CREAMS, 1889.

Milwaukee Brewers
Western League, 1898–1900; renamed franchise. Had been MILWAUKEE CREAMS, 1896–1897. American League, 1901; charter franchise. Became ST. LOUIS BROWNS, 1902.

MILWAUKEE BREWERS
American Association, 1891; new franchise. Western League, 1892; expansion franchise. Disbanded with league during 1892 season.

Milwaukee Brewers
Western League, 1894–1895; charter franchise. Renamed MILWAUKEE CREAMS, 1896.

Milwaukee Brewers
American Association (A), 1903–1907; (AA), 1908–1945; (AAA), 1946–1952; charter franchise. Disbanded after 1952 season.

MILWAUKEE BREWERS
American League, 1970–(still in existence as of 5-1-92); relocated franchise. Had been SEATTLE PILOTS, 1969.

Milwaukee Chicks
All-American Girls Professional Baseball League, 1944; new franchise. Became GRAND RAPIDS CHICKS, 1945.

MILWAUKEE CREAM CITY
Alternate name for MILWAUKEE BREWERS, 1884.

Milwaukee Cream Citys
Western League, 1885; charter franchise. Northwestern League, 1886–1887; charter franchise. Disbanded with league after 1887 season.

Milwaukee Creams
Western Association, 1889–1891; renamed franchise. Had been MILWAUKEE BREWERS, 1888. Disbanded after 1891 season.

Milwaukee Creams
Western League, 1896–1897; renamed franchise. Had been MILWAUKEE BREWERS, 1894–1895. Renamed MILWAUKEE BREWERS, 1898.

Milwaukee Creams
Western League (A), 1902–1903; new franchise. Disbanded after 1903 season.

Milwaukee Creams
Wisconsin–Illinois League (D), 1913; new franchise. Became FOND DU LAC MOLLS, mid-1913.

MILWAUKEE GRAYS
Alternate name for MILWAUKEE BREWERS, 1884.

MILWAUKEE WEST ENDS
Keystone Association, 1877; charter franchise. Disbanded with association after 1877 season.

MINATITLAN, VER, MEXICO

Minatitlan Oilers
Mexican Southeast League (A), 1968; new franchise. Disbanded after 1968 season.

Minatitlan Reds
Mexican Southeast League (A), mid-1969; relocated franchise. Had been LAS CHOAPAS REDS, 1969. Disbanded after 1969 season.

MINERAL WELLS, TX

Mineral Wells
Texas–Oklahoma League (D), mid-1921; relocated franchise. Had been GRAHAM HIJACKERS, 1921. Disbanded after 1921 season.

Mineral Wells Resorters
West Texas League (D), 1920–mid-1921; charter franchise. Became BALLINGER BEARCATS, mid-1921.

MINERSVILLE, PA

Minersville
Central Pennsylvania League, 1887; charter franchise. Disbanded during 1887 season.

MINNEAPOLIS, KS

Minneapolis
Kansas State League, 1896; new franchise. Disbanded with league after 1896 season.

Minneapolis
Kansas State League, 1905; new franchise. Disbanded with league after 1905 season.

Minneapolis
Central Kansas League (D), mid-1912; relocated franchise. Had been NEWTON RAILROADERS, 1912. Disbanded with league after 1912 season.

Minneapolis Minnies
Central Kansas League (D), 1908–1909; new franchise. Disbanded after 1909 season.

MINNEAPOLIS, MN

Minneapolis
Keystone Association, 1877; charter franchise. Disbanded during 1877 season.

Minneapolis
Northwestern League, 1884; new franchise. Disbanded with league after 1884 season.

Minneapolis
Northwestern League, 1886–1887; charter franchise. Disbanded with league after 1887 season.

Minneapolis
Western League, 1901; charter franchise. Disbanded after 1901 season.

Minneapolis
Northern League (C), 1913; charter franchise. Disbanded after 1913 season.

Minneapolis Millerettes
All-American Girls Professional Baseball League; new franchise, 1944. Disbanded after 1944 season.

Minneapolis Millers
Western Association, 1889–1891/League, 1892–1899; new franchise. American League, 1900; charter franchise. Became CHICAGO WHITE SOX, 1901.

Minneapolis Millers
American Association (A), 1903–1907; (AA), 1908–1945; (AAA), 1946–1960; charter franchise. Became PHOENIX GIANTS, 1958; replaced by SAN FRANCISCO SEALS. Disbanded after 1960 season.

Minneapolis Minnies
Western Association, 1888; new franchise. Became DAVENPORT, mid-1888.

MINNESOTA TWINS
American League, 1961–(still in existence as of 5-1-92); relocated franchise. Played in Bloomington, MN, 1961–1981; from 1982–present plays in Minneapolis. Had been WASHINGTON SENATORS, 1957–1960.

MINOT, ND

Minot Magicians
North Dakota League (D), 1923; charter franchise. Disbanded with league during 1923 season.

Minot Mallards
Northern League (C), 1958–1960; new franchise. Disbanded after 1960 season.

Minot Mallards
Northern League (C), 1962; new franchise. Disbanded after 1962 season.

Minot Why-Nots
Northern League (D), 1917; new franchise. Disbanded with league during 1917 season.

MISSION, TX

Mission Grapefruiters
Gulf Coast League (D), mid-1926; relocated franchise. Had been KINGSVILLE JERSEYS, 1926. Texas Valley League (D), 1927–1928; charter franchise. Disbanded with league after 1928 season.

MISSOULA, MT

Missoula
Montana State League, 1892; charter franchise. Disbanded with league after 1892 season.

Missoula
Union Association (C), 1911 (D), 1912–1913; charter franchise. Disbanded after 1913 season.

Missoula Timberjacks
Pioneer League (C), 1956–1960; new franchise. Disbanded after 1960 season.

MITCHELL, SD

Mitchell Kernels
South Dakota League (D), 1920; charter franchise. Dakota League (D), 1921–1923; charter franchise. Disbanded with league after 1923 season.

Mitchell Kernels
Nebraska State League (D), 1936–1937; new franchise. Disbanded after 1937 season.

Mitchell Kernels
Western League (D), 1939; charter franchise. Disbanded after 1939 season.

Mitchell Kernels
Western League (D), mid-1940; relocated franchise. Had been SIOUX CITY COWBOYS, 1939–mid-1940. Disbanded after 1940 season.

MOBILE, AL

Mobile
Southern League, mid-1895; relocated franchise. Had been CHATTANOOGA WARRIORS, 1895. Disbanded after 1895 season.

Mobile A's
Southern League (AA), 1966; new franchise. Disbanded after 1966 season.

Mobile Bears
Southern League, mid-1889; relocated franchise. Had been BIRMINGHAM MAROONS, 1888–mid-1889. Disbanded with league after 1889 season.

Mobile Bears
Southern Association (A), 1918–1930; renamed franchise. Had been MOBILE SEA GULLS, 1908–1917. Disbanded after 1930 season.

Mobile Bears
Southern Association (A1), mid-1944–1945; (AA), 1946–1961; relocated franchise. Had been KNOXVILLE SMOKIES, 1925–mid-1944. Disbanded with league after 1961 season.

Mobile Blackbirds
Southern League, 1892–1893; charter franchise. Renamed MOBILE BLUEBIRDS, 1894.

Mobile Blackbirds
Southern League, mid-1898–1899; relocated franchise. Had been BIRMINGHAM REDS, 1898. Disbanded with league after 1899 season.

Mobile Bluebirds
Southern League, 1894; renamed franchise. Had been MOBILE BLACKBIRDS, 1892–1893. Became ATLANTA ATLANTAS, mid-1894.

Mobile Gulls
Alternate name for MOBILE SEA GULLS.

Mobile Marines
Southern Association (A), 1931; new franchise. Became KNOXVILLE SMOKIES, mid-1931.

Mobile Red Warriors
Southeastern League (D), 1932; charter franchise. Disbanded with league after 1932 season.

Mobile Sea Gulls (aka Gulls)
Cotton States League (D), mid-1905–1907; relocated franchise. Had been NATCHEZ HILL CLIMBERS, 1902–mid-1905. Disbanded with league after 1907 season.

Mobile Sea Gulls (aka Gulls)
Southern Association (A), 1908–1917; relocated franchise. Had

been SHREVEPORT PIRATES, 1901–1907. Renamed MOBILE BEARS, 1918.

Mobile Skippers
Southeastern League (D), 1937–1942; charter franchise. Disbanded with league after 1942 season.

Mobile Swamp Angels
Southern League, 1887; new franchise. Disbanded after 1887 season.

Mobile White Sox
Southern League (AA), 1970; new franchise. Disbanded with league after 1970 season.

MODESTO, CA

Modesto A's
California League (A), 1975–(still in existence as of 5-1-92); renamed franchise. Had been MODESTO REDS, 1972–1974.

Modesto Cardinals
California League (A), 1971; renamed franchise. Had been MODESTO REDS, 1966–1970. Renamed MODESTO REDS, 1972.

Modesto Colt '45s
California League (A), 1962–1964; renamed franchise. Had been MODESTO REDS, 1946–1961. Disbanded after 1964 season.

Modesto Reds
California State League (D), 1914; new franchise. Disbanded with league during 1914 season.

Modesto Reds
California League (A), 1946–1961; charter franchise. Renamed MODESTO COLT '45S, 1962.

Modesto Reds
California League (A), 1966–1970; new franchise. Renamed MODESTO CARDINALS, 1971.

Modesto Reds
California League (A), 1972–1974; renamed franchise. Had

been MODESTO CARDINALS, 1971. Renamed MODESTO A'S, 1975.

MOLINE, IL
(In conjunction with Bettendorf, IA–Davenport, IA–Rock Island, IL)

Quad Cities Angels
Midwest League (A), 1962–1978; renamed franchise. Had been QUAD CITIES BRAVES, 1960–1961. Renamed QUAD CITIES CUBS, 1979.

Quad Cities Angels
Midwest League (A), 1985–(still in existence as of 5-1-92); renamed franchise. Had been QUAD CITIES CUBS, 1979–1984.

Quad Cities Braves
Midwest League (A), 1960–1961; new franchise. Renamed QUAD CITY ANGELS, 1962.

Quad Cities Pirates
Three I League (B), 1949; renamed franchise. Had been QUAD CITY CUBS, 1946–1948. Renamed QUAD CITY QUADS, 1950.

Quad Cities Quads
Three I League (B), 1950; renamed franchise. Had been DAVENPORT PIRATES, 1948–1949. Renamed QUAD CITIES TIGERS, 1951.

Quad Cities Tigers
Three I League (B), 1951; renamed franchise. Had been QUAD CITIES QUADS, 1950. Disbanded after 1952 season.

Quad City Cubs
Three I League (B), 1946–1948; charter franchise. Renamed QUAD CITIES PIRATES, 1949.

Quad City Cubs
Midwest League (A), 1979–1984; charter franchise. Renamed QUAD CITIES ANGELS, 1985.

MOLINE, IL
(See also DAVENPORT, IA; BETTENDORF IL)

Moline
Western Association, mid-1894; relocated franchise. Had been ROCK ISLAND–MOLINE ISLANDERS, 1893–mid-1894. Disbanded after 1894 season.

Moline A's
Central Association (D), 1947–mid-1948; charter franchise. Became KEWANEE A'S, mid-1948.

Moline Plowboys
Illinois–Iowa–Indiana League (B), mid-1914–1917; relocated franchise. Had been DANVILLE SPEAKERS, 1910–mid-1914. Disbanded with league during 1917 season.

Moline Plowboys
Illinois–Iowa–Indiana League (B), 1919–1923; charter franchise. Mississippi Valley League (D), 1924–1932; new franchise. Disbanded after 1932 season.

Moline Plowboys (aka Plows)
Three I League (B), 1937–1941; charter franchise. Disbanded after 1941 season.

Moline Plows
Alternate name for MOLINE PLOWBOYS, 1937–1941.

MOLINE–
ROCK ISLAND, IL
(See also ROCK ISLAND, IL)

Moline
Illinois–Iowa League, 1892; new franchise. Disbanded with league after 1892 season.

MONAHANS, TX

Monahans Trojans
West Texas–New Mexico League (D), 1937; charter franchise. Disbanded after 1937 season.

MONCLOVA– COAHUILA–SABINAS, MEXICO
(See also COAHUILA, MEXICO and SABINAS, MEXICO)

Monclova–Coahuila Acereros (Steelers)
Mexican League (AAA), 1974–1980; new franchise. Disbanded after 1980 season.

Monclova–Coahuila Acereros (Steelers)
Mexican League (AAA), 1982– (still in existence as of 5-1-92); renamed franchise. Had been MONCLOVA–COAHUILA WHITE DEVILS, 1982.

Monclova–Coahuila White Devils
Mexican League (AAA), 1982; new franchise. Renamed MONCLOVA–COAHUILA ACEREROS (Steelers), 1982.

MONCTON, NEW BRUNSWICK, CANADA

Moncton
New Brunswick League, 1890; charter franchise. Disbanded with league after 1890 season.

MONESSEN, PA

Monessen Cardinals
Pennsylvania State Association (D), 1937; renamed franchise. Had been MONESSEN INDIANS, 1936. Disbanded after 1937 season.

Monessen Indians
Pennsylvania State Association (D), mid-1934; charter franchise. Renamed MONESSEN LITTLE REDS, 1935.

Monessen Indians
Pennsylvania State Association (D), 1936; renamed franchise. Had been MONESSEN LITTLE REDS, 1935.

Renamed MONESSEN CARDINALS, 1937.

Monessen Little Reds
Pennsylvania State Association (D), 1935; renamed franchise. Had been MONESSEN INDIANS, mid-1934. Renamed MONESSEN INDIANS, 1936.

MONETT, MO

Monett Red Birds
Arkansas–Missouri League (D), 1936–1939; charter franchise. Disbanded after 1939 season.

MONMOUTH, IL

Monmouth Browns
Illinois–Missouri League (D), 1908–1909; charter franchise. Central Association (D), 1910–1913; new franchise. Disbanded after 1913 season.

Monmouth Maple Cities
Central Inter-State League, mid-1889; relocated franchise. Had been DAVENPORT, 1888–mid-1889. Illinois–Iowa League, 1890; charter franchise. Disbanded after 1890 season.

MONROE, LA

Monroe
Cotton States League (D), 1902–1904; expansion franchise. Disbanded after 1904 season.

Monroe
Arkansas States League (D), 1909; new franchise. Became BATESVILLE–NEWPORT, mid-1909.

Monroe Drillers
Cotton States League (D), 1924–mid-1932; new franchise. Disbanded with league during 1932 season.

MONROE MONARCHS
Negro Southern League, 1932; charter franchise. Disbanded with league after 1932 season.

Monroe Municipals
Gulf Coast League (D), 1907; charter franchise. Cotton States League (D), 1908; new franchise. Disbanded after 1908 season.

Monroe Sports
Cotton States League (C), 1950–1953; new franchise. Renamed TWIN CITIES SPORTS, 1954.

Monroe Twins
Cotton States League (C), 1937; new franchise. Renamed MONROE WHITE SOX, 1938.

Monroe White Sox
Cotton States League (C), 1938–1941; renamed franchise. Had been MONROE TWINS, 1937. Disbanded with league after 1941 season.

MONROE– WEST MONROE, LA

Monroe Twins
Evangeline League (C), 1956; new franchise. Disbanded after 1956 season.

Twin Cities Sports
Cotton States League (C), 1954–1955; renamed franchise. Had been MONROE SPORTS, 1950–1953. Disbanded with league after 1955 season.

MONROE, NC

Monroe Indians
Western Carolinas League (A), mid-1969; relocated franchise. Had been STATESVILLE INDIANS, 1969. Disbanded after 1969 season.

Monroe Pirates
Western Carolinas League (A), 1971; new franchise. Disbanded after 1971 season.

MONTERREY, NUEVO LEON, MEXICO

Monterrey A's
Mexican Center League (A), 1970–1971; new franchise. Renamed MONTERREY INDIANS, 1972.

Monterrey Indians
Mexican Center League (A), 1972; renamed franchise. Had been MONTERREY A'S, 1970–1971. Disbanded after 1972 season.

Monterrey Industriales (Industrials)
Mexican League (AAA), 1971– (still in existence as of 5-1-92); new franchise.

Monterrey Monjes Grises (Gray Monks)
Mexican League (AAA), 1991– (still in existence as of 5-1-92); new franchise.

Monterrey Sultanes (Sultans)
Mexican League (AA), 1955–1966; (AAA), 1967–(still in existence as of 5-1-92); charter franchise.

MONTESANO, WA

Montesano
Washington State League (D), 1910; charter franchise. Disbanded with league during 1910 season.

Montesano
Southwest Washington League (D), 1905; new franchise. Disbanded after 1905 season.

Montesano
Washington State League (D), 1910; charter franchise. Disbanded after 1910 season.

MONTGOMERY, AL

Arkansas Travelers
Southern Association (AA), 1956; relocated franchise. Had been ARKANSAS/LITTLE ROCK TRAVELERS,

1955. Became ARKANSAS/LITTLE ROCK, 1957.

Montgomery Billikens
Southern Association (A), 1911; renamed franchise. Had been MONTGOMERY CLIMBERS, 1909–1910. Renamed MONTGOMERY REBELS, 1912.

Montgomery Black Sox
Southern Association (A), 1903–mid-1915; relocated franchise. Had been CHATTANOOGA LOOKOUTS, 1901–1902. Became ARKANSAS (aka Little Rock) TRAVELERS, mid-1915.

Montgomery Bombers
Southeastern League (C), 1937–1938; charter franchise. Renamed MONTGOMERY REBELS, 1939.

Montgomery Capitals
Southeastern League (B), 1932; charter franchise. Disbanded during 1932 season.

Montgomery Climbers
Southern Association (A), 1909–1910; renamed franchise. Had been MONTGOMERY SENATORS, 1904–1908. Renamed MONTGOMERY BILLIKENS, 1911.

Montgomery Colts
Southern League, 1893; renamed franchise. Had been MONTGOMERY LAMBS, 1892. Disbanded after 1893 season.

Montgomery Grays
Southern League, 1895–1896; new franchise. Disbanded with league after 1896 season.

Montgomery Grays
South Atlantic League (A), 1952–1953; renamed franchise. Had been MONTGOMERY REBELS, 1939–1943; 1946–1952. Renamed MONTGOMERY REBELS, 1954.

MONTGOMERY GREY SOX
Negro Southern League, 1932; charter franchise. Disbanded with league after 1932 season.

Montgomery Lambs
Southern League, 1892; charter franchise. Renamed MONTGOMERY COLTS, 1893.

Montgomery Lions
Southeastern League (D), 1926–1930; charter franchise. Disbanded with league after 1930 season.

Montgomery Rebels
South Atlantic League (C), 1916–mid-1917; new franchise. Disbanded with league during 1917 season.

Montgomery Rebels
Southern Association (A), 1912–1915; renamed franchise. Had been MONTGOMERY BILLIKENS, 1911. Became ARKANSAS/LITTLE ROCK, mid-1915.

Montgomery Rebels
Southeastern League (B), 1939–1942; renamed franchise. Had been MONTGOMERY BOMBERS, 1937–1939. Suspended operations with league after 1942 season.

Montgomery Rebels
Southern Association (A1), mid-1943; relocated franchise. Had been CHATTANOOGA LOOKOUTS, 1910–mid-1943. Suspended operations, 1944–1945. Southeastern League (B), 1946–1950; charter franchise. South Atlantic League (A), 1951; new franchise. Renamed MONTGOMERY GRAYS, 1952.

Montgomery Rebels
South Atlantic League (A), 1954–mid-1956; renamed franchise. Had been MONTGOMERY GRAYS, 1952–1953. Became KNOXVILLE SMOKIES, mid-1956.

Montgomery Rebels
Alabama–Florida League (D), 1957–1962; new franchise. Disbanded with league after 1962 season.

Montgomery Rebels
Southern League (AA), 1965–1970; new franchise. Dixie Association (C), 1971; charter franchise. Southern League (AA), 1972–1980; charter franchise. Disbanded after 1980 season.

Montgomery Senators
Southern League, 1898–mid-1899; charter franchise. Became DALLAS-FORT WORTH, mid-1899.

Montgomery Senators
Southern Association (A), 1904–1908; renamed franchise. Had been MONTGOMERY BLACK SOX, 1903. Renamed MONTGOMERY CLIMBERS, 1909.

MONTGOMERY, AR
(See LITTLE ROCK, AR)

MONTGOMERY, WV

Montgomery Miners
Virginia Valley League (D), 1910; charter franchise. Mountain States League (D), 1911; charter franchise. Disbanded during 1911 season.

Montgomery Miners
Mountain States League (D), mid-1912; relocated franchise. Had been MIDDLEPORT-POMEROY, mid-1911–mid-1912. Disbanded with league after 1912 season.

MONTPELIER, VT
(See also BARRE, VT)

Montpelier
Northern League (D), 1905; new franchise. Disbanded with league after 1905 season.

Montpelier Capital Citys
Northeastern League, 1887; charter franchise. Disbanded during 1887 season.

Montpelier Goldfish
Quebec–Ontario–Vermont League (B), 1924; charter franchise. Disbanded with league after 1924 season.

MONTREAL, QUEBEC, CANADA

Montreal
International League, mid-1890; charter franchise. Had been HAMILTON BLACKBIRDS, 1890.

Montreal
International League, 1890; relocated franchise. Had been BUFFALO BISONS, mid-1890. Became GRAND RAPIDS, mid-1890.

Montreal
Eastern International League, 1895; charter franchise. Disbanded with league during 1885 season.

MONTREAL EXPOS
National League, 1969–(still in existence as of 5-1-92); expansion franchise.

Montreal Jingos
Eastern League, mid-1897–1900; relocated franchise. Had been ROCHESTER BROWNIES, 1895–mid-1897. Renamed MONTREAL ROYALS, 1901.

Montreal Royals
Eastern League, 1901; (A), 1902; renamed franchise. Had been MONTREAL JINGOS, 1897–1900. Disbanded after 1902 season.

Montreal Royals
Eastern League (A), mid-1903–1907; (AA), 1908–1911; renamed franchise. Had been WORCESTER RIDDLES, 1903. International League (AA), 1912–1917; charter franchise. Disbanded after 1917 season.

Montreal Royals
Eastern Canada League (B), 1922–mid-1923; charter franchise. Disbanded during 1923 season.

Montreal Royals
Eastern Canada League (B), mid-1923; relocated franchise. Had been THREE RIVERS TRIOS, 1922–mid-1923. Quebec–Ontario–Vermont League (B), 1924; charter franchise. Disbanded with league after 1924 season.

Montreal Royals
International League (AA), 1928–1945; (AAA), 1946–1960; new franchise. Disbanded after 1960 season.

MOOREHEAD, MN

Moorehead
Red River Valley League, 1897; charter franchise. Disbanded with league during 1897 season.

MOORESVILLE, NC

Mooresville Moors
North Carolina State League (D), 1937–1942; 1945–1952; charter franchise. Tar Heel League (D), 1953; charter franchise. Disbanded after 1953 season.

MOOSE JAW, SASKATCHEWAN, CANADA
(See also SASKATOON, CANADA)

Moose Jaw Millers
Western Canada League (B), 1921; renamed franchise. Had been MOOSE JAW ROBIN HOODS, 1919–1920. Disbanded with league after 1921 season.

Moose Jaw Robin Hoods
Western Canada League (D), 1909–1911; charter franchise. Disbanded after 1911 season.

Moose Jaw Robin Hoods
Western Canada League (D), 1913–1914; new franchise. Disbanded with league after 1914 season.

Moose Jaw Robin Hoods
Western Canada League (C), 1919, (B), 1920; charter franchise. Renamed MOOSE JAW MILLERS, 1921.

MOREHEAD, MN
(See FARGO, ND)

MORGAN CITY, LA
Morgan City Oyster Shockers
Gulf Coast League (D), 1908; new franchise. Disbanded with league after 1908 season.

MORGANTOWN, NC
Morgantown Aggies
Western Carolina League (D), 1948–1952; charter franchise. Disbanded with league after 1952 season.

MOROLEON, MX
Moroleon
Mexican Center League (A), 1975; new franchise. Disbanded with league after 1975 season.

MORRISTOWN, TN
Morristown Cubs
Appalachian League (D), 1959–1961; new franchise. Disbanded after 1961 season.

Morristown Jobbers
Southeastern League (D), 1910; charter franchise. Appalachian League (D), 1911–1912; charter franchise. Became ROME ROMANS, 1913.

Morristown Jobbers
Appalachian League (D), 1913–mid-1914; relocated franchise. Had been CLEVELAND COUNTS, 1911–1912. Disbanded with league during 1914 season.

Morristown Red Sox
Mountain States League (D), 1948–mid-1954; charter franchise. Disbanded during 1954 season.

Morristown Roosters
Appalachian League (D), 1923–mid-1925; expansion franchise. Disbanded with league during 1925 season.

Morristown Twins
Mountain States League (D), mid-1954; relocated franchise. Had been MARYVILLE–ALCOA TWINS, 1953–mid-1954. Disbanded with league after 1954 season.

MOULTRIE, GA
Moultrie Athletics
Georgia–Florida League (D), 1948–1949; renamed franchise. Had been MOULTRIE PACKERS, 1941–1942; 1946–1947. Renamed MOULTRIE CUBS, 1950.

Moultrie Colt .22s
Georgia–Florida League (D), 1962; (A), 1963; new franchise. Disbanded with league after 1963 season.

Moultrie Cubs
Georgia–Florida League (D), 1950; renamed franchise. Had been MOULTRIE ATHLETICS, 1948–1949. Renamed MOULTRIE TO-BAKS, 1951.

Moultrie Giants
Georgia–Florida League (D), 1952; renamed franchise. Had been MOULTRIE TO-BAKS, 1951. Disbanded after 1952 season.

Moultrie Packers
Dixie League (D), 1916–1917; charter franchise. Disbanded with league during 1917 season.

Moultrie Packers
Georgia–Florida League (D), 1936–1942; 1946–1947; renamed franchise. Had been MOULTRIE STEERS, 1935. Renamed MOULTRIE ATHLETICS, 1948.

Moultrie Phillies
Georgia–Florida League (D), 1957; renamed franchise. Had been MOULTRIE GIANTS, 1955–1956. Became BRUNSWICK PHILLIES, mid-1957.

Moultrie Reds
Georgia–Florida League (D), 1955–1956; new franchise. Renamed MOULTRIE PHILLIES, 1957.

Moultrie Steers
Georgia–Florida League (D), 1935; charter franchise. Renamed MOULTRIE PACKERS, 1936.

Moultrie To–baks
Georgia–Florida League (D), 1951; renamed franchise. Had been MOULTRIE CUBS, 1950. Renamed MOULTRIE GIANTS, 1952.

MOUNT AIRY, NC
Mount Airy Graniteers
Bi-State League (NC–VA), (D), mid-1934; expansion franchise. Renamed MOUNT AIRY REDS, 1935.

Mount Airy Graniteers
Bi-State League (NC–VA), (D), 1939–1941; renamed franchise. Had been MOUNT AIRY REDS, 1935–1938. Disbanded after 1941 season.

Mount Airy Graniteers
Blue Ridge League (D), 1946–1950; charter franchise. Disbanded with league after 1950 season.

Mount Airy Reds
Bi-State League (NC–VA), (D), 1935–1938; renamed franchise. Had been MOUNT AIRY GRANITEERS, mid-1934. Renamed MOUNT AIRY GRANITEERS, 1939.

MOUNT CARMEL, PA
Mount Carmel
Central Pennsylvania League, 1887–1888; charter franchise. Dis-

banded with league during 1888 season.

Mount Carmel
Central Pennsylvania League, 1896; charter franchise. Became ASHLAND, mid-1896.

Mount Carmel
Pennsylvania State League (D), mid-1916; relocated franchise. Had been LEBANON, 1916. Disbanded with league after 1916 season.

Mount Carmel
Keystone League (D), 1935; charter franchise. Disbanded with league after 1935 season.

Mount Carmel
Anthracite League (D), 1928; charter franchise. Disbanded with league during 1928 season.

Mount Carmel Reliance
Central Pennsylvania League, 1887–1888; charter franchise. Disbanded with league after 1888 season.

MOUNT CLEMENS, MI

Mount Clemens
Border League (D), 1912; charter franchise. Disbanded with league during 1912 season.

Mount Clemens
Border League (D), 1913; charter franchise. Disbanded with league during 1913 season.

Mount Clemens Bathers
Southern Michigan Association (C), 1906–1907; charter franchise. Disbanded after 1907 season.

Mount Clemens Bathers
Eastern Michigan League (D), mid-1914; relocated franchise. Had been LANSING SENATORS, 1907–mid-1914. Disbanded with league during 1914 season.

MOUNT PLEASANT, TX

Mount Pleasant Cats (aka Long Cats)
East Texas League (D), 1923–1925; charter franchise. Merged with LONGVIEW CANNIBALS, 1926.

Mount Pleasant Long Cats
Alternate name for MOUNT PLEASANT CATS.

MOUNT STERLING, KY

Mount Sterling Essex
Blue Grass League (D), 1922–1923; charter franchise. Disbanded after 1923 season.

Mount Sterling Orphans
Blue Grass League (D), mid-1912; relocated franchise. Had been NICHOLASVILLE, 1912. Disbanded with league after 1912 season.

MOUNT VERNON, IL

Mount Vernon
Southern Illinois (D), 1910; charter franchise. Disbanded with league during 1910 season.

Mount Vernon Braves
Illinois State League (B), 1947–1948; charter franchise. Disbanded with league after 1948 season.

Mount Vernon Kings
MOV League (D), 1949–1954; charter franchise. Disbanded after 1954 season.

Mount Vernon Merchants
Southern Illinois League (D), 1910; charter franchise. Disbanded with league after 1910 season.

MOUNT VERNON, OH

Mount Vernon Clippers
Ohio–Pennsylvania League (D), 1905; charter franchise. Disbanded with league after 1905 season.

MULBERRY, KS

Mulberry
Southeast Kansas League (D), 1911; charter franchise. Disbanded with league after 1911 season.

MUNCIE, IN

Muncie
Indiana State League, 1890; charter franchise. Disbanded with league after 1890 season.

Muncie
Indiana State League, 1900–1901; charter franchise. Disbanded with league after 1901 season.

Muncie
Inter-State Association (C), 1906; charter franchise. Disbanded with league after 1906 season.

Muncie Fruit Jars
Indiana–Ohio League (D), 1907; charter franchise. Disbanded with league after 1907 season.

Muncie Hoosiers
Indiana–Illinois League, 1899; charter franchise. Became CRAWFORDSVILLE ORPHANS, mid-1899.

Muncie Packers
Ohio–Indiana League (D), 1948; new franchise. Renamed MUNCIE REDS, 1949.

Muncie Reds
Ohio State League (D), 1947; new franchise. Became MUNCIE PACKERS, 1948.

Muncie Reds
Ohio–Indiana League (D), 1949–1950; renamed franchise. Had been MUNCIE PACKERS, 1948. Disbanded after 1950 season.

MURRAY, UT

Murray Infants
Union Association (D), 1914; new franchise. Disbanded during 1914 season.

MUSCATINE, IA

Muscatine Camels
Central Association (D), 1911; new franchise. Renamed MUSCATINE WALLOPERS, 1912.

Muscatine Muskies
Central Association (D), 1915–1916; renamed franchise. Had been MUSCATINE WALLOPERS, 1912–1914. Disbanded after 1916 season.

Muscatine Pearl Finders
Northern Association of Baseball (C), 1910; (D), mid-1910; charter franchise. Disbanded with association after 1910 season.

Muscatine Wallopers
Central Association (D), 1912–1914; renamed franchise. Had been MUSCATINE CAMELS, 1911. Renamed MUSCATINE MUSKIES, 1915.

MUSKEGON, MI

Muskegon
Northwestern League, 1884; new franchise. Disbanded during 1884 season.

Muskegon
Michigan State League, 1890; new franchise. Disbanded with league during 1890 season.

Muskegon
Michigan State League (D), 1902; charter franchise. Disbanded with league during 1902 season.

Muskegon
Michigan–Ontario League (B), 1923–1924; expansion franchise. Disbanded after 1924 season.

Muskegon Clippers
Central League (D), 1948–1951; charter franchise. Disbanded with league after 1951 season.

Muskegon Daniels
Alternate name for MUSKEGON MUSKIES, 1922.

Muskegon Lassies
All-American Girls Professional Baseball League, 1946; new franchise. Became KALAMAZOO LASSIES, 1951.

Muskegon Muskies
Central League (B), 1917; renamed franchise. Had been MUSKEGON REDS, 1916. Disbanded with league after 1917 season.

Muskegon Muskies (aka Daniels, 1922)
Central League (D), 1920–1922; charter franchise. Disbanded with league after 1920 season.

Muskegon Reds
Central League (B), 1916; new franchise. Renamed MUSKEGON MUSKIES, 1917.

Muskegon Reds
Central League (C), 1926; charter franchise. Michigan State League (B), 1926; charter franchise. Disbanded with league after 1926 season.

Muskegon Reds
Central League (B), 1934; charter franchise. Disbanded during 1934 season.

Muskegon Reds
Michigan State League (D), 1940–1941; charter franchise. Disbanded with league after 1941 season.

Muskegon Speed Boys (aka Speeders)
West Michigan League (D), 1910; charter franchise. Michigan State League (D), 1911–1914; charter franchise. Disbanded with league after 1914 season.

Muskegon Speeders
Alternate name for MUSKEGON SPEED BOYS.

MUSKOGEE, OK

Muskogee
OAK League (D), 1907; charter franchise. Became CHANUTE, mid-1907.

Muskogee
Western Association (D), 1909–mid-1911; new franchise. Disbanded with league during 1911 season.

Muskogee A's
Western Association (C), 1924–1926; new franchise. Renamed MUSKOGEE CHIEFS, 1927.

Muskogee Chiefs
Western Association (B), 1927; (C), mid-1927–1931; renamed franchise. Had been MUSKOGEE A'S, 1924–1926. Renamed MUSKOGEE NIGHTHAWKS, 1932.

Muskogee Giants
Western Association (C), 1951–1954; renamed franchise. Sooner State League (D), 1955–1957; new franchise. Disbanded with league after 1957 season.

Muskogee Indians
South Central League (D), 1906; charter franchise. Disbanded with league after 1906 season.

Muskogee Indians
Oklahoma State League (D), 1912; charter franchise. Disbanded with league after 1912 season.

Muskogee Mets
Western Association (D), 1914–1917; charter franchise. Disbanded after 1917 season.

Muskogee Mets
Southwestern League (D), 1921, (C), 1922–1923; charter franchise. Disbanded with league after 1923 season.

Muskogee Navigators
Oklahoma–Kansas League (D), 1908; charter franchise. Western

Association (D), 1909–mid-1910; new franchise. Became OKMULGEE, mid-1910.

Muskogee Nighthawks
Western Association (C), 1932; renamed franchise. Had been MUSKOGEE CHIEFS, 1927–1931. Became HUTCHINSON WHEATSHOCKERS, mid-1932.

Muskogee Oilers
Western League (A), mid-1933; relocated franchise. Had been WICHITA OILERS, 1933. Disbanded after 1933 season.

Muskogee Reds
Missouri Valley League (D), 1905; new franchise. Disbanded with league after 1905 season.

Muskogee Reds
Western Association (C), 1937–1942; 1946–1950; renamed franchise. Had been MUSKOGEE SEALS, 1936. Renamed MUSKOGEE GIANTS, 1951.

Muskogee Seals
Western Association (C), 1936; renamed franchise. Had been MUSKOGEE TIGERS, 1934–1935. Renamed MUSKOGEE REDS, 1937.

Muskogee Tigers
Western Association (C), 1934–1935; new franchise. Renamed MUSKOGEE SEALS, 1936.

MYRTLE BEACH, SC

Myrtle Beach Blue Jays
South Atlantic League (A), 1987–1990; new franchise. Renamed MYRTLE BEACH HURRICANES, 1991.

Myrtle Beach Hurricanes
South Atlantic League (A), 1991– (still in existence as of 5-1-92); renamed franchise. Had been MYRTLE BEACH BLUE JAYS, 1987–1990.

NACOGDOCHES, TX

Nacogdoches
East Texas League (D), 1916; charter franchise. Disbanded with league after 1916 season.

NAPA, CA

Napa
Central California Baseball League (D), 1910; charter franchise. Disbanded after 1910 season.

NARANJOS, MEXICO

Naranjos Valles
Mexican Center League (A), 1973; new franchise. Disbanded after 1973 season.

NARROWS– PEARLSBURG, VA
(See also PEARLSBURG, VA)

Narrows Rebels
Appalachian League (D), 1946–1950; expansion franchise. Disbanded after 1950 season.

NASHUA, NH

Nashua
New Hampshire State League, 1886; charter franchise. Disbanded with league after 1886 season.

Nashua
New England Inter-State Association, 1888; charter franchise. Disbanded with association after 1888 season.

Nashua
New England League, 1901; (B), 1902–1905; charter franchise. Disbanded after 1905 season.

Nashua
New England League (B), mid-1933; relocated franchise. Had been QUINCY, 1933. Became BROCKTON, mid-1933.

Nashua Angels
Eastern League (AA), 1983; new franchise. Renamed NASHUA PIRATES, 1984.

Nashua Dodgers
New England League (B), 1946–1949; charter franchise. Disbanded with league after 1949 season.

Nashua Millionaires
New England League (B), 1926–mid-1927; charter franchise. Disbanded during 1927 season.

Nashua Millionaires
New England League (B), mid-1929–1930; relocated franchise. Had been LOWELL MILLERS, 1929. Disbanded with league after 1930 season.

Nashua Pirates
Eastern League (AA), 1984–1986; renamed franchise. Had been NASHUA ANGELS, 1983. Disbanded after 1986 season.

Nashua Rainmakers
New England Association, 1895; charter franchise. Disbanded with association after 1895 season.

NASHVILLE, TN

Nashville Americans
Southern League, 1885–1886; charter franchise. Renamed NASHVILLE BLUES, 1887.

Nashville Blues
Southern League, 1887; renamed franchise. Had been NASHVILLE AMERICANS, 1885–1886. Disbanded after 1887 season.

NASHVILLE ELITE GIANTS
Negro National League, 1930; new franchise. Disbanded after 1930 season. Negro Southern League, 1932; charter franchise. Disbanded with league after 1932 season. Negro National League, 1933–

1934; new franchise. Disbanded after 1934 season.

Nashville Seraphs
Southern League, 1895; renamed franchise. Had been NASHVILLE TIGERS, 1893–1894. Disbanded with league after 1895 season.

Nashville Sounds
Southern League (AA), 1978–1984; new franchise. Became HUNTSVILLE STARS, 1985.

Nashville Sounds
American Association (AAA), 1986–(still in existence as of 5-1-92); new franchise.

Nashville Tigers
Southern League, 1893–1894; new franchise. Renamed NASHVILLE SERAPHS, 1895.

Nashville Vols
Alternate name for NASHVILLE VOLUNTEERS.

Nashville Volunteers (aka Vols)
Southern Association, 1901; (A), 1902–1934; (A1), 1935–1945; (AA), 1946–1961; charter franchise. Disbanded after 1961 season.

NATCHEZ, MS

Natchez Giants
Evangeline League (D), 1942; 1946–1947; renamed franchise. Had been NATCHEZ PILGRIMS, mid-1940–1941. Became NATCHEZ INDIANS, 1948.

Natchez Hill Climbers
Cotton States League (D), 1904–mid-1905; renamed franchise. Had been NATCHEZ INDIANS, 1902–1903. Became MOBILE SEA GULLS, mid-1905.

Natchez Indians
Cotton States League (D), 1902–1903; charter franchise. Renamed NATCHEZ HILL CLIMBERS, 1904.

Natchez Indians
Cotton States League (C), 1948–1953; expansion franchise. Disbanded after 1953 season.

Natchez Pilgrims
Evangeline League (D), mid-1940–1941; relocated franchise. Had been HOUMA BUCCANEERS, 1940. Renamed NATCHEZ GIANTS, 1942.

NAVOJOA, MEXICO

Navojoa
Mexican Pacific League (AAA), 1976; charter franchise. Disbanded with league after 1976 season.

NAZARETH, PA

Nazareth Barons
North Atlantic League (D), 1948–1950; renamed franchise. Had been NAZARETH TIGERS, 1947. Disbanded with league after 1950 season.

Nazareth Cement Dusters
North Atlantic League (D), 1946; charter franchise. Renamed NAZARETH TIGERS, 1947.

Nazareth Tigers
North Atlantic League (D), 1947; renamed franchise. Had been NAZARETH CEMENT DUSTERS, 1946. Renamed NAZARETH BARONS, 1948.

NEBRASKA CITY, NE

Nebraska City Forresters
MINK League (D), 1910–1913; charter franchise. Disbanded with league after 1913 season.

NEGAUNEE, MI
(See also ISHPEMING, MI)

Negaunee
Upper Peninsula League, 1895; charter franchise. Disbanded with league during 1895 season.

NEOSHO, MO

Neosho Night Hawks
Arkansas–Missouri League (D), 1937; new franchise. Renamed NEOSHO YANKEES, 1938.

Neosho Yankees
Arkansas–Missouri League (D), 1938–1940; renamed franchise. Had been NEOSHO NIGHT HAWKS, 1937. Disbanded with league after 1940 season.

NEVADA, MO

Nevada Lunatics
Missouri Valley League (D), 1901–mid-1903; charter franchise. Became WEBB CITY, mid-1903.

NEWARK, NJ

Newark
Atlantic League, 1896; charter franchise. Disbanded after 1896 season.

Newark
Atlantic League (D), 1907; charter franchise. Disbanded with league after 1907 season.

Newark Bears
International League (AA), 1917–1919; renamed franchise. Had been NEWARK INDIANS, mid-1915–1916. Disbanded after 1919 season.

Newark Bears
International League (AA), 1921–mid-1925; new franchise. Became PROVIDENCE GRAYS, mid-1925.

Newark Bears
International League (AA), 1926–1945; (AAA), 1946–1949; relocated franchise. Had been PROVIDENCE GRAYS, mid-1925. Disbanded after 1949 season.

NEWARK BROWNS
East–West League, 1932; charter franchise. Disbanded with league during 1932 season.

Newark Colts
Atlantic League, 1896–1900; charter franchise. Disbanded with league after 1900 season.

Newark Cubans
Atlantic League (D), 1914; charter franchise. Became LONG BRANCH CUBANS, mid-1914.

NEWARK DODGERS
Negro National League, 1934–1935; new franchise. Disbanded after 1935 season.

Newark Domestics
Eastern League, 1884–1885; charter franchise. Renamed NEWARK LITTLE GIANTS, 1886.

NEWARK EAGLES
Negro League, 1936–1948; relocated franchise. Had been BROOKLYN EAGLES, 1935. Disbanded after 1948 season.

NEWARK FEDS
Alternate name for NEWARK PEPPERS, 1915.

Newark Giants
International League, 1887; new franchise. Disbanded after 1887 season.

Newark Indians
Eastern League (AA), 1908–1911; renamed franchise. Had been NEWARK SAILORS, 1902–1907. International League (AA), 1912–mid-1915; charter franchise. Became HARRISBURG SENATORS, mid-1915.

Newark Indians
International League (AA), mid-1915–1916; new franchise. Renamed NEWARK BEARS, 1917.

NEWARK JERSEYMEN
Alternate name for NEWARK PEPPERS, 1915.

Newark Little Giants
Eastern League, 1886; new franchise. Disbanded after 1886 season.

Newark Little Giants
Atlantic Association, 1889–1890; charter franchise. Disbanded with association after 1890 season.

NEWARK NEWFEDS
Alternate name for NEWARK PEPPERS, 1915.

NEWARK PEPPERS (aka Feds, Jerseymen, Newfeds)
Federal League, 1915; relocated franchise. Had been INDIANAPOLIS HOOSIERS, 1914. Disbanded with league after 1915 season.

Newark Sailors
Eastern League (A), 1902–1907; charter franchise. Renamed NEWARK INDIANS, 1908.

NEWARK STARS
Eastern Colored League, 1926; new franchise. Disbanded during 1926 season.

Newark Trunkmakers
Central League, 1888; charter franchise. Disbanded with league during 1888 season.

NEWARK, NY

Newark Co-Pilots
New York–Pennsylvania League (A), 1968–1979; expansion franchise. Disbanded after 1979 season.

Newark Orioles
New York–Pennsylvania League (A), 1983–1987; new franchise. Disbanded after 1987 season.

NEWARK, OH

Newark
Ohio State League, 1889; charter franchise. Disbanded with league after 1889 season.

Newark
Ohio–Pennsylvania League, 1900; charter franchise. Disbanded with league after 1900 season.

Newark
Buckeye League (D), 1915; charter franchise. Disbanded with league after 1915 season.

Newark Cotton Tops
Ohio–Pennsylvania League (D), 1906; renamed franchise. Had been NEWARK IDLEWILDS, 1905. Renamed NEWARK NEWKS, 1907.

Newark Idlewilds
Ohio–Pennsylvania League (D), 1905; charter franchise. Renamed NEWARK COTTON TOPS, 1906.

Newark Moundsmen
Ohio State League (D), 1944–1947; charter franchise. Disbanded after 1947 season.

Newark Newks
Ohio–Pennsylvania League (D), 1907; renamed franchise. Had been NEWARK COTTON TOPS, 1906. Ohio State League (D), 1908–1910; (C), 1911; charter franchise. Became PIQUA PICKS, mid-1911.

Newark Skeeters
Central League (D), mid-1911; relocated franchise. Had been GRAND RAPIDS RAIDERS, 1910–mid-1911. Ohio State League (D), 1912; new franchise. Disbanded after 1912 season.

Newark Yankees
Ohio–Indiana League (D), 1948–1951; new franchise. Disbanded with league during 1951 season.

NEW BEDFORD, MA

New Bedford
New England League, 1878; new franchise. Disbanded with league during 1878 season.

New Bedford
New England League (B), mid-1903; relocated franchise. Had been BROCKTON, 1903.

New Bedford Millmen
New England League (B), 1929–1930; new franchise. Disbanded with league after 1930 season.

New Bedford Whalers
New England League, 1895–mid-1898; new franchise. Became WORCESTER, mid-1898.

New Bedford Whalers
New England League (B), 1903–1913; new franchise. Colonial League (C) 1914–1915; charter franchise. Disbanded with league after 1915 season.

New Bedford Whalers
New England League (B), 1933; charter franchise. Northeastern League (A), mid-1934; charter franchise. Disbanded with league after 1934 season.

NEW BERN, NC

New Bern
Eastern Carolina League (D), 1908; charter franchise. Disbanded after 1908 season.

New Bern Bears
Coastal Plain League (D), 1937–1941; 1946–1952; charter franchise. Disbanded with league after 1952 season.

New Bern Truckers
North Carolina League (D), 1902; charter franchise. Disbanded during 1902 season.

NEW BRIGHTON, PA

New Brighton
Iron & Oil Association, 1884, charter franchise. Became JOHNSTOWN, mid-1884.

NEW BRITAIN, CT

New Britain
Connecticut League, 1884; charter franchise. Southern New England League, 1885; charter franchise. Disbanded with league during 1885 season.

New Britain
Connecticut League, 1894; relocated franchise. Had been WATERBURY, mid-1894.

New Britain
Eastern Association (B), 1914; new franchise. Disbanded with league after 1914 season.

New Britain Perfectos
Connecticut State League (B), 1908–mid-1912; new franchise. Became WATERBURY SPUDS, mid-1912.

New Britain Rangers
Naugatuck Valley League, 1898; charter franchise. Disbanded with league during 1898 season.

New Britain Red Sox
Eastern League (AA), 1983–(still in existence as of 5-1-92); new franchise.

NEW BRUNSWICK, NJ

New Brunswick Hubs
Colonial League (B), 1948; new franchise. Became KINGSTON CO-LONIALS, mid-1948.

NEWBURGH, NY

Newburgh Cobblestone Throwers
Hudson River League, 1886; charter franchise. Disbanded with league after 1886 season.

Newburgh Dutchmen
New York–New Jersey League (D), 1913; charter franchise. Atlantic League (D), 1914; charter franchise. Disbanded with league after 1914 season.

Newburgh Hill Climbers
Hudson River League (D), 1906–1907; renamed franchise. Had been NEWBURGH TAYLOR-MADES, 1903–1905. Disbanded with league after 1907 season.

Newburgh Hummingbirds
North Atlantic League (D), 1946; charter franchise. Became WALDEN HUMMINGBIRDS, mid-1946.

Newburgh Taylor-mades
Hudson River League (D), 1903–1905; charter franchise. Renamed NEWBURGH HILL CLIMBERS, 1906.

NEWBURYPORT, MA

Newburyport
Eastern New England League, mid-1885; relocated franchise. Had been BIDDEFORD, 1885. Disbanded with league during 1895 season.

Newburyport Clamdiggers
New England League, 1886; charter franchise. Became LYNN YANKS, mid-1886.

NEW CASTLE, PA

New Castle
Ohio–Pennsylvania League (D), 1912; new franchise. Disbanded with league after 1912 season.

New Castle Chiefs
Middle Atlantic League (C), 1948; new franchise. Renamed NEW CASTLE NATS, 1949.

New Castle Indians
Middle Atlantic League (C), 1951; renamed franchise. Had been NEW CASTLE NATS, 1949–1950. Disbanded with league after 1951 season.

New Castle Nashannocks
Iron and Oil Association, 1884/League, 1885; charter franchise. Disbanded with league after 1885 season.

New Castle Nats (aka Senators)
Middle Atlantic League (C), 1949–1950; renamed franchise. Had been NEW CASTLE CHIEFS,

1948. Renamed NEW CASTLE INDI-
ANS, 1951.

New Castle Nocks

Ohio–Pennsylvania League (D),
1907–mid-1911; renamed franchise. Had been NEW CASTLE OUT-
LAWS, 1906. Became SHARON
TRAVELERS, mid-1912.

New Castle Outlaws

Ohio–Pennsylvania League (D),
1906; new franchise. Renamed
NEW CASTLE NOCKS, 1907.

New Castle Quakers (aka Yanigans, 1899)

Inter-State League, 1896–1900;
charter franchise. Disbanded with
league after 1900 season.

New Castle Senators

Alternate name for NEW CASTLE
NATS, 1949–1950.

New Castle Yanigans

Alternate name for NEW CASTLE
QUAKERS, 1896–1900.

NEW CUMBERLAND, PA

New Cumberland

Ohio Valley League, 1891; charter
franchise. Disbanded with league
after 1891 season.

NEW HAVEN, CT

New Haven

Connecticut League, 1894; charter
franchise. Disbanded with league
during 1894 season.

New Haven

Eastern Association (B), 1913–
1914; charter franchise. Colonial
League (C), 1915; charter franchise. Eastern League (B), 1916–
1918; charter franchise. Renamed
NEW HAVEN WEISSMEN, 1919.

New Haven

Atlantic Association (D), 1896;
charter franchise. Became LANCAS-
TER MAROONS, mid-1896.

New Haven

Atlantic Association, 1889–1890;
charter franchise. Disbanded with
association after 1890 season.

New Haven Black Crows

Connecticut League (B), 1909; renamed franchise. Had been NEW
HAVEN BLUES, 1899–1908. Renamed NEW HAVEN PRAIRIE HENS, 1910.

New Haven Bluebirds

Naugatuck Valley League, 1898;
charter franchise. Renamed NEW
HAVEN BLUES, 1899.

New Haven Blues

Connecticut League, 1899–1901;
(B), 1902–1908; renamed fran-
chise. Had been NEW HAVEN BLUE-
BIRDS, 1898. Renamed NEW HAVEN
BLACK CROWS, 1909.

New Haven Bulldogs

Eastern League (A), 1931–1932;
new franchise. Disbanded with
league after 1932 season.

New Haven Elm City

Eastern League, 1887; new franchise. Disbanded with league after
1887 season.

NEW HAVEN ELM CITYS

National Association, 1875; expansion franchise. Disbanded during 1875 season.

New Haven Indians

Eastern League (A), 1921–1922;
renamed franchise. Had been NEW
HAVEN WEISSMEN, 1919. Renamed
NEW HAVEN PROFS, 1923.

New Haven Murlins

Connecticut League (B), 1911–
1912; renamed franchise. Had been
NEW HAVEN PRAIRIE HENS, 1910.
Disbanded with league after 1912
season.

New Haven Nutmegs

Eastern Association, 1891/League,
1892; charter franchise. Disbanded
with league after 1892 season.

New Haven Prairie Hens

Connecticut State League (B),
1910; renamed franchise. Had been
NEW HAVEN BLACK CROWS, 1909.
Renamed NEW HAVEN MURLINS,
1911.

New Haven Profs

Eastern League (A), 1923–mid-
1930; renamed franchise. Had been
NEW HAVEN INDIANS, 1921–1922.
Disbanded during 1930 season.

New Haven Students

Atlantic League, 1896; charter
franchise. Became LANCASTER MA-
ROONS, mid-1896.

New Haven Weissmen

Eastern League (B), 1919–1920;
Named franchise. Renamed NEW
HAVEN INDIANS, 1921.

NEW IBERIA, LA

New Iberia Cardinals

Evangeline League (D), 1934–
1942; 1946; charter franchise. Renamed NEW IBERIA PELICANS, 1947.

New Iberia Cardinals

Evangeline League (D), 1940–
1942; (C), 1946–1948; renamed
franchise. Had been NEW IBERIA
PELICANS, 1934–1939. Renamed
NEW IBERIA REBELS, 1949.

New Iberia Indians

Evangeline League (C), 1956; renamed franchise. Had been NEW
IBERIA PELICANS, 1951–1955. Disbanded after 1956 season.

New Iberia Pelicans

Evangeline League (D), 1947–
1949; renamed franchise. Had been
NEW IBERIA CARDINALS, 1934–
1942; 1946. Renamed NEW IBERIA
REBELS, 1950.

New Iberia Pelicans

Evangeline League (C), 1951–
1955; renamed franchise. Had been
NEW IBERIA REBELS, 1949–1951.

Renamed NEW IBERIA INDIANS, 1956.

New Iberia Rebels
Evangeline League (C), 1950; renamed franchise. Had been NEW IBERIA PELICANS, 1944–1949. Renamed NEW IBERIA PELICANS, 1951.

New Iberia Sugar Boys
Louisiana State League (D), 1920; charter franchise. Disbanded with league after 1920 season.

NEWINGTON, NH

Newington
New Hampshire League (D), 1907; charter franchise. Disbanded with league after 1907 season.

NEW LONDON, CT

New London
Eastern Association (B), 1913–1914; charter franchise. Disbanded with league after 1914 season.

New London Colts
Connecticut League, 1898; charter franchise. Renamed NEW LONDON WHALERS, 1899.

New London Planters
Eastern League (B), 1916–1918; charter franchise. Disbanded after 1918 season.

New London Raiders
Colonial League (B), 1947; charter franchise. Disbanded after 1947 season.

New London Whalers
Connecticut League, 1899–1901; (B), 1902–1907; renamed franchise. Had been NEW LONDON COLTS, 1898. Disbanded after 1907 season.

New London Whalers
Connecticut Association (D), 1910; charter franchise. Disbanded with league after 1910 season.

NEWNAN, GA

Newnan Brownies
Georgia–Alabama League (D), 1946–1950; charter franchise. Disbanded after 1950 season.

Newnan Cowetas
Georgia–Alabama League (C), 1913–1916; charter franchise. Disbanded after 1916 season.

NEW ORLEANS, LA
(See also ST. LOUIS, MO)

New Orleans Little Pels
Cotton States League (D), 1912; new franchise. Became YAZOO CITY ZOOS, mid-1912.

New Orleans Pelicans
Southern League, 1887–mid-1888; new franchise. Texas League, mid-1888; expansion franchise. Southern League, 1889; new franchise. Disbanded with league after 1889 season.

New Orleans Pelicans
Southern League, 1892–1896; charter franchise. Disbanded with league after 1896 season.

New Orleans Pelicans
Southern League, 1898–1899; charter franchise. Disbanded with league after 1899 season.

New Orleans Pelicans
Southern Association, 1901; (A), 1902–1934; (A1), 1935–1945; (AA), 1946–1959; charter franchise. Disbanded after 1959 season.

New Orleans Pelicans
American Association (AAA), 1977; relocated franchise. Has been Tulsa Oilers, 1932–1942; 1946–1976. Disbanded after 1977 season.

NEW PHILADELPHIA, OH

New Philadelphia Red Birds
Ohio State League (D), 1936; charter franchise. Disbanded during 1936 season.

NEWPORT, AR
(See also BATESVILLE, AR)

Newport Cardinals
Northeast Arkansas League (D), 1936–1938; charter franchise. Renamed NEWPORT TIGERS, 1939.

Newport Dodgers
Northeast Arkansas League (D), 1940–1941; renamed franchise. Had been NEWPORT TIGERS, 1939. Disbanded with league after 1941 season.

Newport Pear Diggers
Arkansas State League (D), 1908; charter franchise. Northeast Arkansas League (D), 1909; charter franchise. Disbanded after 1909 season.

Newport Tigers
Northeast Arkansas League (D), 1939; renamed franchise. Had been NEWPORT CARDINALS, 1936–1938. Renamed NEWPORT DODGERS, 1940.

NEWPORT, KY

Newport
Ohio State League (D), mid-1914; new franchise. Became PARIS, mid-1914.

NEWPORT, RI

Newport Colts (aka Dudes)
New England League, 1897–1899; new franchise. Disbanded during 1899 season.

Newport Dudes
Alternate name for NEWPORT COLTS.

Newport Ponies
Atlantic Association (D), 1908; new franchise. Disbanded with league during 1908 season.

NEWPORT, TN

Newport Canners
Appalachian League (D), 1937–mid-1940; charter franchise. Be-

came MARYVILLE CANNERS, mid-1940.

Newport Canners
Appalachian League (D), mid-1940–mid-1942; charter franchise. Had been MARYVILLE CANNERS, mid-1940. Disbanded during 1942 season.

Newport Canners
Mountain States League (D), 1948–1950; charter franchise. Disbanded after 1950 season.

Newport Canners
Mountain States League (D), 1954; new franchise. Disbanded with league after 1954 season.

NEWPORT NEWS, VA
(See also HAMPTON, VA)

Newport News
Southeast Virginia League, 1897; charter franchise. Disbanded with league after 1897 season.

Newport News Dodgers
Piedmont League (B), 1944–1955; new franchise. Disbanded with league after 1955 season.

Newport News Pilots
Virginia League (C), 1941–1942; expansion franchise. Disbanded with league after 1942 season.

Newport News Shipbuilders
Virginia League, 1900; charter franchise. Virginia–North Carolina League, 1901; charter franchise. Became TARBORO TARHEELS, mid-1901.

Newport News Shipbuilders
Virginia League (B), 1912–mid-1917; new franchise. Disbanded with league during 1917 season. Virginia League (B), 1918; new franchise. Disbanded with league during 1918 season. Virginia League (B), 1919–1922; new franchise. Became PETERSBURG TRUNKMAKERS, 1923.

NEWPORT NEWS–HAMPTON, VA
(See also HAMPTON, VA)

Newport News–Hampton, VA)
Virginia League, mid-1894; relocated franchise. Had been STAUNTON VALLEYITES (aka Hayseeds), 1894. Disbanded with league during 1894 season.

NEW ROCKFORD–CARRINGTON, ND
(See also CARRINGTON, ND)

New Rockford–Carrington Twins
North Dakota League (D), 1923; charter franchise. Became VALLEY CITY, mid-1923.

NEWTON, KS

Newton
Western League, mid-1888; relocated franchise. Had been LINCOLN TREEPLANTERS, 1886–1888. Disbanded with league after 1888 season.

Newton Browns
Kansas State League (D), 1909; charter franchise. Renamed NEWTON RAILROADERS, 1910.

Newton Railroaders
Kansas State League (D), 1910–1911; renamed franchise. Had been NEWTON BROWNS, 1909. Central Kansas League (D), 1912; new franchise. Became MINNEAPOLIS, mid-1912.

Newton Railroaders
Southwestern League (D), 1924; charter franchise. Became BLACKWELL GASSERS, mid-1924.

Newton Railroaders
Southwestern League (D), 1924; relocated franchise. Had been OTTAWA, mid-1924. Disbanded after 1924 season.

NEWTON–CONOVER, NC

Newton–Conover Twins
North Carolina State League (D), 1937–1938; charter franchise. Tar Heel League (D), 1939–1940; charter franchise. Disbanded with league after 1940 season.

Newton–Conover Twins
Western Carolina League (D), 1948–1951; charter franchise. Disbanded after 1951 season.

Newton–Conover Twins
Western Carolinas League (D), 1960–1962; charter franchise. Disbanded with league after 1962 season.

NEWTON, NE

Newton
Western League, mid-1888; relocated franchise. Had been LINCOLN TREEPLANTERS, 1886–mid-1888. Disbanded with league after 1888 season.

NEW WATERFORD, NOVA SCOTIA, CANADA

New Waterford Dodgers
Cape Breton Colliery League (D), 1937–1938, (C), 1939; charter franchise. Disbanded with league after 1939 season.

NEW WESTMINSTER, BRITISH COLUMBIA, CANADA

New Westminster Frasers
Northwest League (A), 1974; new franchise. Disbanded after 1974 season.

NEW YORK, NY

New York
Keystone Association, 1877; charter franchise. Disbanded with association after 1877 season.

New York
United States League, 1912; charter franchise. Disbanded with league after 1912 season.

NEW YORK BLACK YANKEES
Negro National League, mid-1936; renamed franchise. Had been NEW YORK CUBANS, 1935–mid-1936. Disbanded after 1948 season.

NEW YORK CUBANS
Negro National League, 1935–mid-1936; new franchise. Renamed NEW YORK BLACK YANKEES, mid-1936.

NEW YORK CUBANS
Negro National League, 1948–1950; new franchise. Disbanded with league after 1950 season.

NEW YORK GIANTS
National League, 1885–1957; renamed franchise. Had been NEW YORK GOTHAMS, 1883–1884. Became SAN FRANCISCO GIANTS, 1958.

NEW YORK GIANTS
Players' League, 1890; charter franchise. Disbanded with league after 1890 season.

NEW YORK GOTHAMS
National League, 1883–1884; relocated franchise. Had been TROY TROJANS, 1879–1882. Renamed NEW YORK GIANTS, 1885.

NEW YORK HIGHLANDERS (aka Hilltoppers)
American League, 1903–1912; relocated franchise. Had been BALTIMORE ORIOLES, 1901–1902. Renamed NEW YORK YANKEES, 1913.

NEW YORK HILLTOPPERS
Alternate name for NEW YORK HIGHLANDERS, 1903–1912.

New York Metropolitans
Eastern Association, 1881; charter franchise. Disbanded with association after 1881 season.

NEW YORK METROPOLITANS
American Association, 1883–1885; new franchise. Became SCRANTON INDIANS, 1886.

New York Metropolitans
Atlantic League, 1896; charter franchise. Became PHILADELPHIA, mid-1896.

NEW YORK METS
National League, 1962–(still in existence as of 5-1-92); expansion franchise.

NEW YORK MUTUALS
National League, 1876; charter franchise. Disbanded after 1876 season.

New York New Yorks
Eastern Association, 1881; charter franchise. Disbanded with league after 1881 season.

New York Quicksteps
Eastern Association, 1881; charter franchise. Disbanded with league after 1881 season.

NEW YORK YANKEES
American League, 1913–(still in esistence as of 5-1-92); renamed franchise. Had been NEW YORK HIGHLANDERS, 1903–1912.

NEW YORK– BROOKLYN, NY
(See also BROOKLYN, NY)

NEW YORK MUTUALS
National Association, 1871–1875; charter franchise. Disbanded during 1875 season.

NIAGARA FALLS, NY

Niagara Falls
International League (D), 1908; charter franchise. Disbanded with league after 1908 season.

Niagara Falls Citizens
Middle Atlantic League (C), 1950–1951; new franchise. Disbanded with league after 1951 season.

Niagara Falls Frontiers
Middle Atlantic League (C), 1946–1947; charter franchise. Disbanded after 1947 season.

Niagara Falls Pirates
New York–Pennsylvania League (A), 1970–1979; new franchise. Disbanded after 1979 season.

Niagara Falls Rainbows
PONY League (D), 1939–1940; charter franchise. Merged with JAMESTOWN, as NIAGARA FALLS–JAMESTOWN, 1940. Disbanded after 1940 season.

Niagara Falls Rapids
New York–Pennsylvania League (AA), 1990–(still in existence as of 5-1-92); renamed franchise. Had been NIAGARA FALLS TIGERS, 1989.

Niagara Falls Tigers
New York–Pennsylvania League (AA), 1989; new franchise. Renamed NIAGARA FALLS RAPIDS, 1990.

Niagara Falls White Sox
New York–Pennsylvania League (A), 1982–1985; new franchise. Disbanded after 1985 season.

NIAGARA FALLS– JAMESTOWN, NY

Niagara Falls–Jamestown Falcons
PONY League (D), 1940; relocated franchise. Had been JAMESTOWN FALCONS, 1939. Renamed JAMESTOWN FALCONS, 1941.

NICHOLASVILLE, KY

Nicholasville
Blue Grass League (D), 1912; relocated franchise. Had been WINCHESTER HUSTLERS, 1908–1912. Became MOUNT STERLING ORPHANS, mid-1912.

NILES, MI

Niles Blues
Indiana–Michigan League (D), 1910; charter franchise. Disbanded with league during 1910 season.

NILES, OH

Niles Corwites
Ohio–Pennsylvania League (D), 1905; charter franchise. Disbanded with league after 1905 season.

NOGALES, AZ

Nogales Internationals
Arizona–Texas League (D), 1931; charter franchise. Disbanded after 1931 season.

Nogales Internationals
Arizona–Mexico League (C), 1958; new franchise. Disbanded with league after 1958 season.

Nogales Red Devils
Arizona–Mexico League (C), 1956; renamed franchise. Had been NOGALES YAQUIS, 1954–1955. Disbanded after 1956 season.

Nogales Yaquis
Arizona–Texas League (C), 1954–1955; expansion franchise. Renamed NOGALES RED DEVILS, 1956.

NOGALES, SONOMA, MEXICO

Nogales Internationals
Mexican Northern League (A), 1968–1969; charter franchise. Disbanded with league after 1969 season.

Nogales Internationals
Mexican Northern League (A), 1971; new franchise. Disbanded after 1971 season.

NORFOLK, NE

Norfolk Drummers
Nebraska State League (D), 1914–1915; new franchise. Disbanded with league during 1915 season.

Norfolk Elk Horns
Nebraska State League (D), 1922–1923; charter franchise. Tri-State League (D), 1924; charter franchise. Disbanded with league after 1924 season.

Norfolk Elk Horns
Alternate name for NORFOLK ELKS, 1928–1938.

Norfolk Elks (aka Elk Horns)
Nebraska State League (D), 1928–1938; charter franchise. Western League (D), 1939; charter franchise. Renamed NORFOLK YANKEES, 1940.

Norfolk Yankees
Western League (D), 1940–1941; renamed franchise. Had been NORFOLK ELKS, 1928–1939. Suspended operations with league after 1941 season, and did not rejoin when league resumed operations in 1947.

NORFOLK, VA

Norfolk
Eastern League, 1885; new franchise. Became WATERBURY, mid-1885.

Norfolk
Virginia League, 1885–1886; charter franchise. Disbanded with league during 1886 season.

Norfolk Clams
Virginia League, 1895–1896; renamed franchise. Had been NORFOLK OYSTERMEN, 1894. Disbanded with league after 1896 season.

Norfolk Jewels
Atlantic League, 1897–1898; charter franchise. Disbanded with league during 1898 season.

Norfolk Mary Janes
Virginia League, 1900; charter franchise. Disbanded with league after 1900 season.

Norfolk Mary Janes
Virginia League (D), 1918, (C), 1919, (B), 1920; charter franchise. Renamed NORFOLK TARS, 1921.

Norfolk Oystermen
Virginia League, 1894; charter franchise. Renamed NORFOLK CLAMS, 1895.

Norfolk Skippers
Virginia–North Carolina League (D), 1901; charter franchise. Disbanded with league after 1901 season.

Norfolk Tars
Virginia League (C), 1906–mid-1917; charter franchise. Disbanded with league during 1917 season.

Norfolk Tars
Virginia League (B), 1921–mid-1928; renamed franchise. Had been NORFOLK MARY JANES, 1918–1920. Disbanded with league during 1928 season.

Norfolk Tars
Eastern League (A), 1931–1932; new franchise. Disbanded with league during 1932 season.

Norfolk Tars
Piedmont League (B), 1934–1955; relocated franchise. Had been DURHAM BULLS, 1920–1933. Disbanded during 1955 season.

NORFOLK–PORTSMOUTH, VA
(See also PORTSMOUTH, VA)

Tidewater Tides
Carolina League (B), 1966–1968; renamed franchise. Represented PORTSMOUTH TIDES, 1963–1965. International League (AAA),

1969–(still in existence as of 5-1-92); new franchise.

NORRISTOWN, PA

Norristown
Schuykill Valley League, 1896; charter franchise. Disbanded with league after 1896 season.

Norristown
Inter-State League (D), 1932; charter franchise. Became ST. CLAIR, mid-1932.

NORTHAMPTON, MA

Northampton Meadowlarks
Connecticut State League (B), 1909–1911; new franchise. Disbanded during 1911 season.

NORTHAMPTON, VA

Northampton Red Sox
Eastern Shore League (D), mid-1927; relocated franchise. Had been DOVER SENATORS, 1926–mid-1927. Disbanded after 1927 season.

NORTH BEND–COOS BAY, OR

North Bend–Coos Bay Athletics
Northwest League (A), 1970–1972; expansion franchise. Disbanded with league after 1972 season.

NORTH PLATTE, NE

North Platte Buffaloes
Nebraska State League (D), 1928–1932; charter franchise. Disbanded after 1932 season.

North Platte Indians
Nebraska State League (D), 1956–1959; charter franchise. Disbanded with league after 1959 season.

NORTH WILKESBORO, NC

North Wilkesboro Flashers
Blue Ridge League (D), 1948–1950; new franchise. Disbanded with league after 1950 season.

NORTH YAKIMA, WA

North Yakima Braves
Western Tri-State League (C), 1913; (D), 1914; new franchise. Disbanded with league after 1914 season.

NORTON, KS

Norton Jayhawks
Nebraska State League (D), 1929–1930; new franchise. Disbanded after 1930 season.

NORTON, VA

Norton Braves
Mountain States League (D), 1951–1953; new franchise. Disbanded after 1953 season.

NORWALK, CT

Norwalk
Connecticut State League, 1888; charter franchise. Middle States League, 1889; expansion franchise. Atlantic Association, 1889; charter franchise. Disbanded during 1889 season.

NORWICH, CT

Norwich
Connecticut State League, 1888; charter franchise. Disbanded with league after 1888 season.

Norwich
Connecticut League (B), mid-1904; relocated franchise. Had been WORCESTER, 1904.

Norwich Bonbons
Connecticut Association (D), 1910; charter franchise. Became MERIDEN DOUBLINS, mid-1910.

Norwich Champions
Connecticut League (B), 1907; new franchise. Had been NORWICH REDS, 1903–1906. Disbanded after 1907 season.

Norwich Reds
Connecticut League (B), 1902/Connecticut Valley League (B), 1903–1906; renamed franchise. Disbanded after 1903 season.

Norwich Witches
Connecticut League, 1899–1900/Connecticut State League, 1901; new franchise. Renamed NORWICH REDS, 1902.

NORWICH, NY

Norwich
Central New York League, 1886; charter franchise. Disbanded with league after 1886 season.

NUEVO LAREDO, TAMAULIPAS, MEXICO

Nuevo Laredo Broncos
Mexican Center League (A), 1968; new franchise. Disbanded after 1968 season.

Nuevo Laredo Tecolotes (Owls)
Mexican League (AAA), 1976–(still in existence as of 5-1-92); new franchise.

Nuevo Laredo Tecolotes (Owls)
Mexican League (AA), 1955–1959; charter franchise. Disbanded after 1959 season.

NUEVO LEON, MEXICO
(See MONTERREY, MEXICO)

NYACK, NY

Nyack Rockies
Alternate name for NYACK ROCKLANDS.

Nyack Rocklands (aka Rockies)
North Atlantic League (D), 1946–1948; charter franchise. Disbanded after 1948 season.

OAKDALE, LA

Oakdale Lumberjacks
Louisiana State League (D), 1920; charter franchise. Disbanded with league after 1920 season.

OAKLAND, CA

Oakland
California State League (D), 1915; new franchise. Disbanded with league after 1915 season.

Oakland Acorns
Pacific Coast League (O), 1952–1955; renamed franchise. Had been OAKLAND OAKS, 1903–1951. Became VANCOUVER MOUNTIES, 1956.

OAKLAND A'S

American League, 1968–1986; relocated franchise. Had been KANSAS CITY A'S, 1962–1967. Renamed OAKLAND ATHLETICS, 1987.

OAKLAND ATHLETICS

American League, 1987–(still in exsistence as of 5-1-92); renamed franchise. Had been OAKLAND A'S, 1968–1986.

Oakland Basches
Central California Baseball League (D), mid-1910; new franchise. Became MERCED, mid-1910.

Oakland Clamdiggers
California State League, 1896–1902; charter franchise. Disbanded with league after 1902 season.

Oakland Colonels
California League, 1889–1893; renamed franchise. Had been OAKLAND GREENHOOD & MORANS, 1886–1888. Disbanded after 1893 season.

Oakland Colts
Pacific Coast League, 1898; charter franchise. Disbanded with league after 1898 season.

Oakland Commuters
California State League (C), 1906–1907; new franchise. Disbanded after 1907 season.

Oakland Emery Arms
Central California Baseball League (D), mid-1911; relocated franchise. Had been ELMHURST, 1910–mid-1911. Disbanded with league after 1911 season.

Oakland Greenhood & Morans
California State League, 1887; charter franchise. California League, 1888; charter franchise. Renamed OAKLAND COLONELS, 1889.

Oakland Invaders
Central California Baseball League (D), mid-1910; relocated franchise. Had been ALAMEDA, 1910. Became BERKELEY CLARIONS, mid-1910.

Oakland Monday Models
Central California Baseball League (D), mid-1911; relocated franchise. Had been FRUITVALE, mid-1910–mid-1911. Disbanded with league after 1911 season.

Oakland Oaks
Pacific Coast League (A), 1903–1907; (AA), 1908–1945; (AAA), 1946–1951; charter franchise. Renamed OAKLAND ACORNS, 1952.

Oakland Reliances
Pacific States League, 1898; charter franchise. Disbanded with league after 1898 season.

OAK RIDGE, TN

Oak Ridge Bombers
Mountain States League (D), 1948; charter franchise. Became HAZARD BOMBERS, mid-1948.

Oak Ridge Pioneers
Mountain States League (D), 1954; new franchise. Disbanded with league after 1954 season.

OBREGON, SONORA, MEXICO

Obregon Lobos
Mexican Pacific League (A), 1976; charter franchise. Disbanded with league after 1976 season.

OCALA, FL

Ocala
Florida State League, 1892; charter franchise. Disbanded with league after 1892 season.

Ocala Yearlings
Florida State League (D), 1940–1941; new franchise. Suspended operations after 1941 season, and did not rejoin when league resumed in 1946.

OCONTO, WI

Oconto Log Lumbermen
Wisconsin State League, 1891; charter franchise. Disbanded with league after 1891 season.

ODESSA, TX

Odessa Dodgers
Sophomore League (D), 1959–1960; new franchise. Disbanded after 1960 season.

Odessa Eagles
Longhorn League (C), 1955; renamed franchise. Had been ODESSA OILERS, 1947–1954. Disbanded with league after 1955 season.

Odessa Oilers
West Texas–New Mexico League (D), 1937; charter franchise. Disbanded during 1937 season.

Odessa Oilers
West Texas–New Mexico League (D), mid-1940; relocated franchise. Had been BIG SPRING BARONS, 1938–mid-1940. Became BIG SPRING BOMBERS, 1941.

Odessa Oilers
Longhorn League (D), 1947–1954; charter franchise. Renamed ODESSA EAGLES, 1955.

OGDEN, UT

Ogden
Inter-Mountain League, 1901; charter franchise. Disbanded with league after 1901 season.

Ogden
Pacific National League (D), 1905; new franchise. Disbanded with league after 1905 season.

Ogden A's
Pacific Coast League (AAA), 1979–1980; relocated franchise. Had been SAN JOSE MISSIONS, 1977–1978. Became EDMONTON TRAPPERS, 1981.

Ogden Canners
Union Association (D), 1912–1914; new franchise. Disbanded with league after 1914 season.

Ogden Dodgers
Pioneer League (R), 1966–1973; new franchise. Renamed OGDEN SPIKERS, 1974.

Ogden Gunners
Utah–Idaho League (C), 1926–1928; charter franchise. Disbanded with league after 1928 season.

Ogden Reds
Pioneer League (C), 1939–1942; 1946–1955; charter franchise. Disbanded after 1955 season.

Ogden Spikers
Pioneer League (R), 1974; renamed franchise. Had been OGDEN DODGERS, 1966–1973. Disbanded after 1974 season.

OGDENSBURG, NY
(See also OTTAWA, ONTARIO, CANADA)

Ogdensburg Colts
Canadian–American League (C), 1936–1940; charter franchise. Renamed OTTOWA–OGDENSBURG SENATORS (though still playing in Ogdensburg, NY). Disbanded after 1940 season.

Ogdensburg Maples
Border League (C), 1946–mid-1951; charter franchise. Disbanded with league during 1951 season.

OIL CITY, PA

Oil City
Iron and Oil Association, 1884; charter franchise. Disbanded with association after 1884 season.

Oil City
Iron & Oil League, 1898; charter franchise. Became DUNKIRK, mid-1898.

Oil City
Inter-State League (D), 1908; charter franchise. Disbanded with league during 1908 season.

Oil City A's
Middle Atlantic League (C), mid-1951; relocated franchise. Had been YOUNGSTOWN ATHLETICS, 1949–mid-1951. Disbanded with league after 1951 season.

Oil City Hecker's Hitters
Iron and Oil League, 1895; charter franchise. Disbanded with league after 1895 season.

Oil City Oilers
Pennsylvania State Association (D), mid-1940–1942; relocated franchise. Had been MCKEESPORT LITTLE BRAVES, 1939–mid-1940.

Middle Atlantic League (C), 1946; charter franchise. Renamed OIL CITY REFINERS, 1947.

Oil City Oseejays
Inter-State League (D), 1906; new franchise. Became JAMESTOWN OSEEJAYS, mid-1906.

Oil City Refiners
Middle Atlantic League (C), 1947–1950; renamed franchise. Had been OIL CITY OILERS, 1946. Disbanded after 1950 season.

OKLAHOMA CITY, OK

Oklahoma City Boosters (aka Senators, 1915)
Western Association (D), 1914–mid-1917; charter franchise. Became HUTCHINSON SALT PACKERS, mid-1917.

Oklahoma City '89ers
American Association (AAA), 1962; new franchise. Pacific Coast League (AAA), 1963–1968; expansion franchise. American Association (AAA), 1969–(still in existence as of 5-1-92); charter franchise.

Oklahoma City Indians
Texas League (C), 1909–1910; (B), 1911; new franchise. Became BEAUMONT OILERS, 1912.

Oklahoma City Indians
Western League (A), mid-1918–1932; relocated franchise. Had been HUTCHINSON WHEATSHOCKERS, mid-1917–mid-1918. Texas League (A), 1933–1935; (A1), 1936–1942; (AA) 1946–1957; new franchise. Became CORPUS CHRISTI GIANTS, 1958.

Oklahoma City Mets
Southwestern League (D), 1904; charter franchise. Western Association (C), mid-1905–1908; relocated franchise. Had been AUSTIN

SENATORS, 1905. Disbanded after 1908 season.

Oklahoma City Senators
Oklahoma State League (D), 1912; charter franchise. Disbanded with league during 1912 season.

Oklahoma City Senators
Alternate name for OKLAHOMA BOOSTERS, 1915.

OKMULGEE, OK

Okmulgee
Western Association (D), mid-1910; relocated franchise. Had been MUSKOGEE NAVIGATORS, 1908–mid-1910. Disbanded after 1910 season.

Okmulgee Drillers
Western Association (D), 1920–1921; (C), 1922–1926; (B), 1927; (C), mid-1927; new franchise. Disbanded after 1927 season.

Okmulgee Glassblowers
Oklahoma State League (D), 1912; charter franchise. Disbanded with league during 1912 season.

OLD ORCHARD BEACH, ME

Maine Guides
International League (AAA), 1984–1987; new franchise. Renamed MAINE PHILLIES, 1988.

Maine Phillies
International League (AAA), 1988; renamed franchise. Had been MAINE GUIDES, 1984–1987. Disbanded after 1988 season.

OLD TOWN, ME

Old Town
Northern Maine League (D), 1902; charter franchise. Disbanded with league after 1902 season.

OLEAN, NY

Olean
New York–Pennsylvania League, 1890–1891; charter franchise. Disbanded with league after 1891 season.

Olean
Iron & Oil League, 1898; charter franchise. Disbanded with league during 1898 season.

Olean
Inter-State League (D), 1905–mid-1908; new franchise. Disbanded with league during 1908 season.

Olean Athletics
New York–Pennsylvania League (D), 1959; renamed franchise. Had been OLEAN OILERS, 1957–1958. Disbanded after 1959 season.

Olean Giants
PONY League (D), 1954; renamed franchise. Had been OLEAN YANKEES, 1952–1953. Renamed OLEAN OILERS, 1955.

Olean Oilers
PONY League (D), 1939–1951; charter franchise. Renamed OLEAN YANKEES, 1952.

Olean Oilers
PONY League (D), 1955–1956; renamed franchise. Had been OLEAN GIANTS, 1954. New York–Pennsylvania League (D), 1957–1958; new franchise. Renamed OLEAN ATHLETICS, 1959.

Olean Red Sox
New York–Pennsylvania League (D), 1961–1962; expansion franchise. Disbanded after 1962 season.

Olean Refiners
Inter-State League (D), mid-1914; charter franchise. Renamed OLEAN WHITE SOX, 1915.

Olean White Sox
Inter-State League (D), 1915–1916; renamed franchise. Had been

OLEAN REFINERS, mid-1914. Disbanded with league after 1916 season.

Olean Yankees
PONY League (D), 1952–1953; renamed franchise. Had been OLEAN OILERS, 1939–1951. Renamed OLEAN GIANTS, 1954.

OLYMPIA, WA

Olympia Senators
Southwest Washington League (D), 1903–1904; charter franchise. Dissbanded with league during 1904 season.

OMAHA, NE

Omaha
Nebraska State League (D), 1932; new franchise. Became BEATRICE BLUES, mid-1932.

Omaha Babes
Western League, 1898; new franchise. Became ST. JOSEPH SAINTS, mid-1898.

Omaha Buffaloes (aka Burchers)
Western League (A), 1921–1927; renamed franchise. Had been OMAHA ROURKES, 1905–1920. Renamed OMAHA CRICKETS, 1928.

Omaha Burchers
Alternate name for OMAHA BUFFALOES, 1921–1927.

Omaha Burch Reds
Alternate name for OMAHA BUFFALOS, 1921.

Omaha Cardinals
Western League (A), 1947–1954; charter franchise. American Association (AAA), 1955–1959; expansion franchise. Disbanded after 1959 season.

Omaha Crickets
Western League (A), 1928–1929; renamed franchise. Had been

OMAHA BUFFALOES, 1921–1927. Renamed OMAHA PACKERS, 1930.

Omaha Dodgers
American Association (AAA), 1961–1962; new franchise. Disbanded with league after 1962 season.

Omaha Green Stockings
Northwestern League, 1879; charter franchise. Disbanded with league during 1879 season.

Omaha Indians
Alternate name for OMAHA OMAHOGS, 1895.

Omaha Indians (aka Kidnappers and Omahogs)
Western League (A), 1900–1903; charter franchise. Renamed OMAHA RANGERS, 1904.

Omaha Kidnappers
Alternate name for OMAHA OMAHOGS, 1900–1903.

Omaha Lambs
Western League, 1892; charter franchise. Disbanded during 1892 season.

Omaha Omahogs
Western League, 1885; charter franchise. Became KEOKUK KEOKUKS, mid-1885.

Omaha Omahogs (aka Indians, 1895)
Western Association, 1894–1895; charter franchise. Became DENVER GRIZZLIES, mid-1895.

Omaha Omahogs
Alternate name for OMAHA INDIANS, 1900–1903.

Omaha Omahosses
Western Association, 1888–1892; new franchise. Disbanded with league after 1892 season.

Omaha Packers
Western League (A), 1930–mid-1935; renamed franchise. Had been OMAHA CRICKETS, 1928–1929. Became COUNCIL BLUFFS RAILS, mid-1935.

Omaha Rangers
Western League (A), 1904; renamed franchise. Had been OMAHA OMAHOGS, 1900–1903. Became OMAHA ROURKES, 1905–1920.

Omaha Robin Hoods
Western League (A), 1936; new franchise. Became ROCK ISLAND ROBIN HOODS, mid-1936.

Omaha Rourke Family
Alternate name for OMAHA ROURKES, 1905–1920.

Omaha Rourkes (aka Rourke Family)
Western League (A), 1905–1920; renamed franchise. Had been OMAHA RANGERS, 1904. Renamed OMAHA BUFFALOES, 1921.

Omaha Royals
American Association (AAA), 1969–(still in existence as of 5-1-92); charter franchise.

Omaha Union Pacifics
Western League, 1887; expansion franchise. Disbanded after 1887 season.

Oneida
Central New York League, 1886; charter franchise. Disbanded with league after 1886 season.

Oneida
New York State League, 1889; new franchise. Disbanded after 1889 season.

Oneida
Empire State League (NY), (C), 1905; charter franchise. Disbanded during 1905 season.

Oneida
Central New York League (D), 1910; charter franchise. Disbanded with league after 1910 season.

Oneonta
New York–Pennsylvania League (B), mid-1924; relocated franchise. Had been UTICA UTES, 1924. Disbanded after 1924 season.

Oneonta Indians
New York State League, 1890; new franchise. Disbanded with league after 1890 season.

Oneonta Indians
Canadian–American League (C), 1940–1942; relocated franchise. Had been CORNWALL MAPLE LEAFS, 1939. Disbanded after 1942 season.

Oneonta Red Sox
Canadian–American League (C), 1946–1951; charter franchise. Disbanded with league after 1951 season.

Oneonta Yankees
New York–Pennsylvania League (A), 1966–(still in existence as of 5-1-92); new franchise.

Ontario Orioles
Sunset League (C), 1947; charter franchise. Disbanded after 1947 season.

Opelika Opelicans
Georgia–Alabama League (D), 1913; charter franchise. Renamed OPELIKA PELICANS, 1914.

Opelika Owls
Georgia–Alabama League (D), 1946–1951; charter franchise. Disbanded with league after 1951 season.

Opelika Pelicans
Georgia–Alabama League (D), 1914; renamed franchise. Had been OPELIKA OPELICANS, 1913. Disbanded after 1914 season.

OPELOUSAS, LA

Opelousas
Cotton States League (D), 1932; new franchise. Disbanded with league during 1932 season.

Opelousas Indians
Gulf Coast League (D), 1907; charter franchise. Disbanded after 1907 season.

Opelousas Indians
Evangeline League (D), 1934–1941; charter franchise. Suspended operations with league after 1941 season, and did not rejoin when league resumed in 1946.

OPP, AL

(See ANDALUSIA–OPP, AL)

ORANGE, TX

Orange Hoo-Hoos
Gulf Coast League (D), 1907–1908; charter franchise. Disbanded with league after 1908 season.

ORANGEBURG, SC

Orangeburg Cardinals
Western Carolinas League (A), 1973; new franchise. Renamed ORANGEBURG DODGERS, 1974.

Orangeburg Cotton Pickers
South Carolina League (D), 1907–1908; charter franchise. Disbanded with league after 1908 season.

Orangeburg Dodgers
Western Carolinas League (A), 1974; renamed franchise. Had been ORANGEBURG CARDINALS, 1973. Disbanded after 1974 season.

ORIZABA, VERACRUZ, MEXICO

Orizaba Cerveceros (Brewers)
Mexican Southeast League (A), 1966; new franchise. Renamed ORIZABA CHARROS, 1967.

Orizaba Charros (Chapmen)
Mexican Southeast League (A), 1967; renamed franchise. Had been ORIZABA CERVECEROS, 1966. Disbanded after 1967 season.

ORLANDO, FL

Orlando Bulldogs
Florida State League (C), 1922–mid-1924; renamed franchise. Had been ORLANDO TIGERS, 1921. Disbanded with league during 1924 season.

Orlando Caps
Florida State League (D), 1919–1920; charter franchise. Renamed ORLANDO TIGERS, 1921.

Orlando C. B.'s
Florida State League (D), 1955; renamed franchise. Had been ORLANDO SENATORS, 1938–1941; 1946–1954. Renamed ORLANDO SERTOMAS, 1956.

Orlando Colts
Florida State League (C), 1926–mid-1928; charter franchise. Disbanded with league during 1928 season.

Orlando Dodgers
Florida State League (D), 1959–1961; renamed franchise. Had been ORLANDO FLYERS, 1957–1958. Disbanded after 1961 season.

Orlando Flyers
Florida State League (D), 1957–1958; renamed franchise. Had been ORLANDO SERTOMAS, 1956. Renamed ORLANDO DODGERS, 1959.

Orlando Gulls
Florida State League (D), 1937; new franchise. Renamed ORLANDO SENATORS, 1938.

Orlando Juice
Senior Professional Baseball Association, 1989–1990; charter franchise. Disbanded after 1989–1990 season.

Orlando O-Twins
Alternate name for ORLANDO TWINS.

Orlando Senators
Florida East Coast League (D). Scheduled to begin play in 1942, but did not assemble a team.

Orlando Senators
Florida State League (D), 1938–mid-1942; 1946–1954; renamed franchise. Had been ORLANDO GULLS, 1937. Renamed ORLANDO C. B.'S, 1955.

Orlando Sertomas
Florida State League (D), 1956; renamed franchise. Had been ORLANDO C. B.'S, 1955. Renamed ORLANDO FLYERS, 1957.

Orlando Sunrays
Southern League (AA), 1990– (still in existence as of 5-1-92); renamed franchise. Had been ORLANDO TWINS, 1963–1989.

Orlando Tigers
Florida State League (D) 1921; renamed franchise. Had been ORLANDO CAPS, 1919–1920. Renamed ORLANDO BULLDOGS, 1922.

Orlando Twins (aka O-Twins)
Florida State League (A), 1963–1973; new franchise. Southern League (AA), 1974–1989; new franchise. Renamed ORLANDO SUN RAYS, 1990.

OROVILLE, CA

Oroville Red Sox
Far West League (D), 1948; charter franchise. Disbanded after 1948 season.

OSCEOLA, AR

Osceola Indians
Northeast Arkansas League (D), 1936–1937; charter franchise. Disbanded after 1937 season.

OSCEOLA, FL
(See KISSIMMEE, FL)

OSCEOLA, IA

Osceola
Southwest Iowa League (D), 1903; charter franchise. Disbanded with league during 1903 season.

OSHKOSH, WI

Oshkosh
Northwestern League, 1886–1887; charter franchise. Disbanded with league after 1887 season.

Oshkosh Giants
Wisconsin State League (D), 1941–1942; 1946–1953; new franchise. Disbanded with league after 1953 season.

Oshkosh Indians
Wisconsin State League, 1891; charter franchise. Michigan–Wisconsin League, 1892; charter franchise. Disbanded with league after 1892 season.

Oshkosh Indians
Wisconsin State League (D), 1905–1906; charter franchise. Wisconsin–Illinois League (D), 1907–1908; charter franchise. Wisconsin State League (D), 1909; charter franchise. Wisconsin–Illinois League (D), 1910, (C), 1911–1914; charter franchise. Disbanded with league after 1914 season.

OSKALOOSA, IA

Oskaloosa Quakers
Iowa State League (D), 1904–1907; charter franchise. Central Association (D), 1908; charter

franchise. Disbanded after 1908 season.

OSSINING, NY

Ossining
Hudson River League (D), 1903; charter franchise. Became CATSKILL, mid-1903.

OSWEGO, NY

Oswego
Eastern International League, 1888; charter franchise. Disbanded with league during 1888 season.

Oswego
Central New York League (C), 1910; charter franchise. Disbanded with league after 1910 season.

Oswego Netherlands
Canadian–American League (C), 1936–1940; charter franchise. Became PITTSFIELD ELECTRICS, 1941.

Oswego Starch Boxes
International League, 1886–mid-1887; charter franchise. Became SCRANTON MINERS, mid-1887.

Oswego Starchmakers
New York State League, 1898–1900; new franchise. Became ELMIRA, mid-1900.

Oswego Starchmakers
Empire State League (NY), (C), 1905–1907; charter franchise. Disbanded with league after 1907 season.

Oswego Sweegs
New York State League, 1885; charter franchise. Disbanded with league during 1885 season.

OTTAWA, IL

Ottawa Crows
Illinois–Iowa League, 1890; charter franchise. Renamed OTTAWA MODOCS, 1891.

Ottawa Indians
Illinois–Missouri League (D), 1914; new franchise. Bi-State League (WI–IL), (D), 1915; charter franchise. Disbanded with league after 1915 season.

Ottawa Modocs
Illinois–Iowa League, 1891; renamed franchise. Had been OTTAWA CROWS, 1890. Disbanded after 1891 season.

OTTAWA, KS

Ottawa
Kansas State League, 1898; charter franchise. Disbanded with league during 1898 season.

Ottawa
Southwestern League (D), mid-1924; relocated franchise. Had been BLACKWELL GASSERS, mid-1924. Became NEWTON RAILROADERS, mid-1924.

OTTAWA, ONTARIO, CANADA

Ottawa
Eastern International League, 1895; charter franchise. Disbanded with league during 1895 season.

Ottawa
Eastern League, mid-1898; relocated franchise. Had been ROCHESTER PATRIOTS, 1898. Disbanded after 1898 season.

Ottawa
Canadian League (C), 1905; charter franchise. Disbanded with league after 1905 season.

Ottawa Athletics
International League (AAA), 1951–1954; renamed franchise. Had been OTTAWA NATIONALS, 1950. Disbanded after 1954 season.

Ottawa Braves
Canadian–American League (C), 1937–1938; renamed franchise. Had been OTTAWA SENATORS, 1936. Renamed OTTAWA SENATORS, 1939.

Ottawa Canadiens
Eastern Canada League (B), 1922–1923; charter franchise. Disbanded with league after 1923 season.

Ottawa Giants
International League (AAA), 1951; relocated franchise. Had been JERSEY CITY LITTLE GIANTS, 1937–1950. Renamed OTTAWA ATHLETICS, 1952.

Ottawa Nationals
Border League (C), 1947; new franchise. Renamed OTTAWA SENATORS, 1948.

Ottawa Nationals
Border League (C), 1950; renamed franchise. Had been OTTAWA SENATORS, 1948–1949. Became OTTAWA GIANTS, 1951.

Ottawa Senators
Canadian League (C), 1912–mid-1914; (B), mid-1914–1915; new franchise. Disbanded with league after 1915 season.

Ottawa Senators
Canadian–American League (C), 1936; charter franchise. Renamed OTTAWA BRAVES, 1937.

Ottawa Senators
Canadian–American League (C), 1939; renamed franchise. Had been OTTAWA COLTS, 1937–1938. Became OTTAWA–OGDENSBURG SENATORS, 1940.

Ottawa Senators
Border League (C), 1949; renamed franchise. Had been OTTAWA NATIONALS, 1947–1948. Renamed OTTAWA NATIONALS, 1950.

OTTAWA–HULL, ONTARIO, CANADA

Ottawa–Hull Senators
Quebec–Ontario–Vermont League (B), 1924; charter franchise. Disbanded with league after 1924 season.

OTTAWA, ONTARIO, CANADA–OGDENSBURG, NY
(See also Ogdensburg, NY)

Ottawa–Ogdensburg Senators
Canadian–American League (C), mid-1940; renamed franchise. Had been OTTAWA SENATORS, 1939. Disbanded during 1940 season.

OTTUMWA, IA

Ottumwa
Central Association (D), mid-1916; relocated franchise. Had been BURLINGTON PATHFINDERS, 1908–1916. Disbanded after 1916 season.

Ottumwa Cardinals
Mississippi Valley League (D), 1922–1925; charter franchise. Renamed OTTUMWA PACKERS, 1926.

Ottumwa Champs
Central League/Association (D), 1906; renamed franchise. Had been OTTUMWA SNAPPERS. Renamed OTTUMWA PACKERS, 1907.

Ottumwa Coal Barons
Illinois–Iowa League, 1891; renamed franchise. Had been OTTUMWA COAL PALACE KINGS, 1890. Disbanded after 1891 season.

Ottumwa Coal Barons
Eastern Iowa League, 1895; charter franchise. Disbanded with league after 1895 season.

Ottumwa Coal Palace Giants
Western Association, 1898–1899; relocated franchise. Had been DES MOINES PROHIBITIONISTS (aka Indians), 1894–1897. Disbanded after the 1899 season.

Ottumwa Coal Palace Kings
Illinois–Iowa League, 1890; charter franchise. Renamed OTTUMWA COAL BARONS, 1891.

Ottumwa Packers
Central League/Association (D), 1907–1910; renamed franchise. Had been OTTUMWA CHAMPS, 1906. Renamed OTTUMWA SPEED BOYS, 1911.

Ottumwa Packers
Mississippi Valley League (D), 1926–1928; renamed franchise. Had been OTTUMWA CARDINALS, 1922–1925. Disbanded after 1928 season.

Ottumwa Snappers
Central League/Association (D), 1905; renamed franchise. Had been OTTUMWA STANDPATTERS, 1904. Renamed OTTUMWA CHAMPS, 1906.

Ottumwa Speed Boys
Central League/Association (D), 1911–mid-1914; renamed franchise. Had been OTTUMWA PACKERS, 1907–1910. Became ROCK ISLAND ISLANDERS, mid-1914.

Ottumwa Standpatters
Iowa State League (D), 1904; charter franchise. Renamed OTTUMWA SNAPPERS, 1905.

OUTREMONT, QUEBEC, CANADA

Outremont Canadiens
Quebec–Ontario–Vermont League (B) 1924; charter franchise. Disbanded with league after 1924 season.

OWENSBORO, KY

Owensboro
Kentucky–Indiana League, 1896; charter franchise. Disbanded with league during 1896 season.

Owensboro
KITTY League (D), mid-1916; charter franchise. Disbanded with league after 1916 season.

Owensboro Distillers
KITTY League (D), 1913–1914; new franchise. Disbanded with league after 1914 season.

Owensboro Oilers
KITTY League (D), mid-1936–1942; 1946–1955; renamed franchise. Had been PORTAGEVILLE PIRATES, mid-1935–mid-1936. Disbanded with league after 1955 season.

Owensboro Pirates
KITTY League (D), 1936; new franchise. Renamed OWENSBORO OILERS, 1937.

OWOSSO, MI

Owosso
Michigan State League, 1893; charter franchise. Disbanded during 1893 season.

Owosso Colts
Michigan State League, 1895; new franchise. Disbanded during 1895 season.

OZARK, AL

Ozark Cardinals
Alabama–Florida League (D), 1936–mid-1937; charter franchise. Became EVERGREEN GREENIES, mid-1937.

Ozark Dodgers
Alabama–Florida League (D), 1962; new franchise. Became ANDALUSIA DODGERS, mid-1962.

Ozark Eagles
Alabama State League (D), 1946–1950; charter franchise. Alabama–Florida League (D), 1951–1952; charter franchise. Disbanded after 1952 season.

OZARK, AR

Ozark
West Arkansas League (D), 1924; charter franchise. Disbanded with league after 1924 season.

PADUCAH, KY

Paducah
Central League, 1897; charter franchise. Disbanded with league after 1897 season.

Paducah Chiefs
KITTY League (D), 1903–1906; charter franchise. Disbanded with league after 1906 season.

Paducah Chiefs
KITTY League (D), 1910–1914; charter franchise. Disbanded with league after 1914 season.

Paducah Chiefs
KITTY League (D), 1922–1923; charter franchise. Disbanded after 1923 season.

Paducah Chiefs
MOV League (D), 1949–1950; charter franchise. KITTY League (D), 1951–1955; new franchise. Disbanded with league after 1955 season.

Paducah Indians
KITTY League (D), 1936–1941; renamed franchise. Had been PADUCAH RED BIRDS, 1935. Disbanded after 1941 season.

Paducah Red Birds
KITTY League (D), 1935; charter franchise. Renamed PADUCAH INDIANS, 1936.

PAINTSVILLE, KY

Paintsville Brewers
Appalachian League (R), 1983–1984; renamed franchise. Had been PAINTSVILLE YANKEES, 1979–1982. Disbanded after 1984 season.

Paintsville Hilanders
Appalachian League (R), 1978; new franchise. Renamed PAINTSVILLE YANKEES, 1979.

Paintsville Yankees
Appalachian League (R), 1979–1982; renamed franchise. Had been PAINTSVILLE HILANDERS, 1978. Renamed PAINTSVILLE BREWERS, 1983.

PALATKA, FL

Palatka Azaleas
Florida State League (D), 1936–1939; charter franchise. Disbanded after 1939 season.

Palatka Azaleas
Florida State League (D), 1946–mid-1953; charter franchise. Became LAKELAND PILOTS, mid-1953.

Palatka Cubs
Florida State League (D), 1962; renamed franchise. Had been PALATKA RED LEGS, 1957–1961. Disbanded after 1962 season.

Palatka Red Legs
Florida State League (D), 1957–1961; renamed franchise. Had been PALATKA TIGERS, 1956. Renamed PALATKA CUBS, 1962.

Palatka Tigers
Florida State League (D), 1956; new franchise. Renamed PALATKA RED LEGS, 1957.

PALESTINE, TX

Palestine Browns
East Texas League (D), 1916; charter franchise. Disbanded with league after 1916 season.

Palestine Pals
Texas Association (D), 1925–1926; relocated franchise. Had been MARLIN BATHERS, 1923–mid-1925. Lone Star League (D), 1927–

1929; charter franchise. Disbanded with league after 1929 season.

Palestine Pals
West Dixie League (C), 1934–1935; charter franchise. East Texas League (C), 1936–1940; charter franchise. Disbanded with league after 1940 season.

PALMYRA, NY

Palmyra
Empire State League (D), 1905; charter franchise. Disbanded during 1905 season.

Palmyra Mormons
New York State League, 1897–1898; charter franchise. Disbanded during 1898 season.

PALM SPRINGS, CA

Palm Springs Angels
California League (A), 1986–(still in existence as of 5-1-92); new franchise.

PAMPA, TX

Pampa Oilers
West Texas–New Mexico League (D), 1939–1942; (C), 1946–1955; new franchise. Southwestern League (B), 1956–mid-1957; charter franchise. Became SAN ANGELO COLTS, mid-1957.

PANA, IL

Pana Coal Miners
Eastern Illinois League (D), 1907–mid-1908; charter franchise. Became LINTON, mid-1908.

PANAMA CITY, FL

Panama City Fliers
Alabama–Florida League (D), 1951–1961; charter franchise. Disbanded after 1961 season.

Panama City Papermakers
Alabama–Florida League (D), 1936; charter franchise. Renamed PANAMA CITY PELICANS, 1937.

Panama City Pelicans
Alabama–Florida League (D), 1937; renamed franchise. Had been PANAMA CITY PAPERMAKERS, 1936. Renamed PANAMA CITY PELICANS, 1938.

Panama City Pelicans
Alabama–Florida League (D), 1939; renamed franchise. Had been PANAMA CITY PILOTS, 1938. Disbanded with league after 1939 season.

Panama City Pilots
Georgia–Florida League (D), 1935; charter franchise. Disbanded after 1935 season.

Panama City Pilots
Alabama–Florida League (D), 1938; renamed franchise. Had been PANAMA CITY PELICANS, 1937. Renamed PANAMA CITY PELICANS, 1939.

PANAMA CITY, PANAMA

Panama City Bankers
Inter-American League (AAA), 1979: charter franchise. Disbanded with league during 1979 season.

PARAGOULD, AR

Paragould
Northeast Arkansas League (D), 1909–1911; charter franchise. Disbanded with league after 1911 season.

Paragould Broncos
Northeast Arkansas League (D), 1939–1941; renamed franchise. Had been PARAGOULD REBELS, 1936–1938. Disbanded with league after 1941 season.

Paragould Rebels
Northeast Arkansas League (D), 1936–1938; charter franchise. Renamed PARAGOULD BRONCOS, 1939.

PARIS, AR

Paris
West Arkansas League (D), 1924; charter franchise. Disbanded with league after 1924 season.

PARIS, IL

Paris
Southwestern League, 1898; charter franchise. Disbanded with league during 1898 season.

Paris Colts
Eastern Illinois League (D), mid-1907; relocated franchise. Had been CENTRALIA WHITE STOCKINGS, 1907. Renamed PARIS PARISIANS, 1908.

Paris Lakers
MOV League (D), 1950–1955; new franchise. Midwest League (D), 1956–1959; charter franchise. Disbanded after 1959 season.

Paris Parisians
Eastern Illinois League (D), 1908; renamed franchise. Had been PARIS COLTS, mid-1907. Disbanded with league after 1908 season.

PARIS, KY

Paris
Ohio State League (D), mid-1914; relocated franchise. Had been NEWPORT, 1914. Disbanded after 1914 season.

Paris Bourbonites
Blue Grass League (D), 1909–1912; new franchise. Disbanded with league after 1912 season.

Paris Bourbons
Blue Grass League (D), 1922–1924; charter franchise. Disbanded with league after 1924 season.

PARIS, TN

Paris Parisians
KITTY League (D), 1923–1924; renamed franchise. Had been PARIS TRAVELERS, 1922. Disbanded with league after 1924 season.

Paris Travelers
KITTY League (D), 1922; charter franchise. Renamed PARIS PARISIANS, 1923.

PARIS, TX

Paris
Texas League (D), 1903; new franchise. Became WACO STEERS, mid-1903.

Paris
East Texas League (D), 1931; charter franchise. Disbanded with league during 1931 season.

Paris A's
Western Association (D), 1915–1917; new franchise. Became ARDMORE ARDMORITES, mid-1917.

Paris Bearcats
East Texas League (D), 1925–1926; renamed franchise. Had been PARIS NORTH STARS, 1924. Disbanded with league after 1926 season.

Paris Eisenfelder's Homeseekers (named for owner C. W. Eisenfelder)
Texas League (D), 1902; charter franchise. Became GALVESTON SANDCRABS, 1903.

Paris Grays
East Texas League (D), 1923; charter franchise. Renamed PARIS NORTH STARS, 1924.

Paris Hustlers (aka Colts)
Lone Star League (D), 1928; renamed franchise. Had been PARIS SNAPPERS, 1927. Disbanded after 1928 season.

Paris Indians
Big State League (B), 1952–1953; renamed franchise. Disbanded after 1953 season.

Paris North Stars
East Texas League (D), 1924; renamed franchise. Had been PARIS GRAYS, 1923. Renamed PARIS BEARCATS, 1925.

Paris Orioles
Sooner State League (D), 1955–1957; new franchise. Disbanded with league after 1957 season.

Paris Panthers
Big State League (B), 1948; renamed franchise. Had been PARIS RED PEPPERS, 1947. East Texas League (C), 1949–1950; charter franchise. Disbanded with league after 1950 season.

Paris Parasites
Texas League (D), 1904; new franchise. Became ARDMORE INDIANS, mid-1904.

Paris Parisians
North Texas League (D), 1907; new franchise. Disbanded with league after 1907 season.

Paris Pirates
West Dixie League (C), 1934; charter franchise. Became LUFKIN LUMBERMEN, mid-1934.

Paris Red Peppers
East Texas League (C), 1946; charter franchise. Big State League (B), 1947–1948; charter franchise. Renamed PARIS PANTHERS, 1949.

Paris Snappers
South Central League (D), 1912; charter franchise. Texas–Oklahoma League (D), 1913–1914; new franchise. Disbanded with league after 1914 season.

Paris Snappers
Texas–Oklahoma League (D), 1921–1922; charter franchise. Dis-

banded with league after 1922 season.

Paris Snappers
Lone Star League (D), 1927; charter franchise. Renamed PARIS HUSTLERS (aka Colts), 1928.

Texas Midland Tigers
Texas Southern League, mid-1896; relocated franchise. Had been SHERMAN STUDENTS, 1896. Texas League, 1897; charter franchise. Disbanded after 1897 season.

PARK CITY, UT

Park City
Inter-Mountain League, 1901; charter franchise. Disbanded with league after 1901 season.

PARKERSBURG, WV

Parkersburg
Ohio–West Virginia League, 1897; charter franchise. Disbanded with league after 1897 season.

Parkersburg
Pennsylvania–West Virginia League (D), mid-1909; relocated franchise. Had been CHARLEROI, 1908–mid-1909. Virginia Valley League (D), 1910; charter franchise. Disbanded with league after 1910 season.

Parkersburg Parkers
Middle Atlantic League (D), mid-1931; relocated franchise. Had been HAGERSTOWN HUBS, 1931. Became YOUNGSTOWN TUBERS, mid-1931.

PARKSLEY, VA

Parksley Spuds
Eastern Shore League (D), 1922–mid-1928; charter franchise. Disbanded with league during 1928 season.

PARRAS, MEXICO

Parras Saraperos
Mexican Center League (A), 1974; new franchise. Disbanded after 1974 season.

PARSONS, KS

Parsons
Kansas State League (D), 1906; new franchise. Oak League (D), 1907; charter franchise. Disbanded with league after 1907 season.

Parsons
Southwestern League (D), 1921; charter franchise. Became CUSHING, mid-1921.

Parsons
Missouri Valley League (D), 1905; charter franchise. Disbanded with league after 1905 season.

PASADENA, CA

Pasadena
Southern California League (D), 1913; charter franchise. Became SANTA BARBARA, mid-1913.

Pasadena Silk Sox
Southern California Trolley League (D), 1910; charter franchise. Disbanded with league after 1910 season.

PASCO, WA

(See KENNEWICK, WA)

PATERSON, NJ

Paterson Champions
Atlantic League, 1896; charter franchise. Renamed PATERSON SILK WEAVERS, 1897.

Paterson Giants
Atlantic League, 1899; renamed franchise. Had been PATERSON SILK WEAVERS, 1897–1898. Disbanded after 1899 season.

Paterson Intruders
Hudson River League (C), 1904–1907; new franchise. Disbanded with league after 1907 season.

Paterson Silk City
Atlantic League (D), 1914; charter franchise. Disbanded with league after 1914 season.

Paterson Silk Weavers
Atlantic League, 1897–1898; renamed franchise. Had been PATERSON CHAMPIONS, 1896. Renamed PATERSON GIANTS, 1899.

PATTON, PA

Patton
Inter-State League (D), mid-1906; relocated franchise. Had been HORNELL, 1906. Disbanded with league after 1906 season.

PAULS VALLEY, OK

Pauls Valley Raiders
Sooner State League (D), 1948–1954; new franchise. Disbanded after 1954 season.

PAWHUSKA, OK

Pawhuska
Oklahoma State League (D), mid-1924; relocated franchise. Had been ARDMORE BEARCATS, mid-1924. Disbanded with league after 1924 season.

Pawhuska Huskers
Western Association (D), 1920–1921; charter franchise. Renamed PAWHUSKA OSAGES, 1922.

Pawhuska Osages
Western Association (D), 1922; renamed franchise. Had been PAWHUSKA HUSKERS, 1920–1921. Disbanded after 1922 season.

PAWTUCKET, RI

Pawtucket
New England League, 1892; new franchise. Disbanded during 1892 season.

Pawtucket Clam Eaters (aka Maroons)
New England League, 1894–1895; charter franchise. Renamed PAWTUCKET PHENOMS, 1896.

Pawtucket Colts
Atlantic Association (D), 1908; charter franchise. Disbanded with association during 1908 season.

Pawtucket Indians
Eastern League (AA), 1966–1967; new franchise. Disbanded after 1967 season.

Pawtucket Maroons
Alternate name for PAWTUCKET CLAM EATERS.

Pawtucket Maroons
New England League, 1899; charter franchise. Disbanded during 1899 season.

Pawtucket Phenoms
New England League, 1896–1897; charter franchise. Had been PAWTUCKET TIGERS, 1894–1895. Renamed PAWTUCKET TIGERS, 1898.

Pawtucket Red Sox
Eastern League (AA), 1970–1972; new franchise. International League (AAA), 1973–1975; new franchise. Renamed RHODE ISLAND REDS, 1976.

Pawtucket Red Sox
International League (AAA), 1977–(still in existence as of 5-1-92); renamed franchise. Had been RHODE ISLAND REDS, 1976.

Pawtucket Slaters
New England League (B), 1946–1949; charter franchise. Disbanded with league after 1949 season.

Pawtucket Tigers
New England League, 1898; renamed franchise. Had been PAWTUCKET PHENOMS, 1896–1897. Disbanded with league during 1898 season.

Pawtucket Tigers
Colonial League (C), 1914–1915; charter franchise. Disbanded with league after 1915 season.

Rhode Island Reds
International League (AAA), 1976; renamed franchise. Had been PAWTUCKET RED SOX, 1970–1975. Renamed PAWTUCKET RED SOX, 1977.

PEARLSBURG, VA
(See also NARROWS, VA)

Narrows Rebels
Appalachian League (D), 1946–1950; new franchise. Disbanded after 1950 season.

PEEKSKILL, NY

Peekskill
Hudson River League, 1888; charter franchise. Disbanded with league during 1888 season.

Peekskill
Hudson River League (D), 1903; charter franchise. Disbanded after 1903 season.

Peekskill
Hudson River League (C), 1905; new franchise. Disbanded after 1905 season.

Peekskill Highlanders
North Atlantic League (D), 1946–1949; charter franchise. Disbanded after 1949 season.

PEKIN, IL

Pekin Celestials
Illinois–Missouri League (D), 1909–mid-1913; new franchise. Disbanded during 1913 season.

PENDLETON, OR

Pendleton
Pacific Inter-State League, 1891; charter franchise. Disbanded with league after 1891 season.

Pendleton Buckaroos
Western Tri-State League (C), 1913; (D), 1914; charter franchise. Disbanded with league after 1914 season.

Pendleton Pets
Inland Empire League (D), 1902; charter franchise. Disbanded with league after 1902 season.

PENNINGTON GAP, VA

Pennington Gap Lee Bears
Appalachian League (D), 1937–1939; charter franchise. Renamed PENNINGTON MINERS, 1940.

Pennington Gap Miners
Appalachian League (D), 1940; renamed franchise. Had been PENNINGTON GAP BEARS, 1937–1939. Disbanded after 1940 season.

Pennington Gap Miners
Mountain States League (D), 1948–1951; charter franchise. Disbanded after 1951 season.

PENN YAN, NY

Penn Yan
New York State League, 1888; charter franchise. Disbanded after 1888 season.

Penn Yan
Empire State League (NY), (D), 1906; new franchise. Became SYRACUSE, mid-1906.

PENSACOLA, FL

Pensacola
Southern League, mid-1893; relocated franchise. Had been BIR-

MINGHAM PETS, 1893. Disbanded with league during 1893 season.

Pensacola
Cotton States League (D), 1913; new franchise. Disbanded with league during 1913 season.

Pensacola Angels
Alabama–Florida League (D), 1960–1961; renamed franchise. Had been PENSACOLA DONS, 1957–1959. Renamed PENSACOLA SENATORS, 1962.

Pensacola Dons
Alabama–Florida League (D), 1957–1959; new franchise. Renamed PENSACOLA ANGELS, 1960.

Pensacola Pilots
Southeastern League (D), 1927–1930; new franchise. Disbanded with league after 1930 season.

Pensacola Pilots
Southeastern League (B), 1937–1942; 1946–1950; charter franchise. Disbanded with league after 1950 season.

Pensacola Senators
Alabama–Florida League (D), 1962; renamed franchise. Had been PENSACOLA ANGELS, 1960–1961. Disbanded with league after 1962 season.

PEORIA, AZ

Peoria Padres
Arizona League (R), 1990–(still in existence as of 5-1-92); new franchise.

PEORIA, IL

Peoria Canaries
Central Inter-State League, 1888–1889; charter franchise. Western Inter-State League, 1890; charter franchise. Northwestern League, 1891; charter franchise. Inter-State League, 1891; charter franchise. Il-

linois–Iowa League, 1892; new franchise. Became AURORA HOODOOS, mid-1892.

Peoria Chiefs
Three I League (B), 1953–1957; new franchise. Disbanded after 1957 season.

Peoria Chiefs
Midwest League (A), 1984–(still in existence as of 5-1-92); renamed franchise. Had been PEORIA SUNS, 1983.

Peoria Blackbirds (aka Distillers, 1895)
Western Association, 1894–mid-1898; charter franchise. Disbanded with league during 1898 season.

Peoria Distillers
Alternate name for PEORIA BLACKBIRDS, 1895.

Peoria Distillers
Central League, 1900; charter franchise. Disbanded with league after 1900 season.

Peoria Distillers
Western League (A), 1902–1903; new franchise. Disbanded after 1903 season.

Peoria Distillers
Central Association (D), mid-1904; relocated franchise. Had been MARION OILWORKERS, 1904. Became MARION OILWORKERS, 1904.

Peoria Distillers
Ilinois–Iowa–Indiana League (B), 1905–mid-1917; new franchise. Disbanded during 1917 season.

Peoria Distillers
Central League (B), mid-1917; relocated franchise. Had been SOUTH BEND BENDERS, 1916–mid-1917. Disbanded with league after 1917 season.

Peoria Reds
Northwestern League, 1883–1884; charter franchise. Disbanded with league after 1884 season.

Peoria Reds
Three I League (B), 1937; charter franchise. Disbanded after 1937 season.

Peoria Redwings
All-American Girls Professional Baseball League, 1946–1951; new franchise. Disbanded after 1951 season.

Peoria Suns
Midwest League (A), 1983; new franchise. Renamed PEORIA CHIEFS, 1984.

Peoria Tractors
Illinois–Iowa–Illinois League (B), 1919–mid-1932; charter franchise. Mississippi Valley League (B), 1933; charter franchise. Central League (B), 1934; charter franchise. Three I League (B), 1935; charter franchise. Disbanded with league after 1935 season.

PERTH AMBOY, NJ

Perth Amboy Pacers
Atlantic League (D), 1914; charter franchise. Disbanded with league after 1914 season.

PERTH, ONTARIO, CANADA

Perth Blue Cats
Canadian–American League (C), mid-1936; charter franchise. Renamed PERTH ROYALS during 1936 season.

Perth Royals
Canadian–American League (C), mid-1936; renamed franchise. Had been PERTH BLUE CATS, 1936. Renamed PERTH BRAVES (see PERTH–CORNWALL), 1937.

PERTH–CORNWALL, ONTARIO, CANADA
(See also CORNWALL, ONTARIO, CANADA)

Perth Bisons
Alternate name for PERTH BRAVES.

Perth Braves (aka Bisons)
Canadian–American League (C), 1937; renamed franchise. Had been PERTH BLUE CATS, 1936. Disbanded after 1937 season.

PERU, IN

Peru
Indiana State League, 1890; charter franchise. Disbanded with league after 1890 season.

PETALUMA, CA

Petaluma
Central California Baseball League (D), 1910; charter franchise. Became ELMHURST, mid-1910.

PETERSBORO ONTARIO, CANADA

Petersboro Petes
Canadian League (C), 1913–mid-1914; (B), mid-1914; renamed franchise. Had been PETERSBOROUGH WHITECAPS, 1912. Disbanded after 1914 season.

PETERSBOROUGH, ONTARIO, CANADA

Petersborough Whitecaps
Canadian League (C), 1912; new franchise. Renamed PETERSBORO PETES, 1913.

PETERSBURG, VA
(See also COLONIAL HEIGHTS, VA)

Petersburg
Virginia League, 1885–1886; charter franchise. Disbanded with league after 1886 season.

Petersburg
Virginia State League, 1900; charter franchise. Disbanded during 1900 season.

Petersburg Broncos
Virginia League (B), 1926–mid-1928; new franchise. Disbanded with league during 1928 season.

Petersburg Champs
Virginia League, 1894; charter franchise. Renamed PETERSBURG FARMERS, 1895.

Petersburg Farmers
Virginia League, 1895–mid-1896; renamed franchise. Had been PETERSBURG CHAMPS, 1894. Became HAMPTON, mid-1896.

Petersburg Generals
Virginia League (C), 1948–1950; charter franchise. Became COLONIAL HEIGHTS–PETERSBURG GENERALS, 1951.

Petersburg Goobers (aka Hustlers, 1911)
Virginia League (C), mid-1910–mid-1917; relocated franchise. Had been PORTSMOUTH TRUCKERS, 1906–mid-1910. Disbanded with league during 1917 season. Virginia League (D), 1918; new franchise. Disbanded with league during 1918 season. Virginia League (C); 1919 (B), 1920; new franchise. Renamed PETERSBURG TRUNKMAKERS, 1921.

Petersburg Goobers
Virginia League (B), 1924; renamed franchise. Had been PETERSBURG TRUNKMAKERS, 1923. Disbanded after 1924 season.

Petersburg Hustlers
Alternate name for PETERSBURG GOOBERS, 1911.

Petersburg Rebels
Virginia League (C), 1941–1942; expansion franchise. Suspended operations with league after 1942 season, and did not rejoin when league resumed in 1948.

Petersburg Rebels
Alternate name for PETERSBURG GENERALS.

Petersburg Trunkmakers
Virginia League (B), 1921; renamed franchise. Had been PETERSBURG GOOBERS, 1910–1920. Became TARBORO TARBABIES, mid-1921.

Petersburg Trunkmakers
Virginia League (B), 1923–1924; relocated franchise. Had been NEWPORT NEWS SHIPBUILDERS, 1912–1922. Renamed PETERSBURG GOOBERS, 1924.

PHILADELPHIA, PA

ATHLETICS OF PHILADELPHIA
National Association, 1871–mid-1875; charter franchise. Disbanded during 1875 season.

CENTENNIAL OF PHILADELPHIA
National Association, 1875; expansion franchise. Disbanded during 1875 season.

Philadelphia
Pennsylvania League, 1879; charter franchise. National Association, 1880; new franchise. Disbanded with association after 1880 season.

Philadelphia
League Alliance, 1882; charter franchise. Disbanded during 1882 season.

Philadelphia
Eastern League, 1892; charter franchise. Disbanded after 1892 season.

Philadelphia
Atlantic League, mid-1896–1897; relocated franchise. Had been NEW YORK METROPOLITANS, 1896. Disbanded with league after 1897 season.

Philadelphia
Atlantic League, 1900; new franchise. Became HARRISBURG, mid-1901.

PHILADELPHIA ATHLETICS
National Association, 1871–mid-1875; charter franchise. Disbanded with league during 1875 season.

PHILADELPHIA ATHLETICS
National League, 1876; charter franchise. Disbanded after 1876 season.

Philadelphia Athletics
Keystone Association, 1877; charter franchise. Disbanded after 1877 season.

Philadelphia Athletics
Eastern Association, 1881; charter franchise. Disbanded after 1881 season.

Philadelphia Athletics
American Association, 1882–1891; charter franchise. Disbanded with association after 1891 season.

Philadelphia Athletics
Pennsylvania State League, 1896; new franchise. Disbanded during 1896 season.

PHILADELPHIA ATHLETICS
American League, 1901–1954; charter franchise. Became KANSAS CITY ATHLETICS, 1955.

PHILADELPHIA BLUE JAYS
National League, 1943–1944; renamed franchise. Had been PHILADELPHIA PHILLIES, 1883–1942. Renamed PHILADELPHIA PHILLIES, 1945.

Philadelphia Colts
Pennsylvania State League, mid-1894; relocated franchise. Had

been EASTON COLTS, mid-1894. Disbanded after 1894 season.

Philadelphia Giants
Middle States League, 1889; charter franchise. Disbanded with league after 1889 season.

PHILADELPHIA KEYSTONES
Union Association, 1884; charter franchise. Disbanded during 1884 season.

PHILADELPHIA PHILADELPHIAS
National Association, 1872; expansion franchise. Renamed PHILADELPHIA WHITES, 1873.

PHILADELPHIA PHILLIES
National League, 1890–1943; renamed franchise. Had been PHILADELPHIA QUAKERS, 1883–1889. Renamed PHILADELPHIA BLUE JAYS, 1943–1944.

PHILADELPHIA PHILLIES
National League, 1945–(still in existence as of 5-1-92); renamed franchise. Had been PHILADELPHIA BLUE JAYS, 1943–1944.

PHILADELPHIA QUAKERS
National League, 1883–1889; relocated franchise. Had been WORCESTER BROWN STOCKINGS, 1880–1882. Renamed PHILADELPHIA PHILLIES, 1890.

PHILADELPHIA QUAKERS
Players' League, 1890; charter franchise. Disbanded with league after 1890 season.

PHILADELPHIA STARS
Negro National League, 1934–1948; relocated franchise. Had been DETROIT STARS, 1920–1931; 1933. Negro American League, 1949–mid-1950; new franchise. Disbanded during 1950 season.

PHILADELPHIA WHITES
National Association, 1873–mid-1875; renamed franchise. Had been PHILADELPHIA PHILADELPHIAS, 1972. Disbanded with league during 1875 season.

PHILIPSBURG, MT

Philipsburg
Montana State League, 1892; charter franchise. Disbanded with league after 1892 season.

PHILIPSBURG, PA

Philipsburg
Mountain League, 1887; charter franchise. Disbanded with league after 1887 season.

PHILLIPSBURG, NJ
(See EASTON, PA)

PHOENIX, AZ

Phoenix Firebirds
Pacific Coast League (AAA), 1986–(still in existence as of 5-1-92); renamed franchise. Had been PHOENIX GIANTS, 1966–1985.

Phoenix Giants
Pacific Coast League (AAA), 1958–1959; relocated franchise. Had been MINNEAPOLIS MILLERS, 1902–1957. Became TACOMA GIANTS, 1960.

Phoenix Giants
Pacific Coast League (AAA), 1966–1985; relocated franchise. Had been TACOMA GIANTS, 1960–1965. Renamed PHOENIX FIREBIRDS, 1986.

Phoenix Senators
Rio Grande Valley Association (D), 1915; charter franchise. Disbanded with league after 1915 season.

Phoenix Senators
Arizona State League (D), 1928–1930; charter franchise. Arizona–

Texas League (D), 1931–1932; charter franchise. Disbanded with league after 1932 season.

Phoenix Senators
Arizona–Texas League (C), 1947–1950; charter franchise. Southwest International League (C), 1951; charter franchise. Arizona–Texas League (C), 1952–1953; charter franchise. Renamed PHOENIX STARS, 1954.

Phoenix Stars
Arizona–Texas League (C), 1954; renamed franchise. Arizona–Mexico League (C), 1955–1957. Disbanded with league after 1957 season.

PIEDMONT, WV

Piedmont
POM League (D), mid-1906; relocated franchise. Had been BUTLER, 1906. Became CHARLEROI, mid-1906.

Piedmont
Western Pennsylvania League (D), mid-1907; relocated franchise. Had been CUMBERLAND ROOTERS, mid-1907. Became SOMERSET, mid-1907.

Piedmont Drybugs
Potomac League (D), 1916; charter franchise. Disbanded with league after 1916 season.

Piedmont Drybugs
Blue Ridge League (D), 1918; new franchise. Disbanded with league during 1918 season.

PIKEVILLE, KY

Pikeville Brewers
Appalachian League (R), 1982; new franchise. Renamed PIKEVILLE CUBS, 1983.

Pikeville Cubs
Appalachian League (R), 1983–1984; renamed franchise. Had been

PIKEVILLE BREWERS, 1982. Disbanded after 1984 season.

PINE BLUFF, AR

Pine Bluff
Arkansas–Texas League (D), 1906; new franchise. Disbanded with league during 1906 season.

Pine Bluff Cardinals
Cotton States League (C), 1948–1949; expansion franchise. Renamed PINE BLUFF JUDGES, 1950.

Pine Bluff Infants
Southwestern League, 1887; charter franchise. Disbanded with league after 1887 season.

Pine Bluff Judges
Cotton States League (D) 1930–mid-1932; new franchise. Disbanded with league during 1932 season.

Pine Bluff Judges
Dixie League (C), mid-1933; relocated franchise. Had been WACO CUBS, 1933. East Dixie League (C), 1934–1935; charter franchise. Cotton States League (C); 1936–1940; charter franchise. Disbanded after 1940 season.

Pine Bluff Judges
Cotton States League (C), 1950–mid-1955; renamed franchise. Had been PINE BLUFF CARDINALS, 1948–1949. Became MERIDIAN MILLERS, mid-1955.

Pine Bluff Lumbermen
Cotton States League (D), 1903–1904; expansion franchise. Disbanded after 1904 season.

Pine Bluff Pine Knotts
Arkansas State League (D), 1908; charter franchise. Disbanded after 1908 season.

PINE TREE, ME

Pine Tree
Maine State League (D), 1907; charter franchise. Disbanded with league after 1907 season.

PINEVILLE, KY

Pineville
Appalachian League (D), 1914; relocated franchise. Had been ROME ROMANS, 1913. Became HARRIMAN BOOSTERS, 1914.

PIQUA, OH

Piqua Picks
Ohio State League (D), mid-1911; relocated franchise. Had been NEWARK NEWKS, 1908–mid-1911. Disbanded after 1911 season.

PITTSBURG, CA

Pittsburg Diamonds
Far West League (D), 1948; charter franchise. Became ROSEVILLE DIAMONDS, mid-1948.

Pittsburg Diamonds
Far West League (D), 1949–mid-1951; new franchise. Disbanded during 1951 season.

PITTSBURG, KS

Pittsburg
Southwestern League, 1891; charter franchise. Disbanded with league after 1891 season.

Pittsburg
Missouri Valley League (C), 1903; (D), 1904–1905; charter franchise. Disbanded with league after 1905 season.

Pittsburg
Southeast Kansas League (D), 1911; charter franchise. Missouri–Kansas League (D), 1912; charter franchise. Disbanded with league after 1912 season.

Pittsburg Browns
Kansas–Oklahoma–Missouri League (D), 1946–1951; charter franchise. Disbanded after 1951 season.

Pittsburg Champions
Kansas State League (D), mid-1906; new franchise. Became VINITA, 1905–mid-1906.

Pittsburg Pirates
Western Association (C), 1909; new franchise. Disbanded after 1909 season.

Pittsburg Pirates
Southwestern League (D), 1921; charter franchise. Disbanded after 1921 season.

Pittsburg Pirates
Kansas–Oklahoma–Missouri League (D), mid-1952; renamed franchise. Had been BATESVILLE PIRATES, 1949–mid-1952. Disbanded with league after 1952 season.

PITTSBURGH, PA

Pittsburgh
League Alliance, 1877; charter franchise. Disbanded with league after 1877 season.

Pittsburgh
Pennsylvania State League, 1892; charter franchise. Became WILKESBARRE, mid-1892.

PITTSBURGH ALLEGHENIES
International Association, 1877–1878; charter franchise. National Association, 1879; new franchise.

PITTSBURGH ALLEGHENIES
American Association, 1882–1886; charter franchise. National League, 1887–1889; new franchise. Renamed PITTSBURGH INNOCENTS, 1890.

PITTSBURGH BURGHERS
Players' League, 1890; charter franchise. Disbanded with league after 1890 season.

PITTSBURGH CRAWFORDS
Negro National League, 1933–1938; new franchise. Disbanded after 1938 season.

PITTSBURGH INNOCENTS
National League, 1890; renamed franchise. Had been named PITTSBURGH ALLEGHENIES, 1887–1889. Became PITTSBURGH PIRATES, 1891.

PITTSBURGH PIRATES
National League, 1891–(still in existence as of 5-1-92); renamed franchise. Had been named PITTSBURGH INNOCENTS, 1890.

PITTSBURGH PITTSFEDS
Alternate name for the PITTSBURGH STOGIES.

PITTSBURGH POTATO BUGS
Alternate name for the PITTSBURGH ALLEGHENIES.

PITTSBURGH REBELS
Alternate name for the PITTSBURGH STOGIES.

PITTSBURGH SMOKED ITALIANS
Alternate name for the PITTSBURGH ALLEGHENIES.

PITTSBURGH STOGIES
Union Association, mid-1884; relocated franchise. Had been CHICAGO, 1884. Disbanded with league after 1884 season.

PITTSBURGH STOGIES (aka Rebels and Pittsfeds)
Federal League, 1913–1915; charter franchise. Disbanded with league after 1915 season.

Pittsburgh Zulus
Alternate name for the PITTSBURGH ALLEGHENIES.

PITTSFIELD, MA

Pittsfield Brewers
Eastern League (AA), 1976; renamed franchise. Had been PITTS-FIELD RANGERS, 1972–1975. Disbanded after 1976 season.

Pittsfield Cubs
Eastern League (AA), 1985–1989; relocated franchise. Had been BUFFALO BISONS, 1979–1984. Renamed PITTSFIELD METS, 1989.

Pittsfield Electrics
Eastern Association (B), 1913–1914; charter franchise. Disbanded with league after 1914 season.

Pittsfield Electrics (aka Ponies, 1941)
Canadian–American League (C) 1941–1942; 1946–1948; relocated franchise. Had been OSWEGO NETHERLANDS, 1936–1940. Renamed PITTSFIELD INDIANS, 1949.

Pittsfield Hillies
Hudson River League (C), mid-1905; relocated franchise. Had been SAUGERTIES, 1903–mid-1905. Disbanded after 1905 season.

Pittsfield Hillies
Eastern League (A), 1919–1930; new franchise. Disbanded after 1930 season.

Pittsfield Indians
Canadian–American League (C), 1949–1950; renamed franchise. Had been PITTSFIELD ELECTRICS, 1941–1942; 1946–1948. Renamed PITTSFIELD PHILLIES, 1951.

Pittsfield Mets
New York–Pennsylvania League (A), 1989–(still in existence as of 5-1-92); renamed franchise. Had been PITTSFIELD CUBS, 1985–1988.

Pittsfield Phillies
Canadian–American League (C), 1951; renamed franchise. Had been PITTSFIELD INDIANS, 1949–1950. Disbanded after 1951 season.

Pittsfield Ponies
Alternate name for PITTSFIELD ELECTRICS, 1941.

Pittsfield Rangers
Eastern League (AA), 1972–1975; renamed franchise. Had been PITTSFIELD SENATORS, 1970–1971. Renamed PITTSFIELD BREWERS, 1976.

Pittsfield Red Sox
Eastern League (AA), 1965–1971; new franchise. Renamed PITTSFIELD RANGERS, 1972.

Pittsfield Senators
Eastern League (AA), 1970–1971; renamed franchise. Had been PITTSFIELD RED SOX, 1965–1969. Renamed PITTSFIELD RANGERS, 1972.

PLAINFIELD, NJ

Plainfield
Central New Jersey League, 1892; charter franchise. Disbanded with league after 1892 season.

PLAINVIEW, TX

Plainview Athletics
Sophomore League (D), 1958–1959; charter franchise. Disbanded after 1959 season.

Plainview Ponies
West Texas–New Mexico League (B), 1953–1955; relocated franchise. Had been LAMESA LOBOS, 1946–1952. Southwestern League (D), 1956–1957; charter franchise. Disbanded with league after 1957 season.

PLATTSBURGH, NY

Plattsburgh Brewers
New Hampshire State League (D), mid-1907; relocated franchise. Had been LACONIA, 1907. Disbanded with league during 1907 season.

PLATTSMOUTH, NE

Plattsmouth Indians
Nebraska State League, 1892; charter franchise. Disbanded with league after 1892 season.

POCATELLO, ID

Gate City Giants
Pioneer League (R), 1990–(still in existence as of 5-1-92); renamed franchise. Had been POCATELLO GIANTS, 1987–1989.

Pocatello Athletics
Pioneer League (C), 1957–1959; renamed franchise. Had been POCATELLO BANNOCKS, 1952–1956. Renamed POCATELLO GIANTS, 1960.

Pocatello Bannocks
Utah–Idaho League (C), 1926–1928; charter franchise. Disbanded with league after 1928 season.

Pocatello Bannocks
Pioneer League (C), 1952–1956; renamed franchise. Had been POCATELLO CARDINALS, 1939–1942, 1946–1951. Renamed POCATELLO ATHLETICS, 1957.

Pocatello Bannocks
Pioneer League (C), 1961; renamed franchise. Had been POCATELLO GIANTS, 1960. Renamed POCATELLO CHIEFS, 1962.

Pocatello Cardinals
Pioneer League (C), 1939–1942, 1946–1951; charter franchise. Renamed POCATELLO BANNOCKS, 1952.

Pocatello Chiefs
Pioneer League (C), 1962–1965; renamed franchise. Had been POCATELLO BANNOCKS, 1961. Disbanded after 1965 season.

Pocatello Gems
Pioneer League (R), 1984–1985; new franchise. Disbanded after 1985 season.

Pocatello Giants
Pioneer League (C), 1960; renamed franchise. Had been POCATELLO ATHLETICS, 1957–1959.

Renamed POCATELLO BANNOCKS, 1961.

Pocatello Giants
Pioneer League (R), 1987–1989; new franchise. Renamed GATE CITY GIANTS, 1990.

POCOMOKE CITY, MD

Pocomoke City Chicks
Eastern Shore League (D), 1940; renamed franchise. Had been POCOMOKE CITY RED SOX, 1937–1939. Disbanded after 1940 season.

Pocomoke City Red Sox
Eastern Shore League (D), 1937–1939; charter franchise. Renamed POCOMOKE CITY CHICKS, 1940.

Pocomoke City Salamanders
Eastern Shore League (D), 1922; charter franchise. Disbanded after 1922 season.

POINT PLEASANT–GALLIPOLIS, OH

Point Pleasant–Gallipolis
Virginia Valley League (D), 1910; charter franchise. Mountain States League (D), 1911; charter franchise. Became MIDDLEPORT–POMEROY, mid-1911.

POMEREY, OH
(See MIDDLEPORT, OH)

POMONA, CA

Pomona
California League (D), mid-1929; relocated franchise. Had been ORANGE COUNTY, 1929. Became CORONADO ARABS, mid-1929.

POMPANO BEACH, FL
(See also DEERFIELD BEACH, FL)

Pompano Beach Cubs
Florida State League (A), 1976–1978; new franchise. Disbanded after 1978 season.

Pompano Beach Mets
Florida State League (A), 1969–1973; new franchise. Disbanded after 1973 season.

PONCA CITY, OK

Ponca City
Oklahoma State League (D), mid-1923–1924; relocated franchise. Had been DRUMWRIGHT, 1923. Disbanded with league after 1924 season.

Ponca City Angels
Western Association (C), 1934–1938; charter franchise. Disbanded after 1938 season.

Ponca City A's
Western Association (D), 1915; new franchise. Disbanded after 1915 season.

Ponca City Cubs
Sooner State League (D), mid-1955–1957; relocated franchise. Had been GAINESVILLE OWLS, 1953–mid-1955. Disbanded with league after 1957 season.

Ponca City Dodgers
KOM League (D), 1947–1952; new franchise. Disbanded with league after 1952 season.

Ponca City Jets
Western Association (C), 1954; new franchise. Disbanded with association after 1954 season.

Ponca City Poncans
Southwestern League (D), mid-1926; relocated franchise. Had been EUREKA OILERS, 1926. Disbanded with league after 1926 season.

PONTIAC, MI

Pontiac
Border League (D), 1912; charter franchise. Disbanded with league during 1912 season.

Pontiac
Border League (D), 1913; charter franchise. Disbanded with league during 1913 season.

POPLAR BLUFF, MO

Poplar Bluff
Arkansas State League (D), 1908; charter franchise. Became BRINK-LEY, mid-1908.

PORTAGEVILLE, MO

Portageville Pirates
KITTY League (D), mid-1935–mid-1936; charter franchise. Became OWENSBORO OILERS, mid-1936.

PORT ARTHUR, ONTARIO, CANADA
(See FORT WILLIAM, ONTARIO, CANADA)

PORT ARTHUR, TX

Port Arthur Chieftans
Big State League (B), 1956; renamed franchise. Had been PORT ARTHUR SEA HAWKS, 1955. Renamed PORT ARTHUR REDLEGS, 1957.

Port Arthur Redlegs
Big State League (B), 1957; renamed franchise. Had been PORT ARTHUR SEA HAWKS, 1955–1956. Became TEMPLE REDLEGS, mid-1957.

Port Arthur Refiners
Cotton States League (D), 1932; new franchise. Became DEQUINCY RAILROADERS, mid-1932.

Port Arthur Sea Hawks
Gulf Coast League (C), 1950; (B), 1951–1953; charter franchise. Evangeline League (C), 1954; expansion franchise. Big State League (B), 1955; new franchise. Renamed PORT ARTHUR CHIEFTANS, 1956.

Port Arthur Tarpons
Evangeline League (D), 1940–1942; new franchise. Suspended operations with league after 1942 season, and did not rejoin when league resumed in 1946.

PORT CHARLOTTE, FL

Port Charlotte Rangers
Florida State League (A), 1988–(still in existence as of 5-1-92); new franchise.

PORT CHESTER, NY

Port Chester Clippers
Colonial League (B), 1947–1948; charter franchise. Disbanded after 1948 season.

PORTERVILLE, CA
(See also RIVERSIDE, CA)

Porterville Packers
Sunset League (C), 1949–1950; new franchise. Disbanded with league after 1950 season.

Porterville Padres
Southwest International League (C), 1952; relocated franchise. Had been RIVERSIDE–PORTERVILLE PADRES, mid-1952. Disbanded with league after 1952 season.

PORT HURON, MI

Port Huron
Michigan State League, 1890; new franchise. Disbanded with league during 1890 season.

Port Huron
Michigan State League, 1897; charter franchise. Disbanded during 1897 season.

Port Huron Braves
Canadian League, 1899; new franchise. Disbanded during 1899 season.

Port Huron Independents
Border League (D), 1912; charter franchise. Disbanded with league during 1912 season.

Port Huron Independents
Border League (D), 1913; charter franchise. Disbanded with league during 1913 season. Eastern Michigan League (D), 1914; charter franchise. Disbanded with league during 1914 season.

Port Huron Marines
Michigan State League, 1895; new franchise. Disbanded during 1895 season.

Port Huron Saints
Michigan–Ontario League (B), 1921; new franchise. Became PORT HURON–SARNIA SAINTS, 1922.

Port Huron Saints
Michigan–Ontario League (B), 1926; new franchise. Michigan State League (D), mid-1926; charter franchise. Disbanded with league after 1926 season.

Port Huron Tunnelites
International League, 1900; charter franchise. Disbanded with league during 1900 season.

PORT HURON, MI–SARNIA, ONTARIO, CANADA

Port Huron–Sarnia Saints
Michigan–Ontario League (B), 1922; renamed franchise. Had been PORT HURON SAINTS, 1921. Disbanded after 1922 season.

PORTLAND, CT

Portland
Connecticut State League, 1891; charter franchise. Disbanded with league during 1891 season.

PORTLAND, IN

Portland Jay Birds
Ohio–Indiana League (D), 1907; charter franchise. Disbanded with league after 1907 season.

PORTLAND, ME

Portland
Eastern New England League, 1885; charter franchise. New England League, 1886; charter franchise. Disbanded with league during 1886 season.

Portland
New England League, 1886–mid-1888; charter franchise. Became PORTSMOUTH LILLIES, mid-1888.

Portland
New England Inter-State League, 1888; charter franchise. Disbanded with league after 1888 season.

Portland
New England League, 1891–1896; charter franchise. Maine State League, 1897; charter franchise. Disbanded with league after 1897 season.

Portland Blue Sox
Maine State League (D), 1907; charter franchise. Atlantic Association (D), 1908; new franchise. Disbanded with association after 1908 season.

Portland Blue Sox
New England League (B), 1919; charter franchise. Disbanded with league after 1919 season.

Portland Duffs
New England League (B), 1913–1915; new franchise. Eastern League (B), 1916; charter franchise. Renamed PORTLAND PARAMOUNTS, 1917.

Portland Eskimos
New England League (B), 1926–1927; charter franchise. Renamed PORTLAND MARINERS, 1928.

Portland Gulls
New England League (B), 1946; charter franchise. Renamed PORTLAND PILOTS, 1947.

Portland Mariners
New England League (B), 1928–1929; renamed franchise. Had been PORTLAND ESKIMOS, 1926–1927. Disbanded with league after 1929 season.

Portland Paramounts
Eastern League (B), 1917; renamed franchise. Had been PORTLAND DUFFS, 1913–1916. Disbanded after 1917 season.

Portland Phenoms
New England League, 1899–1901; charter franchise. Disbanded after 1901 season.

Portland Pilots
New England League (B), 1947–1949; renamed franchise. Had been PORTLAND GULLS, 1946. Disbanded with league after 1949 season.

PORTLAND, OR

Portland
New Pacific League, 1896; charter franchise. Disbanded with league during 1896 season.

Portland Beavers
Pacific Coast League (A), 1906–1907; (AA), 1908–1917; renamed franchise. Had been PORTLAND GIANTS, 1905. Became PORTLAND BUCKAROOS, 1918.

Portland Beavers (aka Ducks, 1933; Lucky Beavers, 1952–1954)
Pacific Coast League (AA), 1919–1945; (AAA), 1946–1951; (O), 1952–1957; (AAA), 1958–1972; expansion franchise. Had been PORTLAND BUCKAROOS, 1918. Renamed PORTLAND MAVERICKS, 1973.

Portland Beavers
Pacific Coast League (AAA), 1978–(still in existence as of 5-1-92); new franchise. Had been PORTLAND MAVERICKS, 1973–1977.

Portland Browns
Pacific Coast League (A), 1904; charter franchise. Renamed PORTLAND GIANTS, 1905.

Portland Buckaroos
Pacific Coast International League (B), 1918; charter franchise. Became PORTLAND BEAVERS, 1919.

Portland Colts
Northwestern League (B), 1909; new franchise. Disbanded after 1913 season.

Portland Colts
Northwestern League (B), 1912–mid-1914; renamed franchise. Had been PORTLAND PIPPINS, 1911. Became BALLARD COLTS, mid-1914.

Portland Ducks
Alternate name for PORTLAND BEAVERS, 1933.

Portland Giants
Pacific Coast League (A), 1905; renamed franchise. Had been PORTLAND BROWNS, 1904. Renamed PORTLAND BEAVERS, 1906.

Portland Gladiators
Pacific Northwest League, 1890–1892; charter franchise. Disbanded with league after 1892 season.

Portland Gladiators
Pacific Northwest League, 1898; charter franchise. Disbanded with league after 1898 season.

Portland Green Gages
Pacific National League (A), 1903; charter franchise. Became SALT LAKE CITY ELDERS, mid-1903.

Portland Lucky Beavers
Alternate name for PORTLAND BEAVERS, 1952–1954.

Portland Mavericks
Northwest League (A), 1973–1977; new franchise. Became PORTLAND BEAVERS, 1978.

Portland Pippins
Northwestern League (B), 1911–1913; new franchise. Renamed PORTLAND COLTS, 1912.

Portland Webfoots
Pacific Northwest League, 1901; (D), 1902; charter franchise. Became PORTLAND GREEN GAGES, 1903.

PORTSMOUTH, NH

Portsmouth Lillies
New England Inter-State League, mid-1888; relocated franchise. Had been PORTLAND, 1886–mid-1888. Disbanded with league during 1888 season.

PORTSMOUTH, OH

Portsmouth A's
Ohio–Indiana League (D), 1948–1950; new franchise. Disbanded after 1950 season.

Portsmouth Cobblers
Ohio State League (D), mid-1908–1916; relocated franchise. Had been SPRINGFIELD, 1906–mid-1908. Disbanded with league after 1916 season.

Portsmouth Pirates
Middle Atlantic League (D), 1935–1936; new franchise. Renamed PORTSMOUTH RED BIRDS, 1937.

Portsmouth Red Birds
Middle Atlantic League (D), 1937–1940; renamed franchise. Had been PORTSMOUTH PIRATES, 1935–1936. Disbanded after 1940 season.

Portsmouth Riversides
Tri-State League, 1894; charter franchise. Disbanded with league during 1894 season.

PORTSMOUTH, VA

Portsmouth
Virginia–North Carolina League, 1901; charter franchise. Became CHARLOTTE HORNETS, mid-1901.

Portsmouth
International League (AAA), 1973–1985; new franchise. Disbanded after 1985 season.

Portsmouth Browns
Virginia League, 1896; renamed franchise. Had been PORTSMOUTH TRUCKERS, 1895. Disbanded with league during 1896 season.

Portsmouth Cubs
Piedmont League (B), 1936–1952; renamed franchise. Had been PORTSMOUTH TRUCKERS, 1935. Renamed PORTSMOUTH MERRIMACKS, 1953.

Portsmouth Merrimacs
Piedmont League (B), 1953–1955; renamed franchise. Had been PORTSMOUTH CUBS, 1937–1952. Disbanded with league after 1955 season.

Portsmouth Olympics
Southeast Virginia League, 1897; charter franchise. Disbanded with league during 1897 season.

Portsmouth Pirates
Virginia League, 1900; charter franchise. Disbanded with league after 1900 season.

Portsmouth Pirates
Virginia League (C), 1912–1913; new franchise. Renamed PORTSMOUTH TRUCKERS, 1914.

Portsmouth Truckers
Virginia State League, 1895–1896; charter franchise. Renamed PORTSMOUTH BROWNS, 1896.

Portsmouth Truckers
Virginia League (C), 1906–mid-1910; charter franchise. Became PETERSBURG GOOBERS, mid-1910.

Portsmouth Truckers
Virginia League (C), 1914–mid-1917; new franchise. Had been PORTSMOUTH PIRATES, 1912–1913. Disbanded with league during 1917 season.

Portsmouth Truckers
Virginia League (C), 1919; (B), 1920–mid-1928; new franchise. Disbanded during 1928 season.

Portsmouth Truckers
Piedmont League (B), 1935; new franchise. Renamed PORTSMOUTH CUBS, 1936.

Tidewater Tides
Carolina League (B), 1963–1965; renamed franchise. Had been PORTSMOUTH TIDES, 1961–1962. Represented Norfolk–Portsmouth, Va, 1966.

PORTSMOUTH–NORFOLK, VA
(See also NORFOLK, VA)

Portsmouth–Norfolk Tides
South Atlantic League (A), 1961–1962; new franchise. Renamed TIDEWATER TIDES, 1963.

PORT ST. LUCIE, FL

Port St. Lucie Mets
Florida State League (A), 1988– (still in existence as of 5-1-92); new franchise.

POTSDAM, NY

Potsdam
Northern New York League (D), 1902; charter franchise. Disbanded with league after 1902 season.

POTTSTOWN, PA

Pottstown
Schuykill Valley League, 1896; charter franchise. Disbanded with league during 1896 season.

Pottstown Dukes (aka Legionnaires)
Inter-State League (D), 1932; charter franchise. Disbanded with league during 1932 season.

POTTSVILLE, PA

Pottsville
Central Pennsylvania League, 1897; new franchise. Became SHAMOKIN, mid-1897.

Pottsville
Atlantic League (D), 1907–1908; charter franchise. Disbanded with league after 1908 season.

Pottsville
Keystone League (D), 1935; charter franchise. Disbanded with league after 1935 season.

Pottsville Anthracites
Inter-State Association, 1883–1884; charter franchise. Disbanded with league during 1884 season.

Pottsville Colts
Pennsylvania State League, 1894–mid-1895; new franchise. Became ALLENTOWN GOOBERS, mid-1895.

Pottsville Lambs
Pennsylvania State League, mid-1896; relocated franchise. Had been CARBONDALE ANTHRACITES, 1895–mid-1896. Disbanded with league during 1896 season.

POUGHKEEPSIE, NY

Poughkeepsie
Hudson River League, 1886; charter franchise. Disbanded with league after 1886 season.

Poughkeepsie
New York State League, 1894; charter franchise. Disbanded after 1894 season.

Poughkeepsie Chiefs
Colonial League (B), 1948–mid-1950; renamed franchise. Had been POUGHKEEPSIE GIANTS, 1947. Disbanded with league during 1950 season.

Poughkeepsie Colts
Hudson River League (D), 1903–1907; charter franchise. Disbanded with league after 1907 season.

Poughkeepsie Giants
Colonial League (B), 1947; charter franchise. Renamed POUGHKEEPSIE CHIEFS, 1948.

Poughkeepsie Honey Bugs
New York–New Jersey League (D), 1913; charter franchise. Atlantic League (D), 1914; charter franchise. Disbanded with league after 1914 season.

POZA RICA, VERACRUZ, MEXICO

Poza Rica Petroleros (Oilers)
Mexican League (AA), 1958–1966; (AAA), 1967–1983; new franchise. Disbanded after 1983 season.

PRESQUE ISLAND, ME
(See CARIBOU, ME)

PRINCETON, IN

Princeton Infants
KITTY League (D), 1905; new franchise. Disbanded with league during 1905 season.

PRINCETON, WV

Princeton Patriots
Appalachian League (R), 1990– (still in existence as of 5-1-92); renamed franchise. Had been PRINCETON PIRATES, 1989.

Princeton Pirates
Appalachian League (R), 1989; renamed franchise. Had been PRINCETON REDS, 1988. Renamed PRINCETON PATRIOTS, 1990.

Princeton Reds
Appalachian League (R), 1988; new franchise. Renamed PRINCETON PIRATES, 1989.

PROVIDENCE, RI

Providence Chiefs
New England League (B), 1946–1948; charter franchise. Renamed PROVIDENCE GRAYS, 1949.

Providence Clamdiggers
Eastern League (A), 1905; renamed franchise. Had been PROVIDENCE GRAYS, 1892–1904. Renamed PROVIDENCE GRAYS, 1906.

PROVIDENCE GRAYS
National League, 1879–1885; new franchise. Had been PROVIDENCE RHODE ISLANDERS, 1878. Eastern League, 1886; new franchise. Disbanded during 1886 season.

Providence Grays
Eastern Association, 1891; charter franchise. Disbanded during 1891 season.

Providence Grays
Eastern League, 1892–1904; charter franchise. Renamed PROVIDENCE CLAMDIGGERS, 1905.

Providence Grays
Eastern League (A), 1906–1907; (AA), 1908–1911; renamed franchise. Had been PROVIDENCE CLAMDIGGERS, 1905. Interna-

tional League (AA), 1912–1917; charter franchise. Eastern League (B), 1918; (A), 1919–mid-1925; new franchise. Disbanded during 1925 season.

Providence Grays
International League (AA), mid-1925; relocated franchise. Had been NEWARK BEARS, 1921–mid-1925. Became NEWARK BEARS, 1926.

Providence Grays
Eastern League (A), 1927–mid-1930; renamed franchise. Had been PROVIDENCE RUBES, 1926. Disbanded during 1930 season.

Providence Grays
New England League (B), 1949; renamed franchise. Had been PROVIDENCE CHIEFS, 1946–1948. Disbanded during 1949 season.

Providence Rhode Islanders
League Alliance, 1877; charter franchise. Disbanded after 1877 season.

PROVIDENCE RHODE ISLANDERS
National League, 1878; new franchise. Renamed PROVIDENCE GRAYS, 1879.

Providence Rubes
Eastern League (A), 1926; new franchise. Renamed PROVIDENCE GRAYS, 1927.

PUEBLA, PUEBLA, MEXICO

Puebla Angeles (Angels)
Mexican League (AAA), 1976–1980; renamed franchise. Had been PUEBLA PERICOS (Parrots), 1972–1975. Disbanded after 1980 season.

Puebla Angeles Negros (Black Angels)
Mexican League (AAA), 1985–(still in existence as of 5-1-92); new franchise.

Puebla Pericos (Parrots)
Mexican League (AA), 1960–1966; (AAA), 1967–1969; new franchise. Disbanded after 1969 season.

Puebla Pericos (Parrots)
Mexican League (AAA), 1972–1975; new franchise. Renamed PUEBLA ANGELS, 1976.

PUEBLO, CO

Pueblo
Colorado State League, 1898; new franchise. Disbanded with league during 1898 season.

Pueblo
Western Association, 1901; charter franchise. Disbanded with association after 1901 season.

Pueblo Braves
Western League (A), 1930–1932; renamed franchise. Had been PUEBLO STEELWORKERS, 1928–1930. Disbanded after 1932 season.

Pueblo Bruins
Western League (A), 1957–1958; renamed franchise. Had been PUEBLO DODGERS, 1947–1956. Disbanded with league after 1958 season.

Pueblo Dodgers
Western League (A), 1947–1956; charter franchise. Became PUEBLO BRUINS, 1957.

Pueblo Indians
Western League (A), 1900; charter franchise. Disbanded after 1900 season.

Pueblo Indians
Western League (A), 1905–1909; relocated franchise. Had been COLORADO SPRINGS MILLIONAIRES, 1901–1904. Disbanded after 1909 season.

Pueblo Indians
Western League (A), mid-1911; relocated franchise. Had been WICHITA JOBBERS, 1909–1911. Disbanded after 1911 season.

Pueblo Pastimes
Colorado League, 1885; charter franchise. Disbanded with league after 1885 season.

Pueblo Ponies
Colorado State League, 1889; charter franchise. Disbanded with league after 1889 season.

Pueblo Rollers
Western League (D), 1941; new franchise. Disbanded after 1941 season.

Pueblo Rovers
Colorado State League, 1896; new franchise. Disbanded with league during 1896 season.

Pueblo Steelworkers
Western League (A), 1928–1930; new franchise. Renamed PUEBLO BRAVES, 1931.

PUERTO PENASCO, SONORA, MEXICO

Puerto Penasco Navegantes (Sharks)
Mexican Northern League (A), 1969–1971; new franchise. Disbanded after 1971 season.

PUERTO RICO

Puerto Rico
Inter-American League (AAA), 1979; charter franchise. Disbanded with league during 1979 season.

PULASKI, TN

Pulaski
Tennessee–Alabama League (D), 1903; charter franchise. Disbanded after 1903 season.

PULASKI, VA

Pulaski Braves
Appalachian League (R), 1982–
(still in existence as of 5-1-92); new
franchise.

Pulaski Counts
Virginia League (D), 1942; 1946–
1950; new franchise. Disbanded
after 1950 season.

Pulaski Cubs
Appalachian League (D), 1957–
1958; charter franchise. Disbanded
after 1958 season.

Pulaski Phillies
Appalachian League (D), 1952–
1955; new franchise. Disbanded
with league after 1955 season.

Pulaski Phillies
Appalachian League (R), 1969–
1976; ("Summer Class A") 1977;
new franchise. Disbanded after
1976 season.

PUNXSUTAWNEY, PA

Punxsutawney
Inter-State League (D), 1906; new
franchise. Disbanded with league
after 1906 season.

QUEBEC, QUEBEC, CANADA

Quebec
International League, mid-1890;
relocated franchise. Had been
GRAND RAPIDS, mid-1890. Disbanded with league after 1890 season.

Quebec Alouettes (aka Larks)
Canadian–American League (C),
1946–1948; charter franchise. Renamed QUEBEC BRAVES, 1949.

Quebec Athletics
Quebec Provincial League (B),
1940; charter franchise. Canadian–
American League (C), 1941–1942;

new franchise. Disbanded with
league after 1942 season.

Quebec Braves
Canadian–American League (C),
1949–1950; renamed franchise.
Had been QUEBEC ALOUETTES,
1946–1948. Provincial League
(C), 1951–1955; expansion franchise. Disbanded with league after
1955 season.

Quebec Bulldogs
Eastern Canada League (B), 1923;
new franchise. Quebec–Ontario–
Vermont League (B), 1924; charter
franchise. Disbanded with league
after 1924 season.

Quebec Carnavals
Eastern League (AA), 1971–mid-
1975; new franchise. Renamed
QUEBEC METROS, mid-1975.

Quebec Larks
Alternate name for QUEBEC AL-
OUETTES.

Quebec Metros
Eastern League (AA), mid-1975–
1977; renamed franchise. Had
been QUEBEC CARNAVALS, 1971–
mid-1975. Disbanded after 1977
season.

QUEEN ANNE, MD
(See CENTREVILLE, MD)

QUERETARO, MEXICO
(See CELAYA, MEXICO)

QUINCY, IL

Quincy
Northwestern League, 1883–1884;
charter franchise. Disbanded with
league after 1884 season.

Quincy
Western Association, 1899; new
franchise. Became DUBUQUE, mid-
1899.

Quincy
Mississippi Valley League (B),
1933; charter franchise. Disbanded
with league after 1933 season.

Quincy Advertisers
Illinois–Iowa–Indiana League (B),
1917; renamed franchise. Had been
QUINCY GEMS, 1913. Disbanded
with league during 1917 season.

Quincy Blue Birds
Western Association, 1896; re-
named franchise. Had been
QUINCY BROWNS, 1895. Renamed
QUINCY LITTLE GIANTS, 1897.

Quincy Browns
Western Association, 1895; re-
named franchise. Had been
QUINCY RAVENS (aka Canaries),
1894. Renamed QUINCY BLUE
BIRDS, 1896.

Quincy Crybabies
Alternate name for QUINCY IN-
FANTS, 1911.

Quincy Cubs
Midwest League (A), 1965–1973;
renamed franchise. Had been
QUINCY GEMS, 1964. Disbanded
after 1973 season.

Quincy Debutantes
Alternate name for QUINCY IN-
FANTS, 1911.

Quincy Gems
Iowa State League (D), 1907; new
franchise. Central Association
(D), 1908; charter franchise. Renamed QUINCY VETS, 1909.

Quincy Gems
Illinois–Iowa–Indiana League (B),
1913–1916; renamed franchise.
Had been QUINCY OLD SOLDIERS,
1912. Renamed QUINCY ADVERTIS-
ERS, 1917.

Quincy Gems
Three I League (B), 1946–1956;
charter franchise. Disbanded after
1956 season.

Quincy Gems
Midwest League (A), 1964; renamed franchise. Had been QUINCY JETS, 1962–1963. Renamed QUINCY CUBS, 1965.

Quincy Giants
Midwest League (D), 1960–1961; new franchise. Renamed QUINCY JETS, 1962.

Quincy Indians
Illinois–Iowa–Indiana League (B), 1928–mid-1932; renamed franchise. Had been QUINCY RED BIRDS, 1925–1927. Disbanded with league during 1932 season.

Quincy Infants (aka Debutantes and Crybabies)
Illinois–Iowa–Indiana League (B), 1911; new franchise. Renamed QUINCY OLD SOLDIERS, 1912.

Quincy Jets
Midwest League (D), 1962; (A), 1963; renamed franchise. Had been QUINCY GIANTS, 1960–1961. Renamed QUINCY GEMS, 1964.

Quincy Little Giants
Western Association, 1897; renamed franchise. Had been QUINCY BLUE BIRDS, 1896. Renamed QUINCY LULUS (aka Gem City), 1898.

Quincy Lulus (aka Gem City)
Western Association, 1898; renamed franchise. Had been QUINCY LITTLE GIANTS, 1897. Disbanded after 1898 season.

Quincy Old Soldiers
Illinois–Iowa–Indiana League (B), 1912; renamed franchise. Had been QUINCY INFANTS, 1911. Renamed QUINCY GEMS, 1913.

Quincy Ravens
Central Inter-State League, 1889; new franchise. Western Inter-State League, 1890; charter franchise. Illinois–Iowa League, 1891–1892;

new franchise. Disbanded with league after 1892 season.

Quincy Ravens (aka Canaries)
Western Association, 1894; charter franchise. Renamed QUINCY BROWNS, 1895.

Quincy Red Birds
Illinois–Iowa–Indiana League (B), 1925–1927; new franchise. Renamed QUINCY INDIANS, 1928.

Quincy Vets
Central Association (D), 1909–1910; renamed franchise. Had been QUINCY GEMS, 1907–1908. Disbanded after 1910 season.

QUINCY, MA

Quincy
New England League (B), 1933; charter franchise. Became NASHUA, mid-1933.

QUITMAN, GA

Quitman
Dixie League (D), 1916–1917; charter franchise. Disbanded with league during 1917 season.

RACINE, WI

Racine Belles (aka Malted Milks)
Wisconsin–Illinois League (D), 1909–1914; new franchise. Bi-State League (WI–IL), (D), 1915; charter franchise. Disbanded with league during 1915 season.

Racine Belles
All-American Girls Professional Baseball League, 1943–1950; charter franchise. Became BATTLE CREEK BELLES, 1951.

Racine Malted Milks
Alternate name for RACINE BELLES, 1909–1911; 1914.

RADFORD, VA

Radford Rockets
Blue Ridge League (D), 1946–1950; charter franchise. Disbanded with league after 1950 season.

RALEIGH, NC

Raleigh Capitals
North Carolina State League (D), 1913–mid-1917; new franchise. Disbanded with league during 1917 season.

Raleigh Capitals
Piedmont League (C), 1922–1928, 1930–1932; renamed franchise. Had been RALEIGH RED BIRDS, 1921. Disbanded after 1932 season.

Raleigh Capitals
Carolina League (B), 1958–1962; new franchise. Renamed RALEIGH METS, 1963.

Raleigh Capitals (aka Caps, 1947–1948)
Carolina League (C), 1945–1953; charter franchise. Disbanded after 1953 season.

Raleigh Caps
Alternate name for RALEIGH CAPITALS, 1947–1948.

Raleigh Cardinals
Carolina League (A), 1964–1965; renamed franchise. Had been RALEIGH METS, 1963. Renamed RALEIGH PIRATES, 1966.

Raleigh Lobsters
Alternate name for RALEIGH RED BIRDS, 1902.

Raleigh Mets
Carolina League (A), 1963; renamed franchise. Had been RALEIGH CAPITALS, 1958–1962. Renamed RALEIGH CARDINALS, 1964.

Raleigh Nats
Piedmont League (D), 1920; charter franchise. Renamed RALEIGH RED BIRDS, 1921.

Raleigh Pirates
Carolina League (A), 1963–1967; renamed franchise. Had been RALEIGH CARDINALS, 1964–1965. Became RALEIGH–DURHAM METS, 1968.

Raleigh Red Birds (aka Lobsters)
North Carolina League (D), 1902; charter franchise. Disbanded during 1902 season.

Raleigh Red Birds
Eastern Carolina League (D), 1908–1911; charter franchise. Disbanded with league after 1911 season.

Raleigh Red Birds
Piedmont League (C), 1921; renamed franchise. Had been RALEIGH NATS, 1920. Renamed RALEIGH CAPITALS, 1922.

Raleigh Senators
Virginia–North Carolina League, 1901; charter franchise. Disbanded with league after 1901 season.

RALEIGH–DURHAM, NC
(See also DURHAM, NC)

Raleigh–Durham Mets
Carolina League (A), 1968; renamed/relocated franchise. Had been RALEIGH PIRATES, 1963–1967 and DURHAM BULLS, 1945–1967. Renamed RALEIGH–DURHAM PHILS, 1969.

Raleigh–Durham Phils
Carolina League (A), 1969; renamed franchise. Had been RALEIGH–DURHAM METS, 1968. Renamed RALEIGH–DURHAM TRIANGLES, 1970.

Raleigh–Durham Triangles
Carolina League (A), 1970–1971; renamed franchise. Had been RALEIGH–DURHAM PHILS, 1969. Disbanded after 1971 season.

RANGER, TX

Ranger Nitros
West Texas League (D), 1920–1922; charter franchise. Disbanded after 1922 season.

RAYMOND, WA

Raymond Venetians
Washington State League (D), 1910–1911; charter franchise. Disbanded with league after 1911 season.

RAYNE, LA

Rayne Red Sox
Evangeline League (D), 1934; charter franchise. Renamed RAYNE RICE BIRDS, 1935.

Rayne Rice Birds
Louisiana State League (D), 1920–1922; charter franchise. Disbanded with league after 1922 season.

Rayne Rice Birds
Evangeline League (D), 1935–1941; renamed franchise. Had been RAYNE RED SOX, 1934. Suspended operations with league, 1942, and did not resume when league resumed in 1946.

READING, PA

Reading
Pennsylvania State League, mid-1893–1895; relocated franchise. Had been DANVILLE, 1892–mid-1893. Disbanded during 1895 season.

Reading
Pennsylvania State League, mid-1896; relocated franchise. Had been SHAMOKIN, 1896. Disbanded after 1896 season.

Reading Aces
New International League (AA), 1921–1922; renamed franchise. Had been READING MARINES, 1920.

Renamed READING KEYSTONES, 1923.

Reading Actives
Inter-State Association, 1883; charter franchise. Eastern League, 1884; charter franchise. Disbanded during 1884 season.

Reading Actives
Middle States League, 1889; charter franchise. Disbanded with league after 1889 season.

Reading Actives
Pennsylvania State League, mid-1895; relocated franchise. Had been ALLENTOWN GOOBERS, mid-1895. Renamed READING INDIANS, mid-1895.

Reading Anthracites
Pennsylvania State Association, 1887; new franchise. Disbanded with association after 1887 season.

Reading Anthracites
Pennsylvania State League (D), 1902; charter franchise. Disbanded with league after 1902 season.

Reading Brooks
New York–Pennsylvania League (A), 1933–1935; renamed franchise. Had been READING RED SOX, 1933–1934. Became ALLENTOWN BROOKS, mid-1935.

Reading Brooks
Inter-State League (B), 1941; renamed franchise. Had been READING CHICKS, 1940. Disbanded after 1941 season.

Reading Chicks
Inter-State League (B), 1940; expansion franchise. Renamed READING BROOKS, 1941.

Reading Coal Barons
(New) International League (AA), 1919; new franchise. Renamed READING MARINES, 1920.

Reading Coal Heavers
Atlantic League, 1897–1900; new franchise. Disbanded with league after 1900 season.

Reading Dutchmen
Alternate name for READING PRETZELS, 1909.

Reading Indians
Pennsylvania State League, mid-1895–1896; renamed franchise. Had been READING ACTIVES, mid-1895. Disbanded during 1896 season.

Reading Indians
Eastern League (A), 1952–1961; relocated franchise. Had been WILKES-BARRE BARONS, 1950–1951. Disbanded after 1961 season.

Reading Indians
Eastern League (AA), 1965; renamed franchise. Had been READING RED SOX, 1963–1964. Disbanded after 1965 season.

Reading Keystones
International League (AA), 1923–mid-1932; renamed franchise. Had been READING ACES, 1921–1922. Became ALBANY SENATORS, mid-1932.

Reading Marines
New International League (AA), 1920; renamed franchise. Had been READING COAL BARONS, 1919. Renamed READING ACES, 1921.

Reading Phillies
Eastern League (AA), 1967–(still in existence as of 5-1-92); new franchise.

Reading Pretzels (aka Dutchmen, 1909)
Tri-State League (D), mid-1907–1911; relocated franchise. Had been YORK RED ROSES, 1907. Disbanded with league after 1911 season.

Reading Pretzels (aka Dutchmen, 1909)
Tri-State League (D), mid-1912; relocated franchise. Had been ALTOONA RAMS, 1910–mid-1912. Disbanded after 1912 season.

Reading Pretzels (aka Dutchmen, 1909)
Tri-State League (D), 1914; new franchise. Disbanded with league after 1914 season.

Reading Pretzels
Pennsylvania State League (D), 1916; relocated franchise. Had been ALBANY SENATORS, 1899–mid-1916. Disbanded with league after 1916 season.

Reading Red Roses
Atlantic League (D), 1907; charter franchise. Disbanded after 1907 season.

Reading Red Sox
International League (AA), 1933–1934; new franchise. Renamed READING BROOKS, 1935.

Reading Red Sox
Eastern League (AA), 1963–1964; new franchise. Renamed READING INDIANS, 1965.

RED CLOUD, NE

Red Cloud
Nebraska State League (D), 1910; charter franchise. Disbanded after 1910 season.

RED DEER, ALBERTA, CANADA

Red Deer Eskimos
Western Canada League (D), 1912; new franchise. Disbanded after 1912 season.

REDDING, CA

Redding Browns
Far West League (D), 1948–1951; charter franchise. Disbanded with league after 1951 season.

REDFIELD, SD

Redfield
South Dakota League (D), 1920; charter franchise. Dakota League (D), 1921; charter franchise. Disbanded after 1921 season.

RED OAK, IA

Red Oak
Southwest Iowa League, 1903; charter franchise. Disbanded with league during 1903 season.

REDONDO BEACH, CA

Redondo Beach Sand Dabs
Southern California Trolley League (D), 1910; charter franchise. Disbanded with league after 1910 season.

RED SPRINGS, NC

Red Springs Red Robins
Tobacco State League (D), 1947–1949; new franchise. Became RED SPRINGS–LAURINBURG RED ROBINS, 1950.

Red Springs Twins
Carolina League (A), 1969; new franchise. Disbanded after 1969 season.

RED SPRINGS–LAURINBURG, NC

Red Springs–Laurinburg Red Robins
Tobacco State League (D), 1950; renamed/relocated franchise. Had been RED SPRINGS RED ROBINS, 1947–1949. Disbanded with league after 1950 season.

RED WING, MN

Red Wing Manufacturers
Minnesota–Wisconsin League (D), 1910; (C), 1911; charter franchise. Disbanded during 1911 season.

REED CITY, MI

Reed City
Northern Michigan League, 1897; charter franchise. Disbanded during 1897 season.

REFUGIO, TX

Refugio Oilers
Texas Valley League (D), 1938; charter franchise. Disbanded after 1938 season.

REGINA, SASKATCHAWAN, CANADA

Regina Bonepilers
Western Canada League (D), 1909–mid-1910; charter franchise. Disbanded during 1910 season.

Regina Red Sox
Western Canada League (D), 1913–1914; new franchise. Disbanded after 1914 season.

Regina Senators
Western Canada League (C), 1919, (B), 1920–mid-1921; charter franchise. Disbanded with league during 1921 season.

REHOBOTH BEACH, DE

Rehoboth Beach Pirates
Eastern Shore League (D), 1947–1949; new franchise. Renamed REHOBOTH BEACH SEA HAWKS, 1949.

Rehoboth Beach Sea Hawks
Eastern Shore League (D), 1949; renamed franchise. Had been REHOBOTH BEACH PIRATES, 1947–1948. Disbanded with league after 1949 season.

REIDSVILLE, NC

Reidsville Luckies
Bi-State League (NC–VA), (D), 1935–1940; new franchise. Disbanded after 1940 season.

Reidsville Luckies
Tri-State League (B), 1947; new franchise. Carolina League (B), 1948–1954; new franchise. Renamed REIDSVILLE PHILLIES, 1955.

Reidsville Phillies
Carolina League (B), 1955; renamed franchise. Had been REIDSVILLE LUCKIES, 1947–1954. Became WILSON TOBS, 1956.

RENO, NV

Reno Padres
California League (A), 1982–1987; renamed franchise. Had been RENO SILVER SOX, 1966–1981. Renamed RENO SILVER SOX, 1988.

Reno Silver Sox
Sunset League (C), 1947–1949; charter franchise. Far West League (D), 1950–1951; new franchise. Disbanded with league after 1951 season.

Reno Silver Sox
California League (C), mid-1955–1964; relocated franchise. Had been CHANNEL CITIES OILERS, 1954–mid-1955. Disbanded after 1964 season.

Reno Silver Sox
California League (A), 1966–1981; new franchise. Renamed RENO PADRES, 1982.

Reno Silver Sox
California League (A), 1988–(still in existence as of 5-1-92); renamed franchise. Had been RENO PADRES, 1982–1987.

REYNOSA, TAMAULIPAS, MEXICO

Reynosa Braves
Mexican League (AAA), 1971–1976; renamed franchise. Had been REYNOSA BRONCOS, 1963–1970. Disbanded after 1976 season.

Reynosa Broncos
Mexican League (AA), 1963–1966; (AAA), 1967–1970; new franchise. Renamed REYNOSA BRAVES, 1971.

Reynosa Broncos
Mexican League (AAA), 1980–1982; new franchise. Disbanded after 1982 season.

RICHLAND, WA
(See KENNEWICK, WA)

RICHMOND, CA

Richmond Merchants
Central California Baseball League (D), 1910–1911; charter franchise. Disbanded with league after 1911 season.

RICHMOND, IN

Richmond Quakers
Indiana–Ohio League (D), 1908; charter franchise. Disbanded after 1908 season.

Richmond Quakers
Central League (B), 1917; new franchise. Disbanded with league after 1917 season.

Richmond Roses
Central League (B), 1930; charter franchise. Disbanded with league after 1930 season.

Richmond Roses
Ohio State League (D), 1946–1947; new franchise. Ohio–Indiana League (D), 1948; charter franchise. Renamed RICHMOND TIGERS, 1949.

Richmond Tigers
Ohio–Indiana League (D), 1949–1951; renamed franchise. Had been RICHMOND ROSES, 1946–1948. Disbanded with league after 1951 season.

RICHMOND, KY

Richmond Pioneers
Blue Grass League (D), 1908–1912; charter franchise. Disbanded with league after 1912 season.

RICHMOND, VA

Richmond
Virginia League, 1900; charter franchise. Disbanded during 1900 season.

Richmond
Virginia–North Carolina League, 1901; charter franchise. Disbanded during 1901 season.

Richmond Bluebirds
Alternate name for RICHMOND COLTS, 1894–1898.

Richmond Bluebirds
Virginia League, 1895–1896; renamed franchise. Had been RICHMOND COLTS, 1894. Atlantic League, 1897–1899; new franchise. Disbanded after 1899 season.

Richmond Braves
International League (AAA), 1966–(still in existence as of 5-1-92); new franchise.

Richmond Byrds
Eastern League (A), 1931–mid-1932; new franchise. Disbanded with league during 1932 season.

Richmond Climbers
International League (AA), 1915; relocated franchise. Had been BALTIMORE ORIOLES, 1912–1914. Became BALTIMORE ORIOLES, 1916.

Richmond Colts
Virginia League, 1894; charter franchise. Renamed RICHMOND BLUEBIRDS, 1895.

Richmond Colts
Virginia League (C), 1906–1914; charter franchise. Disbanded after 1914 season.

Richmond Colts
Virginia League (B), 1918; expansion franchise. Disbanded during 1918 season.

Richmond Colts
Virginia League (B), 1919–mid-1928; charter franchise. Disbanded with league during 1928 season.

Richmond Colts
Eastern League (A), 1932; charter franchise. Piedmont League (B), 1933–1953; new franchise. Disbanded after 1953 season.

RICHMOND VIRGINIANS

American Association, mid-1884; relocated franchise. Had been WASHINGTON NATIONALS, 1884. Virginia League, 1885–1886; charter franchise. Disbanded with league after 1886 season.

Richmond Virginians
International League (AAA), 1955–1964; renamed franchise. Had been RICHMOND VIRGINIAS, 1954. Disbanded after 1964 season.

Richmond Virginias
International League (AAA), 1954–1964; new franchise. Renamed RICHMOND VIRGINIANS, 1955.

RIDGWAY, PA

Ridgway
Mountain League, 1887; charter franchise. Disbanded with league during 1887 season.

Ridgway
Inter-State League (D), 1916; new franchise. Disbanded with league after 1916 season.

RIVERSIDE, CA

High Desert Mavericks
California League (A), 1991; renamed franchise. Had been RIVERSIDE RED WAVE, 1988–1990.

Riverside Dons
Sunset League (C), 1947; charter franchise. Renamed RIVERSIDE RUBES, 1948.

Riverside Reds
California League (C), 1941; charter franchise. Disbanded after 1941 season.

Riverside Red Wave
California League (A), 1988–1990; relocated franchise. Had been SALINAS SPURS, 1982–1987. Became HIGH DESERT MAVERICKS, 1991.

Riverside Rubes
Sunset League (C), 1948–1950; renamed franchise. Had been RIVERSIDE DONS, 1947. Disbanded with league after 1950 season.

RIVERSIDE–ENSENADA, CA
(See also ENSENADA, CA)

Riverside–Ensenada Padres
Southwest International League (C), 1952; new franchise. Became RIVERSIDE–PORTERVILLE PADRES, mid-1952.

RIVERSIDE–PORTERVILLE, CA
(See also PORTERVILLE, CA)

Riverside–Porterville Padres
Southwest International League (C), mid-1952; renamed franchise. Had been RIVERSIDE–ENSENADA PADRES. Became PORTERVILLE PADRES, mid-1952.

ROANOKE, VA

Roanoke
Virginia League (C), mid-1916; relocated franchise. Had been HOPEWELL POWDER PUFFS, 1916. Disbanded after 1916 season.

Roanoke Braves (aka Magicians)
Virginia League, 1894–1895; charter franchise. Renamed ROANOKE GOATS, 1896.

Roanoke Goats (aka Magicians)
Virginia League, 1896; renamed franchise. Had been ROANOKE BRAVES, 1894–1895. Disbanded during 1896 season.

Roanoke Magicians
Alternate name for ROANOKE BRAVES, 1894–1895; ROANOKE GOATS, 1896.

Roanoke Tigers
Virginia League (C), 1906–1914; charter franchise. Disbanded after 1914 season.

ROANOKE–SALEM, VA
(See also SALEM, VA)

Roanoke–Salem Friends
See Salem–Roanoke Friends.

Roanoke–Salem Red Sox
Alternate name for ROANOKE–SALEM RO-SOX.

Roanoke–Salem Red Sox
Piedmont League (B), 1943–1950; new franchise. Had been SALEM-ROANOKE FRIENDS, 1939–1942. Renamed ROANOKE–SALEM RO-SOX, 1951.

Roanoke–Salem Ro-Sox
Piedmont League (B), 1951–mid-1953; renamed franchise. Had been ROANOKE–SALEM RED SOX, 1943–1950. Disbanded during 1953 season.

ROANOKE RAPIDS, NC

Roanoke Rapids Blue Jays
Coastal Plain League (D), 1947; new franchise. Renamed ROANOKE RAPIDS JAYS, 1948.

Roanoke Rapids Jays
Coastal Plain League (D), 1948–1950; renamed franchise. Had been ROANOKE RAPIDS BLUE JAYS, 1947. Disbanded with league after 1950 season.

ROBSTOWN, TX

Robstown Cardinals
Rio Grande Valley League (C), 1949; charter franchise. Renamed ROBSTOWN REBELS, 1950.

Robstown Rebels
Rio Grande Valley League (C), 1950; renamed franchise. Had been ROBSTOWN CARDINALS, 1949. Disbanded with league after 1950 season.

ROCHESTER, MN

Rochester Bears
Minnesota–Wisconsin League (C), 1911; renamed franchise. Had been ROCHESTER ROOSTERS, 1910. Renamed ROCHESTER BUGS, 1912.

Rochester Bugs
Minnesota–Wisconsin League (D), 1912; renamed franchise. Had been ROCHESTER BEARS, 1911. Disbanded with league after 1912 season.

Rochester Roosters
Minnesota–Wisconsin League (D), 1910; new franchise. Renamed ROCHESTER BEARS, 1911.

ROCHESTER–WINONA, MN
(See also WINONA, MN)

Rochester A's
Three I League (B), 1958; new franchise. Became WINONA A'S, mid-1958.

ROCHESTER, NH

Rochester
New England Inter-State League, 1888; charter franchise. Disbanded with league during 1888 season.

ROCHESTER, NY

Rochester Beau Brummels
Alternate name for ROCHESTER BRONCHOS, 1905, 1908.

Rochester Bronchos (aka Beau Brummels, 1905, 1908; Hustlers, 1909)
Eastern League, 1899–1901; (A), 1902–1907; (AA), 1908–1911; new franchise. Became ROCHESTER HUSTLERS, 1912.

Rochester Brownies (aka Browns)
Eastern League, 1895–1897; new franchise. Became MONTREAL JINGOS, 1897.

Rochester Colts
International League (AA), 1921; renamed franchise. Had been ROCHESTER HUSTLERS, 1918–1920. Became ROCHESTER THE TRIBE, 1922.

ROCHESTER HOP-BITTERS
American Association, 1890; new franchise. International League, 1891; new franchise. Eastern League, 1892; charter franchise. Disbanded after 1892 season.

Rochester Hustlers
Alternate name for ROCHESTER BRONCHOS, 1909.

Rochester Hustlers
(New) International League (AA), 1912–1920; renamed franchise. Had been ROCHESTER BROWNIES, 1897–1911. Became ROCHESTER COLTS, 1921.

Rochester Jingoes
International Association, 1888–1889; charter franchise. Disbanded with association during 1889 season.

Rochester Maroons
International League, 1886–1887; charter franchise. Had been ROCHESTER ROCHESTERS, 1885. Became ROCHESTER JINGOES, 1888.

Rochester Patriots
Eastern League, 1898; relocated franchise. Had been SCRANTON MINERS, 1897. Had been ROCHES-

TER BROWNIES, 1895–1897. Became OTTAWA, mid-1898.

Rochester Red Wings
International Association, 1877–1878; charter franchise. Disbanded after 1878 season.

Rochester Red Wings
National Association, mid-1879; relocated franchise. Had been ALBANY, 1879. Disbanded with association after 1879 season.

Rochester Red Wings
International League (AA), 1928–1945; (AAA), 1946–(still in existence as of 5-1-92); relocated franchise. Had been SYRACUSE STARS, 1920–1927.

Rochester Rochesters
New York State League, 1885; charter franchise. Renamed ROCHESTER BRONCOS, 1886.

Rochester The Tribe
International League (AA), 1922–1927; renamed franchise. Had been ROCHESTER COLTS, 1921. Disbanded after 1927 and replaced by ROCHESTER RED WINGS, 1928.

ROCKFORD, IL

Forest City of Rockford
National Association, 1871; charter franchise. Disbanded after 1871 season.

Rockford (two separate clubs)
Northwestern League, 1869–1870; charter franchises. Each disbanded after 1870 season.

Rockford
Central Inter-State League, 1888; charter franchise. Disbanded after 1888 season.

Rockford Bells
Alternate name for ROCKFORD ROX, 1919–1923.

Rockford Expos
Midwest League (A), 1988–(still in existence as of 5-1-92); new franchise.

ROCKFORD FOREST CITY
Alternate name for FOREST CITY OF ROCKFORD, 1871.

Rockford Forest City
Western Association, 1895–1898; new franchise. Became ROCKFORD ROUGH RIDERS, 1899.

Rockford Hottentots
Alternate name for ROCKFORD REDS, mid-1908.

Rockford Hustlers
Illinois–Iowa League, 1891–1892; new franchise. Disbanded with league after 1892 season.

Rockford Indignants
Wisconsin–Illinois League (D), 1911; renamed franchise. Had been ROCKFORD REDS, 1908–1910. Renamed ROCKFORD WOLVERINES, 1912.

Rockford Indignants
Wisconsin–Illinois League (D), 1913; renamed franchise. Had been ROCKFORD WOLVERINES, 1912. Renamed ROCKFORD WOLVES, 1914.

Rockford Nicol Platers
Alternate name for ROCKFORD REDS, 1895.

Rockford Peaches
All-American Girls Professional Baseball League, 1943–1954; charter franchise. Disbanded with league after 1954 season.

Rockford Reds (aka Rockford Hottentots, mid-1908)
Wisconsin–Illinois League (D), 1908–1910; new franchise. Renamed ROCKFORD INDIGNANTS, 1911.

Rockford Reds (aka Nicol Platers)
Western Association, 1895; new franchise. Renamed ROCKFORD FOREST CITY, 1896.

Rockford Red Sox
Illinois–Iowa–Indiana League, 1901; (B), 1902–1904; charter franchise. Disbanded after 1904 season.

Rockford Rocks
Alternate name for ROCKFORD ROX, 1919–1923; 1947–1949.

Rockford Rough Riders
Western Association, 1899; renamed franchise. Had been Rockford Forest City, 1895–1898. Disbanded after 1899 season.

Rockford Rox
Alternate name for ROCKFORD WAKES, 1917.

Rockford Rox (aka Bells and Rocks)
Illinois–Iowa–Indiana League (B), 1919–1923; charter franchise. Disbanded after 1923 season.

Rockford Rox (aka Rocks)
Central Association (C), 1947–1949; new franchise. Disbanded with league after 1949 season.

Rockford Wakes (aka Rox, 1917)
Illinois–Iowa–Indiana League (B), 1915–mid-1917; new franchise. Disbanded with league during 1917 season.

Rockford White Stockings
Northwestern League, 1879; charter franchise. Disbanded with league after 1879 season.

Rockford Wolverines
Wisconsin–Illinois League (D), 1912; renamed franchise. Had been ROCKFORD INDIGNANTS, 1911. Renamed ROCKFORD INDIGNANTS (aka Drys), 1913.

Rockford Wolves
Wisconsin–Illinois League (D), 1914; renamed franchise. Had been ROCKFORD INDIGNANTS, 1913. Dis-

banded with league after 1914 season.

ROCK HILL, SC

Rock Hill Cardinals
Western Carolinas League (A), 1964–1966; renamed franchise. Had been ROCK HILL WRENS, 1963. Renamed ROCK HILL INDIANS, 1967.

Rock Hill Catawbas
South Carolina State League (D), 1908; charter franchise. Disbanded with league after 1908 season.

Rock Hill Chiefs
Tri-State League (B), 1947–1955; new franchise. Disbanded with league after 1955 season.

Rock Hill Indians
Western Carolinas League (A), 1967; renamed franchise. Had been ROCK HILL CARDINALS, 1964–1966. Renamed ROCK HILL SPINNERS, 1968.

Rock Hill Spinners
Western Carolinas League (A), 1968; renamed franchise. Had been ROCK HILL INDIANS, 1967. Disbanded after 1968 season.

Rock Hill Wrens
Western Carolinas League (A), 1963; charter franchise. Renamed ROCK HILL CARDINALS, 1964.

ROCKINGHAM, NC

Rockingham Eagles
Tobacco State League (D), 1950; new franchise. Disbanded after 1950 season.

ROCK ISLAND, IL
(with Bettendorf, IA–Davenport, IA–Moline, IL)

Quad Cities Angels
Midwest League (A), 1962–1978; renamed franchise. Had been

QUAD CITIES BRAVES, 1960–1961. Renamed QUAD CITIES CUBS, 1979.

Quad Cities Angels
Midwest League (A), 1985–(still in existence as of 5-1-92); renamed franchise. Had been QUAD CITIES CUBS, 1979–1984.

Quad Cities Blue Sox
Three I League (B), 1952; renamed franchise. Had been QUAD CITIES TIGERS, 1951. Disbanded after 1952 season.

Quad Cities Braves
Midwest League (A), 1960–1961; new franchise. Renamed QUAD CITIES ANGELS, 1962.

Quad Cities Cubs
Midwest League (A), 1979–1984; renamed franchise. Had been QUAD CITIES ANGELS, 1962–1978. Renamed QUAD CITIES ANGELS, 1985.

Quad Cities Pirates
Three I League (B), 1949; renamed franchise. Had been QUAD CITY CUBS, 1946–1948. Renamed QUAD CITY QUADS, 1950.

Quad Cities Quads
Three I League (B), 1950; renamed franchise. Had been DAVENPORT PIRATES, 1948–1949. Renamed QUAD CITIES TIGERS, 1951.

Quad Cities Tigers
Three I League (B), 1951; renamed franchise. Had been QUAD CITIES QUADS, 1950. Renamed QUAD CITIES BLUE SOX, 1952.

Quad City Cubs
Three I League (B), 1946–1948; charter franchise. Renamed QUAD CITIES PIRATES, 1949.

ROCK ISLAND, IL

Rock Island
Illinois–Iowa League, 1891; charter franchise. Became ROCK ISLAND–MOLINE TWINS, 1892.

Rock Island
Eastern Iowa League, 1895; charter franchise. Disbanded with league after 1895 season.

Rock Island Islanders
Central Association (D), mid-1914; relocated franchise. Had been OTTUMWA SPEED BOYS, 1914. Became GALESBURG, mid-1914,

Rock Island Islanders
Western Association, 1898; new franchise. Disbanded with league during 1898 season.

Rock Island Islanders
Illinois–Iowa–Indiana League, 1901; (B), 1902–1911; charter franchise. Disbanded after 1911 season.

Rock Island Islanders
Illinois–Iowa–Indiana League (B), 1916–mid-1917; new franchise. Disbanded with league during 1917 season.

Rock Island Islanders
Illinois–Iowa–Indiana League (B), 1920–1921; new franchise. Mississippi Valley League (D) 1922–1933; charter franchise. Disbanded with league after 1933 season.

Rock Island Islanders
Western League (A), 1934–mid-1935; new franchise. Disbanded during 1935 season.

Rock Island Islanders
Western League (A), 1937; renamed franchise. Had been ROCK ISLAND ROBIN HOODS, mid-1936. Disbanded during 1937 season.

Rock Island Robin Hoods
Western League (A), mid-1936; relocated franchise. Had been OMAHA ROBIN HOODS, 1936. Renamed ROCK ISLAND ISLANDERS, 1937.

Rock Island Rocks
Western League (A), 1936; new franchise. Disbanded during 1936

season, and replaced by ROCK IS-LAND ROBIN HOODS, mid-1936.

ROCK ISLAND–MOLINE, IL
(See also MOLINE, IL)

Rock Island–Moline Islanders
Western Association, 1893–mid-1894; charter franchise. Became MOLINE, mid-1894.

Rock Island–Moline Twins
Illinois–Iowa League, 1892; renamed franchise. Had been ROCK ISLAND, 1891. Disbanded with league during 1892 season.

ROCKLAND, ME

Rockland
Connecticut League, 1884; charter franchise. Disbanded with league after 1884 season.

Rockland
Maine State League, 1897; charter franchise. Disbanded with league after 1897 season.

ROCK RAPIDS, IA

Rock Rapids
Iowa–South Dakota League (D), 1902; charter franchise. Disbanded after 1902 season.

ROCKY MOUNT, NC

Rocky Mount
Eastern Carolina League (D), 1928–1929; charter franchise. Disbanded with league after 1929 season.

Rocky Mount Athletics
Coastal Plain League (D), 1949–1952; renamed franchise. Had been ROCKY MOUNT LEAFS, 1948. Disbanded after 1952 season.

Rocky Mount Bronchos
Virginia League (C), 1924–1925; renamed franchise. Had been ROCKY MOUNT TAR HEELS, 1920–1923. Disbanded with league after 1925 season.

Rocky Mount Buccaneers
Piedmont League (C), 1927; new franchise. Eastern Carolina League (D), 1928–1929; charter franchise. Disbanded with league after 1929 season.

Rocky Mount Carolinians
Virginia League (C), 1915; expansion franchise. Renamed ROCKY MOUNT TAR HEELS, 1916.

Rocky Mount Downhomers
Alternate name for ROCKY MOUNT TAR HEELS.

Rocky Mount Leafs
Coastal Plain League (D), 1941; new franchise. Had been ROCKY MOUNT RED SOX, 1936–1940. Became GREENSBORO RED SOX, 1942.

Rocky Mount Leafs
Coastal Plain League (D), 1947–1948; renamed franchise. Had been ROCKY MOUNT ROCKS, 1946. Renamed ROCKY MOUNT ATHLETICS, 1949.

Rocky Mount Leafs
Carolina League (B), 1962; (A), 1963; new franchise. Renamed ROCKY MOUNT SENATORS, 1964.

Rocky Mount Leafs
Carolina League (A), 1965–1972; renamed franchise. Had been ROCKY MOUNT SENATORS, 1964. Renamed ROCKY MOUNT PHILLIES, 1973.

Rocky Mount Phillies
Carolina League (A), 1973–1975; renamed franchise. Had been ROCKY MOUNT LEAFS, 1965–1972. Disbanded after 1975 season.

Rocky Mount Pines
Carolina League (A), 1980; new franchise. Disbanded after 1980 season.

Rocky Mount Railroaders
Eastern Carolina League (D), 1909–1911; new franchise. Disbanded with league after 1911 season.

Rocky Mount Red Sox
Piedmont League (B), 1936–1940; new franchise. Renamed ROCKY MOUNT LEAFS, 1941.

Rocky Mount Rocks
Bi-State League (D), 1942; new franchise. Disbanded after 1942 season.

Rocky Mount Rocks
Coastal Plain League (D), 1946; charter franchise. Renamed ROCKY MOUNT LEAFS, 1947.

Rocky Mount Senators
Carolina League (A), 1964; renamed franchise. Had been ROCKY MOUNT LEAFS, 1962–1963. Renamed ROCKY MOUNT LEAFS, 1965.

Rocky Mount Tar Heels (aka Downhomers)
Virginia League (C), 1916–mid-1917; renamed franchise. Had been ROCKY MOUNT CAROLINIANS, 1915. Disbanded with league during 1917 season.

Rocky Mount Tar Heels
Virginia League (C), 1920–1923; expansion franchise. Renamed ROCKY MOUNT BRONCHOS, 1924.

ROGERS, AR

Rogers Cardinals
Arkansas State League (D), 1935; renamed franchise. Had been ROGERS RUSTLERS, 1934. Renamed ROGERS LIONS, 1936.

Rogers Lions
Arkansas–Missouri League (D), 1936–1937; charter franchise. Had been ROGERS CARDINALS, 1935. Renamed ROGERS REDS, 1938.

Rogers Reds
Arkansas–Missouri League (D), 1938; renamed franchise. Had been ROGERS LIONS, 1937. Disbanded after 1938 season.

Rogers Rustlers
Arkansas State League (D), 1934; charter franchise. Renamed ROGERS CARDINALS, 1935.

ROGUE VALLEY, WA

Rogue Valley Dodgers
Northwest League (D), 1969; new franchise. Disbanded after 1969 season.

ROME, GA

Rome
Georgia State League (D), 1920–1921; charter franchise. Disbanded with league after 1921 season.

Rome Hillites
Southeastern League (D), 1910–1912; renamed franchise. Had been ROME ROMANS, 1910–mid-1911. Disbanded with league during 1912 season.

Rome Red Sox
Georgia–Alabama League (D), 1950–1951; new franchise. Disbanded with league after 1951 season.

Rome Romans
Southeastern League (D), 1910–mid-1911; charter franchise. Renamed ROME HILLITES, mid-1911.

Rome Romans
Appalachian League (D), 1913; relocated franchise. Had been MORRISTOWN JOBBERS, 1911–1912. Became PINEVILLE, 1914.

ROME–LINDALE, GA
(See also LINDALE, GA)

Rome–Lindale
Georgia–Alabama League (D), 1914–mid-1917; new franchise. Disbanded with league during 1917 season.

ROME, NY

Rome
Empire State League (NY), (C), 1905; charter franchise. Disbanded during 1905 season.

Rome
New York State League (B), 1909; new franchise. Central New York League (C), 1910; charter franchise. Disbanded with league after 1910 season.

Rome Colonels
Canadian–American League (C), 1937–1942; 1946–1951; charter franchise. Disbanded with league after 1951 season.

Rome Noble Romans
New York State League, 1898; new franchise. Renamed ROME ROMANS, 1899.

Rome Romans
New York State League, 1899–1901; renamed franchise. Had been ROME NOBLE ROMANS, 1898. Disbanded after 1901 season.

ROSEVILLE, CA

Roseville Diamonds
Far West League (D), mid-1948; relocated franchise. Had been PITTSBURG DIAMONDS, 1948. Disbanded after 1948 season.

ROSSLAND, BRITISH COLUMBIA, CANADA

Rossland
Washington State League, 1897; charter franchise. Disbanded with league after 1897 season.

ROSWELL, NM

Roswell Giants
Panhandle Pecos Valley League (D), 1923; charter franchise. Disbanded with league after 1923 season.

Roswell Pirates
Sophomore League (D), mid-1959; relocated franchise. Had been SAN ANGELO PIRATES, 1958–mid-1959. Disbanded after 1959 season.

Roswell Rockets
Longhorn (D), 1949–1950, (C), 1951–1955; new franchise. Southwestern League (B), 1956–1957; charter franchise. Disbanded after 1957 season.

Roswell Sunshiners
West Texas–New Mexico League (D), 1937; charter franchise. Disbanded after 1937 season.

ROUSE'S POINT, NY

Rouse's Point
Eastern International League, 1895; charter franchise. Disbanded with league during 1895 season.

ROYERSFORD, PA

Royersford
Schuylkill Valley League, 1896; charter franchise. Disbanded with league during 1896 season.

RUSHVILLE, IN

Rushville
Indiana State League, 1896; charter franchise. Disbanded with league during 1896 season.

RUSK, TX

Rusk
East Texas League (D), 1916; charter franchise. Disbanded with league after 1916 season.

RUSSELLVILLE, AL

Russellville
Alabama–Tennessee League (D), 1921; charter franchise. Disbanded with league after 1921 season.

RUSSELLVILLE, AR

Russellville
West Arkansas League (D), 1924; charter franchise. Disbanded with league after 1924 season.

RUTLAND, VT

Rutland
Northeastern League, 1887; new franchise. Disbanded with league after 1887 season.

Rutland
Northern League (D), 1905; new franchise. Disbanded with league after 1905 season.

Rutland
New Hampshire State League (D), 1907; charter franchise. Disbanded with league after 1907 season.

Rutland Shieks
Quebec–Ontario–Vermont League (B), 1924; charter franchise. Disbanded with league after 1924 season.

SABETHA, KS

Sabetha
Eastern Kansas League (D), 1910; charter franchise. Disbanded after 1910 season.

SABINAS, COAHUILA, MEXICO
(See also MONCLOVA, MEXICO)

Sabinas Pirates
Mexican League (AAA), 1971–1973; new franchise. Disbanded after 1973 season.

SACRAMENTO, CA

Sacramento
California League, mid-1893; relocated franchise. Had been STOCKTON PIRATES (aka Dukes), 1893. Disbanded after 1893 season.

Sacramento
Pacific Coast League, 1898; charter franchise. Pacific States League, mid-1898; charter franchise. Disbanded with league after 1898 season.

Sacramento Altas
California State League, 1887; charter franchise. Disbanded with league after 1887 season.

Sacramento (Baby) Senators
Pacific Coast League (AA), 1910–1911; renamed franchise. Had been SACRAMENTO SACTS, 1909–1910. Renamed SACRAMENTO SACTS, 1912.

Sacramento Gilt Edges
California League, mid-1897–1901; relocated franchise. Had been STOCKTON, 1896–mid-1897. Became SACRAMENTO SACTS, Pacific Coast League, 1903.

Sacramento Sacts
Pacific Coast League (A), 1903; charter franchise. Became TACOMA, 1904.

Sacramento Sacts
Pacific Coast League (A), mid-1905; relocated franchise. Had been TACOMA TIGERS, 1904–1905. Became FRESNO RAISINEATERS, 1906.

Sacramento Sacts
Pacific Coast League (AA), 1909–1914; expansion franchise. Renamed SACRAMENTO (BABY) SENATORS, 1910.

Sacramento Sacts
Pacific Coast League (AA), 1912–1914; renamed franchise. Had been SACRAMENTO (BABY) SENATORS, 1910–1911. Became MISSIONS OF SAN FRANCISCO, mid-1914.

Sacramento Senators
California League, 1889–1891; new franchise. Disbanded after 1891 season.

Sacramento Senators
Pacific Coast League (AA), 1918–1935; new franchise. Renamed SACRAMENTO SOLONS, 1936.

Sacramento Solons
Pacific Coast League (AA), 1936–1945; (AAA), 1946–1960; renamed franchise. Had been SACRAMENTO SENATORS, 1918–1935. Became HAWAII ISLANDERS, 1961.

Sacramento Solons
Pacific Coast League (AAA), 1974–1976; relocated franchise. Had been EUGENE EMERALDS, 1955–1973. Became SAN JOSE MISSIONS, 1977.

SAGINAW– BAY CITY, MI
(See also BAY CITY, MI)

Saginaw–Bay City Hyphens
International League, 1890; charter franchise. Disbanded with league after 1890 season.

SAGINAW, MI

Saginaw
Northwestern League, 1884; charter franchise. Disbanded during 1884 season.

Saginaw
Saginaw Valley League, 1888; charter franchise. Disbanded with league after 1888 season.

Saginaw
Michigan State League, 1889; charter franchise. Disbanded after 1889 season.

Saginaw
International League, 1900; charter franchise. Disbanded during 1900 season.

Saginaw
Michigan State League (D), 1902; charter franchise. Became JACKSON, mid-1902.

Saginaw
Inter-State Association (C), 1906; charter franchise. Disbanded with association after 1906 season.

Saginaw
Southern Michigan League (D), mid-1906; charter franchise. Disbanded with league after 1906 season.

Saginaw Aces
Michigan–Ontario League (B), 1919–mid-1926; charter franchise. Michigan State League (D), 1926; charter franchise. Disbanded with league after 1926 season.

Saginaw Alerts
Ohio–Michigan League, 1893; charter franchise. Disbanded during 1893 season.

Saginaw A's
Michigan State League (D), 1940; charter franchise. Renamed SAGINAW WHITE SOX, 1941.

Saginaw Bears
Central League (D), 1948–1950; charter franchise. Renamed SAGINAW JACKS, 1951.

Saginaw Ducks
Southern Michigan League (C), 1913–1915; charter franchise. Disbanded with league during 1915 season.

Saginaw Jacks
Central League (D), 1951; renamed franchise. Had been SAGINAW BEARS, 1948–1950. Disbanded with league after 1951 season.

Saginaw Krazy Kats
Southern Michigan League (C), 1911; renamed franchise. Had been SAGINAW WA-WAS, 1908–1910. Renamed SAGINAW TRAILERS, 1912.

Saginaw Lumbermen
Inter-State League, 1896; charter franchise. Disbanded during 1896 season.

Saginaw Tigers
Michigan State League, 1897; charter franchise. Disbanded with league during 1897 season.

Saginaw Tigers
Canadian League, 1898; new franchise. Became CHATHAM BABES, mid-1898.

Saginaw Trailers
Southern Michigan Association (C), 1912; renamed franchise. Had been SAGINAW KRAZY KATS, 1911. Became SAGINAW DUCKS, 1913.

Saginaw Wa-was
Southern Michigan League (C), 1908–1910; new franchise. Renamed SAGINAW KRAZY KATS, 1911.

Saginaw White Sox
Michigan State League (D), 1941; renamed franchise. Had been SAGINAW A'S, 1940. Disbanded with league after 1941 season.

ST. ALBANS, VT

St. Albans
Northeastern League, 1887; charter franchise. Disbanded with league during 1887 season.

St. Albans
Eastern International League, 1895; charter franchise. Disbanded with league during 1895 season.

St. Albans
Northern New York League (D), 1902; charter franchise. Disbanded with league after 1902 season.

ST. AUGUSTINE, FL

St. Augustine
Florida State League, 1892; charter franchise. Disbanded with league after 1892 season.

St. Augustine Saints
Southeastern League (D) 1926–mid-1927; charter franchise. Became WAYCROSS, mid-1927.

St. Augustine Saints
Florida State League (D), 1936–1941, 1946–1950; charter franchise. Disbanded after 1950 season.

St. Augustine Saints
Florida State League (D), 1952; new franchise. Disbanded during 1952 season.

ST. BONIFACE, MANITOBA, CANADA

St. Boniface
Northern League (C), 1915; new franchise. Disbanded after 1915 season.

ST. CATHERINES, ONTARIO, CANADA

St. Catherines Blue Jays
New York–Pennsylvania League (A), 1986–(still in existence as of 5-1-92); new franchise.

St. Catherines Brewers
Ontario League (D), 1930; charter franchise. Disbanded during 1930 season.

ST. CLAIR, PA

St. Clair
Interstate League (D), mid-1932; relocated franchise. Had been NOR-

RISTOWN, 1932. Disbanded with league after 1932 season.

ST. CLOUD, MN

St. Cloud
Northern League (C), 1913; charter franchise. Disbanded after 1913 season.

St. Cloud Rox
Northern League (C), 1946–1962; (A), 1963–1971; charter franchise. Disbanded after 1971 season.

ST. CLOUD– BRAINERD, MN
(See also BRAINERD, MA)

St. Cloud–Brainerd
Northern League (C), 1903; new franchise. Became SUPERIOR LONGSHOREMEN, mid-1903.

ST. CROIX, NEW BRUNSWICK, CANADA

St. Croix
New Brunswick–Maine League (D), 1913; charter franchise. Disbanded during 1913 season.

ST. HELENA, CA

St. Helena
Central California Baseball League (D), 1910; charter franchise. Became FRUITVALE, mid-1910.

ST. HYACINTHE, QUEBEC, CANADA

St. Hyacinthe A's
Provincial League (C), 1952–1953; renamed franchise. Had been ST. HYACINTHE SAINTS, 1950–1951. Disbanded after 1953 season.

St. Hyacinthe Saints
Provincial League (B), 1940; charter franchise. Disbanded after 1940 season.

St. Hyacinthe Saints
Provincial League (C), 1950–1951; charter franchise. Renamed ST. HYACINTHE A'S, 1952.

ST. JEAN, QUEBEC, CANADA

St. Jean Braves
Provincial League (C), 1950–1951; charter franchise. Renamed ST. JEAN CANADIANS, 1952.

St. Jean Canadians
Provincial League (C), 1952–1955; charter franchise. Had been ST. JEAN BRAVES, 1950–1951. Disbanded with league after 1955 season.

ST. JOHN, NEW BRUNSWICK, CANADA

St. John
New Brunswick League, 1890; charter franchise. Disbanded with league after 1890 season.

St. John Marathons
New Brunswick–Maine League (D), 1913; charter franchise. Disbanded during 1913 season.

ST. JOSEPH, MI

St. Joseph Autos
Michigan State League (D), 1940–1941; charter franchise. Disbanded with league after 1941 season.

ST. JOSEPH, MO

St. Joseph
Western Association (C), 1906; new franchise. Became HUTCHINSON WHITE SOX, mid-1906.

St. Joseph Angels
Western Association (C), 1939; new franchise. Renamed ST. JOSEPH SAINTS, 1940.

St. Joseph Cardinals
Western Association (C), 1946–1951; charter franchise. Disbanded after 1951 season.

St. Joseph Cardinals
Western Association (C), 1953; new franchise. Renamed ST. JOSEPH SAINTS, 1954.

St. Joseph Clay Eaters
Western Association, 1889; new franchise. Disbanded during 1889 season.

St. Joseph Drummers
Western League (A), 1910–mid-1917; relocated franchise. Became HUTCHINSON WHEATSHOCKERS, mid-1917.

St. Joseph Drummers
Western League (A), 1933–1935; new franchise. Had been ST. JOSEPH SAINTS, 1930–1932. Disbanded after 1935 season.

St. Joseph Josies
Alternate name for ST. JOSEPH SAINTS, 1901 and 1905.

St. Joseph Ponies
Western Association (C), 1941; renamed franchise. Had been ST. JOSEPH SAINTS, 1940. Became CARTHAGE BROWNS, mid-1941.

St. Joseph Red Stockings
Western League, 1886–mid-1887; charter franchise. Disbanded during 1887 season.

St. Joseph Saints
Western Association (C), 1954; renamed franchise. Had been ST. JOSEPH CARDINALS, 1953. Disbanded with league after 1954 season.

St. Joseph Saints (aka Josies, 1901, 1905)
Western League, 1900; charter franchise. Western Association, 1901; charter franchise. Western League (A), 1902–1905; new franchise. Disbanded after 1905 season.

St. Joseph Saints
Western Association, 1894–mid-1898; charter franchise. Disbanded with league during 1898 season.

St. Joseph Saints
Western League, mid-1898; relocated franchise. Had been OMAHA, 1898. Disbanded with league during 1898 season.

St. Joseph Saints
Western League (A), mid-1917–1926; relocated franchise. Had been SIOUX CITY INDIANS, 1914–mid-1917. Became JOPLIN MINERS, 1927.

St. Joseph Saints
Western Association (B), 1927; (C), mid-1927; new franchise. Became JOPLIN MINERS, mid-1927.

St. Joseph Saints
Western League (A), 1930–1932; new franchise. Renamed ST. JOSEPH DRUMMERS, 1933.

St. Joseph Saints
Western Association (C), 1940; renamed franchise. Had been ST. JOSEPH ANGELS, 1939. Renamed ST. JOSEPH PONIES, 1941.

ST. LOUIS, MO
(See also HARRISBURG, PA)

ST. LOUIS BROWNIES
Alternate name for ST. LOUIS TERRIERS.

ST. LOUIS BROWNS
American Association, 1883–1891; renamed franchise. Had been ST. LOUIS BROWN STOCKINGS, 1882. National League, 1892–1898; new franchise. Disbanded after 1898 season.

ST. LOUIS BROWNS
American League, 1902–1953; relocated franchise. Had been MILWAUKEE BREWERS, 1901. Became BALTIMORE ORIOLES, 1954.

ST. LOUIS BROWN STOCKINGS
National Association, 1875; new franchise. National League, 1876–1877; new franchise. Disbanded after 1877 season.

ST. LOUIS BROWN STOCKINGS
American Association, 1882; charter franchise. Renamed ST. LOUIS BROWNS, 1883.

ST. LOUIS CARDINALS
National League, 1900–(still in existence as of 5-1-92); renamed franchise. Had been ST. LOUIS PERFECTOS, 1899.

ST. LOUIS GIANTS
Negro National League, 1920–1921; charter franchise. Renamed ST. LOUIS STARS, 1922.

ST. LOUIS MAROONS
Union Association, 1884; charter franchise. National League, 1885–1886; new franchise. Disbanded after 1886 season.

ST. LOUIS MINERS
Alternate name for ST. LOUIS TERRIERS.

ST. LOUIS PERFECTOS
National League, 1899; Relocated franchise. Had been CLEVELAND BLUES, 1887–1898. Renamed ST. LOUIS CARDINALS, 1900.

ST. LOUIS SLOUFEDS
Alternate name for ST. LOUIS TERRIERS.

ST. LOUIS STARS
Negro National League, 1922–1931; renamed franchise. Had been ST. LOUIS GIANTS, 1920–1921. Disbanded after 1931 season. Negro American League, 1939; new franchise. Disbanded after 1939 season.

St. Louis Terriers
Federal League, 1913; charter franchise.

St. Louis Terriers
Federal League, 1914–1915; charter franchise. Disbanded with league after 1915 season.

St. Louis Whites
Western Association, 1888; charter franchise. Became SIOUX CITY CORN HUSKERS, mid-1888.

ST. LOUIS, MO– NEW ORLEANS, LA
(See also NEW ORLEANS, LA)

ST. LOUIS–NEW ORLEANS STARS
Negro American League, 1941; new franchise. Disbanded after 1941 season.

ST. LUCIE, FL

St. Lucie Legends
Senior Professional Baseball Association, 1989–1990; charter franchise. Disbanded after 1989–90 season.

ST. MARYS, PA

St. Marys
Inter-State League (D), 1916; new franchise. Disbanded with league after 1916 season.

ST. PAUL, MN

St. Paul
Northern League (C), 1913; charter franchise. Became LA CROSSE COLTS, mid-1913.

St. Paul Apostles
Northwestern League, 1884; charter franchise. Became ST. PAUL SAINTS, mid-1884.

St. Paul Apostles
Western Association, 1888–1890; new franchise. Disbanded after 1890 season.

St. Paul Apostles
Western League, 1891; new franchise. Became DULUTH JAYHAWKERS, mid-1891.

St. Paul Apostles

Western League, 1892; expansion franchise. Became FORT WAYNE, mid-1892.

St. Paul Apostles

American Association (A), 1903–1908; (AA), 1909–1914; charter franchise. Renamed ST. PAUL SAINTS, 1915.

St. Paul Freezers

Northwestern League, 1886; charter franchise. Renamed ST. PAUL SAINTS, 1887.

St. Paul Marquettes

Alternate name for ST. PAUL SAINTS, 1901.

St. Paul Red Caps

Keystone Association, 1877; charter franchise. Disbanded after 1877 season.

ST. PAUL SAINTS

Union Association, mid-1884; charter franchise. Had been ST. PAUL APOSTLES, 1884. Disbanded with league after 1884 season.

St. Paul Saints

Northwestern League, 1887; renamed franchise. Had been ST. PAUL FREEZERS, 1886. Disbanded with league after 1887 season.

St. Paul Saints

Western League, 1895–1899; charter franchise. Disbanded with league after 1899 season.

St. Paul Saints (aka Marquettes)

Western League, 1901; expansion franchise. Disbanded after 1901 season.

St. Paul Saints

American Association (AA), 1915–1945; (AAA), 1946–1948; renamed franchise. Had been ST. PAUL APOSTLES, 1902–1914. Renamed ST. PAUL SENATORS, 1949.

St. Paul Saints

American Association (AAA), 1952–1960; renamed franchise. Had been ST. PAUL SENATORS, 1949–1951. Disbanded after 1960 season.

St. Paul Senators

American Association (AAA), 1949–1951; renamed franchise. Had been ST. PAUL SAINTS, 1915–1948. Renamed ST. PAUL SAINTS, 1952.

ST. PETERSBURG, FL

St. Petersburg Cardinals

Florida State League (A), 1966– (still in existence as of 5-1-92); new franchise.

St. Petersburg Pelicans

Senior Professional Baseball Association, 1989; charter franchise. Disbanded during 1989–1990 season.

St. Petersburg Saints

Florida State League (D), 1920; (C), 1921–1923; (D), 1924; expansion franchise. Disbanded with league during 1924 season. Florida State League (D), 1925–1927; charter franchise. Disbanded with league after 1927 season.

St. Petersburg Saints

Florida State League (D), mid-1928; relocated franchise. Had been FORT LAUDERDALE TARPONS, 1928. Disbanded after 1928 season.

St. Petersburg Saints

Florida International League (C), 1947–1948; (B), 1949–mid-1954; new franchise. Disbanded with league during 1954 season.

St. Petersburg Saints

Florida State League (D), 1955–1962; (A), 1963–1965; charter franchise. Renamed ST. PETERSBURG CARDINALS, 1966.

ST. STEPHENS, CANADA

(See CALAIS, CANADA)

ST. THOMAS, ONTARIO, CANADA

St. Thomas

Canadian League (C), 1905; charter franchise. Disbanded with league after 1905 season.

St. Thomas

International League (D), 1908; charter franchise. Disbanded with league after 1908 season.

St. Thomas Blue Sox

Ontario League (D), 1930; charter franchise. Disbanded during the 1930 season.

St. Thomas Saints

Canadian League, 1898–1899; new franchise. Disbanded with league after 1899 season.

St. Thomas Saints

Canadian League (C), 1911; (D), mid-1911; (C), 1912–mid-1914; (B), mid-1914–1915; charter franchise. Disbanded with league after 1915 season.

SALAMANCA, GUANAJUATO, MEXICO

Salamanca Petroleros (Oilers)

Mexican Center League (A), 1975; new franchise. Disbanded after 1975 season.

Salamanca Petroleros (Oilers)

Mexican Center League (D), 1960; (C), 1961–1962; charter franchise. Disbanded after 1962 season.

Salamanca Tigers

Mexican Center League (A), 1964–1965; new franchise. Disbanded after 1965 season.

SALEM, MA

Salem

Massachusetts State Association, 1884; charter franchise. Disbanded with association during 1884 season.

Salem
New England League, 1891–1892; charter franchise. Disbanded with league during 1892 season.

Salem
New England Association, 1895; charter franchise. Became HAVERHILL DUFFERS, mid-1895.

Salem Fairies
New England League, 1887; relocated franchise. Had been LAWRENCE, 1884–mid-1887. Renamed SALEM WITCHES, 1888.

Salem Witches
New England League, 1888; renamed franchise. Had been SALEM FAIRIES, 1887. Disbanded with league during 1888 season.

Salem Witches
New England League (B), mid-1926–1928; relocated franchise. Had been LOWELL, 1926. Disbanded after 1928 season.

Salem Witches
New England League (B), 1930; new franchise. Disbanded with league after 1930 season.

SALEM, NC
(See WINSTON, NC)

SALEM, OH

Salem
Ohio State League, 1898; charter franchise. Disbanded with league during 1898 season.

Salem
Ohio–Pennsylvania League (D), mid-1912; relocated franchise. Had been MCKEESPORT, 1912. Became FAIRMOUNT, mid-1912.

SALEM, OR

Salem Angels
Northwest League (A), 1982–1988; renamed franchise. Had been SALEM SENATORS, 1977–1981. Renamed SALEM DODGERS, 1989.

Salem Dodgers
Northwest League (B), 1961–1965; renamed franchise. Had been SALEM SENATORS, 1940–1942; 1946–1954. Disbanded after 1965 season.

Salem Dodgers
Northwest League (A), 1989; renamed franchise. Had been SALEM ANGELS, 1982–1988. Disbanded after 1989 season.

Salem Raglans
Oregon State League (D), 1904; charter franchise. Disbanded with league during 1904 season.

Salem Senators
Western International League (B), 1940–1942; 1946–1951; (A), 1952–1954; new franchise. Northwest League (B), 1955–1960; charter franchise. Renamed SALEM DODGERS, 1961.

Salem Senators
Northwest League (A), 1977–1981; new franchise. Renamed SALEM ANGELS, 1982.

SALEM, VA

Salem Buccaneers
Carolina League (A), 1987–(still in existence as of 5-1-92); renamed franchise. Had been SALEM REDBIRDS, 1980–1986.

Salem Friends
Virginia League (D), 1940; relocated franchise. Had been SALEM–ROANOKE FRIENDS, 1939. Became SALEM–ROANOKE FRIENDS, 1941.

Salem Giants
Appalachian League (D), 1960; renamed franchise. Had been SALEM REBELS, 1957–1959. Renamed SALEM REBELS, 1961.

Salem Pirates
Appalachian League (R), 1964–1966; renamed franchise. Had been SALEM REBELS, 1961–1963. Renamed SALEM REBELS, 1967.

Salem Pirates
Carolina League (A), 1974–1979; renamed franchise. Had been SALEM REBELS, 1967–1973. Renamed SALEM REDBIRDS, 1980.

Salem Rebels
Appalachian League (D), 1955; new franchise. Disbanded with league after 1955 season.

Salem Rebels
Appalachian League (D), 1957–1959; charter franchise. Renamed SALEM GIANTS, 1960.

Salem Rebels
Appalachian League (D), 1961–1962; (R), 1963; renamed franchise. Had been SALEM GIANTS, 1960. Renamed SALEM PIRATES, 1964.

Salem Rebels
Appalachian League (R), 1967; renamed franchise. Carolina League (A), 1968–1973; new franchise. Had been SALEM PIRATES, 1964–1966. Renamed SALEM PIRATES, 1974.

Salem Redbirds
Carolina League (A), 1980–1986; renamed franchise. Had been SALEM PIRATES, 1974–1979. Renamed SALEM BUCCANEERS, 1987.

SALEM–ROANOKE, VA
(See also ROANOKE, VA)

Salem Friends
Blue Ridge League (D), 1946; charter franchise. Became LENOIR RED SOX, mid-1946.

Salem–Roanoake
Virginia–North Carolina League (D), 1905; charter franchise. Disbanded with league after 1905 season. Disbanded during 1953 season.

Salem–Roanoke Friends
Virginia League (D), 1939; charter franchise. Became SALEM FRIENDS, 1940.

Salem–Roanoke Friends
Virginia League (D), 1941–1942; relocated franchise. Had been SALEM FRIENDS, 1940. Became ROANOKE RO-SO, 1943.

SALINA, KS

Salina
Kansas State League, 1887; charter franchise. Disbanded with league after 1887 season.

Salina
Kansas State League, 1898; charter franchise. Became JUNCTION CITY, mid-1898.

Salina
Kansas State League, mid-1898; relocated franchise. Had been JUNCTION CITY, mid-1898. Disbanded with league after 1898 season.

Salina Blue Jays
Western Association (C), 1946–1952; charter franchise. Disbanded after 1952 season.

Salina Coyotes
Kansas State League (D), 1914; renamed franchise. Had been SALINA INSURGENTS, 1913. Disbanded after 1914 season.

Salina Insurgents
Central Kansas League (D), 1912; new franchise. Kansas State League

(D), 1913; charter franchise. Renamed SALINA COYOTES, 1914.

Salina Millers
Southwestern League (C), 1922–1923, (D), 1924–1926; new franchise. Disbanded with league after 1926 season.

Salina Millers
Western Association (C), 1938–1941; new franchise. Disbanded after 1941 season.

Salina Team Winners
Central Kansas League (D), 1907–1910; charter franchise. Disbanded after 1910 season.

SALINAS, CA

Salinas Angels
California League (A), 1977–1980; renamed franchise. Had been SALINAS PACKERS, 1973–1976. Disbanded after 1980 season.

Salinas Colts
Sunset League (C), 1949; new franchise. Became TIJUANA POTROS (Colts), mid-1949.

Salinas Packers
California League (C), 1954–1958; new franchise. Disbanded after 1958 season.

Salinas Packers
California League (A), 1973–1976; new franchise. Renamed SALINAS ANGELS, 1977.

Salinas Spurs
California League (A), 1982–1987; new franchise. Became RIVERSIDE RED WAVE, 1988.

Salinas Spurs
California League (A), 1989–(still in existence as of 5-1-92); relocated franchise. Had been FRESNO SUNS, 1988.

Salinas Valley Indians
California League (A), 1965; renamed franchise. Had been SALI-

NAS VALLEY METS, 1963–1964. Disbanded after 1965 season.

Salinas Valley Mets
California League (A), 1963–1964; expansion franchise. Renamed SALINAS VALLEY INDIANS, 1965.

SALISBURY, MD

Salisbury A's
Inter-State League (B), 1951; new franchise. Renamed SALISBURY REDS, 1952.

Salisbury Cardinals
Eastern Shore League (D), 1938–1941; 1946–1949; renamed franchise. Had been SALISBURY INDIANS, 1937. Disbanded with league after 1949 season.

Salisbury Indians
Eastern Shore League (D), 1937; charter franchise. Renamed SALISBURY CARDINALS, 1938.

Salisbury Indians
Eastern Shore League (D), 1922–mid-1928; charter franchise. Disbanded with league during 1928 season.

Salisbury Reds
Inter-State League (B), 1952; renamed franchise. Had been SALISBURY A'S, 1951. Disbanded with league after 1952 season.

SALISBURY, NC

Salisbury Astros
Western Carolinas League (A), 1965–1966; renamed franchise. Had been SALISBURY DODGERS, 1963–1964. Disbanded after 1966 season.

Salisbury Bees
North Carolina State League (D), 1937–1938; charter franchise. Renamed SALISBURY GIANTS, 1939.

Salisbury Braves
Western Carolinas League (D), 1960–1962; charter franchise. Renamed SALISBURY DODGERS, 1963.

Salisbury Dodgers
Western Carolinas League (A), 1963–1964; renamed franchise. Had been SALISBURY BRAVES, 1960–1962. Renamed SALISBURY ASTROS, 1965.

Salisbury Giants
North Carolina State League (D), 1939–1942; renamed franchise. Had been SALISBURY BEES, 1937–1938. Suspended operations with league after 1942 season, and resumed as SAILSBURY PIRATES, 1945.

Salisbury Pirates
North Carolina State League (D), 1945–1952; charter franchise. Disbanded with league after 1952 season.

Salisbury Rocots
Tar Heel League (D), 1953; charter franchise. Disbanded after 1953 season.

Salisbury Senators
Western Carolinas League (A), 1968; new franchise. Disbanded after 1968 season.

SALISBURY–SPENCER, NC

Salisbury–Spencer Colonials
Piedmont League (C), 1925–mid-1929; new franchise. Disbanded during 1929 season.

SALTILLO, COAHUILA, MEXICO

Saltillo Parrots
Center Mexican League (C), 1957; renamed franchise. Had been SALTILLO SERAPEROS, 1956. Disbanded after 1957 season.

Saltillo Peroneros (Parrots)
Mexican National League (B), 1946; charter franchise. Disbanded during 1946 season.

Saltillo Seraperos
Center Mexican League (C), 1956; new franchise. Renamed SALTILLO PARROTS, 1957.

Saltillo Saraperos (Sarapemen)
Mexcian League (AAA) 1970– (still in existence as of 5-1-92); new franchise.

Saltillo Sultans
Mexican Center League (A), 1964; new franchise. Disbanded after 1964 season.

Saltillo Tigres (Tigers)
Mexican Center League (A), 1967–1969; new franchise. Disbanded after 1969 season.

SALT LAKE CITY, UT

Salt Lake City
Inter-Mountain League, 1901; charter franchise. Disbanded with league after 1901 season.

Salt Lake City
Inter-Mountain League (D), 1909; charter franchise. Became LIVINGSTON, mid-1909.

Salt Lake City Angels
Pacific Coast League (AAA), 1971–1974; renamed franchise. Had been SALT LAKE CITY PADRES, 1969–1970. Renamed SALT LAKE CITY GULLS, 1975.

Salt Lake City Angels
Pacific Coast League (AAA), 1970–1984; relocated franchise. Had been VANCOUVER MOUNTIES, 1965–1969. Became CALGARY CANNONS, 1985.

Salt Lake City Bees
Pacific Coast League (AA), 1915–1925; relocated franchise. Had been MISSIONS OF SAN FRANCISCO, 1915. Became HOLLYWOOD STARS, 1926.

Salt Lake City Bees
Utah–Idaho League (C), 1926–1928; charter franchise. Disbanded with league after 1928 season.

Salt Lake City Bees
Pioneer League (C), 1939–1942; 1946–1957; charter franchise. Disbanded after 1957 season and replaced by relocated HOLLYWOOD STARS. Pacific Coast League (AAA), 1958–1965; new franchise. Disbanded after 1965 season.

Salt Lake City Elders
Pacific National League (A) mid-1903; (B), 1904; relocated franchise. Had been PORTLAND GREEN GAGES, 1903. Disbanded with league after 1904 season.

Salt Lake City Giants
Pioneer League (R), 1967–1968; new franchise. Renamed SALT LAKE CITY PADRES, 1969.

Salt Lake City Gulls
Pacific Coast League (AAA), 1975–1984; renamed franchise. Had been SALT LAKE CITY ANGELS, 1971–1974. Became SALT LAKE CITY TRAPPERS, 1985.

Salt Lake City Padres
Pioneer League (R), 1969; renamed franchise. Had been SALT LAKE CITY GIANTS, 1967–1968. Pacific Coast League (AAA), 1970; new franchise. Renamed SALT LAKE CITY ANGELS, 1971.

Salt Lake City Skyscrapers
Union Association (C), 1911–1912; (D), 1913–1914; charter franchise. Disbanded with league after 1914 season.

Salt Lake City Trappers
Pioneer League (A), 1985–(still in existence as of 5-1-92); new franchise. Had been SALT LAKE CITY GULLS, 1975–1984.

SAN ANGELO, TX

San Angelo Bronchos
West Texas League (D), 1921–1922; new franchise. Disbanded with league after 1922 season

San Angelo Colts
Longhorn League (D), 1947–1950; (C), 1951–1955; charter franchise. Southwestern League (B), 1956; charter franchise. Disbanded after 1956 season.

San Angelo Colts
Southwestern League (B), mid-1957; relocated franchise. Had been PAMPA OILERS, 1956–mid-1957.

San Angelo Pirates
Sophomore League (D), 1958–mid-1959; charter franchise. Became ROSWELL PIRATES, mid-1959.

San Angelo Red Snappers
West Texas League (D), 1928; charter franchise. Renamed SAN ANGELO SHEEP HERDERS, 1929.

San Angelo Sheep Herders
West Texas League (D), 1929; renamed franchise. Had been SAN ANGELO RED SNAPPERS, 1928. Disbanded with league after 1929 season.

SAN ANTONIO, TX

San Antonio Bears
Texas League (B), 1920; (A), 1921–1928; renamed franchise. Renamed SAN ANTONIO INDIANS, 1929.

San Antonio Brewers
Texas League (AA), 1972–1976; renamed franchise. Had been SAN ANTONIO MISSIONS, 1968–1971. Renamed SAN ANTONIO DODGERS, 1977.

San Antonio Bronchos
Texas League, 1896–1899; charter franchise. Disbanded with league after 1899 season.

San Antonio Bronchos (aka Broncos)
South Texas League (D), 1903–1906; charter franchise. Texas League (C), 1907–1910; (B), 1911–1919; new franchise. Renamed SAN ANTONIO BEARS, 1920.

San Antonio Bullets
Texas League (AA), 1964; renamed franchise. Had been SAN ANTONIO MISSIONS, 1933–1963. Disbanded after 1964 season.

San Antonio Cowboys
Texas League, 1888; charter franchise. Disbanded during 1888 season.

San Antonio Dodgers
Texas League (AA), 1977–1988; renamed franchise. Had been SAN ANTONIO BREWERS, 1972–1976. Became SAN ANTONIO MISSIONS, 1989.

San Antonio Indians
Texas League (A), 1929–1932; renamed franchise. Had been SAN ANTONIO BEARS, 1921–1928. Disbanded after 1932 season.

San Antonio Missions
Texas League, mid-1888; relocated franchise. Had been AUSTIN SENATORS, 1888.

San Antonio Missions
Texas League, mid-1892; relocated franchise. Had been FORT WORTH, 1892. Disbanded with league after 1892 season.

San Antonio Missions
Texas Southern League, 1895; charter franchise. Became SAN ANTONIO BRONCHOS, 1896–1899.

San Antonio Missions
Texas League (A1), 1933–1942; (AA), 1946–1963; relocated franchise. Had been LONGVIEW BROWNS, 1932. Renamed SAN ANTONIO BULLETS, 1964.

San Antonio Missions
Texas League (AA), 1968–1970; new franchise. Dixie Association (AA), 1971; charter franchise. Became SAN ANTONIO BREWERS, 1972.

San Antonio Missions
Texas League (AA), 1989–(still in existence as of 5-1-92); renamed franchise. Had been SAN ANTONIO DODGERS, 1977–1988.

SAN BENITO, TX
(See HARLINGEN, TX)

SAN BERNARDINO, CA

San Bernardino Kittens
Southern California League (D), 1913; charter franchise. Disbanded with league after 1913 season.

San Bernardino Padres
California State League (D), 1929; charter franchise. Disbanded with league during 1929 season.

San Bernardino Pioneers
Sunset League (C), 1949–1950; charter franchise. Had been SAN BERNARDINO VALENCIAS, mid-1948. Disbanded with league after 1950 season.

San Bernardino Pride
Senior Professional Baseball Association, 1990; expansion franchise. Disbanded with league during 1990–1991 season.

San Bernardino Spirit
California League (A), 1987–(still in existence as of 5-1-92); relocated franchise. Had been VENTURA COUNTY GULLS, 1986.

San Bernardino Stars
California League (C), 1941; charter franchise. Disbanded during 1941 season.

San Bernardino Valencias
Sunset League (C), mid-1948; relocated franchise. Had been ANAHEIM VALENCIAS, 1947–mid-1948. Renamed SAN BERNARDINO PIONEERS, 1949.

SANDERSVILLE, GA

Sandersville Giants
Georgia State League (D), 1955–1956; renamed franchise. Had been SANDERSVILLE WACOS, 1953–1954. Disbanded with league after 1956 season.

Sandersville Wacos
Georgia State League (D), 1953–1954; new franchise. Renamed SANDERSVILLE GIANTS, 1955.

SAN DIEGO, CA

San Diego
Southern California Trolley League (D), 1910; charter franchise. Disbanded with league after 1910 season.

San Diego Aces
California State League (D), 1929; charter franchise. Disbanded with league after 1929 season.

San Diego Bears
Southern California League (D), 1913; charter franchise. Disbanded with league after 1913 season.

San Diego Padres
Pacific Coast League (AA), 1936–1945; (AAA), 1946–1951; (O), 1952–1957; (AAA), 1958–1967; relocated franchise. Had been HOLLYWOOD STARS, 1926–1935. Disbanded after 1968 season.

SAN DIEGO PADRES
National League, 1969–(still in existence as of 5-1-92); expansion franchise.

SANDUSKY, OH

Sandusky Fisheaters
Tri-State League, 1888; charter franchise. Disbanded during 1888 season.

Sandusky Maroons (aka Sands; Suds)
Ohio State League, 1887; charter franchise. Disbanded with league after 1887 season.

Sandusky Sailors
Ohio State League (D), 1936–mid-1937; charter franchise. Became MARION PRESIDENTS, mid-1937.

Sandusky Sandies
Ohio–Michigan League, 1893; charter franchise. Disbanded with league after 1893 season.

Sandusky Sands
Alternate name for SANDUSKY MAROONS.

Sandusky Suds
Alternate name for SANDUSKY MAROONS.

SANFORD, FL

Sanford
Florida State League (C), 1922; new franchise. Disbanded after 1922 season.

Sanford Cardinals
Florida State League (D), 1953; 1955; renamed franchise. Had been SANFORD SEMINOLE BLUES, 1952. Disbanded after 1955 season.

Sanford Celeryfeds
Florida State League (D), 1919–1920; charter franchise. Disbanded with league after 1920 season.

Sanford Celeryfeds
Florida State League (D), 1925–mid-1928; new franchise. Disbanded with league during 1928 season.

Sanford Celeryfeds
Florida State League (D), 1946–1947; charter franchise. Renamed SANFORD GIANTS, 1948.

Sanford Giants
Florida State League (D), 1948–1951; renamed franchise. Had been SANFORD CELERYFEDS, 1946–1947. Renamed SANFORD SEMINOLE BLUES, 1952.

Sanford Greyhounds
Florida State League (D), 1959–1960; new franchise. Disbanded after 1960 season.

Sanford Lookouts
Florida State League (D), 1936–1939; charter franchise. Renamed SANFORD SEMINOLES, 1940.

Sanford Seminole Blues
Florida State League (D), 1952; renamed franchise. Had been SANFORD GIANTS, 1948–1951. Renamed SANFORD CARDINALS, 1953.

Sanford Seminoles
Florida State League (D), 1940–mid-1941; charter franchise. Had been SANFORD LOOKOUTS, 1936–1939. Disbanded during 1941 season.

SANFORD, NC

Sanford Spinners
Bi-State League (NC–VA), (D), 1941–1942; new franchise. Disbanded with league after 1942 season.

Sanford Spinners
Tobacco State League (D), 1946–1950; charter franchise. Disbanded with league after 1950 season.

SAN FRANCISCO, CA

Missions of San Francisco
Pacific Coast League (AA), mid-1914–1915; relocated franchise. Had been SACRAMENTO SACTS, 1909–mid-1914. Became SALT LAKE CITY BEES, 1916.

Missions of San Francisco
Pacific Coast League (AA), 1926; relocated franchise. Had been VER-

NON TIGERS, 1915–1925. Became HOLLYWOOD STARS, 1937.

San Francisco
California State League (D), mid-1915; relocated franchise. Had been BERKELEY, 1915. Disbanded with league after 1915 season.

San Francisco A's
California League, mid-1898–1899; renamed franchise. Had been SAN FRANCISCO OLYMPICS, 1898. Renamed SAN FRANCISCO BREWERS, 1900.

San Francisco Baby Seals
California Baseball League (B), 1910; charter franchise. Disbanded with league after 1910 season.

San Francisco Brewers
California State League, 1900–1901; renamed franchise. Had been SAN FRANCISCO A'S, mid-1898–1899. Disbanded with league after 1901 season.

San Francisco Friscoes
California League, 1891–1893; renamed franchise. Had been SAN FRANCISCO HAVERLYS, 1887–1890. Disbanded after 1893 season.

SAN FRANCISCO GIANTS
National League, 1958–(still in existence as of 5-1-92); relocated franchise. Had been NEW YORK GIANTS, 1885–1957. (Scheduled to become SAN JOSE GIANTS, 1996.)

San Francisco Haverlys
California State League, 1887/California League, 1888–1890; charter franchise. Renamed SAN FRANCISCO FRISCOES, 1891.

San Francisco Nationals
Alternate name for SAN FRANCISCO PIRATES, 1903.

San Francisco Olympics
California League, 1897–mid-1898; new franchise. Renamed SAN FRANCISCO A'S, mid-1898.

San Francisco Pacifics
California State League, 1896; charter franchise. Disbanded with league after 1896 season.

San Francisco Pioneers
California State League, 1887/California League, 1888; charter franchise. Disbanded after 1888 season.

San Francisco Pirates (aka Nationals)
Pacific National League (A), 1903; charter franchise. Disbanded during 1903 season.

San Francisco Seals
Pacific Coast League (A), 1903–1907; (AA), 1908–1945; (AAA), 1946–1951; (O), 1952–1957; charter franchise. Became MINNEAPOLIS MILLERS, 1958.

SAN JOSE, CA

San Jose
California State League, 1896; charter franchise. Disbanded with league after 1896 season.

San Jose
California State League (B), 1910; charter franchise. Disbanded with league after 1910 season.

San Jose Beachcombers
Pacific States League, 1898; charter franchise. Renamed SAN JOSE BREWERS, 1899.

San Jose Bears
California State League (D), 1913–1915; charter franchise. Disbanded with league after 1915 season.

San Jose Bees
California League (C), 1962; (A), 1963–1969; new franchise. Renamed SAN JOSE ROYAL BEES, 1970.

San Jose Bees
California League (A), 1975–1976; renamed franchise. Had been SAN JOSE ROYAL BEES, 1970–1974.

Renamed SAN JOSE MISSIONS, 1977.

San Jose Bees
California League (A), 1983–1987; renamed franchise. Had been SAN JOSE EXPOS, 1982. Renamed SAN JOSE GIANTS, 1988.

San Jose Brewers
Pacific States League, 1899; renamed franchise. Had been SAN JOSE BEACHCOMBERS, 1898. Disbanded after 1899 season.

San Jose Dukes
California League, 1892; renamed franchise. Had been SAN JOSE GARDENERS, 1891. Disbanded after 1892 season.

San Jose Expos
California League (A), 1982; renamed franchise. Had been SAN JOSE MISSIONS, 1977–1981. Renamed SAN JOSE BEES, 1983.

San Jose Florists
California State League, 1898–1899; charter franchise. Disbanded with league after 1899 season.

San Jose Gardeners
California League, 1891; new franchise. Renamed SAN JOSE DUKES, 1892.

San Jose Giants
California League (A), 1988–(still in existence as of 1-1–92); renamed franchise. Had been SAN JOSE BEES, 1983–1987.

San Jose JoSox
California League (C), 1956–1957; renamed franchise. Had been SAN JOSE RED SOX, 1947–1955. Renamed SAN JOSE PIRATES, 1958.

San Jose Missions
California League (A), 1977–1981; renamed franchise. Had been SAN JOSE BEES, 1975–1976. Renamed SAN JOSE EXPOS, 1982.

San Jose Missions
Pacific Coast League (AAA), 1977–1978; relocated franchise. Had been SACRAMENTO SOLONS, 1974–1976. Became OGDEN A'S, 1979.

San Jose Owls
California League (C), 1942; new franchise. Disbanded with league after 1942 season.

San Jose Pirates
California League (C), 1958; renamed franchise. Had been SAN JOSE JOSOX, 1956–1957. Became LAS VEGAS PIRATES, mid-1958.

San Jose Red Sox
California League (C), 1947–1955; new franchise. Renamed SAN JOSE JOSOX, 1956.

San Jose Royal Bees
California League (A), 1970–1974; renamed franchise. Had been SAN JOSE BEES, 1962–1969. Renamed SAN JOSE BEES, 1975.

San Jose Silver Stars
Pacific Coast League, 1898; charter franchise. Disbanded with league after 1898 season.

SAN JUAN, PUERTO RICO

San Juan Marlins
International League (AAA), 1961; new franchise. Became CHARLESTON MARLINS, mid-1961.

San Juan Natives
Inter-American League (R), 1979; charter franchise. Disbanded with league during 1979 season.

SAN LEANDRO, CA

San Leandro
Central California Baseball League (D), mid-1910–1911; relocated franchise. Had been HEALDSBURG, 1910. Disbanded with league after 1911 season.

SAN LUIS POTOSI, MEXICO
(See also EBANO, MEXICO)

San Luis Potosi Cactus
Mexican Center League (A), 1969; new franchise. Renamed SAN LUIS POTOSI TUNEROS, 1970.

San Luis Potosi Indians
Alternate name for SAN LUIS POTOSI REDS, 1963.

San Luis Potosi Reales (Royals)
Mexican League (AAA), 1987–1988; new franchise. Disbanded after 1988 season.

San Luis Potosi Reds (aka Indians)
Mexican Center League (A), 1963–1966; renamed franchise. Had been SAN LUIS POTOSI TUNEROS, 1960–1962. Disbanded after 1966 season.

San Luis Potosi Tuneros
Mexican Center League (D), 1960; (C), 1961–1962; charter franchise. Renamed SAN LUIS POTOSI REDS, 1963.

San Luis Potosi Tuneros
Mexican Center League (A), 1970–1971; renamed franchise. Had been SAN LUIS POTOSI CACTUS, 1969. Disbanded after 1971 season.

San Luis Potosi Tuneros (Tunamen)
Meixcan League (AAA), 1990– (still in existence as of 5-1-92); new franchise.

SAN LUIS RIO COLORADO, MEXICO

San Luis Rio Colorado Cottongrowers
Mexican Northern League (A), 1968–1969; charter franchise. Disbanded with league after 1969 season.

SAN PEDRO DE LAS COLONIAS, MEXICO

San Pedro de las Colonias Algodoneros
Mexican Center League (A), 1974; new franchise. Disbanded after 1974 season.

SAN RAFAEL, CA

San Rafael
Central California Baseball League (D), 1910; charter franchise. Became HAYWARD CUBS, mid-1910.

SANTA ANA, CA

Orange County
California State League (D), 1929; charter franchise. Became POMONA, mid-1929.

Santa Ana Walnut Growers
Southern California Trolley League (D), 1910; charter franchise. Disbanded with league after 1910 season.

SANTA BARBARA, CA

Santa Barbara
Southern California League (D), mid-1913; relocated franchise. Had been PASADENA, 1913. Disbanded with league after 1913 season.

Santa Barbara Dodgers
California League (C), 1946–1953; charter franchise. Disbanded after 1953 season.

Santa Barbara Dodgers
California League (A), 1964–1967; renamed franchise. Had been SANTA BARBARA RANCHEROS, 1963. Disbanded after 1967 season.

Santa Barbara Mets
California League (C), 1962; new franchise. Renamed SANTA BARBARA RANCHEROS, 1963.

Santa Barbara Rancheros
California League (A), 1963; renamed franchise. Had been SANTA BARBARA DODGERS, 1964.

Santa Barbara Saints
California League (C), 1941–1942; charter franchise. Disbanded with league after 1942 season.

SANTA BARBARA–VENTURA, CA
(See also VENTURA, CA)

Channel Cities Oilers
California League (C), 1954–mid-1955; renamed/relocated franchise. Had been VENTURA OILERS, 1953. Became RENO SILVER SOX, mid-1955.

SANTA CLARA, CA

Santa Clara Padres
California League (A), 1979; new franchise. Disbanded after 1979 season.

SANTA CRUZ, CA

Santa Cruz
Pacific States League, 1898; charter franchise.

Santa Cruz Sand Crabs
Pacific Coast League, 1898; charter franchise. California League, 1899; charter franchise. Disbanded with league after 1899 season.

SANTA ROSA, CA

Redwood Pioneers
California League (A), 1980–1985; new franchise. Disbanded after 1985 season.

Santa Rosa
Central California Baseball League (D), 1910; charter franchise. Became ALAMEDA, mid-1910.

Santa Rosa Cats
Far West League (D), 1949; renamed franchise. Had been SANTA

ROSA PIRATES, 1948. Disbanded after 1949 season.

Santa Rosa Pirates
Far West League (D), 1948; charter franchise. Renamed SANTA ROSA CATS, 1949.

SANTO DOMINGO, DOMINICAN REPUBLIC

Santo Domingo Sharks
Inter-American League (A), 1979; charter franchise. Renamed SANTO DOMINGO SUGARMAKERS, mid-1979.

Santo Domingo Sugarmakers
Inter-American League (A), mid-1979; renamed franchise. Had been SANTO DOMINGO SHARKS, 1979. Disbanded with league during 1979 season.

SAPULPA, OK

Sapulpa Oilers
Western Association (D), mid-1909–mid-1911; relocated franchise. Had been WEBB CITY WEBFEET (aka Ducklings), 1909. Disbanded with league during 1911 season.

Sapulpa Sappers
Southwestern League (C), 1921–1922; charter franchise. Had been SAPULPA YANKS, 1923.

Sapulpa Yanks
Southwestern League (C), 1923; renamed franchise. Had been SAPULPA SAPPERS, 1921–1922. Disbanded after 1923 season.

SARASOTA, FL
(See also GULF COAST, FL)

Sarasota
Gulf Coast League (R), 1968–1971; new franchise. Disbanded after 1971 season.

Sarasota Astros
Gulf Coast League (R), 1987; new franchise. Became GULF COAST ASTROS, 1988.

Sarasota Dodgers
Gulf Coast League (R), 1987; new franchise. Became GULF COAST DODGERS, 1988.

Sarasota Gulls
Florida State League (D), 1927; new franchise. Renamed SARASOTA TARPONS, 1927.

Sarasota Reds
Gulf Coast League (R), 1987; new franchise. Became GULF COAST REDS, 1988.

Sarasota Royals
Gulf Coast League (R), 1987; new franchise. Became GULF COAST ROYALS, 1988.

Sarasota Sun Sox
Florida State League (D), 1961–1962; (A), 1963–1965; new franchise. Disbanded after 1965 season.

Sarasota Tarpons
Florida State League (D), 1927; renamed franchise. Had been SARASOTA GULLS, 1926. Disbanded with league after 1927 season.

Sarasota White Sox
Gulf Coast League (R), 1987; new franchise. Became GULF COAST WHITE SOX, 1988.

Sarasota Yankees
Gulf Coast League (R), 1987; new franchise. Became GULF COAST YANKEES, 1988.

SARATOGA SPRINGS, NY
(See also GLENS FALLS, NY)

Saratoga Springs
Hudson River League, 1886; charter franchise. Disbanded with league after 1886 season.

SARNIA, ONTARIO, CANADA
(See PORT HURON, MI)

SASKATCHEWAN, CANADA
(See also MOOSE JAW, CANADA; SASKATOON, CANADA; and REGINA, CANADA)

SASKATOON, SASKATCHEWAN, CANADA

Saskatoon Berry Pickers
Western Canada League (D), mid-1910; relocated franchise. Had been MEDICINE HAT MAD HATTERS, 1909–mid-1910. Renamed SASKATOON QUAKERS, 1911.

Saskatoon Quakers
Western Canada League (D), 1911; renamed franchise. Had been SASKATOON BERRY PICKERS, 1910. Disbanded during 1911 season.

Saskatoon Quakers
Western Canada League (D), 1913; new franchise. Renamed SASKATOON SHEIKS, 1914.

Saskatoon Quakers
Western Canada League (D), 1919–1921; charter franchise. Disbanded with league after 1921 season.

Saskatoon Sheiks
Western Canada League (D), 1914; renamed franchise. Had been SASKATOON QUAKERS, 1913. Disbanded with league after 1914 season.

SAUGERTIES, NY

Saugerties
Hudson River League (D), 1903–mid-1905; charter franchise. Became PITTSFIELD HILLIES, mid-1905.

SAULT SAINT MARIE, ONTARIO, CANADA

Sault Saint Marie Soos
Copper County League (D), 1905; charter franchise. Disbanded during 1905 season.

SAVANNAH, GA

Savannah
Southern League, 1886–1887; new franchise. Disbanded during 1887 season.

Savannah
Southern League, 1898; charter franchise. Disbanded during 1898 season.

Savannah Athletics
South Atlantic League (A), 1955; renamed franchise. Had been SAVANNAH INDIANS, 1946–1954. Renamed SAVANNAH REDLEGS, 1956.

Savannah Braves
Dixie Association (C), 1971; charter franchise. Had been SAVANNAH INDIANS, 1970. Southern League (AA), 1972–1983; charter franchise. Renamed SAVANNAH REDBIRDS, 1984.

Savannah Cardinals
South Atlantic League (A), 1987– (still in existence as of 5-1-92); renamed franchise. Had been SAVANNAH REDBIRDS, 1984–1986.

Savannah Colts
South Atlantic League (C), 1913–1915; renamed franchise. Had been SAVANNAH SCOUTS, 1911–1912. Disbanded after 1915 season.

Savannah Electrics
Southern League, 1893; new franchise. Disbanded with league dring 1893 season.

Savannah Indians
Southeastern League (B), 1926; mid-1929; charter franchise. Disbanded during 1929 season.

Savannah Indians
South Atlantic League (A), 1936–1942; 1946–1954; new franchise. Renamed SAVANNAH ATHLETICS, 1955.

Savannah Indians
Southern League (AA), 1970; renamed franchise. Had been SAVANNAH SENATORS, 1968–1969. Became SAVANNAH BRAVES, 1971.

Savannah Modocs
Southern League, 1894; charter franchise. Had been SAVANNAH ELECTRICS, 1893. Disbanded during 1894 season.

Savannah Pathfinders
South Atlantic League (C), 1904–1910; charter franchise. Renamed SAVANNAH SCOUTS, 1911.

Savannah Pirates
South Atlantic League (A), 1960; renamed franchise. Had been SAVANNAH REDS, 1959. Disbanded after 1960 season.

Savannah Redbirds
South Atlantic League (A), 1984–1986; renamed franchise. Had been SAVANNAH BRAVES, 1971–1983. Renamed SAVANNAH CARDINALS, 1987.

Savannah Redlegs
South Atlantic League (A), 1956–1958; renamed franchise. Had been SAVANNAH ATHLETICS, 1955. Renamed SAVANNAH REDS, 1959.

Savannah Reds
South Atlantic League (A), 1960; renamed franchise. Had been SAVANNAH REDLEGS, 1956–1958. Renamed SAVANNAH PIRATES, 1960.

Savannah Scouts
South Atlantic League (C) 1911–1912; renamed franchise. Had been SAVANNAH PATHFINDERS, 1904–1910. Renamed SAVANNAH COLTS, 1913.

Savannah Senators
Southern League (AA), 1968–1969; new franchise. Renamed SAVANNAH INDIANS, 1970.

Savannah White Sox
South Atlantic League (AA), 1962; renamed franchise. Had been SAVANNAH PIRATES, 1960. Became LYNCHBURG WHITE SOX, mid-1962.

SCAMMON, KS

Scammon
Southeast Kansas League (D), 1911; charter franchise. Disbanded with league after 1911 season.

SCHENECTADY, NY

Schenectady Blue Jays (aka Phillies)
Canadian–American League (C), 1946–1950; charter franchise. Disbanded after 1950 season

Schenectady Blue Jays
Eastern League (A), 1951–1957; relocated franchise. Had been UTICA BLUE SOX, mid-1944–1950. Disbanded after 1957 season.

Schenectady Electricians
New York State League, 1899–1901; new franchise. Renamed SCHENECTADY FROG ALLEY BUNCH, 1902.

Schenectady Electrics
New York State League, 1895; new franchise. Disbanded with league after 1895 season.

Schenectady Frog Alley Bunch
New York State League (B), 1902–mid-1904; renamed franchise. Had been SCHENECTADY ELECTRICIANS, 1899–1901. Became SCRANTON MINERS, mid-1904.

Schenectady Phillies
Alternate name for SCHENECTADY BLUE JAYS, 1946–1957.

SCHOOLFIELD, VA
(See DANVILLE, VA)

SCHULENBERG, TX

Schulenberg
Middle Texas League, 1915; new franchise. Disbanded with league during 1915 season.

SCOTTDALE, PA

Scottdale
Western Pennsylvania Association, 1889; charter franchise. Disbanded with association after 1889 season.

Scottdale Giants
Western Pennsylvania League (D), 1907; charter franchise. Pennsylvania–West Virginia League (D), 1908; charter franchise. Became GRAFTON, mid-1908.

Scottdale Scotties
Middle Atlantic League (D), 1925–1931; charter franchise. Disbanded after 1931 season.

SCRANTON, PA

Scranton
Atlantic League, 1899; new franchise. Disbanded during 1899 season.

Scranton
Atlantic League, 1900; new franchise. Disbanded with league duing 1900 season.

Scranton
Pennsylvania State League (D), 1902; charter franchise. Disbanded with league after 1902 season.

Scranton Electrics
Eastern League, 1896; renamed franchise. Had been SCRANTON QUAKERS, 1895. Renamed SCRANTON MINERS, 1897.

Scranton Indians
Pennsylvania State Association, 1886–1887; charter franchise. Had been NEW YORK METROPOLITIANS, 1883–1885. Disbanded with association during 1887 season.

Scranton Indians
Pennsylvania State League, mid-1892–mid-1894; relocated franchise. Had been HARRISBURG PONIES, 1892. Became SHENANDOAH–MAHANOY CITY HUNS, mid-1894.

Scranton Miners
International League, mid-1887; relocated franchise. Had been OSWEGO STARCH BOXES, 1886–mid-1887. Central League, 1888; charter franchise. Eastern Inter-State League, 1889; charter franchise. Disbanded with league after 1889 season.

Scranton Miners
New York State League (B), mid-1904–1917; relocated franchise. Had been SCHENECTADY FROG ALLEY BUNCH, 1902–mid-1904. Disbanded with league during 1917 season.

Scranton Miners
Eastern League, 1897; renamed franchise. Had been SCRANTON ELECTRICS, 1894–1896. Became ROCHESTER PATRIOTS, 1898.

Scranton Miners
New York–Pennsylvania League (B), 1923–1932; (A), 1933–mid-1937; charter franchise. Became HARTFORD LAURELS, mid-1937.

Scranton Miners
Eastern League (A), 1944–1945; renamed franchise. Had been SCRANTON RED SOX, 1939–1943. Renamed SCRANTON RED SOX, 1946.

Scranton Miners
Eastern League (A), 1952–1953; renamed franchise. Had been SCRANTON RED SOX, 1939–1951. Disbanded after 1953 season.

Scranton Quakers
Eastern League, mid-1894–1895; relocated franchise. Had been TROY WASHERWOMEN, 1894. Renamed SCRANTON ELECTRICS, 1896.

Scranton Red Sox
Eastern League (A), 1939–1943; relocated franchise. Had been HAZLETON RED SOX, 1938. Renamed SCRANTON MINERS, 1944.

Scranton Red Sox
Eastern League (A), 1946–1951; renamed franchise. Had been SCRANTON MINERS, 1944–1945. Renamed SCRANTON MINERS, 1952.

SCRANTON– WILKES-BARRE, PA
(See also WILKES-BARRE, PA)

Scranton–Wilkes-Barre Red Barons
International League (AAA), 1989–(still in existence as of 5-1-92); new franchise.

SEAFORD, DE

Seaford Eagles
Eastern Shore League (D), 1946–1949; charter franchise. Disbanded with league after 1949 season.

SEATTLE, WA

Seattle
Pacific Northwest League, 1890–1892; charter franchise. Disbanded with league after 1892 season.

Seattle
New Pacific League, 1896; charter franchise. Disbanded with league during 1896 season.

Seattle
Pacific International League (aka International Northwest League) (B), 1919; charter franchise. Disbanded with league during 1919 season.

Seattle
Northwest League (A), 1973–1976; new franchise. Disbanded after 1976 season.

Seattle Angels
Pacific Coast League (AAA), 1965–1968; renamed franchise. Had been SEATTLE RAINIERS, 1938–1964. Disbanded after 1968 season.

Seattle Babies
Pacific Northwest League, 1896; charter franchise. Disbanded with league after 1896 season.

Seattle Chinooks
Pacific National League (A), 1903; charter franchise. Had been SEATTLE CLAMDIGGERS, 1901–1902. Disbanded after 1903 season.

Seattle Clamdiggers
Pacific Northwest League, 1901; (C), 1902; charter franchise. Became SEATTLE CHINOOKS, 1903.

Seattle Giants
Northwestern League (B), 1910–1917; renamed franchise. Had been SEATTLE TURKS, 1909. Pacific Coast International League (B), 1918; charter franchise. Disbanded after 1918 season.

Seattle Giants
Pacific International League, 1919–1920; charter franchise. Disbanded after 1920 season.

Seattle Indians
Pacific Coast League (AA), 1922–1937; renamed franchise. Had been SEATTLE RAINIERS, 1920–21. Renamed SEATTLE RAINIERS, 1938.

SEATTLE MARINERS
American League, 1977–(still in existence as of 5-1-92); expansion franchise.

SEATTLE PILOTS
American League, 1969; expansion franchise. Became MILWAUKEE BREWERS, 1970.

Seattle Purple Sox
Pacific Coast League (AA), 1919; new franchise. Renamed SEATTLE RAINIERS, 1920.

Seattle Rainiers
Pacific Coast League (AA), 1920–1921; renamed franchise. Had been SEATTLE PURPLE SOX, 1919. Renamed SEATTLE INDIANS, 1922.

Seattle Rainiers
Pacific Coast League (AA), 1938–1945; (AAA), 1946–1951; (O), 1952–1957; (AAA), 1958–1964; renamed franchise. Had been SEATTLE INDIANS, 1922–1937. Became SEATTLE ANGELS, 1965.

Seattle Rainiers
Northwest League (A), 1972–1976; new franchise. Disbanded after 1976 season.

Seattle Siwashes
Pacific Coast League (A), 1903–1906; charter franchise. Northwestern League (B), 1907–1908; new franchise. Renamed SEATTLE TURKS, 1909.

Seattle Turks
Northwestern League (B), 1909; renamed franchise. Had been SEATTLE SIWASHES, 1903–1908. Renamed SEATTLE GIANTS, 1910.

SEBRING, OH
(See ALLIANCE, OH)

SEDALIA, MO

Sedalia Cubs
Missouri State League (D), 1911; charter franchise. Disbanded during 1911 season.

Sedalia Goldbugs
Missouri Valley League, 1901; (D), 1902–1904; charter franchise. Western Association (D), 1905; charter franchise. Disbanded after 1905 season.

SEGUIN, TX

Seguin Toros
Gulf States League (A), 1976; charter franchise. Disbanded with league after 1976 season.

SELMA, AL

Selma Centralites
Southeastern League (D), 1911–1912; charter franchise. Cotton States League (D), 1913; new franchise. Disbanded with league after 1913 season.

Selma Christians
Southern Association, 1901; charter franchise. Became ATLANTA FIREMEN, 1902.

Selma Cloverleafs
Southeastern League (B), 1928–1930; renamed franchise. Had been SELMA SELMIANS, 1927. Disbanded with league after 1930 season.

Selma Cloverleafs
Southeastern League (B), 1932; charter franchise. Disbanded during 1932 season.

Selma Cloverleafs
Southeastern League (C), 1937–1941; (B), 1946–1947; charter franchise. Renamed SELMA CUBS, 1948.

Selma Cloverleafs
Southeastern League (B), 1949–1950; renamed franchise. Had been SELMA CUBS, 1948. Disbanded with league after 1950 season.

Selma Cloverleafs
Alabama–Florida League (D), 1957–1962; new franchise. Disbanded with league after 1962 season.

Selma Cubs
Southeastern League (B), 1948; renamed franchise. Had been SELMA CLOVERLEAFS, 1937–1947. Renamed SELMA CLOVERLEAFS, 1949.

Selma Riverrats
Georgia–Alabama League (C), 1914; new franchise. Disbanded after 1914 season.

Selma Selmians
Southeastern League (B), 1927; new franchise. Renamed SELMA CLOVERLEAFS, 1928.

SELMA, NC
(See SMITHFIELD, NC)

SEMINOLE, OK

Seminole
Oklahoma State League (D), 1936; charter franchise. Disbanded with league during 1936 season.

Seminole Ironmen
Sooner State League (D), 1950–1951; renamed franchise. Had been SEMINOLE OILERS, 1947–1948. Disbanded after 1951 season.

Seminole Oilers
Sooner State League (D), 1947–1949; charter franchise. Renamed SEMINOLE IRONMEN, 1950.

Seminole Oilers
Sooner State League (D), 1954–1957; relocated franchise. Had been SHERMAN-DENISON TWINS, 1953. Disbanded with league after 1957 season.

SENECA, KS

Seneca
East Kansas League (D), 1910–1911; charter franchise. Disbanded with league after 1911 season.

SENECA FALLS, NY

Seneca Falls
Empire State League (C), 1905–1907; charter franchise. Disbanded with league after 1907 season.

Seneca Falls Maroons
New York State League, 1888–1889; charter franchise. Disbanded with league after 1889 season.

SEWARD, NE

Seward Statesmen
Nebraska State League (D), 1910–mid-1913; charter franchise. Became BEATRICE, mid-1913.

SHAMOKIN, PA

Shamokin
Pennsylvania State League, 1896; new franchise. Became READING, mid-1896.

Shamokin
Central Pennsylvania League, 1896–mid-1897; relocated franchise. Had been POTTSVILLE, 1897. Became LOCK HAVEN, mid-1897.

Shamokin Indians
New York–Pennsylvania League (B), 1926–1927; renamed franchise. Had been SHAMOKIN SHAMMIES, 1925. Anthracite League (D), 1928; charter franchise. Disbanded with league during 1928 season.

Shamokin Maroons
Central Pennsylvania League, 1887–1888; charter franchise. Disbanded with league after 1888 season.

Shamokin Miners
Pennsylvania State League (D), 1916; charter franchise. Disbanded with league after 1916 season.

Shamokin Shammies
New York–Pennsylvania League (B), 1925; new franchise. Renamed SHAMOKIN INDIANS, 1926.

SHARON, PA

Sharon
Iron & Oil League, 1895; charter franchise. Became ELBERON, mid-1895.

Sharon Giants
Ohio–Pennsylvania League (D), 1907–1908; renamed franchise. Had been SHARON STEELS, 1905–1906. Disbanded after 1908 season.

Sharon Steels
Ohio–Pennsylvania League (D), 1905–1906; charter franchise. Renamed SHARON GIANTS, 1907.

Sharon Travelers
Ohio–Pennsylvania League (D), mid-1911–1912; relocated franchise. Had been NEW CASTLE NOCKS, 1907–mid-1911. Disbanded with league after 1912 season.

SHAWMUT, AL
(See LANNETT, GA)

SHAWNEE, OK

Shawnee
Oklahoma State League (D), 1923–1924; new franchise. Disbanded with league after 1924 season.

Shawnee Blues
South Central League (D), 1906; charter franchise. Disbanded with league during 1906 season.

Shawnee Braves
Southwestern League (D), mid-1925; relocated franchise. Had been ENID BOOSTERS, 1924–mid-1925. Disbanded with league after 1925 season.

Shawnee Browns
Oklahoma State League (D), mid-1904; relocated franchise. Had been CHICKASHA INDIANS, mid-1904. Became EL RENO BROWNS, mid-1904.

Shawnee Hawks
Sooner State League (D), mid-1950–1957; relocated franchise. Had been DUNCAN UTTMEN, 1949–mid-1950. Disbanded with league after 1957 season.

Shawnee Indians
Southwestern League (B), 1904; charter franchise. Became CHICKASHA BROWNS, mid-1904.

Shawnee Orphans
Alternate name for SHAWNEE SEMINOLES, 1904.

Shawnee Robins
Western Association (C), 1929–1930; new franchise. Disbanded after 1930 season.

Shawnee Seminoles (aka Orphans)
Oklahoma State League (D), mid-1904; relocated franchise. Had been EL RENO BROWNS, mid-1904. Disbanded after 1904 season.

SHEBOYGAN, WI

Sheboygan Indians
Wisconsin State League (D), 1940–1942; 1946–1953; charter franchise. Disbanded with league after 1953 season.

SHEFFIELD, AL

Sheffield
Tennessee–Alabama League (D), 1904; charter franchise. Disbanded after 1904 season.

Sheffield
Alabama–Mississippi League (D), 1936; charter franchise. Disbanded with league during 1936 season.

SHEFFIELD–TUSCUMBIA, AL
(See also FLORENCE, AL)

Sheffield–Tuscumbia Twins
Tri-State League (D), 1926; new franchise. Disbanded with league after 1926 season.

SHEFFIELD–TUSCUMBIA–FLORENCE, AL
(See also FLORENCE, AL)

Tri-Cities
Georgia–Alabama League (D), 1917; new franchise. Disbanded with league after 1917 season.

SHELBY, NC

Shelby Cardinals
North Carolina State League (D), 1937–mid-1938; charter franchise. Became GASTONIA CARDINALS, mid-1938.

Shelby Clippers
Tar Heel League (D), 1953–1954; charter franchise. Disbanded with league after 1954 season.

Shelby Colonels
Tar Heel League (D), 1940; renamed franchise. Had been SHELBY NATIONALS, 1939. Disbanded with league after 1940 season.

Shelby Colonels
Western Carolina League (D), 1960–1963; charter franchise. Renamed SHELBY YANKEES, 1964.

Shelby Cubs
Tri-State League (B), 1946; charter franchise. Disbanded after 1946 season.

Shelby Farmers
Western Carolina League (D), 1948–1952; charter franchise. Disbanded with league after 1952 season.

Shelby Mets
South Atlantic League (A), 1981–1982; renamed franchise. Had been

SHELBY PIRATES, 1979–1980. Disbanded after 1982 season.

Shelby Nationals
Tar Heel League (D), 1939; charter franchise. Renamed SHELBY COLONELS, 1940.

Shelby Pirates
Western Carolinas League (A), 1979; renamed franchise. Had been SHELBY REDS, 1977–1978. South Atlantic League (A), 1980; charter franchise. Renamed SHELBY METS, 1981.

Shelby Reds
Western Carolinas League (A), 1977–1978; new franchise. Renamed SHELBY PIRATES, 1979.

Shelby Rebels
Western Carolina League (D), 1965; renamed franchise. Had been SHELBY YANKEES, 1964. Disbanded after 1965 season.

Shelby Senators
Western Carolinas League (A), 1969; new franchise. Disbanded after 1969 season.

Shelby Yankees
Western Carolina League (D), 1964; renamed franchise. Had been SHELBY COLONELS, 1960–1963. Renamed SHELBY REBELS, 1965.

SHELBYVILLE, IL

Shelbyville Queen Citys
Eastern Illinois League (D), 1907–1908; charter franchise. Disbanded with league after 1908 season.

SHELBYVILLE, KS

Shelbyville
Blue Grass League (D), 1908–1909; charter franchise. Disbanded after 1909 season.

SHELBYVILLE, KY

Shelbyville
Blue Grass League (D), 1908–mid-1910; charter franchise. Became MAYSVILLE RIVERMEN, mid-1910.

SHELDON, IA

Sheldon
Iowa–South Dakota League (D), 1902; charter franchise. Disbanded with league after 1902 season.

Sheldon
Iowa–South Dakota League (D), mid-1903; relocated franchise. Had been COUNCIL BLUFFS, 1903. Disbanded with league after 1903 season.

SHELTON, CT

Shelton
Naugatuck Valley League, mid-1898; relocated franchise. Had been DERBY, 1898. Disbanded with league during 1898 season.

SHENANDOAH, IA

Shenandoah
Southwest Iowa League, (D), 1903; charter franchise. Disbanded with league during 1903 season.

Shenandoah Pin Rollers
MINK League (D), 1910–1911; charter franchise. Disbanded after 1911 season.

SHENANDOAH, PA

Shenandoah
Anthracite League (D), 1928; charter franchise. Disbanded with league during 1928 season.

Shenandoah Hungarian Rioters
Central Pennsylvania League, 1888; new franchise. Middle States League, 1889; charter franchise. Disbanded after 1889 season.

SHENANDOAH–MAHANOY CITY, PA
(See also MAHANOY CITY, PA)

Shenandoah–Mahanoy City Huns
Pennsylvania State League, mid-1894–1895; relocated franchise. Had been SCRANTON INDIANS, mid-1892–mid-1894. Disbanded during 1895 season.

SHERBROOKE, QUEBEC, CANADA

Sherbrooke Athletics
Provincial League (D), 1950–1951; charter franchise. Disbanded after 1951 season.

Sherbrooke Braves
Quebec Provincial League (B), 1940; charter franchise. Disbanded after 1940 season.

Sherbrooke Canadiens
Border League (C), 1946; charter franchise. Disbanded after 1946 season.

Sherbrooke Indians
Provincial League (D), 1953–1955; new franchise. Disbanded with league after 1955 season.

Sherbrooke Pirates
Eastern League (AA), 1972–1973; new franchise. Disbanded after 1973 season.

SHERMAN, TX

Sherman
Southwestern League, 1898; charter franchise. Became DALLAS–FORT WORTH, mid-1898.

Sherman
Texas Association (D), 1923; charter franchise. Disbanded after 1923 season.

Sherman Browns
Western Association (D), 1917; renamed franchise. Had been SHERMAN HITTERS, 1915–1916.

Sherman Cubs
Texas–Oklahoma League (D), 1912–1914; new franchise. Disbanded with league after 1914 season.

Sherman Hitters
Western Association (D), 1915–1916; new franchise. Renamed SHERMAN BROWNS, 1917.

Sherman Lions
Texas–Oklahoma League (D), 1921; charter franchise. Renamed SHERMAN RED SOX, 1922.

Sherman Orphans
Texas Southern League, 1895; charter franchise. Renamed SHERMAN STUDENTS, 1896.

Sherman Red Sox
Texas–Oklahoma League (D), 1922; renamed franchise. Had been SHERMAN LIONS, 1921. Disbanded with league after 1922 season.

Sherman Snappers
Lone Star League (D), 1929; new franchise. Disbanded with league after 1929 season.

Sherman Students
Texas League, 1896; expansion franchise. Had been SHERMAN ORPHANS, 1895. Became TEXAS MIDLAND TIGERS, mid-1896.

Sherman Twins
East Texas League (C), 1946; charter franchise. Became SHERMAN-DENISON TWINS, 1947.

SHERMAN–DENISON, TX
(See also DENISON, TX)

Sherman–Denison Students
Texas League (D), 1902; charter franchise. Became TEXARKANA, mid-1902.

Sherman–Denison Twins
Big State League (B), 1947–1951; charter franchise. Sooner State League

(D), 1952–1953; new franchise. Became SEMINOLE OILERS, 1954.

SHREVEPORT, LA

Shreveport Braves
Texas League (AA), 1968–1970; relocated franchise. Had been AUSTIN SENATORS, 1956–1967. Became SHREVEPORT CAPTAINS, 1971.

Shreveport Captains
Dixie Association (C), 1971; relocated franchise. Had been EL PASO SUN KINGS, 1962–1970. Texas League (AA), 1972–1985; new franchise. Renamed SHREVEPORT GIANTS, 1986.

Shreveport Captains
Texas League (AA), 1987–(still in existence as of 5-1-92); renamed franchise. Had been SHREVEPORT GIANTS, 1986.

Shreveport Creoles
Southwestern League, 1898; charter franchise. Disbanded with league during 1898 season.

Shreveport Gassers
Texas League (B), 1915–1920; (A), 1921–1924; relocated franchise. Had been AUSTIN SENATORS, 1911–1914. Became SHREVEPORT SPORTS, 1925.

Shreveport Giants
Southern Association 1901; (A), 1902–1903; charter franchise. Renamed SHREVEPORT PIRATES, 1904.

Shreveport Giants
Texas League (AA), 1986; renamed franchise. Had been SHREVEPORT CAPTAINS, 1971–1985. Renamed SHREVEPORT CAPTAINS, 1987.

Shreveport Grays
Texas Southern League, 1895; charter franchise. Disbanded during 1895 season.

Shreveport Pirates
Southern Association (A), 1904–1907; charter franchise. Became MOBILE SEA GULLS, 1908.

Shreveport Pirates
Texas League (C), 1908–1910; relocated franchise. Had been TEMPLE BOLL WEEVILS, 1905–1907. Became AUSTIN SENATORS, 1911.

Shreveport Sports
Texas League (A), 1925–mid-1932; renamed franchise. Had been SHREVEPORT GASSERS, 1915–1924. Became TYLER SPORTS, mid-1932.

Shreveport Sports
Dixie League (C), 1933; charter franchise. East Dixie League (C), 1934; charter franchise. Became GREENWOOD CHIEFS, mid-1934.

Shreveport Sports
West Dixie League (C), 1935; new franchise. Became GLADEWATER BEARS, mid-1935.

Shreveport Sports
Texas League (A1), 1938–1942; (AA), 1946–1957; relocated franchise. Had been GALVESTON BUCCANEERS, 1931–1937. Disbanded after 1957 season.

Shreveport Sports
Southern Association (AA), 1959–1961; new franchise. Disbanded with league after 1961 season.

Shreveport Tigers
Southern League, 1899; new franchise. Disbanded after 1899 season.

SIDNEY MINES, NOVA SCOTIA, CANADA

Sidney Mines Ramblers
Cape Breton Colliery League (D), 1937–1938, (C), 1939; charter franchise. Disbanded with league after 1939 season.

SILAO, MEXICO

Silao Catarinos
Mexican League (AAA), 1978; new franchise. Disbanded after 1978 season.

SILOAM SPRINGS, AR

Siloam Springs Buffalos
Arkansas State League (D), 1934; charter franchise. Renamed SILOAM SPRINGS TRAVELERS, 1935.

Siloam Springs Cardinals
Arkansas–Missouri League (D), 1940; new franchise. Disbanded with league after 1940 season.

Siloam Springs Travelers
Arkansas State League (D), 1935; renamed franchise. Had been SILOAM SPRINGS BUFFALOS, 1934. Arkansas–Missouri League (D), 1936–1938; charter franchise. Disbanded after 1938 season.

SIOUX CITY, IA

Sioux City Cardinals
Tri-State League (D), 1924; charter franchise. Had been SIOUX CITY PACKERS, 1920–1923. Disbanded with league after 1924 season.

Sioux City Cornhuskers
Western League, mid-1888–1891; relocated franchise. Had been ST. LOUIS WHITES, 1888. Disbanded after 1891 season.

Sioux City Cornhuskers
Western League, 1894; charter franchise. Disbanded after 1894 season.

Sioux City Cowboys
Western League (A), 1934–1937; new franchise. Nebraska State League (D), 1938; new franchise. Became MITCHELL KERNELS, 1939.

Sioux City Cowboys
Western League (D), 1939–mid-1940; charter franchise. Became MITCHELL KERNELS, mid-1940.

Sioux City Cowboys
Western League (D), 1941; new franchise. Disbanded after 1941 season.

Sioux City Indians
Western League (A), 1900; charter franchise. Disbanded after 1900 season.

Sioux City Indians
Western League (A), 1914–mid-1917; renamed franchise. Had been SIOUX CITY PACKERS, 1905–1913. Became ST. JOSEPH DRUMMERS, mid-1917.

Sioux City Indians
Western League (A), 1918–1923; new franchise. Became SIOUX CITY CARDINALS, Tri-State League, 1924.

Sioux City Packers
Western League (A), 1905–1913; renamed franchise. Had been SIOUX CITY SOOS, 1901–1904. Renamed SIOUX CITY INDIANS, 1914.

Sioux City Packers
Western League (A), 1920–1923; renamed franchise. Became SIOUX CITY CARDINALS, 1924.

Sioux City Soos
Western Association, 1901; charter franchise. Iowa–South Dakota League (D), 1902–1903; charter franchise. Western League (A), 1904; new franchise. Renamed SIOUX CITY PACKERS, 1905.

Sioux City Soos
Western League (A), 1947–1958; charter franchise. Three I League (B), 1959–1960; new franchise. Disbanded after 1960 season.

SIOUX FALLS, SD

Sioux Falls
Iowa–South Dakota League (D), 1902–1903; charter franchise. Dis-banded with league after 1903 season.

Sioux Falls Canaries
Tri-State League (D), 1924; charter franchise. Disbanded with league after 1924 season.

Sioux Falls Canaries
Nebraska State League (D), 1933–1938; new franchise. Western League (D), 1939–1941; charter franchise. Northern League (C), 1942; 1946–1953; new franchise. Disbanded after 1953 season.

Sioux Falls Packers
Northern League (A), 1966–1971; new franchise. Disbanded with league after 1971 season.

Sioux Falls Soos
South Dakota League (D), 1920; charter franchise. Dakota League (D), 1921–1922; charter franchise. Disbanded with league after 1923 season.

SLATINGTON, PA

Slatington
Inter-State League (D), mid-1932; relocated franchise. Had been TAMAQUA DUKES, 1932. Disbanded with league after 1932 season.

SMITHFIELD–SELMA, NC

Smithfield–Selma Leafs
Tobacco State League (D), 1946–1950; charter franchise. Disbanded with league after 1950 season.

SMITHS FALLS, ONTARIO, CANADA

Smiths Falls Beavers
Canadian–American League (C), 1937; charter franchise. Became AUBURN BOULEYS, 1938.

SNOW HILL, NC

Snow Hill Billies
Coastal Plain League (D), 1937–1940; charter franchise. Disbanded after 1940 season.

SOMERSET, PA

Somerset
Western Pennsylvania League, mid-1907; relocated franchise. Had been PIEDMONT, mid-1907. Disbanded with league during 1907 season.

SOMERVILLE, NJ

Somerville West Ends
Central New Jersey League, 1892; charter franchise. Disbanded with league during 1892 season.

SONORA, MEXICO

(See CABORCA, MEXICO; CAMPECHE, MEXICO; CANANEA, MEXICO; CARBORCA, MEXICO; EMPALME, MEXICO; NOGALES, MEXICO; OBREGON, MEXICO; PUERTO PENASCO, MEXICO)

SOUTH BEND, IN

South Bend
Indiana State League, mid-1888; relocated franchise. Had been LAFAYETTE, 1888. Disbanded with league after 1888 season.

South Bend Benders
Central League (D), 1912; new franchise. Disbanded after 1912 season.

South Bend Benders
Southern Michigan League (D), 1914–1915; charter franchise. Central League (B), 1916–mid-1917; charter franchise. Became PEORIA DISTILLERS, mid-1917.

South Bend Blue Sox
All-American Girls Professional Baseball League, 1943–1954; char-

ter franchise. Disbanded with league after 1954 season.

South Bend Bronchos
Central League (D), 1910; renamed franchise. Had been SOUTH BEND GREENS, 1903–1909. Disbanded after 1910 season.

South Bend Bux
Central League (D), mid-1911; relocated franchise. Had been EVANSVILLE STRIKERS, 1911. Became GRAND RAPIDS GRADS, mid-1911.

South Bend Greens
Central League (D), 1903–1909; charter franchise. Renamed SOUTH BEND BRONCHOS, 1910.

South Bend Twins
Central League (B), 1932; charter franchise. Disbanded with league after 1932 season.

South Bend White Sox
Midwest League (A), 1988–(still in existence as of 5-1-92); new franchise.

SOUTH BEND, WA

South Bend River Rats
Washington State League (D), 1911; new franchise. Disbanded after 1911 season.

SOUTH BOSTON, VA

South Boston Wrappers
Bi-State League (D), 1940; renamed franchise. Had been SOUTH BOSTON–HALIFAX WRAPPERS, 1938–1939. Disbanded after 1940 season.

SOUTH BOSTON–HALIFAX, VA

South Boston–Halifax Twins
Bi-State League (D), 1937; new franchise. Renamed SOUTH BOSTON–HALIFAX WRAPPERS, 1938.

South Boston–Halifax Wrappers
Bi-State League (D), 1938–1939; renamed franchise. Had been SOUTH BOSTON–HALIFAX TWINS, 1937. Renamed SOUTH BOSTON WRAPPERS, 1940.

SOUTH McALESTER, INDIAN TERRITORY
(later OK)

South McAlester Coal Miners (aka Giants)
Missouri Valley League (D), 1905; new franchise. Became FORT SMITH, mid-1905.

South McAlester Miners
South Central League (D), 1906; charter franchise. Disbanded with league after 1906 season.

SPARTA, GA

Sparta Saints
Georgia State League (D), 1948–1949; charter franchise. Disbanded after 1949 season.

SPARTANBURG, SC

Spartanburg Peaches
Tri-State League (B), 1947–1955; renamed franchise. Had been SPARTANBURG SPARTANS, 1946. Disbanded with league after 1955 season.

Spartanburg Phillies
Western Carolinas League (A), 1963–1979; charter franchise. South Atlantic League (A), 1980; charter franchise. Renamed SPARTANBURG TRADERS, 1981.

Spartanburg Phillies
South Atlantic League (A), 1986–(still in existence as of 5-1-92); renamed franchise. Had been SPARTANBURG SUNS, 1984–1985.

Spartanburg Pioneers
South Atlantic Association (C), 1919–1920; (B) 1921; charter fran-

chise. Renamed SPARTANBURG SPARTANS, 1922.

Spartanburg Red Sox
Carolina Baseball Association (D), 1911–1912; renamed franchise. Had been SPARTANBURG SPARTANS, 1907–1910. Disbanded with league after 1912 season.

Spartanburg Spartans
South Carolina League (D), 1907; charter franchise. Carolina Baseball Association (D), 1908–1910; charter franchise. Renamed SPARTANBURG RED SOX, 1911.

Spartanburg Spartans
South Atlantic Association (B), 1922–1929; renamed franchise. Had been SPARTANBURG PIONEERS, 1919–1921. Disbanded after 1929 season.

Spartanburg Spartans
Palmetto League (D), mid-1931; relocated franchise. Had been ANDERSON ELECTRICIANS, 1931. Disbanded with league during 1931 season.

Spartanburg Spartans
South Atlantic League (C), 1938–mid-1940; new franchise. Became CHARLESTON REBELS, mid-1940.

Spartanburg Spartans
Tri-State League (B), 1946; charter franchise. Renamed SPARTANBURG PEACHES, 1947.

Spartanburg Spinners
South Atlantic League (A), 1983; renamed franchise. Had been SPARTANBURG TRADERS, 1981–1982. Renamed SPARTANBURG SUNS, 1984.

Spartanburg Suns
South Atlantic League (A), 1984–1985; renamed franchise. Had been SPARTANBURG SPINNERS, 1983. Renamed SPARTANBURG PHILLIES, 1986.

Spartanburg Traders
South Atlantic League (A), 1981–1982; renamed franchise. Had been SPARTANBURG PHILLIES, 1963–1980. Renamed SPARTANBURG SPINNERS, 1983.

SPENCER, NC
(See SALISBURY, NC)

SPINDALE, NC
(See FOREST CITY, NC)

SPOKANE, WA

Spokane
Pacific Coast International League (aka International Northwest League) (B), 1920; charter franchise. Disbanded after 1920 season.

Spokane Blue Stockings
Pacific Northwest League, 1901; charter franchise. Renamed SPOKANE SMOKE EATERS, 1902.

Spokane Falls
Washington State League, 1897; charter franchise. Disbanded with league during 1897 season.

Spokane Falls Spokes
Pacific Northwest League, 1890–1892; charter franchise. Disbanded with league after 1890 season.

Spokane Hawks
Western International League (B), 1937–1938; charter franchise. Renamed SPOKANE INDIANS, 1939.

Spokane Indians
Pacific National League (A), 1903; (B), 1904; charter franchise. Disbanded with league after 1904 season.

Spokane Indians
Northwestern League (D), mid-1905–1917; relocated franchise. Had been VICTORIA LEGISLATORS, 1905. Pacific Coast International League (B), 1918; charter franchise. Disbanded after 1918 season.

Spokane Indians
Western International League (B), 1939–1942; 1946–1951; (A), 1952–1954; renamed franchise. Had been SPOKANE HAWKS, 1937–1938. Northwest League (B), 1955–1956; charter franchise. Disbanded after 1956 season.

Spokane Indians
Pacific Coast League (AAA), 1958–1982; relocated franchise. Had been LOS ANGELES ANGELS, 1903–1957. Became LAS VEGAS STARS, 1983.

Spokane Indians
Northwest League (A), 1983–(still in existence as of 5-1-92); new franchise.

Spokane Smoke Eaters
Pacific Northwest League (C), 1902; renamed franchise. Had been SPOKANE BLUE STOCKINGS, 1901. Disbanded after 1902 season.

SPRAY, NC
(See LEAKSVILLE, NC)

SPRINGFIELD, IL

Springfield
Northwestern League, 1883; charter franchise. Disbanded after 1883 season.

Springfield
Western Association, 1895; expansion franchise. Became JACKSONVILLE JACKS, mid-1895.

Springfield
Central League, 1900; charter franchise. Became JACKSONVILLE REDS, mid-1900.

Springfield
Mississippi Valley League (B), 1933; charter franchise. Disbanded with league after 1933 season.

Springfield Browns
Illinois–Iowa–Indiana League (B), mid-1932; relocated franchise. Had

been DANVILLE VETERANS, 1922–mid-1932. Disbanded with league after 1932 season.

Springfield Browns
Three I League (B), 1938–1942; 1946–1949; new franchise. Disbanded after 1949 season.

Springfield Cardinals
Midwest League (A), 1982–(still in existence as of 5-1-92); renamed franchise. Had been SPRINGFIELD RED BIRDS, 1978–1981.

Springfield Foot Trackers
Illinois–Iowa–Indiana League (B), mid-1903; relocated franchise. Had been JOLIET STANDARDS, 1903. Renamed SPRINGFIELD HUSTLERS, 1904.

Springfield Giants
Mississippi–Ohio Valley League (D), 1950; new franchise. Disbanded after 1950 season.

Springfield Hustlers
Illinois–Iowa–Indiana League (B), 1904; renamed franchise. Had been SPRINGFIELD FOOT TRACKERS, 1903. Renamed SPRINGFIELD SENATORS, 1905.

Springfield Red Birds
Central League (B), 1934; charter franchise. Disbanded with league after 1934 season.

Springfield Red Birds
American Association (AAA), 1978–1981; new franchise. Became SPRINGFIELD CARDINALS, 1982.

Springfield Sallies
All-American Girls Professional Baseball League, 1948; new franchise. Disbanded after the 1948 season.

Springfield Senators
Central Inter-State League, 1889; new franchise. Disbanded with league after 1889 season.

Springfield Senators
Illinois–Iowa–Indiana League (B), 1905–1912; renamed franchise. Had been SPRINGFIELD HUSTLERS, 1904. Became DECATUR NOMADS, mid-1911.

Springfield Senators
Illinois–Iowa League (B), 1912; new franchise. Renamed SPRINGFIELD WATCHMAKERS, 1913.

Springfield Senators
Illinois–Iowa–Indiana League (B), 1925–1932; new franchise. Disbanded with league after 1932 season.

Springfield Senators
Illinois–Iowa–Indiana League (B), 1935; charter franchise. Disbanded with league after 1935 season.

Springfield Senators
Western League (A), 1933; new franchise. Disbanded after 1933 season.

Springfield Watchmakers
Illinois–Iowa–Indiana League (B), 1913–1914; renamed franchise. Had been SPRINGFIELD SENATORS, 1912. Disbanded after 1914 season.

SPRINGFIELD, MA

Springfield
Keystone Association, 1878; charter franchise. Disbanded with association after 1878 season.

Springfield
National Association, 1879; new franchise. Disbanded with association after 1879 season.

Springfield
Massachusetts State Association, 1884; charter franchise. Southern New England League, 1885; charter franchise. Disbanded with league during 1885 season.

Springfield
Eastern League, 1887; new franchise. Disbanded after 1887 season.

Springfield Cubs
New England League (B), 1948–1949; new franchise. International League (AAA), 1950–1953; new franchise. Disbanded after 1953 season.

Springfield Giants
Eastern League (A), 1957–1962; (AA), 1963–1965; new franchise. Disbanded after 1965 season.

Springfield Green Sox
Eastern League (B), 1917; renamed franchise. Had been SPRINGFIELD RIFLES, 1916. Renamed SPRINGFIELD RIFLES, 1918.

Springfield Hampdens
Eastern League (A), 1919–1922; renamed franchise. Had been SPRINGFIELD RIFLES, 1918. Renamed SPRINGFIELD PONIES, 1923.

Springfield Hampdens
Eastern League (A), 1931; renamed franchise. Had been SPRINGFIELD PONIES, 1923–1930. Renamed SPRINGFIELD RIFLES, 1932.

Springfield Nationals
Eastern League (A), 1939–1941; new franchise. Renamed SPRINGFIELD RIFLES, 1942.

Springfield Ponies
Eastern League, 1893–1900; new franchise. Disbanded after 1900 season.

Springfield Ponies
Connecticut League (B), 1902; 1904–1912/Valley League (B), 1903; charter franchise. Eastern Association (B), 1913–1914; charter franchise. Disbanded with association after 1914 season.

Springfield Ponies
Eastern League (A), 1923–1930; renamed franchise. Had been SPRINGFIELD HAMPDENS, 1919–

1922. Renamed SPRINGFIELD HAMPDENS, 1931.

Springfield Ponies
Northeastern League (A), 1934; charter franchise. Disbanded with league after 1934 season.

Springfield Rifles
Eastern League (B), 1916; charter franchise. Renamed SPRINGFIELD GREEN SOX, 1917.

Springfield Rifles
Eastern League (B), 1918; renamed franchise. Had been SPRINGFIELD GREEN SOX, 1917. Renamed SPRINGFIELD HAMPDENS, 1919.

Springfield Rifles
Eastern League (A), 1932; renamed franchise. Had been SPRINGFIELD HAMPDENS, 1931. Disbanded with league during 1932 season.

Springfield Rifles
Eastern League (A), 1942–1943; renamed franchise. Had been SPRINGFIELD NATIONALS, 1939–1941. Disbanded after 1943 season.

SPRINGFIELD, MO

Springfield
Western Association (C), 1911; new franchise. Disbanded with association during 1911 season.

Springfield Cardinals
Western Association (C), 1932/League (C), 1933; renamed franchise. Had been SPRINGFIELD RED WINGS, 1931. Renamed SPRINGFIELD RED WINGS, 1934.

Springfield Cardinals
Western Association (C), 1935–1942; renamed franchise. Had been SPRINGFIELD RED WINGS, 1934. Disbanded with association after 1942 season.

Springfield Cubs
Western Association (C), 1948; new franchise. Disbanded after 1948 season.

Springfield Cubs
Western Association (C), 1950; new franchise. Disbanded after 1950 season.

Springfield Highlanders
Western Association (D), 1905; charter franchise. Renamed SPRINGFIELD MIDGETS, 1906.

Springfield Indians
Southwestern League, 1887; charter franchise. Disbanded during 1887 season.

Springfield Merchants
Western Association (B), 1920; charter franchise. Renamed SPRINGFIELD ORIOLES, mid-1920.

Springfield Midgets
Missouri Valley League (D), 1904; renamed franchise. Had been SPRINGFIELD REDS, 1902–1903. Disbanded after 1904 season.

Springfield Midgets
Western Association (C), 1906–1909; renamed franchise. Had been SPRINGFIELD HIGHLANDERS, 1905. Disbanded after 1909 season.

Springfield Midgets
Western Association (B), 1921–1930; renamed franchise. Had been SPRINGFIELD ORIOLES, mid-1920. Renamed SPRINGFIELD RED WINGS, 1931.

Springfield Orioles
Western Association (B), mid-1920; renamed franchise. Had been SPRINGFIELD MERCHANTS, 1920. Renamed SPRINGFIELD MIDGETS, 1921.

Springfield Reds
Missouri Valley League (D), 1902–1903; charter franchise. Renamed SPRINGFIELD MIDGETS, 1904.

Springfield Red Wings
Western Association (B), 1931; renamed franchise. Had been SPRINGFIELD MIDGETS, 1921–1930. Renamed SPRINGFIELD CARDINALS, 1932.

Springfield Red Wings
Western Association (C), 1934; renamed franchise. Had been SPRINGFIELD CARDINALS, 1932–1933. Renamed SPRINGFIELD CARDINALS, 1935

SPRINGFIELD, OH

Springfield
Ohio State Association, 1884; charter franchise. Inter-State League, 1885; charter franchise. Disbanded with league after 1885 season.

Springfield
Tri-State League, mid-1889–1890; relocated franchise. Had been COLUMBUS, mid-1889. Disbanded with league during 1890 season.

Springfield
Ohio State League (D), 1906–mid-1908; charter franchise. Became PORTSMOUTH COBBLERS, mid-1908.

Springfield Babes
Central League (C), 1905–1907; new franchise. Disbanded after 1907 season.

Springfield Blue Sox
Central League (B), 1930; renamed franchise. Had been SPRINGFIELD DUNNMEN, 1929. Disbanded with league after 1930 season.

Springfield Buckeyes
Central League (B), 1928; charter franchise. Renamed SPRINGFIELD DUNNMEN, 1929.

Springfield Cardinals
Middle Atlantic League (C), 1940–1942; renamed franchise.

Had been SPRINGFIELD INDIANS, 1937–1939. Suspended operations after 1942 season, and resumed as the SPRINGFIELD GIANTS, 1944.

Springfield Chicks

Middle Atlantic League (C), 1933; new franchise. Renamed SPRING-FIELD PIRATES, 1934.

Springfield Dunnmen

Central League (B), 1929; charter franchise. Had been SPRINGFIELD BUCKEYES, 1928. Renamed SPRING-FIELD BLUE SOX, 1930.

Springfield Giants

Middle Atlantic League (C), 1944–1947; new franchise. Ohio–Indiana League (D), 1948–1951; charter franchise. Disbanded with league after 1951 season.

Springfield Governors

Inter-State League, 1897–1898; new franchise. Renamed SPRING-FIELD WANDERERS, 1899.

Springfield Indians

Middle Atlantic League (C), 1937–1939; new franchise. Re-named SPRINGFIELD CARDINALS, 1940.

Springfield Pirates

Middle Atlantic League (C), 1934; renamed franchise. Had been SPRINGFIELD CHICKS, 1933. Dis-banded after 1934 season.

Springfield Reapers

Ohio State League (D), 1911; new franchise. Central League (C), 1912–1914; new franchise. Disbanded after 1914 season.

Springfield Reapers

Central League (C), 1916–1917; new franchise. Disbanded with league after 1917 season.

Springfield Wanderers

Inter-State League, 1899; re-named franchise. Had been SPRINGFIELD GOVERNORS, 1897–1898. Disbanded after 1899 season.

SPRINGFIELD, TN

Springfield Blanketmakers

KITTY League (D), 1923; new franchise. Became MILAN–TREN-TON TWINS, mid-1923.

SPRINGFIELD–CHARLESTON, VT

Springfield–Charleston Hyphens

Twin States League (D), 1911; charter franchise. Disbanded with league after 1911 season.

STAMFORD, CT

Stamford

Connecticut State League, mid-1888; relocated franchise. Had been BRIDGEPORT GIANTS, 1886–mid-1888.

Stamford Bombers

Colonial League (B), 1947; charter franchise. Renamed STAMFORD PI-ONEERS, 1948.

Stamford Pioneers

Colonial League (B), 1948–mid-1949; renamed franchise. Had been STAMFORD BOMBERS, 1947. Dis-banded with league during 1949 season.

STAMFORD, TX

Stamford

West Texas League (D), 1922; new franchise. Disbanded with league after 1922 season.

STATESBORO, GA

Statesboro Pilots

Georgia State League (D), 1952–1955; new franchise. Disbanded during 1955 sea-son.

STATESVILLE, NC

Statesville Blues

Tar Heel League (D), 1953; new franchise. Disbanded during 1953 season.

Statesville Colts

Western Carolinas League (D), 1964; renamed franchise. Had been STATESVILLE OWLS, 1960–1963. Disbanded after 1964 season.

Statesville Cubs

North Carolina State League (D), 1945–1946; charter franchise. Re-named STATESVILLE OWLS, 1947.

Statesville Indians

Western Carolinas League (A), 1969; new franchise. Became MON-ROE INDIANS, mid-1969.

Statesville Owls

Tar Heel League (D), 1939–1940; charter franchise. Disbanded with league after 1940 season.

Statesville Owls

North Carolina State League (D), 1942; new franchise. Suspended operations with league after 1942 season, and resumed as STATES-VILLE CUBS, 1945.

Statesville Owls

North Carolina State League (D), 1947–1952; renamed franchise. Had been STATESVILLE CUBS, 1945–1946. Disbanded with league after 1952 season.

Statesville Owls

Western Carolinas League (D), 1960–1963; charter franchise. Re-named STATESVILLE COLTS, 1964.

Statesville Sports

Tar Heel League (D), mid-1953; relocated franchise. Had been LINCOLNTON CARDINALS (aka Cards), 1949–mid-1953. Dis-banded after 1953 season.

Statesville Tigers
Western Carolinas League (A), 1966–1967; new franchise. Disbanded after 1967 season.

STAUNTON, IL

Staunton
Eastern Illinois League (D), mid-1908; relocated franchise. Had been DANVILLE SPEAKERS, 1908. Disbanded with league after 1908 season.

STAUNTON, VA

Staunton
Virginia Mountain League (D), 1914; charter franchise. Became HARRISONBURG, mid-1914.

Staunton Hayseeds
Alternate name for STAUNTON VALLEYITES, 1894.

Staunton Presidents
Virginia League (D), 1939–1942; charter franchise. Disbanded with league after 1942 season.

Staunton Valleyites (aka Hayseeds)
Virginia League, 1894; charter franchise. Became NEWPORT NEWS–HAMPTON, mid-1894.

STERLING, IL

Sterling Infants
Northern Association of Baseball (D), mid-1910; relocated franchise. Had been JOLIET JOLLY-ITES, 1910. Disbanded with league after 1910 season.

Sterling Rag Chewers
Illinois–Iowa League, mid-1890; charter franchise. Became GALESBURG, mid-1890.

STEUBENVILLE, OH

Steubenville
Ohio State League, 1887; charter franchise. Disbanded with league after 1887 season.

Steubenville
POM League (D), 1906–1907; charter franchise. Disbanded with league after 1907 season.

Steubenville Stubs
Western Inter-State League, 1895; charter franchise. Became AKRON AKRONS, mid-1895.

Steubenville Stubs
Ohio–Pennsylvania League (D), 1909; new franchise. Disbanded after 1909 season.

Steubenville Stubs
Ohio–Pennsylvania League (C), 1911; (D), 1912; new franchise. Became FOLLANSBEE, mid-1912.

Steubenville Stubs
Inter-State League (B), 1913; charter franchise. Disbanded during 1913 season.

STILLWATER, MN

Stillwater
Northwestern League, 1884; charter franchise. Disbanded with league after 1884 season.

STOCKTON, CA

Stockton
California League, 1888–1890; charter franchise. Disbanded after 1890 season.

Stockton
California League, 1896–mid-1897; charter franchise. Became SACRAMENTO GILT EDGES, mid-1897.

Stockton
Pacific Coast League, 1898; charter franchise. Disbanded with league after 1898 season.

Stockton
California League, 1900; new franchise. Disbanded after 1900 season.

Stockton Dukes
Alternate name for STOCKTON PIRATES, 1893.

Stockton Fliers
California League (C), 1941; charter franchise. Suspended operations with league after 1941 season, and rejoined as STOCKTON PORTS when league resumed in 1946.

Stockton Mariners
California League (A), 1978; new franchise. Renamed STOCKTON PORTS, 1979.

Stockton Millers (aka Terrors)
California League, 1898; new franchise. Disbanded after 1898 season.

Stockton Millers
California State Baseball League (B), 1910; charter franchise. Disbanded after 1910 season.

Stockton Millers
California State League (D), 1914–1915; renamed franchise. Had been STOCKTON PRODUCERS, 1913. Disbanded with league after 1915 season.

Stockton Mudville Ports
Alternate name for STOCKTON PORTS, 1982.

Stockton Pirates (aka Dukes)
California League, 1893; new franchise. Became SACRAMENTO, mid-1893.

Stockton Ports
California League (C); 1946–1972; charter franchise. Disbanded after 1972 season.

Stockton Ports (aka Mudville Ports, 1982)
California League (A), 1979–(still in existence as of 5-1-92); renamed franchise. Had been STOCKTON MARINERS, 1978.

Stockton Producers
California State League (D), 1913; charter franchise. Renamed STOCKTON MILLERS, 1914.

Stockton Terrors
Alternate name for STOCKTON MILLERS, 1898.

STRATFORD, ONTARIO, CANADA

Stratford Poets
Canadian League, 1899; new franchise. Became WOODSTOCK BAINS, mid-1899.

STREATOR, IL

Streator Boosters
Illinois–Missouri League (D), 1913–1914; renamed franchise. Had been STREATOR SPEEDBOYS, 1912. Bi-State League (WI–IL) (D), 1915; charter franchise. Disbanded with league after 1915 season.

Streator Speedboys
Illinois–Missouri League (D), 1912; new franchise. Renamed STREATOR BOOSTERS, 1913.

STROUDSBURG, PA

Stroudsburg Bluebirds
North Atlantic League (D), 1947; renamed franchise. Had been STROUDSBURG POCONOS, 1946. Renamed STROUDSBURG POCONOS, 1948.

Stroudsburg Poconos
Interstate League (D), 1932; charter franchise. Disbanded with league after 1932 season.

Stroudsburg Poconos
North Atlantic League (D), 1946; charter franchise. Renamed STROUDSBURG BLUEBIRDS, 1947.

Stroudsburg Poconos
North Atlantic League (D), 1948–1950; renamed franchise. Had been STROUDSBURG BLUEBIRDS, 1947. Disbanded with league after 1950 season.

SUFFOLK, VA

Suffolk
Southeast Virginia League, 1897; charter franchise. Disbanded with league during 1897 season.

Suffolk Goobers
Virginia League (D), 1948–1951; charter franchise. Disbanded with league after 1951 season.

Suffolk Nuts
Virginia League (C), 1919, (B), 1920; expansion franchise. Renamed SUFFOLK WILDCATS, 1921.

Suffolk Tigers
Virginia League (C), 1914–1915; new franchise. Disbanded after 1915 season.

Suffolk Wildcats
Virginia League (B), 1921; renamed franchise. Had been SUFFOLK NUTS, 1919–1920. Disbanded after 1921 season.

SULPHUR SPRINGS, TX

Sulphur Springs Lions
East Texas League (D), 1924; charter franchise. Renamed SULPHUR SPRINGS SAINTS, 1924.

Sulphur Springs Saints
East Texas League (D), 1924; renamed franchise. Had been SULPHUR SPRINGS LIONS, 1923. Renamed SULPHUR SPRINGS SPARTANS, 1925.

Sulphur Springs Spartans
East Texas League (D), 1925; renamed franchise. Had been SULPHUR SPRINGS SAINTS, 1924. Disbanded after 1925 season.

SUMTER, SC

Sumter Astros
Western Carolinas League (A), 1971; renamed franchise. Had been SUMTER INDIANS, 1970. Disbanded after 1971 season.

Sumter Chicks
Tri-State League (B), 1949–1950; new franchise. Disbanded after 1950 season.

Sumter Flyers
South Atlantic League (A), 1985–1990; new franchise. Became MACON BRAVES, 1991.

Sumter Gamecocks
South Carolina League (D), 1907–1908; charter franchise. Disbanded with league after 1908 season.

Sumter Indians
Western Carolinas League (A), 1970; new franchise. Renamed SUMTER ASTROS, 1971.

SUNBURY, PA

Sunbury
Central Pennsylvania League, 1887; charter franchise. Disbanded after 1887 season.

Sunbury Athletics
Inter-State League (B), 1950; renamed franchise. Had been SUNBURY REDS, 1948–1949. Renamed SUNBURY GIANTS, 1951

Sunbury Giants
Inter-State League (B), 1951–1952; renamed franchise. Had been SUNBURY ATHLETICS, 1950. Disbanded with league after 1952 season.

Sunbury Indians
Inter-State League (C), 1940; renamed franchise. Had been SUNBURY SENATORS, 1939. Became HAGERSTOWN OWLS, 1941.

Sunbury Red Legs
Piedmont League (B), 1955; new franchise. Disbanded with league after 1955 season.

Sunbury Reds
Inter-State League (B), 1948–1949; renamed franchise. Had been SUNBURY YANKEES, 1946–1947.

Renamed SUNBURY ATHLETICS, 1950.

Sunbury Senators
Inter-State League (C), 1939; charter franchise. Renamed SUNBURY INDIANS, 1940.

Sunbury Yankees
Inter-State League (B), 1946–1947; expansion franchise. Renamed SUNBURY REDS, 1948.

SUN CITY, AZ

Sun City Rays
Senior Professional Baseball Association, 1989–1990; expansion franchise. Disbanded with league during 1990–1991 season.

SUPERIOR, NE

Superior Brickmakers
Nebraska State League (D), 1910–1914; charter franchise. Disbanded after 1914 season.

Superior Senators
Nebraska State League (D), 1956–1958; charter franchise. Disbanded after 1958 season.

SUPERIOR, WI
(See also DELUTH, WI)

Superior Blues
Northern League (D), 1933–1942; 1946–1955; charter franchise. Disbanded after 1955 season.

Superior Boys
Twin Ports League (E), 1943; charter franchise. Disbanded during 1943 season.

Superior Longshoremen
Northern League (C), mid-1903; (D), 1904; relocated franchise. Had been ST. CLOUD–BRAINERD, 1903. Disbanded after 1904 season.

Superior Red Sox
Minnesota–Wisconsin League (D), 1910; (C), 1911; charter fran-

chise. Central International League (D), 1912; charter franchise. Northern League (C), 1913–1916; charter franchise. Disbanded with league after 1916 season.

SWEETWATER, TX

Sweetwater Braves
Longhorn League (C), 1952; renamed franchise. Had been SWEETWATER SWATTERS, 1949–1951. Disbanded after 1952 season.

Sweetwater Sports
Longhorn League (D), 1947–1948; charter franchise. Renamed SWEETWATER SWATTERS, 1949.

Sweetwater Spudders
Longhorn League (C), mid-1954; relocated franchise. Had been WICHITA FALLS, 1947–mid-1954. Disbanded after 1954 season.

Sweetwater Swatters
West Texas League (D), mid-1920–1922; relocated franchise. Had been GORMAN, mid-1920. Disbanded with league after 1922 season.

Sweetwater Swatters
Longhorn League (D), 1949–1950; (C), 1951; renamed franchise. Had been SWEETWATER SPORTS, 1947–1948. Renamed SWEETWATER BRAVES, 1952.

SYDNEY, NOVA SCOTIA, CANADA

Sydney Steel Citians
Cape Breton Colliery League (D), 1937–1938; (C), 1939; charter franchise. Disbanded with league after 1939 season.

SYRACUSE, NY

Syracuse
Empire State League (NY), (C), mid-1906; relocated franchise. Had

been PENN YAN, 1906. Disbanded after 1906 season.

Syracuse Chiefs
International League (AA), 1934–1945; (AAA), 1946–1955; new franchise. Eastern League (A), 1956–mid-1957; new franchise. Became ALLENTOWN CHIEFS, mid-1957.

Syracuse Chiefs
International League (AAA), 1961–(still in existence as of 5-1-92); new franchise.

SYRACUSE STARS
Keystone Association, 1877; charter franchise. Disbanded with association after 1877 season.

SYRACUSE STARS
National League, 1879; new franchise. Disbanded during 1879 season.

SYRACUSE STARS
New York State League, 1885; charter franchise. International League, 1886–1887/Association, 1888–1889; charter franchise. American Association, 1890; new franchise. Eastern Association, 1891–mid-1892; charter franchise. Became UTICA, mid-1892.

Syracuse Stars
Eastern League, 1894–1901; new franchise. Became BROCKTON B'S, mid-1901.

Syracuse Stars
New York State League (B), 1902–1917; new franchise. Disbanded with league after 1917 season.

Syracuse Stars
International League (AA), 1918; new franchise. Became HAMILTON TIGERS, mid-1918.

Syracuse Stars
International League (AA), 1920–1927; new franchise. Became ROCHESTER RED WINGS, 1928.

Syracuse Stars
New York–Pennsylvania League (B), 1928–mid-1929; new franchise. Became HAZLETON MOUNTAINEERS, mid-1929.

TABASCO, VILLAHERMOSA, MEXICO
(See also TABASCO, MEXICO)

Tabasco Bananas
Mexican Southwest League (A), 1964–1969; renamed franchise. Renamed TABASCO TIGERS, 1970.

Tabasco Cardinals
Mexican League (AAA), 1974–1975; new franchise. Disbanded after 1975 season.

Tabasco Ganaderos (Cattlemen)
Mexican League (AAA), 1987–(still in existence as of 5-1-92); renamed franchise. Had been TABASCO PLATANEROS (Planters), 1981–1986.

Tabasco Plataneros (Planters)
Mexican League (AAA), 1981–1986; new franchise. Renamed TABASCO CATTLEMEN, 1987.

Tabasco Tigers
Mexican Southwest League (A), 1970; renamed franchise. Had been TABASCO BANANAS, 1964–1969. Disbanded with league after 1970 season.

TACOMA, WA

Tacoma
New Pacific League, 1896; charter franchise. Disbanded with league after 1896 season.

Tacoma
Washington State League (D), 1910; charter franchise. Disbanded after 1910 season.

Tacoma Cubs
Pacific Coast League (AAA), 1966–1971; new franchise. Renamed TACOMA TWINS, 1972.

Tacoma Daisies
Alternate name for TACOMA TIGERS, 1892.

Tacoma Giants
Pacific Coast League (AAA), 1960–1965; relocated franchise. Had been PHOENIX GIANTS, 1958–1959. Became PHOENIX GIANTS, 1966.

Tacoma Tigers (aka Daisies, 1892)
Pacific Northwest League 1890–1892, 1896, 1901; (C), 1902; charter franchise. Pacific National League (A), 1903; charter franchise. Disbanded after 1903 season.

Tacoma Tigers
Pacific Coast League (A), 1904–mid-1905; relocated franchise. Had been SACRAMENTO SACTS, 1903. Became SACRAMENTO SACTS, mid-1905.

Tacoma Tigers
Northwestern League (B), 1906–mid-1917; new franchise. Disbanded with league during 1917 season.

Tacoma Tigers
Pacific Coast International League (B), 1918; charter franchise. Pacific International League (aka International Northwest League) (B), 1919–1921; charter franchise. Western International League (B), 1922; charter franchise. Disbanded with league during 1922 season.

Tacoma Tigers
Western International League (B), 1937–1942; 1946–1951; charter franchise. Disbanded after 1951 season.

Tacoma Tigers
Pacific Coast League (AAA), 1980–(still in existence as of 5-1-92); Reenamed franchise. Had been TACOMA TUGS, 1979.

Tacoma Twins
Pacific Coast League (AAA), 1972–1977; renamed franchise. Had been TACOMA CUBS, 1966–1971. Became TACOMA YANKEES, 1978.

Tacoma Tugs
Pacific Coast League (AAA), 1979; renamed franchise. Had been TACOMA YANKEES, 1978. Became TACOMA TIGERS, 1980.

Tacoma Yankees
Pacific Coast League (AAA), 1978; renamed franchise. Had been TACOMA TWINS, 1973–1977. Became TACOMA TUGS, 1979.

TAFT, TX

Taft Cardinals
Texas Valley League (D), 1938; charter franchise. Disbanded with league after 1938 season.

TALLADEGA, AL

Talladega Indians
Southeastern League (D), mid-1912; relocated franchise. Had been HUNTSVILLE MOUNTAINEERS, 1912. Georgia–Alabama League (C), 1913–1914; charter franchise. Renamed TALLADEGA TIGERS, 1915.

Talladega Indians
Georgia–Alabama Association (D), mid-1928/League (D), 1929–1930; charter franchise. Disbanded with league after 1930 season.

Talladega Tigers
Georgia–Alabama League (C), 1915–1917; renamed franchise. Had been TALLADEGA INDIANS, 1912–1914. Disbanded with league after 1917 season.

TALLAHASSEE, FL

Tallahassee Capitals (aka Caps, 1942)
Georgia–Florida League (D), 1935–1942; charter franchise. Sus-

pended operation after 1942 season, and resumed as TALLAHASSEE PIRATES, 1946.

Tallahassee Caps
Alternate name for TALLAHASSEE CAPITALS, 1942.

Tallahassee Citizens
Alabama–Florida League (D), 1951; charter franchise. Disbanded after 1951 season.

Tallahassee Rebels
Florida International League (B), 1954; new franchise. Disbanded with league during 1954 season.

Tallahassee Pirates
Georgia–Florida League (D), 1946–1950; charter franchise. Disbanded after 1950 season.

TALLASSEE, AL

Tallassee Cardinals
Georgia–Alabama League (D), 1949; renamed franchise. Had been TALLASSEE INDIANS, 1939–1941; 1946–1948. Disbanded after 1949 season.

Tallassee Indians
Alabama–Florida League (D), 1939; new franchise. Tallassee Alabama State League (D), 1940–1941; charter franchise. Georgia–Alabama League (D), 1946–1948; charter franchise. Renamed TALLASSEE CARDINALS, 1949

TAMAQUA, PA

Tamaqua
Atlantic League (D), 1907; charter franchise. Disbanded after 1907 season.

Tamaqua
Anthracite League (D), 1928; charter franchise. Disbanded with league during 1928 season.

Tamaqua Dukes
Inter-State League (D), 1932; charter franchise. Became SLATINGTON, mid-1932.

TAMAULIPAS, MEXICO
(See CIUDAD MANTE, MEXICO; CIUDAD VICTORIA, MEXICO; NUEVO LAREDO, MEXICO; REYNOSA, MEXICO; TAMPICO, MEXICO; VICTORIA, MEXICO)

TAMPA, FL

Tampa
Florida State League, 1892; charter franchise. Disbanded with league after 1892 season.

Tampa Krewes
Southeastern League (B), 1928; new franchise. Renamed TAMPA SMOKERS, 1929.

Tampa Smokers
Florida State League (D), 1919–1920, (C), 1921–1923, (D), mid-1924; charter franchise. Disbanded with league during 1924 season.

Tampa Smokers
Florida State League (D), 1925–1927; charter franchise. Disbanded after 1927 season.

Tampa Smokers
Southeastern League (B), 1929–1930; renamed franchise. Had been TAMPA KREWES, 1928. Disbanded after 1930 season.

Tampa Smokers
Florida International League (C), 1946–1948; (B), 1949–mid-1954; charter franchise. Disbanded during 1954 season.

Tampa Tarpons
Florida State League (D), 1957–1988; new franchise. Disbanded after 1988 season.

Tampa Yankees
Gulf Coast League (R), 1990–(still in existence as of 5-1-92); new franchise.

TAMPICO, TAMAULIPAS, MEXICO

Tampico Alijadores
Mexican Center League (A), 1970; renamed franchise. Had been TAMPICO ALLIGATORS, 1967–1969. Disbanded after 1970 season.

Tampico Alligators
Mexican Center League (A), 1967–1969; new franchise. Renamed TAMPICO ALIJADORES, 1970.

Tampico Dockworkers
Mexican League (AAA), 1971–1972; renamed franchise. Had been TAMPICO ALIJADORES, 1970. Became TAMPICO–MADERA DOCKWORKERS, 1973.

Tampico Astros
Mexican League (AAA), 1983–1985; new franchise. Disbanded after 1985 season.

TAMPICO–MADERA, MEXICO

Tampico–Madero Alijadores (Woodchoppers)
Mexican League (AAA), 1991–(still in existence as of 5-1-92); new franchise.

Tampico–Madera Alijadores
Mexican League (AAA), 1978; renamed franchise. Had been TAMPICO–MADERA DOCKWORKERS, 1973–1977. Became TAMPICO–MADERA DOCKWORKERS, 1979.

Tampico–Madera Dockworkers
Mexican League (AAA), 1973–1977; renamed/relocated franchise. Had been TAMPICO DOCKWORKERS, 1971–1972. Became TAMPICO–MADERA ALIJADORES, 1978.

Tampico–Madera Dockworkers
Mexican League (AAA), 1979; renamed franchise. Had been TAMPICO–MADERA ALIJADORES, 1978. Disbanded after 1979 season.

TAMUIN, MEXICO

Tamuin Cafeteritos
Mexican Center League (A), 1973; new franchise. Disbanded after 1973 season.

TARBORO, NC

Tarboro Athletics
Coastal Plain League (D), 1949–1951; renamed franchise. Had been TARBORO TARS, 1946–1948. Renamed TARBORO TARS, 1952.

Tarboro Cubs
Coastal Plain League (D), 1940; renamed franchise. Had been TARBORO TARS, 1939. Renamed TARBORO ORIOLES, 1941.

Tarboro Orioles
Coastal Plain League (D), 1941; renamed franchise. Had been TARBORO CUBS, 1940. Suspended operations after 1941 season, and resumed as TARBORO TARS, 1946.

Tarboro Serpents
Coastal Plain League (D), 1937–1938; charter franchise. Renamed TARBORO TARS, 1939.

Tarboro Tarbabies
Virginia League (B), mid-1921; relocated franchise. Had been PETERSBURG TRUNKMAKERS, 1921. Disbanded after 1921 season.

Tarboro Tarheels
Virginia–North Carolina League, mid-1901; relocated franchise. Had been NEWPORT NEWS SHIPBUILDERS, 1900–mid-1901. Disbanded with league after 1901 season.

Tarboro Tars
Coastal Plain League (D), 1939; renamed franchise. Had been TARBORO SERPENTS, 1937–1938. Renamed TARBORO CUBS, 1940.

Tarboro Tars
Coastal Plain League (D), 1946–1948; charter franchise. Renamed TARBORO ATHLETICS, 1949.

Tarboro Tars
Coastal Plain League (D), 1952; renamed franchise. Had been TARBORO ATHLETICS, 1949–1951. Disbanded with league after 1952 season.

TAUNTON, MA

Taunton
New England League (B), mid-1905; relocated franchise. Had been LOWELL, 1902–mid-1905. Disbanded after 1905 season.

Taunton
Colonial League (C), 1914–1915; charter franchise. Disbanded with league after 1915 season.

Taunton Blues
New England League (B), 1933; charter franchise. Disbanded with league after 1933 season.

Taunton Herrings
New England League, 1897–1899; new franchise. Disbanded with league after 1899 season.

TAYLOR, TX

Taylor
Middle Texas League (D), mid-1915; relocated franchise. Had been AUSTIN, 1915. Disbanded with league during 1915 season.

TAYLORVILLE, IL

Taylorville Christians
Illinois–Missouri League (D), 1911; charter franchise. Disbanded after 1911 season.

Taylorville Tailors
Eastern Illinois League (D), 1907–1908; charter franchise. Disbanded with league after 1908 season.

Taylorville Taylored Commies
Northern Association of Baseball (C), mid-1910; (D), mid-1910; relocated franchise. Had been DECATUR COMMIES, 1901–mid-1910. Became DECATUR COMMIES, mid-1910.

TECUMSEH, MI

Tecumseh
Southern Michigan League (D), 1906–1908; charter franchise. Disbanded after 1908 season.

TEMPLE, TX

Temple Boll Weevils
Texas League (D), 1905; (C), 1906–1907; expansion franchise. Became SHREVEPORT PIRATES, 1908.

Temple Eagles
Big State League (B), 1949–1954; new franchise. Disbanded after 1954 season.

Temple Governors
Middle Texas League (D), 1915; renamed franchise. Had been TEMPLE TIGERS, mid-1914. Central Texas League (D), mid-1916; charter franchise. Disbanded during 1916 season.

Temple Governors
Central Texas League (D), mid-1916–mid-1917; charter franchise. Became CORSICANA OILERS, mid-1917.

Temple Redlegs
Big State League (B), mid-1957; relocated franchise. Had been PORT ARTHUR REDLEGS, 1957. Disbanded with league after 1957 season.

Temple Surgeons
Texas Association (D), 1924–1926; new franchise. Disbanded with league after 1926 season.

Temple Tigers
Middle Texas League (D), mid-1914; charter franchise. Renamed TEMPLE GOVERNORS, 1915.

TEOCALTICHE, MEXICO

Teocaltiche Chapulines
Mexican Center League (A), 1977–1978; new franchise. Disbanded after 1978 season.

TERRE HAUTE, IN

Terre Haute
Northwestern League, 1884; new franchise. Disbanded with league after 1884 season.

Terre Haute
Central League, 1897; charter franchise. Disbanded with league after 1897 season.

Terre Haute Browns
Illinois–Iowa–League (B), 1919–1920; charter franchise. Renamed TERRE HAUTE TOTS, 1921.

Terre Haute Coals
Illinois–Iowa–League (B), 1923; renamed franchise. Had been TERRE HAUTE TOTS, 1921–1922. Became TERRE HAUTE TOTS, 1924.

Terre Haute Highlanders
Central League (D), 1915–1916; renamed franchise. Had been TERRE HAUTE TERRE–IRS. Disbanded after 1916 season.

Terre Haute Hoosiers
Central Inter-State League, mid-1888; relocated franchise. Had been CRAWFORDSVILLE HOOSIERS, 1888. Illinois–Indiana League, 1889; charter franchise. Western Inter-State League, 1890; charter franchise.

Terre Haute Hoosiers
Western Inter-State League, 1895; charter franchise. Disbanded with league after 1895 season.

Terre Haute Hottentots
Northwestern League, 1891; charter franchise. Illinois–Iowa League, 1892; new franchise. Disbanded with league after 1892 season.

Terre Haute Hottentots
Indiana–Illinois League, 1899; charter franchise. Central League, 1900; charter franchise. Illinois–Iowa–Indiana League, 1901; (D), 1902; charter franchise. Central League (D), 1903–1909; renamed franchise. Renamed TERRE HAUTE STAGS, 1910.

Terre Haute Huts
Three I League (B), 1956; renamed franchise. Had been TERRE HAUTE TIGERS, 1955. Disbanded after 1956 season.

Terre Haute Miners
Central League (D), 1911; renamed franchise. Had been TERRE HAUTE STAGS, 1910. Renamed TERRE HAUTE TERRE–IRS, 1912.

Terre Haute Phillies
Three I League (B), 1946–1954; charter franchise. Renamed TERRE HAUTE TIGERS, 1955.

Terre Haute Stags
Central League (D), 1910; renamed franchise. Had been TERRE HAUTE HOTTENTOTS, 1899–1909. Renamed TERRE HAUTE MINERS, 1911.

Terre Haute Terre–irs
Central League (D), 1912–1914; renamed franchise. Had been TERRE HAUTE MINERS, 1911. Renamed TERRE HAUTE HIGHLANDERS, 1915.

Terre Haute Terriers
Western League, 1895; relocated franchise. Had been TOLEDO SWAMP ANGELS, 1895. Disbanded after 1895 season.

Terre Haute Tigers
Three I League (B), 1955; renamed franchise. Had been TERRE HAUTE PHILLIES, 1946–1954. Renamed TERRE HAUTE HUTS, 1956.

Terre Haute Tots
Illinois–Iowa–League (B), 1921–1922; renamed franchise. Had been TERRE HAUTE BROWNS, 1919–1920. Renamed TERRE HAUTE COALS, 1923.

Terre Haute Tots
Illinois–Iowa–Indiana League (B), 1924–1932; renamed franchise. Had been TERRE HAUTE COALS, 1923. Disbanded with league after 1932 season.

Terre Haute Tots
Three I League (B), 1935; charter franchise. Disbanded during 1937 season.

Terre Haute Tots
Three I League (B), 1937; charter franchise. Disbanded during 1937 season.

TERRELL, TX

Terrell
Central Texas League (D), 1916/Trolley League (D), 1915; new franchise. Disbanded during 1916 season.

Terrell Red Stockings
North Texas League (D), 1907; charter franchise. Disbanded with league after 1907 season.

Terrell Terrors
Texas Association (D), 1925–1926; new franchise. Disbanded with league after 1926 season.

TEXARKANA, TX

Texarkana
Southwestern League, 1898; charter franchise. Disbanded with league with 1898 season.

Texarkana
Texas League (D), mid-1902; relocated franchise. Had been SHERMAN–DENISON STUDENTS, 1902. Disbanded during 1902 season.

Texarkana
Arkansas–Texas League (D), 1906; new franchise. Disbanded with league during 1906 season.

Texarkana
Arkansas State League (D), 1909; new franchise. Disbanded with league after 1909 season.

Texarkana Bears
East Texas League (C), 1946; charter franchise. Big State League (B), 1947–1953; charter franchise. Disbanded after 1953 season.

Texarkana Liners
East Texas League (C), 1937–1940; new franchise. Cotton States League (C), 1941; new franchise. Disbanded after 1941 season.

Texarkana Nobles
Arkansas State League, 1897; charter franchise. Disbanded with league after 1897 season.

Texarkana Tigers
South Central League (D), 1912; charter franchise. Texas–Oklahoma League (D), 1913–1914; new franchise. Disbanded with league after 1914 season.

Texarkana Twins
East Texas League (D), 1924–1926; new franchise. Lone Star League (D), 1927–1929; charter franchise. Disbanded with league during 1929 season.

TEXAS CITY, TX

Texas City Exporters
Big State League (B), mid-1956; relocated franchise. Had been BEAUMONT ROUGHNECKS, 1950–mid-1956. Became BEAUMONT ROUGHNECKS, mid-1956.

Texas City Hubbers
Big State League (B), mid-1956; relocated franchise. Had been LUBBOCK HUBBERS, 1946–mid-1956. Disbanded during 1956 season.

Texas City Pilots
Evangeline League (C), 1954; expansion franchise. Had been TEXAS CITY TEXANS, 1951–1953. Became THIBODAUX PILOTS, mid-1954.

Texas City Stars
Lone Star League (A), 1977; charter franchise. Disbanded with league after 1977 season.

Texas City Texans
Gulf Coast League (B), 1952–1953; relocated franchise. Had also represented LaMarque, Tx, 1951. Became TEXAS CITY PILOTS, 1954.

Texas City Texans
Big State League (B), 1955; renamed franchise. Disbanded after 1956 season.

TEXAS CITY–LaMARQUE, TX

Texas City Texans
Gulf Coast League (B), 1951; new franchise. Only represented Texas City, 1952.

THETFORD MINES, QUEBEC, CANADA

Thetford Mines Miners
Provincial League (C), 1953–1955; new franchise. Disbanded with league after 1955 season.

Thetford Mines Miners
Eastern League (AA), 1975; renamed franchise. Had been THETFORD MINES PIRATES, 1974. Disbanded after 1975 season.

Thetford Mines Pirates
Eastern League (AA), 1974; new franchise. Renamed THETFORD MINES MINERS, 1975.

THIBODAUX, LA

Thibodaux Giants
Evangeline League (D), 1946–1953; charter franchise. Disbanded after 1953 season.

Thibodaux Pilots
Evangeline League (C), mid-1954; relocated franchise. Had been TEXAS CITY PILOTS, 1954. Disbanded after 1954 season.

Thibodaux Senators
Evangeline League (C), 1956–1957; expansion franchise. Disbanded with league after 1957 season.

THOMASVILLE, GA

Thomasville Dodgers
Georgia–Florida League (D), 1953–1958; renamed franchise. Disbanded with league after 1958 season.

Thomasville Hornets
Empire State League (Ga) (D), 1913; charter franchise. Georgia State League (D), 1914–1915; charter franchise. Disbanded with league after 1915 season.

Thomasville Lookouts
Georgia–Florida League, 1941; renamed franchise. Had been THOMASVILLE TOURISTS, 1940. Suspended operations with league after 1942 season, and resumed as THOMASVILLE TIGERS, 1946.

Thomasville Orioles
Georgia–Florida League (D), 1935–1939; charter franchise. Renamed THOMASVILLE TOURISTS, 1940.

Thomasville Tigers
Georgia–Florida League (D), 1946–1950; charter franchise. Disbanded after 1950 season.

Thomasville Tigers
Georgia–Florida League (D), 1962; (A), 1963; charter franchise. Disbanded with league after 1963 season.

Thomasville Tomcats
Georgia–Florida League (D), 1952; new franchise. Renamed THOMASVILLE DODGERS, 1953.

Thomasville Tourists
Georgia–Florida League, 1940; renamed franchise. Had been THOMASVILLE ORIOLES, 1935–1939. Renamed THOMASVILLE LOOKOUTS, 1941.

THOMASVILLE, NC

Thomasville Chairmakers
North Carolina State League (D), 1937; charter franchise. Renamed THOMASVILLE ORIOLES, 1938.

Thomasville Dodgers
North Carolina State League (D), 1945–1947; charter franchise. Became THOMASVILLE–HIGH POINT HI-TOMS, 1948.

Thomasville Hi-Toms
Western Carolinas League (A), 1965–1966; new franchise. Disbanded after 1966 season.

Thomasville Orioles
North Carolina State League (D), 1938; renamed franchise. Renamed THOMASVILLE TOMMIES, 1939.

Thomasville Tommies
North Carolina State League (D), 1937–1942; charter franchise. Had been THOMASVILLE ORIOLES, 1938. Disbanded after 1942 season.

THOMASVILLE,– HIGH POINT, NC
(See also HIGH POINT, NC)

Thomasville–High Point Hi-Toms
North Carolina State League (D), 1948–1952; renamed franchise. Had been THOMASVILLE DODGERS, 1945–1947. Tar Heel League (D), 1953; charter franchise. Carolina League (B), 1954–1958; new franchise. Disbanded after 1958 season.

Thomasville–High Point Hi-Toms
Carolinas League (A), 1968–1969; new franchise. Disbanded after 1969 season.

THOMSON, GA

Thomson Orioles
Georgia State League (D), 1956; new franchise. Disbanded with league after 1956 season.

THREE RIVERS, QUEBEC, CANADA

Three Rivers Eagles
Eastern League (AA), 1971–1977; new franchise. Disbanded after 1977 season.

Three Rivers Foxes
Quebec Provincial League (B), 1940; charter franchise. Became THREE RIVERS RENARDS, 1941.

Three Rivers Foxes
Canadian–American League (C), 1942; renamed franchise. Had been THREE RIVERS RENARDS, 1941. Suspended operations after 1942 season, and rejoined as THREE RIVERS ROYALS, 1946.

Three Rivers Phillies
Provincial League (C), 1954; renamed franchise. Had been THREE RIVERS ROYALS, 1952–1953. Disbanded with league after 1955 season.

Three Rivers Renards
Canadian–American League (C), 1941; new franchise. Renamed THREE RIVERS FOXES, 1942.

Three Rivers Royals
Canadian–American League (C), 1946–1950; charter franchise. Provincial League (C), 1951; expansion franchise. Renamed THREE RIVERS YANKEES, 1952.

Three Rivers Trios
Eastern Canada League (B), 1922–mid-1923; charter franchise. Became MONTREAL ROYALS, mid-1923.

Three Rivers Yankees
Provincial League (C), 1952–1953; renamed franchise. Had been THREE RIVERS ROYALS, 1946–1950. Renamed THREE RIVERS PHILLIES, 1954.

TIFFIN, OH

Tiffin
Ohio State League, 1889; charter franchise. Disbanded during 1889 season.

Tiffin Mud Hens
Ohio State League (D), 1936–1941; charter franchise. Disbanded with league after 1941 season.

TIFTON, GA

Tifton Blue Sox
Georgia State League (D), 1949–1950; new franchise. Georgia–Florida League (D), 1951–1953; new franchise. Renamed TIFTON INDIANS, 1954.

Tifton Blue Sox
Georgia–Florida League (D), 1955; renamed franchise. Had been TIFTON INDIANS, 1964. Renamed TIFTON PHILLIES, 1956.

Tifton Indians
Georgia–Florida League (D), 1954; renamed franchise. Had been

TIFTON BLUE SOX, 1949–1953. Renamed TIFTON BLUE SOX, 1955.

Tifton Phillies
Georgia–Florida League (D), 1956; renamed franchise. Had been TIFTON BLUE SOX, 1955. Disbanded after 1956 season.

Tifton Tifters
Dixie League (D), 1917; expansion franchise. Disbanded with league during 1917 season.

TIJUANA, BAJA CALIFORNIA, MEXICO

Tijuana Potros (Colts)
Sunset League (C), mid-1949–1950; relocated franchise. Had been SALINAS COLTS, 1949. Southwest International League (C), 1951–1952; charter franchise. Disbanded with league after 1952 season.

Tijuana Potros (Colts)
Arizona–Mexico League (C), 1956; new franchise. Disbanded after 1956 season.

TOLEDO, OH

Toledo Black Pirates
International Association, 1889; new franchise. American Association, 1890; new franchise. Disbanded after 1890 season.

Toledo Black Pirates
Western League, 1892; expansion franchise. Disbanded with league during 1892 season.

Toledo Blue Stockings
Northwestern League, 1883; charter franchise. American Association, 1884; charter franchise. Disbanded after 1884 season.

TOLEDO CRAWFORDS
Negro American League, mid-1939; new franchise. Became INDIANAPOLIS CRAWFORDS, 1940.

Toledo Iron Men
American Association (AA), 1916–1918; new franchise. Renamed TOLEDO MUD HENS, 1919.

Toledo Maumees
Tri-State League, 1888; charter franchise. Disbanded with league after 1888 season.

Toledo Mud Hens (aka Swamp Angels, 1901)
Western League, mid-1896; renamed franchise. Had been TOLEDO SWAMP ANGELS, 1895–mid-1896. Inter-State League, 1896–1900; charter franchise. Western Association, 1901; charter franchise. American Association (A), 1902–1907; (AA), 1908–1913; charter franchise. Southern Michigan League (C), 1914; new franchise. Disbanded after 1914 season.

Toledo Mud Hens
American Association (AA), 1919–1945; (AAA), 1946–1952; renamed franchise. Had been TOLEDO IRON MEN, 1916–1918. Renamed TOLEDO SOX, 1953.

Toledo Mud Hens
International League (AAA), 1965–(still in existence as of 5-1-92); new franchise.

Toledo Sox
American Association (AAA), 1953–1955; renamed franchise. Had been TOLEDO MUD HENS, 1919–1952. Disbanded after 1955 season.

Toledo Swamp Angels
Alternate name for TOLEDO MUD HENS, 1901.

Toledo Swamp Angels (aka Terriers)
Western League, 1895–mid-1896; renamed franchise. Had been TOLEDO WHITE STOCKINGS, 1894. Re-

named TOLEDO MUD HENS, mid-1896.

Toledo Terriers
Alternate name for TOLEDO SWAMP ANGELS, 1895.

Toledo Toledos
Western League, 1885; charter franchise. Disbanded during 1885 season.

Toledo White Stockings
Western League, 1894; new franchise. Renamed TOLEDO SWAMP ANGELS, 1895

TOLUCA, MEXICO

Toluca Osos Negros (Black Bears)
Mexican League (AAA), 1980; new franchise. Disbanded after 1980 season.

Toluca Osos Negros (Black Bears)
Mexican League (AAA), 1984; new franchise. Disbanded after 1984 season.

TOPEKA, KS

Topeka
Kansas State League, 1895–1896; charter franchise. Disbanded with league after 1896 season.

Topeka Athletics
Western League, 1886; charter franchise. Renamed TOPEKA GOLDEN GIANTS, 1887.

Topeka Giants
Kansas State League, 1897–1898; renamed franchise. Had been TOPEKA MAROONS, 1896. Disbanded with league after 1898 season.

Topeka Golden Giants
Western League, 1887; renamed franchise. Had been TOPEKA ATHLETICS, 1886. Disbanded after 1887 season.

Topeka Hawks
Western League (A), 1956–1958; expansion franchise. Three I League (B), 1959; expansion franchise. Renamed TOPEKA REDS, 1960.

Topeka Jayhawks (aka Kaws, 1911)
Western League (A), 1909–1915; expansion franchise. Renamed TOPEKA SAVAGES, 1916.

Topeka Jayhawks
Western Association (B), 1927; (C), mid-1927–1928; relocated franchise. Had been JOPLIN OZARKS, 1926. Disbanded after 1928 season.

Topeka Jayhawks
Western Association (C), mid-1932; relocated franchise. Had been JOPLIN MINERS, 1926–mid-1932. Disbanded with association after 1932 season.

Topeka Kaw-nees
Western League (A), 1918; new franchise. Became HUTCHINSON WHEATSHOCKERS, mid-1918.

Topeka Kaws
Alternate name for TOPEKA JAYHAWKS, 1911.

Topeka Kaws
Southwestern League (C), 1922–1923; new franchise. Disbanded after 1923 season.

Topeka Maroons
Kansas State League, 1896; charter franchise. Renamed TOPEKA GIANTS, 1895.

Topeka Owls
Western Association (C), 1939–1942; 1946–1954; new franchise. Disbanded with league after 1954 season.

Topeka Populists
Western League, 1893; new franchise. Disbanded with league after 1893 season.

Topeka Reds
Three I League (B), 1960–1961; renamed franchise. Had been TOPEKA HAWKS, 1956–1959. Disbanded with league after 1961 season.

Topeka Saints
Missouri Valley League (D), 1904; new franchise. Disbanded after 1904 season.

Topeka Savages
Western League (A), 1916; renamed franchise. Had been TOPEKA JAYHAWKS, 1909–1915. Disbanded after 1916 season.

Topeka Senators
Western Association (C), 1924; new franchise. Southwestern League (D), 1925–1926; new franchise. Disbanded with league after 1926 season.

Topeka Senators
Western League (A), 1929–1931; new franchise. Disbanded after 1931 season.

Topeka Senators
Western League (A), 1933–1934; new franchise. Disbanded after 1934 season.

Topeka White Sox
Western Association (D), 1905; (C), 1906–1908; charter franchise. Disbanded after 1908 season.

TORONTO, ONTARIO, CANADA

Toronto
Ontario League, 1884; charter franchise. Canadian League, 1885; charter franchise.

Toronto Beavers
Canadian League (C), 1914; (B), mid-1914; new franchise. Disbanded after 1914 season.

TORONTO BLUE JAYS
American League, 1977–(still in existence as of 5-1-92); expansion franchise.

Toronto Canadians (aka Red Stockings)
Eastern League, 1895; new franchise. Renamed TORONTO CANUCKS, 1896.

Toronto Canucks
International League, 1886–1887, 1890/Association, 1888–1889; charter franchise. Disbanded with league after 1890 season.

Toronto Canucks
Eastern League, 1896; renamed franchise. Had been TORONTO CANUCKS, 1895. Became ALBANY SENATORS, mid-1896.

Toronto Canucks
Eastern League, mid-1896–1900; relocated franchise. Had been ALBANY SENATORS, mid-1896. Renamed TORONTO ROYALS, 1901.

Toronto Leafs
Alternate name for TORONTO MAPLE LEAFS.

Toronto Maple Leafs (aka Leafs)
Eastern League, (A), 1902–1907; (AA), 1908–1911; renamed franchise. (New) International League (AA), 1912–1945; (AAA), 1946–1967; charter franchise. Disbanded after 1967 season.

Toronto Red Stockings
Alternate name for TORONTO CANADIANS, 1895.

Toronto Royals
Eastern League, 1901; renamed franchise. Had been TORONTO CANUCKS, 1896–1900. Renamed TORONTO MAPLE LEAFS, 1902.

TORREON LAGUNA–ESPERANZA, MEXICO
(See also GOMEZ PALACIO, MEXICO)

Torreon Laguna–Esperanza Laguneros (Lagooners)
Mexican National League (B), 1946; charter franchise. Disbanded during 1946 season.

Torreon Laguna–Esperanza Lagooners (Lagooners)
Mexican League (AAA), 1991– (still in existence as of 5-1-92); new franchise.

TORRINGTON, CT

Torrington
Naugatuck Valley League, 1898; charter franchise. Disbanded with league after 1898 season.

Torrington Braves
Colonial League (B), 1950; new franchise. Disbanded with league during 1950 season.

Torrington Demons
Connecticut League, 1897; charter franchise. Disbanded with league after 1897 season.

TRAVERSE CITY, MI

Traverse City Resorters
West Michigan League (D), 1910; charter franchise. Michigan State League (D), 1911–1914; charter franchise. Disbanded during 1914 season.

TRENTON, NJ

Trenton
Inter-State Association, 1883; charter franchise. Eastern League, 1884–mid-1885; charter franchise. Became JERSEY CITY JERSEYS, mid-1885.

Trenton
New Jersey State, 1897; charter franchise. Disbanded with league after 1897 season.

Trenton Capitols
Alternate name for TRENTON SENATORS, 1936–1937.

Trenton Cuban Giants
Middle States League, 1889; charter franchise. Became HOBOKEN CUBAN GIANTS, mid-1889.

Trenton Giants
Inter-State League (B), 1946–1950; renamed franchise. Had been TRENTON SPARTANS, 1945. Disbanded after 1950 season.

Trenton Packers
Inter-State League (B), 1942–1944; renamed franchise. Had been TRENTON SENATORS, 1939–1941. Renamed TRENTON SPARTANS, 1945.

Trenton Senators (aka Capitols)
New York–Pennsylvania League (A), mid-1936–1937; relocated franchise. Had been YORK WHITE ROSES, 1936. Eastern League (A), 1938; charter franchise. Inter-State League (C), 1939–1941; charter franchise. Renamed TRENTON PACKERS, 1942.

Trenton Spartans
Inter-State League (B), 1945; renamed franchise. Had been TRENTON PACKERS, 1942–1944. Renamed TRENTON GIANTS, 1946.

Trenton Tigers
Tri-State League (B), 1907–1914; charter franchise. Disbanded with league after 1914 season.

TRENTON, TN
(See also MILAN, TN)

Trenton Reds
KITTY League (D), 1922; charter franchise. Disbanded after 1922 season.

TROY, AL

Troy Tigers
Alabama State League (D), 1948–1949; renamed franchise. Had been TROY TROJANS, 1946–1947. Disbanded after 1949 season.

Troy Trojans
Alabama–Florida League (D), 1936–1939; charter franchise. Alabama State League (D), 1940–1941; charter franchise. Disbanded with league after 1941 season.

Troy Trojans
Alabama State League (D), 1946–1947; charter franchise. Renamed TROY TIGERS, 1948.

TROY, NY

HAYMAKERS OF TROY
National Association, 1871–1872; charter franchise. Disbanded after 1872 season.

Troy
League Alliance, 1877; charter franchise. Disbanded with alliance after 1877 season.

Troy Collars
New York State League, 1895; new franchise. Disbanded after 1895 season.

TROY TROJANS
National League, 1879–1882; new franchise. Became NEW YORK GOTHAMS, 1883.

Troy Trojans
International Association, 1888; charter franchise. Disbanded after 1888 season.

Troy Trojans
Hudson River League, 1886; charter franchise. Disbanded with league during 1886 season.

Troy Trojans
New York State League, 1890; new franchise. Eastern Association, 1891/Eastern League, 1892–1893; charter franchise. Renamed TROY WASHERWOMEN, 1894.

Troy Trojans
New York State League, 1900–1901, (B), 1902–1916; new franchise. Had been TROY WASHERWOMEN, 1899. Became HARRISBURG ISLANDERS, mid-1916.

Troy Washerwomen
Eastern League, 1894; renamed franchise. Had been TROY TROJANS, 1890–1893. Became SCRANTON QUAKERS, mid-1894.

Troy Washerwomen
New York State League, mid-1899; relocated franchise. Had been AUBURN PRISONERS, 1899. Renamed TROY TROJANS, 1900.

TUCSON, AZ

Tucson Baby Seals
Alternate name for TUCSON COWBOYS, 1937.

Tucson Cowboys
Arizona State League (D), 1928–1930; charter franchise. Disbanded with league after 1930 season.

Tucson Cowboys (aka Baby Seals, 1937)
Arizona–Texas League (D), 1937–1939; (C), 1940–1941, 1947–1950; charter franchise. Southwest International League (C), 1951; charter franchise. Arizona–Texas League (D), 1952–1954; charter franchise. Arizona–Mexico League (C), 1955–1958; charter franchise. Disbanded after 1958 season.

Tucson Lizards
Arizona–Texas League (D), 1932; renamed franchise. Had been TUCSON MISSION BELLS, 1931. Disbanded with league during 1932 season.

Tucson Mission Bells
Arizona–Texas League (D), 1931; charter franchise. Renamed TUCSON LIZARDS, 1932.

Tucson Old Pueblos
Rio Grande Valley Association (D), 1915; charter franchise. Disbanded with association after 1915 season.

Tucson Toros
Pacific Coast League (AAA), 1969–(still in existence as of 5-1-92); new franchise.

TULARE, CA

Tulare Merchants
San Joaquin Valley League (B), 1910; charter franchise. Disbanded with league after 1910 season.

TULSA, OK

Tulsa Drillers
Texas League (AA), 1977–(still in existence as of 5-1-92); relocated franchise. Had been LAFAYETTE DRILLERS, 1975–1976.

Tulsa Gassers
Missouri Valley League (D), 1905; charter franchise. Disbanded with league after 1905 season.

Tulsa Oilers
South Central League (D), 1906; charter franchise. OAK League (D), 1907; charter franchise. Oklahoma–Kansas League (D), 1908; charter franchise. Disbanded with league after 1908 season.

Tulsa Oilers
Western Association (D), mid-1910; (C), 1911; relocated franchise. Had been GUTHRIE SENATORS, 1910. Disbanded with league after 1911 season.

Tulsa Oilers
Western League (A), 1919–1929; new franchise. Disbanded after 1929 season.

Tulsa Oilers
Western League (A), 1932; new franchise. Texas League (A), 1933–1935; (A1), 1936–1942; (AA), 1946–1965; new franchise. Pacific Coast League (AAA), 1966–1968; new franchise. American Association (AAA), 1969–

1976; charter franchise. Became NEW ORLEANS PELICANS, 1977.

Tulsa Producers
Western Association (A), 1914–1917; new franchise. Disbanded after 1917 season.

Tulsa Terrors
Oklahoma State League (D), 1912; charter franchise. Disbanded with league during 1912 season.

TUPELO, MS

Tupelo Wolves
Tri-State League (D), 1925–1926; charter franchise. Disbanded with league after 1926 season.

TUSCUMBIA, AL
(See FLORENCE, AL; SHEFFIELD, AL)

TWIN FALLS, ID

Magic Valley Cowboys
Pioneer League (C), 1952–1958; renamed franchise. Had been TWIN VALLEY COWBOYS, 1939–1942; 1946–1951. Disbanded after 1958 season.

Magic Valley Cowboys
Pioneer League (C), 1961–1962; (A), 1963; (R), 1964–1970; new franchise. Renamed TWIN FALLS COWBOYS, 1971.

Twin Falls Bruins
Utah–Idaho League (D), 1926–1928; charter franchise. Disbanded during 1928 season.

Twin Falls Cowboys
Pioneer League (R), 1971; renamed franchise. Had been MAGIC VALLEY COWBOYS, 1968–1970. Disbanded after 1971 season.

Twin Falls Cowboys
Pioneer League (C), 1939–1942; 1946–1951; charter franchise. Renamed MAGIC VALLEY COWBOYS, 1952.

TYLER, TX

Tyler
South Central League (D), 1912; charter franchise. Disbanded with league after 1912 season.

Tyler East Texans
Big State League (B), 1951–1955; new franchise. Disbanded after 1955 season.

Tyler Governors
Dixie League (C), 1933; charter franchise. West Dixie League (D), 1934; charter franchise. Renamed TYLER TROJANS, 1935.

Tyler Sports
Texas League (A), mid-1932; relocated franchise. Had been SHREVEPORT SPORTS, 1925–mid-1932. Disbanded after 1932 season.

Tyler Trojans
East Texas League (D), 1924–1926; new franchise. Lone Star League (D), 1927–mid-1929; charter franchise. Disbanded with league during 1929 season.

Tyler Trojans
East Texas League (D), 1931; charter franchise. Disbanded during 1931 season.

Tyler Trojans
West Dixie League (D), 1935; renamed franchise. Had been TYLER GOVERNORS, 1934. East Texas League (C), 1936–1940; 1946; charter franchise. Lone Star League (C), 1947; charter franchise. East Texas League (C), 1949–1950; charter franchise. Disbanded with league after 1950 season.

UNION CITY, TN

Union City Dodgers
KITTY League (D), 1954–1955; renamed franchise. Had been UNION CITY GREYHOUNDS, 1935–

1942; 1946–1953. Disbanded with league after 1955 season.

Union City Greyhounds
KITTY League (D), 1935–1942; 1946–1953; charter franchise. Renamed UNION CITY DODGERS, 1954.

UNION LAGUNA, MEXICO
(See also GOMEZ PALACIO, MEXICO)

Union Laguna Algodoneros (Cottonmen)
Mexican League (AAA), 1975–1979; new franchise. Renamed UNION LAGUNA WHITE DEVILS, 1980.

Union Laguna Cotton Pickers
Mexican League (AAA), 1989–(still in existence as of 5-1-92); renamed franchise. Had been UNION LAGUNA WHITE DEVILS, 1980–1988.

Union Laguna White Devils
Mexican League (AAA), 1980–1988; renamed franchise. Had been UNION LAGUNA ALGODONEROS (Cottonmen), 1975–1979. Renamed UNION LAGUNA COTTON PICKERS, 1989.

UNION SPRINGS, AL

Union Springs Redbirds
Alabama–Florida League (D), 1938; renamed franchise. Had been UNION SPRINGS SPRINGERS, 1936–1937. Disbanded with league after 1938 season.

Union Springs Springers
Alabama–Florida League (D), 1936–1937; charter franchise. Renamed UNION SPRINGS REDBIRDS, 1938

UNIONTOWN, PA

Uniontown
POM League (D), 1906–1907; charter franchise. Pennsylvania–

West Virginia League (D), 1908–1909; charter franchise. Disbanded with league after 1909 season.

Uniontown
Pennsylvania–West Virginia League (D), 1914; charter franchise. Disbanded with league after 1914 season.

Uniontown Coal Barons
Middle Atlantic League (C), 1947–1949; new franchise. Disbanded after 1949 season.

Uniontown Cokers
Middle Atlantic League (D), 1926; expansion franchise. Disbanded after 1926 season.

URBANA, IL
(See CHAMPAIGN, IL)

URIANGATO, MEXICO

Uriangato
Mexican Center League (A), 1975; new franchise. Disbanded with league after 1975 season.

UTICA, NY

Utica
National Association, 1879; charter franchise. Disbanded with association after 1879 season.

Utica
Eastern League, 1892; relocated franchise. Had been SYRACUSE STARS, 1891–mid-1892. Disbanded after 1892 season.

Utica Asylums
Alternate name for UTICA PENT-UPS, 1900.

Utica Blue Jays
New York–Pennsylvania League (A), 1977–1980; new franchise. Renamed UTICA BLUE SOX, 1981.

Utica Blue Sox
Eastern League (A), mid-1944–1950; renamed franchise. Had been

UTICA BRAVES, 1939–mid-1944. Became SCHENECTADY BLUE JAYS, 1951.

Utica Blue Sox
New York–Pennsylvania League (A), 1981–(still in existence as of 5-1-92); renamed franchise. Had been UTICA BLUE JAYS, 1977–1980.

Utica Braves
Canadian–American League (C), 1939–1942; relocated franchise. Had been AUBURN BOULEYS, 1938. Eastern League (A), 1943–mid-1944; new franchise. Renamed UTICA BLUE SOX, mid-1944.

Utica Indians
Alternate name for UTICA UTES, 1911.

Utica Pent-ups
New York State League, 1889–1890; new franchise. Disbanded with league after 1890 season.

Utica Pent-ups
New York State League, 1885; charter franchise. International League, 1886–mid-1887; charter franchise. Became WILKES-BARRE COAL BARONS, mid-1887.

Utica Pent-ups (aka Asylums)
New York State League, 1898–1901; (B), 1902–1909; new franchise. Renamed UTICA UTES, 1910.

Utica Utes
International Association, 1878; charter franchise. Disbanded after 1878 season.

Utica Utes (aka Indians, 1911)
New York State League, 1910–1917; renamed franchise. Had been UTICA PENT-UPS, 1898–1909. Disbanded with league after 1917 season.

Utica Utes
New York–Pennsylvania League (B), 1924; new franchise. Became ONEONTA, mid-1924 season.

VALDOSTA, GA

Valdosta Browns
Georgia–Florida League (D), 1953; renamed franchise. Had been VALDOSTA DODGERS, 1949–1952. Renamed VALDOSTA TIGERS, 1954.

Valdosta Dodgers
Georgia–Florida League (D), 1946–1947; charter franchise. Renamed VALDOSTA PACKERS, 1948.

Valdosta Dodgers
Georgia–Florida League (D), 1949–1952; renamed franchise. Had been VALDOSTA PACKERS, 1948. Renamed VALDOSTA BROWNS, 1953.

Valdosta Millionaires
Empire State League (GA), (D), 1913; charter franchise. Georgia State League (D), 1914–1915; charter franchise. Dixie League (D), mid-1916; charter franchise. Disbanded after 1916 season.

Valdosta Packers
Georgia–Florida League (D), 1948; renamed franchise. Had been VALDOSTA DODGERS, 1946–1947. Renamed VALDOSTA DODGERS, 1949.

Valdosta Stars
Georgia State League (D), 1906; charter franchise. Disbanded during 1906 season.

Valdosta Tigers
Georgia–Florida League (D), 1954–1958; renamed franchise. Had been VALDOSTA BROWNS, 1953. Disbanded with league after 1958 season.

Valdosta Trojans
Georgia–Florida League (D), 1939–1942; expansion franchise. Suspended operations with league after 1942 season, and rejoined as VALDOSTA DODGERS when league resumed in 1946.

VALLEJO, CA

Vallejo
Central California Baseball League (D), 1910–1911; charter franchise. Disbanded with league after 1911 season.

Vallejo Chiefs
Far West League (D), 1949; new franchise. Disbanded after 1949 season.

Vallejo Marines
California State League (D), 1913; charter franchise. Became WATSONVILLE PIPPINS, mid-1913.

VALLEY CITY, ND

Valley City
Dakota League (D), mid-1923; relocated franchise. Had been NEW ROCKFORD–CARRINGTON TWINS, 1923. Disbanded with league after 1923 season.

Valley City Hi-Liners
Dakota League (D), 1922; charter franchise. Became BISMARCK CAPITALS, mid-1922.

VALLEYFIELD, QUEBEC, CANADA

Valleyfield
Eastern Canada League (B), 1922; charter franchise. Became CAP DE LA MADELEINE MADCAPS, mid-1922.

VAN BUREN, AR
(See FORT SMITH, AR)

VANCOUVER, BRITISH COLUMBIA, CANADA
(See also VANCOUVER, WA)

Vancouver
Oregon State League (D), 1904; charter franchise. Became ALBANY ROLLERS, mid-1904.

Vancouver Beavers
Northwestern League (B), 1908–1911; renamed franchise. Had been VANCOUVER HORSE DOCTORS, 1905–1907. Renamed VANCOUVER CHAMPIONS, 1912.

Vancouver Beavers
Northwestern League (B), 1914–1917; renamed franchise. Had been VANCOUVER BEES, 1913. Disbanded after 1917 season.

Vancouver Beavers
Pacific International League (aka International Northwest League) (B), 1919–1922; charter franchise. Disbanded with league during 1922 season.

Vancouver Bees
Northwestern League (B), 1913; renamed franchise. Had been VANCOUVER CHAMPIONS, 1912. Renamed VANCOUVER BEAVERS, 1914.

Vancouver Canadians
Pacific Coast League (AAA), 1978–(still in existence as of 5-1-92); new franchise.

Vancouver Capilanos
Western International League (B), 1939–1942; 1946–1951; (A), 1952–1954; renamed franchise. Had been VANCOUVER MAPLE LEAFS, 1937–1938. Disbanded with league after 1954 season.

Vancouver Champions
Northwestern League (B), 1912; renamed franchise. Had been VANCOUVER BEAVERS, 1905–1907. Renamed VANCOUVER BEES, 1913.

Vancouver Horse Doctors
Northwestern League (B), 1905–1907; charter franchise. Renamed VANCOUVER BEAVERS, 1908.

Vancouver Maple Leafs
Western International League (B), 1937–1938; charter franchise. Re-

named VANCOUVER CAPILANOS, 1939.

Vancouver Mounties
Pacific Coast League (AAA), 1956–1962; relocated franchise. Had been OAKLAND ACORNS, 1952. Disbanded after 1962 season.

Vancouver Mounties
Pacific Coast League (AAA), 1965–1969; new franchise. Became SALT LAKE CITY ANGELS, 1970.

VANCOUVER, BRITISH COLUMBIA, CANADA– VANCOUVER, WA

Vancouver Beavers
Pacific Coast International League (B), 1918; charter franchise. Disbanded with league after 1918 season.

Vancouver Soldiers
Oregon State League (D), 1904; charter franchise. Disbanded with league after 1904 season.

VANDERGRIFT, PA

Vandergrift Pioneers
Middle Atlantic League (C), 1947–1950; expansion franchise. Disbanded after 1950 season.

VAN WERT, OH

Van Wert Buckeyes
Indiana–Ohio League (D), 1908; charter franchise. Disbanded with league after 1908 season.

VARINA, NC
(See ANGIER, NC)

VENICE, CA

Venice Tigers
Pacific Coast League (AA), 1913–mid-1915; relocated franchise. Had been VERNON TIGERS, 1909–1912.

Became VERNON TIGERS, mid-1915.

VENTURA, CA
(See also SANTA BARBARA, CA)

Ventura
California State League (D), 1929; charter franchise. Disbanded with league after 1929 season.

Ventura Braves
California League (C), 1950; renamed franchise. Had been VENTURA YANKEES, 1947–1949. Renamed VENTURA OILERS, 1953.

Ventura County Gulls
California League (A), 1986; new franchise. Became SAN BERNADINO SPIRIT, 1987.

Ventura Oilers
California League (C), 1953; renamed franchise. Had been VENTURA BRAVES, 1950–1952. Renamed CHANNEL CITIES OILERS, 1954–1955.

Ventura Yankees
California League (C), 1947–1949; new franchise. Renamed VENTURA BRAVES, 1950.

VERACRUZ, VERACRUZ, MEXICO
(See also CIUDAD MADERO, MEXICO; COATZACOALCOS, MEXICO; CORDOBA, MEXICO; MADERA, MEXICO; MIGUEL ALEMAN, MEXICO; ORIZABA, MEXICO; POZA RICA, MEXICO)

Veracruz
Mexican League (AAA), 1981–1986; new franchise. Disbanded after 1986 season.

Veracruz Aguilas (Eagles)
Mexican League (AA), 1955–1957; charter franchise. Disbanded after 1957 season.

Veracruz Aguilas (Eagles)
Mexican League (AA), 1959–1966; (AAA), 1967–1968; new franchise. Disbanded after 1968 season.

Veracruz Aguilas (Eagles)
Mexican League (AAA), 1971; new franchise. Disbanded after 1971 season.

Veracruz Aguilas (Eagles)
Mexican League (AAA), 1973; new franchise. Disbanded after 1973 season.

VERNON, CA

Vernon Tigers (aka Villagers, 1911)
Pacific Coast Baseball League (AAA), 1909–1912; expansion franchise. Became VENICE TIGERS, 1913.

Vernon Tigers
Pacific Coast Baseball League (AAA), 1915–1925; relocated franchise. Had been VENICE TIGERS, 1913–1914. Became MISSIONS OF SAN FRANCISCO, 1926.

Vernon Villagers
Alternate name for VERNON TIGERS, 1911.

VERNON, TX

Vernon Dusters
Longhorn League (D), 1947–1950; (C), 1951–1952; charter franchise. Disbanded after 1952 season.

VERO BEACH, FL

Vero Beach Dodgers
Florida State League (A), 1980– (still in existence as of 5-1-92); new franchise.

VERSAILLES, KY

Versailles
Blue Grass League (D), 1908; charter franchise. Became WINCHESTER, mid-1908.

VICKSBURG, MS

Vicksburg Billies
Cotton States League (C), 1955; new franchise. Disbanded with league after 1955 season.

Vicksburg Billies
Southeastern League (B), 1946–1950; charter franchise. Disbanded with league after 1950 season.

Vicksburg Hill Billies
Cotton States League (D), 1902–1908; 1910–1912; charter franchise. Disbanded with league during 1912 season.

Vicksburg Hill Billies
Cotton States League (D), 1922–mid-1923; new franchise. Disbanded during 1923 season. Cotton States League (D), 1924–mid-1932; new franchise. Became JACKSON SENATORS, mid-1932.

Vicksburg Hill Billies
Cotton States League (C), 1941; new franchise. Suspended operations with league after 1941 season, and did not rejoin when league resumed in 1947.

Vicksburg Hill Billies
Cotton States League (C), 1937; new franchise. Disbanded after 1937 season.

Vicksburg Reds
Mississippi League, 1893–1894; charter franchise. Disbanded with league after 1894 season.

VICTORIA, BRITISH COLUMBIA, CANADA

Victoria Athletics
Western International League (B), 1946–1951; charter franchise. Renamed VICTORIA TYEES, 1952.

Victoria Bees
Northwestern League (B), 1911–1915; new franchise. Disbanded after 1915 season.

Victoria Bees
Pacific Coast International League (aka International Northwestern League) (B), 1921; renamed franchise. Had been VICTORIA ISLANDERS, 1919–1920. Disbanded with league after 1921 season.

Victoria Chappies
Pacific Northwest League, 1896; charter franchise. Disbanded with league after 1896 season.

Victoria Islanders
Pacific International League (aka International Northwestern League) (B), 1919–1920; charter franchise. Became VICTORIA BEES, 1921.

Victoria Legislators
Northwestern League (B), 1905; charter franchise. Became SPOKANE INDIANS, mid-1905.

Victoria Mussels
Northwest League (A), 1978–1980; new franchise. Disbanded after 1980 season.

Victoria Tyees
Western International League (A), 1952–1954; renamed franchise. Had been VICTORIA ATHLETICS, 1946–1952. Disbanded after 1954 season.

VICTORIA, TAMAULPAIS, MEXICO

Victoria Braves
Mexican Center League (A), 1971; new franchise. Disbanded after 1971 season.

Victoria Sultancitos (Sultans)
Mexican Center League (A), 1973–1974; new franchise. Disbanded after 1974 season.

Victoria Tuzos (Gophers)
Mexican League (AAA), 1976–1978; new franchise. Disbanded after 1978 season.

VICTORIA, TX

Victoria Cowboys
Gulf States League (A), 1976; charter franchise. Disbanded with league after 1976 season.

Victoria Eagles
Big State League (B), 1956; new franchise. Renamed VICTORIA ROSEBUDS, 1957.

Victoria Giants
Texas League (AA), mid-1961; relocated franchise. Had been RIO GRANDE VALLEY GIANTS, 1960–mid-1961. Disbanded after 1961 season.

Victoria Rosebuds
Southwest Texas League (D), 1910–1911; charter franchise. Disbanded with league after 1911 season.

Victoria Rosebuds
Gulf Coast League (D), 1926; charter franchise. Became EDINBURG BOBCATS, mid-1926.

Victoria Rosebuds
Big State League (B), 1957; renamed franchise. Had been VICTORIA EAGLES, 1956. Texas League (AA), 1958–mid-1961; new franchise. Became ARDMORE ROSEBUDS, mid-1961.

Victoria Rosebuds
Lone Star League (A), 1977; charter franchise. Disbanded with league after 1977 season.

Victoria Toros
Texas League (AA), 1974; relocated franchise. Had been MEMPHIS BLUES, 1972–1973. Became JACKSON METS, 1975.

VIDALIA, GA

Vidalia Indians
Georgia State League (D), 1952–1956; new franchise. Disbanded with league after 1956 season.

VIDALIA–LYONS, GA

Vidalia–Lyons Twins
Georgia State League (D), 1948–1950; charter franchise. Disbanded after 1950 season.

VILLAHERMOSA–TABASCO, MEXICO
(See also TABASCO, MEXICO)

Villahermosa Banana Growers
Mexican League (AAA), 1977; new franchise. Became VILLAHERMOSA PLATANEROS, 1978.

Villahermosa Bananas
Mexican League (AAA), 1968; new franchise. Renamed VILLAHERMOSA TIGRES, 1959.

Villahermosa Plataneros
Mexican League (AA), 1966–mid-1967; renamed franchise. Had been VILLAHERMOSA TIGERS, 1964–1965. Became LAS CHOAPAS REDS, mid-1967.

Villahermosa Plataneros
Mexican League (AAA), 1978–1980; renamed franchise. Had been VILLAHERMOSA BANANA GROWERS, 1977. Disbanded after 1980 season.

Villahermosa Tigers
Mexican League (AA), 1964–1965; new franchise. Renamed VILLAHERMOSA PLATANEROS, 1966.

Villahermosa Tigres
Mexican League (AAA), 1969; renamed franchise. Had been VILLAHERMOSA BANANAS, 1968. Disbanded after 1969 season.

VINCENNES, IN

Vincennes Alice
KITTY League (D), 1905–1906; renamed franchise. Had been VINCENNES REDS, 1904. Disbanded with league after 1906 season.

Vincennes Alice
Eastern Illinois League (D), 1908; new franchise. Disbanded with league after 1908 season.

Vincennes Alice
KITTY League (D), 1910; charter franchise. Renamed VINCENNES HOOSIERS, 1911.

Vincennes Alice
KITTY League (D), 1913; new franchise. Disbanded after 1913 season.

Vincennes Citizens
MOV League (D), 1950; new franchise. Renamed VINCENNES VELVETS, 1951.

Vincennes Hoosiers
KITTY League (D), 1911; renamed franchise. Had been VINCENNES ALICE, 1910. Disbanded after 1911 season.

Vincennes Reds
KITTY League (D), 1904; new franchise. Renamed VICENNES ALICE, 1950.

Vincennes Velvets
MOV League (D), 1951–mid-1952; renamed franchise. Had been VINCENNES CITIZENS, 1950. Became CANTON CITIZENS, mid-1952.

VINITA, OK

Vinita
Missouri Valley League (D), 1905; charter franchise. Disbanded after 1905 season.

Vinita
Kansas State League (D), mid-1906; relocated franchise. Had been PITTSBURG CHAMPIONS, 1906. Disbanded with league after 1906 season.

VIRGINIA, MN

Virginia Ore Diggers
Central International League (C), 1912; charter franchise. Northern League (C), 1913–1916; charter franchise. Disbanded during 1916 season.

VISALIA, CA

Visalia Athletics
California League (B), 1960–1961; renamed franchise. Had been VISALIA REDLEGS, 1957–1959. Renamed VISALIA WHITE SOX, 1962.

Visalia Cubs
California League (C), 1946–1952; new franchise. Renamed VISALIA STARS, 1953.

Visalia Cubs
California League (B), 1954–1956; renamed franchise. Had been VISALIA STARS, 1953. Renamed VISALIA REDLEGS, 1957.

Visalia Mets
California League (A), 1968–1975; new franchise. Disbanded after 1975 season.

Visalia Oaks
California League (A), 1977–(still in existence as of 5-1-92); new franchise.

Visalia Pirates
San Joaquin Valley League (D), 1910; charter franchise. Disbanded with league after 1910 season.

Visalia Redlegs
California League (B), 1957–1959; renamed franchise. Had been VISALIA CUBS, 1954–1956. Renamed VISALIA ATHLETICS, 1960.

Visalia Stars
California League (B), 1953; renamed franchise. Had been VISALIA CUBS, 1946–1952. Renamed VISALIA CUBS, 1954.

Visalia White Sox
California League (B), 1962; renamed franchise. Had been VISALIA ATHLETICS, 1961. Disbanded after 1962 season.

WABASH, IN

Wabash Brownies
Alternate name for WABASH SYCAMORES.

Wabash Rockeries
Northern State of Indiana League (D), 1909; charter franchise. Northern State League of Indiana (D), 1910–1911; charter franchise. Disbanded with league after 1911 season.

Wabash Sycamores (aka Brownies)
Indiana–Illinois League, 1899; charter franchise. Indiana State League, 1900–1901; charter franchise. Disbanded with league after 1901 season.

WACO, TX

Waco
Texas League, mid-1892; relocated franchise. Had been DALLAS–FORT WORTH, 1892. Disbanded with league after 1892 season.

Waco Babies
Texas League, 1889–1890; new franchise. Disbanded during 1890 season.

Waco Cubs
Texas League (A), 1925–1930; relocated franchise. Had been GALVESTON CUBS, 1921–1924. Became GALVESTON BUCCANEERS, 1931.

Waco Cubs
Dixie League (C), 1933; charter franchise. Became PINE BLUFF JUDGES, mid-1933. Disbanded during 1933 season.

Waco Dons
Big States League (B), 1947; charter franchise. Renamed WACO PIRATES, 1948.

Waco Indians
Texas Association (D), 1923–1924; charter franchise. Disbanded after 1924 season.

Waco Navigators
Texas League (C), 1906–1910; (B), 1911–1919; renamed franchise. Had been WACO TIGERS, 1905. Became WICHITA FALLS SPUDDERS, 1920.

Waco Pirates
Big States League (B), 1948–mid-1953; renamed franchise. Had been WACO DONS, 1947. Became LONGVIEW PIRATES, mid-1953.

Waco Pirates
Big States League (B), 1954–1956; new franchise. Had been WACO DONS, 1947. Disbanded after 1956 season.

Waco Steers
Texas League (D), 1903; relocated franchise. Had been PARIS. Disbanded after 1903 season.

Waco Tigers
Texas League, mid-1897; relocated franchise. Had been DENISON TIGERS, 1897. Disbanded after 1897 season.

Waco Tigers
Texas League, 1902; charter franchise. Disbanded during 1902 season.

Waco Tigers
Texas League (D), 1905; expansion franchise. Renamed WACO NAVIGATORS, 1906.

WAHPETON, MN

Wahpeton
Red River Valley League, 1897; charter franchise. Disbanded with league after 1897 season.

WAHPETON–BRECKENRIDGE, MN

Wahpeton–Breckenridge Twins
Dakota League (D), 1921–1922; charter franchise. Disbanded with league after 1922 season.

WALDEN, NY

Walden Hummingbirds
North Atlantic League (D), mid-1946; renamed franchise. Had been NEWBURGH HUMMINGBIRDS, early-1946. Disbanded after 1946 season.

WALLA WALLA, WA

Walla Walla
Pacific Inter-State League, 1891; charter franchise. Disbanded with league after 1891 season.

Walla Walla Bears
Western Tri-State League (C), 1913; (D), 1914; charter franchise. Disbanded with league after 1914 season.

Walla Walla Bears
Northwest League (A), 1969–1971; new franchise. Renamed WALLA WALLA ISLANDERS, 1972.

Walla Walla Bears
Northwest League (A), 1983; renamed franchise. Had been WALLA WALLA PADRES, 1973–1982. Disbanded after 1983 season.

Walla Walla Islanders
Northwest League (A), 1972; renamed franchise. Had been WALLA WALLA BEARS, 1969–1971. Renamed WALLA WALLA PADRES, 1973.

Walla Walla Padres
Northwest League (A), 1973–1982; renamed franchise. Had been WALLA WALLA ISLANDERS, 1972. Renamed WALLA WALLA BEARS, 1983.

Walla Walla Walla Wallans
Inland Empire League (D), 1908. Disbanded with league after 1908 season.

WALTHAM, MA

Waltham
Massachusetts State Association, 1884; charter franchise. Disbanded with association during 1884 season.

Waltham Rosebuds
Northeastern League (A), 1934; charter franchise. Became WORCESTER ROSEBUDS, mid-1934.

Waltham Rosebuds
Northeastern League (A), mid-1934; relocated franchise. Had been WORCESTER ROSEBUDS, mid-1934. Disbanded with league after 1934 season.

WARREN, ND

Warren Wanderers
Northern League (C), 1917; new franchise. Disbanded with league after 1917 season.

WARREN, PA

Warren
Inter-State League (D), 1908; charter franchise. Disbanded with league after 1908 season.

Warren Bingos
Inter-State League (D), mid-1914–1916; charter franchise. Disbanded with league after 1916 season.

Warren Buckeyes
Pennsylvania State Association (D), 1941; renamed franchise. Had been WARREN REDSKINS, 1940. Disbanded with league after 1941 season.

Warren Redskins
Pennsylvania State Association (D), 1940; new franchise. Renamed WARREN BUCKEYES, 1941.

Warren Wonders
Iron & Oil League, 1895; charter franchise. Disbanded with league after 1895 season.

Warren Wonders
Iron & Oil League, 1898; charter franchise. Disbanded with league after 1898 season.

WARSAW, NC

Warsaw Red Sox
Tobacco State League (D), 1947–1948; new franchise. Disbanded after 1948 season.

WASHINGTON, DC

NATIONAL OF WASHINGTON
National Association, mid-1872; renamed franchise. Had been OLYMPIC OF WASHINGTON, 1871–1872. Disbanded after 1873 season.

OLYMPIC OF WASHINGTON
National Association, 1871; charter franchise. Renamed NATIONAL OF WASHINGTON during 1872 season.

WASHINGTON ELITE GIANTS
Negro National League, 1936–1937; relocated franchise. Had been COLUMBUS ELITE GIANTS, 1935. Became BALTIMORE ELITE GIANTS, 1938.

WASHINGTON NATIONALS
Alternate name for WASHINGTON OLYMPICS, 1872.

WASHINGTON NATIONALS
National Association, 1875; new franchise. Disbanded after 1875 season.

WASHINGTON NATIONALS
National Association, 1879–1880; new franchise. Disbanded after 1880 season.

Washington Nationals
Eastern Association, 1881; charter franchise. Became ALBANY CAPITAL CITY, mid-1881.

WASHINGTON NATIONALS (aka QUICKSTEPS)
Union Association, 1884; charter franchise. Eastern League, 1885; new franchise. Disbanded after 1885 season.

WASHINGTON NATIONALS
American Association, 1884; new franchise. Became RICHMOND VIRGINIANS, mid-1884.

WASHINGTON NATIONALS
American League, 1905–1956; renamed franchise. Had been WASHINGTON SENATORS, 1901–1904. Renamed WASHINGTON SENATORS, 1957–1960.

WASHINGTON OLYMPICS (aka NATIONALS)
National Association, 1871–1872; charter franchise. Disbanded after 1872 season.

WASHINGTON QUICKSTEPS
Alternate name for WASHINGTON NATIONALS, 1884.

WASHINGTON RUBY LEGS
National League, 1880–1882; new franchise. Disbanded after 1882 season.

Washington Senators
Atlantic Association, 1890; new franchise. Disbanded with league after 1890 season.

WASHINGTON SENATORS
American League, 1901–1904; charter franchise. Renamed WASHINGTON NATIONALS, 1905–1956.

WASHINGTON SENATORS
National League, 1892–1899; new franchise. Disbanded after 1899 season.

WASHINGTON SENATORS
American League, 1957–1960; renamed franchise. Had been WASHINGTON NATIONALS, 1905–1956. Became MINNESOTA TWINS, 1961.

WASHINGTON SENATORS
American League, 1961–1971; expansion franchise. Became TEXAS RANGERS, 1972.

WASHINGTON STATESMEN
National League, 1886–1889; new franchise. Disbanded after 1889 season.

WASHINGTON STATESMEN
American Association, 1891; new franchise. Disbanded after 1891 season.

WASHINGTON, IN

Washington
Kentucky–Indiana League, 1896; charter franchise. Disbanded with league after 1896 season.

WASHINGTON, NJ

Washington Potomacs
Inter-State League (D), 1932; charter franchise. Disbanded with league after 1932 season.

WASHINGTON, PA

Washington
POM League (D), 1906–1907; charter franchise. Disbanded with league after 1907 season.

Washington Generals
Pennsylvania State Association (D), mid-1934–mid-1936; charter franchise. Disbanded during 1936 season.

Washington Little Senators
Inter-State League, 1896; charter franchise. Disbanded after 1896 season.

Washington Red Birds
Pennsylvania State Association (D), 1939–1942; new franchise. Disbanded with league after 1942 season.

WATERBURY, CT

Waterbury
Connecticut League, 1884; charter franchise. Disbanded with league during 1884 season.

Waterbury
Southern New England League, mid-1885; relocated franchise. Had been NORFOLK, 1885. Eastern League, 1886–1887; new franchise. Connecticut State League, 1888; charter franchise. Disbanded with league after 1888 season.

Waterbury
Connecticut State League, 1891; charter franchise. Disbanded with league after 1891 season.

Waterbury
Connecticut League, 1894; charter franchise. Became NEW BRITAIN, mid-1894.

Waterbury
Connecticut Valley League (B), 1903; charter franchise. Became HOLYOKE, mid-1903.

Waterbury Angels
Eastern League (AA), 1984; renamed franchise. Had been WATERBURY REDS, 1980–1983. Renamed WATERBURY INDIANS, 1985.

Waterbury Authors
Connecticut League (B), 1906–1908; new franchise. Renamed WATERBURY INVINCIBLES, 1909.

Waterbury Brasscos
Eastern League (A), 1920–1928; renamed franchise. Had been WATERBURY NATTATUCKS, 1918–1919. Disbanded after 1928 season.

Waterbury Braves
Alternate name for WATERBURY ROUGH RIDERS.

Waterbury Champs
Connecticut League (B), 1911; renamed franchise. Had been WATERBURY FINNEGANS, 1910. Disbanded after 1911 season.

Waterbury Contenders
Eastern Association (B), 1913; charter franchise. Renamed WATERBURY HUSKIES (aka Frolickers), 1914.

Waterbury Dodgers
Eastern League (AA), 1973–1976; renamed franchise. Had been WATERBURY PIRATES, 1970–1972. Renamed WATERBURY GIANTS, 1977.

Waterbury Finnegans
Connecticut League (B), 1910; renamed franchise. Had been WATERBURY INVINCIBLES, 1909. Renamed WATERBURY CHAMPS, 1911.

Waterbury Frolickers
Alternate name for WATERBURY HUSKIES.

Waterbury Giants
Eastern League (AA), 1966–1967; new franchise. Renamed WATERBURY INDIANS, 1968.

Waterbury Giants
Eastern League (AA), 1977–1978; renamed franchise. Had been WATERBURY DODGERS, 1973–1976. Disbanded after 1978 season.

Waterbury Huskies (aka Frolickers)
Eastern Association (B), 1914; renamed franchise. Had been WATERBURY CONTENDERS, 1913. Disbanded with league after 1914 season.

Waterbury Indians
Eastern League (AA), 1968–1969; renamed franchise. Had been

WATERBURY GIANTS, 1966–1967. Renamed WATERBURY PIRATES, 1970.

Waterbury Indians
Eastern League (AA), 1985–1986; renamed franchise. Had been WATERBURY ANGELS, 1984. Disbanded after 1986 season.

Waterbury Invincibles
Connecticut League (B), 1909; renamed franchise. Had been WATERBURY AUTHORS, 1906–1908. Renamed WATERBURY FINNEGANS, 1910.

Waterbury Nattatucks
Eastern League (B), 1918; (A), 1919; new franchise. Renamed WATERBURY BRASSCOS, 1920.

Waterbury Pirates
Eastern League (AA), 1970–1972; renamed franchise. Had been WATERBURY INDIANS, 1968–1969. Renamed WATERBURY DODGERS, 1973.

Waterbury Ponies
Connecticut State League, 1897; charter franchise. Renamed WATERBURY ROUGH RIDERS, 1898.

Waterbury Reds
Eastern League (AA), 1980–1983; new franchise. Renamed WATERBURY ANGELS, 1984.

Waterbury Rough Riders (aka Braves, 1900)
Connecticut State League, 1898–1902; renamed franchise. Had been WATERBURY PONIES, 1897. Disbanded after 1902 season.

Waterbury Spuds
Connecticut League (B), mid-1912; relocated franchise. Had been NEW BRITAIN, 1911–mid-1912. Disbanded with league after 1912 season.

Waterbury Timers
Colonial League (B), 1947–1950; charter franchise. Disbanded with league during 1950 season.

Waterloo
Eastern Iowa League, 1895; charter franchise. Disbanded with league after 1895 season.

Waterloo Boosters
Illinois–Iowa–Indiana League (B), 1910–1911; new franchise. Disbanded after 1911 season.

Waterloo Cubs
Iowa State League (D), 1907; renamed franchise. Had been WATERLOO MICROBES, 1904–1906. Disbanded with league after 1907 season.

Waterloo Diamonds
Midwest League (A), 1989–(still in existence as of 5-1-92); renamed franchise. Had been WATERLOO INDIANS, 1977–1988.

Waterloo Hawks
Mississippi Valley League (D) 1922–1932; charter franchise. Disbanded with league after 1932 season.

Waterloo Hawks
Western League (A), 1936; new franchise. Renamed WATERLOO REDS, 1937.

Waterloo Hawks
Midwest League (D), 1958–1962; (A), 1963–1971; new franchise. Renamed WATERLOO ROYALS, 1972.

Waterloo Indians
Midwest League (A), 1977–1988; renamed franchise. Had been WATERLOO ROYALS, 1972–1976. Renamed WATERLOO DIAMONDS, 1989.

Waterloo Jays
Central Association (D), 1913–1917; new franchise. Disbanded with league after 1917 season.

Waterloo Lulus
Central Association (D), 1908–1909; charter franchise. Disbanded after 1909 season.

Waterloo Microbes
Iowa State League (D), 1904–1906; charter franchise. Renamed WATERLOO CUBS, 1907.

Waterloo Red Hawks
Three I League (B), 1938–1939; new franchise. Had been WATERLOO REDS, 1937. Renamed WATERLOO WHITE HAWKS, 1940–1942.

Waterloo Reds
Western League (A), 1937; renamed franchise. Had been WATERLOO HAWKS, 1936. Became WATERLOO RED HAWKS, 1938.

Waterloo Royals
Midwest League (A), 1972–1976; renamed franchise. Had been WATERLOO HAWKS, 1958–1971. Renamed WATERLOO INDIANS, 1977.

Waterloo White Hawks
Three I League (B), 1940–1942; 1946–1956; renamed franchise. Had been WATERLOO RED HAWKS, 1938–1939. Disbanded after 1956 season.

WATERLOO, NY

Waterloo
New York State League, 1888; charter franchise. Disbanded after 1888 season.

WATERTOWN, MA

Watertown Townies
Eastern International League, 1888; charter franchise. Disbanded with league after 1888 season.

Watertown Townies
Northeastern League (A), 1934; charter franchise. Disbanded with league after 1934 season.

WATERTOWN, NY

Watertown
Central New York League, 1886; charter franchise. Disbanded with league after 1886 season.

Watertown Athletics
Border League (C), 1946–1951; charter franchise. Disbanded with league during 1951 season.

Watertown Bucks
Alternate name for WATERTOWN GRAYS.

Watertown Grays (aka Bucks)
Canadian–American League (C), 1936; charter franchise. Became BROCKVILLE PIRATES, mid-1936.

Watertown Indians
New York–Pennsylvania League (A), 1989–(still in existence as of 5-1-92); renamed franchise. Had been WATERTOWN PIRATES, 1983–1988.

Watertown Pirates
New York–Pennsylvania League (A), 1983–1988; new franchise. Renamed WATERTOWN INDIANS, 1989.

WATERTOWN, SD

Watertown Cubs
Dakota League (D), 1921–1923; charter franchise. Disbanded with league during 1923 season.

Watertown Expos
Northern League (A), 1970–1971; new franchise. Disbanded with league after 1971 season.

WATSONVILLE, CA

Watersonville Gardiners
Alternate name for WATERSONVILLE HAYSEEDS.

Watersonville Hayseeds (aka Gardiners)
California League, 1899; new franchise. Disbanded after 1899 season.

Watersonville Infants
Pacific Coast League, 1898; relocated franchise. Had been FRESNO, mid-1898. Disbanded after 1898 season.

Watersonville Pippins
California State League (D), mid-1913; relocated franchise. Had been VALLEJO MARINES, 1913. Disbanded after 1913 season.

WATSONVILLE, CA

Watsonville Gardiners
California League, 1899; new franchise. Disbanded after 1899 season.

Watsonville Infants
California State League, mid-1898; relocated franchise. Had been FRESNO TIGERS, 1898. Disbanded after 1898 season

Watsonville Pippins
California State League (D), mid-1913; renamed franchise. Had been VALLEJO MARINES, 1913. Disbanded after 1913 season.

WAUSAU, WI

Wausau Lumberjacks
Wisconsin State League (D), 1905–1906; charter franchise. Wisconsin–Illinois League (D), 1907–1908; charter franchise. Minnesota–Wisconsin League (C), 1909, 1911; (D), 1910, 1912; charter franchise. Wisconsin–Illinois League (D), 1912–1914; new franchise. Disbanded with league after 1914 season.

Wausau Lumberjacks
Northern League (C), 1936–1942; new franchise. Suspended operations with league after 1942 season, and resumed with Wisconsin State League (see below), 1946.

Wausau Lumberjacks
Wisconsin State League (D), 1946–1953; charter franchise. Dis-

banded with league after 1953 season.

Wausau Lumberjacks
Northern League (C), 1956–1957; new franchise. Disbanded after 1957 season.

Wausau Mets
Midwest League (A), 1975–1978; new franchise. Renamed WAUSAU TIMBERS, 1979.

Wausau Timbers
Midwest League (A), 1979–1990; renamed franchise. Had been WAUSAU METS, 1975–1978. Became KANE COUNTY COUGARS, 1990.

WAVERLY, NY

Waverly Wagonmakers
New York State League, mid-1901; relocated franchise. Had been CORTLAND WAGONMAKERS, 1901. Disbanded after 1901 season.

WAXAHACHIE, TX

Waxahachie Athletics
Central Texas Trolley League (D), 1914–1915; charter franchise. Central Texas League (D), 1916–1917; charter franchise. Disbanded with league during 1917 season.

WAYCROSS, GA

Waycross
Southeastern League (B), mid-1927; relocated franchise. Had been ST. AUGUSTINE SAINTS, 1926–mid-1927. Became ST. AUGUSTINE SAINTS, mid-1927.

Waycross Bears
Georgia–Florida League (D), 1939–1942; 1946–1955; expansion franchise. Renamed WAYCROSS BRAVES, 1956.

Waycross Blowhards
Empire State League (D), 1913; charter franchise. Disbanded with league after 1913 season.

Waycross Braves
Georgia–Florida League (A), 1956–1958; renamed franchise. Had been WAYCROSS BEARS, 1939–1942; 1946–1955. Disbanded with league after 1958 season.

Waycross Grasshoppers
Georgia State League (D), 1914; charter franchise. Renamed WAYCROSS MOGULS, mid-1914.

Waycross Machinists
Georgia State League (D), 1906; charter franchise. Disbanded with league during 1906 season.

Waycross Moguls
Georgia State League (D), mid-1914; charter franchise. Had been WAYCROSS GRASSHOPPERS. FLAG League (D), 1915; charter franchise. Disbanded with league after 1915 season.

WAYLAND, MA

Wayland Birds
Northeastern League (A), mid-1934; relocated franchise. Had been CAMBRIDGE CANTABS, 1934. Disbanded with league after 1934 season.

WAYNESBORO, PA

Waynesboro Red Birds
Blue Ridge League (D), 1928–1930; renamed franchise. Had been WAYNESBORO VILLAGERS, 1920–1937. Disbanded with league after 1930 season.

Waynesboro Villagers
Blue Ridge League (D), 1928–1930; charter franchise. Had been WAYNESBORO RED BIRDS, 1920–1927.

WAYNESBURG, PA

Waynesburg
POM League (D), 1906; charter franchise. Disbanded after 1906 season.

WEBB CITY, MO

Webb City
Southwestern League, 1891; charter franchise. Disbanded with league after 1891 season.

Webb City
Missouri Valley League (D), mid-1903; relocated franchise. Had been NEVADA LUNATICS, 1902–mid-1903. Disbanded after 1903 season.

Webb City Ducklings
Alternate name for WEBB CITY WEBFEET, 1909.

Webb City Goldbugs
Missouri Valley League (D), 1905; charter franchise. Western Association (C), 1906–1908; new franchise. Renamed WEBB CITY WEBFEET (aka Ducklings), 1909.

Webb City Missourians
Southwestern League, 1887; charter franchise. Disbanded during 1887 season.

Webb City Webfeet (aka Ducklings)
Western Association (C), 1909; renamed franchise. Had been WEBB CITY GOLDBUGS, 1905–1908. Became SAPULPA OILERS, mid-1909.

WEIR CITY, MO

Weir City Browns
Southwestern League, 1891; charter franchise. Disbanded with league after 1891 season.

WELCH, WV

Welch Miners
Mountain State League (C), 1937–1942; charter franchise. Resumed

operations with Appalachian League (D), 1946–mid-1955; expansion franchise. Became MARION A'S, mid-1955.

WELLAND, ONTARIO, CANADA

Welland Pirates
New York–Pennsylvania League (A), 1989–(still in existence as of 5-1-92); new franchise.

WELLINGTON, KS

Wellington
Kansas State League, 1887; charter franchise. Disbanded with league after 1887 season.

Wellington Dukes
Kansas State League (D), 1909–mid-1911; charter franchise. Became WICHITA WITCHES, mid-1911.

Wellington Dukes
Kansas State League (D), mid-1911; relocated franchise. Had been WICHITA WITCHES, mid-1911. Disbanded with league after 1911 season.

WELLSBURG, WV

Wellsburg
Ohio Valley League, 1891; charter franchise. Disbanded with league after 1891 season.

WELLSVILLE, NY

Wellsville
Western New York League, 1890; charter franchise. Disbanded with league after 1890 season.

Wellsville Braves
New York–Pennsylvania League (D), 1953–1961; renamed franchise. Had been WELLSVILLE ROCKETS, 1951–1952. Disbanded after 1961 season.

Wellsville Nitros
PONY League (D), 1947–1949; renamed franchise. Had been WELLSVILLE YANKEES, 1942–1946. Renamed WELLSVILLE SENATORS, 1950.

Wellsville Rainmakers
Inter-State League (B), mid-1914–1916; charter franchise. Disbanded with league after 1916 season.

Wellsville Rockets
PONY League (D), 1951–1952; renamed franchise. Had been WELLSVILLE SENATORS, 1950. Renamed WELLSVILLE BRAVES, 1953.

Wellsville Senators
PONY League (D), 1950; renamed franchise. Had been WELLSVILLE NITROS, 1947–1949. Renamed WELLSVILLE ROCKETS, 1951.

Wellsville White Sox
New York–Pennsylvania League (A), 1963–1965; new franchise. Disbanded after 1965 season.

Wellsville Yankees
PONY League (D), 1942–1946; new franchise. Renamed WELLSVILLE NITROS, 1947.

WENATCHEE, WA

Wenatchee Chiefs
Western International League (B), 1937–1941; 1946–1951; (A), 1952–1954; charter franchise. Northwest League (B), 1955–1965; charter franchise. Disbanded after 1965 season.

WESLACO, TX
(See DONNA, TX)

WESSINGTON SPRINGS, SD

Wessington Springs
South Dakota League (D), 1920; charter franchise. Disbanded with league after 1920 season.

WESTFIELD, NJ

Westfield
Central New Jersey League, 1892; charter franchise. Disbanded with league during 1892 season.

WEST FRANKFORT, IL

West Frankfort Cardinals
Illinois State League (B), 1947–1948; charter franchise. MOV League (D), 1949–1950; charter franchise. Disbanded after 1950 season.

WEST HAVEN, CT

West Haven A's
Eastern League (AA), 1981–1982; renamed franchise. Had been WEST HAVEN WHITECAPS, 1980. Became ALBANY YANKEES, 1983.

West Haven Whitecaps
Eastern League (AA), 1980; renamed franchise. Had been WEST HAVEN YANKEES, 1972–1979. Renamed WEST HAVEN A'S, 1981.

West Haven Yankees
Eastern League (AA), 1972–1979; new franchise. Renamed WEST HAVEN WHITECAPS, 1980.

WEST MANCHESTER, NH

West Manchester
New Hampshire State League, 1886; charter franchise. Disbanded with league after 1886 season.

West Manchester
New Hampshire State League (D), 1907; charter franchise. Disbanded with league after 1907 season.

WEST MONROE, LA
(See MONROE, LA)

WEST PALM BEACH, FL

West Palm Beach Braves
Florida State League (A), 1965–1968; new franchise. Renamed WEST PALM BEACH EXPOS, 1969.

West Palm Beach Expos
Florida State League (A), 1969–(still in existence as of 5-1-92); renamed franchise. Had been WEST PALM BEACH BRAVES, 1965–1968.

West Palm Beach Indians
Florida East Coast League (D), 1940–mid-1942; charter franchise. Disbanded with league during 1942 season.

West Palm Beach Indians
Florida International League (B), 1946–mid-1954; charter franchise. Disbanded with league during 1954 season.

West Palm Beach Indians
Florida State League (D), 1955; expansion franchise. Renamed WEST PALM BEACH SUN CHIEFS, 1956.

West Palm Beach Sheriffs
Florida State League (D), 1928; new franchise. Disbanded with league during 1928 season.

West Palm Beach Sun Chiefs
Florida State League (D), 1956; renamed franchise. Had been WEST PALM BEACH INDIANS, 1955. Disbanded after 1956 season.

WEST PLAINS, MO

West Plains Badgers
Northeast Arkansas League (D), 1936; charter franchise. Became CARUTHERSVILLE BADGERS, mid-1936.

WEST POINT, GA
(See LANNETT, GA)

WEWOKA, OK

Wewoka
Oklahoma State League (D), mid-1924; relocated franchise. Had been MCALESTER, mid-1924. Disbanded with league during 1924 season.

Wewoka
Oklahoma State League (D), 1936; charter franchise. Disbanded with league during 1936 season.

WHEELING, WV

Wheeling
Ohio State League, 1887; charter franchise. Disbanded with league after 1887 season.

Wheeling
Inter-State League, 1894–1895; charter franchise. Named WHEELING NAILERS, 1896.

Wheeling Mountaineers
Iron & Oil League, 1895; charter franchise. Disbanded with league after 1895 season.

Wheeling Nail City
Alternate name for WHEELING NAILERS, 1890.

Wheeling Nailers (aka Nail City, 1890)
Tri-State League, 1888–1890; charter franchise. Ohio Valley League, 1891; charter franchise. Disbanded with league after 1891 season.

Wheeling Nailers
Inter-State League, 1896–1897; Named franchise. Disbanded after 1897 season.

Wheeling Stogies
Inter-State League, 1899–1900; new franchise. Disbanded with league after 1900 season.

Wheeling Stogies
Western Association, mid-1901; relocated franchise. Had been GRAND RAPIDS WOODWORKERS, 1901. Disbanded after 1901 season.

Wheeling Stogies
Central League (D), 1903–1912; charter franchise. Inter-State League, (B), 1913; charter franchise. Disbanded with league after 1913 season.

Wheeling Stogies
Central League (B), 1915–1916; new franchise. Disbanded after 1916 season.

Wheeling Stogies
Middle Atlantic League (D), mid-1925–1932; 1934; charter franchise. Disbanded after 1934 season.

WHITEVILLE, NC

Whiteville Tobacconists
Tobacco State League (D), mid-1950; relocated franchise. Had been DUNN–ERWIN TWINS, 1946–mid-1950. Disbanded with league after 1950 season.

WICHITA, KS

Wichita Aeros
American Association (AAA), 1970–1984; new franchise. Became BUFFALO BISONS, 1985.

Wichita Aviators
Western League (A), 1929–1932; renamed franchise. Had been WICHITA LARKS, 1927–1928. Renamed WICHITA OILERS, 1933.

Wichita Braves (aka Gold Nuggets)
Western League, 1887; new franchise. Kansas State League, 1887; charter franchise. Disbanded with league after 1887 season.

Wichita Braves
American Association (AAA), 1956–1958; new franchise. Disbanded after 1958 season.

Wichita Gold Nuggets
Alternate name for WICHITA BRAVES, 1887.

Wichita Indians
Western League (A), 1950–1955; expansion franchise. Disbanded after 1955 season.

Wichita Izzies
Western League (A), 1922–1926; renamed franchise. Had been WICHITA WITCHES, 1921–1922. Renamed WICHITA LARKS, 1927.

Wichita Jobbers
Western Association (C), 1905–1908; charter franchise. Disbanded after 1908 season.

Wichita Jobbers
Western League (C), 1909–mid-1911; new franchise. Became PUEBLO INDIANS, mid-1911.

Wichita Jobbers
Western League (A), 1918–1920; renamed franchise. Had been WICHITA WITCHES, 1912–1917. Renamed WICHITA WITCHES, 1921.

Wichita Larks
Western League (A), 1927–1928; renamed franchise. Had been WICHITA IZZIES, 1922–1926. Became WICHITA AVIATORS, 1929.

Wichita Oilers
Western League (A), 1933; renamed franchise. Had been WICHITA AVIATORS, 1929–1932. Became MUSKOGEE OILERS, mid-1933.

Wichita Pilots
Texas League (AA), 1987; relocated franchise. Had been BEAUMONT GOLDEN GATORS, 1983–1986. Renamed WICHITA WRANGLERS, 1988.

Wichita Witches
Western League (A), mid-1911; relocated franchise. Had been WELLINGTON DUKES, 1909–mid-1911. Became WELLINGTON DUKES, mid-1911.

Wichita Witches
Western League (A), 1912–1917; new franchise. Renamed WICHITA JOBBERS, 1918–1920. Disbanded after 1917 season.

Wichita Witches
Western League (A), 1921–1922; renamed franchise. Had been WICHITA JOBBERS, 1920.

Wichita Wolves
Western League (A), 1915–mid-1916; charter franchise. Became COLORADO SPRINGS MILLIONAIRES, mid-1916.

Wichita Wranglers
Texas League (AA), 1988–(still in existence as of 5-1-92); renamed franchise. Had been WICHITA PILOTS, 1987.

WICHITA FALLS, TX

Wichita Falls Drillers
Alternate name for WICHITA FALLS OILERS, 1912.

Wichita Falls Irish Lads
Texas–Oklahoma League (D), 1911; charter franchise. Renamed WICHITA FALLS OILERS (aka Drillers), 1912.

Wichita Falls Oilers (aka Drillers)
Texas–Oklahoma League (D), 1912–mid-1913; renamed franchise. Had been WICHITA FALLS IRISH LADS, 1911. Became HUGO, mid-1913.

Wichita Falls Spudders
Texas League (B), 1920; (A), 1921–mid-1932; relocated franchise. Had been WACO NAVIGATORS, 1911–1919. Became LONGVIEW BROWNS, mid-1932.

Wichita Falls Spudders
West Texas–New Mexico League (D), 1941–mid-1942; new franchise. Became BIG SPRINGS PIRATES, mid-1942.

Wichita Falls Spudders
Big State League (B), 1947–1953; charter franchise. Longhorn League (C); new franchise, 1954. Became SWEETWATER SPUDDERS, mid-1953.

Wichita Falls Spudders
Big State League (B), 1956–1957; new franchise. Disbanded with league after 1957 season.

WILKES-BARRE, PA
(See also SCRANTON, PA)

Wilkes-Barre
Pennsylvania State Association, 1886–mid-1887; charter franchise. Disbanded with association during 1887 season.

Wilkes-Barre
Eastern Inter-State League, 1889; charter franchise. Disbanded with league during 1889 season.

Wilkes-Barre
Pennsylvania State League (D), 1902; charter franchise. Disbanded with league after 1902 season.

Wilkes-Barre Barons
Atlantic Association, 1889; charter franchise. Disbanded after 1889 season.

Wilkes-Barre Barons
New York State League (B), 1905–1917; new franchise. Disbanded with league after 1917 season.

Wilkes-Barre Barons
New York–Pennsylvania League (B), 1923–1937; charter franchise. Eastern League (A), 1938–1948; charter franchise. Renamed WILKES-BARRE INDIANS, 1949.

Wilkes-Barre Barons
Eastern League (A), 1953–mid-1955; new franchise. Became JOHNSTOWN JOHNNIES, mid-1955.

Wilkes-Barre Barons
Eastern League (A), 1950–1951; renamed franchise. Had been WILKES-BARRE INDIANS, 1949. Became READING INDIANS, 1952.

Wilkes-Barre Coal Barons
International Association, mid-1887; new franchise. Had been UTICA PENT-UPS, 1885–mid-1887. Central League, 1888; charter franchise. Disbanded with league after 1888 season.

Wilkes-Barre Coal Barons
Pennsylvania State League, mid-1892; relocated franchise. Had been PITTSBURGH, 1892. Eastern League, 1893–1898; new franchise. Atlantic League, 1899–1900; new franchise. Disbanded with league after 1900 season.

Wilkes-Barre Indians
Eastern League (A), 1949; renamed franchise. Had been WILKES-BARRE BARONS, 1923–1948. Renamed WILKES-BARRE BARONS, 1950.

WILLAMANTIC, CT

Willamantic Colts
Connecticut Association (D), 1910; charter franchise. Disbanded with league during 1910 season.

WILLIAMSON, WV

Williamson
Mountain States League (D), 1912; new franchise. Disbanded with league after 1912 season.

Williamson Colts
Mountain State League (C), 1937–1938; charter franchise. Renamed WILLIAMSON RED BIRDS, 1939.

Williamson Red Birds
Mountain State League (C), 1939–1942; renamed franchise. Had been WILLIAMSON COLTS, 1937–1938.

Disbanded with league after 1942 season.

WILLIAMSPORT, PA

Williamsport
Pennsylvania State League (D), 1902; charter franchise. Disbanded with league after 1902 season.

Williamsport Astros
Eastern League (AA), 1968–1969; renamed franchise. Had been WILLIAMSPORT METS, 1964–1967. New York–Pennsylvania League (A), 1970; new franchise. Renamed WILLIAMSPORT RED SOX, 1971.

Williamsport Athletics
Eastern League (A), 1953; renamed franchise. Had been WILLIAMSPORT TIGERS, 1947–1952. Renamed WILLIAMSPORT GRAYS, 1954.

Williamsport Billies
New York–Pennsylvania League (B), 1923; charter franchise. Renamed WILLIAMSPORT GRAYS, 1924.

Williamsport Bills
Eastern League (AA), 1987–(still in existence as of 5-1-92); new franchise.

Williamsport Champions
Alternate name for WILLIAMSPORT MILLIONAIRES, 1908.

Williamsport Demarests
Central Pennsylvania League, 1897; charter franchise. Disbanded with league after 1897 season.

Williamsport Grays
New York–Pennsylvania League (B), 1924–1937; renamed franchise. Had been WILLIAMSPORT BILLIES, 1923. Eastern League (A), 1938–1942; 1944–1946; charter franchise. Renamed WILLIAMSPORT TIGERS, 1947.

Williamsport Grays
Eastern League (A), 1954–1956; 1958–1962; renamed franchise. Disbanded after 1962 season.

Williamsport Lumber City
Pennsylvania State Association, 1886–1887; charter franchise. Disbanded with league after 1887 season.

Williamsport Mets
Eastern League (AA), 1964–1967; new franchise. Renamed WILLIAMSPORT ASTROS, 1968.

Williamsport Millionaires (aka Champions, 1908)
Tri-State League (D), 1907–1910; charter franchise. Disbanded after 1910 season.

Williamsport Red Sox
New York–Pennsylvania League (A), 1971–1972; renamed franchise. Had been WILLIAMSPORT ASTROS, 1968–1970. Disbanded after 1972 season.

Williamsport Tigers
Eastern League (A), 1947–1952; renamed franchise. Had been WILLIAMSPORT GRAYS, 1924–1942; 1944–1946. Renamed WILLIAMSPORT ATHLETICS, 1953.

Williamsport Tomahawks
Eastern League (AA), 1976; new franchise. Disbanded after 1976 season.

WILLIAMSTON, NC

Williamston Martins
Coastal Plain League (D), 1937–1941; charter franchise. Disbanded after 1941 season.

WILLIMANTIC, CT

Willimantic Colts
Connecticut Association (D), 1910; charter franchise. Disbanded with league after 1910 season.

WILLOWS, CA

Willows Cardinals
Far West League (D), 1948–1950; charter franchise. Disbanded after 1950 season.

WILMINGTON, DE

Wilmington
Middle States League, 1889; charter franchise. Disbanded during 1889 season.

Wilmington Blue Hens
Eastern League, 1885; new franchise. Became ATLANTIC CITY, mid-1885.

Wilmington Blue Rocks
Inter-State League (B), 1940–1952; expansion franchise. Disbanded with league after 1952 season.

Wilmington Chicks
Tri-State League (B), 1911–1914; new franchise. Disbanded with league after 1914 season.

Wilmington Delawareans
Eastern League, 1884; charter franchise. Became WILMINGTON QUICKSTEPS, mid-1884.

Wilmington Peach Growers
Atlantic Association, 1890; new franchise. Disbanded during 1890 season.

Wilmington Peaches
Atlantic League, 1896; charter franchise. Disbanded after 1896 season.

Wilmington Peaches
Tri-State League (D), 1907–1908; charter franchise. Disbanded after 1908 season.

Wilmington Quicksteps
Inter-State Association, 1883; charter franchise. Disbanded with league after 1883 season.

WILMINGTON QUICKSTEPS

Union Association, mid-1884; new franchise. Had been WILMINGTON DELAWAREANS, early 1884. Disbanded after 1884 season.

WILMINGTON, NC

Wilmington
Virginia–North Carolina League, 1901; charter franchise. Disbanded with league after 1901 season.

Wilmington Sailors (aka Sea Gulls)
North Carolina League (D), 1902; charter franchise. Disbanded during 1902 season.

Wilmington Sailors
East Carolina Association (D), 1908–1910; charter franchise. Disbanded with league after 1908 season.

Wilmington Sea Gulls
Alternate name for WILMINGTON SAILORS, 1902.

Wilmington Pirates
East Carolina League (D), 1928–1929; charter franchise. Disbanded with league after 1929 season.

Wilmington Pirates
Piedmont League (B), 1933–1935; renamed franchise. Had been WILMINGTON TWINS, 1932. Disbanded after 1935 season.

Wilmington Pirates
Tobacco State League (D), 1946–1950; charter franchise. Disbanded with league after 1950 season.

Wilmington Twins
Piedmont League (C), 1932; new franchise. Renamed WILMINGTON PIRATES, 1933.

WILSON, NC

Wilson Bugs
Virginia League (B), 1920–1921; expansion franchise. Renamed WILSON TOBACCONISTS, 1922.

Wilson Bugs
Virginia League (B), 1924–1927; renamed franchise. Had been WILSON TOBACCONISTS (aka Tobs), 1922–1923. Disbanded after 1927 season.

Wilson Pennants
Carolina League (A), 1973; new franchise. Disbanded after 1973 season.

Wilson Tobacconists
East Carolina League (D), 1908–1911; charter franchise. Disbanded with league after 1911 season.

Wilson Tobacconists (aka Tobs)
Virginia League (B), 1922–1923; renamed franchise. Had been WILSON BUGS, 1920–1921. Renamed WILSON BUGS, 1924.

Wilson Tobacconists (aka Tobs)
Coastal Plain League (D), 1939–1941; new franchise. Bi-State League (NC–VA), (D), 1942; new franchise. Suspended operations with league after 1942 season, and resumed as WILSON TOBS, 1946.

Wilson Tobs (aka Tobacconists)
Coastal Plain League (D), 1946–1952; charter franchise. Disbanded with league after 1952 season.

Wilson Tobs (aka Tobacconists)
Carolina League (B), 1956; relocated franchise. Had been REIDSVILLE PHILLIES, 1948–1955. Disbanded after 1956 season.

Wilson Tobs (aka Tobacconists)
Carolina League (B), mid-1957–1968; relocated franchise. Had been KINSTON EAGLES, 1956–mid-1957. Disbanded after 1968 season.

WILSON, OK

Wilson Drillers
Oklahoma State League (D), mid-1922; charter franchise. Disbanded after 1922 season.

WINCHESTER, KY

Winchester Dodgers
Blue Grass League (D), 1922–1924; charter franchise. Disbanded with league after 1924 season.

Winchester Hustlers
Blue Grass League (D), mid-1908–mid-1912; relocated franchise. Had been VERSAILLES, 1908. Became NICHOLASVILLE, mid-1912.

WINDSOR, ONTARIO, CANADA

Windsor
Border League (D), 1912–1913; charter franchise. Eastern Michigan League (D), 1914; charter franchise. Disbanded with league during 1914 season.

WINFIELD, KS

Winfield
Kansas State League, 1887; charter franchise. Disbanded with league after 1887 season.

Winfield
Kansas State League (D), mid-1909; relocated franchise. Had been ARKANSAS CITY GRAYS, 1909. Disbanded after 1909 season.

WINK, TX

Wink Spudders
West Texas–New Mexico League (D), 1937–1938; charter franchise. Disbanded after 1938 season.

WINNIPEG, MANITOBA, CANADA

Winnipeg
Red River Valley League, 1891; charter franchise. Disbanded with league after 1891 season.

Winnipeg Gold Eyes
Northern League (C), 1954–1962; (A), 1963–1964; new franchise. Disbanded after 1964 season.

Winnipeg Gold Eyes
Northern League (A), 1969; new franchise. Disbanded after 1969 season.

Winnipeg Maroons (aka Peggers, 1905)
Northern League (C), 1902–1905; charter franchise. Northern Copper County League (C), 1906–1907; charter franchise. Northern League (D), 1908; charter franchise. Western Canada League (D), 1909–1911; charter franchise. Central International League (C), 1912; charter franchise. Northern League (C), 1913–1916; (D), 1917; charter franchise. Disbanded with league during 1917 season.

Winnipeg Maroons
Western Canada League (C), 1919–1921; charter franchise. Disbanded with league after 1921 season.

Winnipeg Maroons
Northern League (D), 1933–1942; charter franchise. Disbanded after 1942 season.

Winnipeg Peggers
Alternate name for WINNIPEG MAROONS, 1905.

Winnipeg Whips
International League (AAA), 1970–1971; relocated franchise. Had been BUFFALO BISONS, 1912–1969. Disbanded after 1971 season.

WINONA, MN
(See also ROCHESTER, MN)

Winona
Keystone Association, 1877; charter franchise. Disbanded with association after 1877 season.

Winona A's
Three I League (B), mid-1958; relocated franchise. Had been ROCHESTER A'S, 1958. Disbanded after 1958 season.

Winona Clippers
Northwestern League, 1884; new franchise. Disbanded with league after 1884 season.

Winona Pirates
Minnesota–Wisconsin League (C), 1909, 1911; (D), 1910, 1912; charter franchise. Northern League (C), 1913–1914; charter franchise. Disbanded after 1914 season.

WINSTEAD, CT

Winstead
Naugatuck Valley League, 1898; charter franchise. Disbanded with league after 1898 season.

WINSTON–SALEM, NC

Winston–Salem
South Atlantic League, 1892; charter franchise. Disbanded with league after 1892 season.

Winston–Salem
Virginia–North Carolina League (D), 1905; charter franchise. Disbanded with league after 1905 season.

Winston–Salem Card(inal)s
Carolina League (C), 1945–1953; charter franchise. Renamed WINSTON–SALEM TWINS, 1954.

Winston–Salem Red Birds
Carolina League (C), 1957–1960; renamed franchise. Had been WINSTON–SALEM TWINS, 1945–1956. Renamed WINSTON–SALEM RED SOX, 1961.

Winston–Salem Red Sox
Carolina League (C), 1961–1983; renamed franchise. Had been WINSTON–SALEM RED BIRDS, 1957–1960. Renamed WINSTON–SALEM SPIRITS, 1984.

Winston–Salem Spirits
Carolina League (A), 1984–(still in existence as of 5-1-92); renamed

franchise. Had been WINSTON-SALEM RED SOX, 1961–1983.

Winston–Salem Twins
Carolina Association (D), 1908–1912; charter franchise. North Carolina State League (D), 1913–1917; charter franchise. Disbanded with league during 1917 season.

Winston–Salem Twins
Piedmont League (D), 1920; (C), 1921–mid-1932; charter franchise. Became HIGH POINT POINTERS, mid-1932.

Winston–Salem Twins
Piedmont League (B), 1933; new franchise. Disbanded after 1933 season.

Winston–Salem Twins
Piedmont League (B), 1937–1942; new franchise. Disbanded after 1942 season.

Winston–Salem Twins
Carolina League (C), 1954–1956; renamed franchise. Had been WINSTON–SALEM CARDINALS, 1945–1953. Renamed WINSTON–SALEM RED BIRDS, 1957.

WINTER HAVEN, FL
(See also BARTOW, FL)

Winter Haven Mets
Florida State League (A), 1967; renamed franchise. Had been WINTER HAVEN WHITE SOX, mid-1966. Disbanded after 1967 season.

Winter Haven Red Sox
Florida State League (A), 1969–(still in existence as of 5-1-92); new franchise.

Winter Haven Super Sox
Senior Professional Baseball Association, 1989–1990; charter franchise. Disbanded after 1989–1990 season.

Winter Haven White Sox
Florida State League (A), mid-1966; relocated franchise. Had been DEER-FIELD BEACH SUN SOX, 1966. Renamed WINTER HAVEN METS, 1967.

WINTERS, TX
(See BALLINGER, TX)

WISCONSIN RAPIDS, WI

Wisconsin Rapids Indians
Wisconsin State League (D), 1942; 1946–1953; renamed franchise. Had been WISCONSIN RAPIDS WHITE SOX, 1940–1941. Disbanded with league after 1953 season.

Wisconsin Rapids Senators
Midwest League (A), 1963; new franchise. Renamed WISCONSIN RAPIDS TWINS, 1964.

Wisconsin Rapids Twins
Midwest League (A), 1964–1983; renamed franchise. Renamed WISCONSIN RAPIDS SENATORS, 1963. Disbanded after 1983 season.

Wisconsin Rapids White Sox
Wisconsin State League (D), 1940–1941; charter franchise. Renamed WISCONSIN RAPIDS INDIANS, 1942.

WOODBRIDGE, VA
(See DALE CITY, VA)

WOODSTOCK, ONTARIO, CANADA

Woodstock Bains
Canadian League, mid-1899; relocated franchise. Had been STRATFORD POETS, 1899. Disbanded with league after 1899 season.

Woodstock Maroons
Canadian League (C), 1905; charter franchise. Disbanded with league after 1905 season.

WOONSOCKET, RI

Woonsocket
New England League, mid-1891; new franchise. Disbanded with league during 1891 season.

Woonsocket
New England League, 1892; new franchise. Disbanded with league after 1892 season.

Woonsocket
New England League (B), mid-1933; relocated franchise. Had been LAWRENCE, mid-1933. Disbanded with league after 1933 season.

Woonsocket Tigers
Colonial League (C), 1914; charter franchise. Disbanded after 1914 season.

Woonsocket Trotters
Atlantic Association (D), 1908; charter franchise. Disbanded with league during 1908 season.

WORCESTER, MA

Worcester
Massachusetts State Association, 1884; charter franchise. Disbanded with association after 1884 season.

Worcester
Atlantic Association, 1889–mid-1890; charter franchise. Became LEBANON, mid-1890.

Worcester
New England League, 1891; charter franchise. Disbanded after 1891 season.

Worcester
New England League, 1894; charter franchise. Disbanded with league after 1894 season.

Worcester
New England League, 1898; relocated franchise. Had been NEW BEDFORD WHALERS, 1895–mid-1898. Disbanded after 1898 season.

Worcester
Connecticut League (B), 1904; new franchise. Became NORWICH, mid-1904.

Worcester Boosters

Eastern League (B), 1918; (A), 1919–mid-1922; charter franchise. Had been WORCESTER BUSTERS, 1906–1917. Became FITCHBURG, mid-1922.

WORCESTER BROWN STOCKINGS

National League, 1880–1882; new franchise. Became PHILADELPHIA PHILLIES, 1883.

Worcester Brown Stockings

New England League, 1888; new franchise. Disbanded after 1888 season.

Worcester Busters

New England League (B), 1906–1915; new franchise. Eastern League (B), 1916–1917; charter franchise. Renamed WORCESTER BOOSTERS, 1918.

Worcester Chiefs

New England League (B), 1933; charter franchise. Disbanded with league after 1933 season.

Worcester Clamdiggers

Alternate name for WORCESTER FARMERS, 1899.

Worcester Coal Heavers

Alternate name for WORCESTER PANTHERS, 1924.

Worcester Farmers (aka Clamdiggers)

Eastern League, 1899–1900; new franchise. Renamed WORCESTER QUAKERS, 1901.

Worcester Hustlers

Eastern League (A), 1902; renamed franchise. Had been WORCESTER QUAKERS, 1901. Became WORCESTER RIDDLES, 1902.

Worcester Panthers (aka Coal Heavers, 1924)

Eastern League (A), 1923–1925; new franchise. Disbanded after 1925 season.

Worcester Quakers

Eastern League, 1901; renamed franchise. Had been WORCESTER FARMERS (aka Clamdiggers, 1899–1901). Renamed WORCESTER HUSTLERS, 1902.

Worcester Riddles

Eastern League (A), 1903; renamed franchise. Had been WORCESTER HUSTLERS, 1902. Became MONTREAL JINGOES, mid-1903.

Worcester Rosebuds

Northeastern League (A), 1934; relocated franchise. Had been WALTHAM ROSEBUDS, mid-1934. Became MALDEN ROSEBUDS, mid-1934.

Worcester Worcesters

National Association, 1879; charter franchise. Disbanded with association after 1879 season.

WORTHINGTON, MN

Worthington Cardinals

Western League (D), 1939–1940; charter franchise. Disbanded after 1940 season.

WYANDOTTE, MI

Wyandotte

Border League (D), 1912; charter franchise. Disbanded with league during 1912 season.

Wyandotte

Border League (D), 1913; charter franchise. Disbanded with league during 1913 season.

Wyandotte

Eastern Michigan League (D), 1914; charter franchise. Disbanded with league during 1914 season.

WYTHEVILLE, VA

Wytheville A's

Appalachian League (R), 1964; renamed franchise. Had been WYTHEVILLE TWINS, 1961–1963. Renamed WYTHEVILLE SENATORS, 1965.

Wytheville Braves

Appalachian League (R), 1971–1973; new franchise. Disbanded after 1973 season.

Wytheville Cardinals

Appalachian League (D), 1957–1959; charter franchise. Renamed WYTHEVILLE SENATORS, 1960.

Wytheville Cubs

Appalachian League (R), 1985–1989; new franchise. Disbanded after 1989 season.

Wytheville Pioneers

Blue Ridge League (D), 1948; new franchise. Renamed WYTHEVILLE STATESMEN, 1949.

Wytheville Reds

Appalachian League (R), 1967; new franchise. Disbanded after 1967 season.

Wytheville Senators

Appalachian League (D), 1960; renamed franchise. Had been WYTHEVILLE CARDINALS, 1957–1959. Renamed WYTHEVILLE TWINS, 1961.

Wytheville Senators

Appalachian League (R), 1965; renamed franchise. Had been WYTHEVILLE A'S, 1964. Disbanded after 1965 season.

Wytheville Senators

Appalachian League (R), 1969; new franchise. Disbanded after 1969 season.

Wytheville Statesmen

Blue Ridge League (D), 1949–mid-1950; renamed franchise. Had been WYTHEVILLE PIONEERS, 1948. Became BASSETT STATESMEN, mid-1950.

Wytheville Statesmen
Appalachian League (D), 1953–1955; new franchise. Disbanded with league after 1955 season.

Wytheville Twins
Appalachian League (D), 1961–1962; (R), 1963; renamed franchise. Had been WYTHEVILLE SENATORS, 1960. Renamed WYTHEVILLE A'S, 1964.

YAKIMA, WA

Yakima Bears
Northwest League (A), 1990–(still in existence as of 5-1-92); new franchise.

Yakima Bears
Western International League (B), 1949–1951; (A), 1952–1954; renamed franchise. Had been YAKIMA PACKERS, 1948. Northwest League (B), 1955–1962; (A) 1963–1964; charter franchise. Renamed YAKIMA VALLEY BRAVES, 1965.

Yakima Indians
Pacific International League (B), 1920–1921; charter franchise. Disbanded with league after 1921 season.

Yakima Packers
Western International League (B), 1948; renamed franchise. Had been YAKIMA STARS, 1946–1947. Renamed YAKIMA BEARS, 1949.

Yakima Pippins
Western International League (B), 1937–1941; charter franchise. Disbanded with league after 1941 season.

Yakima Stars
Western International League (B), 1946–1947; charter franchise. Renamed YAKIMA PACKERS, 1948.

Yakima Valley Braves
Northwest League (A), 1965–1966; renamed franchise. Had been YAKIMA BEARS, 1949–1964. Disbanded after 1966 season.

YAZOO CITY, MS

Yazoo City
Delta League (D), 1904; charter franchise. Disbanded with league after 1904 season.

Yazoo City Zoos
Cotton States League (D), 1910–1911; new franchise. Disbanded after 1911 season.

Yazoo City Zoos
Cotton States League (D), mid-1912; relocated franchise. Had been NEW ORLEANS LITTLE PELS, 1912. Disbanded after 1912 season.

YONKERS, NY

Yonkers
Hudson River League, 1888; charter franchise. Disbanded with league after 1888 season.

Yonkers
Hudson River League (D), 1905; new franchise. Disbanded after 1905 season.

Yonkers
Hudson River League (D), 1907; new franchise. Disbanded with league after 1907 season.

YORK, NE

York Dukes
Nebraska State League (D), 1928–1931; charter franchise. Disbanded after 1931 season.

York Prohibitionists
Nebraska State League (D), 1911–1915; new franchise. Disbanded with league during 1915 season.

YORK, PA

York
Kesytone Association, 1884; charter franchise. Disbanded with association after 1884 season.

York
Eastern League, mid-1884; relocated franchise. Had been HARRISBURG OLYMPICS, 1884.

York
Pennsylvania State League, 1893; charter franchise. Disbanded after 1893 season.

York Bees
Inter-State League (B), 1940; expansion franchise. Became BRIDGEPORT BEES, 1941.

York Hayseeders
Middle States League, 1889; new franchise. Disbanded after 1889 season.

York Monarchs
Pennsylvania State League, 1890; charter franchise. Disbanded with league after 1890 season.

York Pirates
Eastern League (AA), 1968–1969; renamed franchise. Had been YORK WHITE ROSES, 1962–1967. Disbanded after 1969 season.

York Red Roses
Tri-State League (B), 1907; charter franchise. Became READING RED ROSES, mid-1907.

York White Roses
Tri-State League (B), 1909–mid-1914; new franchise. Became LANCASTER RED ROSES, mid-1914.

York White Roses
Pennsylvania State League (D), 1916; charter franchise. Disbanded with league after 1916 season.

York White Roses
New York–Pennsylvania League (B), 1923–1932, (A), 1933; charter franchise. Disbanded after 1933 season.

York White Roses
Inter-State League (B), 1940; expansion franchise. Became BRIDGEPORT BEES, 1941.

York White Roses
Eastern League (A), 1962; (AA), 1963–1967; new franchise. Renamed YORK PIRATES, 1968.

York White Roses
New York–Pennsylvania League (A), 1936; new franchise. Became TRENTON SENATORS, mid-1936.

York White Roses
Inter-State League (B), 1943–1952; relocated franchise. Had been HARRISBURG SENATORS, 1940–1942. Piedmont League (B), 1953–1955; expansion franchise. Disbanded with league after 1955 season.

York White Roses
Eastern League (A), 1958–1959; new franchise. Disbanded after 1959 season.

York Yahoos
Pennsylvania State League, 1896; new franchise. Disbanded with league after 1896 season.

YOUNGSTOWN, OH

Youngstown
Iron & Oil Association, 1884; charter franchise. Inter-State League, 1885; charter franchise. Disbanded with league after 1885 season.

Youngstown Athletics
Middle Atlantic League (C), 1949–mid-1951; renamed franchise. Had been YOUNGSTOWN COLTS, 1948. Became OIL CITY A'S, mid-1951.

Youngstown Browns
Middle Atlantic League (C), 1939–1941; expansion franchise. Disbanded after 1941 season.

Youngstown Buckeyes
Central League (B), 1932; charter franchise. Disbanded with league after 1932 season.

Youngstown Champs
Ohio–Pennsylvania League (C), 1907–1908; renamed franchise. Had been YOUNGSTOWN OHIO WORKS, 1905–1906. Renamed YOUNGSTOWN INDIANS, 1909.

Youngstown Colts
Middle Atlantic League (C), 1947–1948; renamed franchise. Had been YOUNGSTOWN GREMLINS, 1946. Renamed YOUNGSTOWN ATHLETICS, 1949.

Youngstown Giants
Ohio State League, 1889; charter franchise. Tri-State League, 1890; new franchise. Disbanded with league after 1890 season.

Youngstown Giants
Inter-State League, 1899; renamed franchise. Had been YOUNGSTOWN PUDDLERS, 1896–1898. Renamed YOUNGSTOWN LITTLE GIANTS, 1900.

Youngstown Gremlins
Middle Atlantic League (C), 1946; charter franchise. Renamed YOUNGSTOWN COLTS, 1947.

Youngstown Indians
Ohio–Pennsylvania League (C), 1909; renamed franchise. Had been YOUNGSTOWN CHAMPS, 1907–1908. Renamed YOUNGSTOWN STEELMEN, 1910.

Youngstown Little Giants
Inter-State League, 1900; renamed franchise. Had been YOUNGSTOWN GIANTS, 1899. Became MARION, mid-1900.

Youngstown Ohio Works
Ohio–Pennsylvania League (C), 1905–1906; charter franchise. Renamed YOUNGSTOWN CHAMPS, 1907.

Youngstown Puddlers
Inter-State League, 1896–1898; charter franchise. Renamed YOUNGSTOWN GIANTS, 1899.

Youngstown Steelmen
Ohio–Pennsylvania League (C), 1910–1911; renamed franchise. Had been YOUNGSTOWN INDIANS, 1909. Central League (C), 1912; new franchise. Inter-State League (B), 1913; charter franchise. Disbanded with league after 1913 season.

Youngstown Steelmen
Central League (B), 1915; new franchise. Disbanded after 1915 season.

Youngstown Tubers
Middle Atlantic League (D), mid-1931; relocated franchise. Had been PARKERSBURG PARKERS, mid-1931. Disbanded after 1931 season.

YPSILANTI, MI

Ypsilanti
Border League (D), 1913; charter franchise. Disbanded with league during 1913 season.

Ypsilanti
East Michigan League (D), 1914; charter franchise. Disbanded with league during 1914 season.

YUCATAN, MERIDA, YUCATAN, MEXICO
(See also MERIDA, MEXICO)

Yucatan Deer
Mexican Southeast League (A), 1964–1970; charter franchise. Disbanded with league after 1970 season.

Yucatan Leones (Lions)
Mexican League (AA), 1955–1958; charter franchise. Disbanded after 1958 season.

Yucatan Leones (Lions)
Mexican League (AAA), 1973–1974; new franchise. Disbanded after 1974 season.

Yucatan Leones (Lions)
Mexican League (AAA), 1979– (still in existence as of 5-1-92); new franchise.

YUMA, AZ

Yuma Panthers
Sunset League (C), 1950; new franchise. Southwest International League (C), 1951–1952; charter franchise. Disbanded with league after 1952 season.

Yuma Sun Sox
Arizona–Mexico League (C), 1955–1956; charter franchise. Disbanded after 1956 season.

ZACATECAS, MEXICO
(See also FRESNILLO, MEXICO)

Zacatecas Pericos (Parrots)
Mexican Center League (A), 1965–1967; new franchise. Renamed ZACATECAS TUZOS, 1968.

Zacatecas Tuzos (Gophers)
Mexican Center League (A), 1975–1977; new franchise. Disbanded after 1977 season.

Zacatecas Tuzos (Gophers)
Mexican Center League (A), 1968–1973; renamed franchise. Had been ZACATECAS PERICOS (Parrots), 1965–1967. Disbanded after 1973 season.

ZANESVILLE, OH

Zanesville
POM League (D), 1907; new franchise. Disbanded with league after 1907 season.

Zanesville
Ohio–West Virginia League, 1897; charter franchise. Ohio State League, 1898; charter franchise. Disbanded with league after 1898 season.

Zanesville Cubs
Middle Atlantic League (C), 1941–1942; expansion franchise. Suspended operations with league after 1942 season, and did not rejoin when league resumed in 1946.

Zanesville Dodgers
Ohio State League (D), 1944–1947; charter franchise. Ohio–Indiana League (D), 1948; charter franchise. Renamed ZANESVILLE INDIANS, 1949.

Zanesville Flood Sufferers
Inter-State League (B), 1913; charter franchise. Disbanded with league after 1913 season.

Zanesville Grays
Middle Atlantic League (D), 1933–1937; expansion franchise. Disbanded after 1937 season.

Zanesville Indians
Ohio–Indiana League (D), 1949–1950; renamed franchise. Had been ZANESVILLE DODGERS, 1944–1948. Disbanded after 1950 season.

Zanesville Infants
Central League (B), 1908–1909; new franchise. Renamed ZANESVILLE POTTERS, 1910.

Zanesville Kickapoos
Ohio State League, 1887; charter franchise. Tri-State League, 1888; charter franchise. Disbanded after 1888 season.

Zanesville Moguls
Ohio–Pennsylvania League (D), 1905–mid-1906; charter franchise. Became MARION MOGULS, mid-1906.

Zanesville Potters
Central League (B), 1910–1912; renamed franchise. Had been ZANESVILLE INFANTS, 1908–1909. Disbanded after 1912 season.

ZEBULON, NC

Carolina Mudcats
Southern League (AA), 1991– (still in existence as of 5-1-92); relocated franchise. Had been COLUMBUS MUDCATS, 1989–1990.

APPENDIX OF LEAGUES

(Major League and Negro League affiliations are in capital letters. Years in existence follow the league name.)

Alabama–Florida League, 1936–1939; 1951–1962

Alabama State League, 1940–1941; 1946–1950

Alabama–Tennessee League, 1921

All-American Girls Professional Baseball League, 1943–1954

AMERICAN ASSOCIATION, 1882–1884; 1887–1891

American Association, 1903–1962; 1969–(still in existence as of 5-1-92)

AMERICAN LEAGUE, 1900–(still in existence as of 5-1-92)

AMERICAN NEGRO LEAGUE, 1929

Appalachian League, 1911–1914; 1921–1925; 1937–1955; 1957–1963

Arizona League, 1988–(still in existence as of 5-1-92)

Arizona–Mexico League, 1955–1958

Arizona State League, 1928–1930

Arizona–Texas League, 1931–1932; 1937–1941; 1947–1950; 1952–1954

Arkansas League, 1897; 1908

Arkansas–Missouri League, 1936–1939

Arkansas State League, 1934–1935

Arkansas–Texas League, 1905–1906

Atlantic Association, 1889–1890; 1908

Atlantic League, 1896–1900; 1914

Big State League, 1947–1957

Bi–State League, 1915; 1934–1942

Black Hills League, 1891–1892

Blue Grass League, 1908–1912; 1922–1924

Blue Ridge League, 1915–1918; 1920–1930; 1946–1950

Border League, 1912–1913; 1946–1951

California League, 1888–1893; 1899–1900; 1941–1942; 1946–(still in existence as of 5-1-92)

California State League, 1885–1887; 1896; 1898–1899

Canadian–American League, 1936–1942; 1946–1951

Canadian League, 1885–1886; 1896–1899; 1905; 1911–1913; 1915

Cape Bretton Colliery League, 1937–1939

Carolina Association, 1908–1912

Carolina Coast League, 1909

Carolina League, 1945–(still in existence as of 5-1-92)

Central Association, 1888; 1908–1917; 1947–1949

Central International League, 1912

Central Inter-State League, 1888–1889

Central Kansas League, 1908–1912

Central League, 1888; 1897; 1900; 1903–1917; 1920–1922; 1926; 1928–1930; 1932; 1934; 1948–1951

Central Mexican League, 1956–1957

Central New Jersey League, 1892

Central New York League, 1886; 1888; 1910

Central Pennsylvania League, 1886–1888; 1897

Central Texas League, 1914–1917

Coastal Plain League, 1937–1941; 1946–1952

Cocoa Rookie League, 1964

Colonial League, 1914

Colorado League, 1885

Colorado State League, 1889; 1898

Connecticut Association, 1910

Connecticut League, 1884; 1897–1900; 1902–1912

Connecticut State League, 1885; 1888; 1891

Connecticut Valley League, 1902

Copper-Country Soo League, 1905

Cotton States League, 1902–1908; 1910–1913; 1922–1932; 1936–1941; 1947–1955

Cumberland Valley League, 1895–1896

Dakota League, 1921–1922

Delta League, 1904–1905

Dixie Association, 1971

Dixie League, 1916–1917; 1933

East Dixie League, 1934–1935

Eastern Association, 1881; 1884; 1885–1886; 1891–1892; 1913–1914

Eastern Canada League,
 1922–1923
Eastern Carolina League,
 1908–1910; 1928–1929
Eastern Championship
 Association, 1881
EASTERN COLORED
 LEAGUE, 1923–1928
Eastern Illinois League,
 1907–1908
Eastern Inter-State League, 1889
Eastern Iowa League, 1890; 1895
Eastern Kansas League,
 1910–1911
Eastern League, 1884–1887;
 1889–1911; 1916–1932;
 1938–(still in existence as of
 5-1-92)
Eastern New England League,
 1885
Eastern Shore League,
 1922–1928; 1937–1941;
 1946–1949
East Texas League, 1926; 1931;
 1936–1940; 1946; 1949–1950
EAST–WEST LEAGUE, 1932
Empire State League, 1913
Evangeline League, 1934–1942;
 1946–1957

Far West League, 1948–1951
FLAG League: See
 FLORIDA–ALABAMA–GEORGIA
 LEAGUE
Florida–Alabama–Georgia
 (FLAG) League, 1915
Florida East Coast League (D),
 1921; 1940–1942; 1972
Florida International League,
 1946–1954
Florida Rookie League, 1965
Florida State League, 1892;
 1919–1928; 1936–1941;
 1946–(still in existence as of
 5-1-92)
Georgia–Alabama League,
 1913–1917; 1928–1930;
 1946–1951

Georgia–Florida League,
 1935–1942; 1946–1958;
 1962–1963
Georgia State League, 1906;
 1914; 1920–1921; 1948–1956
Gulf Coast League, 1907–1908;
 1926; 1950–1953; 1964–(still
 in existence as of 5-1-92)
Gulf States League, 1976

Hudson River League, 1886;
 1903–1907

Illinois–Indiana League, 1889
Illinois–Iowa–Indiana (Three-I)
 League, 1902–1917;
 1919–1932; 1935; 1937–1942;
 1946–1961
Illinois–Iowa League, 1889–1892
Illinois–Missouri League,
 1908–1914
Illinois State League, 1947–1948
Indiana–Illinois League, 1899
Indiana–Michigan League, 1910
Indiana–Ohio League, 1908
Indiana State League, 1888;
 1890; 1896; 1900
Inland Empire League, 1908
Intermountain League, 1909
International Association,
 1877–1880; 1887–1889
International League,
 1886–1887; 1890; 1898; 1900;
 1908; 1912–(still in existence
 as of 5-1-92)
Inter-State Association
 1883–1884; 1906;
Inter-State Leagues, 1885–1886;
 1889; 1891; 1894–1900; 1903;
 1905–1906; 1908; 1913–1916;
 1932; 1939–1952
Iowa–South Dakota League,
 1902–1903
Iowa State League, 1902;
 1904–1907; 1912
Iron & Oil Association, 1884
Iron & Oil League, 1884–1885;
 1895; 1898

Kansas–Oklahoma–Missouri
 (KOM) League, 1946–1952
Kansas–Missouri League, 1892
Kansas State League, 1887;
 1896–1898; 1905–1906;
 1909–1911; 1913–1914
Kentucky–Illinois–Tennessee
 (KITTY) League, 1903–1906;
 1910–1914; 1916; 1922–1924;
 1935–1942; 1946–1955
Keystone Association, 1884
KITTY League: See
 KENTUCKY–ILLINOIS–
 TENNESSEE (KITTY) LEAGUE
KOM League: See
 KANSAS–OKLAHOMA–
 MISSOURI LEAGUE

Lake Shore League, 1908
Lone Star League, 1927–1929;
 1947–1948
Longhorn League, 1947–1955
Louisiana State League, 1915;
 1920

Maine State League, 1897; 1907
Mexican Center League,
 1960–1975
Mexican League, 1955–(still in
 existence as of 5-1-92)
Mexican National League, 1946
Mexican Pacific League, 1976
Mexican Rookie League, 1968
Mexican Southeast League,
 1964–1970
Michigan–Ontario League,
 1919–1926
Michigan State League,
 1889–1890; 1893–1895; 1897;
 1902; 1911–1914; 1926;
 1940–1941
Michigan–Wisconsin League,
 1892
Middle Atlantic League,
 1925–1942; 1946–1951
Middle State League, 1889–1890
Middle Texas League, 1914–1915

Midwest League, 1956–(still in existence as of 5-1-92)

MINK League: See MISSOURI–IOWA–NEBRASKA–KANSAS LEAGUE

Minnesota–Wisconsin League, 1909–1912

Mississippi–Ohio Valley League, 1949–1955

Mississippi State League, 1921

Mississippi Valley League, 1922–1933

Missouri–Iowa–Nebraska–Kansas (MINK) League, 1910–1913

Missouri–Kansas League, 1912

Missouri State League, 1911

Missouri Valley League, 1902–1905

Montana State League, 1892; 1898–1900

Mountain State League, 1937–1942

Mountain States League, 1911–1912; 1948–1954

NATIONAL ASSOCIATION, 1871–1875; 1879–1880

NATIONAL LEAGUE, 1876–(still in existence as of 5-1-92)

Nebraska State League, 1887; 1892; 1910–1915; 1922–1923; 1928–1938; 1956–1959

NEGRO AMERICAN LEAGUE, 1937–1950

NEGRO NATIONAL LEAGUE, 1920–1948

NEGRO SOUTHERN LEAGUE, 1932

New Brunswick League, 1890

New Brunswick–Maine League, 1913

New England Association, 1895

New England Inter-State League, 1888

New England League, 1877; 1886–1889; 1891–1899; 1902–1915; 1919; 1926–1930; 1933; 1946–1949

New Hampshire State League, 1886; 1907

New York–New Jersey League, 1913

New York–Pennsylvania League, 1890–1891; 1923–1937; 1957–(still in existence as of 5-1-92)

New York State League, 1885; 1888–1890; 1894–1901; 1902–1917

North Atlantic League, 1946–1950

North Carolina Association, 1913

North Carolina League, 1902; 1913–1917

North Carolina State League, 1937–1942; 1945–1952

North Dakota League, 1923

Northeast Arkansas League, 1936–1941

North-Eastern Arkansas League, 1909–1911

Northeastern League, 1934

Northern Association, 1910

Northern Copper Country League, 1906–1907

Northern League, 1902–1905; 1908; 1913–1917; 1933–1942; 1946–1971

Northern New York League, 1902

Northern State League of Indiana, 1909–1911

Northern Utah League, 1921

North Texas League, 1904–1907

Northwestern League, 1879–1881; 1883–1884; 1886–1887; 1891; 1905–1917

Northwest League, 1955–(still in existence as of 5-1-92)

OAK League: See OKLAHOMA–ARKANSAS–KANSAS LEAGUE

Ohio–Indiana League, 1907; 1948–1951

Ohio–Michigan League, 1893

Ohio–Pennsylvania League, 1900; 1905–1912

Ohio State Association, 1884

Ohio State League, 1884; 1887; 1889; 1892–1893; 1895–1896; 1908–1916; 1936–1941; 1944–1947

Ohio Valley League, 1891

Ohio–West Virginia League, 1897

Oklahoma–Arkansas–Kansas (OAK) League, 1907

Oklahoma–Kansas League, 1908

Oklahoma State League, 1912; 1922–1924

Old Dominion League, 1908

Ontario League, 1884

Oregon State League, 1904

Pacific Coast International League, 1918; 1920

Pacific Coast League, 1898; 1903–(still in existence as of 5-1-92)

Pacific Inter-State League, 1891

Pacific National League, 1903–1905

Pacific Northwest League, 1890–1892; 1896

Pacific States League, 1898–1899

Panhandle–Pecos Valley League, 1923

Pennsylvania League, 1879

Pennsylvania–Ohio–Maryland (POM) League, 1906–1907

Pennsylvania–Ontario–New York (PONY) League, 1939–1956

Pennsylvania State Association, 1886–1887; 1889–1890; 1934–1942

Pennsylvania State League, 1890–1896; 1916

Pennsylvania–West Virginia League, 1907–1909; 1914

Permian Basin League, 1934

Piedmont League, 1920–1955

Pioneer League, 1939–1942; 1946–(still in existence as of 5-1-92)

POM League: See
PENNSYLVANIA–OHIO–
MARYLAND LEAGUE
PONY League: See
PENNSYLVANIA–ONTARIO–
NEW YORK LEAGUE
Potomac League, 1916
Provincial League, 1950–1955

Quebec–Ontario–Vermont
League, 1924
Quebec Provincial League, 1940

Rio Grande Association, 1915
Rio Grande Valley League, 1931;
1949–1950

Saginaw Valley League, 1888
San Joaquin Valley League,
1910–1911
Sarasota Rookie League, 1964
Sooner State League, 1947–1957
Sophomore League, 1958–1961
South Atlantic Association,
1919–1930
South Atlantic League, 1892;
1904–1917; 1919; 1936–1942;
1946–1963; 1980–(still in
existence as of 5-1-92)
South Carolina League,
1906–1908
South Central League, 1906; 1912
South Dakota League, 1920; 1923
Southeastern League,
1896–1897; 1910–1912
Southeastern Kansas League, 1911
Southern Association, 1902–1961
Southern California League,
1910; 1913
Southern Illinois League, 1910
Southern League, 1884–1889;
1892–1896; 1898–1899; 1964–
(still in existence as of 5-1-92)
Southern New England League,
1885

Southern Texas League,
1903–1906
South Michigan League,
1906–1915
South Texas League, 1903–1906
Southwestern League, 1887;
1891; 1893; 1895; 1898; 1904;
1921–1926; 1956–1957
Southwest International League,
1951–1952
Southwest Iowa League, 1903
Southwest Texas League,
1910–1911
Southwest Washington League,
1903–1906
Sunset League, 1947–1950

Tar Heel League, 1939–1940;
1953–1954
Tennessee–Alabama League,
1903
Texas Association, 1923–1926
Texas League, 1892; 1902–(still
in existence as of 5-1-92)
Texas–Oklahoma League,
1911–1914; 1921–1922
Texas Valley League,
1901–1908; 1927–1928; 1938
Three I League: See ILLINOIS–
IOWA–INDIANA LEAGUE
Tobacco State League,
1946–1950
Tri-State League, 1888–1891;
1907–1914; 1924–1926;
1946–1955

Union Association, 1911–1914
Upper Peninsula League,
1890–1891
Utah–Idaho League, 1926–1928

Virginia League, 1885–1886;
1894–1896; 1900; 1906–1921;
1923–1928; 1939–1940;
1948–1951

Virginia-Mountain League, 1912;
1914
Virginia–North Carolina League,
1905
Virginia Valley League, 1910

Washington State League, 1897;
1910–1912
West Dixie League, 1934–1935
WESTERN ASSOCIATION,
1888–1891; 1893–1899
Western Association,
1905–1911; 1914–1917;
1920–1932; 1934–1942;
1946–1954
Western Canada League,
1907–1914; 1919–1921
Western Carolina League,
1948–1952; 1960–1962
Western Carolinas League,
1963–1979
Western International League,
1902; 1904–1919; 1922;
1937–1942; 1946–1954
Western Inter-State League,
1890; 1895
Western League, 1882–1883;
1885–1888; 1890–1899;
1901–1937; 1939–1941;
1947–1958;
Western New York League, 1890
Western Ontario League, 1884
Western Pennsylvania
Association, 1889
Western Pennsylvania League, 1907
Western Tri-State League,
1912–1914
West Michigan League, 1910
West Texas League, 1920–1922
West Texas–New Mexico
League, 1937–1942;
1946–1955
West Virginia League, 1910
Wisconsin League, 1907
Wisconsin State League, 1891;
1905–1907; 1940–1942;
1946–1953

BIBLIOGRAPHY

You'll find great discrepancies from one sports book to the next; I suggest that you trust, as I did, the information found most often.

Adelman, Melvin L. *A Sporting Time: New York City and the Rise of Modern Athletics, 1820–70.* Urbana: University of Illinois Press, 1986.

Allen, Lee. *The Cincinnati Reds.* New York: G. P. Putnam's Sons, 1948.

———. *The Giants and the Dodgers: The Fabulous Story of Baseball's Fiercest Feud.* New York: G. P. Putnam's Sons, 1964.

Bailey, Jim. *Arkansas Travelers—79 Years of Baseball.* Little Rock: Arkansas Travelers Baseball Club, 1980.

Beverage, Richard. *The Angels: Los Angeles in the Pacific Coast League, 1919–1957.* Placentia, CA: Deacon Press, 1981.

———. *Hollywood Stars—Baseball and the Pacific Coast League, 1919–1957.* Placentia, CA: Deacon Press, 1984.

Bjarkman, Peter C., ed. *The Encyclopedia of Major League Baseball Histories: Vol. I—The American League.* Westport, CT: Meckler, 1991.

———. *The Encyclopedia of Major League Baseball Histories: Vol. II—The National League.* Westport, CT: Meckler, 1991.

Blake, Mike. *The Minor Leagues—A Celebration of the Little Show.* New York: Wynwood Press, 1991.

Bready, James. *The Home Team: A History of Baseball in Baltimore.* Baltimore: Mono-type Company, 1975.

Brooks, Ken. *The Last Rebel Yell—A History of the Alabama–Florida League.* Lynn Haven, FL: Seneca Park Publishing, 1896.

Chrisman, David F. *This History of the International League.* Bend, OR: Maverick, 1981.

———. *This History of the Piedmont League.* Bend, OR: Maverick, 1986.

———. *This History of the Virginia League.* Bend, OR: Maverick, 1988.

Cohen, Stanley. *The Dodgers—The First Hundred Years.* New York: Birch Lane Press, 1990.

Coombs, Samm, and West, Bob, eds. *Baseball—America's National Game.* San Francisco: Halo, 1991.

Danzig, Allison, and Reichler, Joe. *The History of Baseball: Its Great Players, Teams, and Managers.* Englewood Cliffs: Prentice-Hall, 1959.

DeClerico, James M., and Pavalec, Barry J. *The Jersey Game.* New Brunswick: Rutgers University Press, 1991.

French, Robert. *50 Golden Years in the American Association of Professional Baseball Clubs, 1902–1951.* Minneapolis: Syndicate Printing, 1951.

Goldstein, Richard. *Spartan Seasons—How Baseball Survived the Second World War.* New York: Macmillan, 1980.

Heilbroner Associates. *The Baseball Blue Books, 1909–current.* Ft. Wayne: Heilbroner Baseball Bureau, 1909–current.

Holway, John B. *Blackball Stars—Negro League Pioneers.* New York: Carroll & Graf, 1991.

Lamb, David. *Stolen Season—A Journey through America and Baseball's Minor Leagues.* New York: Random House, 1991.

Levine, Peter. *A. G. Spalding and the Rise of Baseball.* New York: Oxford University Press, 1985.

Linthurst, Randolph. *The Trenton Giants.* Trenton, N.J.: White Eagle Printing, 1982.

Lowenfish, Lee, and Tony Lupien. *The Imperfect Diamond—A History of Baseball's Labor Wars.* New York: Da Capo, 1991.

Mayer, Ronald A. *The 1937 Newark Bears: A Baseball Legend.* Union City, N.J.: William H. Wise, 1980.

Neft, David, ed. *The Sports Encyclopedia of Baseball.* New York: Grosset & Dunlap, 1976.

Obosjski, Robert. *Bush League—A History of Minor League Baseball.* New York: Macmillan, 1975.

O'Neal, Bill. *The Pacific Coast League, 1903–1988.* Austin, TX: Eakin Press, 1990.

————. *The Texas League, 1888–1987.* Austin, TX: Eakin Press, 1987.

Parker, Al. *Baseball Giant Killers—The Spudders of the '20s.* Quanah, TX: Nortex Press, 1976.

Peterson, Robert. *Only the Ball Was White.* New York: McGraw-Hill, 1984.

Phillips, John. *The Spiders—Who Was Who. (revised).* Cabin John, MD: Capital, 1991.

Pietrusza, David. *Baseball's Canadian–American League.* Jefferson, NC: McFarland, 1987.

————. *The Formation, Sometimes Absorption, and Mostly Inevitable Demise of 18 Baseball Organizations.* Jefferson, NC: McFarland, 1991.

Reichler, Joseph L. *The Baseball Encyclopedia.* New York: Macmillan, 1979.

Reidenbaugh, Lowell. *Take Me out to the Ball Park.* St. Louis: The Sporting News, 1983.

Rogosin, Donn. *Invisible Men—Life in Baseball's Negro Leagues.* New York: Atheneum, 1985.

Ruck, Rob. *The Tropic of Baseball: Baseball in the Dominican Republic.* Westport, CT: Meckler, 1991.

Seymour, Harold. *Baseball: The Early Years.* New York: Oxford University Press, 1989.

————. *Baseball: The Golden Age.* New York: Oxford University Press, 1971.

Somers, Dale A. *The Rise of Sports in New Orleans, 1850–1900.* Baton Rouge: Louisiana State University Press, 1972.

Sullivan Neil J. *The Minors.* New York: St. Martin's Press, 1990.

Turkin, Hy, and Thompson, S. C. *The Official Encyclopedia of Baseball.* New York: A. S. Barnes, 1956.

Voigt, David. *American Baseball: From the Gentleman's Sport to the Commissioner System.* University Park: Penn State Press, 1983.

INDEX OF TEAM NICKNAMES

(This Index lists team nicknames alphabetically, followed by city citations. To find an entry in the "Team Listings by City" section, simply look up the city alphabetically and then scan down the list for the team nickname. If a team doesn't have a city name, please refer to the "Key to Teams Without City Names" section. For further information, please consult the "How to Use This Book" section.)

Abc's
  Indianapolis (IN)
Abes
  Lincoln (IL)
Acereros
  Monclova–
  Coahuila (MEXICO)
Aces
  Abilene (TX)
  Alexandria (LA)
  Anaheim (CA)
  Ayden (NC)
  Corpus Christi
  (TX)
  Erwin (TN)
  Huntington (WV)
  Reading (PA)
  Saginaw (MI)
  San Diego (CA)
Acme Colored Giants
  Celeron (NY)
Acorns
  Akron (OH)
  Oakland (CA)
Actives
  Reading (PA)
Admirals
  Daytona Beach
  (FL)
  Decatur (IN)
Adopted Sons
  Fall River (MA)
Adventists
  Battle Creek (MI)
Advertisers
  Quincy (IL)
Aeros
  Wichita (KS)

Aggies
  Morgantown (NC)
Aguilas
  Mexicali
  (MEXICO)
  Mexico City
  (MEXICO)
  Veracruz
  (MEXICO)
Aguiluchos
  Leon (MEXICO)
Akrons
  Akron (OH)
Albemarles
  Elizabeth City
  (TN)
Alcranes
  Campeche
  (MEXICO)
  Durango
  (MEXICO)
Alerts
  London (CANADA)
  Saginaw (MI)
Algodoneros
  Durango
  (MEXICO)
  Guasave
  (MEXICO)
  San Pedro de las
  Colonias
  (MEXICO)
  Union Laguna
  (MEXICO)
Alice
  Vincennes (IN)
Alijadores
  Ciudad Mante

  (MEXICO)
  Tampico (MEX-
  ICO)
  Tampico–Madero
  (MEXICO)
Alleghenies
  Pittsburgh (PA)
Alligators
  Tampico
  (MEXICO)
Alouettes
  Quebec
  (CANADA)
Altas
  Sacramento (CA)
American Giants
  Chicago (IL)
  Cole's (Chicago)
  (IL)
Americans
  Bridgeport (CN)
  Nashville (TN)
Amigos
  Miami (FL)
Amskoegs
  Manchester (NH)
Angeles
  Puebla (MEXICO)
Angeles Negros
  Puebla (MEXICO)
Angels
  California (CA)
  Arizona (AZ)
  Attleboro (MA)
  Brandon (CAN-
  ADA)
  Derby (CT)
  Fayetteville (AR)

Idaho Falls (ID)
  Tri-Cities (Kennewick–
  Richland–Pasco, WA)
  Leadville (CO)
  Leesville (LA)
  Los Angeles (CA)
  Lufkin (TX)
  Maysville (KY)
  Midland (TX)
  Nashua (NH)
  Palm Springs (CA)
  Pensacola (FL)
  Ponca City (OK)
  Puebla (MEXICO)
  Quad Cities (IL, IA)
  St. John (CAN-
  ADA)
  Salem (OR)
  Salinas (CA)
  Salt Lake City (UT)
  Seattle (WA)
  Waterbury (CT)
Anglers
  Leesburg (FL)
Ansons
  Marshalltown (IA)
Antelopes
  Clarinda (IA)
Anthracites
  Carbondale (PA)
  Pottsville (PA)
  Reading (PA)
Apaches
  Abilene (TX)
  Globe–Miami (AZ)
  Laredo (TX)
Appalachians
  Knoxville (TX)

Apostles
  St. Paul (MN)
Arabs
  Coronado (CA)
Ardmorites
  Ardmore (OK)
Aristocrats
  Calumet (MI)
Arrows
  Andalusia (AL)
  Andalusia–Opp
  (AL)
  Flint (MI)
A's
  Abbeville (LA)
  Albany (NY)
  Anderson (SC)
  Auburn (NE)
  Boise (ID)
  Burlington (VT)
  Cordele (GA)
  Corsicana (TX)
  Drummondville
  (CANADA)
  Fargo–Morehead
  (ND)
  Fayetteville (NC)
  Federalsburg (MD)
  Fitzgerald (GA)
  Idaho Falls (ID)
  Kansas City (KS)
  Kewanee (IL)
  Lexington (NC)
  Lincoln (NE)
  Marion (VA)
  Long Island
  (Maspeth, NY)
  Medicine Hat

(CANADA)
Mobile (AL)
Modesto (CA)
Moline (IL)
Monterrey (MEX-ICO)
Muskogee (OK)
Oakland (CA)
Ogden (UT)
Oil City (PA)
Paris (TX)
Ponca City (OK)
Portsmouth (OH)
Rochester–Winona (MN)
Saginaw (MI)
St. Hyacinthe (CANADA)
Salisbury (MD)
San Francisco (CA)
Tri-Cities (Kennewick–Richland–Pasco, WA)
West Haven (CT)
Winona (MN)
Wytheville (VA)
Astros
 Auburn (NY)
 Cedar Rapids (IN)
 Cocoa (FL)
 Columbia (GA)
 Covington (VA)
 Daytona Beach (FL)
 Gulf Coast (FL)
 Houston (TX)
 Osceola (FL)
 Peninsula (PA)
 Salisbury (NC)
 Sarasota (FL)
 Sumter (SC)
 Tampico (MEXICO)
 Williamsport (PA)
Asylums
 Utica (NY)
Athletics
 Abbeville (LA)
 Arizona (AZ)
 Chanute (KS)
 Corning (NY)
 Fayetteville (NC)
 Grand Island (NC)

Indianapolis (IN)
Kansas City (KS)
Leesburg (FL)
Lincoln (NE)
Martinsville (VA)
Mattoon (IL)
Medford (OR)
Middlesboro (KY)
Moultrie (GA)
North Bend–Coos Bay (VA)
Oakland (CA)
Olean (NY)
Ottawa (CANADA)
Philadelphia (PA)
Plainview (TX)
Pocatello (ID)
Quebec (CANADA)
Rocky Mount (NC)
Savannah (GA)
Sherbrooke (CANADA)
Southern Oregon (OR)
Sunbury (PA)
Tarboro (NC)
Topeka (KS)
Victoria (CANADA)
Visalia (CA)
Watertown (NY)
Waxahachie (TX)
Williamsport (PA)
Youngstown (OH)
Atlantas
 Atlanta (GA)
Atlantic(s)
 Brooklyn (NY)
Atoms
 Tri-Cities (Kennewick–Richland–Pasco, WA)
Auctioneers
 Lumberton (NC)
Authors
 Waterbury (CT)
Aviators
 Dayton (OH)
 Wichita (KS)
Azaleas
 Palatka (FL)

Aztecas
 Mexico City (MEXICO)
Aztecs
 Mexico City (MEXICO)

Babes
 Bluffton (IN)
 Charleroi (PA)
 Chatam (CANADA)
 Chicago (IL)
 Chillicothe (OH)
 Lincoln (IL)
 Omaha (NB)
 Springfield (OH)
Babies
 Albany (GA)
 Birmingham (AL)
 Burlington (IA)
 Columbia (GA)
 Cordele (GA)
 Elmira (NY)
 Houston (TX)
 Seattle (WA)
 Waco (TX)
Baby Cardinals
 Laurel (MS)
Baby Seals
 San Francisco (CA)
 Tucson (AZ)
Baby Senators
 Sacramento (CA)
Badgers
 Bakersfield (CA)
 Caruthersville (MO)
 LaCrosse (WI)
 West Plains (MO)
Bains
 Woodstock (NY)
Baltfeds
 Baltimore (MD)
Banana Growers
 Villahermosa (MEXICO)
Bananas
 Tabasco (MEXICO)
 Villahermosa (MEXICO)

Bangors
 Bangor (ME)
Bankers
 Panama City (PANAMA)
Bannocks
 Pocatello (ID)
Barons
 Big Spring (TX)
 Birmingham (AL)
 Bowling Green (KY)
 Nazareth (PA)
 Wilkes-Barre (PA)
Barristers
 Blackstone (VA)
 Lawrence (MA)
Bathers
 Hot Springs (AZ)
 Marlin (TX)
 Mount Carmel (PA)
Bays
 Green Bay (WI)
Beachcombers
 San Jose (CA)
Beagles
 Bradford (PA)
Beaneaters (aka Bean Eaters)
 Boston (MA)
 Lima (OH)
Bearcats
 Ardmore (OK)
 Ballinger (TX)
 Bartlesville (OK)
 Cleveland (OH)
 Coleman (TX)
 Paris (TX)
Bears
 Bakersfield (CA)
 Bridgeport (CT)
 Cleveland (OH)
 Denver (CO)
 Eau Claire (WI)
 Fayetteville (AR)
 Gladewater (TX)
 Globe (AZ)
 Hannibal (MO)
 Janesville (WI)
 Merced (CA)
 Meridian (MS)
 Milwaukee (WI)
 Mobile (AL)

Newark (NJ)
New Bern (NC)
Rochester (MN)
Saginaw (MI)
San Antonio (TX)
San Diego (CA)
San Jose (CA)
Texarkana (TX)
Walla Walla (WA)
Waycross (GA)
Yakima (WA)
Beavers
 Austin (TX)
 Bay City (MI)
 Beaver Falls (PA)
 Kitchner (CANADA)
 Portland (OR)
 Smiths Falls (CANADA)
 Toronto (CANADA)
 Vancouver (CANADA)
 Vancouver (CANADA)–
 Vancouver (WA)
Beay Brummels
 Rochester (NY)
Bees
 Bakersfield (CA)
 Beaver Falls (PA)
 Beeville (TX)
 Bisbee (AZ)
 Boston (MA)
 Bradford (PA)
 Bridgeport (CT)
 Burlington (IA)
 Burlington (NC)
 Clarksburg (WV)
 Cordele (GA)
 Evansville (IN)
 Hartford (CT)
 Huntington (WV)
 Jesup (GA)
 Salisbury (NC)
 Salt Lake City (UT)
 San Jose (CA)
 Vancouver (CANADA)
 Victoria (CANADA)
 York (PA)

Belles
  Battle Creek (MI)
  Racine (WI)
Bellmakers
  Bristol (CT)
Bells
  Rockford (IL)
Benders
  Great Bend (KS)
  South Bend (IN)
Bengals
  Beckley (WV)
  Bloomington (IL)
  Cleveland (MS)
  Columbus (MS)
Bermudas
  Laredo (TX)
Berries
  Hammond (LA)
Berry Pickers
  Saskatoon (CANADA)
Betsy Cubs
  Elizabethton (TN)
Betsy Local
  Elizabethton (TN)
Betsy Red Sox
  Elizabethton (TN)
Bidwells
  Emporia (KS)
Big Benders
  Great Bend (KS)
Billbobs
  Grand Rapids (MI)
Bill-Eds
  Grand Rapids (MI)
Billies
  Clarksville (TN)
  Snow Hill (NC)
  Vicksburg (MS)
  Williamsport (PA)
Billikens
  Bay City (MI)
  Fort Wayne (IN)
  Montgomery (AL)
Bills
  Williamsport (PA)
Biltmores
  Guelph (OH)
Bingers
  Bonham (TX)
Bingling Pans
  Lowell (MA)

Bingos
  Binghamton (NY)
  Warren (PA)
Birdies
  Mattoon–Charleston (IL)
Birds
  Wayland (MA)
Bisons
  Buffalo (NY)
  Cornwall (CANADA)
  Perth (CANADA)
Black Angels
  Puebla (MEXICO)
Black Barons
  Birmingham (AL)
Black Bears
  Toluca (MEXICO)
Blackbirds
  Erie (PA)
  Evansville (IN)
  Grand Rapids (MI)
  Hamilton (CANADA)
  Mobile (AL)
  Peoria (IL)
Black Caps
  Louisville (KY)
Black Cats
  Aberdeen (WA)
Black Crackers
  Atlanta (GA)
Black Crows
  New Haven (CT)
Black Diamonds
  Fairmount (WV)
Blackhawks
  LaCrosse (WI)
  Lincoln (IL)
Black Knights
  Beckley (WV)
Black Pirates
  Toledo (OH)
Black Sox
  Baltimore (MD)
  Battle Creek (MI)
  Evansville (IN)
  Grand Rapids (MI)
  Montgomery (AL)
Black Yankees
  New York (NY)
Blanketeers
  Elkin (NC)

Blanketmakers
  Springfield (TN)
Blazers
  Beeville (TX)
Bloomers
  Bloomington (IL)
Blowhards
  Waycross (GA)
Bluebirds (aka Blue Birds)
  Cleveland (OH)
  Columbus (OH)
  Hartford (CT)
  Henderson (KY)
  Mahanoy City (PA)
  Mobile (AL)
  New Haven (CT)
  Quincy (IL)
  Richmond (VA)
  Stroudsburg (PA)
Blue Cats
  Perth (CANADA)
Blue-Grays
  Bluefield (WV)
Blue Hens
  Laurel (DE)
  Wilmington (DE)
Bluejackets
  Bremerton (WA)
Blue Jays
  Dunedin (FL)
  Florence (SC)
  Green Bay (WI)
  Gulf Coast (FL)
  Jackson (TN)
  Kinston (NC)
  Knoxville (TX)
  Medicine Hat (CANADA)
  Myrtle Beach (SC)
  Philadelphia (PA)
  Roanoke Rapids (NC)
  St. Catherines (CANADA)
  Salina (KS)
  Schenectady (NY)
  Toronto (CANADA)
  Utica (NY)
Blue Ribbons
  Gainesville (TX)

Blue Rocks
  Wilmington (DE)
Blues
  Alton (IL)
  Ardmore (OK)
  Aurora (IL)
  Bartlesville (OK)
  Beatrice (NE)
  Bloomington (IL)
  Boston (MA)
  Brockville (CANADA)
  Buffalo (NY)
  Cassville (MO)
  Cleveland (OH)
  Clinton (NC)
  Ellsworth (KS)
  Eugene (OR)
  Hagerstown (MD)
  Haverhill (MA)
  Hot Springs (CO)
  Hutchinson (KS)
  Jeanerette (LA)
  Kansas City (KS)
  La Junta (MEXICO)
  Leadville (CO)
  Madison (WI)
  Memphis (TN)
  Miami (OK)
  Nashville (TN)
  New Haven (CT)
  Niles (MI)
  Shawnee (OK)
  Statesville (NC)
  Superior (WI)
  Taunton (MA)
Blue Sox
  Abilene (TX)
  Carbondale (PA)
  Davenport (IA)
  Hopewell (VA)
  Huntington (WV)
  LaSalle (IL)
  Manchester (NH)
  Martinsburg (WV)
  Portland (ME)
  St. Thomas (CANADA)
  South Bend (IN)
  Springfield (OH)
  Tifton (GA)
  Toledo (OH)
  Utica (NY)

Blue Stockings
  Spokane (WA)
Blue Wings
  Bradford (PA)
Bobcats
  Edinburg (TX)
  Lubbock (TX)
Bobolinks
  Grand Rapids (MI)
Boers
  Grand Rapids (MI)
Boilermakers
  Kewanee (IL)
Boll Weevils
  Dothan (AL)
  Enterprise (AL)
  Graceville (FL)
  Temple (TX)
Bombers
  Big Spring (TX)
  Bryan (TX)
  Fort Pierce (FL)
  Hazard (KY)
  Montgomery (AL)
  Oakland (CA)
  Stamford (CT)
Bonbons
  Norwich (CT)
Bonepilers
  Regina (CANADA)
Boogers
  Bonham (TX)
Boomers
  Ardmore (OK)
  Kilgore (TX)
Boosters
  Aberdeen (SD)
  Bakersfield (CA)
  Bartlesville (OK)
  Bassano (CANADA)
  Bonham (TX)
  Boyne City (MI)
  Bristol (TN–VA)
  Cherryvale (KS)
  Clarksville (TN)
  Concordia (KS)
  Des Moines (IA)
  Enid (OK)
  Harriman (TN)
  Henryetta (OK)
  Hobbs (NM)
  Huntington (WV)

Marion (IN)
Oklahoma City (OK)
Streator (IL)
Waterloo (IA)
Worcester (MA)
Border Cits
Bristol (TN–VA)
Bouleys
Auburn (NY)
Bourbonites
Paris (KY)
Bourbons
Paris (KY)
Boys
Superior (WI)
Brahman Bulls
Lafayette (LA)
Brakies
Fort Wayne (IN)
Brants
Brantford (CANADA)
Brasscos
Waterbury (CT)
Braves
Anderson (SC)
Atlanta (GA)
Austin (TX)
Bartlesville (OK)
Belton (TX)
Boise (ID)
Boston (MA)
Bridgeport (CT)
Burlington (IA)
Cedar Rapids (IA)
Cedartown (GA)
Ciudad Madero (MEXICO)
Crestview (FL)
Dublin (GA)
Eau Claire (WI)
Evansville (IL)
Fort Lauderdale (FL)
Franklin (PA)
Greenville (SC)
Greenwood (SC)
Gulf Coast (FL)
Hagerstown (MD)
Idaho Falls (ID)
Jacksonville (FL)
Jacksonville (IL)
Jamestown (NY)

Tri-Cities (Kennewick–Richland–Pasco, WA)
Kilgore (TX)
Kingsport (TN)
Lawton (OK)
Leavenworth (KS)
Leesburg (FL)
Leon (MEXICO)
Macon (GA)
Madero (MEXICO)
Mansfield (OH)
Marysville (CA)
McCook (NE)
Midland (TX)
Milwaukee (WI)
Mount Vernon (IL)
North Yakima (WA)
Norton (VA)
Ottawa (CANADA)
Perth (CANADA)
Port Huron (MI)
Pueblo (CO)
Pulaski (VA)
Quad Cities (IA, IL)
Quebec (CANADA)
Reynosa (MEXICO)
Richmond (VA)
Roanoke (VA)
St. Jean (CANADA)
Salisbury (NC)
Savannah (GA)
Shawnee (OK)
Sherbrooke (CANADA)
Shreveport (LA)
Sweetwater (TX)
Torrington (CT)
Utica (NY)
Ventura (CA)
Victoria (MEXICO)
Waterbury (CT)
Waycross (GA)
Wellsville (NY)
West Palm Beach (FL)

Wichita (KS)
Wytheville (VA)
Bravos
Leon (MEXICO)
Brewers
Arizona (AZ)
Beloit (WI)
Brenham (TX)
Erie (PA)
Helena (MT)
Mahanoy City (PA)
Milwaukee (WI)
Paintsville (KY)
Pikeville (KY)
Pittsfield (MA)
Plattsburgh (NY)
St. Catherines (CANADA)
San Antonio (TX)
San Francisco (CA)
San Jose (CA)
Brickmakers
Hastings (NE)
Superior (NE)
Bricks
Coffeyville (KS)
Bridegrooms
Brooklyn (NY)
Brigands
Macon (GA)
Brinies
Fall River (MA)
Bronchos
Calgary (CANADA)
Rochester (NY)
Rocky Mount (NC)
San Angelo (TX)
San Antonio (TX)
South Bend (IN)
Broncos
Aguascalientes (MEXICO)
Bartlesville (OK)
Blackwell (OK)
Cleveland (OH)
Leon (MEXICO)
Nuevo Laredo (MEXICO)
Paragould (AR)

Petersburg (VA)
Reynosa (MEXICO)
San Antonio (TX)
Broncs
Amarillo (TX)
Bartlesville (OK)
Big Spring (TX)
Lewiston (ID)
Lewis–Clark (WA)
Brookfeds
Brooklyn (NY)
Brooks
Allentown (PA)
Reading (PA)
Broom Corn Cutters
Charleston (IL)
Broom Corn Raisers
Mattoon (IL)
Brownies
Brownsville (TX)
Mansfield (OH)
Marshalltown (IA)
Newnan (GA)
Rochester (NY)
St. Louis (MO)
Wabash (IN)
Youngstown (OH)
Browns
Augusta (GA)
Carthage (MO)
Chicago (IL)
Cleveland (OH)
Dallas (TX)
Dothan (AL)
Easton (MD)
El Reno (OK)
Enterprise (AL)
Findlay (OH)
Gastonia (NC)
Globe–Miami (AZ)
Hopkinsville (KY)
Independence (KS)
Lafayette (LA)
Lincoln (NE)
Longview (TX)
Marshall (TX)
Mayfield (KY)
Memphis (TN)
Monmouth (IL)
Newark (NJ)
Newton (KS)
Palestine (TX)
Pittsburg (KS)

Portland (OR)
Portsmouth (VA)
Quincy (IL)
Redding (CA)
Rochester (NY)
St. Louis (MO)
Shawnee (OK)
Sherman (TX)
Springfield (IL)
Terre Haute (IN)
Valdosta (GA)
Weir City (MO)
Brown Stockings
Davenport (IA)
St. Louis (MO)
Worcester (MA)
Bruins
Des Moines (IA)
Pueblo (CO)
Twin Falls (ID)
B's
Brockton (MA)
Buccaneers
Bartlesville (OK)
Galveston (TX)
Houma (LA)
Rocky Mount (NC)
Salem (VA)
Buckaroos
Pendleton (OK)
Portland (OR)
Buckeyes
Akron (OH)
Cincinnati (OH)
Cleveland (OH)
Columbus (OH)
Lima (OH)
Springfield (OH)
Van Wert (OH)
Warren (PA)
Youngstown (OH)
Bucks
Central Oregon (Bend, OR)
Greenville (MS)
Watertown (NY)
Buckshots
Greenville (MS)
Buckskins
Boise (ID)
Johnstown (NY)
Buffalo(e)s
Allentown (PA)
Enid (OK)

Houston (TX)
Jonesboro (AR)
Kearney (NJ)
North Platte (NE)
Omaha (NE)
Siloam Springs
(AR)
Buffeds
Buffalo (NY)
Buffs
Houston (TX)
Bugs
Danville (VA)
Rochester (MN)
Wilson (NC)
Bulldogs
Andalusia (AL)
Clinton (OK)
Fulton (KY)
Meriden (CT)
New Haven (CT)
Orlando (FL)
Quebec
(CANADA)
Bullets
San Antonio (TX)
Bulls
Angier–Fuquay
Springs–Varina
(AL)
Durham (NC)
Lafayette (LA)
Bunnies
Cedar Rapids (IA)
Henderson (NC)
Burchers
Omaha (NE)
Burch Reds
Omaha (NE)
Burghers
Fitchburg (MA)
Burghers
Pittsburgh (PA)
Burley Cubs
Greeneville (TN)
Maysville (KY)
Burros
Attleboro (MA)
Busters
Worcester (MA)
Busy Bees
Berlin (CANADA)
Bux
South Bend (IN)

Byrds
Richmond (VA)

Cabinetmakers
Grand Rapids (MI)
Cachorros
Leon (MEXICO)
Cactus
San Luis Potosi
(MEXICO)
Cafeteritos
Tamuin
(MEXICO)
Cajeteros
Celaya (MEXICO)
Cajuns
Baton Rouge (LA)
Camaraneros
Campeche
(MEXICO)
Camels
Muscatine (IA)
Canadians
Cornwall
(CANADA)
Fort William
(CANADA)
Fort William–Port
Arthur
(CANADA)
St. Jean
(CANADA)
Toronto
(CANADA)
Vancouver
(CANADA)
Canadiens
Ottawa
(CANADA)
Outremont
(CANADA)
Sherbrooke
(CANADA)
Canaries
Cedar Rapids (IA)
Peoria (IL)
Quincy (IL)
Sioux Falls (SD)
Caneros
Ciudad Mante
(MEXICO)
Los Moches
(MEXICO)

Canners
Cambridge (MD)
Maryville (TN)
Newport (TN)
Ogden (UT)
Cannibals
Hannibal (MO)
Longview (TX)
Cannons
Calgary
(CANADA)
Prince William
(Dale City–
Woodbridge, VA)
Cantabs
Cambridge (MA)
Canteens
Canton (IL)
Canucks
Toronto
(CANADA)
Capilanos
Vancouver
(CANADA)
Capital City
Albany (NY)
Capital Citys
Indianapolis (IN)
Montpelier (VT)
Capitals
Bismarck (ND)
Harlingen (TX)
Montgomery (AL)
Raleigh (NC)
Tallahassee (FL)
Capitolites
Jefferson City
(MO)
Capitols
Trenton (NJ)
Caporales
Lagos de Moreno
(MEXICO)
Caps
Tallahassee (FL)
Orlando (FL)
Raleigh (NC)
Captains
Shreveport (LA)
Cardinals
Albany (GA)
Albuquerque (NM)
Allentown (PA)
Americus (GA)

Ardmore (OK)
Arizona (AZ)
Batesville (AL)
Brunswick (GA)
Calgary
(CANADA)
Cambridge (MD)
Carthage (MO)
Cedar Rapids (IA)
Columbia (GA)
Dothan (AK)
Duluth (MN)
Eau Claire (WA)
Erie (PA)
Fostoria (OH)
Fresno (CA)
Gastonia (NC)
Goldsboro (NC)
Grand Island (NC)
Hamilton (CAN-
ADA)
Hannibal (MO)
Hazlehurst–Baxley
(GA)
Hobbs (NM)
Johnson City (TN)
Joplin (MO)
Keokuk (IA)
Lawrenceville
(VA)
Lincolnton (NC)
Lynchburg (VA)
Marion (OH)
Mayfield (KY)
Maysville (KY)
Midland (TX)
Modesto (CA)
Monessen (PA)
New Iberia (LA)
Newport (AR)
Omaha (NE)
Orangeburg (SC)
Ottumwa (IA)
Ozark (AL)
Pine Bluff (AR)
Pocatello (ID)
Raleigh (NC)
Rock Hill (SC)
Rogers (AK)
St. John (CAN-
ADA)
St. Louis (MO)
St. Petersburg (FL)
Salisbury (MD)

Sanford (FL)
Savannah (GA)
Shelby (NC)
Siloam Springs
(AR)
Sioux City (IA)
Springfield (IL)
Springfield (MO)
Springfield (OH)
Tabasco
(MEXICO)
Tacoma (WA)
Taft (TX)
Tallassee (FL)
West Frankfort
(ID)
Willows (CA)
Winston–Salem
(NC)
Worthington
(MN)
Wytheville (VA)
Cards
Allentown (PA)
Carthage (MO)
Cooleemee (NC)
Hamilton
(CANADA)
Lincolnton (NC)
Winston–Salem
(NC)
Carnavals
Quebec
(CANADA)
Carolinians
Rocky Mount
(NC)
Castro
Matamoros
(MEXICO)
Catarinos
Silao (MEXICO)
Catawbas
Rock Hill (SC)
Cats
Ballinger (TX)
Clarksville (TN)
Fort Worth (TX)
Mount Pleasant
(TX)
Santa Rosa (CA)
Cattlemen
Tabasco
(MEXICO)

Colonials
Edenton (TX)
Kingston (NY)
Salisbury–Spencer (NC)

Colt .45s
Houston (TX)
Modesto (CA)

Colts
Allentown (PA)
Angier–Fuquay Springs–Varina (NC)
Atlanta (GA)
Ballard (WA)
Blackwell (OK)
Burlington (IA)
Centreville (MD)
Chicago (IL)
Clay Center (KS)
Colonial Heights–Petersburg (VA)
Columbus (OH)
Cumberland (MD)
Dallas (TX)
Des Moines (IA)
Dubuque (IA)
East Grand Forks (TX)
Easton (MD)
Falls City (ND)
Grand Rapids (MI)
Green Bay (WI)
Haverhill (MA)
Houston (TX)
Jersey City (NJ)
Kitchner (NJ)
LaCrosse (WI)
Lawrence (MA)
Lexington (KY)
Manistee (MI)
McKeesport (PA)
Midland (TX)
Montgomery (AL)
Newark (NJ)
New London (CT)
Newport (RI)
Oakland (CA)
Ogdensburg (NY)
Orlando (FL)
Owosso (MI)
Paris (IL)
Paris (TX)
Pawtucket (RI)

Philadelphia (PA)
Portland (OR)
Pottsville (PA)
Poughkeepsie (NY)
Queen Anne (Centreville, MD)
Richmond (VA)
Rochester (NY)
Salinas (CA)
San Angelo (CA)
Savannah (GA)
Statesville (NC)
Tijuana (MEXICO)
Willamantic (CT)
Williamson (WV)
Willimantic (CT)
Youngstown (OH)

Colt .22s
Moultrie (GA)

Combines
Kokomo (IN)

Comeons
Freeport (NC)

Comers
Columbia (SC)
Gastonia (NC)
Mattoon (IL)

Comets
Kenosha (WI)
Marshall (TX)
Maryville (MO)

Commies
Columbia (SC)
Decatur (IL)

Commissioners
Eau Claire (WI)

Commodores
Decatur (IL)

Commuters
Oakland (CA)

Conchs
Key West (FL)

Confederate Yankees
Augusta (GA)
Columbia (GA)

Contenders
Waterbury (CT)

Convicts
Jackson (MI)
Jefferson City (MO)
Joliet (IL)
Leavenworth (KS)

Cools
Cooleemee (NC)

Co-operatives
Hartford (CT)

Co-Pilots
Newark (NY)

Copper Kings
Bisbee–Douglas (AZ)
Butte (MT)

Corinthians
Corinth (MS)

Cornhuskers
Lincoln (NE)
Sioux City (IA)

Cor-Sox
Corning (NY)

Corwites
Niles (OH)

Cosden Cops
Big Spring (TX)

Cotton Growers (aka Cottongrowers)
Gomez Palacio (MEXICO)
San Luis Rio (CO)

Cottonmen
Union Laguna (MEXICO)

Cotton Pickers
Orangeburg (SC)
Union Laguna (MEXICO)

Cotton Tops
Newark (OH)

Cougars
Baton Rouge (LA)
Hoquiam (WA)
Kane County Cougars (Geneva, IL)

Counts
Cleveland (TN)
Pulaski (VA)

County Gulls
Ventura (CA)

Cowboys
Agua Prieta (MEXICO)
Alpine (TX)
Big Spring (TX)
Burlington (IA)
Del Rio (TX)
El Paso (TX)
Kansas City (KS)

Magic Valley
(Twin Falls, ID)
Midland (TX)
San Antonio (TX)
Sioux City (IA)
Tucson (AZ)
Twin Falls (ID)
Victoria (TX)

Cowetas
Newnan (GA)

Coyotes
Independence (KS)
Salina (KS)

Crabbers
Crisfield (MO)

Crabs
Gulfport (MI)
Gulfport–Biloxi (MI)

Crackers
Atlanta (GA)
Greenwood (MS)

Crawfords
Indianapolis (IN)
Pittsburgh (PA)

Creoles
Shreveport (LA)

Cream City(s)
Milwaukee (WI)

Creams
Detroit (MI)
Milwaukee (WI)

Creoles
Lake Charles (LA)

Crickets
Binghamton (NY)
Omaha (NE)

Crooks
Crookston (MD)

Crows
Ottawa (IL)

Crushers
El Dorado (MEXICO)
Lodi (CA)

Crybabies
Quincy (IL)

C-Sox
Clinton (IA)

Cuban Giants
Ansonia (CT)
Hoboken (NJ)
Trenton (NJ)

Cubans
Havana (CUBA)
Long Branch (NJ)
Newark (NJ)
New York (NY)

Cuban Stars
Cincinnati (OH)

Cubs
Beaumont (TX)
Blackwell (OK)
Bloomington (IL)
Caldwell (ID)
Carthage (MO)
Centralia (IL)
Chicago (IL)
Clarksdale (MI)
Clinton (IA)
Clovis (NM)
Columbus (OH)
Davenport (IA)
Decatur (IL)
Drummondville (CANADA)
Easton (MD)
Elizabethton (TN)
Erwin (TN)
Fayetteville (NC)
Fond du Lac (WI)
Fort Wayne (IN)
Franklin (VA)
Geneva (NY)
Hastings (NY)
Hayward (CA)
Huntington (WV)
Huron (SD)
Hutchinson (KS)
Iola (KS)
Iowa (Des Moines, IA)
Janesville (WI)
Key West (FL)
Lockport (NY)
Lumberton (NC)
Marion (OH)
Midland (TX)
Morristown (TN)
Moultrie (GA)
Palatka (FL)
Pikeville (KY)
Pittsfield (MA)
Pompano Beach (FL)
Ponca City (OK)
Portsmouth (VA)

Pulaski (VA)
Quad Cities (IA-IL)
Quincy (IL)
Sedalia (MO)
Selma (AL)
Shelby (NC)
Sherman (TX)
Springfield (MA)
Springfield (MO)
Statesville (NC)
Tacoma (WA)
Tarboro (NC)
Treasure Valley (ID)
Visalia (CA)
Waco (TX)
Waterloo (IA)
Watertown (SD)
Wytheville (VA)
Zanesville (OH)
Cubsox
  Middlesboro (OH)
Cupids
  Lewiston (ME)
Custers
  Battle Creek (MI)
Cyrians
  Clarksburg (WV)

Daisies
  Denver (CO)
  Fort Wayne (IN)
  Tacoma (WA)
Dandies
  Dunkirk (NY)
Daniels
  Muskegon (MI)
Dans
  Danville (IL)
Dark Blues
  Hartford (CT)
DavSox
  Davenport (IA)
Debutantes
  Quincy (IL)
Deer
  Yucatan (Merida, MEXICO)
Deers
  Dyersburg (TN)
Delawareans
  Wilmington (DE)

Demarests
  Williamsport (PA)
Demons
  Adrian (MI)
  Des Moines (IA)
  Frostburg (MD)
  Torrington (CT)
Desperados
  Corsicana (TX)
Detroits
  Detroit (MI)
Deubers
  Canton (OH)
Diablos
  El Paso (TX)
Diablos Rojos
  Mexico City (MEXICO)
Diablos Verdes
  Leon (MEXICO)
Diamonds
  Pittsburg (CA)
  Roseville (CA)
  Waterloo (IA)
Diggers
  Marion (OH)
  McAlester (OK)
Discoverers
  Columbus (MS)
  Columbus (NE)
  Columbus (OH)
Distillers
  Owensboro (KY)
  Peoria (IL)
Dixie Runners
  Headland (AL)
Dobbins
  Dover (DE)
Dockworkers
  Tampico (MEXICO)
  Tampico–Madero (MEXICO)
Dodgers
  Albuquerque (NM)
  Andalusia (AL)
  Artesia (NM)
  Bakersfield (CA)
  Bellingham (WA)
  Bluefield (WV)
  Brooklyn (NY)
  Cairo (IL)
  Cambridge (MD)
  Clinton (IA)

Danville (IL)
Daytona Beach (FL)
Des Moines (IA)
Eastman (GA)
Elmira (NY)
Fort Dodge (IA)
Grand Forks (ND)
Great Falls (MT)
Green Bay (WI)
Gulf Coast (FL)
Greenwood (MS)
Hazleton (PA)
Hornell (NY)
Jamestown (NY)
Kingsport (TN)
Kingston (NY)
Kokomo (IN)
Lamesa (TX)
Landis (NC)
Leesburg (FL)
Lethbridge (CANADA)
Lodi (CA)
Los Angeles (CA)
Macon (GA)
Medford (OK)
Midwest (Dubuque, IA)
Nashua (NH)
Newark (NJ)
Newport (AR)
Newport News (VA)
New Waterford (CANADA)
Odessa (TX)
Ogden (UT)
Omaha (NE)
Orangeburg (SC)
Orlando (FL)
Ozark (AL)
Ponca City (OK)
Pueblo (CO)
Rogue Valley (WA)
Salem (OR)
Salisbury (NC)
San Antonio (TX)
Santa Barbara (CA)
Sarasota (FL)
Thomasville (GA)
Thomasville (NC)
Union City (TN)

Valdosta (GA)
Vero Beach (FL)
Waterbury (CT)
Winchester (KY)
Zanesville (OH)
Dollies
  Augusta (GA)
Domestics
  Newark (NJ)
Dons
  Albuquerque (NM)
  Pensacola (FL)
  Riverside (CA)
  Waco (TX)
Dorados
  Chihuahua (MEXICO)
Doublins
  Meriden (CT)
Doves
  Boston (MA)
Downeasters
  Calais (ME)
  St. Stephens (CANADA)
Downhomers
  Rocky Mount (IA)
Dragons
  Lindale (GA)
Dregs
  Bluffton (IN)
Drillers
  Artesia (NM)
  Bakersfield (CA)
  Bradford (PA)
  Hobbs (NM)
  Kilgore (TX)
  Lafayette (LA)
  Monroe (LA)
  Okmulgee (OK)
  Tulsa (OK)
  Wichita Falls (KS)
  Wilson (OK)
Drummers
  Drumwright (OK)
  Jackson (MS)
  Norfolk (NE)
  St. John (CANADA)
Drybugs
  Piedmont (WV)
Dubs
  Dubuque (IA)

Ducklings
  Lincoln (NE)
  Webb City (ME)
Ducks
  Dayton (IL)
  Portland (OR)
  Saginaw (MI)
Duck Wallopers
  Green Bay (WI)
Dudes
  Augusta (GA)
  Newport (RI)
Duffers
  Haverhill (MA)
  Portland (ME)
Dukes
  Albuquerque (NM)
  Alexandria (VA)
  Allentown (PA)
  Duluth (MN)
  Duluth (MN)–Superior (WI)
  Lansdale (PA)
  Pottstown (PA)
  San Jose (CA)
  Stockton (CA)
  Tamaqua (PA)
  Wellington (KS)
  York (NE)
Dunnmen
  Springfield (OH)
Dusters
  McAllen (TX)
  Vernon (TX)
Dutchmen
  Newburgh (VA)
  Reading (PA)

Eagles
  Abilene (TX)
  Ballinger–Winters (TX)
  Brooklyn (MA)
  Dallas (TX)
  Fulton (KY)
  Gadsden (AL)
  Houston (TX)
  Kinston (RI)
  Leon (MEXICO)
  Meridian (CT)
  Mexicali (MEXICO)
  Miami (OK)

Newark (NJ)
Odessa (TX)
Ozark (AL)
Rockingham (NC)
Seaford (DE)
Temple (TX)
Three Rivers
(CANADA)
Veracruz
(MEXICO)
Victoria (TX)
East End Stars
East Liverpool
(OH)
East Texans
Tyler (TX)
Eckfords
Brooklyn (NY)
Greenpoint (NY)
Eclipse
Louisville (KY)
Edistoes
Greenville (SC)
Educators
Durant (OK)
Fayetteville (AR)
Egyptians
Cairo (IL)
Memphis (TN)
'89ers
Oklahoma City
(OK)
Eisenfelder's
Homeseekers
Paris (TX)
Elders
Salt Lake City
(UT)
Electricians
Anderson (SC)
Augusta (GA)
Mansfield (OH)
Schenectady (NY)
Electrics
Buffalo (NY)
Fort Smith (AR)
Great Falls (MT)
Pittsfield (MA)
Savannah (GA)
Schenectady (NY)
Scranton (PA)
Elite Giants
Baltimore (MD)
Columbus (OH)

Nashville (TN)
Washington (DC)
Elites
Cleveland (OH)
Elk Horns
Norfolk (NE)
Elks
Hutchinson (KS)
Manhattan (NY)
Norfolk (NE)
Elm City
New Haven (CT)
Emeralds
Eugene (OR)
Emery Arms
Oakland (CA)
Empires
Albany (NY)
Engineers
Altoona (PA)
Eskimos
Edmonton
(CANADA)
Portland (ME)
Red Deer
(CANADA)
Esparza
Matamoros
(MEXICO)
Esquimos
Edmonton
(CANADA)
Essex
Mount Sterling
(KY)
Essos
Baton Rouge (LA)
Evangelists
Charleston (IL)
Enid (OK)
Evas
Evansville (ID)
Explorers
Bradenton (FL)
Daytona Beach
(FL)
Exporters
Beaumont (TX)
Lake Charles (LA)
Texas City (TX)
Expos
Burlington (IA)
Calgary (CAN-
ADA)

Gastonia (NC)
Gulf Coast (FL)
Jacksonville (FL)
Jamestown (NY)
Kinston (RI)
Lethbridge (CAN-
ADA)
Montreal (CAN-
ADA)
Rockford (IL)
San Jose (CA)
Watertown (SD)
West Palm Beach
(FL)
Eyeopeners
Calgary
(CANADA)

Fairbanks
Chicago (IL)
Fairies
Salem (MA)
Falcons
Auburn (NY)
Jamestown (NY)
Farmers
Easton (MD)
Fort Wayne (IN)
Greensboro (NC)
Lafayette (IN)
Las Cruces (NM)
Lawrence (KS)
Lima (OH)
Massillon (OH)
Petersburg (VA)
Shelby (NC)
Worcester (MA)
Favorites
Bonham (TX)
Feds
Brooklyn (NY)
Federalsburg (MD)
Newark (NJ)
Fencevilles
Adrian (MI)
Fever Germs
Memphis (TN)
Fiddlers
Darlington (SC)
Fighters
Lynn (MA)
Finnegans
Waterbury (CT)

Firebirds
Phoenix (AZ)
Firecrackers
Atlanta (GA)
Firemen
Atlanta (GA)
Fisheaters
Sandusky (OH)
Fishermen
Erie (PA)
Flamingos
Greater Miami (FL)
Miami Beach (FL)
Flashers
North Platte (NE)
Fleetwings
Allentown (PA)
Flickertails
Grand Forks (ND)
Fliers
Cocoa (FL)
Gadsden (AL)
Panama City (FL)
Stockton (CA)
Flint Hills
Burlington (IA)
Flints
Burlington (IA)
Flood Sufferers
Zanesville (OH)
Florists
San Jose (CA)
Flyers
Flint (MI)
Orlando (FL)
Sumter (CA)
Fondies
Fond du Lac (WI)
Foot Trackers
Springfield (IL)
Forest City
Cleveland (OH)
Rockford (IL)
Foresters
Lufkin (TX)
Forked Deers
Dyersburg (TN)
Forkers
Grand Forks (ND)
Forresters
Nebraska City
(NE)
Foundlings
Johnstown (NY)

Foutz's Fillies
Brooklyn (NY)
Foxes
Appleton (WI)
Fox Cities (ME)
Aurora (IL)
Columbia (GA)
Fitchburg (MA)
Three Rivers
(CANADA)
Frasers
New Westminster
(CANADA)
Freaks
Fremont (NE)
Freezers
St. Paul (MN)
Friends
Roanoke–Salem
(VA)
Salem (VA)
Friscoes
San Francisco
(CA)
Frog Alley Bunch
Schenectady (NY)
Frogs
Carrollton (GA)
Frolickers
Waterbury (CT)
Frontiers
Niagara Falls (NY)
Fruit Jars
Muncie (IN)
Fruit Pickers
Boise (ID)
Furnituremakers
Bassett (VA)
Grand Rapids (MI)
High Point (NC)

Gamecocks
Columbia (SC)
Henderson (NC)
Sumter (SC)
Ganderos
Tabasco (MEX-
ICO)
Gardeners
San Jose (CA)
Gardiners
Watsonville (CA)

Fremont (OH)
Greensburg (PA)
Hornell (NY)
Springfield (MA)
Green Stockings
Omaha (NE)
Gremlins
Youngstown (OH)
Greyhounds
Boone (IA)
Sanford (FL)
Union City (TN)
Greys
East Saginaw (MI)
Grey Sox
Montgomery (AL)
Griffs
Griffin (GA)
Grizzlies
Denver (CO)
Growers
Bradenton (IL)
Bradentown (FL)
Guides
Maine (Old Or-
chard Beach, ME)
Gulfs
Denver (CO)
Gulls
Charleston (SC)
Mobile (AL)
Orlando (FL)
Portland (ME)
Salt Lake City
(UT)
Sarasota (FL)
Gumbo Busters
Corsicana (TX)
Gunners
Ogden (UT)
Gushers
Kilgore (TX)
Mexia (TX)
Gypsumeaters
Fort Dodge (IA)
Gypsumites
Fort Dodge (IA)

Halligans
Flint (MI)
Hampdens
Springfield (MA)
Hams
Dallas (TX)

Hamilton
(CANADA)
Harvesters
Enid (OK)
Hatters
Danbury (CT)
Medicine Hat
(CANADA)
Hawkeyes
Burlington (IA)
Davenport (IA)
Des Moines (IA)
Hawks
Boise (ID)
Dominion
(CANADA)
Shawnee (OK)
Spokane (WA)
Topeka (AR)
Waterloo (IA)
Haverlys
San Francisco
(CA)
Hay Diggers
Fort Scott (KS)
Haymakers
Mansfield (OH)
Troy (NY)
Hayseeders
York (PA)
Hayseeds
Staunton (VA)
Watsonville (CA)
Hecker's Hitters
Oil City (PA)
Hens
Henderson (KY)
Henryetta (OK)
Heralds
Duluth (MN)
Herefords
Ada (OK)
Herrings
Taunton (MA)
Highlanders
Baton Rouge (LA)
Canton (IL)
Fayetteville (NC)
Greenville (TX)
Lakeland (FL)
Macon (GA)
New York (NY)
Peekskill (NY)

Springfield (MO)
Terre Haute (IN)
Highwaymen
Lowell (MA)
Hijackers
Graham (TX)
Hilanders
Paintsville (KY)
Hi-Liners
Valley City (ND)
Hill Billies
Vicksburg (MS)
Hill Climbers
Jamestown (NY)
Lynchburg (VA)
Natchez (MS)
Newburgh (NY)
Hillies
Gloucester (MA)
Haverhill (MA)
Pittsfield (MA)
Hillites
Rome (GA)
Hilltoppers
New York (NY)
Hi-Toms
Thomasville (NC)
Thomasville–High
Point (NC)
Hitters
Sherman (TX)
Homoners
Grand Rapids (MI)
Honey Bugs
Poughkeepsie (NY)
Hoodoos
Aurora (IL)
Hoofeds
Indianapolis (IN)
Hoo-Hoos
Orange (TX)
Hoosierfeds
Indianapolis (IN)
Hoosiers
Crawfordsville (IN)
Fort Wayne (IN)
Indianapolis (IN)
Muncie (IN)
Terre Haute (IN)
Vincennes (IN)
Hop-Bitters
Rochester (NY)
Hoppers
Hopkinsville (KY)

Hornells
Hornellsville (NY)
Hornets
Carrollton (GA)
Charlotte (NC)
Cleveland (OH)
Greensboro (SC)
Hanover (NH)
Macon (GA)
Thomasville (GA)
Horse Soldiers
Vancouver (CAN-
ADA)
Hottentots
Rockford (IL)
Terre Haute (IN)
Hubbers
Lubbock (TX)
Texas City (TX)
Hubmen
Hattiesburg (MS)
Hubs
Evansville (IN)
Hagerstown (MD)
Harlingen (TX)
Lafayette (LA)
New Brunswick
(NJ)
Hummingbirds
Newburgh (NY)
Walden (MN)
Hungarian Rioters
Shenandoah (PA)
Huns
Shenandoah–
Mahanoy City
(PA)
Hunters
Greenville (TX)
Hurricanes
Myrtle Beach (SC)
Huskies
Waterbury (CT)
Huskers
Pawhuska (OK)
Hustlers
Bridgeport (CT)
Brookfield (MO)
Dubuque (IA)
Durant (OK)
Frederick (MD)
Harrisburg (PA)
Hastings (NY)
Haverhill (MA)

Lowell (MA)
Miami (FL)
Paris (TX)
Petersburg (VA)
Rochester (NY)
Rockford (IL)
Springfield (IL)
Winchester (MA)
Worcester (MA)
Huts
Terre Haute (IN)
Hyphens
Bay City–Saginaw
(MI)
Johnstown–Am-
sterdam–Glovers-
ville (NY)
Mattoon–Charles-
ton (IL)
Springfield–
Charleston (VT)
Idlewilds
Newark (OH)
Imperials
El Centro (CA)
Tri-Cities (Kenne-
wick–Richland–
Pasco, WA)
Imps
El Centro (CA)
Independents
Corning (NY)
Lewiston (PA)
Port Huron (MI)
Indian Chiefs
Greenwood (MS)
Indians
Andalusia–Opp
(AL)
Ardmore (OK)
Bakersfield (CA)
Batavia (NY)
Beatrice (NE)
Brantford (CAN-
ADA)
Bryan (TX)
Burlington (IA)
Burlington (NC)
Butler (PA)
Canton–Akron
(OH)
Cedar Rapids (IA)
Chanute (KS)
Charleston (WV)

Jolly-ites
  Joliet (IL)
Joshers
  Grand Rapids (MI)
Josies
  St. John
  (CANADA)
Josox
  San Jose (CA)
Joy Riders
  Columbus (MS)
Judges
  Pine Bluff (AR)
Juice
  Orlando (FL)
Junior Cardinals
  Laurel (MS)

Kaisers
  Brenham (TX)
Kanks
  Kankakee (IL)
Kapitalists
  Kearney (NE)
Katydids
  Denison (TX)
Kaw-nees
  Topeka (KS)
Kaws
  Topeka (KS)
Kays
  Kankakee (ID)
Kazoos
  Kalamazoo (MI)
Kekiongas
  Fort Wayne (IN)
Kellys
  Cincinnati (OH)
Kennebecs
  Augusta (ME)
Kenties
  Kent (OH)
Keokuks
  Keokuk (IA)
Kernals
  Keokuk (IA)
Kernels
  Mitchell (SD)
Keys
  Frederick (MD)
Keystones
  Philadelphia (PA)
  Reading (PA)

Kickapoos
  Zanesville (OH)
Kickers
  Cedar Rapids (IA)
  Fort Scott (KS)
Kidnappers
  Omaha (NE)
Kids
  Mansfield (OH)
Kildees
  Franklin (VA)
Killers
  Cincinnati (OH)
Kings
  Kent (OH)
  Mount Vernon (IL)
Kittens
  Elgin (IL)
  Marquette (MI)
  San Bernardino
  (CA)
Knickerbockers
  Davenport (IA)
Knights
  Charlotte (NC)
Knox Sox
  Knoxville (TX)
Kolts
  Hamilton (CAN-
  ADA)
Krazy Kats
  Saginaw (MI)
Krewes
  Tampa (FL)
Kubs
  Baker (CANADA)

Ladds
  Harlingen–San
  Benito (TX)
Laguneros
  Torreon Laguna–
  Esperanza (MEX-
  ICO)
Lakers
  Lake Charles (LA)
  Leesburg (FL)
  Paris (IL)
Lakes
  Lake Linden (MI)
Lake Shores
  Cleveland (OH)

Lambs
  Kearney (NE)
  Memphis (TN)
  Montgomery (AL)
  Omaha (NE)
  Pottsville (PA)
Lancers
  Lansing (MI)
Lanks
  Lancaster (OH)
Larks
  Eugene (OR)
  Hutchinson (KS)
  Quebec (CAN-
  ADA)
  Wichita (KS)
Lassies
  Kalamazoo (MI)
  Muskegon (MI)
Laurels
  Hartford (CT)
Lauriers
  Lowell (MA)
Lawmakers
  Albany (NY)
  Frankfort (KY)
  Jackson (MS)
Leafs
  Danville (VA)
  Danville–
  Schoolfield (VA)
  Galax (VA)
  Rocky Mount
  (NC)
  Smithfield–Selma
  (AL)
  Toronto
  (CANADA)
Lechugueros
  Leon (MEXICO)
Lee Bears
  Pennington Gap
  (VA)
Legends
  St. Lucie (FL)
Legionnaires
  Pottstown (PA)
Legislators
  Guthrie (OK)
  Victoria (CAN-
  ADA)
Leonardites
  Lynn (MA)

Leones
  Yucatan (Merida,
  MEXICO)
Lightfoots
  Griffin (GA)
Lillies
  Portsmouth (NH)
Liners
  Texarkana (TX)
Links
  Lincoln (NE)
Lions
  Adrian (MI)
  El Dorado (IL)
  Fort Lauderdale
  (FL)
  Greenville (AL)
  Lodi (CA)
  Lynn (MA)
  Lyons (KS)
  Montgomery (AL)
  Rogers (AR)
  Sherman (TX)
  Sulphur Springs
  (TX)
  Yucatan (Merida,
  MEXICO)
Little A's
  Cleveland (MS)
  Federalsburg (MD)
Little Bisons
  Jeanette (PA)
Little Braves
  McKeesport (PA)
Little Evas
  Evansville (IN)
Little Giants
  Greenwood (MS)
  Jersey City (NJ)
  Newark (NJ)
  Quincy (IL)
  Youngstown (OH)
Little Pels
  New Orleans (LA)
Little Pirates
  Jeanette (PA)
Little Reds
  Monessen (PA)
Little Red Sox
  Clarksdale (MI)
Little Senators
  Washington (PA)
Live Oaks
  Lynn (MA)

Lizards
  Tucson (AZ)
Loboes (aka Lobos)
  Lamesa (AZ)
  Obregon (MEX-
  ICO)
Lobsters
  Raleigh (NC)
Locks
  Lockport (NY)
Logans
  Chillicothe (OH)
Loggers
  Gray's Harbor
  (WA)
Log Lumbermen
  Oconto (WI)
Log Rollers
  Marinette (WI)
Long Cats
  Longview (TX)
  Mount Pleasant
  (TX)
Longhorns
  El Paso (TX)
Longshoremen
  Superior (WI)
Lookouts
  Chattanooga (TN)
  Fulton (KY)
  Sanford (FL)
  Thomasville (GA)
Lord Baltimores
  Baltimore (MD)
Luckies
  Reidsville (NC)
Lucky Beavers
  Portland (OR)
Lulus
  Quincy (IL)
  Waterloo (IA)
Lumber City
  Allentown (PA)
  Williamsport (PA)
Lumberjacks
  Laurel (MS)
  Oakdale (LA)
  Wausau (WI)
Lumbermen
  Lufkin (TX)
  Pine Bluff (AR)
  Saginaw (MI)
Lumber Shovers
  Marinette (WI)

Madisonville (KY)
McAlester (OK)
McLeansboro (IL)
Miami (AZ)
Montgomery (WV)
Pennington Gap
(VA)
St. Louis (MO)
Scranton (PA)
Shamokin (PA)
South McAlester
(INDIAN TERRI-
TORY, later OK)
Terre Haute (IN)
Thetford Mines
(CANADA)
Welch (WV)
Minnies
Minneapolis (MN)
Miracle
Miami (FL)
Misfits
Bridgeport (CT)
Missing Links
Lincoln (NE)
Mission Bells
Tucson (AZ)
Missions
San Francisco
(CA)
San Antonio (TX)
San Jose (CA)
Mississippians
Jackson (MS)
Missourians
Webb City (MO)
Mitten Makers
Gloversville (NY)
Models
Anniston (AL)
Modocs
Ottawa (IL)
Savannah (GA)
Moguls
Waycross (GA)
Zanesville (OH)
Mohawk Colored
Giants
Schenectady (NY)
Molls
Fond du Lac (WI)
Twin Cities
(Marinette, WI–
Menominee, MI)

Molly McGuires
Cleveland (OH)
Monarchs
Kansas City (KS)
Monroe (LA)
York (PA)
Monday Models
Oakland (CA)
Monjes Grises
Monterrey (MEX-
ICO)
Monumentals
Baltimore (MD)
Moonshiners
Ashville (NC)
Moore's Marvels
Houston (TX)
Moors
Mooresville (NJ)
Moran's Colts
Jersey City (NJ)
Mormons
Palmyra (NY)
Moulders
Anniston (AL)
Moundsmen
Newark (OH)
Mountain City
Altoona (PA)
Mountaineers
Altoona (PA)
Ashville (NC)
Boise (ID)
Denver (CO)
Erwin (TN)
Hazleton (PA)
Huntsville (AL)
Kane (PA)
Martinsburg (WV)
Wheeling (WV)
Mounties
Vancouver
(CANADA)
Muckalees
Americus (GA)
Mudcats (aka Mud
Cats)
Carolina (Zebulon,
NC)
Columbia (GA)
Houston (TX)
Mudhens (aka/ Mud
Hens)
Fond du Lac (WI)

Tiffin (OH)
Toledo (OH)
Mudville Ports
Stockton (CA)
Mud Wallopers
Cairo (IL)
Mules
Columbia (TN)
Hannibal (MO)
Municipals
Monroe (LA)
Murlins
New Haven (CT)
Muskies
Madison (WI)
Muscatine (IA)
Muskegon (MI)
Mussels
Victoria
(CANADA)
Mustangs
Bartlesville (OK)
Bentonville (AZ)
Billings (MT)
Brainerd (MN)
Brainerd–Little
(MN)
Mutuals
Brooklyn (NY)
New York (NY)

Nail City
Wheeling (WV)
Nailers
Ironton (OH)
Wheeling (WV)
Naps
Cleveland (OH)
Nashannocks
New Castle (PA)
Nationals
Concord (NC)
Emporia (VA)
Ottawa
(CANADA)
San Francisco
(CA)
Shelby (NC)
Springfield (MA)
Washington (DC)
Natives
San Juan
(PUERTO RICO)

Nats
Emporia (VA)
New Castle (PA)
Raleigh (NC)
Nattatucks
Waterbury (CT)
Natural Gassers
Findlay (OH)
Navegantes
Puerto Penasco
(MEXICO)
Navigators
Dallas (TX)
Muskogee (OK)
Waco (TX)
Netherlands
Oswego (NY)
Newfeds
Newark (NJ)
Newks
Newark (OH)
Newporters
Lake Charles (LA)
New Yorks
New York (NY)
Nicol Platers
Rockford (IL)
Nighthawkes
LaFeria (TX)
Nighthawks (aka
Night Hawks)
Muskogee (OK)
Neosho (MO)
Nine
Church City
(Brooklyn, NY)
Nitros
Ranger (TX)
Wellsville (NY)
Noble Romans
Rome (NY)
Nobles
Anniston (AL)
Texarkana (TX)
Nocks
New Castle (PA)
Nolans
Albany (NY)
Nomads
Decatur (IL)
North Stars
Paris (TX)

Nuggets
Baker (OR)
Medford (OR)
Numexers
Artesia (NM)
Nutmegs
New Haven (CT)
Nuts
Albany (GA)
Suffolk (VA)

Oaks
Des Moines (IA)
Oakland (CA)
Visalia (GA)
Ocampo
Jalapa (MEXICO)
Ocean Parkers
Lynn (MA)
Officeholders
Bentonville (AR)
Ohio Works
Youngstown (OH)
Oil Citys
Corsicana (TX)
Oilers
Bartlesville (OK)
Beaumont (TX)
Channel Cities
(Santa Barbara–
Ventura, CA)
Corsicana (TX)
Duncan (OK)
Ebano (MEXICO)
El Dorado (TX)
Eureka (KS)
Findlay (OH)
Graceville (FL)
Henderson (TX)
Independence (KS)
Lafayette (LA)
Laredo (TX)
Logansport (IN)
Maracaibo (VENE-
ZUELA)
Minatitlan
(MEXICO)
Muskogee (OK)
Odessa (TX)
Oil City (PA)
Olean (NY)
Owensboro (KY)
Pampa (TX)
Poza Rica (MEXICO)

Refugio (TX)
Salamanca (MEX-
ICO)
Sapulpa (OK)
Seminole (OK)
Tulsa (OK)
Ventura (CA)
Wichita (KS)
Wichita Falls (KS)
Oil Gushers
Beaumont (TX)
Oil Workers
Marion (IN)
Old Pueblos
Tucson (AZ)
Old Soldiers
Danville (IL)
Dayton (OH)
Leavenworth (KS)
Quincy (IL)
Old Taylors
Frankfort (KY)
Olympics
Erie (PA)
Harrisburg (PA)
Portsmouth (VA)
San Francisco
(CA)
Washington (DC)
Omahogs
Omaha (NE)
Omahosses
Omaha (NE)
Opelicans
Opelika
(AL)
Orange Growers
Beeville (TX)
Orangepickers
Hermosillo
(MEXICO)
Orators
Bridgeport (CT)
Ore Diggers
Virginia (MN)
Orioles
Americus–Cordele
(GA)
Ashville (NC)
Baltimore (MD)
Bluefield (WV)
Centreville (MD)
Cordele (GA)
Dover (DE)

Dublin (GA)
Erie (PA)
Fitzgerald (GA)
Gulf Coast (FL)
Kingsport (TN)
Lawrence (KS)
Leavenworth
(KS)
Leesburg (FL)
Lodi (CA)
Miami (FL)
Newark (NY)
Ontario (CAN-
ADA)
Paris (TX)
Springfield (MO)
Tarboro (NC)
Thomasville (GA)
Thomasville (NC)
Thomson (GA)
Orions
Lodi (CA)
Orphans
Altus (OK)
Brenham (TX)
Chicago (IL)
Chickasha (OK)
Crawfordsville (IN)
Eau Claire (WI)
Grand Rapids (MI)
Green Bay (WI)
Haverhill (MA)
Ironton (OH)
Lawrence (MA)
Lowell (MA)
Marshall (TX)
Mayodan (NC)
Mesa (AZ)
Mount Sterling
(IL)
Shawnee (OK)
Sherman (TX)
O's
Charlotte (NC)
Osages
Arkansas City
(AR)
Pawhuska (OK)
Oseejays
Jamestown (NY)
Oil City (PA)
Osos Negros
Toluca (MEXICO)

Osteopaths
Kirksville (MO)
Ostineros
Guaymas
(MEXICO)
O-Twins
Orlando (FL)
Outcasts
LaCrosse (WI)
Outlaw Reds
Cincinnati (OH)
Outlaws
New Castle (PA)
Outlaws
Bakersfield (CA)
Owls
Bristol (CT)
Clarksville (TN)
Clinton (IA)
Forest City (NC)
Forest City–
Spindale (NC)
Gainesville (TX)
Hagerstown (MD)
Miami (OK)
Nuevo Laredo
(MEXICO)
Opelika (AL)
Rutherford County
(NC)
San Jose (CA)
Statesville (NC)
Topeka (KS)
Oystermen
Norfolk (VA)
Oyster Shockers
Morgan City (LA)
Ozarks
Joplin (MO)

Pacers
Perth Amboy (NJ)
Pacifics
San Francisco
(CA)
Packers
Dubuque (IA)
El Reno (OK)
Fresno (CA)
Hutchinson (KS)
Kansas City (KS)
Leesburg (FL)
McAllen (TX)

Moultrie (GA)
Muncie (IN)
Omaha (NE)
Ottumwa (IA)
Porterville (CA)
Salinas (CA)
Sioux City (IA)
Sioux Falls (SD)
Trenton (NJ)
Valdosta (GA)
Yakima (WA)
Packets
Hagerstown (MD)
Padres
Arizona (AZ)
Tri-Cities (Kenne-
wick–Richland–
Pasco, WA)
Key West (FL)
Lodi (CA)
Peoria (AZ)
Porterville (CA)
Reno (NA)
Riverside–En-
senada (CA)
Riverside–Porter-
ville (CA)
Salt Lake City
(UT)
San Bernardino
(CA)
San Diego (CA)
Santa Clara (CA)
Walla Walla (WA)
Pallbearers
Americus (GA)
Palmettos
Charleston (SC)
Palms
Fort Meyers (FL)
McAllen (TX)
Pals
Charleston (SC)
Palestine (TX)
Pan Ams
Buffalo (NY)
Pandas
Lima (OH)
Panthers
Fond du Lac (WI)
Fort Worth (TX)
Paris (TX)
Worcester (MA)
Yuma (AZ)

Pantsmakers
Mayfield (OH)
Papermakers
Appleton (WI)
Covington (KY)
Holyoke (MA)
Millinocket (ME)
Panama City (FL)
Paperweights
Holyoke (MA)
Papooses
Lynn (MA)
Paramounts
Portland (ME)
Parasites
Paris (TX)
Pards
Bismarck–Mandan
(ND)
Parisians
Paris (IL)
Paris (TN)
Paris (TX)
Parkers
Parkersburg (WV)
Parrots
Puebla (MEXICO)
Saltillo (MEXICO)
Zacatecas
(MEXICO)
Pastimes
Belfast (ME)
Pueblo (CO)
Pathfinders
Burlington (IA)
Fremont (NE)
Savannah (GA)
Patriots
Brenham (TX)
Charleston (SC)
Gettysburg (PA)
Greensboro (NC)
Lakeland (FL)
Princeton (WV)
Rochester (NY)
Pavers
Galesburg (IL)
Pawnees
Columbus (NE)
Peaches
Macon (GA)
Marysville (CA)
Rockford (IL)

Spartanburg (SC)
Wilmington (DE)
Peach Growers
Wilmington (DE)
Peanuts
Allentown (PA)
Pear Diggers
Newport (AR)
Pearl Finders
Muscatine (IA)
Pedagogues
Georgetown (TX)
Pee Deans
Florence (SC)
Peggers
Winnipeg (CAN-
ADA)
Pelicans
Clearwater (FL)
Corpus Christi
(TX)
New Iberia (LA)
New Orleans (LA)
Opelika (AL)
Panama City (FL)
St. Petersburg (FL)
Pennants
Peninsula (NC)
Wilson (NC)
Pent-ups
Utica (NY)
Pepperells
Lindale (GA)
Peppers
Newark (NJ)
Peps
Ardmore (OK)
Meridian (CT)
Pepsies
Hannibal (MO)
Perfect Gentlemen
Hoquiam (WA)
Perfectos
New Britain (CT)
St. Louis (MO)
Perforadores
Matamoros
(MEXICO)
Pericos
Puebla (MEXICO)
Zacatecas
(MEXICO)
Peroneros
Saltillo (MEXICO)

Petes
Petersboro (CAN-
ADA)
Petroleros
Poza Rica
(MEXICO)
Salamanca
(MEXICO)
Pets
Birmingham (AL)
Centralia (WA)
Fredericton (CAN-
ADA)
Pendleton (OR)
Pheasants
Aberdeen (SD)
Phenoms
Pawtucket (RI)
Portland (ME)
Philadelphias
Philadelphia (PA)
Phillies
Americus (GA)
Auburn (NY)
Bend (OR)
Bradford (PA)
Brunswick (GA)
Clearwater (FL)
Dothan (AL)
Dover (DE)
Granby (CAN-
ADA)
Helena (MT)
Huron (SD)
Johnson City (TN)
Lima (OH)
Maine (Old Or-
chard Beach, ME)
Martinsville (VA)
Mattoon (IL)
Moultrie (GA)
Philadelphia (PA)
Pittsfield (MA)
Pulaski (VA)
Reading (PA)
Reidsville (NC)
Rocky Mount
(NC)
Schenectady (NY)
Spartanburg (SC)
Terre Haute (IN)
Three Rivers
(CANADA)
Tifton (GA)

Phils
Elizabethton (TN)
Raleigh–Durham
(NC)
Picks
Piqua (OH)
Pilgrims
Boston (MA)
Natchez (MS)
Pilots
Batesville (AR)
Boise (ID)
Brunswick (GA)
Caruthersville
(MO)
Clinton (IA)
Gadsden (AL)
Hannibal (MO)
Lakeland (FL)
Newport News
(VA)
Panama City (FL)
Peninsula (Hamp-
ton–Newport
News, VA)
Pensacola (FL)
Portland (ME)
Seattle (WA)
Statesboro (GA)
Texas City (TX)
Thibodaux (LA)
Wichita (KS)
Pimientos
Griffin (GA)
Pine Knots
Pine Bluff (AR)
Pines
Rocky Mount
(NC)
Pinetoppers
Hattiesburg (MS)
Pinks
LaCrosse (WI)
Pin Rollers
Shenandoah (IA)
Pioneer Blues
Carbondale (PA)
Pioneer Red Sox
Elmira (NY)
Pioneers
Americus (GA)
Austin (TX)
Carbondale (PA)
Clovis (NM)

Elmira (NY)
Fitzgerald (GA)
Knoxville (TX)
Mansfield (OH)
Oakland (CA)
Redwood (Santa
Rosa, CA)
Richmond (KY)
San Bernardino
(CA)
San Francisco
(CA)
Redwood (Santa
Rosa, CA)
Spartanburg (SC)
Stamford (CT)
Vandergrift (PA)
Wytheville (VA)
Pipe Makers
Bessemer (AL)
Pipers
Hamlin (TX)
Lynn (MA)
Pippins
Aberdeen (WA)
Portland (OR)
Yakima (WA)
Piratas
Campeche
(MEXICO)
Pirates
Augusta (GA)
Bartlesville (OK)
Batavia (NY)
Beaumont (TX)
Big Spring (TX)
Brockville
(CANADA)
Brunswick (GA)
Bur-Gra (Burling-
ton–Elon–
Graham, NC)
Campeche (MEX-
ICO)
Carthage (MO)
Charleston (SC)
Chicago (IL)
Clinton (IA)
Columbia (GA)
Crookston (MD)
Davenport (IA)
Farnham (CAN-
ADA)
Galveston (TX)

Gastonia (ND)
Greensboro, (NC)
Greenville (AL)
Greenwood (SC)
Gulf Coast (FL)
Hobbs (NM)
Hutchinson (KS)
Keokuk (IA)
Kingsport (TN)
Las Vegas (NV)
Leesburg (FL)
Lodi (CA)
London (CAN-
ADA)
Longview (TX)
Lynn (MA)
Macon (GA)
Monroe (NC)
Nashua (NH)
Niagara Falls (NY)
Owensboro (KY)
Paris (TX)
Pittsburg (KS)
Pittsburgh (PA)
Portageville (MO)
Portsmouth (OH)
Portsmouth (VA)
Princeton (WV)
Prince William
(Dale City–
Woodbridge, VA)
Quad Cities (IA–IL)
Raleigh (NC)
Rehoboth Beach
(DE)
Roswell (NM)
Sabinas (MEXCO)
Salem (VA)
Salisbury (NC)
San Angelo (TX)
San Francisco
(CA)
San Jose (CA)
Santa Rosa (CA)
Savannah (GA)
Shelby (NC)
Sherbrooke (CAN-
ADA)
Shreveport (LA)
Stockton (CA)
Tallahassee (FL)
Thetford Mines
(CANADA)
Visalia (CA)

Dothan (AL)
Douglas (GA)
Emporia (VA)
Hickory (NC)
LaGrange (GA)
Lannett (AL)
Montgomery (AL)
Narrows (Pearls-
burg, VA)
New Iberia (LA)
Paragould (AR)
Petersburg (VA)
Pittsburgh (PA)
Salem (VA)
Shelby (NC)
Tallahassee (FL)
Valley (Lannett–
Langdale–Fairfax–
Shawmut, AL–
West Point, GA)
Red Barons
Scranton–Wilkes-
Barre (PA)
Red Birds (aka Red-
birds)
Columbia (GA)
Columbus (OH)
Elmira (NY)
Fostoria (OH)
Geneva (AL)
Geneva (NY)
Grand Island (NE)
Hamilton (CAN-
ADA)
Huntington (WV)
Huntsville (AR)
Lima (OH)
Louisville (KY)
Monett (MO)
New Philadelphia
(OH)
Paducah (KY)
Portsmouth (OH)
Quincy (IL)
Raleigh (NC)
Salem (VA)
Savannah (GA)
Springfield (IL)
Union Springs (AL)
Washington (PA)
Waynesboro (PA)
Williamson (WV)
Winston–Salem
(NC)

Red Bulls
Durham (NC)
Red Caps
Boston (MA)
Jacksonville (FL)
St. Paul (MN)
Red Devils
Leon (MEXICO)
Mexico City
(MEXICO)
Nogales (AZ)
Red Hats
Deland (FL)
Red Hawks
Waterloo (IA)
Red Jackets
Calumet (MI)
Redlegs (aka Red
Legs)
Cincinnati (OH)
Clovis (NM)
Fitzgerald (GA)
Geneva (NY)
Hornell (NY)
Palatka (FL)
Port Arthur (FL)
Savannah (GA)
Sunbury (PA)
Temple (TX)
Visalia (CA)
Red Links
Lincoln (NE)
Red Peppers
Paris (TX)
Red Raiders
Cedar Rapids (IA)
Red Robins
Red Springs (NC)
Red Springs–
Laurinburg (NC)
Red Roses
Lancaster (PA)
Reading (PA)
York (PA)
Reds
Abilene (KS)
Alexandria (LA)
Andalusia (AL)
Bartlesville (OK)
Batavia (NY)
Birmingham (AL)
Bloomington (IL)
Boston (MA)
Brewton (AL)

Caborca (MEX-
ICO)
Cedar Rapids (IA)
Central City (KY)
Chatam (CAN-
ADA)
Cincinnati (OH)
Columbia (SC)
Columbus (OH)
Cordele (GA)
Dayton (OH)
Deland (FL)
Douglas (GA)
Ebano (MEXICO)
Fremont (OH)
Fresnillo
(MEXICO)
Gulf Coast (FL)
Hastings (NY)
Jacksonville (IL)
Jeanette (PA)
Jersey City (NJ)
Knoxville (TX)
Las Choapas
(MEXICO)
Lawton (OK)
Leavenworth (KS)
Lenoir (NC)
Lexington (KY)
Lima (OH)
Lockport (NY)
Memphis (TN)
Mexico City
(MEXICO)
Minatitlan
(MEXICO)
Modesto (CA)
Moultrie (GA)
Mount Airy (NC)
Muncie (IN)
Muskegon (MI)
Muskogee (OK)
Norwich (CT)
Ogden (UT)
Peoria (IL)
Princeton (WV)
Rhode Island
(Pawtucket, RI)
Riverside (CA)
Rockford (IL)
Rogers (AR)
Salisbury (MD)
San Luis Potosi
(MEXICO)

Sarasota (FL)
Savannah (GA)
Shelby Springfield
(MO)
Sunbury (PA)
Topeka (KS)
Trenton (TN)
Vermont
(Burlington, VT)
Vicksburg (MS)
Vincennes (IN)
Waterbury (CT)
Waterloo (IA)
Wytheville (VA)
Redskins
Warren (PA)
Red Snappers
San Angelo
(TX)
Red Socks
Granby
(CANADA)
Hazlehurst–Baxley
(CANADA)
Red Sox
Abbeville (AL)
Abilene (KS)
Allentown (PA)
Baxley (GA)
Boston (MA)
Brantford (CAN-
ADA)
Bristol (CT)
Centreville (MD)
Clarksdale (MI)
Cleveland (OH)
Corning (NY)
Covington (VA)
Danville (VA)
Elmira (NY)
Granby (CAN-
ADA)
Greensboro, (NC)
Greensburg (PA)
Greenville (SC)
Gulf Coast (FL)
Harlan (KY)
Hazlehurst–Baxley
(GA)
Hazleton (PA)
Jackson (MS)
Johnstown (PA)
Lafayette (IN)
Lancaster (PA)

Lenoir (NC)
Lexington (NE)
Lexington (NC)
Lynchburg (VA)
Lynn (MA)
Mansfield (OH)
Marion (OH)
Memphis (TN)
Middletown (OH)
Milford (DE)
Morristown (TN)
New Britain (CT)
Northampton
(Cape Charles,
VA)
Olean (NY)
Oneonta (NY)
Oroville (CA)
Pawtucket (RI)
Pittsfield (MA)
Pocomoke City
(MD)
Rayne (LA)
Reading (PA)
Regina (CAN-
ADA)
Roanoke–Salem
(VA)
Rockford (IL)
Rocky Mount
(NC)
Rome (GA)
San Jose (CA)
Scranton (PA)
Sherman (TX)
Spartanburg (SC)
Superior (WI)
Warsaw (NC)
Williamsport (PA)
Winston–Salem
(NC)
Winter Haven (FL)
Wisconsin Rapids
(WI)
Red Stars
Auburn (NY)
Red Sticks
Baton Rouge (LA)
Red Stockings
Amsterdam (NY)
Boston (MA)
Cincinnati (OH)
Dubuque (IA)
Houston (TX)

Memphis (TN)
St. John
(CANADA)
Terrell (TX)
Toronto (CAN-
ADA)
Red Warriors
Mobile (AL)
Red Wave
Riverside (CA)
Red Wings
Elmira (NY)
Greensburg (PA)
Hamilton
(CANADA)
Peoria (IL)
Rochester (NY)
Springfield (MO)
Refiners
Coffeyville (KS)
Cushing (OK)
Oil City (PA)
Olean (NY)
Port Arthur (TX)
Reformers
Mansfield (OH)
Reliance(s)
Mount Carmel
(PA)
Oakland (CA)
Renards
Three Rivers
(CANADA)
Reserves
Boston (MA)
Denver (CO)
Resolutes
Brooklyn (NY)
Elizabeth (NJ)
Resorters
Mineral Wells
(TX)
Traverse City (MI)
Rhode Islanders
Providence (RI)
Ribboners
Meridian (CT)
Rice Birds
Crowley (LA)
Rayne (LA)
Rice Eaters
Bay City (TX)
Riddles
Worcester (MA)

Riders
Bay City (MI)
Rieteros
Aguascalientes
(MEXICO)
Rifles
Springfield (MA)
Rippers
Gastonia (NC)
Rivermen
Maysville (KY)
River Rats (aka
Riverrats)
Burlington (IA)
Davenport (IA)
Evansville (IL)
Selma (AL)
South Bend (WA)
Riversides
Portsmouth (OH)
River Snipes
Columbia (GA)
Robin Hoods
Moose Jaw
(CANADA)
Omaha (NE)
Rock Island (IL)
Robins
Brooklyn (NY)
Geneva (NY)
Greenville (NC)
Lawrenceville
(VA)
Shawnee (OK)
Rochesters
Rochester (NY)
Rockeries
Wabash (IN)
Rockets
Albermarle (NC)
Cedar Rapids (IA)
Gastonia (NC)
McAlester (OK)
Middletown (OH)
Radford (VA)
Roswell (NM)
Wellsville (NY)
Rockies
Colorado
(Denver, CO)
Nyack (NY)
Rocklands
Nyack (NY)

Rocks
Rockford (IL)
Rock Island (IL)
Rocky Mount
(NC)
Rocots
Salisbury (NC)
Rogues
Medford (OR)
Rojos
Fresnillo (MEX-
ICO)
Mexico City
(MEXICO)
Rollers
Albany (OR)
Pueblo (CO)
Romans
Rome (GA)
Rome (NY)
Roosters
Morristown (TN)
Rochester (MN)
Rooters
Cumberland (MD)
Rosebuds (aka Rose
Buds)
Ardmore (OK)
Little Rock (AR)
Malden (MA)
Victoria (TX)
Waltham (MA)
Worcester (MA)
Roses
Jacksonville (FL)
Richmond (IN)
Ro-Sox
Roanoke–Salem
(VA)
Roughnecks
Beaumont (TX)
Rough Riders
Rockford (IL)
Waterbury (CT)
Rourke Family
Omaha (NE)
Rourkes
Omaha (NE)
Rovers
Pueblo (CO)
Rox
Rockford (IL)
St. Cloud (MN)

Royal Bees
San Jose (CA)
Royal Giants
Brooklyn (NY)
Royals
Baseball City (FL)
Charleston (SC)
Corning (NY)
Drummondville
(CANADA)
Elmira (NY)
Fort Meyers (FL)
Gulf Coast (FL)
Kansas City (KS)
Kingsport (TN)
Montreal (CAN-
ADA)
Omaha (NE)
Perth (CANADA)
Sarasota (FL)
Three Rivers
(CANADA)
Toronto
(CANADA)
Waterloo (IA)
Rubbermen
Akron (OH)
Rubbernecks
Akron (OH)
Rubes
Providence (RI)
Riverside (CA)
Ruby Legs
Washington (DC)
Rugmakers
Amsterdam (NY)
Russets
Idaho Falls (ID)
Rustlers
Birmingham (AL)
Boston (MA)
Canandaigua (NY)
Grand Rapids (MI)
Rogers (AR)

Sacts
Sacramento (CA)
Sailors
Butler (PA)
Erie (PA)
Girard (PA)
Lynn (MA)
Newark (NJ)

Sandusky (OH)
Wilmington (NC)
Saints
Port Huron (MI)
Port Huron–Sarnia
(CANADA)
St. Augustine (FL)
St. Hyacinthe
(CANADA)
St. John (CAN-
ADA)
St. Paul (MN)
St. Petersburg (FL)
St. Thomas (CAN-
ADA)
Santa Barbara
(CA)
Sparta (GA)
Sulphur Springs
(TX)
Topeka (KS)
Salamanders
Pocomoke City
(MD)
Sallies
Springfield (IL)
Salt Miners
Hutchinson (KS)
Salt Packers
Hutchinson (KS)
Sampson Blues
Clinton (NC)
Sandcrabs (aka Sand
Crabs)
Galveston (TX)
Santa Cruz (CA)
Sand Dabs
Redondo Beach
(CA)
Sand Fleas
Gary (IN)
Sandies
Sandusky (OH)
Sandlappers
Columbia (SC)
Sandpipers
Milford (DE)
Sands
Sandusky (OH)
Sappers
Sapulpa (OK)
Saraperos
Parras (MEXICO)

Savages
  Coalinga (CA)
  Erie (PA)
  Topeka (KS)
Scorpions
  Durango
  (MEXICO)
  Durango–Laguna
  (MEXICO)
Scotties
  Fayetteville (NC)
  Fort Scott (KS)
  Scottsdale (PA)
Scouts
  Cisco (TX)
  Greenwood (MS)
  Jacksonville (FL)
  Savannah (GA)
Scrappers
  Dallas (TX)
  Meridian (CT)
Sea Birds
  Jacksonville Beach
  (FL)
Sea Cows
  Cedartown (GA)
Seagulls (aka Sea
  Gulls)
  Asbury Park (NJ)
  Charleston (SC)
  Corpus Christi
  (TX)
  Mobile (AL)
  Wilmington (NC)
Seahawks (aka Sea
  Hawks)
  Corpus Christi
  (TX)
  Port Arthur (TX)
  Rehoboth Beach
  (DE)
Seals
  Muskogee (OK)
  San Francisco
  (CA)
Seaporters
  Helena (AR)
Selectrics
  Great Falls (MT)
Selmians
  Selma (AL)
Seminole Blues
  Sanford (FL)

Seminoles
  Donalsonville
  (GA)
  Miami (FL)
  Sanford (FL)
  Shawnee (OK)
Senators
  Albany (NY)
  Anderson (SC)
  Austin (TX)
  Baton Rouge (LA)
  Burlington (NC)
  Charleston (WV)
  Columbia (SC)
  Columbus (OH)
  Dover (DE)
  Erie (PA)
  Geneva (NY)
  Greensburg (PA)
  Guthrie (OK)
  Harrisburg (PA)
  Hartford (CT)
  Helena (MT)
  Jackson (MS)
  Jefferson City
  (MO)
  Landis (NC)
  Lansing (MI)
  Lincoln (NE)
  Little Rock (AR)
  Lynchburg (VA)
  Madison (WI)
  Mayodan (NC)
  Middlesboro (OH)
  Montgomery (AL)
  New Castle (PA)
  Oklahoma City
  (OK)
  Olympia (WA)
  Orlando (FL)
  Ottawa
  (CANADA)
  Ottawa–Hull
  (CANADA)
  Ottawa–Ogdens-
  burg (CANADA)
  Peninsula (VA)
  Pensacola (FL)
  Phoenix (AZ)
  Pittsfield (MA)
  Raleigh (NC)
  Regina (CAN-
  ADA)
  Rocky Mount

(NC)
  St. Paul (MN)
  Salem (OR)
  Salisbury (NC)
  Savannah (GA)
  Shelby (NC)
  Springfield (IL)
  Sunbury (PA)
  Superior (NE)
  Thibodaux (LA)
  Topeka (KS)
  Trenton (NJ)
  Washington (DC)
  Wellsville (NY)
  Wisconsin Rapids
  (WI)
  Wytheville (VA)
Sens
  Landis (NC)
Seraperos
  Saltillo (MEXICO)
Seraphs
  Nashville (TN)
Serpents
  Anaconda (MT)
  Tarboro (NC)
Sertomas
  Orlando (FL)
Shammies
  Shamokin (PA)
Shamrocks
  Dubuque (IA)
Shaners
  Fairbury (NE)
Sharks
  Gainesville (FL)
  Puerto Penasco
  (MEXICO)
  Santo Domingo
  (DOMINICAN
  REPUBLIC)
Sheep Herders
  San Angelo (TX)
Sheiks
  Hollywood (CA)
  Rutland (VT)
  Saskatoon (CAN-
  ADA)
Sheriffs
  West Palm Beach
  (FL)
Shipbuilders
  Hampton–New-
  port News (VA)

Newport News
  (VA)
Shoemakers
  Brockton (MA)
  Leon (MEXICO)
  Lynchburg (VA)
  Lynn (MA)
Shrimpers
  Carmen (MEX-
  ICO)
Sighs
  McAlester (OK)
Silk Citys
  Paterson (NJ)
Silk Socks
  Pasadena (CA)
Silk Weavers
  Paterson (NJ)
Silverites
  Meriden (CT)
Silver Sox
  Reno (NV)
Silver Stars
  San Jose (CA)
Siwashers
  Seattle (WA)
Skeeters
  Jersey City (NJ)
  Newark (OH)
Skippers
  Lake Charles (LA)
  Mobile (AL)
  Norfolk (VA)
Skylanders
  Ashville (NC)
Skylarks
  Hendersonville
  (NC)
Skyscrapers
  Columbia (SC)
  Salt Lake City
  (UT)
Sky Sox
  Colorado Springs
  (CO)
Slate Pickers
  Bangor–Berwick
  (PA)
Slaters
  Bangor (ME)
  Pawtucket (RI)
Sloufeds
  St. Louis (MO)

Sluggers
  Abbeville (LA)
  Hot Springs (AR)
Smeltermen
  Douglas (AZ)
Smoked Italians
  Pittsburgh (PA)
Smoke Eaters
  Butte (MT)
  Spokane (WA)
Smokers
  Tampa (FL)
Smokestackers
  Everett (WA)
Smokies
  Harlan (KY)
  Knoxville (TX)
Snappers
  Ardmore (OK)
  Marshall (TX)
  Marshalltown (IA)
  Ottumwa (IA)
  Paris (TX)
  Sherman (TX)
Soldiers
  Johnson City (NY)
  Junction City (KS)
  Vancouver (CAN-
  ADA)–Vancouver
  (WA)
Solis
  Denver (CO)
Solons
  Baton Rouge (LA)
Somersets
  Boston (MA)
Sonics
  Amarillo (TX)
Sooner States
  Ada (OK)
Soos
  Sault Saint Marie
  (CANADA)
  Sioux City (IA)
  Sioux Falls (SD)
Sounds
  Nashville (TN)
Sox
  Knoxville (TX)
  Toledo (OH)
Spartans
  Spartanburg (SC)
  Sulphur Springs

Tate Stars
  Cleveland (OH)
Taylored Commies
  Taylorville (IL)
Taylor-mades
  Newburgh (NY)
Team Winners
  Salina (KS)
Tecolotes
  Nuevo Laredo
  (MEXICO)
Tecumsehs
  London (CAN-
  ADA)
Teddies
  Clinton (IA)
Tennesseens
  Dyersburg (TN)
Terrapins
  Baltimore (MD)
  LaGrange (GA)
Terre-irs
  Terre Haute (IN)
Terriers
  Canton (OH)
  Hagerstown (MD)
  Kitchner (CAN-
  ADA)
  Lima (OH)
  St. Louis (MO)
  Terre Haute (IN)
  Toledo (OH)
Terrors
  Stockton (CA)
  Terrell (TX)
  Tulsa (OK)
Texans
  Amarillo (TX)
  El Paso (TX)
  Longview (TX)
  Texas City (TX)
  Texas City–LaM-
  arque (TX)
Textiles
  Manchester (NH)
Third Citys
  Hastings (NY)
Tides
  Portsmouth–Nor-
  folk (VA)
  Tidewater (Nor-
  folk–Portsmouth,
  VA)

Tiftons
  Tifton (GA)
Timberjacks
  Hattiesburg (MS)
  Missoula (MT)
Timbers
  Wausau (WI)
Timers
  Waterbury (CT)
Tigers
  Aguascalientes
  (MEXICO)
  Alamance (Bur-
  lington, NC)
  Anderson (SC)
  Augusta (GA)
  Blytheville ()
  Bonham (TX)
  Bristol (TN–VA)
  Brockton (MA)
  Burlington (IA)
  Butler (PA)
  Caborca (MEX-
  ICO)
  Cassville (MO)
  Charleroi (PA)
  Cincinnati (OH)
  Dallas (TX)
  Denison (TX)
  Detroit (MI)
  Drummondville
  (CANADA)
  Dubuque (IA)
  Eau Claire (WI)
  Ennis (TX)
  Ensenada (MEX-
  ICO)
  Erie (PA)
  Fresno (CA)
  Fulton (KY)
  Gastonia (NC)
  Green Bay (WI)
  Greenville (MS)
  Greenwood (SC)
  Griffin (GA)
  Hamilton (CAN-
  ADA)
  Jamestown (NY)
  Lakeland (FL)
  Lincoln (NE)
  London (CAN-
  ADA)
  Lowell (MA)
  Lynn (MA)

Macon (GA)
Mansfield (OH)
Marshall (TX)
Mexico City
  (MEXICO)
Miami Beach (FL)
Muskogee (OK)
Nashville (TN)
Nazareth (PA)
Newport (AR)
Niagara Falls (NY)
Orlando (FL)
Palatka (FL)
Pawtucket (RI)
Quad Cities
  (IL) Richmond
  (IN)
Roanoke (VA)
Saginaw (MI)
Saginaw (MI)
Salamanca
  (MEXICO)
Saltillo (MEXICO)
Shreveport (LA)
Statesville (NC)
Suffolk (VA)
Tabasco
  (MEXICO)
Tacoma (WA)
Talladega (AL)
Temple (TX)
Terre Haute (IN)
Texarkana (TX)
Texas Midland Ti-
  gers (Paris, TX)
Thomasville (GA)
Trenton (NJ)
Troy (AL)
Valdosta (GA)
Venice (CA)
Vernon (CA)
Villahermosa
  (MEXICO)
Waco (TX)
Williamsport (PA)
Woonsocket (RI)
Tigres
  Aguascalientes
  (MEXICO)
  Caborca
  (MEXICO)
  Ensenada
  (MEXICO)
  Mexico City

(MEXICO)
  Saltillo (MEXICO)
Tabasco
  (MEXICO)
Villahermosa
  (MEXICO)
Timber Hawks
  Bend (OR)
Tip-Tops
  Brooklyn (NY)
Tobacconists
  Danville (VA)
  Greenville (NC)
  Whiteville (NC)
  Wilson (NC)
Tobs
  Wilson (NC)
To-baks
  Moultrie (GA)
Togs
  Greenville (TX)
Toledos
  Toledo (OH)
Tomahawks
  Williamsport (PA)
Tomcats
  Thomasville (GA)
Tommies
  Thomasville (NC)
Toros
  Seguin (TX)
  Tucson (AZ)
  Victoria (TX)
Tots
  Terre Haute (IN)
Tourists
  Ashville (NC)
  Augusta (GA)
  Miami (FL)
  Thomasville (GA)
Towerlers
  Kannapolis (NC)
Towlers
  Fieldale (VA)
Townies
  Watertown (MA)
Tractorites
  Charles City (IA)
Tractors
  Peoria (IL)
Traders
  Emporia (KS)
  Spartanburg (SC)

Trailers
  Saginaw (MI)
Tramps
  Bristol (CT)
Trappers
  Edmonton (CAN-
  ADA)
  Salt Lake City
  (UT)
Travelers
  Albany (GA)
  Arkansas (AR)
  Chickasha (OK)
  Little Rock (AR)
  Little Rock–Mont-
  gomery (AR)
  Paris (TN)
  Sharon (PA)
  Siloam Springs
  (AR)
Treeplanters
  Lincoln (NE)
Triangles
  Raleigh–Durham
  (NC)
Tribe
  Rochester (NY)
Trilbies
  Fitchburg (MA)
Trios
  Three Rivers
  (CANADA)
Triple Cities
  Easton (MD)
Triplets
  Binghamton (NY)
  Evansville (IL)
  Leaksville (NC)
  Tri-Cities (AL)
  Tri-Cities (Kenne-
  wick–Richland–
  Pasco, WA)
  Tri-City (Leaks-
  ville–Spray–
  Draper, NC)
  Triple Cities (NY)
Trips
  Tri-City (Leaks-
  ville–Spray–
  Draper, NC)
Trojans
  Batavia (NY)
  Douglas (GA)
  Dublin (GA)

Wheatshockers
    Hutchinson (KS)
Wheelers
    Charleston (WV)
Whips
    Peninsula (VA)
    Winnipeg
    (CANADA)
White Caps (aka
    Whitecaps)
    Galveston (TX)
    Logansport (IN)
    Michigan City
    (IN)
    Petersboro
    (CANADA)
    West Haven (CT)
White Devils
    Monclova–
    Coahuila
    (MEXICO)
    Union Laguna
    (MEXICO)
White Hawks
    Waterloo (IA)
White Ribbons
    Meridian (CT)
White Roses
    York (PA)
Whites
    Philadelphia (PA)
    St. Louis (MO)
White Socks
    Lockport (NY)
White Sox
    Alexandria (LA)
    Bangor (ME)
    Batesville (AR)
    Butler (PA)
    Charleston (SC)
    Chicago (IL)
    Coffeyville (KS)
    Columbia (GA)
    Cordele (GA)

Duluth (MN)
Duluth–Superior (MN)
Evansville (IL)
Glens Falls (NY)
Gulf Coast (FL)
Holdrege (NE)
Hutchinson (KS)
Jonesboro (AR)
Kalamazoo (MI)
Kingsport (TN)
Knoxville (TX)
Lafayette (LA)
Lockport (LA)
Lynchburg (VA)
Mobile (AL)
Monroe (LA)
Niagara Falls (NY)
Olean (NY)
Peninsula (Ham-
    ton–Newport
    News, VA)
Saginaw (MI)
Sarasota (FL)
Savannah (GA)
South Bend (IN)
Topeka (KS)
Visalia (CA)
Wellsville (NY)
Winter Haven (FL)
Wisconsin Rapids
    (WI)
White Stockings
    Centralia (IL)
    Chicago (IL)
    Rockford (IL)
    Toledo (OH)
Whitewings
    Rio Grande Valley
    (TX)
Why-Nots
    Minot (ND)
Wildcats
    Kokomo (IN)
    Suffolk (VA)

Windjammers
    Atlanta (GA)
Wings
    Dayton (OH)
Witches
    Norwich (CT)
    Salem (MA)
    Wichita (KS)
Wolverines
    Detroit (MI)
    Grand Rapids (MI)
    Jackson (MI)
    Menominee (MI)
    Rockford (IL)
Wolves
    Augusta (GA)
    Bay City (MI)
    Rockford (IL)
    Tupelo (MS)
    Wichita (KS)
Wonders
    Brooklyn (NY)
    Warren (PA)
Woodchoppers
    Bristol (CT)
    Tampico
    (MEXICO)
    Tampico–Madero
    (MEXICO)
Wooden Nutmegs
    Hartford (CT)
Wooden Shoes
    Holland (MI)
Woodpeckers
    Hattiesburg (MS)
    Leavenworth (KS)
Woodworkers
    Grand Rapids (MI)
Worcesters
    Worcester (MA)
Worthies
    Ellsworth (KS)

Wranglers
    Las Vegas (NV)
    Wichita (KS)
Wrappers
    South Boston (VA)
    South Boston–Hal-
    ifax (VA)
Wrens
    Rock Hill (SC)

Yahoos
    York (PA)
Yanigans
    New Castle (PA)
Yankees
    Akron (OH)
    Albany–Colonie
    (NY)
    Auburn (NY)
    Bellingham (WA)
    Boise (ID)
    Bradford (PA)
    Butler (PA)
    Easton (MD)
    Erie (PA)
    Evansville (IL)
    Fort Lauderdale
    (FL)
    Greensboro (NC)
    Gulf Coast (FL)
    Harlan (KY)
    Idaho Falls (ID)
    Independence
    (KS)
    Johnson City (TN)
    Kearney (NE)
    Kinston (NC)
    Manchester (NH)
    Neosho (MO)
    Newark (OH)
    New York (NY)
    Norfolk (NE)
    Olean (NY)
    Oneonta (NY)

Paintsville (KY)
Prince William
    (Dale City–
    Woodbridge, VA)
Sarasota (FL)
Shelby (NC)
Sunbury (PA)
Tacoma (WA)
Tampa (FL)
Three Rivers
    (CANADA)
Ventura (CA)
Wellsville (NY)
West Haven (CT)
Yanks
    Bisbee (AZ)
    Bisbee–Douglas
    (AZ)
    Lynn (MA)
    Sapulpa (OK)
Yaquis
    Nogales (AZ)
Yearlings
    Ocala (FL)
Yeggs
    Adrian (MI)
    Jackson (MI)
Young Giants
    Manchester (NH)
Young Yanks
    Chambersburg
    (PA)

Zenith City
    Duluth (MN)
Zephyrs
    Denver (CO)
Zeros
    Centralia (IL)
Zoos
    Yazoo City (MS)
Zulus
    Pittsburgh (PA)